The First Night
GILBERT
and
SULLIVAN

CENTENNIAL EDITION

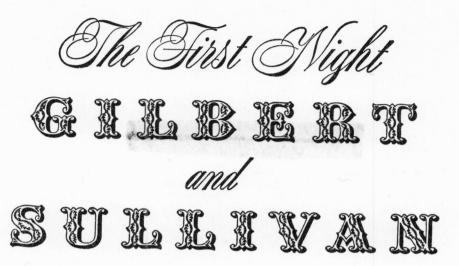

The First Night
GILBERT
and
SULLIVAN

CONTAINING

Complete Librettos of the Fourteen Operas,

Exactly as presented at their Première Performances

Edited, with a Prologue and Copious Descriptive Particulars,

by REGINALD ALLEN;

and a Foreword by BRIDGET D'OYLY CARTE.

Illustrated with Contemporary Drawings.

CHAPPELL & CO. LTD.

LONDON

This revised Centennial Edition is published by arrangement with
The Cardavon Press, Inc., Avon, Connecticut

ISBN 0 903443 10 4

Printed in England by Westerham Press Limited

IN 1901, IN SUBURBAN PHILADELPHIA, a young doctor of twenty-five organized a club for the amateur production of Gilbert and Sullivan operas, of which he was doubly a devotee. His keen creative wit and articulate interest in the theatre combined with unusual natural musical gifts to make him a peculiarly understanding and discriminating votary of W. S. Gilbert and Arthur Sullivan, individually and collaboratively. He was the life and soul of the Savoy Opera Company, as his company was named. He not only trained and directed the cast and chorus, but he conducted the orchestra. Following the success of a modest initial *Trial by Jury,* the second production was planned to be *The Sorcerer.* This meant expanding the club membership to get more men and girls for the chorus: Rollicking Buns and Gay Sally Lunns, they called themselves. One of them, a Gay Sally Lunn of twenty-two, attracted something more than the young doctor's musical and dramatic notice. He fell in love with her during those *Sorcerer* rehearsals. They became engaged during *Pinafore* rehearsals the following year, and were married.

The Philadelphia Savoy Opera Company, now in its seventy-fifth year, remains an enduring monument to the young doctor's enthusiasm for Gilbert and Sullivan opera, even though his own mortal career terminated abruptly in the Argonne, 1918. His Gay Sally Lunn has joined him, some years since. But, as they were my father and mother, they have left behind in me a demonstrably prenatal addiction. I cannot remember the time I did not know and love the operas of Gilbert and Sullivan.

REGINALD ALLEN
June, 1975

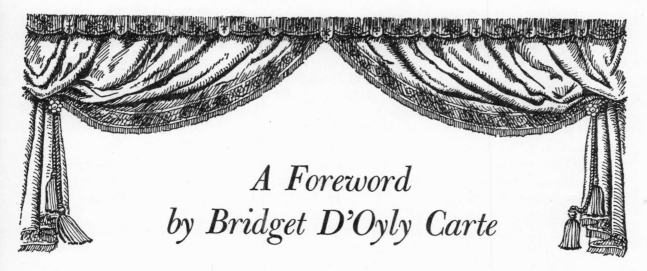

A Foreword
by Bridget D'Oyly Carte

REGINALD ALLEN once made it clear to me, in one of his long and demanding, but quite irresistible, letters, that the wear and tear which I should have to sustain if I were willing to help him with his research work for this book would be a good example of the "sins" of the fathers being visited upon the children, unto the third generation. Certainly, in my effort to write this Foreword, I feel as if the labours if not the "sins" of my grandfather, Richard D'Oyly Carte, had descended upon me. But I have to confess that since the correspondence started between Mr. Allen and myself, I have learned much more about my illustrious grandfather than I ever knew before. Indeed, had it not been for Mr. Allen's determination, the dusty bundles of papers which I have had to turn out and read for him would probably have remained undisturbed for many years to come. Yet, in view of his great knowledge of the subject, my task has not been so much to discover fresh material for him, or to tell him anything new, as to help him in the work of checking the facts and in confirming the truth of his suppositions.

Gilbert, Sullivan, and D'Oyly Carte correspondence between England and America has a long tradition; and the many letters that have passed between Reginald Allen and myself would seem to be the inevitable continuation of that tradition. My grandfather began his theatrical adventures in America in the 1870's, and the correspondence between the various parties concerned on both sides of the Atlantic soon became voluminous. The handwritten copies of these early letters, now in my possession, are extremely difficult to read. They are faded and discoloured by time, and many of them were badly damaged during the war. But they do give one an interesting and often an amusing picture of what was happening at the time. They give, too, considerable insight into the characters of the persons who wrote them and to whom they were written.

In a letter from D'Oyly to his business associate Michael Gunn, addressed from New York to London in 1882, there is for instance this interesting comment on the production of *Patience* and its coincidence with Oscar Wilde's lecture tours in America: "*Patience* is still playing to fair business. Wilde has given it a fresh spurt and it has simply made him. His business is *enormous*." *Patience* had opened the Savoy Theatre the year before, and the following reference to that occasion appears in a letter from D'Oyly, then in London, to Helen Lenoir in New York: "The new theatre is a colossal success, the loveliest theatre *in the world* all the critics say and everyone. Acoustics marvelous. In the top gallery every whisper is heard. Electric light in the auditorium only—stage will be lighted next week with it. At the end of the show the top gallery as *cool* as a sitting room with two wax candles."

Some of the letters contain scraps of the curious secret codes which D'Oyly and Gilbert used when sending cables about "takings," salaries, and other confidential and complicated business matters. I have a strong feeling that both Gilbert and my grandfather greatly enjoyed contriving these code messages and the conspiratorial atmosphere they created.

Undoubtedly the early productions of the Savoy operas in America established a close connection between England and America from the very beginning; and it is evident that the operas themselves have remained the joint possession of the two countries ever since. I think it would be true to say that my grandfather's part in bringing this about was one of the great contributions he made to the Gilbert, Sullivan, and D'Oyly Carte partnership. He not only fully appreciated America's theatrical potentialities, he loved the country and enjoyed adventuring there. America offered him new and splendid opportunities—for the business of touring a theatrical company in America was a speculation and a challenge then, as it is today.

Although he was an Englishman he would, I think, have made quite a satisfactory American. Indeed, it is plain that he possessed many qualities that we in England now have come to regard as exclusive to the American—although I am inclined to think that they never were so at any time. He had boundless energy and imagination, and the determination to carry out what he imagined. He had faith in the future and in new ideas. He would never accept the second-rate; and his confidence was such that he would battle to realise his ideas regardless of difficulties and opposition. Above all, he had an outstanding sense of showmanship. I very much regret that he died before I was born, for I should like to have known him.

Fortunately, however, living and working with my father, Rupert D'Oyly Carte, as I did for so many years until his death in 1948, I had the opportunity to learn a great deal from him about these early ventures and what they must have meant, particularly as my father had a very deep affection for his father and for his stepmother Helen. But my father was a rather shy person, and being himself so much a part of this history, it was not always easy to get him to speak of it. He seemed to assume that one already knew all about it, as a kind of natural inheritance. His great admiration for his stepmother, who, as Helen Lenoir, managed my grandfather's many companies both here and abroad, was very understandable. She must have been a woman of exceptional intelligence and charm, both tactful and determined. Although she was frail and physically very small, she was, for her time, a woman of great courage, independence, and organizing ability. Indeed, only a strong character could have successfully managed my grandfather's theatrical affairs as she did, both in England and in America. Yet this strength in her character was by no means obvious to me when, as a child, I was once taken to see her at the Savoy Hotel, where she then lived.

I had been given a bunch of Parma violets to present to her, and I remember the hot, airless room where I found her lying upon a sofa propped up with cushions. She looked to me exactly like some kind of very fragile small bird. I was about four or five years old, and somewhat overawed by the whole occasion. But I must admit that the most memorable thing about that day happened when I left her and was taken down to the car waiting to carry me home. On the floor of the car there was an enormous sugared cake, which she had arranged to have there as a present for me. It had been splendidly decorated in the Savoy kitchens, and I shall never forget the pink and white wonder of it lying there wrapped in transparent tissue paper.

But I should not digress from my present purpose—which is simply to say how truly glad I have been to contribute even a little to the work that has gone into the making of this book. Reginald Allen has brought together and presented in a unique way information concerning the first nights of the Savoy operas that will surely delight and interest Gilbert and Sullivan enthusiasts on both sides of the Atlantic.

Contents

Acknowledgments

THE LIVING THEATRE of an era has so much of the quality of journalism, that its most faithful likeness is, perhaps, best mirrored by its own press. I have sought to preserve in this edition of Gilbert and Sullivan first nights not only the facts and flavor, but the point of view and idiom of their time. So, wherever possible, my quoted sources are contemporary reviews, diaries, and letters—in fact, you will find that the introductory description preceding each first-night text is largely a mosaic of excerpts, quoted from these eye-witness sources.

For the press coverage from which I have derived whatever vividness of detail and depth of understanding these descriptions possess, I am indebted beyond gratitude to Miss Bridget D'Oyly Carte. She sent me from London not one or two or three notices for each of the opening nights, but a dozen and more, many carefully briefed to give me the descriptive kernel I sought. Then there were unpublished correspondence of Richard D'Oyly Carte and his two partners, pre-publication prompt-copies of *Pirates* librettos, and three of the first-night programs that I have found in no other collection but hers; all these and more Miss D'Oyly Carte turned over to me. Her judgment and her sense of humor in commenting on each sheaf of photostats and in her long, patient replies to my endless questions, were a continuing challenge and spur to my own work. The generous abandon with which she gave of her time and thought in behalf of this enterprise makes her in every sense my collaborator. So, if there is any special charm of intimacy to be drawn from these first-night descriptions, mark it down to the good fortune I have enjoyed in working with Richard D'Oyly Carte's granddaughter, the closest living direct descendant of any member of that wonder-working triumvirate.

"Soon after he landed in America [i.e. in December 1879] Sullivan began to keep a diary, and he kept these diaries carefully until his death." For such intimate information on the composer's life and for many quoted passages from his diaries and letters, I have drawn on the excellent biography of Arthur Sullivan written by his nephew, the late Herbert Sullivan and Sir Newman Flower.

Gilbert kept a diary, of a sort, only for the year 1878 and part of 1879, in the period covered by this work. "A good diarist is interested either in himself or in other people; a great diarist is interested in both; Gilbert was interested in neither." For this pithy appraisal of Gilbert as diarist and for the opportunity to quote both from Gilbert's diary and from several of his unpublished letters, I am grateful to Hesketh Pearson's *Gilbert, His Life and Strife*.

I am particularly thankful to Leslie Baily, whose *The Gilbert and Sullivan Book* has proved most stimulating and useful, and to Thomas F. Dunhill, whose approach to the evaluation of Sullivan as a composer (*Sullivan's Comic Operas, A Critical Appreciation*) has been an important aid.

A number of letters of both Gilbert and Sullivan quoted in this volume come originally from my own collection and from that of the late Carroll A. Wilson, and are here made available for the first time by the Pierpont Morgan Library. I am most grateful to Frederick Adams, director, and to the staff of the Pierpont Morgan Library for this and other invaluable help in all phases of my work on this edition.

De mortuis . . . Were they now living I should wish to thank: Miss Nancy McIntosh, last of the Gilbert and Sullivan leading ladies, and Mrs. Elena Bashford, widow of Herbert Sullivan, for treasured moments of reminiscence they gave me; Townley Searle, without whose inter-bellum collecting of librettos and programs, and their subsequently derived bibliography, much of my source material might have been pulped or blitzed before I could have got to it; my friend Carroll Wilson, whose collection and bibliographic studies made available to me by his widow, Jean Shelly Wilson, have been both aid and inspiration; my fellow-American Savoyard, Isaac Goldberg, whose work on Gilbert and Sullivan more than thirty years ago is still in many respects unrivaled.

For generous material assistance I am indebted to the British Museum (Bertram Schofield and Alec King), the Enthoven Collection of the Victoria and Albert Museum (George W. Nash), the office of the Lord Chamberlain, the office staff of the D'Oyly Carte Opera Company, and the Harvard College Library (William Jackson, William Van Lennep, and Miss Mary Reardon).

Other individuals and libraries to whom I am grateful include Jacques Barzun, Miss Ruth Bashford, the Boston Athenaeum (Miss Margaret Hackett), the Brander Matthews Collection of the Columbia University Library (Henry Wells), the Century Association (Theodore Bolton), Cecil Hopkinson, the Huntington Library (Robert Schad), the Library of Congress (William Lichtenwanger), the Museum of the City of New York (Miss May Seymour), the New York Historical Society (Louis H. Fox), the New York Public Library (George Freedley and Carleton Sprague Smith), Miss Mabel Zahn, Ruth Thompson (my secretary), and, from beginning to end, to my wife—wedded to "the cause" as well as to me.

For the preparation of this Centennial Edition I have received additional valuable help from the following:

In England: Albert Truelove of Bridget D'Oyly Carte Ltd., Derek Hudson, Colin Prestige, Terence Rees, Cyril Rollins, and R. John Witts.

In America: Charles Ryskamp, Director of the Pierpont Morgan Library, and my colleagues Herbert Cahoon and Mrs. Gale D'Luhy; the Beinecke Library, Yale University; Professor Jane Stedman of Roosevelt University, Chicago; and John Wolfson of New York.

A complete list of the newspapers, weeklies, monthly magazines, and published works which have been my sources for both text and illustrations, will be found beginning on page 462.

R.A.

Prologue

How MANY have dreamed enviously, as I have, of those incredible occasions, the first-night performances of the Gilbert and Sullivan operas! Oh, to have savored just once with those fortunate few this veritable quintessence of the Victorian Era!

"A first night at Mr. D'Oyly Carte's small but sumptuous house," wrote a morning-after reviewer, "differs from others very materially; in fact we may go further and say it is unique. A Lyceum production [i.e., one of Henry Irving's] draws together all that is celebrated or notorious in the world of drama: and a new opera at Covent Garden causes a brilliant gathering of musical people. But in Gilbert and Sullivan openings [these] two large sections of the public meet on common ground."

Never before in recorded time, and never since, has civilization provided the stellar phenomenon of the leading wit and dramatist, the leading composer, and the leading impresario in happy conjunction. The miracle of it was early recognized. There was something more than the usual anticipation in the air at the launching of *The Sorcerer,* the third collaboration. The *Sunday Times* critic Herman Klein wrote in 1925 of his happy recollection at being present on that occasion, "the first of the long succession of world-renowned comic operas created by the twin geniuses." Perhaps he is the one I most envy, for he continued, "It was subsequently my unique privilege—unique, I believe, for a working journalist still in the flesh—to attend and criticize every first performance of the now historic series from 1878 down to 1896." This record gave Klein twelve of the fourteen nights that shook the world with laughter.

I doubt that anyone but the two creators themselves had them all. D'Oyly Carte probably had thirteen, for there is no reason to believe that he attended the first night of *Thespis.* François Cellier—who recalled seeing *Thespis* at a later performance—might also have had thirteen except that he certainly missed *Iolanthe,* for he was con-

ducting the simultaneous American première. So —if I am ever in the good graces of a *genie* who offers me one of those who-would-you-like-to-be choices—until I can find the man who had a good stall seat to all fourteen, I shall answer, Herman Klein.

But with practicing *genii* scarcer these days even than comic-opera rivals to Gilbert and Sullivan, it has seemed more practical to try to recreate, insofar as is possible in a word-picture, the experience of attending each of those exciting evenings. For my eye-witness descriptions I have concentrated on the writings of the working press as they appeared, usually from a few hours to thirty-six hours after the final curtain. In so doing I hope to have avoided the well-intentioned, sentimental inaccuracies that invariably color autobiographies and personal reminiscences written in the dimming light of fifty or more years. Let me give you one example (the culprits are that adored—and, I am sure, adorable—Jessie Bond and, aiding and abetting, an unnamed "first nighter" from faraway Glenorchy, Victoria, Australia):

I had overlooked in one of the closing chapters of her *Life and Reminiscences* (published in 1930 when she was seventy-seven years old) a quotation from a letter Miss Bond had received from a man who owned to having attended the first night of *The Gondoliers.* William Lichtenwanger of the Library of Congress, Music Division, called my attention to this passage and to its startling intelligence: "Perhaps you will remember that, on the night of the production of *The Gondoliers,* the two kings sang the duet 'Replying we sing as one individual' as a *duet,* and not in the comical way they afterwards sang it." I had already finished my introduction to *The Gondoliers* and this was news to me, exactly the kind of performance detail I wanted this edition to contain—IF it really happened that way. I rushed an urgent letter of inquiry across the Atlantic to the harassed Miss D'Oyly Carte. Her reply characteristically enclosed several press excerpts specifically describing the Palmieri brothers as singing this song in alternate lines rather than as a duet. *Q.E.D.*

Gilbert self-caricature, from a letter to Arthur Pinero.

THE AUTHOR

"For, look you, there is humour in all things + the truest philosophy is that which teaches us to find it and make the most of it."

W. S. Gilbert.

WILLIAM SCHWENCK GILBERT was born in Southampton Street, Strand, London, November 18, 1836. His father was ex-naval surgeon, William Gilbert; his mother, Scottish Anne Morris. He attended London University and worked as a clerk six years to 1862 in the Office of the Privy Council. During the latter part of this period he became a weekly contributor to the comic magazine, *Fun,* for which he drew his beguiling sketches signed "Bab" and wrote both prose and verse. Some of these verses he named "Bab Ballads." They were collected and published in 1869, and more of them were published in the '70's. "All Gilbert is in 'The Bab Ballads,'" said the *Times,* "as all the flower is in the bud." These delightful satiric rhythmic creations with their improbable "Bab" illustrations are the fountainhead of topsy-turviness in many of Gilbert's opera plots and characters. In 1866 he wrote his first dramatic work, *Dulcamara,* a burlesque. In 1867 he married Lucy Turner, who survived him by twenty-five years to 1936. They had no children, but the American-born singer, Nancy McIntosh, lived with them as their adopted daughter from 1893. The immortal collaboration with Arthur Sullivan spanned the twenty-five years from 1871 to 1896. Gilbert was

knighted by Edward VII in 1907. He died on May 29, 1911, at the age of seventy-four.

The London *Times* published the following eulogy:

He was one of the very few really original figures in our recent dramatic history, and partly through his own genius, and partly through the fortunate accident of his finding a perfect musical collaborator and exponent in Sir Arthur Sullivan, he long ago secured a position in the public consciousness which has been obtained by no other dramatist for many a long year.

He would no more utter a hackneyed witticism than he would publish a clumsy rhyme. Everything came fresh from his mint. Nor, though he is classed with the satirists, was he always satirical. *Patience* is, perhaps, the only one of his operas which has a definitely satirical theme, and there the excellent fooling is perfectly good-natured. . . . It is commonly said that in conversation Gilbert was not amiable in his treatment of the follies of his contemporaries, and yet certainly, in his ballads and plays, our modern embodiment of the comic spirit was as genial as Molière. For that reason, and because of the beauty and appropriateness of his collaborator's music, his best works will live perhaps longer than any other plays of the Victorian era.

In these days, when events and their interpretations follow one another with a swiftness such as has never been known before, it is foolish to predict immortality for any work or any reputation; but if originality, humour, and wide outlook, and the gift of happy expression count for anything, the name of W. S. Gilbert ought long to remain, unsubmerged by the waters of oblivion.

G.B.S., in the fire of his critical Irish youth, was inclined to be prickly with Gilbert's (to him) old-guard formulae and perhaps even a bit jealous of his reputation as a humorist: "Mr. Gilbert's paradoxical wit, astonishing to the ordinary Englishman, is nothing to me," he wrote at the time of *The Gondoliers* in 1889. "Nature has cursed me with a facility for the same trick; and I could paradox Mr. Gilbert's head off were I not convinced that such trifling is morally unjustifiable." But he set aside such mock-humane scruples a few years later and fired a characteristically Shavian epigrammatic burst toward Gilbert when discoursing on the need for sentimental relief at the Savoy in the fall of 1892. Shaw wrote that the Savoy needed "relief from Mr. Gilbert, whose great fault was that he began and ended with himself [G.B.S. could recognize that trait from close at home], and gave no really congenial opportunities to the management and the composer. He exploited their unrivalled *savoir faire* to his head's content; but he starved their genius, possibly because he did not give them credit for possessing any."

The North Pole and the South Pole have many imposing superficialities in common, but one is land and one is water and they are a whole world apart. So let it be with Gilbert and Shaw. One fact remains which in the language of the theatre speaks louder than a Stentor or a G.B.S.: For twenty-four years—from the production of *The Vivandiere* at the Queen's Theatre, Longacre, in 1868, to the end of the run of *The Gondoliers* at the Savoy in 1891—Gilbert's name was never out of the London playbills.

THE COMPOSER

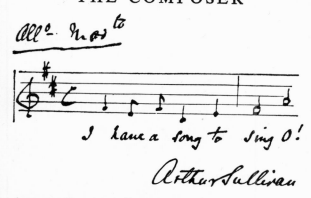

ARTHUR SEYMOUR SULLIVAN was born in Bolwell Terrace, Lambeth, London, on May 13, 1842. His father was an Irish military bandmaster. His

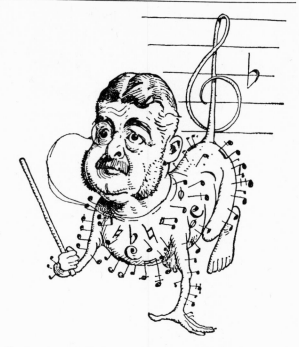

Caricature of Sullivan from MR. PUNCH'S ANIMAL LAND, *by E. P. Reed.*

mother was of Italian lineage, artistic and sensitive. At the age of eight he composed his first anthem. He became a choir boy at Chapel Royal in 1854. Two years later, at fourteen, he became the first winner of the Mendelssohn Scholarship, and in 1858 went to Leipzig for his advanced musical education. His *Music to Shakespeare's Tempest,* 1861, was his first important work. In December 1867, with Francis Burnand as librettist, Sullivan composed his first comic opera. He edited two large hymn collections at this time and wrote a number of original hymn tunes including (in 1872) the famous setting for "Onward! Christian Soldiers." He was appointed Principal of the National Training School of Music (precursor of The Royal College of Music) in 1876, the same year in which Cambridge made him an Honorary Mus. Doc. He was knighted by Queen Victoria in 1883. In the period from 1871 to 1896 he collaborated with W. S. Gilbert in fourteen comic operas. During that time Sullivan composed several major choral works, including *The Light of the World, The Martyr of Antioch,* and *The Golden Legend.* His lone grand opera, *Ivanhoe,* was produced in 1891. Sir Arthur never married, but from 1877 enjoyed the company of his nephew, Herbert Sullivan, as his adopted son. He died on November 22, 1900, at the age of fifty-eight.

Sir Arthur Sullivan [wrote G.B.S. in 1891] made his reputation as a composer of comic operas by a consummate *savoir faire* which was partly, no doubt, a personal and social talent, but which had been cultivated musically by a thorough technical training in the elegant and fastidious school of Mendelssohn, and by twenty years' work in composing for the drawing room, the church, the festival, and the concert room. In 1875, when he composed *Trial by Jury,* no manager would have dreamt of approaching him with a commission for an Offenbachian opera: he was pre-eminently a sentimental and ecclesiastical composer. . . . When he plunged into the banalities and trivialities of Savoy opera he carried his old training with him. He taught the public to understand orchestral fun; but his instrumental jokes, which he never carried too far, were always in good taste; and his workmanship was unfailingly skillful and refined, even when the material was of the cheapest.

Two sides traditionally make an argument, and Sullivan had this schizoid requirement highly developed. The genius vs. society darling, the serious composer vs. popular balladist, the Verdi vs. Offenbach in him—all invited disagreement. Shaw was willing to overlook one Sullivan while admiring certain attributes of the other.

Perhaps in the analysis of Thomas F. Dunhill one finds the fairest, clearest presentation of the two Sullivans:

> Sullivan was, quite frankly, a tantalizing mixture of talent and genius. His talent was dated: his genius is for all time. His talent concerned itself with the making of serious music, an occupation in which—as a leader in his profession—he was naturally anxious to prove his efficiency: his genius took wing and lightly skimmed on the surface of the waters into which his talent plunged. In serious music-making, despite skill and sincerity, he was not strong enough to break away from the fashions of a peculiarly narrow age in our English art—the age of cumbersome oratorios, sugary anthems and hymns, and a species of domestic music which hovered between flowery elegance and insipid pathos.
>
> Even the comic operas, which are the fruits of his genius, did not wholly emancipate themselves from the sentimentalities which so many people, in those days, craved for; but in spite of occasional lapses they most assuredly possess the spark of independent life, a spark kindled anew every time they are performed.

Dr. Dunhill advocated disregarding Sullivan's serious music altogether (which is what G.B.S. did) as belonging irrecoverably to the past. But on the other side, "A comic genius is a rarity—the combination of two comic geniuses in almost perfect accord, the one the complement of the other, is probably unique." Ergo, "His comic operas alone belong to the present and the future."

THE IMPRESARIO

RICHARD D'OYLY CARTE was born in Soho, London, May 3, 1844. He was the son of a flautist, a partner in the firm of Rudall, Carte & Co., musical instrument makers. After graduating from London University in 1861 he entered his father's business, while in his spare time he composed operetta music. In 1870 he formed his own lecture and concert agency. He managed the farewell tour of Mario, one of the greatest tenors of his day, and also made the lecture bookings for such public figures as Matthew Arnold and Oscar Wilde. As manager of the Royalty Theatre in 1875 he brought together Gilbert and Sullivan in *Trial by Jury,* the first of thirteen comic operas in which his name and theirs were associated. D'Oyly Carte organized and managed touring companies in all parts of the world for the performance of Gilbert and Sullivan and other comic operas in English. In 1881 he built the Savoy Theatre, and later the Savoy Hotel. In 1891 he built the Royal English Opera House (now the Palace Theatre), which was opened with Sullivan's grand opera *Ivanhoe.* Carte's former secretarial assistant, Helen Couper-Black (known as Helen Lenoir), became his second wife in 1888; she was his virtual partner till his death on April 3, 1901, at the age of fifty-seven, after which she assumed the management of his companies. She married Stanley Carr Boulter, and retired in 1909 at the expiration of her Savoy Theatre tenancy. She died in 1913, leaving the stewardship of the D'Oyly Carte Opera Company in the hands of her stepson, Rupert D'Oyly Carte. He, in turn, died in 1948. Rupert's daughter, Bridget D'Oyly Carte, now heads the Company.

Wrote G.B.S. in September 1892—"Mr. and Mrs. D'Oyly Carte have unmistakable genius for management: their stage pictures are as recognizable by the style alone as a picture by Watteau or Monticelli." Herman Klein, long-time music critic for the *Sunday Times,* knew D'Oyly Carte from his Comedy Opera Company days in 1877. His appraisal of Carte's importance in the triumvirate with Gilbert and Sullivan was unequivocally admiring. "I was in a position to appreciate from actual observation the valuable work he had accomplished in—what shall I say?—not 'exploiting' but in consolidating, assimilating, and reinforcing the united labours of his gifted collaborators. For they were, these three men, a truly interdependent trio. The work of each was essential to the other. If it was Gilbert and Sullivan who supplied the incomparable 'bricks and mortar,' the substance and form of the amazing structure, then it was D'Oyly Carte who furnished the finished product with living shape and colour, who set it before the world with taste and elegance to the greatest benefit of all concerned."

In *Punch* appeared repeated praise for those attributes of Gilbert and Sullivan operas that could be most readily ascribed to D'Oyly Carte rather than to Gilbert. The production values, *mise en scène,* costumes, the perfection guaranteed by long and expensive weeks of rehearsal—all were often lauded by *Punch* while the author was being accused of plagiarism, or simply of not having written a good enough libretto. At the outset of his career Gilbert had thrown in with *Punch*'s rival comic weekly, *Fun,* so there was little reason in those days for it to be pro-Gilbert. But Francis Burnand, Sullivan's comic-opera collaborator before Gilbert, was on the staff of *Punch* and later became its head. *Unhappy Thought*: It has always seemed to me that Burnand's envy of Gilbert at the height of the latter's career was a permeating influence of *Punch*'s anti-Gilbert policy from which D'Oyly Carte benefited. Showing between the lines

of these jibes was a suggestion of "There but for the grace of God is any other competent librettist, perhaps Frank Burnand." His one chance to prove this, came with the ill-fated production of *The Chieftain* (Burnand-Sullivan) in December 1894. It was a warmed-over rewrite of their twenty-seven-year-old *Contrabandista,* far too late for both of them.

D'Oyly Carte was an innovator of courage and imagination. It was he who first lighted a theatre entirely by electricity. He is credited with having started the queue system for London theatres. He was in the forefront of managers who abolished the tipping nuisance. He first conceived the idea of printing a sectional seating-plan on the stub of each Savoy ticket, with the specific location of that particular seat clearly indicated—just as is now printed on the stubs of most outdoor sports arenas. His sense of publicity and promotion was astute yet in impeccable taste, and D'Oyly Carte theatres and companies were never the hub of business or personal scandals. Richard D'Oyly Carte was a great showman and a great businessman.

THE COLLABORATION

"THE FIRST BLOSSOM on an immortal tree, *Thespis, or The Gods Grown Old . . .* is all but completely forgotten," began the London *Times* in its panoramic appraisal of Gilbert's collaboration with Sullivan. "Its successor, *Trial by Jury . . .* is one of the most characteristic things we possess. Its lightning sarcasm, the extraordinary freedom and finesse of its versification, the choice of our legal procedure as a mark for the author's satire, and the exquisite absurdity of the whole treatment make it only describable by the word that has enriched our language for the purpose: 'Gilbertian.'

"In 1877 Mr. D'Oyly Carte produced *The Sorcerer* at the Opéra Comique; some six months later came *H.M.S. Pinafore* at the same theatre, and its two years' run established the fortunes of the most extraordinary combination of talent that English opera, that any opera, serious or comic, has ever seen. The most extraordinary combination; there have been greater writers, though possibly none more individual, than Gilbert, and greater musicians than Sir Arthur Sullivan; there has never been regular collaboration between a poet and musician who could play so unerringly into each other's hands. The 'lyrics,' unlike those of our later librettists, were always written first, and the music fitted to them afterwards . . . but it may be questioned whether any composer but Sir Arthur Sullivan could have fitted it so well. He had a fertility, an ease, a melody which matched those of Gilbert. He had, too, a musical humour of his own that could reinforce Gilbert's poetical humour, could actually

D'Oyly Carte cartoon from THE FIGARO.

increase its effect, without ever straining or superseding it, and a musical pathos, if the phrase may be allowed, which exactly hit the tone of the rare but beautiful elegiac or love songs. If [they] give exquisite pleasure in themselves, they give still more when heard or remembered to the music from which it is now almost impossible to dissociate them."

The Gilbert and Sullivan method of collaboration appears to have followed the following pattern: First the author described to the composer his idea for a plot, or he read him a plot outline. Then, if Sullivan responded with enthusiasm, Gilbert wrote out a complete story-line, without dialog and without lyrics. (That of *Utopia Limited* is thirty-six pages long.) Next, working painstakingly through trial and error on scores of copybook pages, he roughed out his libretto, including the lyrics, which he sent to Sullivan for setting as fast as they were finished. Sequence was of no concern to either collaborator.

In Gilbert's own words, when interviewed by William Archer:

"The verse always preceded the music, or even any hint of it. Sometimes—very rarely—Sullivan would say of some song I had given him, 'My dear fellow, I can't make anything of this'—and then I would rewrite it entirely—never tinker at it. But, of course, I don't mean to say that I 'invented' all the rhythms and stanzas in the operas. Often a rhythm would be suggested by some old tune or other running in my head, and I would fit my words to it more or less exactly. When Sullivan knew I had done so, he would say, 'Don't tell me what the tune is, or I shan't be able to get it out of my head.'"

It was Gilbert's habit to work at night, a detail he recorded with dry humor in a letter to Frank Holl, R.A., in November 1886, when that eminent artist was—on Lucy Gilbert's instigation—commissioned to paint his portrait. Holl evidently had suggested that Gilbert be painted in the clothes he normally wore while writing. The author replied: "My usual writing dress would hardly do for exhibition—consisting, as it does, of a nightshirt & dressing gown—for I only write after 11 P.M. when everyone has gone to bed."

In an age of cheap labor and before the perfection of the typewriter, Gilbert had found early in his career that librettos "printed as manuscript" more readily won favor with managers, were easier for him to work with while making daily changes, and were clearer and more accurate than copyists' drafts for use at rehearsal. So, as soon as he completed a manuscript libretto, it was invariably set in type. From then on, author's alterations involved endless resetting. In other words there were many different proof-copies pulled by the printer for the author's and company's use before eventual publication day. But the fact that I have seen only one such prepublication proof-copy of a Gilbert and Sullivan libretto outside of the files of the D'Oyly Carte Opera Company (and, of course, the Lord Chamberlain's vault) is testimony to the rigid discipline that must have controlled their return by cast members and by the press. In fact, the late Miss Nancy McIntosh—Gilbert's adopted daughter, who generously gave me her treasured manuscript notebook of his *Utopia* (*Limited*) story-line—told me that he never kept any of his preliminary material once a new production was launched. Except for his early trial jottings preserved in a number of copybooks, his own archive, now in the British Museum, does not contain prepublication proof-copies or in most instances even the earliest issues of first editions of his opera li-

THE FIRST RUNS

Thespis	December 26, 1871,	to March	8, 1872	64 performances
Trial by Jury	March 25, 1875,	to December	18, 1875	175 performances*
The Sorcerer	November 17, 1877,	to May	22, 1878	175 performances
H.M.S. Pinafore	May 25, 1878,	to March	20, 1880	700 performances
Pirates of Penzance				
PAIGNTON	December 30, 1879			1 performance
NEW YORK	December 31, 1879,	to June	5, 1880	100 performances*
LONDON	April 3, 1880,	to April	2, 1881	363 performances
Patience	April 23, 1881,	to November	22, 1882	578 performances
Iolanthe	November 25, 1882,	to January	1, 1884	398 performances
Princess Ida	January 5, 1884,	to October	9, 1884	246 performances
Mikado	March 14, 1885,	to January	19, 1887	672 performances
Ruddygore	January 22, 1887,	to November	5, 1887	288 performances
Yeomen of the Guard	October 3, 1888,	to November	30, 1889	423 performances
Gondoliers	December 7, 1889,	to June	20, 1891	554 performances
Utopia (*Limited*)	October 7, 1893,	to June	9, 1894	245 performances
The Grand Duke	March 7, 1896,	to July	10, 1896	123 performances

* Not consecutive

brettos. Most of his personal copies of the operas are later issues or editions in which he has made manuscript revisions for revivals in the '90's and early 1900's that have become the texts of still later printings.

Although fundamentally we must concentrate more on the author than on the composer (because this edition cannot include the scores), the importance of Arthur Sullivan to the development of the operas, from his first contact with Gilbert's germinal plot, cannot be underestimated. The Sullivan method he described in detail to his friend and first biographer, Arthur Lawrence. It appeared to begin at the point that Gilbert's lyrics arrived, one by one.

"The first thing I have to decide upon is the rhythm," Sullivan said, "and I arrange the rhythm before I come to the question of melody." He then illustrated for Lawrence a number of possible rhythmic patterns for one well-known lyric. "You see that five out of six methods were commonplace," he continued, "and my first aim has always been to get as much originality as possible in the rhythm, approaching the question of melody afterwards. . . . It is only after I have decided the rhythm that I proceed to the notation.

"My first work—the jotting down of the melo-

dies—I term 'sketches.' They are hieroglyphics which, possibly, would seem undecipherable. It is my musical shorthand, and, of course, it means much to me. When I have finished these sketches the creative part of my work is completed." This meant, Sullivan explained, the writing, rewriting, and alterations of every description. The work was then "drawn out in so-called 'skeleton score,' that is, with all the vocal parts, rests for symphonies, &c., completed, but without a note of accompaniment or instrumental work of any kind, although naturally I have all that in mind. Then the voice parts are written out by the copyist, and the rehearsals begin. . . . It is not until the music has been thoroughly learnt, and the rehearsals on the stage with the necessary action and 'business' are well advanced, that I begin orchestration."

THE FIRST-NIGHT TEXTS

IT MIGHT SEEM AMAZING that so relatively few people are familiar with the first-night texts of the Gilbert and Sullivan operas, until one considers several excellent explanations. Their first published appearances are all scarce, and some by any standard are even rare. At this writing I know of no other complete sets of Gilbert and Sullivan first issues except those collected by me and by my friend, the late bibliographic scholar, Carroll A. Wilson. Secondly, there has never been an adequate bibliography from which one could, with certainty, identify the true first issues. The late Townley Searle published a bibliography in 1931, but even then it was unreliable; now it is confusing and out-of-date. Thirdly, until this edition of the operas, it has never been clear that the texts as first published were, indeed, the texts of the first-night performances (excluding, as we shall see, the more complicated *Pirates of Penzance*). So it naturally follows that, as these original first-night texts have never before been properly identified, they have certainly never before been collected and published in one volume.

As our concern in this edition is to present the texts as actually performed on the first nights, we are fortunately relieved of the complex considerations educed by prepublication librettos. Gilbert all too frequently made important changes at the last moment, rewrote or excised complete lyrics within a day or two of first-night curtain-time. His nimble publishers could evidently keep up with him on twenty-four hours' notice. But for our purposes these changes of creative fancy, however fascinating, are like authors' manuscript drafts and never of first-night textual significance. What! Never? Well, hardly ever!—as you will see. There was one exception, *The Pirates of Penzance,* which alone of all the operas had its first public run in America and had no published libretto for many months thereafter. So its first-night text was, of necessity, a prepublication text and differed considerably from the first published version.

The first American librettos of other Gilbert and Sullivan operas after *The Pirates of Penzance* (whether pirated or authorized) were textually at least as early as the London first-night librettos, and in some instances were based on even earlier Gilbert drafts. This is readily understood when one recognizes that a transatlantic crossing for the manuscript took ten or twelve days, the American printer required time for setting and his or Carte's lawyer time for copyright registry, and the American company at least a couple of weeks for rehearsal, if the first New World performance was to follow closely the London première. So it is not improbable that the manuscript for the first American libretto was a month earlier than Chappell & Company's final proofs—and in a month's time during rehearsals Gilbert could do an amazing amount of rewriting. Thus, the earliest American printing of *Patience, Princess Ida, The Gondoliers, Utopia* (*Limited*), and *The Grand Duke* discloses material that never appeared in published British librettos, showing clearly their origin in Gilbert's prepublication manuscript proofs.

That published librettos were available and important to the first-nighters of all fourteen operas except *The Pirates of Penzance* is evident from press commentary. Neither gaslighting nor the pioneer electric lighting permitted dimming down the house-lights completely as they are today. During performance there was always sufficient light for reading; so the Gilbert and Sullivan faithful followed their librettos assiduously, even noisily. "Throughout the opera, the audience is nose-deep in the book; and the music is interrupted with a periodic hiss of printed leaves," was the way the reviewer for the *Illustrated London News* described this phenomenon at the *Ruddygore* première. First-night critics frequently quoted entire verses of lyrics—from their librettos, not from memory.

In fact it was their predilection for quoting lyrics, or at least mentioning them by their first lines, that has enabled me to state with certainty that songs which have hitherto either been overlooked altogether or assumed cut out at final rehearsal, were actually sung in the first-night performances. For example, you will have the advantage over the Savoy first-nighters at *Utopia* (*Limited*), for your text herein contains Princess Zara's solo—"Youth is a boon avowed"—which the press recorded was sung by Miss McIntosh that night, but which did not appear in the published libretto. This is the only instance in which I have added to the published text of a first performance.

The actual texts I have used are those from librettos in my own collection now in the Pierpont Morgan Library in New York. I have endeavored to correct all typographic and metrical errors that are clearly due to careless proofreading; but I have not incorporated in these texts any of the later improvements, however obvious, found in subsequent editions. Therefore, these texts cannot be used for identification of first-edition bibliographic minutiae, nor do they pretend to be facsimiles of the original librettos. For example, the Dramatis Personae pages of both *Pinafore* and *Patience* in the actual first-edition librettos omit the names of cast. In this edition I have included these names to be consistent with the other twelve operas and for the convenience of the reader.

POSTSCRIPT

THIS IS NOT A BIBLIOGRAPHY. But I have assumed that, with respect to the lyrics, interested readers will wish to correlate these first-night texts with those of standard current usage, particularly for following disc or tape recordings of the operas, or their radio and television performances. For this reason each first-night text is followed by a

DAYS WITH CELEBRITIES. (77.)
MR. W. S. GILBERT.

DAYS WITH CELEBRITIES. (71.)
DR. SULLIVAN.

Postscript, a capsule comparison to the text in most recent librettos. It would require the scope of a variorum edition to apply these *Postscript* references to dialog as well as lyrics; so for the most part, dialog changes have been ignored. And even in the area of lyrics many small alterations are not noted. On the other hand, whenever the changes in a rewritten verse seem too complex for easily followed description, you will find the entire revised verse requoted. In a few instances I have yielded to the blandishments of Gilbert's wit and included in its appropriate *Postscript* a lyric from an early draft which was neither published in the libretto nor sung in the first-night performance.

In the case of *Trial by Jury,* as there is no spoken dialog, I have treated the text as though it were one long lyric. Thus its *Postscript* provides in detail the changes between the first night's performance and what one might hear today. *The Pirates of Penzance,* for reasons already mentioned, will be found to differ in many more respects than the few changes that I have described. You will wonder about those extra "tarantara's" in the Policemen's Song and about numerous other points of difference between this synthesized first-night text and the libretto you are accustomed to hear. The latter-day texts of *The Sorcerer, Patience,* and *Iolanthe* are readily extracted from the first-night libretto by indicated eliminations or replacements. *Pinafore* and *Princess Ida* have survived the years with negligible alterations—as, of course, has *Thespis* by the dubious expedient of not having survived at all as living theatre. Important transpositions will be noted as the chief distinction of *The Mikado* in its revised form, but there is also a different finale involving a familiar reprise. *Ruaaigore* of today, as opposed to *Ruddygore* of the première, has monumental changes in dialog in the second act, but as we are ignoring dialog variations we can fortunately by-pass these. On the other hand both *The Yeomen of the Guard* and *The Gondoliers* are exactly the reverse; both have suffered relatively few dialog changes but

many revisions in lyrics. So the *Postscript* for each of these involves greater detail. For *Utopia (Limited)* and *The Grand Duke*—both never revived and not yet recorded by a professional company —there is no current reference point. *Utopia* in later editions of the libretto was given a different finale, which I have included in its *Postscript. The Grand Duke*'s many cuts and omissions between first-night and second-edition texts receive only brief mention, but sufficient to show where a reader may expect to find the major points of difference.

* * *

IT IS INTERESTING that *Punch* chose not a world première of a new opera, but the first full-fledged Gilbert and Sullivan revival—in November 1884 —as the occasion for the following unusually friendly and perceiving comment:

It is difficult to classify these Gilbert-Sullivan Operas. They are not, strictly speaking, Comic Operas, they are not operettas, they are not exactly German Reed Entertainment, nor Extravaganzas, nor Burlesques. Yet they contain something of all of these. What are they? They are perfectly original, and Messrs. Gilbert and Sullivan have founded a school of their own. "Once upon a time" Messrs. Bunn and Balfe were the chief Professors of a style of entertainment called "Ballad Operas." Now, as the plots of *The Sorcerer, Pinafore, Patience,* and *Pirates,* remind me of the grotesque humour of the *Bab Ballads,* I should suggest that the Gilbert-Sullivan series should be known as "The Bab Ballad Operas." . . .

Their union is their strength, yet if truth be told . . . so absolutely does the Gilbertian humour in these Bab-Ballad Operas depend upon the masterly Sullivanian illustrations, that it would be true for their worshippers . . . without irreverence, or disrespect to the religion of Islam, to exclaim,

"There is one Gilbert, and Sullivan is his profit!"

Advertisement for first G. & S. first night, in THE TIMES *of London, December 26, 1871.*

CURTAIN GOING UP!

THESPIS

Introduction

THE FIRST NIGHT of Gilbert and Sullivan first nights had probably the largest audience of them all. But then, the Gaiety, with a capacity of over fifteen hundred, was the largest of the five theatres to house Gilbert and Sullivan premières. The lead-sentence of the London *Times* review carried the success story: "This theatre enjoyed a share of public patronage which was not to be measured by the actual numbers present, for the fortunate seatholders who had engaged their places beforehand met, as they mounted the stairs on their entrance, a descending crowd, hardly less numerous, composed of the disappointed, for whom there was not even standing room in any part of the house."

It was properly topsy-turvy and Gilbertian that the debut of the most successful partnership in the history of the stage took place to STANDING ROOM ONLY, in a larger than average theatre, and with a better than average press, for a run of sixty-four performances—only to be forgotten almost immediately thereafter by most followers of the theatre, its score never published and lost forever. Such an ingenious paradox is the short life-story of *Thespis: or, The Gods Grown Old,* the first collaboration of Gilbert and Sullivan.

One understands and excuses more readily the frequent blunder of a legion of books and articles on the Gilbert and Sullivan operas in naming *Trial by Jury* as the starting-point of the collaboration, and thirteen the total number of their joint works. Only six years after the final curtain had been rung down for all time on *Thespis,* the critic for the London *Globe* in his review of the first night of *Pinafore* wrote: "This is the third work by the same authors, and in many of its features it bears resemblance to *Trial by Jury* and *The Sorcerer.*"

The common ingredient of the theatrical be-

ginnings of both Gilbert and Sullivan had been impresario German Reed. As lessee of St. George's Hall in December 1867, he had commissioned composer Sullivan's first two-act comic opera, *The Contrabandista,* with libretto by Frank Burnand, with whom Sullivan had collaborated a year and a half earlier in a highly successful trifle, *Cox and Box.* As proprietor of the Royal Gallery of Illustration in March of 1869 he had produced author Gilbert's "Entirely New Entertainment," *No Cards,* appropriately sharing the program with *Cox and Box,* and had thereby become, unwittingly, the first manager to have the names of Gilbert and Sullivan on the same playbill.

In November of that year German Reed had induced Gilbert to collaborate with composer Fred Clay, close friend of Arthur Sullivan, in *Ages Ago,* a one-act opera that was to provide the germ of *Ruddygore* some seventeen years later. It was Clay who has been credited with introducing Mr. Gilbert to Mr. Sullivan, a portentous meeting that took place in 1869 at a rehearsal of *Ages Ago.* Sullivan told Arthur Lawrence: "I was introduced to him [Gilbert] by Frederic Clay at one of the

German Reed entertainments. Of course he had done a good deal of work, and I knew him by name very well before that occasion." Shortly thereafter, Reed wrote to Sullivan: "Gilbert is doing a comic one-act entertainment for me—soprano-contralto-tenor-baritone and bass. Would you like to compose the music? Reply at once, as I want to get the piece going without loss of time." But this deal was never consummated; it was left for another to be the producer of the first Gilbert and Sullivan opera. That other was John Hollingshead.

The Gaiety Theatre, with front entrance in the Strand and stage entrance round the corner on Wellington Street, near the Lyceum, had been built and opened by John Hollingshead in December 1868, with a triple bill that featured Gilbert's "Original Operatic Extravaganza," *Robert the Devil*. The following year he produced the same author's first "Original Comedy-Drama," *An Old Score*. So the house of Hollingshead was neither inappropriate nor unlikely for a Gilbert and Sullivan collaboration. There was even an obscure tie between the Gaiety's staff and Sullivan's professional circle at that time. One Mr. J. Pittman, listed as in charge of chorus and vocal music at the Gaiety, was the same Josiah Pittman who at that period had been co-editor with Sullivan in some twenty-six of *Boosey's Standard Operas,* an early potboiler activity that had given the twenty-nine-year-old composer the operatic background for his genius at musical parody.

For Hollingshead the business arrangements with Gilbert and Sullivan had certainly begun well before October 30, 1871, on which date Gilbert's literary agent, Edward English, wrote a letter to manager R. M. Field, of the Boston Museum Theatre, containing the following earliest mention of their first collaboration: "At Xmas will be produced at the Gaiety Theatre, a new and original Opera Bouffe in English, by W. S. Gilbert, Esq., & Arthur Sullivan, Esq. does the new music. It is expected to be a *Big Thing*—and the purport of my present letter to you is—first—to send you (this day) rough sketch of the piece *for your own reading,* and secondly to ask you—if you care and will cause the piece to be rightly protected—with a view to sale in all places possible in the United States. . . . Messrs. G. & S. are now hard at work on said piece."

Gilbert recalled of *Thespis,* in his autobiographic contribution to the *Theatre* in April 1883, that "it was put together in less than three weeks, and was produced at the Gaiety Theatre after a week's rehearsal." Almost twenty years later, in 1902, he wrote to a friend: "The piece was produced under stress of tremendous hurry. It was invented, written, composed, rehearsed, and pro-

duced within five weeks." Manager Field's correspondence file in the Harvard Theatre Collection shows that Gilbert was inaccurate, at least to the extent that these four or five weeks of *Thespis* preparation were not consecutive. Although Field was sent a "rough sketch" as early as October 30, agent English was still promising "will send you the M.S. of 'Gilbert & Sullivan' piece as soon as I get it" as late as December 12. It was not until December 28, two days after the first night, that English wrote Field, "Enclosed I send you assignment of piece by Gilbert and Sullivan. It is called here at the Gaiety *Thespis*. I have been expecting the M.S. as per Mr. Gilbert's promise for some days past. Instant I get it, will forward to you . . ."

But at the top of the first text-page of the *Thespis* libretto was printed: "Caution to American Pirates.—The Copyright of the Dialogue and Music of this Piece, for the United States and Canada, has been assigned to Mr. Field, of the Boston Museum, by agreement, dated 7th December, 1871." Agent English's two letters of transmission are clear that it was the assignment of the American rights to *Pygmalion and Galatea,* that was mailed to Field on that date (Gilbert's extremely successful Mythological Comedy was to open at the Haymarket Theatre in two days, December 9), and that the assignment of *Thespis* was not sent to Field till three weeks later. During this pre-Christmas period there seems no doubt the libretto of *Thespis* was published and circulated. Its content of Christmas seasonal advertising would testify to this, as well as evidence that it was certainly in the audience's hands the night of the 26th. (Where else could the *Daily News* reviewer have found the four-verse lyric that he quoted?) Yet as late as the 28th, agent English wrote he still did not have the "M.S." to send Field.

These contradictions add up to only one conclusion: Gilbert must have changed his mind at some time during November and must have decided to hedge on tying up *Thespis* with Field. Yet he must have wished to give the appearance of having some protection of his American rights in the work while he held back or negotiated with others: hence the bogus notice of American rights in a printed libretto that could perfectly well have been sent to Field, in lieu of manuscript, days, if not a couple of weeks, before December 26.

It is more than coincidence that Gilbert had both his mythological brain-children gestating simultaneously—*Pygmalion and Galatea* and *Thespis*—and it is entirely probable that intimate classical preoccupation with the *agora* of one led him to the Olympus of the other. His "tremendous hurry" in putting together *Thespis* as a finished two-act opera was no exaggeration; it was, in fact, amply sustained by Hollingshead's remark in

Gaiety Chronicles that his leading comedian, J. L. Toole, "returned again [i.e. to London] December 18, 1871, appearing in some of the old pieces while the operatic extravaganza of *Thespis* was being rehearsed." This gave Gilbert exactly the one week's rehearsal he had recollected. How different were to be the atmosphere and working conditions that he, Sullivan, and D'Oyly Carte were to evolve in less than a decade . . . and how different the result!

A full-page illustration purporting to be one of those rare rehearsals of *Thespis* was used by Hollingshead in *Gaiety Chronicles* in 1898, after twenty-six years had dulled his memory. He did not identify its source, but he did identify himself, Gilbert, and stage-manager Robert Soutar (who played Tipseion in *Thespis*) in the background. The original of this drawing actually had nothing whatsoever to do with *Thespis,* and the presence of Gilbert, Soutar, and himself betrayed Hollingshead into giving it a false significance. The original, entitled "The New Burlesque—An Un-

dress Rehearsal," was drawn by Gordon Thomson for the Christmas Number of the *Graphic,* which —though dated December 25, 1871—was published at least two or three weeks ahead of that date (as was, and is, the practice with such special issues) and therefore well in advance of the first *Thespis* rehearsal. Artist Thomson made no mention of the Gaiety or of *Thespis,* either in his title or in the accompanying article. The seasonal appropriateness of this as a subject was probably to suggest the unprepossessing larval state of that spectacularly beautiful butterfly, the London Christmas pantomime. If the artist happened to have been a Gaiety habitué, the drawing could have been done from memory. The inclusion of those particular three recognizable theatrical figures certainly provided a clue to the theatre in mind; but a maiden in chains, a knight errant, and a fearsome dragon cannot be found to suit the casting of any piece at the Gaiety during the whole month of December 1871, and is particularly inappropriate to *Thespis.* The rehearsal scene as illustrated may

"The New Burlesque"—an 1871 rehearsal scene; Hollingshead and Gilbert (with sideburns) at left.

Interior of the Gaiety Theatre at the time of its opening, three years before THESPIS.

never have taken place anywhere except in the artist's eye—a burlesque version of the St. George-and-the-dragon theme.

December 26—Boxing Night—at the Gaiety was neither the ideal time nor place for a Gilbert and Sullivan opera. The Gaiety was known chiefly as a burlesque house, and the Boxing Night audience that crammed its every available space was out for a good time, the less subtle the better. (Even so the *Morning Advertiser* commented that the reputation of composer and author had helped pack the theatre.) The *Times* reviewer noted, "The dialogue throughout is superior in ability and point to that with which ordinary burlesque and extravaganza have familiarized us; so much so, in fact, that it was a daring experiment to produce such a piece on such a night. It met, however, with an excellent reception, and on any other

occasion than Boxing Night the numerous merits of the piece cannot fail to secure for it in the public estimation a high place among the novelties of the season." The critic continued, "In honour of the occasion Mr. Sullivan conducted the orchestra in person, and was warmly applauded on taking his seat for that purpose." This Gaiety program, undiscovered till 1960, contains identifying data not found in any later *Thespis* program. It notes the performance as "First Time," that Arthur Sullivan conducted, that *Dearer than Life* was brother Fred's London stage debut, and it adds to the D.P. the short-lived role of Venus played by Miss Jolly.

The bill that night commenced at seven o'clock with a three-act drama by H. J. Byron, *Dearer than Life,* of course starring Johnnie Toole. The carriage-call, noted in the program, was for eleven.

The ghastly fact that the second act of *Thespis* was still playing at midnight was obvious—and, it must be admitted, even justified—grounds for a mixed audience reaction. The *Morning Advertiser,* representing the opposition, described the experience as "a dreary, tedious two-act rigmarole of a plot . . . grotesque without wit, and the music thin without liveliness . . . however, not entirely devoid of melody. . . . The curtain falls before a yawning and weary audience."

The *Daily Telegraph,* in a long and favorable account of the proceedings, made it clear that the show was better than it seemed as played that night to that particular audience:

> Possibly a holiday audience is disinclined to dive into the mysteries of heathen mythology, and does not care to exercise the requisite intellect to unravel an amusing, and by no means intricate, plot. . . . Certain it is, however, that the greeting which awaited *Thespis, or The Gods Grown Old,* was not so cordial as might have been expected. The story, written by Mr. W. S. Gilbert in his liveliest manner, is so original, and the music contributed by Mr. Arthur Sullivan so pretty and fascinating, that we are inclined to be disappointed when we find the applause but fitful, the laughter scarcely spontaneous, and the curtain falling not without sounds of disapprobation. Such a fate as this was certainly not deserved, and the verdict of last evening cannot be taken as final. *Thespis* is too good to be put on one side and cold-shouldered in this fashion: and we anticipate that judicious curtailment and constant rehearsal will enable us shortly to tell a very different tale.

The *Standard*'s review praised Hollingshead for judiciously calling on Gilbert to furnish him with an original opera-extravaganza and entrusting its musical setting to Arthur Sullivan. "From the association of these two names the most pleasing result has for some weeks past been anticipated, which the success of last evening fully justified." The *Standard* then obscured in words, as though it were a virtue, what was to be one of the most sensitive points of Gilbert and Sullivan association for the next twenty-five years: "Mr. Gilbert in *Thespis* has happily [sic] provided the composer with everything he could desire, mastering the character of opera-extravaganza, which precludes the exercise of the highest flights of genius of which a musician is capable, and sets a limit to the exercise of his talents."

The *Daily Telegraph* described Sullivan as having "not marred the effect by ambitious music." And then this critic went on to describe his detailed reaction to music that can never again be heard: "Tuneful throughout, always pretty, frequently suggestive, the songs and dances are quite

in character with the author's design." And he prophesied:

> Some of the numbers will certainly live, and the impression caused by the music as a whole is that it will have far more than a passing interest. For instance, the quaint lyric sung by Miss Farren, "Oh! I'm the Olympian drudge," is suited with a very pretty minor tune, extremely taking. The song was deservedly encored. With the public no doubt the musical gem will be a ballad called "Cousin Robin"—pathetic and tender words, with a dreamy and somewhat Gounodish air. So sweetly was this sung by Mdlle. Clary that another encore was inevitable. [This, in fact, was the only surviving number from *Thespis,* published in late 1872 by J. B. Cramer & Co. as "Little Maid of Arcadee."] . . . A ludicrous ballad for Mr. Toole, commencing, "I once knew a chap who discharged a function on the North-South-Eastern-Diddlesex Junction" [sic], is quite in the spirit of the well-known compositions of "Bab," and, as it has been fitted with a lively tune and a rattling chorus, a hearty encore was inevitable. Though the ditty was long, the audience would have been well content to hear it all over again.

From *Punch*'s account it would seem that Toole obliged with a one-verse encore. The accompaniment "consisted of railway noises."

> Musicians will not improbably turn with more affection [continued the *Daily Telegraph*] to Mr. J. G. Taylor's song at the commencement of the second act—"What is the use of being Gods?" a very pretty and refined air—to the dance tunes, the waltz, and some of the concerted music in the last act. The acting, except for the tardy taking up of points . . . is scarcely less commendable than the libretto and the music. . . . Had the audience not been wearied towards the close, greater attention would have been paid to the eccentric fooling of our popular comedian Mr. Toole when trying to pooh-pooh the ugly truth contained in the petitions from earth. With Mdlle. Clary, Miss Constance Loseby, and Miss Tremaine to sing, with Miss Farren to bring with her the familiar spriteliness and fun as Mercury, with Miss L. Wilson and Miss Rose Behrend to fascinate the susceptible portion of the audience, and with such clever supports as Mr. Maclean, Mr. J. G. Taylor, and Mr. Robert Soutar [he might also have mentioned Arthur Sullivan's brother Frederic, in the role of Apollo], there is surely sufficient acting material for justice eventually to be done to *Thespis* and to make a struggle to obtain a better-tempered and less sleepy audience than that of last evening.

Only this once, in Gilbert and Sullivan productions, did a woman take a man's role. (There were American and German productions later in which Ralph Rackstraw and Nanki-Poo were played by women, but these were beyond the jurisdictional lightnings of the author.) In *Thespis* little Nelly Farren, famed for her vivacious personality and for her beautiful legs, was cast as Mercury and she wore a tight-fitting silver costume which displayed these latter attributes to advantage. (The illustration on page 10 shows Nelly, not in her Mercury costume but, as Aladdin, on Christmas eve, 1881.) When Hollingshead first signed her as a member of the Gaiety company he remarked, "I had secured my priceless burlesque boy, my equally priceless chambermaid, in the person of Miss Ellen Farren." She was in private life the wife of stage-manager Robert Soutar, but to her producer-employer "she was the brightest boy-girl or girl-boy that ever graced the stage." But he said of her voice: "Neither Mr. J. L. Toole nor Miss Nelly Farren could be called 'singers' even in the most elastic English."

No vocal score of *Thespis* was ever published, and the manuscript score and parts that existed as late as mid-1879 (on the evidence of a letter from Sullivan to Hollingshead) have long since disappeared. When asked in later years why the *Thespis* music was never published, Sullivan answered with a laugh that he had saved up its tunes for other operas. An example was the transfer of both words and music of the entrance chorus of Thespis' company—"Climbing over rocky mountain"—to the first act of *The Pirates of Penzance;* and from its rhythmic structure it seems certain that the musical setting for the chorus (page 134):

> Here's a pretty tale for future Iliads and
>   Odysseys,
> Mortals are about to personate the gods and
>   goddesses

was appropriated for the original finale to the second act of the same opera:

> At length we are provided, with unusual fa-
>   cility,
> To change piratic crime for dignified respect-
>   ability.

The music to this *Pirates* castoff has also been lost.

The *Daily News,* in a brief notice, held that "the burlesque on the whole was fairly successful and will doubtless amuse the public for some time to come." The *Observer* felt that Gilbert and Sullivan had "attempted, with not a little success, to imitate French comic opera. . . . It is not disagreeable to find we have authors and musicians as delightful as our neighbours." And the *Times'* closing comment was, "The piece, as a whole, deserves high praise."

But there is no question, the lack of adequate preparation was the main flaw in that long-drawn-out first performance. Gilbert was never again to let himself be at this disadvantage. The production credo for his thirteen subsequent collaborations with Sullivan was to be thoroughness of preparation regardless of cost—and in D'Oyly Carte he was to find a business partner who required the same high standards—with the result that repeatedly a first-night press comment of a Gilbert and Sullivan opera was that it went as smoothly as though it had been the hundredth performance. Not so, however, on that Tuesday evening, December 26, 1871.

> That the grotesque opera was sufficiently rehearsed cannot be allowed [remarked the *Daily Telegraph*'s critic, who had obviously enjoyed the performance and stayed to the bitter end], and to this cause must be ascribed the frequent waits, the dragging effect, and the indisposition to take up points which, recurring so frequently, nullified the pleasant effect of Mr. Sullivan's music and destroyed the pungency of Mr. Gilbert's humour. . . . It is more satisfactory for many reasons to look upon the performance last evening as a full-dress rehearsal, and to look forward to brighter days ahead for *Thespis.* There are audiences in the future who will cheerfully take another and more favourable view of the piece. A story so pointed and happy, music so satisfactory and refined, a spectacle so beautiful and artists so clever deserve a better reward than a curtain falling in silence and in the absence of those familiar calls and greetings which are so pleasant. It must be remembered that it was past midnight when the curtain descended, and the audience was in a fidgety state to get away. When *Thespis* ends at the orthodox Gaiety closing hour, and the opera has been energetically rehearsed, few happier entertainments will be found.

I have rarely seen anything so beautifully put upon the stage. The first night I had a great reception, but the music went badly, and the singer sang half a tone sharp, so that the enthusiasm of the audience did not sustain itself towards me. Last night I cut out the song, the music went very well, and consequently I had a hearty call before the curtain at the end of Act II.

FROM ARTHUR SULLIVAN'S LETTER TO HIS
MOTHER, 28TH DECEMBER, 1871.

An Entirely Original Grotesque Opera,

IN TWO ACTS,

THESPIS

OR,

THE GODS GROWN OLD.

Dramatis Personae.

GODS.

JUPITER		MR. JOHN MACLEAN.
APOLLO		MR. F. SULLIVAN.
MARS	*Aged Deities*	MR. WOOD.
DIANA		MRS. H. LEIGH.
MERCURY		MISS E. FARREN.

THESPIANS.

THESPIS	MR. J. L. TOOLE.
SILLIMON	MR. J. G. TAYLOR.
TIMIDON	MR. MARSHALL.
TIPSEION	MR. ROBERT SOUTAR.
PREPOSTEROS	MR. H. PAYNE.
STUPIDAS	MR. F. PAYNE.
SPARKEION	MDLLE. CLARY.
NICEMIS	MISS CONSTANCE LOSEBY.
PRETTEIA	MISS BEREND.
DAPHNE	MISS ANNIE TREMAINE.
CYMON	MISS L. WILSON.

ACT I. — Ruined Temple on the Summit of Olympus.

ACT II. — The same Scene, with the Ruins Restored.

THESPIS

OR,

THE GODS GROWN OLD.

ACT I.

SCENE. — *The ruins of The Temple of the Gods on summit of Mount Olympus. Picturesque shattered columns, overgrown with ivy, with entrances to temple (ruined). Fallen columns on the stage. Three broken pillars. At the back of stage is the approach from the summit of the mountain. In the distance are the summits of adjacent mountains. At first all this is concealed by a thick fog, which clears presently.*

Enter (through fog) Chorus of Stars, coming off duty, as fatigued with their night's work.

CHORUS OF STARS.

Throughout the night,
　The constellations
Have given light
　From various stations.
When midnight gloom
　Falls on all nations,
We will resume
　Our occupations.

SOLO.

Our light, it's true,
　Is not worth mention,
What can we do
　To gain attention,
When, night and noon,
　With vulgar glaring,
A great big Moon
　Is *always* flaring?

CHORUS.　Throughout the night, &c.

During Chorus enter DIANA, *an elderly Goddess. She is carefully wrapped up in Cloaks, Shawls, etc. A hood is over her head, a respirator in her mouth, and galoshes on her feet. During the chorus she takes these things off, and discovers herself dressed in the usual costume of the Lunar Diana, the Goddess of the Moon.*

DIANA (*shuddering*).　Ugh! How cold the nights are! I don't know how it is, but I seem to feel the night air a great deal more than I used to. But it is time for the sun to be rising. (*Calls.*) Apollo.

APOLLO (*within*).　Hollo!

DIANA.　I've come off duty—it's time for you to be getting up.

Enter APOLLO. *He is an elderly "buck" with an air of assumed juvenility, and is dressed in dressing gown and smoking cap.*

APOLLO (*yawning*).　I shan't go out to-day. I was out yesterday and the day before and I want a little rest. I don't know how it is, but I seem to feel my work a great deal more than I used to.

DIANA.　I'm sure these short days can't hurt you. Why, you don't rise till six and you're in bed again by five: you should have a turn at *my* work and see how you like that—out all night!

APOLLO.　My dear sister, I don't envy you—though I remember when I did—. But that was when I was a younger sun. I don't think I'm quite well. Perhaps a little change of air will do me good. I've a great mind to show myself in London this winter; they'll be very glad to see me. No! I shan't go out to-day. I shall send them this fine thick wholesome fog and they won't miss me. It's the best substitute for a blazing sun—and like most substitutes, nothing at all like the real thing. (*To fog.*) Be off with you.

(*Fog clears away and discovers the scene described.*)

Hurried music. MERCURY *shoots up from behind precipice at back of stage. He carries several parcels afterwards described. He sits down, very much fatigued.*

MERCURY. Home at last! A nice time I've had of it.

DIANA. You young scamp, you've been down all night again. This is the third time you've been out this week.

MERCURY. Well, *you're* a nice one to blow me up for that.

DIANA. *I* can't help being out all night.

MERCURY. And I can't help being down all night. The nature of Mercury requires that he should go down when the sun sets, and rise again, when the sun rises.

DIANA. And what have you been doing?

MERCURY. Stealing on commission. There's a set of false teeth and a box of Life Pills—that's for Jupiter—. An invisible peruke and a bottle of hair dye—that's for Apollo—. A respirator and a pair of galoshes—that's for Cupid—. A full-bottomed chignon, some auricomous fluid, a box of pearl-powder, a pot of rouge, and a hare's foot—that's for Venus.

DIANA. Stealing! you ought to be ashamed of yourself!

MERCURY. Oh, as the god of thieves I must do something to justify my position.

DIANA *and* APOLLO (*contemptuously*). Your position!

MERCURY. Oh I know it's nothing to boast of, even on earth. Up here, it's simply contemptible. Now that you gods are too old for your work, you've made me the miserable drudge of Olympus—groom, valet, postman, butler, commissionaire, maid of all work, parish beadle, and original dustman.

APOLLO. Your Christmas boxes ought to be something considerable.

MERCURY. They ought to be, but they're not. I'm treated abominably. I make everybody and I'm nobody—I go everywhere and I'm nowhere—I do everything and I'm nothing. I've made thunder for Jupiter, odes for Apollo, battles for Mars, and love for Venus. I've married couples for Hymen, and six weeks afterwards, I've divorced them for Cupid—and in return I get all the kicks while they pocket the halfpence. And in compensation for robbing me of the halfpence in question, what have they done for me?

APOLLO. Why they've—ha! ha! they've made you the god of thieves!

MERCURY. Very self-denying of them—there

isn't one of them who hasn't a better claim to the distinction than I have.

SONG — MERCURY.

Oh, I'm the celestial drudge,
    From morning to night I must stop at it,
On errands all day I must trudge,
    And I stick to my work till I drop at it!
In summer I get up at one,
    (As a good-natured donkey I'm ranked for
        it),
Then I go and I light up the Sun,
    And Phœbus Apollo gets thanked for it!
            Well, well, it's the way of the world,
                And will be through all its futurity;
            Though noodles are baroned and
                earled,
                There's nothing for clever ob-
                    scurity!

I'm the slave of the gods, neck and heels,
    And I'm bound to obey, though I rate at 'em;
And I not only order their meals,
    But I cook 'em, and serve 'em, and wait at
        'em.
Then I make all their nectar—I do—
    (Which a terrible liquor to rack us is)
And whenever I mix them a brew,
    Why all the thanksgivings are Bacchus's!
            Well, well, it's the way of the world, &c.

Then reading and writing I teach,
    And spelling books many I've edited!
And for bringing these arts within reach,
    That donkey Minerva gets credited.

Then I scrape at the stars with a knife,
  And plate-powder the moon (on the days for
    it),
And I hear all the world and his wife
  Awarding Diana the praise for it!
    Well, well, it's the way of the world, &c.

*(After song—very loud and majestic music is
heard.)*

DIANA *and* MERCURY *(looking off).* Why, who's
this? Jupiter, by Jove!

Enter JUPITER, *an extremely old man, very decrepit with very thin straggling white beard. He
wears a long braided dressing gown, handsomely
trimmed, and a silk night-cap on his head.* MER-
CURY *falls back respectfully as he enters.*

JUPITER. Good day, Diana—ah, Apollo— Well,
well, well, what's the matter? what's the matter?

DIANA. Why, that young scamp Mercury says
that we do nothing, and leave all the duties of
Olympus to him! Will you believe it, he actually
says that our influence on earth is dropping down
to *nil.*

JUPITER. Well, well—don't be hard on the lad—
to tell you the truth, I'm not sure that he's very far
wrong. Don't let it go any further, but, between
ourselves, the sacrifices and votive offerings have
fallen off terribly of late. Why, I can remember the
time when people offered us human sacrifices—.
No mistake about it—human sacrifices! think of
that!

DIANA. Ah! those good old days!

JUPITER. Then it fell off to oxen, pigs, and sheep.

APOLLO. Well, there are worse things than oxen,
pigs, and sheep!

JUPITER. So I've found to my cost. My dear sir—
between ourselves it's dropped off from one thing
to another until it has positively dwindled down to
preserved Australian beef! What do you think of
that?

APOLLO. I don't like it at all.

JUPITER. You won't mention it—it might go further—

DIANA. It couldn't fare worse.

JUPITER. In short, matters have come to such a
crisis that there's no mistake about it—something
must be done to restore our influence, the only
question is, *What?*

QUARTETTE.

MERCURY *(coming forward in great alarm).*

Enter MARS.

Oh incident unprecedented!
  I hardly can believe it's true!

MARS. Why bless the boy, he's quite demented!
  Why, what's the matter, sir, with
you?

APOLLO. Speak quickly, or you'll get a warning!

MERCURY. Why mortals up the mount are
swarming,
  Our temple on Olympus storming,
    In hundreds—aye in thousands,
too!

ALL.   Goodness gracious,
          How audacious!
          Earth is spacious,
            Why come here?
          Our impeding
          Their proceeding
          Were good breeding,
            That is clear!

DIANA.   Jupiter, hear my plea,
            Upon the mount if *they* light,
          There'll be an end of me,
            I won't be seen by daylight!

APOLLO.   Tartarus is the place
            These scoundrels you should send
to—
          Should they behold my face
            My influence there's an end to!

JUPITER *(looking over precipice).* What fools to
            give themselves so much
              exertion!

DIANA.   " " A government survey, I'll
              make assertion!

APOLLO. " " Perhaps the Alpine club at
              their diversion!

MERCURY. " " They seem to be more like
              a "Cook's Excursion."

ALL.   Goodness gracious, &c.

APOLLO.   If, mighty Jove, you value your exist-
            ence,
          Send them a thunderbolt with your
            regards!

JUPITER. My thunderbolts, though valid at a
            distance,
          Are not effective at a hundred
            yards.

MERCURY. Let the moon's rays, Diana, strike 'em
            flighty,
          Make 'em all lunatics in various
            styles!

DIANA.   My Lunar rays unhappily are mighty
          Only at many hundred thousand
            miles.

ALL.   Goodness gracious, &c.

(*Exeunt* JUPITER, APOLLO, DIANA, *and* MERCURY *into ruined temple.*)

Enter SPARKEION *and* NICEMIS *climbing mountain at back.*

SPARKEION.　Here we are at last on the very summit and we've left the others ever so far behind! Why, what's this?

NICEMIS.　A ruined Palace! A Palace on the top of a mountain. I wonder who lives here? Some mighty king I dare say, with wealth beyond all counting, who came to live up here—

SPARKEION.　To avoid his creditors! It's a lovely situation for a country house, though it's very much out of repair.

NICEMIS.　Very inconvenient situation.

SPARKEION.　Inconvenient?

NICEMIS.　Yes—how are you to get butter, milk and eggs up here? No pigs—no poultry—no postman. Why, I should go mad.

SPARKEION.　What a dear little practical mind it is! What a wife you will make!

NICEMIS.　Don't be too sure—we are only partly married—the marriage ceremony lasts all day.

SPARKEION.　I've no doubt at all about it. We shall be as happy as a king and queen, though we are only a strolling actor and actress.

NICEMIS.　It's very kind of Thespis to celebrate our marriage day by giving the company a picnic on this lovely mountain.

SPARKEION.　And still more kind to allow us to get so much ahead of all the others. Discreet Thespis! (*Kissing her.*)

NICEMIS.　There now, get away, do! Remember the marriage ceremony is not yet completed.

SPARKEION.　But it would be ungrateful to Thespis's discretion not to take advantage of it by improving the opportunity.

NICEMIS.　Certainly not; get away.

SPARKEION.　On second thoughts, the opportunity's so good it don't admit of improvement. There! (*Kisses her.*)

NICEMIS.　How dare you kiss me before we are quite married.

SPARKEION.　Attribute it to the intoxicating influence of the mountain air.

NICEMIS.　Then we had better go down again. It is not right to expose ourselves to influences over which we have no control.

DUET — SPARKEION *and* NICEMIS.

SPARKEION.　Here far away from all the world,
　　　　Dissension and derision,
　　　　With Nature's wonders all unfurled

To our delighted vision,
　With no one here
　　(At least in sight)
　To interfere
　With our delight,
And two fond lovers sever,
　Oh do not free,
　　Thine hand from mine,
　I swear to thee
　　My love is thine,
For ever and for ever!

NICEMIS.　On mountain top the air is keen,
　　　　And most exhilarating,
　　　　And we say things we do not mean
　　　　In moments less elating.
　　　　So please to wait;
　　　　　For thoughts that crop
　　　　En tête-à-tête,
　　　　　On mountain top,
　　　　May not exactly tally
　　　　With those that you
　　　　　May entertain,
　　　　Returning to
　　　　　The sober plain
　　　　Of yon relaxing valley.

SPARKEION.　Very well—if you won't have anything to say to me, I know who will.

NICEMIS.　Who will?

SPARKEION.　Daphne will.

NICEMIS.　Daphne would flirt with anybody.

SPARKEION.　Anybody would flirt with Daphne. She is quite as pretty as you and has twice as much back-hair.

NICEMIS.　She has twice as much money, which may account for it.

SPARKEION.　At all events *she* has appreciation. *She* likes good looks.

NICEMIS.　We all like what we haven't got.

SPARKEION.　*She* keeps her eyes open.

NICEMIS.　Yes—one of them.

SPARKEION.　Which one?

NICEMIS.　The one she doesn't wink with.

SPARKEION.　Well, I was engaged to her for six months, and if she still makes eyes at me, you must attribute it to force of habit. Besides, remember—we are only half-married at present.

NICEMIS.　I suppose you mean that you are going to treat me as shamefully as you treated her. Very well, break it off if you like. *I* shall not offer any objection. Thespis used to be very attentive to me, and I'd just as soon be a manager's wife as a fifth-rate actor's!

Chorus heard, at first below, then enter DAPHNE, PRETTEIA, PREPOSTEROS, STUPIDAS, TIPSEION,

CYMON, *and other members of* THESPIS'S *company climbing over rocks at back. All carry small baskets.*

CHORUS — *with dance.*

Climbing over rocky mountain,
Skipping rivulet and fountain,
Passing where the willows quiver,
By the ever-rolling river,
　Swollen with the summer rain,
Threading long and leafy mazes,
Dotted with unnumbered daisies,
Scaling rough and rugged passes,
Climb the hardy lads and lasses,
　Till the mountain top they gain.

FIRST VOICE.   Fill the cup and tread the measure,
　Make the most of fleeting leisure,
　Hail it as a true ally,
　Though it perish bye and bye!

SECOND VOICE.   Every moment brings a treasure
　Of its own especial pleasure;
　Though the moments quickly die,
　Greet them gaily as they fly!

THIRD VOICE.   Far away from grief and care,
　High up in the mountain air,
　Let us live and reign alone
　In a world that's all our own.

FOURTH VOICE.   Here enthroned in the sky,
　Far away from mortal eye,
　We'll be gods and make decrees,
　Those may honour them who please.

CHORUS.   Fill the cup and tread the measure, &c.

After CHORUS *and* COUPLETS, *enter* THESPIS *climbing over rocks.*

THESPIS.   Bless you, my people, bless you. Let the revels commence. After all, for thorough, unconstrained, unconventional enjoyment give me a picnic.

PREPOSTEROS (*very gloomily*).   Give him a picnic, somebody!

THESPIS.   Be quiet, Preposteros—don't interrupt.

PREPOSTEROS.   Ha! ha! shut up again! But no matter.

STUPIDAS *endeavours, in pantomime, to reconcile him. Throughout the scene* PREPOSTEROS *shows symptoms of breaking out into a furious passion and* STUPIDAS *does all he can to pacify and restrain him.*

THESPIS.   The best of a picnic is that everybody contributes what he pleases, and nobody knows what anybody else has brought till the last mo-ment. Now, unpack everybody, and let's see what there is for everybody.

NICEMIS.   I have brought you—a bottle of soda water—for the claret cup.

DAPHNE.   I have brought you—a lettuce for the lobster salad.

SPARKEION.   A piece of ice—for the claret cup.

PRETTEIA.   A bottle of vinegar—for the lobster salad.

CYMON.   A bunch of burrage for the claret cup!

TIPSEION.   A hard-boiled egg—for the lobster salad!

STUPIDAS.   One lump of sugar for the claret cup!

PREPOSTEROS.   He has brought one lump of sugar for the claret cup! Ha! ha! ha! (*Laughing melodramatically.*)

STUPIDAS.   Well, Preposteros, and what have *you* brought?

PREPOSTEROS.   *I* have brought *two* lumps of the very best salt for the lobster salad.

THESPIS.   Oh—is that all?

PREPOSTEROS.   All! Ha! Ha! He asks if it is all! (STUPIDAS *consoles him.*)

THESPIS.   But I say—this is capital, as far as it goes—nothing could be better, but it don't go far enough. The claret, for instance! I don't insist on claret—or a lobster—. I don't insist on lobster, but a lobster salad without a lobster, why it isn't lobster salad. Here, Tipseion!

TIPSEION (*a very drunken bloated fellow, dressed however with scrupulous accuracy and wearing a large medal round his neck*). My master? (*Falls on his knees to* THESPIS *and kisses his robe.*)

THESPIS.   Get up—don't be a fool—. Where's the claret? We arranged last week that you were to see to that?

TIPSEION.   True, dear master—. But then I was a drunkard!

THESPIS.   You were.

TIPSEION.   You engaged me to play convivial parts on the strength of my personal appearance.

THESPIS.   I did.

TIPSEION.   You then found that my habits interfered with my duties as low comedian.

THESPIS.   True—

TIPSEION.   You said yesterday that unless I took the pledge you would dismiss me from your company.

THESPIS.   Quite so.

TIPSEION.   Good. I have taken it. It is all I have taken since yesterday. My preserver! (*Embraces him.*)

THESPIS.   Yes, but where's the wine?

TIPSEION. I left it behind, that I might not be tempted to violate my pledge.

PREPOSTEROS. Minion! (*Attempts to get at him—is restrained by* STUPIDAS.)

THESPIS. Now, Preposteros, what *is* the matter with you?

PREPOSTEROS. It is enough that I am downtrodden in my profession. I will not submit to imposition out of it. It is enough that as your heavy villain I get the worst of it every night in a combat of six. I will *not* submit to insult in the day time. I have come out, ha! ha! to enjoy myself!

THESPIS. But look here, you know—virtue only triumphs at night from seven to ten—vice gets the best of it during the other twenty-one hours. Won't that satisfy you? (STUPIDAS *endeavours to pacify him.*)

PREPOSTEROS (*irritated, to* STUPIDAS). Ye are odious to my sight! get out of it!

STUPIDAS (*in great terror*). What have I done?

THESPIS. Now *what* is it, Preposteros, *what* is it?

PREPOSTEROS. I a—hate him and would have his life!

THESPIS (*to* STUPIDAS). That's it—he hates you and would have your life—now go and be merry.

STUPIDAS. Yes, but why does he hate me?

THESPIS. Oh—exactly. (*To* PREPOSTEROS.) Why do you hate him?

PREPOSTEROS. Because he is a minion!

THESPIS. He hates you because you are a minion. It explains itself. Now go and enjoy yourselves. Ha! ha! It is well for those who *can* laugh—let them do so—there is no extra charge. The light-hearted cup and the convivial jest for them—but for me—what is there for me?

SILLIMON. There is some claret cup and lobster salad (*handing some*).

THESPIS (*taking it*). Thank you. (*Resuming.*) What is there for me but anxiety—ceaseless gnawing anxiety that tears at my very vitals and rends my peace of mind asunder? There is nothing whatever for me but anxiety of the nature I have just described. The charge of these thoughtless revellers is my unhappy lot. It is not a small charge and it is rightly termed a lot, because they are many. Oh why did the gods make me a manager?

SILLIMON (*as guessing a riddle*). *Why* did the gods make him a manager?

SPARKEION. Why did the *gods* make him a manager?

DAPHNE. Why did the gods make *him* a manager?

PRETTEIA. Why did the gods make him a *manager*?

THESPIS. No—no—what are you talking about? what do you mean?

DAPHNE. I've got it—don't tell us—

ALL. No—no—because—because—

THESPIS (*annoyed*). It isn't a conundrum—it's a misanthropical question. Why cannot I join you? (*Retires up centre.*)

DAPHNE (*who is sitting with* SPARKEION *to the annoyance of* NICEMIS, *who is crying alone*). I'm sure I don't know. We do not want you. Don't distress yourself on our account—we are getting on very comfortably—aren't we, Sparkeion?

SPARKEION. We are so happy that we don't miss the lobster or the claret. What are lobster and claret compared with the society of those we love! (*Embracing* DAPHNE.)

DAPHNE. Why, Nicemis, love, you are eating nothing. Aren't you happy, dear?

NICEMIS (*spitefully*). *You* are *quite* welcome to *my* share of *everything.* I intend to console *myself* with the society of my manager. (*Takes* THESPIS's *arm affectionately.*)

THESPIS. Here, I say—this won't do, you know—I can't allow it—at least before my company—besides, you are half-married to Sparkeion. Sparkeion, here's your half-wife impairing my influence before my company. Don't you know the story of the gentleman who undermined his influence by associating with his inferiors?

ALL. Yes, yes,—we know it.

PREPOSTEROS (*furiously*). *I* do not know it! It's ever thus! Doomed to disappointment from my earliest years— (STUPIDAS *endeavours to console him.*)

THESPIS. There—that's enough. Preposteros—you *shall* hear it.

SONG — THESPIS.

I once knew a chap who discharged a function
On the North South East West Diddlesex junction,
He was conspic*uous* exceeding,
For his affable ways and his easy breeding.
Although a Chairman of Directors,
He was hand in glove with the ticket inspectors,
He tipped the guards with bran-new fivers,
And sang little songs to the engine drivers.
 'Twas told to me with great compunction,
 By one who had discharged with unction,
 A Chairman of Directors' function,
 On the North South East West Diddlesex
  junction.
  Fol diddle, lol diddle, lol lol lay.

Each Christmas day he gave each stoker
A silver shovel and a golden poker,

He'd button-hole flowers for the ticket sorters,
And rich Bath-buns for the outside porters.
He'd mount the clerks on his first-class hunters,
And he built little villas for the road-side shun-
    ters,
And if any were fond of pigeon shooting,
He'd ask them down to his place at Tooting.
    'Twas told to me, &c.

In course of time there spread a rumour
That he did all this from a sense of humour,
So instead of signaling and stoking,
They gave themselves up to a course of joking.
Whenever they knew that he was riding,
They shunted his train on a lonely siding,
Or stopped all night in the middle of a tunnel,
On the plea that the boiler was a-coming through
    the funnel.
    'Twas told to me, &c.

If he wished to go to Perth or Stirling,
His train through several counties whirling,
Would set him down in a fit of larking,
At four a.m. in the wilds of Barking.
This pleased his whim and seemed to strike it,
But the general Public did not like it.
The receipts fell, after a few repeatings,
And he got it hot at the Annual meetings.
    'Twas told to me, &c.

He followed out his whim with vigour,
The shares went down to a nominal figure.
These are the consequences all proceeding
From his affable ways and his easy breeding!
The line, with its rails and guards and peelers,
Was sold for a song to marine-store dealers,
The shareholders are all in the work'us,
And he sells pipe-lights in the Regent Circus.
    'Twas told to me with much compunction,
    By one who had discharged with unction,
    A Chairman of Directors' function,
    On the North South East West Diddlesex
        junction,
    Fol diddle, lol diddle, lol lol lay!

(After song.)

THESPIS.   It's very hard. As a man I am naturally of an easy disposition. As a manager, I am compelled to hold myself aloof, that my influence may not be deteriorated. As a man, I am inclined to fraternize with the pauper—as a manager I am compelled to walk about like this: Don't know yah! Don't know yah! don't know yah! *(Strides haughtily about the stage.)*

JUPITER, MARS, *and* APOLLO, *in full Olympian costume, appear on the three broken columns. Thespians scream.*

JUPITER, MARS, and APOLLO *(in recitative).* Presumptuous mortal!

THESPIS *(same business).* Don't know yah! Don't know yah!

JUPITER, MARS, *and* APOLLO *(seated on three broken pillars, still in recit.).* Presumptuous mortal!

THESPIS. I do not know you, I do not know you.

JUPITER, MARS, *and* APOLLO *(standing on ground, recit.).* Presumptuous mortal!

THESPIS *(recit.).* Remove this person! (STUPIDAS and PREPOSTEROS *seize* APOLLO *and* MARS.)

JUPITER *(speaking).* Stop, you evidently *don't* know me. Allow me to offer you my card. *(Throws flash paper.)*

THESPIS. Ah, yes, it's very pretty, but we don't want any at present. When we do our Christmas piece I'll let you know. *(Changing his manner.)* Look here, you know, this is a private party and we haven't the pleasure of your acquaintance. There are a good many other mountains about, if you must have a mountain all to yourself. Don't make me let myself down before my company. *(Resuming.)* Don't know yah! Don't know yah!

JUPITER. I am Jupiter, the King of the Gods. This is Apollo. This is Mars. *(All kneel to them except* THESPIS.)

THESPIS. Oh, then as I'm a respectable man, and rather particular about the company I keep, I think I'll go.

JUPITER. No—no—. Stop a bit. We want to consult you on a matter of great importance. There! Now we are alone. Who are you?

THESPIS. I am Thespis of the Thessalian Theatres.

JUPITER. The very man we want. Now as a judge of what the public likes, are you impressed with my appearance as the father of the gods?

THESPIS. Well, to be candid with you, I am not. In fact I'm disappointed.

JUPITER. Disappointed?

THESPIS. Yes, you see you're so much out of repair. No, you don't come up to my idea of the part. Bless you, I've played you often.

JUPITER. You have!

THESPIS. To be sure I have.

JUPITER. And how have you dressed the part?

THESPIS. Fine commanding party in the prime of life. Thunderbolt—full beard—dignified manner —. A good deal of this sort of thing: "Don't know yah! Don't know yah! Don't know yah!" *(Imitating.)*

JUPITER *(much affected).* I—I'm very much obliged to you. It's very good of you. I—I—I used to be like that. I can't tell you how much I feel it.

And do you find I'm an impressive character to play?

THESPIS. Well, no, I can't say you are. In fact we don't use you much out of burlesque.

JUPITER. Burlesque! (*Offended, walks up.*)

THESPIS. Yes, it's a painful subject; drop it, drop it. The fact is, you are not the gods you were—you're behind your age.

JUPITER. Well, but what are we to do? We feel that we ought to do something, but we don't know what.

THESPIS. Why don't you all go down to Earth, incog, mingle with the world, hear and see what people think of you, and judge for yourselves, as to the best means to take to restore your influence.

JUPITER. Ah, but what's to become of Olympus in the meantime?

THESPIS. Lor' bless you, don't distress yourself about that. I've a very clever company, used to take long parts on the shortest notice. Invest us

with your powers and we'll fill your places till you return.

JUPITER (*aside*). The offer is tempting. But suppose you fail?

THESPIS. Fail! Oh, we never fail in our profession. We've nothing but great successes!

JUPITER. Then it's a bargain?

THESPIS. It's a bargain. (*They shake hands on it.*)

JUPITER. And that you may not be entirely without assistance, we will leave you Mercury, and whenever you find yourself in a difficulty you can consult him.

Enter MERCURY *through trap.*

QUARTETTE.

JUPITER. So that's arranged—you take my place, my boy,
  While we make trial of a new existence.
 At length I shall be able to enjoy
  The pleasures I have envied from a distance.

MERCURY. Compelled upon Olympus here to stop,
        While other gods go down to play the hero,
Don't be surprised if on this mountain top,
        You find your Mercury is down at zero!

APOLLO. To earth away! to join in mortal acts,
        And gather fresh materials to write on,
Investigate more closely several facts,
        That I for centuries have thrown some light
            on!

DIANA. I, as the modest moon with crescent bow,
        Have always shown a light to nightly scandal,
I must say I should like to go below,
        And find out if the game is worth the candle!

Enter all the Thespians, summoned by MERCURY.

MERCURY. Here come your people!
THESPIS. People better now!

AIR — THESPIS.

While mighty Jove goes down below
        With all the other deities,
I fill his place and wear his "clo,"
        The very part for me it is.
To mother earth to make a track,
        They all are spurred and booted, too,
And you will fill, till they come back,
        The parts you best are suited to.

CHORUS. Here's a pretty tale for future Iliads and
        Odysseys:
Mortals are about to personate the gods and
        goddesses.
Now to set the world in order, we will work in
        unity;
Jupiter's perplexity is Thespis' opportunity.

SOLO — SPARKEION.

Phœbus am I, with golden ray,
        The God of Day, the God of Day.
When shadowy night has held her sway,
        I make the goddess fly.
'Tis mine the task to wake the world,
        In slumber curled, in slumber curled;
By me her charms are all unfurled,
        The God of Day am I!

CHORUS. The God of Day, the God of Day,
        That part shall our Sparkeion play.
            Ha! ha! &c.
        The rarest fun and rarest fare,
        That ever fell to mortal share!
            Ha! ha! &c.

SOLO — NICEMIS.

I am the Moon, the lamp of night.
        I show a light—I show a light.
With radiant sheen I put to flight

The shadows of the sky.
By my fair rays, as you're aware,
        Gay lovers swear—gay lovers swear,
While graybeards sleep away their care,
        The lamp of night am I!

CHORUS. The lamp of night—the lamp of night,
        Nicemis plays, to her delight,
            Ha! ha! ha! ha!
        The rarest fun and rarest fare
        That ever fell to mortal share,
            Ha! ha! ha! ha!

SOLO — TIMIDON.

Mighty old Mars, the God of War,
        I'm destined for—I'm destined for—
A terribly famous conqueror,
        With sword upon his thigh.
When armies meet with eager shout,
        And warlike rout, and warlike rout,
You'll find me there without a doubt.
        The God of War am I!

CHORUS. The God of War, the God of War,
        Great Timidon is destined for!
            Ha! ha! ha! ha!
        The rarest fun and rarest fare,
        That ever fell to mortal share.
            Ha! ha! ha! ha! &c.

SOLO — DAPHNE.

When, as the fruit of warlike deeds,
        The soldier bleeds, the soldier bleeds,
Calliope crowns heroic deeds,
        With immortality.
From mere oblivion I reclaim
        The soldier's name, the soldier's name,
And write it on the roll of fame,
        The Muse of Fame, am I!

CHORUS. The Muse of Fame, the Muse of Fame,
        Calliope is Daphne's name,
            Ha! ha! ha! ha!
        The rarest fun and rarest fare,
        That ever fell to mortal share!
            Ha! ha! ha! ha!

TUTTI. Here's a pretty tale!

*Enter procession of old Gods. They come down
very much astonished at all they see, then, passing
by, ascend the platform that leads to the
descent at the back.*

GODS (JUPITER, DIANA, *and* APOLLO, *in corner
together*).   We will go,
                Down below,
                Revels rare,
                We will share.
                    Ha! ha! ha!

With a gay
Holiday,
All unknown,
And alone.
Ha! ha! ha!

TUTTI.   Here's a pretty tale!

The Gods, including those who have lately entered in procession, group themselves on rising ground at back. The Thespians (kneeling) bid them farewell.

CURTAIN.

ACT II.

SCENE. — *The same scene as in Act I, with the exception that in place of the ruins that filled the foreground of the stage, the interior of a magnificent temple is seen, showing the background of the scene of Act I, through the columns of the portico at the back. High throne* L.U.E. *Low seats below it. All the substitute gods and goddesses (that is to say, Thespians) are discovered grouped in picturesque attitudes about the stage, eating, drinking, and smoking, and singing the following verses:*

CHORUS.

Of all symposia,
    The best by half,
        Upon Olympus, here, await us,
We eat Ambrosia,
    And nectar quaff—
        It cheers but don't inebriate us.
We know the fallacies
    Of human food,
        So please to pass Olympian rosy,
We built up palaces,
    Where ruins stood,
        And find them much more snug
        and cosy.

SOLO — SILLIMON.

To work and think, my dear,
    Up here, would be,
        The height of conscientious folly,
So eat and drink, my dear—
    I like to see,
        Young people gay—young people
        jolly!
Olympian food my love,
    I'll lay long odds,
        Will please your lips—those rosy
        portals.
What is the good, my love,
    Of being gods,
        If we must work like common
        mortals?

CHORUS.   Of all symposia, &c.

Exeunt all but NICEMIS, *who is dressed as* DIANA, *and* PRETTEIA *who is dressed as* VENUS. *They take* SILLIMON'S *arm and bring him down.*

SILLIMON.   Bless their little hearts, I can refuse them nothing. As the Olympian stage-manager I ought to be strict with them and make them do their duty, but I can't. Bless their little hearts, when I see the pretty little craft come sailing up to me with a wheedling smile on their pretty little figure-heads, I can't turn my back on 'em. I'm all bow, though I'm sure I try to be stern!

PRETTEIA.   You certainly are a dear old thing.

SILLIMON.   She says I'm a dear old thing! Deputy Venus says I'm a dear old thing!

NICEMIS.   It's her affectionate habit to describe everybody in those terms. *I* am more particular, but still even *I* am bound to admit that you are certainly a very dear old thing.

SILLIMON.   Deputy Venus says I'm a dear old thing, and deputy Diana, who is much more particular, endorses it! Who could be severe with such deputy divinities!

PRETTEIA.   Do you know, I'm going to ask you a favour.

SILLIMON.   Venus is going to ask me a favour!

PRETTEIA.   You see, I am Venus.

SILLIMON.   No one who saw your face would doubt it.

NICEMIS (*aside*).   No one who knew her *character* would!

PRETTEIA.   Well, Venus, you know, is married to Mars.

SILLIMON.   To Vulcan, my dear, to Vulcan. The exact connubial relation of the different gods and goddesses is a point on which we must be extremely particular.

PRETTEIA.   I beg your pardon—Venus is married to Mars.

NICEMIS. If she isn't married to Mars, she ought to be.

SILLIMON. Then that decides it—call it married to Mars.

PRETTEIA. Married to Vulcan or married to Mars, what does it signify?

SILLIMON. My dear, it's a matter on which I have no personal feeling whatever.

PRETTEIA. So that she is married to some one!

SILLIMON. Exactly, so that she is married to some one. Call it married to Mars.

PRETTEIA. Now here's my difficulty. Presumptios takes the place of Mars, and Presumptios is my father!

SILLIMON. Then why object to Vulcan?

PRETTEIA. Because Vulcan is my grandfather!

SILLIMON. But my dear, what an objection. You are playing a part till the real gods return. That's all! Whether you are supposed to be married to your father—or your grandfather, what does it matter? This passion for realism is the curse of the stage!

PRETTEIA. That's all very well, but I can't throw myself into a part that has already lasted a twelve-month, when I have to make love to my father. It interferes with my conception of the characters. It spoils the part.

SILLIMON. Well, well, I'll see what can be done. (*Exit* PRETTEIA.) That's always the way with beginners, they've no imaginative power. A true artist ought to be superior to such considerations. (NICEMIS *comes down.*) Well, Nicemis—I should say Diana—what's wrong with you? Don't you like your part?

NICEMIS. Oh, immensely! It's great fun.

SILLIMON. Don't you find it lonely out by yourself all night?

NICEMIS. Oh, but I'm *not* alone all night!

SILLIMON. But—I don't want to ask any injudicious questions—but who accompanies you?

NICEMIS. Who? why Sparkeion, of course.

SILLIMON. Sparkeion? Well, but Sparkeion is Phœbus Apollo. (*Enter* SPARKEION.) He's the Sun, you know.

NICEMIS. Of course he is. I should catch my death of cold, in the night air, if he didn't accompany me.

SPARKEION. My dear Sillimon, it would never do for a young lady to be out alone all night. It wouldn't be respectable.

SILLIMON. There's a good deal of truth in that. But still—the Sun—at night—I don't like the idea. The original Diana always went out alone.

NICEMIS. I hope the original Diana is no rule for *me*. After all, what *does* it matter?

SILLIMON. To be sure—what *does* it matter?

SPARKEION. The sun at night, or in the daytime!

SILLIMON. So that he shines. That's all that's necessary. (*Exit* NICEMIS.) But poor Daphne, what will she say to this?

SPARKEION. Oh, Daphne can console herself, young ladies soon get over this sort of thing. Did you never hear of the young lady who was engaged to cousin Robin?

SILLIMON. Never.

SPARKEION. Then I'll sing it to you.

SONG — SPARKEION.

> Little maid of Arcadee
> Sat on Cousin Robin's knee,
> Thought in form and face and limb,
> Nobody could rival him.
> He was brave and she was fair.
> Truth, they made a pretty pair,
> Happy little maiden, she!
> Happy maid of Arcadee.
>
> Moments fled as moments will,
> Happily enough, until,
> After, say, a month or two,
> Robin did as Robins do.
> Weary of his lover's play,
> Jilted her and went away.
> Wretched little maiden, she—
> Wretched maid of Arcadee!
>
> To her little home she crept,
> There she sat her down and wept.
> Maiden wept as maidens will—
> Grew so thin and pale—until
> Cousin Richard came to woo!
> Then again the roses grew!
> Happy little maiden, she—
> Happy maid of Arcadee!

(*Exit* SPARKEION.)

SILLIMON. Well, Mercury, my boy, you've had a year's experience of us up here. How do we do it? I think we're rather an improvement on the original gods—don't you?

MERCURY. Well, you see, there's a good deal to be said on both sides of the question. You are certainly younger than the original gods, and, therefore, more active. On the other hand, they are certainly older than you, and have, therefore, more experience. On the whole, I prefer you, because your mistakes amuse me.

SONG — MERCURY.

Olympus is now in a terrible muddle,
  The deputy deities all are at fault;

They splutter and splash like a pig in the puddle,
　And dickens a one of 'em's earning his salt.
For Thespis as Jove is a terrible blunder,
　Too nervous and timid—too easy and weak—
Whenever he's called on to lighten or thunder,
　The thought of it keeps him awake for a week!

Then mighty Mars hasn't the pluck of a parrot,
　When left in the dark he will quiver and quail;
And Vulcan has arms that would snap like a
　carrot,
　Before he could drive in a tenpenny nail!
Then Venus's freckles are very repelling.
　And Venus should *not* have a squint in her
　eyes;
The learned Minerva is weak in her spelling,
　And scatters her h's all over the skies.

Then Pluto, in kindhearted tenderness erring,
　Can't make up his mind to let anyone die—
The *Times* has a paragraph ever recurring,
　"Remarkable instance of longevi*ty*."
On some it has come as a serious onus,
　To others it's quite an advantage—in short,
While ev'ry Life Office declares a big bonus,
　The poor undertakers are all in the court!

Then Cupid the rascal, forgetting his trade is
　To make men and women impartially smart;
Will only shoot at pretty young ladies,
　And never takes aim at a bachelor's heart.
The results of this freak—or whatever you term
　it—
　Should cover the wicked young scamp with
　disgrace;
While ev'ry young man is as shy as a hermit,
　Young ladies are popping all over the place!

This wouldn't much matter—for bashful and
　shy men,
　When skilfully handled, are certain to fall,
But alas that determined young bachelor Hymen
　Refuses to wed anybody at all!
He swears that Love's flame is the vilest of
　arsons,
　And looks upon marriage as quite a mistake;
Now what in the world's to become of the
　parsons,
　And what of the artist who sugars the cake?

In short, you will see from the facts that I'm
　showing,
　The state of the case is exceedingly sad.
If Thespis's people go on as they're going,
　Olympus will certainly go to the bad!
From Jupiter downwards there isn't a dab in it,
　All of 'em quibble and shuffle and shirk;
A premier in Downing Street forming a cabinet,
　Couldn't find people less fit for their work!

Enter THESPIS.

THESPIS. Sillimon, you can retire.

SILLIMON. Sir, I—

THESPIS. Don't pretend you can't when I say you can. I've seen you do it, go. (*Exit* SILLIMON *bowing extravagantly.* THESPIS *imitates him.*) Well, Mercury, I've been in power one year to-day.

MERCURY. One year to-day. How do you like ruling the world?

THESPIS. Like it! Why it's as straightforward as possible. Why there hasn't been a hitch of any kind since we came up here. Lor'! The airs you gods and goddesses give yourselves, are perfectly sickening. Why it's mere child's play!

MERCURY. Very simple, isn't it?

THESPIS. Simple! Why I could do it on my head!

MERCURY. Ah—I daresay you will do it on your head very soon.

THESPIS. What do you mean by *that,* Mercury?

MERCURY. I mean that when you've turned the world *quite* topsy-turvy you won't know whether you're standing on your head or your heels.

THESPIS. Well, but Mercury, it's all right at present.

MERCURY. Oh yes—as far as we know.

THESPIS. Well, but you know, we know as much as anybody knows, you know. I believe that the world's still going on.

MERCURY. Yes—as far as we can judge—much as usual.

THESPIS. Well, then, give the father of the Drama his due, Mercury. Don't be envious of the father of the Drama.

MERCURY. Well, but you see you leave so much to accident.

THESPIS. Well, Mercury, if I do, it's my principle. I am an easy man, and I like to make things as pleasant as possible. What did I do the day we took office? Why, I called the company together and I said to them: "Here we are, you know, gods and goddesses, no mistake about it, the real thing. Well, we have certain duties to discharge; let's discharge them intelligently. Don't let us be hampered by routine and red tape and precedent; let's set the original gods an example, and put a liberal interpretation on our duties. If it occurs to any one to try an experiment in his own department, let him try it; if he fails there's no harm done; if he succeeds it is a distinct gain to society. Take it easy," I said, "and at the same time, make experiments. Don't hurry your work, do it slowly and do it well." And here we are after a twelvemonth, and not a single complaint or a single petition has reached me.

MERCURY. No—not yet.

THESPIS. What do you mean by "no, not yet"?

MERCURY. Well, you see, you don't understand these things. All the petitions that are addressed by men to Jupiter pass through my hands, and it's my duty to collect them and present them once a year.

THESPIS. Oh, only once a year?

MERCURY. Only once a year.

THESPIS. And the year is up—?

MERCURY. To-day.

THESPIS. Oh, then I suppose there are *some* complaints.

MERCURY. Yes, there *are some*.

THESPIS (*disturbed*). Oh. Perhaps there are a good many?

MERCURY. There are, a good many.

THESPIS. Oh. Perhaps there are a thundering lot?

MERCURY. There are a thundering lot.

THESPIS (*very much disturbed*). Oh!

MERCURY. You see you've been taking it so very easy—and so have most of your company.

THESPIS. Oh, who has been taking it easy?

MERCURY. Well, all except those who have been trying experiments.

THESPIS. Well, but I suppose the experiments are ingenious?

MERCURY. Yes, they are ingenious, but on the whole ill-judged. But it's time to go and summon your court.

THESPIS. What for?

MERCURY. To hear the complaints. In five minutes they will be here. (*Exit.*)

THESPIS (*very uneasy*). I don't know how it is, but there is something in that young man's manner that suggests that the Father of the gods has been taking it *too* easy. Perhaps it would have been better if I hadn't given my company so much scope. I wonder what they've been doing. I think I will curtail their discretion; though none of them appear to have much of the article it seems a pity to deprive 'em of what little they have.

Enter DAPHNE, *weeping.*

THESPIS. Now, then, Daphne, what's the matter with you?

DAPHNE. Well, you know how disgracefully Sparkeion—

THESPIS (*correcting her*). Apollo—

DAPHNE. Apollo, then—has treated me. He promised to marry me years ago, and now he's married to Nicemis.

THESPIS. Now look here. I can't go into that.

You're in Olympus now and must behave accordingly. Drop your Daphne—assume your Calliope.

DAPHNE. Quite so. That's it! (*Mysteriously.*)

THESPIS. Oh—that is it? (*Puzzled.*)

DAPHNE. That is it, Thespis. I am Calliope the Muse of Fame. Very good. This morning I was in the Olympian library, and I took down the only book there. Here it is.

THESPIS (*taking it*). Lemprière's Classical Dictionary. The Olympian Peerage.

DAPHNE. Open it at Apollo.

THESPIS (*opens it*). It is done.

DAPHNE. Read.

THESPIS. "Apollo was several times married, among others to Issa, Bolina, Coronis, Chymene, Cyrene, Chione, Acacallis, and Calliope."

DAPHNE. *And* Calliope.

THESPIS (*musing*). Ha! I didn't know he was *married* to them.

DAPHNE (*severely*). Sir! This is the Family Edition.

THESPIS. Quite so.

DAPHNE. You couldn't expect a lady to read any other?

THESPIS. On no consideration. But in the original version—

DAPHNE. I go by the Family Edition.

THESPIS. Then by the Family Edition, Apollo is your husband.

Enter NICEMIS *and* SPARKEION.

NICEMIS. Apollo *your* husband? He is *my* husband.

DAPHNE. I beg your pardon. He is *my* husband.

NICEMIS. Apollo is Sparkeion and he's married to *me*.

DAPHNE. Sparkeion is Apollo and he's married to *me*.

NICEMIS. He's my husband.

DAPHNE. He's your brother.

THESPIS. Look here, Apollo, whose husband are you? Don't let's have any row about it; whose husband are you?

SPARKEION. Upon my honour I don't know. I'm in a very delicate position, but I'll fall in with any arrangement Thespis may propose.

DAPHNE. I've just found out that he's my husband and yet he goes out every evening with that "thing"!

THESPIS. Perhaps he's trying an experiment.

DAPHNE. I don't like my husband to make such experiments. The question is, who are we all and what is our relation to each other?

QUARTETTE.

SPARKEION.   You're Diana, I'm Apollo—
        And Calliope is she.

DAPHNE.   He's your brother,

NICEMIS.   You're another.
        He has fairly married me.

DAPHNE.   By the rules of this fair spot,
        I'm his wife and you are not—

SPARKEION and DAPHNE.   By the rules of this fair
        spot,
        I'm } his wife and you are not.
        She's }

NICEMIS.   By this golden wedding ring,
        I'm his wife and you're a "thing."

DAPHNE, NICEMIS, and SPARKEION.   By this
        golden wedding ring,
        I'm } his wife and you're a "thing."
        She's }

ALL.   Please will some one kindly tell us,
        Who are our respective kin?
        All of { us } are very jealous,
               { them }
        Neither of { us } will give in.
                   { them }

NICEMIS.   He's my husband, I declare,
        I espoused him properlee.

SPARKEION.   That is true for I was there,
        And I saw her marry me.

DAPHNE.   He's your brother—I'm his wife,
        If we go by Lemprière.

SPARKEION.   So she is, upon my life,
        Really that seems very fair.

NICEMIS.   You're my husband and no other,

SPARKEION.   That is true enough, I swear,

DAPHNE.   I'm his wife and you're his brother,

SPARKEION.   If we go by Lemprière.

NICEMIS.   It will surely be unfair,
        To decide by Lemprière (crying).

DAPHNE.   It will surely be quite fair,
        To decide by Lemprière,

SPARKEION and THESPIS.   How you settle I don't
        care,
        Leave it all to Lemprière.
        (Spoken). The Verdict:
        As Sparkeion is Apollo
            Up in this Olympian clime,
        Why, Nicemis, it will follow,
            He's her husband, for the time—
                        (indicating DAPHNE).
        When Sparkeion turns to mortal,
            Joins once more the sons of men,
        He may take you to his portal
                        (indicating NICEMIS).

He will be your husband then.
That, oh that is my decision,
    'Cording to my mental vision.
Put an end to all collision,
    That, oh that is my decision.
My decision—my decision,

ALL.   That, oh that is his decision,
        His decision—his decision! &c.

(Exeunt SPARKEION with DAPHNE, NICEMIS
                weeping with THESPIS.)

Mysterious music. Enter JUPITER, APOLLO, and
MARS, from below, at the back of stage. All wear
    cloaks as disguise and all are masked.

RECITATIVE.

Oh rage and fury! Oh shame and sorrow!
We'll be resuming our ranks to-morrow.
Since from Olympus we have departed,
We've been distracted and brokenhearted.
Oh wicked Thespis! Oh villain scurvy;
Through him Olympus is topsy-turvy!
Compelled to silence, to grin and bear it!
He's caused our sorrow, and he shall share it.
Where is the monster! Avenge his blunders;
He has awakened Olympian thunders.

Enter MERCURY.

JUPITER (recit.).   Oh Monster!

APOLLO (recit.).   Oh Monster!

MARS (recit.).   Oh Monster!

MERCURY (in great terror).   Please, sir, what have
I done, sir?

JUPITER.   What did we leave you behind for?

MERCURY.   Please, sir, that's the question I asked
when you went away.

JUPITER.   Was it not that Thespis might consult
you whenever he was in a difficulty?

MERCURY.   Well, here I've been, ready to be consulted, chock-full of reliable information—running over with celestial maxims—advice gratis ten
to four—after twelve ring the night bell in cases
of emergency.

JUPITER.   And hasn't he consulted you?

MERCURY.   Not he—he disagrees with me about
everything.

JUPITER.   He must have misunderstood me. I told
him to consult you whenever he was in a fix.

MERCURY.   He must have thought you said insult.
Why, whenever I open my mouth he jumps down
my throat. It isn't pleasant to have a fellow constantly jumping down your throat—especially
when he always disagrees with you. It's just the
sort of thing I can't digest.

JUPITER (in a rage).   Send him here. I'll talk to
him!

Enter THESPIS. *He is much terrified.*

JUPITER (*recit.*). Oh Monster!

APOLLO " Oh Monster!

MARS " Oh Monster!

THESPIS *sings in great terror, which he endeavours to conceal.*

JUPITER. Well, sir, the year is up to-day.

APOLLO. And a nice mess you've made of it.

MARS. You've deranged the whole scheme of society!

THESPIS (*aside*). There's going to be a row! (*Aloud and very familiarly.*) My dear boy—I do assure you—

JUPITER (*in recit.*). Be respectful!

APOLLO " Be respectful!

MARS " Be respectful!

THESPIS. I don't know what you allude to. With the exception of getting our scene painter to "run up" this temple, because we found the ruins draughty, we haven't touched a thing.

JUPITER (*in recit.*). Oh, story-teller!

APOLLO " Oh, story-teller!

MARS " Oh, story-teller!

THESPIS. My dear fellows, you're distressing yourselves unnecessarily. The court of Olympus is about to assemble to listen to the complaints of the year, if any. But there are none, or next to none. Let the Olympians assemble!

Enter THESPIANS. THESPIS *takes chair.* JUPITER, APOLLO, *and* MARS *sit below him.*

THESPIS. Ladies and gentlemen. It seems that it is usual for the gods to assemble once a year to listen to mortal petitions. It don't seem to me to be a good plan, as work is liable to accumulate, but as I'm particularly anxious not to interfere with Olympian precedent, but to allow everything to go on as it has always been accustomed to go, why we'll say no more about it. (*Aside.*) But how shall I account for your presence?

JUPITER. Say we are gentlemen of the press.

THESPIS. That all our proceedings may be perfectly open and above-board I have communicated with the most influential members of the Athenian press, and I beg to introduce to your notice three of its most distinguished members. They bear marks emblematic of the anonymous character of modern journalism. (*Business of introduction.* THESPIS *very uneasy.*) Now, then, if you're all ready we will begin.

MERCURY (*brings tremendous bundles of petitions*). Here is the agenda.

THESPIS. What's that? The petitions?

MERCURY. Some of them. (*Opens one and reads.*) Ah, I thought there'd be a row about it.

THESPIS. Why, what's wrong now?

MERCURY. Why, it's been a foggy Friday in November for the last six months and the Athenians are tired of it.

THESPIS. There's no pleasing some people. This craving for perpetual change is the curse of the country. Friday's a very nice day.

MERCURY. So it is, but a Friday six months long —it gets monotonous.

JUPITER, APOLLO, *and* MARS (*in recit., rising*). It's perfectly ridiculous.

THESPIS (*calling them*). It shall be arranged. Cymon!

CYMON (*as Time, with the usual attributes*). Sir!

THESPIS (*introducing him to three gods*). Allow me—Father Time—rather young at present but even Time must have a beginning. In course of Time, Time will grow older. Now then, Father Time, what's this about a wet Friday in November for the last six months?

CYMON. Well, the fact is, I've been trying an experiment. Seven days in the week is an awkward number. It can't be halved. Two's into seven won't go.

THESPIS (*tries it on his fingers*). Quite so—quite so.

CYMON. So I abolished Saturday.

JUPITER, APOLLO, *and* MARS. Oh, but— (*rising*).

THESPIS. Do be quiet. He's a very intelligent young man and knows what he is about. So you abolished Saturday. And how did you find it answered?

CYMON. Admirably.

THESPIS. You hear? He found it answered admirably.

CYMON. Yes, only Sunday refused to take its place.

THESPIS. Sunday refused to take its place?

CYMON. Sunday comes after Saturday—Sunday won't go on duty after Friday, Sunday's principles are very strict. That's where my experiment sticks.

THESPIS. Well, but why November? Come! why November?

CYMON. December can't begin till November has finished. November can't finish because he's abolished Saturday. There again my experiment sticks.

THESPIS. Well, but why wet? Come, now, why wet?

CYMON. Ah, that's your fault. You turned on the rain six months and you've forgot to turn it off again.

JUPITER, MARS, *and* APOLLO (*rising—recit.*). Oh, this is monstrous!

ALL. Order, order!

THESPIS. Gentlemen, pray be seated. (*To the others.*) The liberty of the press, one can't help it. (*To the three gods.*) It is easily settled. Athens has had a wet Friday in November for the last six months. Let them have a blazing Tuesday in July for the next twelve.

JUPITER, MARS, *and* APOLLO. But—

ALL. Order, order!

THESPIS. Now, then, the next article.

MERCURY. Here's a petition from the Peace Society. They complain that there are no more battles.

MARS (*springing up*). What!

THESPIS. Quiet there! Good dog—soho; Timidon!

TIMIDON (*as* MARS). Here.

THESPIS. What's this about there being no battles?

TIMIDON. I've abolished battles; it's an experiment.

MARS (*springing up*). Oh, come, I say—

THESPIS. Quiet, then! (*To* TIMIDON.) Abolished battles?

TIMIDON. Yes, you told us on taking office to remember two things, to try experiments and to take it easy. I found I couldn't take it easy while there are any battles to attend to, so I tried the experiment and abolished battles. And then I took it easy. The Peace Society ought to be very much obliged to me.

THESPIS. Obliged to you? Why, confound it! since battles have been abolished war is universal.

TIMIDON. War universal?

THESPIS. To be sure it is! Now that nations can't fight, no two of 'em are on speaking terms. The dread of fighting was the only thing that kept them civil to each other. Let battles be restored and peace reign supreme.

MERCURY (*reads*). Here's a petition from the associated wine merchants of Mytilene.

THESPIS. Well, what's wrong with the associated wine merchants of Mytilene? Are there no grapes this year?

MERCURY. Plenty of grapes, more than usual.

THESPIS (*to the gods*). You observe, there's no deception, there are more than usual.

MERCURY. There are plenty of grapes, only they are full of ginger beer.

THREE GODS. Oh, come, I say (*rising, they are put down by* THESPIS).

THESPIS. Eh? what? (*Much alarmed.*) Bacchus?

TIPSEION (*as* BACCHUS). Here!

THESPIS. There seems to be something unusual with the grapes of Mytilene, they only grow ginger beer.

TIPSEION. And a very good thing too.

THESPIS. It's very nice in its way, but it is not what one looks for from grapes.

TIPSEION. Beloved master, a week before we came up here, you insisted on my taking the pledge. By so doing you rescued me from my otherwise inevitable misery. I cannot utter my thanks. Embrace me! (*Attempts to embrace him.*)

THESPIS. Get out, don't be a fool. Look here, you know you're the God of Wine.

TIPSEION. I am.

THESPIS (*very angry*). Well, do you consider it consistent with your duty as the God of Wine to make the grapes yield nothing but ginger beer?

TIPSEION. Do you consider it consistent with my duty as a total abstainer, to grow anything stronger than ginger beer?

THESPIS. But your duty as the God of Wine—

TIPSEION. In every respect in which my duty as the God of Wine can be discharged consistently with my duty as a total abstainer, I will discharge it. But when the functions clash, everything must give way to the pledge. My preserver! (*Attempts to embrace him.*)

THESPIS. Don't be a confounded fool! This can be arranged. We can't give over the wine this year, but at least we can improve the ginger beer. Let all the ginger beer be extracted from it immediately.

JUPITER, MARS, *and* APOLLO (*aside*). We can't stand this,
We can't stand this,
It's much too strong,
We can't stand this.
It would be wrong,
Extremely wrong,
If we stood this,
If we stand this,
If we stand this,
We can't stand this.

DAPHNE, SPARKEION, *and* NICEMIS. Great Jove, this interference,
Is more than we can stand;
Of them make a clearance,
With your majestic hand.

JUPITER. This cool audacity, it beats us hollow! (*Removing mask.*) I'm Jupiter!

MARS.   I'm Mars!

APOLLO.   I'm Apollo!

Enter DIANA, *and all the other Gods and Goddesses.*

ALL (*kneeling with their foreheads on the ground*).
   Jupiter, Mars, and Apollo,
     Have quitted the dwellings of men;
   The other gods quickly will follow,
     And what will become of us then.

   Oh pardon us, Jove and Apollo,
     Pardon us, Jupiter, Mars;
   Oh, see us in misery wallow,
     Cursing our terrible stars.

Enter other Gods.

CHORUS AND BALLET.

ALL THE THESPIANS. Let us remain, we beg of you pleadingly!

THREE GODS. Let them remain, they beg of us pleadingly!

THESPIANS. Life on Olympus suits us exceedingly,

GODS. Life on Olympus suits them exceedingly.

THESPIANS. Let us remain, we pray in humility,

GODS. Let 'em remain, they pray in humility.

THESPIANS. If we have shown some little ability—

GODS. If they have shown some little ability—

ALL. Let us remain, &c.

JUPITER. Enough, your reign is ended;
     Upon this sacred hill
   Let him be apprehended,
     And learn our awful will.
Away to earth, contemptible comedians,
   And hear our curse, before we set you free;

You shall all be eminent tragedians,
   Whom no one ever, ever goes to see!

ALL. We go to earth, contemptible comedians,
     We hear his curse before he sets us free,
   We shall all be eminent tragedians,
     Whom no one ever ever goes to see!

SILLIMON.   Whom no one—

SPARKEION.   Whom no one—

THESPIS.   Whom *no* one—

ALL.   Ever, ever goes to see.

The Thespians are driven away by the Gods, who group themselves in attitudes of triumph.

BALLET DIVERTISSEMENT.

THESPIS. Now here you see the arrant folly
   Of doing your best to make things jolly.
   I've ruled the world like a chap in his senses;
   Observe the terrible consequences.
   Great Jupiter, whom nothing pleases,
   Splutters and swears and kicks up breezes,
   And sends us home, in a mood avengin',
   In double quick time like a railroad engine.

   All this he does without compunction,
   Because I have discharged with unction
   A highly complicated function,
   Complying with his own injunction.
        Fol, lol, lay.

CHORUS. All this he does, &c.

The Gods drive the Thespians away. The Thespians prepare to descend the mountain as the

CURTAIN FALLS.

Postscript

THE FIRST ISSUE of the first edition of this earliest Gilbert and Sullivan collaboration is among the most difficult to find of all their first-night librettos. All early issues of *Thespis* manifest extremely careless printing. Even the production date on both cover and title-page is incorrect—"Tuesday, December 23rd, 1871"—and it was never changed.

Almost twenty years after the launching of *Thespis,* Gilbert made belated excuses for the condition of this libretto. In so doing, although he failed to absolve himself, he uncovered a fascinating problem for the biographer: not merely a "lost weekend" but an entire "lost" month—a round trip to America, unknown to literature.

In a letter to Percy Strzelecki dated April 23, 1890, about the *Thespis* libretto he wrote: "I was in the United States when it was published & I had no opportunity of correcting proofs. This will explain the presence of innumerable typographical & other errors." Townley Searle, who first ci-

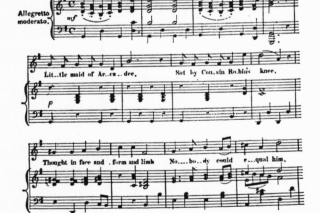

The only THESPIS *sheet-music survivor, a reprint of "Little Maid of Arcadee."*

ted this letter of Gilbert's, accepted its contents without question, even though there had been no mention of any kind by any writer on Gilbert and Sullivan establishing the fact that Gilbert made his first trip to America prior to 1879; nor, on the authority of Hesketh Pearson, is there any evidence of such a trip in Gilbert's personal records.

However, doubts of the validity of Gilbert's alibi have arisen from a study of the correspondence between his agent, Edward English, and R. M. Field, manager of the Boston Museum Theatre (see page 2). The search that followed turned up an article in the New York *Sun* of February 16, 1879, and one in the New York *Times* of November 6, the same year, each mentioning an earlier American visit by Gilbert "seven or eight years ago." This would have been 1871 or 1872. The *Sun* placed the month as August and the trip as secretly made. The *Times* described the stay in this country as of only five days' duration, two of which were spent in Boston, and intimated that New York was not visited. No further information has as yet been forthcoming. But the evidence of the English-Field correspondence would seem to rule out 1871; and if it was mid-1872—as is probably the case—then it could not possibly have been during the period of the *Thespis* proofs. Gilbert's memory on this point must have been faulty.

Between December 1871 and March 1872 there were four issues of the original first edition wherein the text remained virtually unchanged. It was not like the later Gilbert to refrain from making prodigious alterations from issue to issue of an already published libretto. He seems clearly to have written off this *Thespis* text as unworthy of his further effort. For example: Sullivan in the letter to his mother describing the second night's performance (see page 6) referred to a song that he cut out after the première. What song? And if so important a change was made in subsequent performances, why was the libretto not made to conform? There was opportunity enough to change pages of its advertising in later issues, why not its text? If Gilbert had cared he would certainly have seen that this libretto was corrected.

Introduction

EASTERTIDE, 1875, IN LONDON held more than the season's customary significance—a rebirth neither Christian nor pagan, and of theatrical rather than religious import. After a winter of almost exactly three years, the springtime of a new and incredibly fruitful collaboration was heralded by the flowering of "the operatic trifle which Mr. W. S. Gilbert and Mr. Arthur Sullivan have perfected at the Royalty," as the event was reported in the *Pictorial World*'s column of "Theatrical and Musical Chat."

Gilbert had planted the seed of this gay harbinger in the Easter issue of *Fun* Magazine, April 11, 1868—a one-page skit entitled "TRIAL BY JURY. An Operetta." illustrated with five characteristic Bab drawings. Publisher Dalziel had paid him £1 5s. 6d. for the literary effort and an additional £1 5s. for the art work, totaling a munificent £2 10s. 6d. (a little more than twelve dollars at the then current exchange). The seedling from which were to burgeon a dozen comic operas, including the most popular in the English language, was assuredly a bargain in immortality.

It was not until late 1873 that Gilbert considered his five-year-old skit in *Fun* as material for expansion into a theatrical product. In an interview for the January 3, 1876, *Illustrated Sporting & Dramatic News* he recalled: "More than two years ago I arranged with M. Carl Rosa to write it [*Trial by Jury*] for the company with which he then intended to open Drury Lane Theatre for a season of English Opera, a scheme which fell through owing to the lamented death of Madame Parepa Rosa." Carl Rosa liked Gilbert's expanded libretto so much, particularly for the opportunities it seemed to hold out for his wife, that he had decided to set the music to it himself. After the death of Parepa Rosa and the collapse

of plans for a Gilbert–Rosa collaboration, it is interesting but not significant that Gilbert did not, apparently, immediately consider Arthur Sullivan to take Carl Rosa's place. Since their *Thespis* collaboration, Sullivan had concentrated on popular ballads, church music, a Festival *Te Deum,* incidental music to *The Merry Wives of Windsor,* and his oratorio *The Light of the World,* to the exclusion of the stage; while Gilbert in the same period had busied himself with miscellaneous farces, comedies, plays, and the publication of his second volume of *Bab Ballads.* They had certainly not avoided each other, but simply had moved busily in different worlds. In fact, on one occasion their worlds had coincided to produce "The Distant Shore," a song with words by Gilbert and music by Sullivan, published in December 1874 by Chappell & Company.

But even with this recent Sullivan contact, Gilbert had not apparently thought to enlist his aid in reactivating *Trial by Jury.* It required the introduction of a third member to this potential author-composer combination to bring about a successful producing team. Such a human catalyst was Richard D'Oyly Carte, young lecture bureau and concert agency executive, who at thirty-one was also serving as manager of the Royalty Theatre for

[27]

Directress Selina Dolaro. Gilbert is said to have dropped in on D'Oyly Carte one day in mid-January 1875, when Dolaro's program, featuring her in Offenbach's popular *La Périchole,* was in rehearsal for the opening of the Royalty on January 30. Carte was alert to pick up good material for use either as curtain raisers or afterpieces for the changes on this bill. Gilbert had showed him the original libretto he had prepared for Carl Rosa, and this had swiftly captured D'Oyly Carte's keen imagination, ending in his suggestion that Sullivan was the man who should set it. A few days later, according to Sullivan's biographers, Gilbert "went down to Sullivan's flat with the manuscript in his pocket and read it to him." Sullivan vividly recalled the occasion: "He read it through, as it seemed to me, in a perturbed sort of way, with a gradual crescendo of indignation, in the manner of a man considerably disappointed with what he had written. As soon as he had come to the last word he closed up the manuscript violently, apparently unconscious of the fact that he had achieved his purpose so far as I was concerned, inasmuch as I was screaming with laughter the whole time. The words were written, and the rehearsals completed, within the space of three weeks' time."

The first announcement in the *Times,* on January 23, omitted the name of Gilbert entirely: "In Preparation, a New Comic Opera composed expressly for this theatre by Mr. Arthur Sullivan, in which Madame Dolaro and Nelly Bromley will appear." This notice ran for five days between January 23 and 30. According to S. J. Adair Fitz-Gerald there was a similar announcement in the Royalty program, which was changed shortly afterward (*very* shortly, it may be imagined) to include Gilbert's name, but written "W. C. Gilbert," and with only Nelly Bromley's name appearing in the cast. There was no further advertisement of the new work until March 20 and 24, when the *Times* notice did contain Gilbert's name, properly initialed. But, one cannot help wondering if the words that Gilbert undoubtedly had in January with Directress Dolaro on the billing error may not have led to her withdrawal from his rehearsal jurisdiction, particularly as she had no way of knowing at that time how this modest afterpiece was destined to run away with the show. It is not unlikely speculation, as, if one pursues these intramural relations further, one learns (also on the authority of Fitz-Gerald) that "in a month's time, for reasons unexplained—except it was darkly hinted that little, pretty, fiery Selina Dolaro objected to big, beautiful Nelly Bromley—Nelly Bromley gave place to Linda Verner, who was Selina Dolaro's particular friend." This exaggerated the brevity of Miss Bromley's participation,

as she actually finished the Spring run through June 12, after which the Royalty closed down for the summer. Linda Verner did not assume the role of the Plaintiff until the theatre's reopening on October 11.

During the preparation for the play an amusing incident occurred, retold by Kate Field in her interview with Gilbert for *Scribner's Monthly* (September 1879): "On the occasion of the first dress rehearsal, every man in the cantata appeared made up for Dr. Kenealy! The stage swarmed with the Tichborne champion, much to the disgust of every individual actor who thought he had conceived an original idea." And what a rollicking surprise that sight must have been on the Royalty Theatre stage!—a jury-boxful of bushy-bearded veniremen, each the comic caricature of Edward Vaughn Kenealy, erstwhile counsel for the claimant in the sensational Tichborne case, whose spectacled face and round full-beard with bare upper and lower lip were as well known as that of Mr. Punch and an easy mark for imitative make-up. (The joke was especially timely since in February Dr. Kenealy, the redoubtable disbarred loser in the famous trial, had defeated both Liberal and Conservative candidates in a by-election for the Stoke-upon-Trent seat in Commons, and so was back in the news.)

"The little house in Dean Street, Soho—which was often referred to as the Soho Theatre," as Adair Fitz-Gerald described the Royalty Theatre, was at that time leased by journalist Henry Labouchere's actress-wife, Henrietta Hodson. (She was destined to tangle with Gilbert two years later in a legal action that secured for her an apology for charges of professional damage.) Manager D'Oyly Carte and Selina Dolaro had assembled a good evening's entertainment in addition to *Trial by Jury.* In the words of the *Morning Advertiser* for Easter-even, March 27, "The Royalty Programme is a highly attractive one for the Easter holidays, including as it does *La Périchole.* . . . Messrs. Edgar and Collette's farce with the weird name *Cryptoconchoidsyphonostomata* begins the entertainment." But, as the *Daily Telegraph* put it, it was "the Easter novelty at this house" that was "a really divertising trifle—a burlesque of the wildest character," in which it was reserved for Mr. W. S. Gilbert "to discover 'fresh fields and pastures new' in a court of justice." *Fun* Magazine found *Trial by Jury* "extremely funny and admirably composed. For once we have an original notion brought to a satisfactory conclusion." In this issue, dated April 10, 1875, *Fun* did not mention that the same notion had been "original" in the *Fun* issue just one day short of seven years before, April 11, 1868.

Even *Punch*'s Our Representative Man gave

54   FUN.   [APRIL 11, 1868.

TRIAL BY JURY.

AN OPERETTA.

SCENE.—*A Court of Law at Westminster.*
Opening Chorus of Counsel, Attorneys, and Populace.

HARK! The hour of ten is sounding,
  Hearts with anxious hopes are bounding,
  Halls of Justice crowds surrounding,
    Breathing hope and fear—
For to-day in this arena
Summoned by a stern subpœna
EDWIN, sued by ANGELINA,
    Shortly will appear!

Chorus of Attorneys.
Attorneys are we
And we pocket our fee,
Singing so merrily, "Trial la law!"
  With our merry ca. sa.,
  And our jolly fi. fa.
Worshipping verily Trial la law!
    Trial la law!
    Trial la law!
Worshipping verily Trial la law!

Chorus of Barristers.
Barristers we,
With demurrer and plea,
Singing so merrily, "Trial la law!"
  Be-wigged and be-gowned
  We rejoice at the sound
Of the several syllables "Trial by law!"
    Trial la law!
    Trial la law!
Singing so merrily Trial la law!

Recitative.
Usher.—Silence in court, and all attention lend!
  Behold the Judge! In due submission bend.

(The Judge enters and bows to the Bar. The Bar returns the compliment.)
Recitative.
Counsel for Plaintiff.—May it please you, my lud!
  Gentlemen of the Jury!

Aria.
With a sense of deep emotion
  I approach this painful case,
For I never had a notion
  That a man could be so base.
    Or deceive a girl confiding,
    Vows, *et cætera*, deriding!
All.—He deceived a girl confiding,
    Vows, *et cætera*, deriding!

Counsel.—See my interesting client,
    Victim of a heartless wile,
  See the traitor all defiant
    Wear a supercilious smile:
      Sweetly smiled my client on him,
      Coyly woo'd and gently won him!
All.—Sweetly smiled the plaintiff on him,
    Coyly woo'd and gently won him!

Counsel.—Swiftly fled each honied hour
    Spent with this unmanly male,
  Camberwell became a bower,
    Peckham an Arcadian vale;
      Breathing concentrated otto!
      An existence *à la Watteau!*
All.—Bless us, concentrated otto!
    An existence *à la Watteau!*

Counsel.—Picture, then, my client naming
    And insisting on the day,
  Picture him excuses framing,
    Going from her far away.
      Doubly criminal to do so
      For the maid had bought her trousseau!
All.—Doubly criminal to do so
    For the maid had bought her trousseau!

Recitative.
Counsel.—Angelina!
(Angelina steps into the witness box.)
Solo.

Judge.—In the course of my career
    As a judex, sitting here,
  Never, never, I declare,
  Have I see a maid so fair!
All.—Ah! Sly dog!

Judge.—See her sinking on her knees
  In the Court of Common Pleas—
  Place your briefs upon the shelf
  I will marry her myself!

(He throws himself into her arms.)
All.—Ah! Sly dog!
Recitative.
Judge.—Come all of you—the breakfast I'll prepare—
  Five hundred and eleven, Eaton Square!
Final Chorus.
Trial la law! Trial la law!
Singing so merrily, Trial la law!
    CURTAIN.

rival *Fun*-man Gilbert a good review: "In *Trial by Jury* (Librettist, W. S. Gilbert; composer, Arthur Sullivan) both Mr. Words and Mr. Music have worked together, and for the first quarter of an hour the Cantata (as they've called it) is the funniest bit of nonsense your representative has seen for a considerable time." *Punch*'s criticism was only that it was too short. "But I must draw a veil," Our Representative Man concluded, "and finish by advising those whom Providence has blessed with affluence and a good digestive, to leave their pleasant dinner-table, and for the sake of a hearty laugh . . . to visit the Royalty. . . ."

Not every London newspaper by any means carried a review of this momentous first night. Easter entertainment did not in those days rate serious critical coverage. But, although as a creative team they had yet to win their own following, as creative individuals they were so well known that, even in a forty-five-minute afterpiece not scheduled to begin till ten fifteen, "the popularity attaching to the names of the authors" (in the words of the *Times*) attracted more than usual attention. Gilbert, for example, was hailed by the *Daily News* in this fashion: "In whimsical invention and eccentric humour Mr. W. S. Gilbert has no living rival among our dramatic writers, and never has his peculiar vein of drollery and satire been more conspicuous than in a little piece entitled *Trial by Jury,* produced at the Royalty Theatre on Thursday evening." And the same reviewer (reaching into I Corinthians XIII, perhaps in deference to the season) added: "Mr. Gilbert was himself an extravaganza writer in his early days, but he has learnt to put away these childish things."

On the composer's side, the *Daily Telegraph* declared: *"Trial by Jury* is a Cantata, and, as such, is the work of . . . Mr. Sullivan, who, by the way, conducted the performance on Thursday night with his usual great tact and skill. After but one hearing of the piece it is scarcely possible to decide upon the precise merits of Mr. Sullivan's latest work, so much is every faculty absorbed by the fun of the dialogue and situations. Nevertheless, we believe it will be found that the music to *Trial by Jury* is worthy the composer of *Cox and Box:* and, consequently, that it illustrates Mr. Sullivan's great capacity for dramatic writing of the lighter class." The *Times* enlarged on this last thought: *"Cox and Box* and *The Contrabandista,* in the concoction of which Mr. Sullivan was associated with Mr. Burnand, proved his ability to cope with the most admired French composers of burlesque, while, at the same time, better provided in a strictly musical sense than any of them."

Even at this virtual debut of their serious collaboration, the miracle of the Gilbert and Sullivan talents in combination was not lost to the press. The *Daily News* wrote: "On this occasion the dramatist and the musical composer have worked together; and so completely is each imbued with the same spirit that it would be as difficult to conceive the existence of Mr. Gilbert's verses without Mr. Sullivan's music, as of Mr. Sullivan's music without Mr. Gilbert's verses. Each gives each a double charm." And the *Times* bestowed a classic accolade: "It seems, as in the great Wagnerian operas, as though poem and music had proceeded simultaneously from one and the same brain."

The Royalty Theatre program for that night carried no indication of day or date, nor that the afterpiece was to be conducted by the composer. (Even so, there is no question of which is the first-night program because only on the evening of Thursday, March 25, did the triple bill at the Royalty consist of *Cryptoconchoidsyphonostomata, La Périchole,* and *Trial by Jury.* This was the last performance for the long-named curtain-raiser, which was replaced on Saturday, March 27, by *A Good Night's Rest.* The Royalty had been dark on Good Friday, March 26.) Sullivan's name preceded Gilbert's in the billing, as it did in the libretto. There were numerous typographic errors that, by their being corrected in later issues, serve to help establish priority. So comparatively little fanfare attended this première, and so soon was the curtain raiser changed and the *Trial by Jury* cast slightly altered, that biographers and historians of Gilbert and Sullivan have unintentionally woven a fabric of error and confusion as to the correct program and proper cast. One particular bacterial cause of this state of ferment has been an elaborately illustrated program showing cartoons of Gilbert and Sullivan as cupids on either side of a large central medallion portrait of Selina Dolaro, and below a tiny portrait head of Offenbach. This design was used by Adair Fitz-Gerald for illustration in his *Story of the Savoy Opera* (1924). Unhappily someone had written, with more enthusiasm than accuracy, at the top of this program the words *"March 25/75 FIRST NIGHT."* The fact that its cast did not tally with the first-night cast reviewed by the press, and that it did not carry the proper curtain raiser was overlooked. Isaac Goldberg, usually very dependable, was deceived by this. In *The Story of Gilbert and Sullivan* he refers to the program as having "an intentional symbolic touch." But if really issued for the first night, it would have been more than symbolic, it would have been illogically and fantastically prophetic. Clearly no one until the final curtain could have been so certain of the huge success that *Trial by Jury* would enjoy. This program was for a later evening when the curtain raiser was a farce entitled *The Secret,* by which time the success of the afterpiece was no secret, and the symbolism of the triumph of Gilbert and Sullivan over Jacques Offenbach was not only intentional but meaningful in the program cover design (see illustration on page 32).

Next to Gilbert, Sullivan, and D'Oyly Carte, the first night of *Trial by Jury* was a triumph for the composer's older brother Frederick in the role of the Judge. He had played the part of Apollo in *Thespis,* but had not until that night shown his true potential as a comedian. The *Daily Telegraph* stated that "the greatest 'hit' was made by Mr. F. Sullivan, whose blending of official dignity, condescension, and, at the right moment, extravagant humour, made the character of the Judge stand out with all requisite prominence, and added much to the interest of the piece." And the *Times* agreed: "Mr. F. Sullivan's impersonation of the learned and impressionable Judge deserves a special word of praise for its quiet and natural hu-

Fred Sullivan as The Learned Judge, after a cabinet photograph he presented to Gilbert, August 1875.

mour." *Punch* praised his delivery of "When I, good friends, first came to the bar"—"of which Mr. Frederic Sullivan does not allow the audience to miss a syllable in four or five verses."

The rest of the cast received more cursory attention. The *Daily Telegraph* thought that "Miss Nelly Bromley made the Plaintiff as interesting and attractive as possible." The *Daily News* remarked of her: "Miss Nellie Bromley, as the Bride, sings with more taste than voice," and continued, "and the same remark applies, under the circumstances already mentioned, to Mr. Walter Fisher, as the Defendant; but both in their acting entered fully into the spirit of the piece." (The "circumstance" referred to by the *Daily News* critic was the fact that Mr. Fisher had sung the

Chorus.

And now if you please, he's ready to try this Breach of Promise of marriage.

Arthur Sullivan

chief male role in the longer and more demanding *La Périchole* preceding *Trial by Jury,* and "had unfortunately exerted himself too much to have any voice left for Mr. Sullivan's service.") For the record and the enlightenment of posterity, the *Daily Telegraph* noted that "Mr. Hollingsworth did good service as the Counsel; nor should the efforts of Mr. Kelleher (Foreman) and Mr. Pepper (Usher) pass unrecognized."

"The little piece is briskly acted. . . . The music is fresh and effective always," was the opinion of the *Pictorial World,* adding: "The piece is an undoubted success." The *Daily News'* enthusiastic reviewer declared: "Laughter more frequent or more hearty was never heard in any theatre than that which more than once brought the action of the 'dramatic cantata' on Thursday evening to a temporary standstill."

ROYALTY.—Trial by Jury, *the joint production of Messrs. W. S. Gilbert and Arthur Sullivan, is a pleasant addition to the bill of fare at Madame Selina Dolaro's pretty theatre in Soho. Its success on Thursday night, when Mr. Sullivan himself directed the orchestra, and both he and his colleague were summoned at the descent of the curtain, was thoroughly genuine. None could feel surprise at such result. . . .*

THE TIMES, MARCH 29, 1875

A Novel and Entirely Original
Dramatic Cantata,

TRIAL
BY JURY

Dramatis Personae.

THE LEARNED JUDGE	MR. F. SULLIVAN.
COUNSEL FOR THE PLAINTIFF	MR. HOLLINGSWORTH.
THE DEFENDANT	MR. W. FISHER.
FOREMAN OF THE JURY	MR. KELLEHER.
USHER	MR. PEPPER.

and

THE PLAINTIFF	MISS NELLY BROMLEY.

BRIDESMAIDS

GENTLEMEN OF THE JURY.

SCENE. — A Court of Justice.

SCENE. — *A Court of Justice. Associate, Barristers, Attorneys, and Jurymen discovered, with* USHER.

CHORUS.

Hark, the hour of ten is sounding;
Hearts with anxious fears are bounding,
Hall of Justice crowds surrounding,
　　Breathing hope and fear—
For to-day in this arena,
Summoned by a stern subpœna,
Edwin, sued by Angelina—
　　Shortly will appear.

The Usher marshals the Jury into Jury-box. Ladies and Barristers cross over and sit on Counsel's benches.

SOLO — USHER.

Now, Jurymen, hear my advice—
All kinds of vulgar prejudice
　　I pray you set aside:
With stern judicial frame of mind,
From bias free of every kind,
　　This trial must be tried!

CHORUS.

From bias free of every kind,
This trial must be tried.

During Choruses, USHER *says* fortissimo, *"Silence in Court!"*

USHER.　Oh listen to the plaintiff's case:
Observe the features of her face—
　　The brokenhearted bride.
Condole with her distress of mind:
From bias free of every kind,
　　This trial must be tried!

CHORUS.　From bias free, &c.

USHER.　And when amid the plaintiff's shrieks,
The ruffianly defendant speaks—
　　Upon the other side;

What *he* may say you needn't mind—
From bias free of every kind,
　　This trial must be tried.

CHORUS.　From bias free, &c.

Enter DEFENDANT *with guitar.*

RECITATIVE — DEFENDANT.

Is this the Court of the Exchequer?

ALL.　It is!

DEFENDANT (*aside*).　Be firm, my moral pecker,
　　Your evil star's in the ascendant!

ALL.　Who are you?

DEFENDANT.　I'm the Defendant!

CHORUS OF JURYMEN.

Monster, dread our damages!
　　We're the jury,
　　Dread our fury!

DEFENDANT.　Hear me, hear me, if you please
　　These are very strange proceedings—
For permit me to remark
　　On the merits of my pleadings,
You're at present in the dark.

DEFENDANT *beckons to* JURYMEN—*they leave the box and gather round him as they sing the following:*

Ha! ha! ha!
That's a very true remark—
　　On the merits of your pleadings
We're entirely in the dark!
Ha! ha!—ha! ha!

SONG — DEFENDANT.

When first my old, old love I knew,

My bosom swelled with joy;
My riches at her feet I threw—
    I was a lovesick boy!
No terms seemed extravagant
    Upon her to employ—
I used to mope and sigh and pant,
    Just like a lovesick boy!
        Tink-a-Tank—Tink-a-Tank.

But joy incessant palls the sense;
    And love, unchanged, will cloy,
And she became a bore intense
    Unto her lovesick boy!
With fitful glimmer burnt my flame,
    And I grew cold and coy.
At last, one morning, I became
    Another's lovesick boy!
        Tink-a-Tank—Tink-a-Tank.

CHORUS OF JURYMEN (*advancing stealthily*).
    Oh, I was like that when a lad!
    A shocking young scamp of a rover,
    I behaved like a regular cad;
    But that sort of thing is all over.
    I'm now a respectable chap
    And shine with a virtue resplendent,
    And therefore, I haven't a scrap
    Of sympathy with the defendant!
        He shall treat us with awe,
        If there isn't a flaw,
    Singing so merrily—Trial-la-law!
    Trial-la-law—Trial-la-law!
    Singing so merrily—Trial-la-law!

RECITATIVE — USHER (*on Bench*).

Silence in Court and all attention lend.
Behold your Judge! In due submission bend!

Enter JUDGE *on Bench.*

CHORUS.

    All hail, great judge!
        To your bright rays
    We never grudge
        Ecstatic praise.
            All hail!

    May each decree
        As statute rank,
    And never be
    Reversed in banc.
            All hail!

RECITATIVE — JUDGE.

For these kind words accept my thanks, I pray.
A Breach of Promise we've to try to-day.
But firstly, if the time you'll not begrudge,
I'll tell you how I came to be a judge.

ALL.   He'll tell us how he came to be a judge!

JUDGE.   Let me speak.

ALL.   Let him speak.

JUDGE.   Let me speak.

ALL.   Let him speak. Hush! hush!! hush!!!
    (*Fortissimo.*) He'll tell us how he came to be a
    judge!

SONG — JUDGE.

When I, good friends, was called to the bar,
    I'd an appetite fresh and hearty,
But I was as many young barristers are,
    An impecunious party.
I'd a swallow-tail coat of a beautiful blue—
    A brief which I bought of a booby—
A couple of shirts and a collar or two,
    And a ring that looked like a ruby!

CHORUS.   A couple of shirts, &c.

JUDGE.   In Westminster Hall I danced a dance,
    Like a semi-despondent fury;
For I thought I never should hit on a chance
    Of addressing a British jury—
But I soon got tired of third-class journeys,
    And dinners of bread and water;
So I fell in love with a rich attorney's
    Elderly, ugly daughter.

CHORUS.   So he fell in love, &c.

JUDGE.   The rich attorney he jumped with joy,
    And replied to my fond professions:
"You shall reap the reward of your pluck, my
        boy,
    At the Bailey and Middlesex Sessions.
You'll soon get used to her looks," said he,
    "And a very nice girl you'll find her!
She may very well pass for forty-three
    In the dusk, with a light behind her!"

CHORUS.   She may very well, &c.

JUDGE.   The rich attorney was good as his word:
        The briefs came trooping gaily,
    And every day my voice was heard
        At the Sessions or Ancient Bailey,
    All thieves who could my fees afford
        Relied on my orations,
    And many a burglar I've restored,
        To his friends and his relations.

CHORUS.   And many a burglar &c.

JUDGE.   At length I became as rich as the
            Gurneys—
        An incubus then I thought her,
    So I threw over that rich attorney's
        Elderly ugly daughter.
    The rich attorney my character high
        Tried vainly to disparage—

And now if you please, I'm ready to try
This breach of promise of marriage!

CHORUS.   And now if you please &c.

JUDGE.   For now I am a Judge!

ALL.   And a good Judge too!

JUDGE.   Yes, now I am a Judge!

ALL.   And a good Judge too!

JUDGE.   Though all my law is fudge
Yet I'll never, never budge,
But I'll live and die a Judge!

ALL.   And a good Judge too!

JUDGE (*pianissimo*).   It was managed by a job—

ALL.   And a good job too!

JUDGE.   It was managed by a job!

ALL.   And a good job too!

JUDGE.   It is patent to the mob,
That my being made a nob
Was effected by a job.

ALL.   And a good job too!

Enter COUNSEL *for* PLAINTIFF. *He takes his place
in front row of Counsel's Seats.*

RECITATIVE — COUNSEL.

Swear thou the Jury!

USHER.   Kneel, Jurymen, oh! kneel!

All the JURY *kneel in the Jury-box, and so are
hidden from audience.*

USHER.   Oh will you swear by yonder skies,
Whatever question may arise,
'Twixt rich and poor—'twixt low and high,
That you will well and truly try.

JURY (*raising their hands, which alone are visible*).
To all of this we make reply,

By the dull slate of yonder sky:
That we will well and truly try.

(*All rise with the last note, both hands in air.*)

USHER. This blind devotion is indeed a crusher—
Pardon the tear-drop of the simple usher!
(*He weeps.*)

COUNSEL. Call the plaintiff.

USHER. Oh Angelina! Angelina!! Come thou into
Court;

Enter the BRIDESMAIDS, *each bearing two palm
branches, their arms crossed on their bosoms, and
rose-wreaths on their arms.*

CHORUS OF BRIDESMAIDS.

Comes the broken flower—
Comes the cheated maid—
Though the tempest lower,
Rain and cloud will fade!
Take, oh maid, these posies:
Though thy beauty rare
Shame the blushing roses—
They are passing fair!
Wear the flowers till they fade:
Happy be thy life, oh maid!

The JUDGE *having taken a great fancy to* 1st
BRIDESMAID, *sends her a note by* USHER, *which
she reads, kisses rapturously, and places in
her bosom.*

SOLO — ANGELINA.

O'er the season vernal,
Time may cast a shade;
Sunshine, if eternal,
Makes the roses fade:
Time may do his duty;
Let the thief alone—
Winter hath a beauty,
That is all his own.
Fairest days are sun and shade:
I am no unhappy maid!

(*By this time the* JUDGE *has transferred his
admiration to* ANGELINA.)

CHORUS OF BRIDESMAIDS.

Comes the broken flower, &c.

During chorus ANGELINA *collects wreaths of roses
from* BRIDESMAIDS *and gives them to the* JURY,
*who put them on and wear them during the rest
of the piece.*

JUDGE (*to* ASSOCIATE). Oh never, never, never,
since I joined the human race:
Saw I so exquisitely fair a face.

THE JURY (*shaking their forefingers at him*). Ah,
sly dog!

JUDGE (*to* JURY). How say you—is she not designed for capture?

FOREMAN (*after consulting with the* JURY). We've
but one word, my lord, and that is—
Rapture!

PLAINTIFF (*curtseying*). Your kindness, gentlemen, quite overpowers!

THE JURY. We love you fondly and would make
you ours!

THE BRIDESMAIDS (*shaking their forefingers at*
JURY). Ah, sly dogs!

RECITATIVE — COUNSEL *for* PLAINTIFF.

May it please you, my lud!
Gentlemen of the jury!

ARIA.

With a sense of deep emotion,
I approach this painful case;
For I never had a notion

That a man could be so base,
Or deceive a girl confiding,
Vows *etcetera* deriding!

ALL. He deceived a girl confiding,
Vows *etcetera* deriding.

PLAINTIFF *falls sobbing on* COUNSEL'S *breast and
remains there.*

COUNSEL. See my interesting client,
Victim of a heartless wile!
See the traitor all defiant
Wear a supercilious smile!
Sweetly smiled my client on him,
Coyly woo'd and gently won him.

ALL. Sweetly smiled, &c.

COUNSEL. Swiftly fled each honeyed hour
Spent with this unmanly male!
Camberwell became a bower,
Peckham an Arcadian Vale,
Breathing concentrated otto!—
An existence *à la* Watteau.

ALL. Bless us, concentrated otto! &c.

COUNSEL (*coming down with* PLAINTIFF, *who is
still sobbing on his breast*).

Picture then my client naming
And insisting on the day:
Picture him excuses framing—
Going from her far away;
Doubly criminal to do so,
For the maid had bought her *trousseau!*

ALL. Doubly criminal, &c.

COUNSEL (*to* PLAINTIFF, *who weeps*). Cheer up,
my pretty—oh cheer up!

JURY. Cheer up, cheer up, we love you!

COUNSEL *leads* PLAINTIFF *fondly into Witness-
box; he takes a tender leave of her and resumes his
place in Court.* PLAINTIFF *reels as if about
to faint.*

JUDGE. That she is reeling
Is plain to me!

FOREMAN. If faint you're feeling,
Recline on me!

(*She falls sobbing on to the* FOREMAN'S *breast.*)

PLAINTIFF (*feebly*). I shall recover
If left alone.

ALL (*shaking their fists at* DEFENDANT). Atone!
atone!

FOREMAN. Just like a father
I wish to be! (*Kissing her.*)

JUDGE (*approaching her*). Or, if you'd rather,
Recline on me!

She staggers on to Bench, sits down by the JUDGE,
and falls sobbing on his breast.

COUNSEL. Oh! fetch some water
Far from Cologne!

ALL. For this sad slaughter
Atone! atone!

JURY (*shaking fists at* DEFENDANT). Monster,
monster, dread our fury,
There's the Judge, and we're the Jury!

SONG — DEFENDANT.

Oh, gentlemen, listen, I pray, I pray,
Though I own that my heart has been
ranging,
Of Nature the laws I obey,
For nature is constantly changing.
The moon in her phases is found,
The time and the wind and the weather,
The months in succession come round,
And you don't find two Mondays together.
Consider the moral, I pray,
Nor bring a young fellow to sorrow,
Who loves this young lady to-day,
And loves that young lady to-morrow.

You cannot eat breakfast all day,
Nor is it the act of a sinner,
When breakfast is taken away,
To turn your attention to dinner;
And it's not in the range of belief,
That you could hold him as a glutton,
Who, when he is tired of beef,
Determines to tackle the mutton.
Consider the moral, I pray, &c.

Oh, beware a dilemma so strange,
    It will soon play the deuce with your dollars,
It will soon be illegal to change
    Your money, your mind, or your collars;
A singer must sing the same song
    From the time of his youth to his latter days;
'Twill be eight o'clock all the day long,
    And the week will be nothing but Saturdays!
    But this I am ready to say,
        If it will appease their sorrow,
    I'll marry one lady to-day,
        And I'll marry the other to-morrow!

RECITATIVE.

JUDGE. That seems a reasonable proposition,
    To which, I think, your client may agree.

ALL. Oh, Judge discerning!

COUNSEL. But, I submit, my lord, with all
    submission,
    To marry two at once is Burglaree!
                (*Referring to law book.*)

In the reign of James the Second,
It was generally reckoned
As a very serious crime
To marry two wives at one time.
    (*Hands book up to* JUDGE, *who reads it.*)

ALL. Oh, man of learning!

QUARTETTE.

JUDGE. A nice dilemma we have here,
    That calls for all our wit:

COUNSEL. And at this stage, it don't appear
    That we can settle it.

DEFENDANT (*in Witness-box*). If I to wed the girl
    am loth
    A breach 'twill surely be—

PLAINTIFF. And if he goes and marries both,
    It counts as Burglaree!

ALL. A nice dilemma, &c.

DUET — PLAINTIFF *and* DEFENDANT.

PLAINTIFF (*embracing him rapturously*). I love
    him—I love him—with fervour unceasing,
I worship and madly adore;
My blind adoration is always increasing,
    My loss I shall ever deplore.
Oh, see what a blessing, what love and caressing
    I've lost, and remember it, pray,
When you I'm addressing, are busy assessing
    The damages Edwin must pay.

DEFENDANT (*repelling her furiously*). I smoke
    like a furnace—I'm always in liquor,
    A ruffian—a bully—a sot.

I'm sure I should thrash her, perhaps I should
    kick her,
    I am such a very bad lot!
I'm not prepossessing, as you may be guessing,
    She couldn't endure me a day.
Recall my professing, when you are assessing
    The damages Edwin must pay!
    (*She clings to him passionately; he drags her
    round stage and flings her to the ground.*)

JURY. We would be fairly acting,
    But this is most distracting!

RECITATIVE.

JUDGE. The question, gentlemen, is one of liquor;
    You ask for guidance—this is my reply:
If he, when tipsy, would assault and kick her,
    Let's make him tipsy, gentlemen, and try!

COUNSEL. With all respect
             I do object!

ALL. With all respect
             We do object!

DEFENDANT. I don't object!

ALL.   We do object!

JUDGE (*tossing his books and papers about.*) All
    the legal furies seize you!
No proposal seems to please you,
I can't stop up here all day;
I must shortly go away.
Barristers, and you, attorneys,
Set out on your homeward journeys;
Put your briefs upon the shelf,
I will marry her myself!

(He comes down from Bench to floor of Court.
He embraces ANGELINA.)

FINALE.

PLAINTIFF. Oh, joy unbounded!
　　　With wealth surrounded,
　　　The knell is sounded

　　　　　　　Of grief and woe.

COUNSEL. With love devoted,
　　　On you he's doated,
　　　To castle moated

　　　　　　　Away they go.

DEFENDANT. I wonder whether
　　　They'll live together
　　　In marriage tether

　　　　　　　In manner true?

USHER. It seems to me, sir,
　　　Of such as she, sir,
　　　A judge is he, sir,

　　　　　　　A good judge too.

CHORUS. It seems to me, sir, &c.

JUDGE. Oh, yes, I am a Judge.

ALL. And a good judge too!

JUDGE. Oh, yes, I am a Judge.

ALL. And a good judge too!

JUDGE. Though homeward as you trudge,
　　　You declare my law is fudge,
　　　Yet of beauty I'm a judge.

ALL. And a good judge too!

JUDGE *and* PLAINTIFF *dance back, hornpipe step,
and get on to the Bench—the* BRIDESMAIDS *take
the eight garlands of Roses from behind* JUDGE'S
*desk and draw them across floor of Court, so that
they radiate from the desk. Two plaster Cupids in
bar wigs descend from flies. Red fire.*

CURTAIN.

Postscript

THE AUDIENCE at the Royalty Theatre on the night of March 25, 1875, had an eighteen-page libretto in glossy, vivid blue paper wrappers. Sullivan's name preceded Gilbert's on the title-page. On the Dramatis Personae page, under the headline "Characters," this first edition listed Mr. Kelleher as Foreman of the Jury, Mr. Pepper as the Usher, and Mr. Campbell as first of the Gentlemen of the Jury. There was no such character as that of Associate, a role added later.

The original cast of *Trial by Jury* has suffered from inaccurate representation of one sort or another (particularly involving these characters) from the earliest books on Gilbert and Sullivan operas, as far back as the 1890's. In part, this has stemmed from the use of programs of later performances, or the D.P. page of later-issue librettos, as source. In addition there has been a bibliographic low blow in the fact that the first edition of the vocal score—because it was published considerably later than the first night—does not give the proper original cast.

But the most important distinguishing feature of the first-edition libretto—used on the first night—is the presence of a third verse to the Defendant's Song on page 40, beginning:

Oh, beware a dilemma so strange,
It will soon play the deuce with your dollars . . .

That this was sung by Mr. Walter Fisher, at least on the first night, is fortunately recorded by the critic for the *Pictorial World,* who quoted a portion of this very verse in his review. It is found only in the first edition of the libretto and nowhere else.

As *Trial by Jury* is sung from beginning to end with no spoken dialog, it seems appropriate to indicate here the major changes that followed its first published form, as though it were one long lyric. Not only were there immediate variations from the libretto text in the first edition of the vocal score, but in the joint revival of *Trial by Jury* and *The Sorcerer* in 1884, and in subsequent editions, further changes were introduced and consolidated into what now survives as the current text.

On page 35 "Be firm, my moral pecker" was altered in the vocal score to "Be firm, be firm, my pecker." On page 36 the Defendant's bosom "welled" instead of "swelled" with joy. And on the same page, for metrical purposes, "No terms seemed too extravagant" replaced "No terms seemed extravagant." All these small changes stemming from the first vocal score are found in modern usage.

On page 36, the lines between "I'll tell you how I came to be a judge" and the beginning of the Judge's song are frequently condensed to:

ALL.   He'll tell us how he came to be a Judge!
JUDGE.   Let me speak.
ALL.   Let him speak.

But these lines were omitted altogether in the 1884 revival.

On page 38, the recitative for the Usher ("This blind devotion . . .") is dropped, and the immediately following Recitative of the Counsel becomes

Where is the Plaintiff?
Let her now be brought.

—after which the Usher's summoning recitative is changed to

Oh Angelina! Come thou into Court! Angelina! Angelina!

On page 38, after the Jury has sung "We love you fondly and would make you ours!" and before the Counsel's recitative, both the vocal score and the later librettos have made the following addition:

THE BRIDESMAIDS (*shaking their forefingers at Jury*).
Ah, sly dogs! Ah, sly dogs!
THE JURY (*shaking their fists at Defendant*).
Monster! Monster! Dread our fury!
There's the Judge and we're the Jury!
Come, substantial damages!
Substantial damages!
Damages! dam—
USHER.
Silence in Court!

On page 39, after the Plaintiff has sung "I shall recover if left alone," a line is added to the court's denunciation and it now reads

Oh, perjured lover,
Atone! atone!

The Defendant's cheerful solution to his problem as stated in the chorus of his song becomes "I'll marry this lady today" instead of ". . . one lady today."

On page 40, after the Defendant has sung the

line, "The damages Edwin must pay!" the Jury's comment has been expanded to read:

> We would be fairly acting,
> But this is most distracting!
> If, when in liquor, he would kick her,
>   That is an abatement.

and the court, picking up the Plaintiff's previous fervent declaration, joins in: "She loves him, and madly adores, &c."

In the Judge's next recitative, the line "If he, when tipsy . . ." is changed to "He says, when tipsy, he would thrash and kick her."

Minor changes in the Judge's next song make two lines read: "I must shortly get away" and "Get you on your homeward journeys."

Immediately thereafter the following couplet is added:

> Gentle, simple-minded usher,
> Get you, if you like, to Russ*her*!
>   [Vocal score spelling: Russia.]

And the Finale in its later form ends with the following added lines which had been in the vocal score from the earliest edition:

JUDGE.	Though defendant is a snob.
ALL.	And a great snob too!
JUDGE.	Though defendant is a snob, I'll reward him from my fob.
ALL.	So we've settled with the job, And a good job too!

Gong for Change

#

GRAND TRANSFORMATION SCENE!

JUDGE.
Oh, yes, I am a Judge.
ALL.
And a good Judge too!
JUDGE.
Oh, yes, I am a Judge.
ALL.
And a good Judge too!
JUDGE.
Though homeward as you trudge,
You declare my law is fudge,
Yet of beauty I'm a judge.
ALL.
And a good Judge too!

CURTAIN.

Red fire

[handwritten: Judge. Defendant is a snob / All. And a great snob too / Judge. Tho' Deft is a snob / All. And a great snob too / Judge. Tho' Deft is a snob / I'll reward him from my fob / So we've settled with the job / And a good job too. / Picture & Curtain / Red fire R & L / 8 pairs on each side]

Alterations in Gilbert's own prompt copy, though not in his hand. (The stage direction written on opposite page of this prompt copy—now in the British Museum— will be found on page 457.)

THE SORCERER

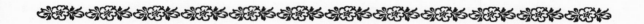

Introduction

THE SORCERER, in a manner of speaking, was initially a three-act opera, and the first act, a "Prelude," was written in 1876 by D'Oyly Carte, with helpful suggestions from Gilbert. Sullivan never set Carte's words to music, but they proved later to be music to his ears and Gilbert's nonetheless. This opus of Carte's was in essence the plan for a Comedy Opera Company which would enable him to achieve two objectives: First, to become an independent producer-manager, his fervent ambition; and second, to meet the insistence of Gilbert and Sullivan that they be paid a guarantee in advance on their next collaboration.

The necessity for sufficient capital to insure this latter arrangement was made urgent in March of 1876, at which time Gilbert in as many words insisted that he and Sullivan must "receive a sum down, before putting pen to paper," and made clear that they would sign up with another manager if one would comply to these terms. There was no other answer but for D'Oyly Carte to write his "Prelude" to *The Sorcerer* there and then—a Prospectus to raise capital—and this work was largely completed by the end of the year.

Gilbert, on his part, had written a short story for the Christmas number of the *Graphic,* entitled "An Elixir of Love," with illustrations by the then-seldom-heard-from artist Bab, and drawing economically on his own *Bab Ballad,* "The Rival Curates," for basic material. It may well be that the businessman's prospectus and the humorist's description of the effect of a love-philtre on the population of Ploverleigh, were read by some Londoners on the same December day, 1876 . . . certainly without associating the one with the other.

Arthur Sullivan, on the other hand, in the latter part of that same month was concerned neither with Carte's capital nor with Gilbert's "Elixir."

His brother Fred, of *Trial by Jury* fame, had been taken seriously ill. By mid-January 1877 he was dead—and Sullivan, having borne "The Lost Chord" out of the depths of suffering at his brother's deathbed, had written "his last composition for many months."

Carte's Comedy Opera Company, Ltd., at that stage was a syndicate with four directors: Frank Chappell and George Metzler (partners in the latter's music publishing firm, which had published the vocal score of *Trial by Jury*), Collard Augustus Drake (secretary of the company, also associated with Metzler), and Edward Hodgson Bayley (known as "Water-cart Bayley" because, according to Isaac Goldberg, he held a virtual monopoly on the sprinkling of London's streets). Carte himself was not a director at the outset, but became one a year later. He appears to have been still looking for further capital in early 1877, as at that time he sent an unidentified nobleman a detailed letter soliciting his interest. It is noteworthy that in this letter he wrote: ". . . and propose to produce, in the first instance, a new 'opera comique,' by Messrs. W. S. Gilbert and Arthur Sullivan, which they have talked over." There was still outstanding that most important negotiatory feature, an arrangement of terms with his author and composer. This detail was not resolved till June 5, according to Sullivan's letter of that date to D'Oyly Carte:

> My dear Carte,   Gilbert and myself are quite willing to write a two-act piece for you on the following terms:
> 1. Payment to us of two hundred guineas (£210) on delivery of the MS. words and music—that is to say, before the piece is produced.
> 2. Six guineas a performance (£6.6) to be paid to us for the run of the piece in London, from this will be deducted the two hundred guineas paid in advance so that the payment of the six guineas a performance will not really commence until about the 33rd or 34th performance.
> 3. We reserve the country right, your right to play it in London on these terms to extend only to the end of your season.
> The piece would be of a musical comedy character and could be ready for performance by the end of September. If this outline of terms is agreed to, we could prepare a proper agreement upon this basis.
>
> Yours truly
> Arthur Sullivan

In July the memorandum of agreement was signed incorporating all the foregoing details as well as the following paragraph indicating that already postponement had become necessary:

> The said Arthur Sullivan and W. S. Gilbert undertake to deliver the manuscript (words and music) in installments as completed in sufficient time for the production of the piece on Monday, October 29, 1877, the whole of the manuscript to be delivered not later than the 15th October 1877. The said R. D'Oyly Carte undertakes to produce the said opera on or about the 29th of October, 1877.

The libretto, at least of an early version of the opera, based on "An Elixir of Love," from all accounts was already in Sullivan's hands in April. The matter of a suitable theatre had given Carte some difficulty as none was available for his new company; so he had to lease the Opéra Comique —"a distinctly second-rate one," in the memory of Sir George Douglas; although Carte, naturally enough, in approaching potential investors referred to it as "an excellent West-end theatre."

The Opéra Comique, Jessie Bond described as being "in what was then a most unsavoury neighbourhood; the theatre was small, poor, and incon-venient, even according to the standards of those days." Rutland Barrington recalled that "though giving from the auditorium a sense of elegance and plenty of room," it was in reality one of the most cramped theatres in his experience. "It was like a rabbit-warren for entrances, having three or four in as many different streets, and from the principal one, which was in the Strand, there was an excessively long and narrow tunnel to traverse before arriving at the stalls, which would have been an awful place in case of fire or any panic." Backstage, "with the exception of one or two little cabins, more resembling stoke-holes, below the level of the stage, occupied by the ladies and the tenor," Barrington continues, "all the dressing-rooms were upstairs in houses along Holywell Street . . . and reached from the stage by a flight of some thirty very steep stone steps commencing almost at the street door," which François Cellier remembered as a narrow, dingy doorway in Wych Street.

If Gilbert's libretto was really ready in April, Sullivan must have required five months to get fully out of his despondency and into the mood necessary for setting comic lyrics. "The fires were slow to rise," as his biographers put it. But they have confused the record by suggesting he was finishing *The Sorcerer* by mid-August whereas in reality he had not yet begun it, even though Carte's original schedule for the première was Monday, September 3. The Sullivan biographers have mistakenly identified as *The Sorcerer* the unnamed work which, in a letter of August 18, he wrote he was about to finish "by Tuesday or Wednesday [August 21 or 22]. It comes out Monday week." But a newly discovered Sullivan letter dated August 21 to his musician friend A. A. Visetti makes clear it is the *Henry VIII* music he was finishing in late August. The letter concludes: "I am going to work now on a new 2 act piece with W. S. Gilbert, to come out on Nov: 1, so I have not *too* much time to spare!" This underestimate was emphasized two months later when, on November 1, he wrote: "I am just putting the last few bars to my opera, and tomorrow begin the scoring. I have been slaving at this work, and hope it will be a success. Everything at present promises very well. The book is brilliant, and the music I think very pretty and good. All the company are good and like it very much." So, the delay formerly attributed to casting problems probably was due to no other reason than a very late start.

The *Daily News* mentioned "Mr. Sullivan's temporary illness" as the alleged cause of the postponement, but this is not substantiated by his biography. And until now it has been hard to credit that the casting problems of *The Sorcerer* became so snarled. Whether Gilbert and

One of the Opéra Comique's several entrances.

Sullivan began too late, or whether they suffered initial delays and disappointments, is not evident in the record. It is known that they were both determined to avoid engaging already-established popular favorites of the London stage, a relatively small and concentrated group, selection from which would not have been too time-consuming. Instead they combed the larger and more scattered legion of provincial players, entertainers, and professional beginners. By August they had secured a particularly helpful member, Mrs. Howard Paul, an experienced actress with her own touring company. Directly and indirectly through her, Gilbert and Sullivan obtained their two most important Savoyards-to-be: Directly, because she made it mandatory in her contract that they engage one of her young actors named Rutland Barrington; indirectly, because, when a young touring entertainer, George Grossmith, Jr., was vacillating in his decision to accept Gilbert and Sullivan's offer, it was her astute—almost clairvoyant—letter of advice that tipped the scales:

My dear Brother George,   May I claim the privilege of an old friend, and be impertinent enough to make a suggestion and give my opinion?—which is as follows: First, that, under any circumstances, and at some sacrifice, you do not fail to accept the part of the "Magician" in Gilbert and Sullivan's new play. It is a splendid part—better than you

think, I fancy—and the "patter" song is great in its way. . . . I think, if you will arrange, it will be a new and *magnificent introduction* for you, and be of great service afterwards. I am sure the part will suit you exactly. . . .

Years later George Grossmith admitted, "This was a great comfort to me. . . . I wrote Mrs. Howard Paul that I had decided to take the engagement; and on the 5th of November, 1877, she, Barrington and myself, and a few others, celebrated the event in the back garden at Bedford Park [Mrs. Paul's home] with a display of fireworks." Had Gilbert, Sullivan, and D'Oyly Carte been as clairvoyant as Isabella Paul, there would certainly have been a simultaneous celebration, also with fireworks, at 24, The Boltons, South Kensington— home and castle to W. S. Gilbert.

Uncertainties that plagued the casting also hounded the libretto till late into October. Sullivan made this clear in a revealing letter to Mrs. Paul dated October 23:

Dear Mrs. Paul,   I do not send you any music by post because as you are coming back on Thursday I would rather you read it all through with me first.

That of the first Act is quite done. The second of course will be far the more important now you are going to take the part of the Spirit Fiend.

Could you and Mr. Barrington come and have a quiet run through the music with me before the Rehearsal is called for principals? Thursday or Friday morning I shall be at home. The Principals are called for first rehearsal for Saturday morning.

"The part of the Spirit Fiend"—his satanic majesty Ahrimanes to whom Sorcerer Wells owed allegiance —can be found only in a preproduction promptbook. It is a role unlikely to win actresses. So perhaps Mrs. Paul's reaction helped speed its disappearance, save for one lone mention by Wells near the end.

Exhaustively thorough rehearsing, for which Gilbert was already known, occupied the first half of November, culminating in the final dress rehearsal on Friday night, the 16th. Then, on Saturday evening November 17, at eight o'clock, the Opéra Comique curtain rose on the forepiece, *Dora's Dream,* an operetta by Arthur Cecil and Alfred Cellier (conducted on that occasion by Cellier himself) that had won favor four years earlier at the Gallery of Illustration. The *Times* remarked that "this pleasant and sparkling *bagatelle* at once put the house in a good humour." It was close to nine o'clock before the capacity audience burst into applause for composer Sullivan as he made his way to the conductor's desk in the pit.

The *Daily News* reported: "The opera is preceded by a light and melodious orchestral introduction . . ." but this critic either did not recognize or at least did not specify what was noted sourly by the *Figaro:* "Mr. Sullivan has not deemed it worth while to write an overture, but has, it is said, borrowed his prelude from his *Henry VIII* incidental music" (which had first been heard at Manchester that August).

The general tone of press reaction, from the start, was warmly favorable and reflected a real anticipation. "Messrs. W. S. Gilbert and Arthur Sullivan have once again combined their efforts with the happiest result," was the opinion of the *Times.* "*The Sorcerer,* produced at the Opéra Comique on Saturday night before an audience that crowded the theatre in every part, achieved a genuine success, and moreover, a success in every respect deserved." "The production of the new opera," added the *Daily News,* "has been for some time looked forward to with much interest. . . . The new work . . . was brought out . . . with a result that fulfilled the most sanguine anticipations."

"We have not space to enumerate the numerous encores," wrote the *Observer*'s critic, "but we are glad to say that this specimen of genuine comic opera was received with enthusiastic applause by a brilliant and crowded audience." The first of the encores appears to have been "Oh, happy young heart!" sung by Miss Alice May, which, according to the *Daily Telegraph,* "deserved the encore [it] received." A few moments later, "Welcome joy," sung by Richard Temple and Mrs. Paul, and described by the *Daily News* as "a cleverly written duet . . . capitally sung and acted, . . . was the second encore of the evening." The *Echo* confusingly reported this number as "the minuet" which "had to be repeated, in order that the audience might witness Mr. Temple's and Mrs. Howard Paul's caricature of the old style of dancing." But the reviewer was obviously recalling Gilbert's courtly stage-business rather than Sullivan's 4-4 time. The real *minuetto* (3-4) had been heard earlier, just before Aline's entrance, as background music to Dr. Daly's spoken lines "May fortune bless you!" George Grossmith naturally was encored for his "rattling 'patter' song for J. W. Wells." The only encored number noted in the second act was the Quintet, "I rejoice that it's decided," which, according to the *Daily News,* was "one of the successes of the evening, and had to be repeated." To the *Observer* it was "simply delicious and will be hailed with delight wherever piquant melody and exquisite counterpoint are appreciated."

Musically, the press in general praised the finales of both acts—"scholarly as well as charming," wrote the *Hornet.* The finale to Act I was considered by the *Observer* "a masterly work, worthy of Auber himself." The *Daily News,* using the same adjective, found it "masterly in its choral and orchestral combinations and the distinctive treatment of the vocal solo portions." The second-act finale, according to the *Daily Telegraph,* "though not equal to its predecessor, has merits of a high order."

For the production as a whole the *Times* had unusual praise: "A more careful first performance of a new work of its kind has rarely been witnessed [shades of the *Thespis* first night!]. The orchestra and chorus were excellent, and quite strong enough for the size of the theatre—the former numbering nearly thirty, the latter upwards of forty. The leading singers . . . were also thoroughly efficient, every one of them doing all that was practicable to insure an effective 'ensemble,' and succeeding in proportion." Of these principals, the two who achieved the best press acclaim were Grossmith and Barrington. Of the former all the reviews were favorable and many were raves. This was his debut on the dramatic stage, and—as the *Figaro* commented—"We were glad to see Mr. Grossmith's remarkable talents as an actor appreciated as they deserve to be; he is at once the least self-conscious and most humorous of all entertainers." *Punch* went all-out in his behalf: "Mr. George Grossmith as *Wellington Wells* is the Sorcerestest Sorcerer that ever I did see or hear. His incantation scene, his clear and intelligible patter song, and his squatter's-run, are things which alone would repay a second visit to the Opéra Comique . . ."

"Rutland Barrington," exclaimed the *Hornet,* "won the chief honours of the evening, by his unforced, self-controlled, and quietly humorous acting as the Vicar. His voice is a most agreeable baritone of charming quality, well-trained and flexible." And the *Figaro* added the laurel most relaxing to both Gilbert and Barrington: "By his good taste and freedom from exaggeration, he preserved the character of the Vicar from any suspicion of impropriety; . . . he will certainly make his mark on the stage."

George Bentham, the tenor from Her Majesty's Opera Company, had the role of Alexis. According to the *Figaro* he was "laboring under the disadvantage of a swollen face and a sore throat, but he scarcely needed the apology made for him; his dialogue was as clear and artistically rendered as his recitative." (Whether this apology was in the form of an announcement from the stage or by a printed slip in the program is not clear; but if the latter, no copy has apparently survived.) The

Observer thought Richard Temple "both dramatically and vocally good as Sir Marmaduke"; and *Figaro* wrote that "he promises to be a most valuable addition to the scanty list of singers who can act as well as sing."

"Amongst the ladies," in the opinion of the *Observer,* "Miss May carried off the chief honours." The *Hornet* found her "a trifle too exuberant in style" and that she "has a habit of flinging her music at her audience." But, as the *Daily News* put it, "Miss May was an attractive and graceful Aline, and her brilliant and extensive soprano voice told with much effect." The *Figaro's* reviewer, with heavy sarcasm wrote that "she earned her first laurels . . . on the vast continent of Australia; and, apparently, she has not yet learned to modify the scale of her accomplishments to the requirements of this very limited island."

"Mrs. Howard Paul, who had a warm reception," noted the *Daily Telegraph,* "was excellent from a dramatic point of view as Lady Sangazure." The *Figaro* was more direct and less gallant to this aging actress: "Mrs. Howard Paul's voice is not all that it was, but her artistic skill is sufficient to cover any defects of physical strength; she looked and acted her part most charmingly." By bibliographic good fortune the *Daily News* reporter mentioned by name the ballad, "In days gone by," which she sang at this first-night performance, but which was later cut from the libretto.

As Constance, Miss Giulia Warwick (who was a member of the Carl Rosa Opera Company) "sang delightfully," according to the *Hornet,* "and would, had she shown the possession of any dramatic talent, have been perfectly successful." Miss Harriet Everard, "appropriately demure as the pew-opener" (*Daily News*), was reported by the *Hornet* to be "as good as usual, which is saying no little." *Punch* singled her out for special commendation: "Too much praise cannot be awarded to Miss Everard for her demure Pew-opener: like Mr. Grossmith, she enters thoroughly into the eccentric seriousness of the Author's grotesque idea."

The program in the hands of the audience that night appears to have varied only in minor points from that used early the following week, beginning "Saturday, November 17th, and every evening . . ." There is no mention of the fact that Sullivan conducted.

The *Times* found the libretto "an extravaganza of the best, set forth in Mr. Gilbert's raciest manner, full of genial humour and such droll fancies as come to him so readily." And the same critic wrote of Sullivan's contribution: "Above all, the music is spontaneous, appearing invariably to spring out of dramatic situations. . . . It is also distinguished by marked character and skillfully

varied in accordance with the nature of the incidents its composer has had to illustrate. . . . Enough that by this new effort Mr. Sullivan has certainly not deteriorated from, but, on the contrary, added to his well-earned repute."

In opposition, the *Figaro* felt that both author and composer were prostituting their gifts of genius. For Gilbert the charge was: "Originality is a great gift; but success may tempt its possessor to reproduce the original so often, that the charm of novelty becomes merged in the greater charm of familiarity." For Sullivan this *Figaro* critic had a more serious charge which—in one form or another—was to plague him the rest of his career:

There is nothing whatever in Mr. Sullivan's score which any theatrical conductor engaged at a few pounds a week could not have written equally well. . . . The music is neither that of opera nor of *opéra bouffe,* but it misses the dramatic feeling of the one and the sparkle of the other, while it preserves the dull respectability of the former and the triviality of the latter. . . . We trust Mr. Sullivan is more proud of it than we can pretend to be. But we must confess to a sense of disappointment at the downward art course Mr. Sullivan appears to be now drifting into. . . . [He] has all the ability to make him a great composer, but he wilfully throws his opportunity away. A giant may play at times, but Mr. Sullivan is always playing. . . . [He]

George Grossmith as J. Wellington Wells.

possesses all the natural ability to have given us an English opera, and, instead, he affords us a little more-or-less excellent fooling. . . . The result is disheartening to us all, but if the lesson be well marked and inwardly digested, *The Sorcerer* will not have been written in vain.

But the gentleman from the *Figaro* was seriously outnumbered at the Opéra Comique that night. Critic Herman Klein in his memoirs has described "the series of tremendous ovations . . . when first the author and composer, then the manager by himself, came in front of the curtain. . . . I had seldomed witnessed anything to equal it," he recalled, "and no one witnessing it then could possibly have dreamt that there was to be a repetition of the same tableau, with the same enthusiasm more or less, every year for twenty years to come." The reviewer from the *Times* wrote that Mr. Sullivan and Mr. Gilbert were "called before the lamps at the conclusion, amid applause, the genuine nature of which could never once have been mistaken. In short, the audience had been diverted from the rise of the curtain to the fall, and the laughter was incessant." Over to you, Mr. *Figaro!*

In the words of the *Echo:* "To say that a great success was achieved is only to record that that which was anticipated was realised."

22 Nov. 1877—I had a long rehearsal beginning at 7:30 on Friday, & heaps of little things—cuts &c, to arrange on Saturday [Nov. 17] so that it was absolutely impossible for me to come to your father. . . . We are doing tremendous business at the Op: Comique I am glad to say. I was on the stage last night and heard three *encores before I left. If it is a great success it is another nail in the coffin of Opera Bouffe from the French. . . .*

LETTER FROM SULLIVAN TO HIS FRIEND, ALAN COLE,
SON OF SIR HENRY COLE, K.C.B.

An Entirely New and Original Modern Comic Opera,

IN TWO ACTS,

THE SORCERER

Dramatis Personae.

Sir Marmaduke Pointdextre, *An Elderly Baronet*	Mr. Temple.
Alexis, *of the Grenadier Guards—His Son*	Mr. George Bentham.
Dr. Daly, *Vicar of Ploverleigh*	Mr. Rutland Barrington.
Notary	Mr. Clifton.
John Wellington Wells, *of J. W. Wells & Co., Family Sorcerers*	Mr. George Grossmith.
Lady Sangazure, *A Lady of Ancient Lineage*	Mrs. Howard Paul.
Aline, *Her Daughter—betrothed to Alexis*	Miss Alice May.
Mrs. Partlet, *A Pew-Opener*	Miss Everard.
Constance, *Her Daughter*	Miss Giulia Warwick.

Chorus of Peasantry.

Act I. — Grounds of Sir Marmaduke's Mansion.

Act II. — Market-Place of Ploverleigh.

(*Half-an-hour is supposed to elapse between Acts I. and II.*)

Time. — The Present Day.

THE SORCERER

ACT I.

SCENE. — *Garden of Sir Marmaduke's Elizabethan Mansion. The end of a large marquee, open, and showing portion of table covered with white cloth, on which are joints of meat, tea-pots, cups, bread and butter, jam, &c. A park in the background, with spire of church seen above the trees.*

CHORUS OF PEASANTRY.

Ring forth, ye bells,
  With clarion sound—
Forget your knells,
  For joys abound.
Forget your notes
  Of mournful lay,
And from your throats
  Pour joy to-day.

For to-day young Alexis—young Alexis Pointdextre
Is betrothed to Aline—to Aline Sangazure,
And that pride of his sex is—of his sex is to be next her,
  At the feast on the green—on the green, oh be sure!
    Ring forth, ye bells, &c.

(*At the end of chorus, exeunt the men into house.*)

Enter Mrs. PARTLET, *meeting* CONSTANCE, *her daughter.*

RECITATIVE.

MRS. PARTLET. Constance, my daughter, why this strange depression?
The village rings with seasonable joy,
Because the young and amiable Alexis,
Heir to the great Sir Marmaduke Pointdextre,
Is plighted to Aline, the only daughter
Of Annabella, Lady Sangazure.
You, you alone are sad and out of spirits;
What is the reason? Speak, my daughter, speak!

CONSTANCE. Oh, mother, do not ask! If my complexion
From red to white should change in quick succession—
And then from white to red, oh, take no notice!
If my poor limbs shall tremble with emotion,
Pay no attention, mother—it is nothing!
If long and deep-drawn sighs I chance to utter,
Oh, heed them not—their cause must ne'er be known!

MRS. PARTLET. My child, be candid—think not to deceive
The eagle-eyed pew-opener—. You love!

CONSTANCE (*aside*). How guessed she that, my heart's most cherished secret?
  (*Aloud*). I *do* love—fondly—madly—hopelessly!

ARIA — CONSTANCE.

When he is here,
  I sigh with pleasure—
When he is gone,
  I sigh with grief.
My hopeless fear
  No soul can measure—
His love alone
  Can give my aching heart relief!
When he is cold,
  I weep for sorrow—
When he is kind,
  I weep for joy.
My grief untold
  Knows no to-morrow—

My woe can find
  No hope, no solace, no alloy!

When I rejoice,
  He shows no pleasure.
When I am sad,
  It grieves him not.
His solemn voice
  Has tones I treasure—
My heart they glad,
  They solace my unhappy lot!
When I despond,
  My woe they chasten—
When I take heart,
  My hope they cheer;
With folly fond
  To him I hasten—
From him apart,
  My life is very sad and drear!

At the end of the song, MRS. PARTLET *silently motions to women to leave them together. Exeunt chorus.*

MRS. PARTLET. Come, tell me all about it! Do not fear—
  I, too, have loved; but that was long ago!
  Who is the object of your young affections?

CONSTANCE. Hush, mother! He is here!

Enter DR. DALY. *He is pensive and does not see them.*

MRS. PARTLET (*amazed*).   Our reverend vicar!

CONSTANCE. Oh pity me, my heart is almost broken!

MRS. PARTLET. My child, be comforted. To such an union
  I shall not offer any opposition.
  Take him—he's yours! May you and he be happy!

CONSTANCE. But, mother dear, he is not yours to give!

MRS. PARTLET.   That's true, indeed!

CONSTANCE.   He might object!

MRS. PARTLET.   He might.
  But come—take heart—I'll probe him on the subject.
  Be comforted—leave this affair to me.

RECITATIVE — DR. DALY.

The air is charged with amatory numbers—
  Soft madrigals, and dreamy lovers' lays.
Peace, peace, old heart! Why waken from its slumbers
  The aching memory of the old, old days?

BALLAD.

Time was, when Love and I were well acquainted.
  Time was, when we walked ever hand in hand,
A saintly youth, with worldly thought untainted—
  None better-loved than I in all the land!
Time was, when maidens of the noblest station,
  Forsaking even military men,
Would gaze upon me, rapt in adoration—
  Ah me, I was a fair young curate then!

Had I a headache? sighed the maids assembled;
  Had I a cold? welled forth the silent tear;
Did I look pale? then half a parish trembled;
  And when I coughed all thought the end was near!
I had no care—no jealous doubts hung o'er me—
  For I was loved beyond all other men.
Fled gilded dukes and belted earls before me—
  Ah me, I was a pale young curate then!

At the conclusion of the ballad, MRS. PARTLET *comes forward with* CONSTANCE.

MRS. PARTLET. Good day, reverend sir.

DR. DALY. Ah, good Mrs. Partlet, I am glad to see you. And your little daughter, Constance! Why, she is quite a little woman, I declare!

CONSTANCE (*aside*). Oh mother, I cannot speak to him!

MRS. PARTLET. Yes, reverend sir, she is nearly

eighteen, and as good a girl as ever stepped. (*Aside to* DR. DALY). Ah, sir, I'm afraid I shall soon lose her!

DR. DALY (*aside to* MRS. PARTLET). Dear me, you pain me very much. Is she delicate?

MRS. PARTLET. Oh, no, sir—I don't mean that—but young girls look to get married.

DR. DALY. Oh, I take you. To be sure. But there's plenty of time for that. Four or five years hence, Mrs. Partlet, four or five years hence. But when the time *does* come, I shall have much pleasure in marrying her myself—

CONSTANCE (*aside*). Oh mother!

DR. DALY. To some strapping young fellow in her own rank of life.

CONSTANCE (*in tears*). He does *not* love me!

MRS. PARTLET. I have often wondered, reverend sir (if you'll excuse the liberty), that *you* have never married.

DR. DALY (*aside*). Be still, my fluttering heart!

MRS. PARTLET. A clergyman's wife does so much good in a village. Besides that, you are not so young as you were, and before very long you will want somebody to nurse you, and look after your little comforts.

DR. DALY. Mrs. Partlet, there is much truth in what you say. I am indeed getting on in years, and a helpmate would cheer my declining days. Time was when it might have been; but I have left it too long—I am an old fogy now, am I not, my dear? (*to* CONSTANCE)—a very old fogy indeed. Ha! ha! No, Mrs. Partlet, my mind is quite made up. I shall live and die a solitary old bachelor.

CONSTANCE. Oh mother, mother! (*Sobs on* MRS. PARTLET'S *bosom*.)

MRS. PARTLET. Come, come, dear one, don't fret. At a more fitting time we will try again—we will try again.

(*Exeunt* MRS. PARTLET *and* CONSTANCE.)

DR. DALY (*looking after them*). Poor little girl! I'm afraid she has something on her mind. She is rather comely. Time was when this old heart would have throbbed in double-time at the sight of such a fairy form! But tush! I am puling! Here comes the young Alexis with his proud and happy father. Let me dry this tell-tale tear!

Enter SIR MARMADUKE *and* ALEXIS.

RECITATIVE.

DR. DALY.   Sir Marmaduke—my dear young friend, Alexis—
On this most happy—most auspicious plighting—
Permit me, as a true old friend, to tender
My best, my very best congratulations!

SIR MARMADUKE. Sir, you are most obleeging!
ALEXIS.   Dr. Daly,
My dear old tutor, and my valued pastor,
I thank you from the bottom of my heart!

Spoken through music.

DR. DALY. May fortune bless you! may the middle distance
Of your young life be pleasant as the foreground—
The joyous foreground! and, when you have reached it,
May that which now is the far-off horizon,
But which will then become the middle distance,
In fruitful promise be exceeded only
By that which will have opened, in the meantime,
Into a new and glorious horizon!

SIR MARMADUKE. Dear sir, that is an excellent example
Of an old school of stately compliment
To which I have, through life, been much addicted.
Will you obleege me with a copy of it,
In clerkly manuscript, that I myself
May use it on appropriate occasions?

DR. DALY. Sir, you shall have a fairly-written copy
Ere Sol has sunk into his western slumbers!
(*Exit.*)

SIR MARMADUKE (*to* ALEXIS, *who is in a reverie*).
Come, come, my son—your *fiancée* will be here in five minutes. Rouse yourself to receive her.

ALEXIS (*rising*). Oh rapture!

SIR MARMADUKE. Yes, you are a fortunate young fellow, and I will not disguise from you that this union with the House of Sangazure realizes my fondest wishes. Aline is rich, and she comes of a sufficiently old family, for she is the seven thousand and thirty-seventh in direct descent from Helen of Troy. True, there was a blot on the escutcheon of that lady—that affair with Paris—but where is the family, other than my own, in which there is no flaw? You are a lucky fellow, sir—a very lucky fellow!

ALEXIS. Father, I am welling over with limpid joy! No sicklying taint of sorrow overlies the lucid lake of liquid love upon which, hand-in-hand, Aline and I are to float into eternity!

SIR MARMADUKE. Alexis, I desire that of your love for this young lady you do not speak so openly. You are always singing ballads in praise of her beauty, and you expect the very menials who wait behind your chair, to chorus your ecstasies. It is not delicate.

ALEXIS. Father, a man who loves as I love—

SIR MARMADUKE. Pooh pooh, sir! Fifty years ago I madly loved your future mother-in-law, the lady Sangazure, and I have reason to believe that she returned my love. But were we guilty of the indelicacy of publicly rushing into each other's arms, exclaiming—

RECITATIVE.

"Oh my adored one!" "Beloved boy!"
"Ecstatic rapture!" "Unmingled joy!"

which seems to be the modern fashion of love-making? No! it was "Madam, I trust you are in the enjoyment of good health"—"Sir, you are vastly polite, I protest I am mighty well"—and so forth. Much more delicate—much more respectful. But see—Aline approaches—let us retire, that she may compose herself for the interesting ceremony in which she is to play so important a part.

(*Exeunt* SIR MARMADUKE *and* ALEXIS.)

Enter ALINE, *on terrace, preceded by Chorus of girls.*

CHORUS OF GIRLS.

With heart and with voice
　Let us welcome this mating:
To the youth of her choice,
　With a heart palpitating,
　　Comes the lovely Aline!

May their love never cloy!
　May their bliss be unbounded!
With a halo of joy
　May their lives be surrounded!
　Heaven bless our Aline!

RECITATIVE — ALINE.

My kindly friends, I thank you for this greeting,
And as you wish me every earthly joy,
I trust your wishes may have quick fulfilment!

ARIA — ALINE.

Oh, happy young heart!
　Comes thy young lord a-wooing,
With joy in his eyes,
　And pride in his breast—
Make much of thy prize,
　For he is the best
That ever came a-suing.
　Yet—yet we must part,
　　　　　Young heart!
　Yet—yet we must part!

Oh, merry young heart,
　Bright are the days of thy wooing!
But happier far
　The days untried—
No sorrow can mar,
　When Love has tied
The knot there's no undoing.
　Then, never to part,
　　　　　Young heart!
　Then, never to part!

Enter LADY SANGAZURE.

RECITATIVE — LADY SANGAZURE.

My child, I join in these congratulations:
Heed not the tear that dims this aged eye!
Old memories crowd upon me. Though I
　sorrow,
'Tis for myself, Aline, and not for thee!

BALLAD — LADY SANGAZURE.

In days gone by, these eyes were bright,
　This bosom fair, these cheeks were rosy,
This faded brow was snowy white,
　These lips were fresh as new-plucked posy;
My girlish love he never guessed,
　Until the day when we were parted;
I treasured it within my heart,
　And lived alone and broken-hearted.

These cheeks are wan with age and care,
　These weary eyes have done their duty,
As white as falling snow my hair,
　And faded all my girlish beauty.
I see my every charm depart;
　But Memory's chain I cannot sever,
For ah, within my poor old heart
　The fire of love burns bright as ever!

Enter ALEXIS, *preceded by Chorus of Men.*

CHORUS OF MEN AND WOMEN.

With heart and with voice
   Let us welcome this mating;
To the maid of his choice,
   With a heart palpitating,
      Comes Alexis the brave!

SIR MARMADUKE *enters.* LADY SANGAZURE *and he exhibit signs of strong emotion at the sight of each other, which they endeavour to repress.* ALEXIS *and* ALINE *rush into each other's arms.*

RECITATIVE.

ALEXIS.   Oh, my adored one!
ALINE.   Beloved boy!
ALEXIS.   Ecstatic rapture!
ALINE.   Unmingled joy!
                              (*They retire.*)

DUET — SIR MARMADUKE *and* LADY SANGAZURE.

SIR MARMADUKE (*with stately courtesy*).
   Welcome joy, adieu to sadness!
      As Aurora gilds the day,
   So those eyes, twin orbs of gladness,
      Chase the clouds of care away.
   Irresistible incentive
      Bids me humbly kiss your hand;
   I'm your servant most attentive—
      Most attentive to command!

         (*Aside, with frantic vehemence.*)
   Wild with adoration!
   Mad with fascination!
   To indulge my lamentation
      No occasion do I miss!
   Goaded to distraction
   By maddening inaction,
   I find some satisfaction
      In apostrophe like this:
   "Sangazure immortal,
      Sangazure divine,

   Welcome to my portal,
      Angel, oh be mine!"

         (*Aloud, with much ceremony.*)
   Irresistible incentive
      Bids me humbly kiss your hand;
   I'm your servant most attentive—
      Most attentive to command!

LADY SANGAZURE.   Sir, I thank you most politely
   For your graceful courtesee;
   Compliment more true and knightly
      Never yet was paid to me!
   Chivalry is an ingredient
      Sadly lacking in our land—
   Sir, I am your most obedient,
      Most obedient to command!

         (*Aside, with great vehemence.*)
   Wild with adoration!
   Mad with fascination!
   To indulge my lamentation
      No occasion do I miss!
   Goaded to distraction
   By maddening inaction,
   I find some satisfaction
      In apostrophe like this:
   "Marmaduke immortal,
      Marmaduke divine,
   Take me to thy portal,
      Loved one, oh be mine!"

         (*Aloud, with much ceremony.*)
   Chivalry is an ingredient
      Sadly lacking in our land;
   Sir, I am your most obedient,
      Most obedient to command!

During this duet the COUNSEL *has entered, and prepares marriage contract.*

RECITATIVE — COUNSEL.

All is prepared for sealing and for signing,
   The contract has been drafted as agreed;

Approach the table, oh ye lovers pining,
With hand and seal come execute the deed!

ALEXIS *and* ALINE *advance and sign,* ALEXIS *supported by* SIR MARMADUKE, ALINE *by her Mother.*

CHORUS.

See they sign, without a quiver, it
Then to seal proceed.
They deliver it—they deliver it
As their act and deed!

ALEXIS. I deliver it—I deliver it
As my act and deed!

ALINE. I deliver it—I deliver it
As my act and deed!

CHORUS. With heart and with voice
Let us welcome this mating;
Leave them here to rejoice.
With true love palpitating,
Alexis the brave,
And the lovely Aline!
(*Exeunt all but* ALEXIS *and* ALINE.)

ALEXIS. At last we are alone! My darling, you are now irrevocably betrothed to me. Are you not very, very happy?

ALINE. Oh, Alexis, can you doubt it? Do I not love you beyond all on earth, and am I not beloved in return? Is not true love, faithfully given and faithfully returned, the source of every earthly joy?

ALEXIS. Of that there can be no doubt. Oh, that the world could be persuaded of the truth of that maxim! Oh, that the world would break down the artificial barriers of rank, wealth, education, age, beauty, habits, taste, and temper, and recognise the glorious principle, that in marriage alone is to be found the panacea for every ill.

ALINE. Continue to preach that sweet doctrine, and you will succeed, O evangel of true happiness!

ALEXIS. I hope so, but as yet the cause progresses but slowly. Still, I have made some converts to the principle that men and women should be coupled in matrimony without distinction of rank. I have lectured on the subject at Mechanics' Institutes, and the Mechanics were unanimous in favour of my views. I have preached in workhouses, beershops, and Lunatic Asylums, and I have been received with enthusiasm. I have addressed navvies on the advantages that would accrue to them if they married wealthy ladies of rank, and not a navvy dissented!

ALINE. Noble fellows! And yet there are those who hold that the uneducated classes are not open to argument! And what do the countesses say?

ALEXIS. Why, at present, it can't be denied, the aristocracy hold aloof.

ALINE. The working man is the true Intelligence after all!

ALEXIS. He is a noble creature when he is quite sober. Yes, Aline, true happiness comes of true love, and true love should be independent of external influences. It should live upon itself and by itself—in itself love should live for love alone!

BALLAD — ALEXIS.

Love feeds on many kinds of food, I know—
  Some love for rank, and some for duty:
Some give their hearts away for empty show,
  And others love for youth and beauty.
To love for money all the world is prone:
  Some love themselves, and live all lonely:
Give me the love that loves for love alone—
  I love that love—I love it only!

What man for any other joy can thirst,
  Whose loving wife adores him duly?
Want, misery, and care may do their worst,
  If loving woman loves you truly.
A lover's thoughts are ever with his own—
  None truly loved is ever lonely:
Give me the love that loves for love alone—
  I love that love—I love it only!

ALINE. Oh, Alexis, those are noble principles!

ALEXIS. Yes, Aline, and I am going to take a desperate step in support of them. Have you ever heard of the firm of J. W. Wells & Co., the old-established Family Sorcerers, in St. Mary Axe?

ALINE. I have seen their advertisement.

ALEXIS. They have invented a philtre which, if report may be believed, is simply infallible. I intend to distribute it through the village, and within half-an-hour of my doing so, there will not be an adult in the place who will not have learnt the secret of pure and lasting happiness. What do you say to that?

ALINE. Well, dear, of course a filter is a very useful thing in a house; quite indispensable in the present state of Thames water; but still I don't quite see that it is the sort of thing that places its possessor on the very pinnacle of earthly joy.

ALEXIS. Aline, you misunderstand me. I didn't say a filter—I said philtre.

ALINE. So did I, dear. *I* said a filter.

ALEXIS. No, dear, you said a filter. I don't mean a filter—I mean a philtre,—oh, you know.

ALINE (*alarmed*). You don't mean a love-potion?

ALEXIS. On the contrary—I *do* mean a love-potion.

ALINE. Oh, Alexis, I don't think it would be right. I don't indeed. And then—a real magician! Oh, it would be downright wicked.

ALEXIS. Aline, is it, or is it not, a laudable object to steep the whole village up to its lips in love, and to couple them in matrimony without distinction of age, rank, or fortune?

ALINE. Unquestionably, but—

ALEXIS. Then, unpleasant as it must be to have recourse to supernatural aid, I must nevertheless pocket my aversion, in deference to the great and good end I have in view. (*Calling.*) Hercules.

Enter a PAGE.

PAGE. Yes, sir.

ALEXIS. Is Mr. Wells there?

PAGE. He's in the tent, sir—refreshing.

ALEXIS. Ask him to be so good as to step this way.

PAGE. Yes, sir. (*Exit.*)

ALINE. Oh, but Alexis! A real Sorcerer! Oh, I shall be frightened to death!

ALEXIS. I trust my Aline will not yield to fear while the strong right arm of her Alexis is here to protect her.

ALINE. It's nonsense, dear, to talk of your protecting me with your strong right arm, in face of the fact that this Family Sorcerer could change me into a guinea-pig before you could turn round.

ALEXIS. He *could* change you into a guinea-pig, no doubt, but it is most unlikely that he would take such a liberty. It's a most respectable firm, and I am sure he would never be guilty of so untradesmanlike an act.

Enter MR. WELLS.

MR. WELLS. Good day, sir. (ALINE *much terrified.*)

ALEXIS. Good day—I believe you are a Sorcerer.

MR. WELLS. Yes, sir, we practice Necromancy in all its branches. We've a choice assortment of wishing-caps, divining-rods, amulets, charms, and counter-charms. We can cast you a nativity at a low figure, and we have a horoscope at three-and-six that we can guarantee. Our Abudah chests, each containing a patent Hag who comes out and prophesies disasters, with spring complete, are strongly recommended. Our Aladdin lamps are very chaste, and our Prophetic Tablets, foretelling everything—from a change of Ministry down to a rise in Turkish Stock—are much enquired for. Our penny Curse—one of the cheapest things in the trade—is considered infallible. We have some very superior Blessings, too, but they're very little asked for. We've only sold one since Christmas—to a gentleman who bought it to send to his mother-in-law—but it turned out that he was afflicted in the head, and it's been returned on our hands. But our sale of penny Curses, especially on Saturday nights, is tremendous. We can't turn 'em out fast enough.

SONG — MR. WELLS.

Oh! my name is John Wellington Wells,
I'm a dealer in magic and spells,
  In blessings and curses,

And ever-filled purses,
In prophecies, witches, and knells.

If you want a proud foe to "make tracks"—
If you'd melt a rich uncle in wax—
   You've but to look in
   On our resident Djinn,
Number seventy, Simmery Axe.

We've a first-class assortment of magic;
  And for raising a posthumous shade
With effects that are comic or tragic,
  There's no cheaper house in the trade.
Love-philtre—we've quantities of it!
  And for knowledge if any one burns,
We keep an extremely small prophet
  Who brings us unbounded returns:

   Oh! he can prophesy
   With a wink *of* his eye,
   Peep with security
   Into futurity,
   Sum up your history,
   Clear up a mystery,
   Humour proclivity
   For a nativity—for a nativity;
   Mirrors so magical,
   Tetrapods tragical,
   Bogies spectacular,
   Answers oracular,
   Facts astronomical,
   Solemn or comical,
   And, if you want it, he
Makes a reduction on taking a quantity!

   Oh!
If anyone anything lacks,
He'll find it all ready in stacks,
   If he'll only look in
   On the resident Djinn,
Number seventy, Simmery Axe!

   He can raise you hosts
     Of ghosts,
And that, without reflectors;
   And creepy things
     With wings,
And gaunt and grisly spectres;
   He can fill you crowds
     Of shrouds,
And horrify you vastly;
   He can rack your brains
     With chains,
And gibberings grim and ghastly!

   Then, if you plan it, he
   Changes organity,
   With an urbanity
   Full of Satanity,
   Vexes humanity
   With an inanity

   Fatal to vanity—
Driving your foes to the verge of insanity!

   Barring tautology,
   In demonology,
   'Lectro-biology,
   Mystic nosology,
   Spirit philology,
   High-class astrology,
   Such is his knowledge, he
Isn't the man to require an apology!

   Oh!
My name is John Wellington Wells,
I'm a dealer in magic and spells,
   In blessings and curses,
   And ever-filled purses—
In prophecies, witches, and knells.

   If anyone anything lacks,
   He'll find it all ready in stacks,
     If he'll only look in
     On the resident Djinn,
   Number seventy, Simmery Axe!

ALEXIS. I have sent for you to consult you on a very important matter. I believe you advertise a Patent Oxy-Hydrogen Love-at-first-sight Philtre?

MR. WELLS. Sir, it is our leading article (*producing a phial*).

ALEXIS. Now I want to know if you can confidently guarantee it as possessing all the qualities you claim for it in your advertisement?

MR. WELLS. Sir, we are not in the habit of puffing our goods. Ours is an old-established house with a large family connection, and every assurance held out in the advertisement is fully realised (*hurt*).

ALINE (*aside*). Oh, Alexis, don't offend him! He'll change us into something dreadful—I know he will!

ALEXIS. I am anxious from purely philanthropical motives to distribute this philtre, secretly, among the inhabitants of this village. I shall of course require a quantity. How do you sell it?

MR. WELLS. In buying a quantity, sir, we should strongly advise your taking it in the wood, and drawing it off as you happen to want it. We have it in four-and-a-half- and nine-gallon casks—also in pipes and hogsheads for laying down, and we deduct 10 per cent for prompt cash.

ALINE. Oh, Alexis, surely you don't want to lay any down!

ALEXIS. Aline, the villagers will assemble to carouse in a few minutes. Go and fetch the tea-pot.

ALINE. But, Alexis—

ALEXIS. My dear, you must obey me, if you please. Go and fetch the tea-pot.

ALINE (*going*). I'm sure Dr. Daly would disapprove of it. (*Exit.*)

ALEXIS.   And how soon does it take effect?

MR. WELLS.   In half-an-hour. Whoever drinks of it falls in love, as a matter of course, with the first lady he meets who has also tasted it, and his affection is at once returned. One trial will prove the fact.

Enter ALINE *from tent with large tea-pot.*

ALEXIS. Good: then, Mr. Wells, I shall feel obliged if you will at once pour as much philtre into this tea-pot as will suffice to affect the whole village.

ALINE. But bless me, Alexis, many of the villagers are married people.

MR. WELLS. Madam, this philtre is compounded on the strictest principles. On married people it has no effect whatever. But are you quite sure that you have nerve enough to carry you through the fearful ordeal?

ALEXIS.   In the good cause I fear nothing.

MR. WELLS.   Very good, then, we will proceed at once to the Incantation.

The stage grows dark.

INCANTATION.

MR. WELLS.   Sprites of earth and air—
Fiends of flame and fire—
Demon souls,
Come here in shoals,
This dreadful deed inspire!
Appear, appear, appear!

MALE VOICES.   Good master, we are here!

MR. WELLS.   Noisome hags of night—
Imps of deadly shade—
Pallid ghosts,
Arise in hosts,
And lend me all your aid.
Appear, appear, appear!

FEMALE VOICES.   Good master, we are here!

ALEXIS (*aside*).   Hark, they assemble,
These fiends of the night!

ALINE (*aside*).   Oh Alexis, I tremble,
Seek safety in flight!

ARIA — ALINE.

Let us fly to a far-off land
Where peace and plenty dwell—

Where the sigh of the silver strand
  Is echoed in every shell.
To the joy that land will give,
  On the wings of Love we'll fly;
In innocence there to live—
  In innocence there to die!

CHORUS OF SPIRITS.

Too late—too late—
  It may not be!
That happy fate
  Is not for thee!

ALEXIS, ALINE, and MR. WELLS.

Too late—too late,
  That may not be!
That happy fate
  Is not for $\left\{\begin{array}{l}\text{me!}\\\text{thee!}\end{array}\right.$

MR. WELLS.

Now shrivelled hags, with poison bags,
  Discharge your loathsome loads!
Spit flame and fire, unholy choir!
  Belch forth your venom, toads!
Ye demons fell, with yelp and yell,
  Shed curses far a-field—
Ye fiends of night, your filthy blight
  In noisome plenty yield!

MR. WELLS (*pouring vial into tea-pot—flash*).
Number One!

CHORUS. It is done!

MR. WELLS (*same business*). Number Two!
                                    (*Flash.*)

CHORUS. One too few!

MR. WELLS (*same business*). Number Three!
                                    (*Flash.*)

CHORUS. Set us free!
      Set us free—our work is done,
        Ha! ha! ha!
      Set us free—our course is run!
        Ha! ha! ha!

ALINE and ALEXIS (*aside*).

Let us fly to a far-off land
  Where peace and plenty dwell,
Where the sigh of the silver strand
  Is echoed in every shell.

CHORUS OF FIENDS.

Ha! ha! ha! ha! ha! ha! ha! ha! ha! ha!

Stage grows light. MR. WELLS *beckons villagers.*

*Enter villagers and all the dramatis personæ, danc-
ing joyously.* SIR MARMADUKE *enters with* LADY
SANGAZURE. VICAR *enters, absorbed in thought.
He is followed by* CONSTANCE. COUNSEL *enters,
followed by* MRS. PARTLET. MRS. PARTLET *and*
MR. WELLS *distribute tea-cups.*

CHORUS.

Now to the banquet we press;
  Now for the eggs, the ham.
Now for the mustard and cress,
  Now for the strawberry jam!
Now for the tea of our host,
  Now for the rollicking bun,
Now for the muffin and toast,
  Now for the gay Sally Lunn!

WOMEN. The eggs and the ham, and the straw-
          berry jam!

MEN. The rollicking bun, and the gay Sally Lunn!
        The rollicking, rollicking bun!

RECITATIVE — SIR MARMADUKE.

Be happy all—the feast is spread before ye,
  Fear nothing, but enjoy yourselves, I pray!
Eat, aye and drink—be merry, I implore ye,
  For once let thoughtless Folly rule the day!

TEA-CUP BRINDISI.

Eat, drink, and be gay,
  Banish all worry and sorrow,
Laugh gaily to-day,
  Weep, if you're sorry, to-morrow!
Come, pass the cup round—
  I will go bail for the liquor;
It's strong, I'll be bound,
  For it was brewed by the vicar!

CHORUS. None so knowing as he
          At brewing a jorum of tea,
              Ha! ha!
          A pretty stiff jorum of tea.

TRIO.
MR. WELLS, ALINE, and ALEXIS (*aside*).

See—see—they drink—
  All thought unheeding,
The tea-cups clink,
  They are exceeding!
Their hearts will melt
  In half-an-hour—
Then will be felt
  The potion's power!

During this verse CONSTANCE *has brought a small*

tea-pot, kettle, caddy, and cosy to DR. DALY. *He makes tea scientifically.*

BRINDISI, *2nd Verse* — DR. DALY (*with the tea-pot*).

Pain, trouble, and care,
    Misery, heart-ache, and worry,
Quick, out of your lair!
    Get you all gone in a hurry!
Toil, sorrow, and plot,
    Fly away quicker and quicker—
Three spoons to the pot—
    That is the brew of your vicar!

CHORUS.   None so cunning as he
    At brewing a jorum of tea,
                    Ha! ha!
    A pretty stiff jorum of tea!

DR. DALY *places tea-pot on tray held by* CONSTANCE. *He covers it with the cosy. She takes tray into the house.*

ENSEMBLE — ALEXIS *and* ALINE (*aside*).

Oh, love, true love—unworldly, abiding!
    Source of all pleasure—true fountain of joy—
Oh, love, true love—divinely confiding,
    Exquisite treasure that knows no alloy!
Oh love, true love, rich harvest of gladness,
    Peace-bearing tillage—great garner of bliss—
Oh love, true love, look down on our sadness—
    Dwell in this village—oh hear us in this!

It becomes evident, by the strange conduct of the characters, that the charm is working. All rub their eyes.

TUTTI (*aside*).

Oh marvellous illusion!
    Oh terrible surprise!
What is this strange confusion
    That veils my aching eyes?
I must regain my senses,
    Restoring Reason's law,
Or fearful inferences
    The company will draw!

ALEXIS, MR. WELLS, *and* ALINE (*aside*).

A marvellous illusion—
    A terrible surprise
Excites a strange confusion
    Within their aching eyes—
They must regain their senses,
    Restoring Reason's law,
Or fearful inferences
    The company will draw!

Those who have partaken of the philtre struggle against its effects, and resume the Brindisi with a violent effort.

TUTTI.

Eat, drink, and be gay,
    Banish all worry and sorrow—
Laugh gaily to-day—
    Weep, if you're sorry, to-morrow.
Come, pass the cup round—
    We will go bail for the liquor;
It's strong, I'll be bound,
    For it was brewed by the vicar!
None so cunning as he
    At brewing a jorum of tea.
                    Ha! ha!
    At brewing a jorum of tea!

ACT-DROP.

ACT II.

SCENE. — *Market Place in the Village. Enter* PEASANTS *dancing, coupled two and two: an old man with a young girl, then an old woman with a young man, then other ill-assorted couples.*

OPENING CHORUS.

Happy are we in our loving frivolity,
Happy and jolly as people of quality;
Love is the source of all joy to humanity,
Money, position, and rank are a vanity;
Year after year we've been waiting and tarrying,
Without ever dreaming of loving and marrying.
Though we've been hitherto deaf, dumb, and blind to it,
It's pleasant enough when you've made up your mind to it.

Enter CONSTANCE, *leading* NOTARY.

ARIA — CONSTANCE.

Dear friends, take pity on my lot,
    My cup is not of nectar!
I long have loved—as who would not?—
    Our kind and reverend rector.
Long years ago my love began
    So sweetly—yet so sadly—
But when I saw this plain old man,
Away my old affection ran—
    I found I loved him madly.
        Oh!

(*To* NOTARY.)

You very, very plain old man,
   I love, I love you madly!

CHORUS.   You very, very plain old man,
   She loves, she loves you madly!

NOTARY.   I am a very deaf old man,
   And hear you very badly.

CONSTANCE.   I know not why I love him so;
   It is enchantment, surely!
He's dry and snuffy, deaf and slow,
   Ill-tempered, weak, and poorly!
He's ugly, and absurdly dressed,
   And sixty-seven nearly,
He's everything that I detest,
But if the truth must be confessed,
   I love him very dearly!
      Oh!

         (*To* NOTARY.)

You're everything that I detest,
   But still I love you dearly!

CHORUS.   You're everything that girls detest,
   But still she loves you dearly!

NOTARY.   I caught that line, but for the rest
   I did not hear it clearly!

During this verse ALINE *and* ALEXIS *have entered at back, unobserved.*

      ALINE *and* ALEXIS.

ALEXIS.   Oh joy! oh joy!
   The charm works well,
      And all are now united.

ALINE.   The blind young boy
   Obeys the spell,
      Their troth they all have plighted!

(*All, except* ALEXIS *and* ALINE, *dance off to symphony.*)

ALINE.   How joyful they all seem in their new-found happiness! The whole village has paired off in the happiest manner. And yet not a match has been made that the hollow world would not consider ill-advised!

ALEXIS.   But we are wiser—far wiser—than the world. Observe the good that will become of these ill-assorted unions. The miserly wife will check the reckless expenditure of her too frivolous consort—the wealthy husband will shower innumerable bonnets on his penniless bride, and the young and lively spouse will cheer the declining days of her aged partner with comic songs unceasing!

ALINE.   What a delightful prospect for him!

ALEXIS.   But one thing remains to be done, that my happiness may be complete. We must drink the philtre ourselves, that I may be assured of your love for ever and ever.

                     ENSEMBLE.

ALINE *and* ALEXIS.	CONSTANCE.	NOTARY.

Oh joy! oh joy!
   The charm works well,
      And all are now united!
	Oh, bitter joy!
	   No words can tell
	      How my poor heart is
	         blighted!
		Oh joy! oh joy!
		   No words can tell,
		      My state of mind delighted.

The blind young boy,
   Obeys the spell,
      Their troth they all have
         plighted.
	They'll soon employ
	   A marriage bell,
	      To say that we're united.
		They'll soon employ
		   A marriage bell,
		      To say that we're united!

True happiness
   Reigns everywhere,
      And dwells with both the
         sexes,
	I do confess
	   A sorrow rare
	      My humbled spirit vexes,
		True happiness
		   Reigns everywhere,
		      And dwells with both the
		         sexes,

And all will bless
   The thoughtful care
      Of their beloved Alexis!
	And none will bless
	   Example rare
	      Of their beloved Alexis!
		And all will bless
		   Example rare
		      Of their beloved Alexis!

ALINE. Oh Alexis, do you doubt me? Is it necessary that such love as ours should be secured by artificial means? Oh, no, no, no!

ALEXIS. My dear Aline, time works terrible changes, and I want to place our love beyond the chance of change.

ALINE. Alexis, it is already far beyond that chance. Have faith in me, for my love can never, never change!

ALEXIS. Then you absolutely refuse?

ALINE. I do. If you cannot trust me, you have no right to love me—no right to be loved *by* me.

ALEXIS. Enough, Aline, I shall know how to interpret this refusal.

BALLAD — ALEXIS.

Thou hast the power thy vaunted love
To sanctify, all doubt above,
    Despite the gathering shade:
To make that love of thine so sure
That, come what may, it must endure
    Till time itself shall fade.
        Thy love is but a flower
        That fades within the hour!
        If such thy love, oh shame!
        Call it by other name—
           It is not love!

Thine is the power, and thine alone!
To place me on so proud a throne
    That kings might envy me!
A priceless throne of love untold,
More rare than orient pearl and gold.
    But no! Thou wouldst be free!
        Such love is like the ray
        That dies within the day:
        If such thy love, oh shame!
        Call it by other name—
           It is not love! (*They retire.*)

Enter DR. DALY.

DR. DALY (*musing*). It is singular—it is very singular. It has overthrown all my calculations. It is distinctly opposed to the doctrine of averages. I cannot understand it.

ALINE. Dear Dr. Daly, what has puzzled you?

DR. DALY. My dear, this village has not, hitherto, been addicted to marrying and giving in marriage. Hitherto the youths of this village have not been enterprising, and the maidens have been distinctly coy. Judge then of my surprise when I tell you that the whole village came to me in a body just now, and implored me to join them in matrimony with as little delay as possible. Even your excellent father has hinted to me that before very long it is not unlikely that he, also, may change his condition.

ALINE. Oh Alexis—do you hear that? Are you not delighted?

ALEXIS. Yes. I confess that a union between your mother and my father would be a happy circumstance indeed. (*Crossing to* DR. DALY.) My dear sir—the news that you bring us is very gratifying.

DR. DALY. Yes—still, in my eyes, it has its melancholy side. This universal marrying recalls the happy days—now, alas, gone for ever—when I myself might have—but tush! I am puling. I am too old to marry—and yet, within the last half-hour, I have greatly yearned for companionship. I never remarked it before, but the young maidens of this village are very comely. So likewise are the middle-aged. Also the elderly. All are comely—and (*with a deep sigh*) all are engaged!

ALINE. Here comes your father.

Enter SIR MARMADUKE *with* MRS. PARTLET, *arm-in-arm.*

ALINE *and* ALEXIS (*aside*). Mrs. Partlet!

SIR MARMADUKE. Dr. Daly, give me joy. Alexis, my dear boy, you will, I am sure, be pleased to hear that my declining days are not unlikely to be solaced by the companionship of this good, virtuous, and amiable woman.

ALEXIS (*rather taken aback*). My dear father, this is not altogether what I expected. I am certainly taken somewhat by surprise. Still, it can hardly be necessary to assure you that any wife of yours is a mother of mine. (*Aside to* ALINE.) It is not quite what I could have wished.

MRS. PARTLET (*crossing to* ALEXIS). Oh, sir, I entreat your forgiveness. I am aware that socially I am not everything that could be desired, nor am I blessed with an abundance of worldly goods, but I can at least confer on your estimable father the great and priceless dowry of a true, tender, and loving heart.

ALEXIS (*coldly*). I do not question it. After all, a faithful love is the true source of every earthly joy.

SIR MARMADUKE. I knew that my boy would not blame his poor father for acting on the impulse of a heart that has never yet misled him. Zorah is not perhaps what the world calls beautiful—

DR. DALY. Still, she is comely—distinctly comely! (*Sighs and retires.*)

ALINE. Zorah is very good, and very clean, and honest; and quite, quite sober in her habits, and that is worth far more than beauty, dear Sir Marmaduke.

DR. DALY (*coming down*). Yes; beauty will fade and perish, but personal cleanliness is practically undying, for it can be renewed whenever it discovers symptoms of decay. My dear Sir Marmaduke, I heartily congratulate you. (*Sighs.*)

QUINTETTE.

ALEXIS, ALINE, SIR MARMADUKE, ZORAH, *and* DR. DALY.

ALEXIS.   I rejoice that it's decided,
Happy now will be his life,
For my father is provided
With a true and tender wife!

ENSEMBLE.   She will tend him, nurse him, mend him,
Air his linen, dry his tears.
Bless the thoughtful fates that send him
Such a wife to soothe his years!

ALINE.   No young giddy thoughtless maiden,
Full of graces, airs, and jeers—
But a sober widow, laden
With the weight of fifty years!

SIR MARMADUKE.   No high-born exacting beauty
Blazing like a jewelled sun—
But a wife who'll do her duty,
As that duty should be done!

MRS. PARTLET.   I'm no saucy minx and giddy—
Hussies such as they abound—
But a clean and tidy widdy
Well be-known for miles around!

DR. DALY.   All the village now have mated,
All are happy as can be—
I to live alone am fated:
No one's left to marry me!

ENSEMBLE.   She will tend him, etc.

(*Exeunt* SIR MARMADUKE, MRS. PARTLET, ALINE, *and* ALEXIS. DR. DALY *looks after them sentimentally, then exit with a sigh.*)

MR. WELLS, *who has overheard part of this Quintette, and who has remained concealed behind the market cross, comes down as they go off.*

RECITATIVE — MR. WELLS.

Oh, I have wrought much evil with my spells!
An ill I can't undo!
This is too bad of you, J. W. Wells—
What wrong have they done you?
And see—another love-lorn lady comes—
Alas, poor stricken dame!
A gentle pensiveness her life benumbs—
And mine, alone, the blame!
                    (*Sits at foot of market cross.*)

LADY SANGAZURE *enters. She is very melancholy.*

LADY SANGAZURE.   Alas! ah me! and well-a-day!
I sigh for love, and well I may,
For I am very old and gray.
But stay!

(*Sees* MR. WELLS *and becomes fascinated by him.*)

RECITATIVE.

LADY SANGAZURE.   What is this fairy form I see before me?
MR. WELLS.   Oh, horrible!—she's going to adore me!
This last catastrophe is overpowering!
LADY SANGAZURE.   Why do you glare at one with visage lowering?
For pity's sake recoil not thus from me!
MR. WELLS.   My lady, leave me—this may never be!

DUET — LADY SANGAZURE *and* MR. WELLS.

MR. WELLS.   Hate me! I drop my H's—have through life!
LADY SANGAZURE.   Love me! I'll drop them too!
MR. WELLS.   Hate me! I always eat peas with a knife!
LADY SANGAZURE.   Love me! I'll eat like you!
MR. WELLS.   Hate me! I spend the day at Rosherville!
LADY SANGAZURE.   Love me! that joy I'll share!
MR. WELLS.   Hate me! I often roll down One Tree Hill!
LADY SANGAZURE.   Love me! I'll join you there!
LADY SANGAZURE.   Love me! my prejudices I will drop!
MR. WELLS.   Hate me! that's not enough!
LADY SANGAZURE.   Love me! I'll come and help you in the shop!
MR. WELLS.   Hate me! the life is rough!
LADY SANGAZURE.   Love me! my grammar I will all forswear!
MR. WELLS.   Hate me! abjure my lot!
LADY SANGAZURE.   Love me! I'll stick sunflowers in my hair!
MR. WELLS.   Hate me! they'll suit you not!

RECITATIVE — MR. WELLS.

At what I'm going to say be not enraged—
I may not love you—for I am engaged!

LADY SANGAZURE (*horrified*).   Engaged!

MR. WELLS.   Engaged!
To a maiden fair,
With bright brown hair,
And a sweet and simple smile,
Who waits for me
By the sounding sea,
On a South Pacific isle.

MR. WELLS (*aside*). A lie! No maiden waits me there!

LADY SANGAZURE (*mournfully*). She has bright brown hair!

MR. WELLS (*aside*). A lie! No maiden smiles on me!

LADY SANGAZURE (*mournfully*). By the sounding sea!

ENSEMBLE.

LADY SANGAZURE.	MR. WELLS.

Oh agony, rage, despair!
The maiden has bright brown hair,
  And mine is as white as snow!
False man, it will be your fault,
If I go to my family vault,
  And bury my life-long woe!
	Oh agony, rage, despair!
	Oh where will this end —oh where?
	  I should like very much to know!
	It will certainly be my fault,
	If she goes to her family vault,
	  To bury her life-long woe!

BOTH. The family vault—the family vault.

It will certainly be $\left\{ \begin{array}{c} \text{your} \\ \text{my} \end{array} \right\}$ fault,

If $\left\{ \begin{array}{c} \text{I go} \\ \text{she goes} \end{array} \right\}$ to $\left\{ \begin{array}{c} \text{my} \\ \text{her} \end{array} \right\}$ family vault,

To bury $\left\{ \begin{array}{c} \text{my} \\ \text{her} \end{array} \right\}$ life-long woe!

(*Exit* LADY SANGAZURE *in great anguish.*)

RECITATIVE — MR. WELLS.

Oh, hideous doom—to scatter desolation,
  And sow the seeds of sorrow far and wide!
To foster *mésalliances* through the nation,
  And drive high-born old dames to suicide!
Shall I subject myself to reprobation
  By leaving her in solitude to pine?
No! come what may, I'll make her reparation,
  So, aged lady, take me!—I am thine! (*Exit.*)

Enter ALINE.

ALINE. This was to have been the happiest day of my life—but I am very far from happy! Alexis insists that I shall taste the philtre—and when I try to persuade him that to do so would be an insult to my pure and lasting love, he tells me that I object because I do not desire that my love for him shall be eternal. Well (*sighing, and producing a phial*), I can at least prove to him that, in that, he is unjust!

RECITATIVE.

Alexis! Doubt me not, my loved one! See
Thine uttered will is sovereign law to me!
All fear—all thought of ill I cast away!
It is my darling's will, and I obey!
    (*She drinks the philtre.*)

  The fearful deed is done,
    My love is near!
  I go to meet my own
    In trembling fear!
  If o'er us aught of ill
    Should cast a shade,
  It was my darling's will,
  And I obeyed!

As ALINE *is going off, she meets* DR. DALY, *entering pensively. He is playing on a flageolet. Under the influence of the spell she at once becomes strangely fascinated by him, and exhibits every symptom of being hopelessly in love with him.*

SONG — DR. DALY.

Oh, my voice is sad and low,
And with timid step I go—
For with load of love o'erladen
I enquire of every maiden,
"Will you wed me, little lady?
Will you share my cottage shady?"
  Little lady answers "No!
  Thank you for your kindly proffer—
  Good your heart, and full your coffer;
  Yet I must decline your offer—
  I'm engaged to so-and-so!"
    So-and-so!
    So-and-so! (*Flageolet.*)
  She's engaged to so-and-so!
What a rogue young hearts to pillage!
What a worker on Love's tillage!
Every maiden in the village
  Is engaged to so-and-so!
    So-and-so!
    So-and-so! (*Flageolet.*)
  All engaged to so-and-so!

At the end of the song DR. DALY *sees* ALINE, *and, under the influence of the potion, falls in love with her.*

ENSEMBLE — ALINE *and* DR. DALY.

Oh, joyous boon! oh, mad delight!
Oh, sun and moon! oh, day and night!
  Rejoice, rejoice with me!
Proclaim our joy, ye birds above—
Ye brooklets, murmur forth our love,
  In choral ecstasy:

ALINE. Oh, joyous boon!
DR. DALY. Oh, mad delight!

ALINE. Oh, sun and moon!

DR. DALY. Oh, day and night!

BOTH.   Ye birds, and brooks, and fruitful trees,
    With choral joy delight the breeze—
      Rejoice, rejoice with me!

Enter ALEXIS.

ALEXIS (*with rapture*). Aline, my only love, my
    happiness!
    The philtre—you have tasted it?

ALINE (*with confusion*). Yes! yes!

ALEXIS. Oh, joy! mine, mine for ever, and for
    aye! (*Embraces her.*)

ALINE. Alexis, don't do that—you must not!
      (DR. DALY *interposes between them.*)

ALEXIS (*amazed*).   Why?

DUET — ALINE and DR. DALY.

ALINE. Alas! that lovers thus should meet:
    Oh pity, pity me!
  Oh, charge me not with cold deceit;
    Oh pity, pity me!
  You bade me drink—with trembling awe
  I drank, and, by the potion's law,
  I loved the very first I saw!
    Oh pity, pity me!

DR. DALY. My dear young friend, consolèd be—
    We pity, pity you.
  In this I'm not an agent free—
    We pity, pity you.
  Some most extraordinary spell,
  O'er us has cast its magic fell—
  The consequence I need not tell.
    We pity, pity you.

ENSEMBLE.

Some most extraordinary spell,

O'er $\left\{ \begin{array}{c} us \\ them \end{array} \right\}$ has cast its magic fell—

The consequence $\left\{ \begin{array}{c} we \\ they \end{array} \right\}$ need not tell.

$\left\{ \begin{array}{c} We \\ They \end{array} \right\}$ pity, pity $\left\{ \begin{array}{c} thee! \\ me! \end{array} \right\}$

ALEXIS (*furiously*). False one, begone—I spurn
    thee!
    To thy new lover turn thee!
    Thy perfidy all men shall know.

ALINE (*wildly*). I could not help it!

ALEXIS (*calling off*). Come one, come all!

DR. DALY. We could not help it!

ALEXIS (*calling off*). Obey my call!

ALINE (*wildly*). I could not help it!

ALEXIS (*calling off*). Come, hither, run!

DR. DALY. We could not help it!

ALEXIS (*calling off*). Come, every one!

Enter all the characters, except LADY SANGAZURE
and MR. WELLS.

CHORUS.

Oh, what is the matter, and what is the clatter?
  He's glowering at her, and threatens a blow!
Oh, why does he batter the girl he did flatter?
  And why does the latter recoil from him so?

RECITATIVE — ALEXIS.

Prepare for sad surprises—
My love Aline despises!
No thought of sorrow shames her—
Another lover claims her!
Be his, false girl, for better or for worse—
But, ere you leave me, may a lover's curse—

DR. DALY (*coming forward*). Hold! Be just.
This poor child drank the philtre at your instance.
She hurried off to meet you—but, most unhappily, she met me instead. As you had administered the potion to both of us, the result was inevitable. But fear nothing from me—I will be no
man's rival. I shall quit the country at once—and
bury my sorrow in the congenial gloom of a Co-
lonial Bishopric.

ALEXIS. My excellent old friend! (*Taking his
hand—then turning to* MR. WELLS, *who has entered with* LADY SANGAZURE.) Oh, Mr. Wells,
what, what is to be done!

MR. WELLS. I do not know—and yet—there is
one means by which this spell may be removed.

ALEXIS. Name it—oh, name it!

MR. WELLS. Or you or I, must yield up his life
to Ahrimanes. I would rather it were you. I
should have no hesitation in sacrificing my own
life to spare yours, but we take stock next week,
and it would not be fair on the Co.

ALEXIS. True. Well, I am ready!

ALINE. No, no—Alexis—it must not be! Mr.
Wells, if he must die that all may be restored to
their old loves, what is to become of me? I should
be left out in the cold, with no love to be restored
to!

MR. WELLS. True—I did not think of that. (*To
the others.*) My friends, I appeal to you, and I
will leave the decision in your hands.

FINALE.

MR. WELLS.   Or I, or he
               Must die!
              Which shall it be?
               Reply!

SIR MARMADUKE. Die thou!

Thou art the cause of all offending!

LADY SANGAZURE.   Die thou!
    Yield thou to this decree unbending!

ALL.   Die thou!

MR. WELLS.   So be it! I submit! My fate is sealed.
    To popular opinion thus I yield!
                       (*Falls on trap.*)
    Be happy all—leave me to my despair—
    I go—it matters not with whom—or where!
                           (*Gong.*)

All quit their present partners, and rejoin their old lovers. SIR MARMADUKE *leaves* MRS. PARTLET, *and goes to* LADY SANGAZURE. ALINE *leaves* DR. DALY, *and goes to* ALEXIS. DR. DALY *leaves* ALINE, *and goes to* CONSTANCE. NOTARY *leaves* CONSTANCE, *and goes to* MRS. PARTLET. *All the Chorus make a corresponding change.*

ALL.

GENTLEMEN.   Oh my adored one!

LADIES.   Unmingled joy!

GENTLEMEN.   Ecstatic rapture!

LADIES.   Beloved boy!
                    (*They embrace.*)

SIR MARMADUKE.   Come to my mansion, all of you! At least
    We'll crown our rapture with another feast!

ENSEMBLE.

SIR MARMADUKE, LADY SANGAZURE, ALEXIS,
and ALINE.

Now to the banquet we press—
    Now for the eggs and the ham—
Now for the mustard and cress—
    Now for the strawberry jam!

CHORUS.   Now to the banquet, etc.

DR. DALY, CONSTANCE, NOTARY, *and*
MRS. PARTLET.

Now for the tea of our host—
    Now for the rollicking bun—
Now for the muffin and toast—
    Now for the gay Sally Lunn!

CHORUS.   Now for the tea, etc.

General dance. During the symphony MR. WELLS
sinks through grave trap, amid red fire.

CURTAIN.

Postscript

THE FIRST-NIGHT TEXT contains a second verse to Constance's aria on page 54, starting "When I rejoice, He shows no pleasure." This verse appears in both issues of the first edition but in no other reprints of this opera. The same is true of a ballad in two verses of eight lines each, sung by Lady Sangazure, immediately following her opening recitative beginning, "In days gone by, these eyes were bright." Not only was this ballad sung on opening night but under the title "In days gone by" it appeared in the "List of music in *The Sorcerer* published separately," and persisted in this list through the first issue of the second edition, when the ballad had already been dropped from the text itself.

Seven years later, on October 11, 1884, D'Oyly Carte revived this opera along with *Trial by Jury* in a double bill at the Savoy Theatre. For this revival the libretto of *The Sorcerer* was considerably tightened and amended to the textual status in which it appears today. The Tutti which ends Act I, "Eat, drink, and be gay," was eliminated, and the act ended with the Company falling insensible on the stage instead of continuing to dance the Brindisi at the curtain (see accompanying illustration from an 1884 souvenir program).

Both librettist and composer radically changed the opening to the second act, omitting the eight-line chorus "Happy are we in our loving frivolity" and in its place substituting a page and a half of new text before the entrance of Constance with the Notary (see page 63):

ACT II.

SCENE.—*Exterior of* SIR MARMADUKE'S *mansion by moonlight. All the peasantry are discovered asleep on the ground, as at the end of Act I. Enter* MR. WELLS, *on tiptoe, followed by* ALEXIS *and* ALINE. MR. WELLS *carries a dark lantern.*

TRIO—ALEXIS, ALINE, *and* MR. WELLS.

> 'Tis twelve, I think,
>   And at this mystic hour
> The magic drink
>   Should manifest its power.
> Oh slumbering forms,
>   How little have ye guessed
> The fire that warms
>   Each apathetic breast!

ALEXIS.   But stay, my father is not here!

ALINE.   And pray where is my mother dear?

MR. WELLS.   I did not think it meet to see
A dame of lengthy pedigree,
A Baronet and K.C.B.,
A Doctor of Divinity,
And that respectable Q. C.,
All fast asleep, al-fresco-ly,
And so I had them taken home
And put to bed respectably!
I trust my conduct meets your approbation.

ALEXIS.   Sir, you acted with discrimination,
And showed more delicate appreciation
Than we expect in persons of your station.

MR. WELLS.   But soft—they waken, one by one—
The spell has worked—the deed is done!
I would suggest that we retire
While Love, the Housemaid, lights her kitchen fire!

Exeunt MR. WELLS, ALEXIS, *and* ALINE, *on tiptoe, as the villagers stretch their arms, yawn, rub their eyes, and sit up.*

MEN.   Why, where be oi, and what be oi a doin',
A-sleepin' out, just when the dews du rise?

GIRLS.   Why that's the very way your health to ruin,
And don't seem quite respectable likewise!

MEN (*staring at girls*).   Eh, that's you!
Only think o' that, now!

GIRLS (*coyly*).   What may you be at, now?
Tell me, du!

MEN (*admiringly*).   Eh, what a nose,
And eh, what eyes, miss!
Lips like a rose,
And cheeks likewise, miss!

GIRLS (*coyly*).   Oi tell you true,
Which I've never done, sir,
Oi loike you
As I never loiked none, sir!

ALL.   Eh, but oi du loike you!

MEN.   If you'll marry me, I'll dig for you and rake for you!

GIRLS.   If you'll marry me, I'll scrub for you and bake for you!

MEN.   If you'll marry me, all

	others I'll forsake for you!
ALL.	All this will I du, if you'll marry me!
GIRLS.	If you'll marry me, I'll cook for you and brew for you!
MEN.	If you'll marry me, I'll take you in and du for you!
GIRLS.	If you'll marry me, I'll take you in and du for you!

ALL.	All this will I du, if you'll marry me! Eh, but oi du loike you!

Country Dance. At end of dance, enter CONSTANCE *in tears, leading* NOTARY, *who carries an ear trumpet.*

Later in the act the Recitative of Mr. Wells on page 67, "Oh hideous doom—to scatter desolation," as well as Aline's monologue immediately following, were both dropped, and have remained out of subsequent texts.

H.M.S. PINAFORE

Introduction

THE KEEL PLATE of Literature's greatest shipbuilding venture since Argus the Thespian hewed the *Argo* from timbers of Mt. Pelion, was laid without ceremony in December 1877. W. S. Gilbert, a somewhat different Thespian, had used ideas and characters from three *Bab Ballads*—"Captain Reece," "Joe Go-Lightly," and "The Bumboat Woman's Story"—as the success-seasoned main timbers of an Entirely Original Nautical Comic Opera, a wonder-craft which was to secure for its three latter-day Argonauts a veritable golden fleece.

The Sorcerer was only a month and ten days old at the Opéra Comique, when Gilbert wrote his composer-colleague:

Dear Sullivan   I send you herewith a sketch plot of the proposed opera. I hope and think you will like it. I called on you two days ago (not knowing you had gone abroad) to consult you about it before drawing it up in full. I have very little doubt whatever but that you will be pleased with it. I should have liked to have talked it over with you, as there is a good deal of fun in it which I haven't set down on paper. Among other things a song (kind of "Judge's song") for the First Lord —tracing his career as office-boy in cotton-broker's office, clerk, traveller, junior partner, and First Lord of Britain's Navy.

I think a splendid song can be made of this. Of course there will be no *personality* in this—the fact that the First Lord in the Opera is a *Radical* of the most pronounced type will do away with any suspicion that W. H. Smith is intended. [Gilbert could not have seriously believed this, but as W. H. Smith was Disraeli's First Lord appointee, he was probably trying to allay any potential fears Sullivan might have that offense might be given in high places.] Barrington will be a capital captain, and Grossmith a first-rate First Lord. The uniforms of the officers and crew will be effective—the chorus will look like sailors, and we will ask to have their uniforms *made for them* at Portsmouth.

I shall be anxious to know what you think of the plot. It seems to me that there is plenty of story in it (*The Sorcerer* rather lacks story) with good musical situations. Josephine can have two good ballads, and so can Ralph.

I hope you will have fine weather and that the change will do you a lot of good. As soon as I hear from you that the plot will do, I will set to work, sending you the first act as soon as it is finished.

Sullivan had received this letter and enclosure in Paris on December 29. His reaction to the sketch plot had been instantly favorable. He started back to London on the 31st and arrived home on New Year's Day, 1878. The following day Gilbert had noted in his diary: "Met Carte in Strand. Directors of Opera Co'y want to reduce guarantee on new piece. Absolutely declined, as not having heard from them for four weeks, concluded proposition accepted." This was an early indication of the reefs and shoals of a business nature that were to beset the course of Her Majesty's Ship *Pinafore* even, in a manner of speaking, before she left the ways. The Directors of the Opéra Comique had begun—shortly after the opening of *The Sorcerer,* their first corporate theatrical venture—to harass D'Oyly Carte with vacillating threats of closing-down every time the box office revenue declined. This must have accounted for the urgency with which Gilbert had approached the preparation of a new opera, literally within a month of the very successful reception of its predecessor. And after his conversation with Carte on January 2, he pressed on so that by mid-month he had read the plot of the new opera to Carte, who, according to Hesketh Pearson, "was much pleased with it."

The christening of the good ship, like the keel-laying, had proceeded without fanfare. Gilbert in an interview a year later admitted that the title "was suggested entirely by rhyme" . . . something to rhyme with "and three cheers more" . . . something like "semaphore," which was the first idea, later changed, at the suggestion of Arthur Sullivan (according to Blanche Roosevelt's recollection) to "Pinafore."

H.M.S. Pinafore can be said to be the first of the pure-bred Gilbert and Sullivan operas—the first to be conceived and written with an existing company in mind, already selected by the three partners. Isaac Goldberg made the distinction that *Thespis* and *Trial by Jury* had both been written for the companies of other impresarios. In *The Sorcerer* the Gilbert and Sullivan formula had emerged, cast and rehearsed by the author, composer, and manager themselves. It was for this truly Gilbert and Sullivan opera company that *Pinafore* had been prepared, even tailored.

Gilbert had made clear in his letter to Sullivan in Paris that in the earliest sketch plot he had Grossmith and Barrington in mind for specific form-fitting roles. Probably Little Buttercup's part similarly had been created to fit Harriet Everard, and it has been assumed—largely on the basis of Jessie Bond's reminiscences at the age of seventy-five—that the original Hebe was designed to have been Mrs. Howard Paul. Three of these four principals, along with Richard Temple and Fred Clifton, by their very existence under contract had helped Gilbert fashion his libretto. And in a negative sense this was probably also true of Mrs. Paul.

In her interview for the *Sphere* fifty years afterward, Jessie Bond's recollection was understandably inaccurate. "Clearly *H.M.S. Pinafore* was written with a view to providing Mrs. Paul with a 'fat' part," recalled Miss Bond, "and there was

to be an opportunity for her to interpolate her own turns, a latitude the collaborators never dreamed later of allowing to any of their principals. But when at rehearsals she was told that a Miss Bond, a mere unknown, was to be her understudy, her dignity was so offended that then and there she walked out of the Opéra Comique." Fact, as well as surmise, is against this anecdote. Sullivan, as early as February 5, had written D'Oyly Carte from Nice the simple statement: "There will be no part for Mrs. Paul I believe in the new piece." In another letter to Carte on April 23 he expressed his regrets that there was *"absolutely nothing* for her to do."

It is improbable to the point of being downright unbelievable that Gilbert would ever countenance and even prearrange an actor's own interpolations. Mrs. Paul, an experienced actress, would scarcely have expected to be understudied by one of similar experience; but she might well have been surprised to find her understudy years younger, far prettier, and possessor of a well-trained voice. Mrs. Paul's vocal ability was described in the *Figaro*'s review of *The Sorcerer* as "not all that it was." It seems abundantly clear that Gilbert, far from writing a fat part for Mrs. Paul, intentionally wrote her out of the script, and that he employed this indirect means of causing a waning and probably domineering star to leave the company of her own accord.

Gilbert, suffering from intermittent headaches perhaps of sinus origin and from the early pangs of gout, which was to plague him the rest of his life, worked hard at the lyrics of the new opera and at rehearsing his play *The Ne'er-do-Weel* (a failure under both its original title and its secondtry title, *The Vagabond.*) Sullivan on the other hand had returned to the Continent. He had been undergoing acute physical torments, the agony of a kidney ailment that was to be his almost constant companion. In the letter he had written D'Oyly Carte from Nice on February 5 he had revealed his state of mind: "Is *The Sorcerer* seriously on the wane—I mean is business bad? I hope not for I am not in very good cue yet for writing anything fresh and bright. I think the new piece ought to be very funny. . . ." His nephew cited him in later years as recollecting: "It is, perhaps, rather a strange fact that the music to *Pinafore,* which was thought to be so merry and spontaneous, was written while I was suffering agonies from a cruel illness. I would compose a few bars, and then be almost insensible from pain. When the paroxysm was passed, I would write a little more, until the pain overwhelmed me again. Never was music written under such distressing conditions." Gilbert's diary shows that he and Sullivan had spent April 13 in Portsmouth, checking meticulously the nautical detail of their forthcoming production. A week later Sullivan had written his mother: "Everyone is out of town for Easter except myself. . . . I haven't been out this week except to dine, as I am in the full swing of my new work. It will be bright and probably more popular than *The Sorcerer,* but it is not so clever. . . ."

On May 3 (according to Pearson, who gleaned it from Gilbert's diary) he completed the dialogue of *Pinafore* and sent Sullivan the changes he had made in the lyrics. "Thereafter he was rehearsing and rewriting the opera at the same time." On May 24, the day before the première, Gilbert rehearsed in the morning, staying at the theatre till five thirty p.m. He returned for a night dress rehearsal: "everything smooth—dresses all right—remained there till 3.35 a.m.—then to Beefsteak [Club] for supper—then home at 4.30." This was sixteen hours before the advertised curtain-time of the first night.

The Opéra Comique on the night of Saturday, April 25, had "a great house. . . . All seats were sold out days beforehand, and a crowd,—far greater than the unreserved seats could accom-

modate—was turned away." The *Figaro* reported otherwise in a review so scathingly hostile as to weaken its credibility in the face of the generally friendly press: "It is curious that, whereas at the first performance of *The Sorcerer* a seat could not be had for love or money, on the afternoon of the first performance of the *Pinafore* burlesque an applicant at the box office was told 'Plenty of seats, sir. I can give you one in the first row, in the third row, or at the back.'" This effort to minimize the box-office success was not justified by the *Times* account: "The performance—conducted on the first night by the composer himself—was received by a crowded audience with every sign of satisfaction."

The program for the occasion was printed to serve both the first and second performances and so bears "Saturday, May 25th, and Monday, May 27th" on front cover and inside, but gave no mention of the composer conducting.

There was neither forepiece nor afterpiece that night. Arthur Sullivan, according to the *Era,* "previously to the rise of the curtain, treated his admirers to a light and sparkling little overture." With

From an early PINAFORE *poster. The original is in full color.*

the curtain up, the *Daily News* described the setting as "a beautiful scene of the quarter-deck of the ship and Portsmouth in the distance (painted by Messrs. Gordon and Harford)." The critic of the *Standard* was more detailed in his enthusiasm: "So perfect a quarter-deck as that of *H.M.S. Pinafore* has assuredly never been put upon the stage. Every block and rope to the minutest detail is in its place, in fact it is an exact model of what it represents; and thanks no doubt to the untiring diligence of the author the piece is admirably represented all round. Here we find that marvel of marvels, a chorus that acts, and adds to the reality of the illusion." The *Era* found that "the caricature of official routine was very droll indeed, and must be seen to be appreciated as it deserves. The dresses were remarkably bright and attractive, and the opera was in every way well placed upon the stage by Mr. D'Oyly Carte, who had evidently spared no pains to make the representation as complete as possible."

At least five selections were encored, and there were probably others not specifically identified by the press. The first noted by the *Standard* was the Captain's opening song: "Upon the Captain's arrival comes what will be one of the songs of the piece—a ditty which on Saturday evening evoked a hearty encore." The *Era* reported that George Grossmith was so successful in "When I was a lad I served a term" that "it was obliged to be repeated." And the *Daily News* recorded that the latter part of "the very spirited ensemble at the close of the first act" was encored. In the second act the same reviewer noted the concluding portion of "the sprightly trio, 'Never mind the why and wherefore,'" was encored, as indeed it has been perennially ever since, complete with much of the same stage business described by the critic of the *Standard*—"a movement in E so vivacious and tuneful that even the First Lord has to retire at intervals behind the wardroom skylight and relieve his feelings by a dance, in which his dignified playfulness is delightful to behold." The *Daily News* added that the Boatswain's solo—"He is an Englishman!"—"forcibly declaimed by Mr. Clifton," was encored.

For the cast there was uniform approbation led by the *Times'* praise for the three principal veterans: "Few theatres can boast of such a trio of genuine humorists as are Mr. G. Grossmith (Sir Joseph Porter), Mr. Rutland Barrington (the philanthropic captain), and Miss Everard (Little Buttercup). The vocal achievements of these are not of the highest order, but their *parlato* style does full justice to the humorous sallies of Mr. Gilbert." The *Era* found Grossmith's Sir Joseph "a very effective study of a British Admiral. Whether purposely imitated or not, there was a

PUNCH *cartoon portrait of Arthur Sullivan by Linley Sambourne, October 30, 1880.*

certain resemblance to the portraits of Nelson in Mr. Grossmith's makeup." (This may well have been contrived deliberately by Gilbert as a red-herring to avoid any charge that the characterization was W. H. Smith.) Rutland Barrington suffered that night from a severe cold; but even with this handicap which rendered his voice "practically useless" the press praised his performance of Captain Corcoran. The *Daily News* mentioned that "an apology was made" for him, which would seem to indicate that there was an "indulgence slip" in the program, although no copy appears to have survived. That Barrington made a good show of a difficult situation is evident from the fact that his opening song was encored. In the *Daily News'* opinion, "Miss Everard gave a very clever interpretation of the character assigned her," and the *Era* added that her quaint humour as Little Buttercup "was frequently rewarded with laughter and applause as cordial as it was deserved. The mysterious duet with the Captain on the moonlit deck was an excellent example of Miss Everard's drollery, which in this scene will be more prominent still when Mr. Barrington is able to render greater assistance."

Miss Emma Howson received a press agent's dream of good notices. To cite just a few: Her "accession to the Opéra Comique company is an event of importance" (*Globe*); "A singer of decided promise. Her voice is a light soprano of an agreeable quality, and her singing betrays musical intelligence and dramatic instinct" (*Times*); and "Miss Emma Howson, who made her first appearance in this country, is one of the brightest, liveliest little ladies imaginable. She has a voice of charming quality, pure, sweet, and admirably in tune. Her singing at once established her in the good graces of the audience, and her acting was full of intelligence and comic talent. Her debut was a complete success" (*Era*). Only *Figaro* was in opposition: "The heroine, Josephine, is a silly and a colorless character, and its exponent has a curiously unsympathetic and harsh-speaking voice."

Mr. George Power as Ralph, the *Daily News* commented, "in his ballad and concerted pieces, displayed a light tenor voice of very agreeable quality, and acted the part of the sentimental lover well." The *Times* critic found his intonation "a little uncertain" on the first night. The *Era* felt that Richard Temple "made a great deal of Dick Deadeye . . . both in acting and singing." The same critic thought "Mr. Clifton deserved great praise for his humour in more than one scene" and particularly cited the encore he won for his rendering of "A British tar is a soaring soul."

Little Jessie Bond—who was to win lavish lineage from the Press in her many subsequent roles —had to be content with a mere mention in most reviews on this her Gilbert and Sullivan debut. She "played and sang with agreeable vivacity as the First Lord's favourite cousin," wrote the critic of the *Standard;* and the *Era* found that "Miss Jessie Bond in the little character of Hebe was agreeable." Two "agreeables" was not much of a score for Jessie.

"The curtain fell amidst enthusiastic applause," in the detailed description of the *Era,* "and Messrs. Gilbert and Sullivan and the principal performers were called to the footlights, and greeted most heartily, a compliment most thoroughly deserved, for the success of the comic opera and the genuine enjoyment the audience had derived from it was unquestionable. The performance was for a first night capital."

The press in general was warmly favorable, with the particular exceptions of the *Daily Telegraph* and *Figaro*. Gilbert, perhaps, fared better than Sullivan. His *Bab Ballads,* burlesques, and comedies had stamped him in the public eye first-and-foremost as a humorist. There was no body of critical public to deplore the loss of his services to the cause of serious drama every time he wrote a comic libretto, even though in the eight years preceding *Pinafore* he had written eight successfully produced serious plays. Arthur Sullivan, on the other hand, was regarded by most musically sophisticated Englishmen as the nation's hope for an outstanding composer. His *Tempest* music, oratorios, overtures, a masque, and a symphony had dictated for him—as far as the public was concerned—the role of premier British exponent of serious music, even though he had written a half-dozen comic works for the stage and a legion of popular ballads and hymns, in those same eight years.

So it was: the *Globe* thought Gilbert's libretto the best he had ever written. The *Illustrated Sporting and Dramatic News* found it "irresistibly comical." *Touchstone; or, The New Era* expatiated: "As a humorous effort we consider that *H.M.S. Pinafore* surpasses its predecessor. . . . There is a perfect proportion. The humour is sustained throughout, and the circumstance . . . that there is no superfluous dialogue shows how artistically Mr. Gilbert has performed his share of the undertaking. One can read the libretto with thorough enjoyment before the curtain rises. . . . Mr. Gilbert and Mr. Sullivan have worked together in the true spirit of collaboration. The former has not simply provided jingle for pretty tunes; his words are really wedded to the music, not sacrificed to it. Mr. Sullivan has entered thoroughly into the spirit of the jest. . . ."

"With Mr. Gilbert a plot is seldom more than a lay figure which he delights in dressing in the fantastic garb of his wit and imagination," explained the *Times*. "We hardly become conscious of the absence of any kind of human interest. The audience, therefore, have little reason to complain of Mr. Gilbert. But the musician has. His true field of action is after all genuine emotion. . . . The manner in which Mr. Sullivan accepts the difficult position thus prepared for him by his collaborator is worthy of the highest commendation. Whenever he finds that Mr. Gilbert's humour cannot be aided by musical means he lets well alone and retires to modest recitative. On the other hand, he loses no opportunity to emphasize comic points or to indicate hidden irony by a slight touch of exaggeration. A very unsophisticated audience might accept, for instance, Ralph's ballad, 'A maiden fair to see,' as the real sentiment of which it is an admirable caricature. . . ." And the *Times* then pressed home to Sullivan's most sensitive spot: "While recording this decided success of Mr. Sullivan's new work we cannot suppress a word of regret that the composer on whom before all others the chance of a national school of music depends should confine himself, or be confined by circumstances, to a class of production which, however attractive, is hardly worthy of the efforts of an accomplished and serious artist."

The *Sunday Times* argued along the same lines:

"It is not a reassuring circumstance to see a representative dramatist and a representative musician unable or unwilling to give us anything better than fare which is toothsome but not filling. . . . There is funny material in this ridiculous plot, but not of the sort to allow a musician much chance of distinction. . . . Mr. Sullivan cannot give us music which is otherwise than flowing and pleasing, but perhaps he has attempted less in the present comic opera than in any he has yet done. . . . It is not an effort of high art; but it is a good representation of what a really clever musician can do in what Beethoven called his 'unbuttoned' moments." And the *Illustrated Sporting and Dramatic News* hedged as it summed up: "It is not likely to enhance his fame, yet it is not entirely unworthy of his pen. . . . Mr. Sullivan is capable of infinitely better things."

The two principal comic weeklies of the day were obviously split wide apart. Gilbert-loving *Fun*—the alma mater of the *Bab Ballads*—in its June 5 issue ruled: *"H.M.S. Pinafore* is a great hit, and will add to the repute of W. S. Gilbert and Arthur Sullivan as authors of a style of production peculiarly their own. . . . We can say that the fun and subtle humour of the piece is in the author's happiest vein, and that the music is in every way worthy of the composer, full of beauty and freshness, and much of it with that charm that at once fixes it on the mind of the hearer." Gilbert-baiting *Punch* displayed its editorial policy by ignoring the merest mention of the name *Pinafore* until October 5 (and then it was only a word in the dialog of a comic story, "How I couldn't find Stanley"). The *Figaro*'s column, "Before and Behind the Curtain," excoriated both Gilbert and Sullivan, Grossmith, and every feature of the first night that had found favor in most other eyes. There was so much venom and so little apparent factual reporting in the *Figaro* review that one wonders whether to believe such

vivid details as—"After one of Mr. Sullivan's dreary ditties in the second act, a cry was raised in the gallery, 'We don't want any more shop ballads.' " And *Figaro* enlarged on this with a bit of insinuative shop-criticism: "It is impossible to resist the conclusion that Messrs. Gilbert and Sullivan have not in *Pinafore* given us their best, and that they have been fain to write down to the level of the artists, and to the wishes or necessities of that heterogeneous quintet of music publishers and amateurs, the Opéra Comique directors. The fact that three of the five directors are in some way or other connected with the firm of music publishers who publish the burlesque will explain the presence in the score of so many shop ballads, to be sung by a company whose strong point is certainly not vocal."

Certainly there were many professionals among those who attended that epochal first night who agreed with the *Era:* "We feel confident that an entertainment so bright, witty, and amusing will attract large audiences for a long time to come." It was indeed a night to remember, particularly a scant year thence, when every major city in America had—or was threatened by—at least one *Pinafore* company! On the fiftieth anniversary of that May 25 evening, in 1928, Sir George Douglas in a tribute to the occasion recalled the wonder of being among those fortunate few: "I was present that night in the amphitheatre of the Opéra Comique. . . . It was all too soon . . . that, amid cheers, the curtain fell—to be raised again presently to allow the tall, erect figure of the author and the shorter and stouter one of the composer to march upon the stage and bow their acknowledgments, though without speeches."

The *Globe* closed its enthusiastic notice with this sentence: "The success of the opera was genuine and complete, and it will probably be a long time before *H.M.S. Pinafore* is laid up in dock." It may well be centuries.

MAY 25 (SATURDAY) 1878. *Went to Opéra Comique to superintend scene—remained there till 6:30 working at it—Wiseman helping. Then went to Beefsteak to dine and dress. To theatre at 8—put finishing touches &c. Rowdy gallery, singing songs &c. Piece went extremely well. I went in and out three or four times during the evening. Enthusiastic call for self and Sullivan. Then to Beefsteak. Great meeting—Beaufort, Yardley, Lyttleton, F. Locker, Labouchere, Kendal, Marshall, &c. Arranged to dine with Locker on Monday.*
                                      W. S. GILBERT'S DIARY

An Entirely Original Nautical Comic Opera,

IN TWO ACTS,

H.M.S. PINAFORE

OR,

THE LASS THAT LOVED A SAILOR.

Dramatis Personae.

THE RT. HON. SIR JOSEPH PORTER, K.C.B., *First Lord of the Admiralty*	MR. GEO. GROSSMITH, JUN.
CAPT. CORCORAN, *Commanding H.M.S. Pinafore*	MR. RUTLAND BARRINGTON.
RALPH RACKSTRAW, *Able Seaman*	MR. POWER.
DICK DEADEYE, *Able Seaman*	MR. R. TEMPLE.
BILL BOBSTAY, *Boatswain's Mate*	MR. CLIFTON.
BOB BECKET, *Carpenter's Mate*	MR. DYMOTT.
TOM TUCKER, *Midshipmite*	MR. FITZALTAMONT.
SERGEANT OF MARINES	MR. TALBOT.
JOSEPHINE, *The Captain's Daughter*	MISS E. HOWSON.
HEBE, *Sir Joseph's First Cousin*	MISS JESSIE BOND.
LITTLE BUTTERCUP, *A Portsmouth Bumboat Woman*	MISS EVERARD.

FIRST LORD'S SISTERS, HIS COUSINS, HIS AUNTS, SAILORS, MARINES, &C.

SCENE. — Quarter-deck of H.M.S. *Pinafore,* off Portsmouth.

ACT I. — Noon.   ACT II. — Night.

H.M.S. PINAFORE

OR,

THE LASS THAT LOVED A SAILOR.

ACT I.

SCENE. — *Quarter-deck of H.M.S. Pinafore. View of Portsmouth in distance. Sailors, led by* BOATSWAIN, *discovered cleaning brasswork, splicing rope, &c.*

CHORUS.

We sail the ocean blue,
 And our saucy ship's a beauty,
We're sober men, and true,
 And attentive to our duty.
When the balls whistle free o'er the bright
  blue sea,
 We stand to our guns all day;
When at anchor we ride on the Portsmouth
  tide,
 We have plenty of time for play.

Enter LITTLE BUTTERCUP, *with large basket
on her arm.*

RECITATIVE.

Hail, men-o'-wars' men—safeguards of your
 nation,
Here is an end, at last, of all privation;
You've got your pay—spare all you can afford
To welcome Little Buttercup on board.

ARIA.

For I'm called Little Buttercup—dear Little
 Buttercup,
 Though I could never tell why,
But still I'm called Buttercup—poor Little But-
 tercup,
 Sweet Little Buttercup, I.

I've snuff and tobaccy and excellent jacky,
 I've scissors, and watches, and knives;

I've ribbons and laces to set off the faces
 Of pretty young sweethearts and wives.

I've treacle and toffee and excellent coffee,
 Soft tommy and succulent chops;
I've chickens and conies and pretty polonies,
 And excellent peppermint drops.

Then buy of your Buttercup—dear Little But-
 tercup,
 Sailors should never be shy;
So, buy of your Buttercup—poor Little Butter-
 cup,
 Come, of your Buttercup buy!

BOATSWAIN. Aye, Little Buttercup—and well called—for you're the rosiest, the roundest and the reddest beauty in all Spithead.

BUTTERCUP. Red, am I? and round—and rosy! Maybe, for I have dissembled well! But hark ye, my merry friend—hast ever thought that beneath a gay and frivolous exterior there may lurk a canker-worm which is slowly but surely eating its way into one's very heart?

BOATSWAIN. No, my lass, I can't say I've ever thought that.

Enter DICK DEADEYE. *He pushes through sailors,
and comes down.*

DICK. *I* have thought it often. (*All recoil from him.*)

BUTTERCUP. Yes, you look like it! What's the matter with the man? Isn't he well?

BOATSWAIN. Don't take no heed of *him,* that's only poor Dick Deadeye.

DICK. I say—it's a beast of a name, ain't it—Dick Deadeye?

BUTTERCUP. It's not a nice name.

DICK. I'm ugly too, ain't I?

BUTTERCUP. You are certainly plain.

DICK. And I'm three-cornered too, ain't I?

BUTTERCUP. You are rather triangular.

DICK. Ha! ha! That's it. I'm ugly and they hate me for it; for you all hate me, don't you?

BOATSWAIN. Well, Dick, we wouldn't go for to hurt any fellow creetur's feelings, but you can't expect a chap with such a name as Dick Deadeye to be a popular character—now, can you?

DICK. No.

BOATSWAIN. It's asking too much, ain't it?

DICK. It is. From such a face and form as mine the noblest sentiments sound like the black utterances of a depraved imagination. It is human nature—I am resigned.

RECITATIVE.

BUTTERCUP (*looking down hatchway*). But, tell me—who's the youth whose faltering feet
With difficulty bear him on his course?

BOATSWAIN. That is the smartest lad in all the fleet—
Ralph Rackstraw!

BUTTERCUP. Ha! that name! Remorse! remorse!

Enter RALPH RACKSTRAW *from hatchway.*

MADRIGAL — RALPH.

The Nightingale
Loved the pale moon's bright ray,
And told his tale

In his own melodious way!
He sang "Ah, well-a-day!"

ALL. He sang "Ah, well-a-day!"

The lowly vale
For the Mountain vainly sighed;
To his humble wail
The echoing hills replied.
They sang "Ah well-a-day!"

ALL. They sang "Ah well-a-day!"

RECITATIVE.

I know the value of a kindly chorus,
But choruses yield little consolation
When we have pain and trouble too before us!
I love—and love, alas, above my station!

BUTTERCUP (*aside*). He loves—and loves a lass above his station!

ALL (*aside*). Yes, yes, the lass is much above his station.

BALLAD — RALPH.

A maiden fair to see,
The pearl of minstrelsy,
A bud of blushing beauty;
For whom proud nobles sigh,
And with each other vie
To do her menial's duty.

ALL. To do her menial's duty.

RALPH. A suitor, lowly born,
With hopeless passion torn,
And poor beyond concealing,
Has dared for her to pine
At whose exalted shrine
A world of wealth is kneeling!

ALL.   A world of wealth is kneeling!

RALPH.   Unlearned he in aught
    Save that which love has taught
      (For love had been his tutor);
    Oh, pity, pity me—
    Our captain's daughter she,
      And I that lowly suitor!

ALL.   And he that lowly suitor!
          (*Exit* LITTLE BUTTERCUP.)

BOATSWAIN.   Ah, my poor lad, you've climbed too high: our worthy captain's child won't have nothin' to say to a poor chap like you. Will she, lads?

DICK.   No, no, captains' daughters don't marry foremast jacks.

ALL (*recoiling from him*).   Shame! shame!

BOATSWAIN.   Dick Deadeye, them sentiments o' yourn are a disgrace to our common natur'.

RALPH.   But it's a strange anomaly, that the daughter of a man who hails from the quarter-deck may not love another who lays out on the fore-yard arm. For a man is but a man, whether he hoists his flag at the main-truck or his slacks on the main deck.

DICK.   Ah, it's a queer world!

RALPH.   Dick Deadeye, I have no desire to press hardly on you, but such a revolutionary sentiment is enough to make an honest sailor shudder.

BOATSWAIN (*who has gone on poop-deck, returns*).   My lads, our gallant captain has come on deck. Let us greet him as so brave an officer and so gallant a seaman deserves.

Enter CAPTAIN CORCORAN.

RECITATIVE.

CAPTAIN.   My gallant crew, good morning.

ALL (*saluting*).   Sir, good morning!

CAPTAIN.   I hope you're all well.

ALL (*as before*).   Quite well, and you, sir?

CAPTAIN.   I am in reasonable health, and happy
    To meet you all once more.

ALL (*as before*).   You do us proud, sir!
          (*All hitch their trousers.*)

SONG — CAPTAIN CORCORAN.

CAPTAIN.   I am the Captain of the Pinafore!

ALL.   And a right good captain, too!

CAPTAIN.   You're very, very good,
    And be it understood,
    I command a right good crew.

ALL.   We're very, very good,
    And be it understood,
    He commands a right good crew.

CAPTAIN.   Though related to a peer,

    I can hand, reef, and steer,
      And ship a selvagee;
    I am never known to quail
    At the fury of a gale,
      And I'm never, never sick at sea!

ALL.   What, never?

CAPTAIN.   No, never!

ALL.   What, *never?*

CAPTAIN.   Hardly ever!

ALL.   He's hardly ever sick at sea!
    Then give three cheers, and one cheer more
    For the hardy Captain of the Pinafore!

CAPTAIN.   I do my best to satisfy you all—

ALL.   And with you we're quite content.

CAPTAIN.   You're exceedingly polite,
    And I think it only right
    To return the compliment.

ALL.   We're exceedingly polite,
    And he thinks it only right
    To return the compliment.

CAPTAIN.   Bad language or abuse,
    I never, never use,
    Whatever the emergency;
      Though "bother it" I may
      Occasionally say,
    I never use a big, big D—

ALL.   What, never?

CAPTAIN.   No, never!

ALL.   What, *never?*

CAPTAIN.   Hardly ever!

ALL.   Hardly ever swears a big, big D—
    Then give three cheers, and one cheer more,
    For the well-bred Captain of the Pinafore!
(*After song, exeunt all but* CAPTAIN CORCORAN.)

Enter LITTLE BUTTERCUP.

RECITATIVE.

BUTTERCUP.   Sir, you are sad—the silent eloquence
    Of yonder tear that trembles on your eyelash
    Proclaims a sorrow far more deep than common;
    Confide in me—fear not—I am a mother!

CAPTAIN.   Yes, Little Buttercup, I'm sad and sorry:
    My daughter, Josephine, the fairest flower
    That ever blossomed on ancestral timber,
    Is sought in marriage by Sir Joseph Porter,
    Our Admiralty's First Lord, but for some reason
    She does not seem to tackle kindly to it.

BUTTERCUP (*with emotion*).   Ah, poor Sir Joseph!
    Ah, I know too well
    The anguish of a heart that loves but vainly!
    But see—here comes your most attractive daughter

I go—Farewell!   (*Exit.*)

CAPTAIN (*looking after her*). A plump and
pleasing person!

Enter JOSEPHINE, *twining some flowers which she
carries in a small basket.*

BALLAD — JOSEPHINE.

Sorry her lot who loves too well,
    Heavy the heart that hopes but vainly,

Sad are the sighs that own the spell,
    Uttered by eyes that speak too plainly;
        Heavy the sorrow that bows the head
        When love is alive and hope is dead!

Sad is the hour when sets the sun—
    Dark is the night to earth's poor daughters,
When to the ark the wearied one
    Flies from the empty waste of waters!
        Heavy the sorrow that bows the head
        When love is alive and hope is dead!

CAPTAIN. My child, I grieve to see that you are
a prey to melancholy. You should look your best
to-day, for Sir Joseph Porter, K.C.B., will be here
this afternoon to claim your promised hand.

JOSEPHINE. Ah, father, your words cut me to the
quick. I can esteem—reverence—venerate Sir Joseph, for he is a great and good man; but oh, I
cannot love him! My heart is already given.

CAPTAIN (*aside*). It is then as I feared. (*Aloud.*)
Given? And to whom? Not to some gilded lordling?

JOSEPHINE. No, father—the object of my love is
no lordling. Oh, pity me, for he is but a humble
sailor on board your own ship!

CAPTAIN. Impossible!

JOSEPHINE. Yes, it is true—too true!

CAPTAIN. A common sailor? Oh fie!

JOSEPHINE. I blush for the weakness that allows
me to cherish such a passion. I hate myself when
I think of the depth to which I have stooped in
permitting myself to think tenderly of one so ignobly born, but I love him! I love him! I love
him! (*Weeps.*)

CAPTAIN. Come, my child, let us talk this over.
In a matter of the heart I would not coerce my
daughter—I attach but little value to rank or
wealth, but the line must be drawn somewhere.
A man in that station may be brave and worthy,
but at every step he would commit solecisms that
society would never pardon.

JOSEPHINE. Oh, I have thought of this night and
day. But fear not, father, I have a heart, and therefore I love; but I am your daughter, and therefore
I am proud. Though I carry my love with me to the
tomb, he shall never, never know it.

CAPTAIN. You *are* my daughter, after all. But
see, Sir Joseph's barge approaches, manned by
twelve trusty oarsmen and accompanied by the
admiring crowd of female relatives that attend him
wherever he goes. Retire, my daughter, to your
cabin—take this, his photograph, with you—it
may help to bring you to a more reasonable frame
of mind.

JOSEPHINE. My own thoughtful father. (*Exit.*)

BARCAROLLE (*invisible*).

Over the bright blue sea
Comes Sir Joseph Porter, K.C.B.
Wherever he may go,
Bang-bang the loud nine-pounders go!
Shout o'er the bright blue sea
For Sir Joseph Porter, K.C.B.

During this the crew have entered on tip-toe,
listening attentively to the song.

CHORUS OF SAILORS.

We sail the ocean blue,
    And our saucy ship's a beauty,
We're sober men and true,
    And attentive to our duty.
We're smart and sober men,
    And quite devoid of fe-ar,
In all the Royal N.
    None are so smart as we are.

Enter SIR JOSEPH'S FEMALE RELATIVES. *They*
dance round stage.

RELATIVES. Gaily tripping,
    Lightly skipping,
Flock the maidens to the shipping.
SAILORS. Flags and guns and pennants dipping!
    All the ladies love the shipping.
RELATIVES. Sailors sprightly,
    Always rightly,
Welcome ladies so politely;
SAILORS. Ladies who can smile so brightly,
    Sailors welcome most politely.

Enter SIR JOSEPH *with* COUSIN HEBE.

CAPTAIN (*from poop*). Now give three cheers,
    I'll lead the way,
ALL. Hurrah! hurrah! hurrah! hurray!

SONG — SIR JOSEPH.

I am the monarch of the sea,
    The ruler of the Queen's navee.
Whose praise Great Britain loudly chaunts.
HEBE. And we are his sisters, and his cousins,
    and his aunts.
RELATIVES. And we are his sisters, and his cou-
    sins, and his aunts!
SIR JOSEPH. When at anchor here I ride,
    My bosom swells with pride,
And I snap my fingers at a foeman's taunts;
HEBE. And so do his sisters, and his cousins, and
    his aunts!
ALL. And so do his sisters, and his cousins, and
    his aunts!
SIR JOSEPH. But when the breezes blow,

I generally go below,
    And seek the seclusion that a cabin grants!
HEBE. And so do his sisters, and his cousins, and
    his aunts!
ALL. And so do his sisters, and his cousins, and
    his aunts!
His sisters and his cousins
Whom he reckons up by dozens,
    And his aunts!

SONG — SIR JOSEPH.

When I was a lad I served a term
As office boy to an Attorney's firm.
I cleaned the windows and I swept the floor,
And I polished up the handle of the big front
    door.
    I polished up that handle so carefullee
    That now I am the Ruler of the Queen's
        Navee!

CHORUS.   He polished, &c.

As office boy I made such a mark
That they gave me the post of a junior clerk.
I served the writs with a smile so bland,
And I copied all the letters in a big round
    hand—
    I copied all the letters in a hand so free,
    That now I am the Ruler of the Queen's
        Navee!

CHORUS.   He copied, &c.

In serving writs I made such a name
That an articled clerk I soon became;
I wore clean collars and a bran-new suit
For the pass examination at the Institute.
    And that pass examination did so well for me,
    That now I am the Ruler of the Queen's
        Navee!

CHORUS.   And that pass examination, &c.

Of legal knowledge I acquired such a grip
That they took me into the partnership,
And that junior partnership I ween
Was the only ship that I ever had seen.
    But that kind of ship so suited me,
    That now I am the Ruler of the Queen's
        Navee!

CHORUS.   But that kind, &c.

I grew so rich that I was sent
By a pocket borough into Parliament.
I always voted at my party's call,
And I never thought of thinking for myself at
    all.
    I thought so little, they rewarded me,
    By making me the Ruler of the Queen's
        Navee!

CHORUS.   He thought so little, &c.

Now landsmen all, whoever you may be,
If you want to rise to the top of the tree,
If your soul isn't fettered to an office stool,
Be careful to be guided by this golden rule—
   Stick close to your desks and never go to sea,
   And you all may be Rulers of the Queen's
        Navee!

CHORUS.   Stick close, &c.

SIR JOSEPH.   You've a remarkably fine crew, Captain Corcoran.

CAPTAIN.   It *is* a fine crew, Sir Joseph.

SIR JOSEPH (*examining a very small midshipman*). A British sailor is a splendid fellow, Captain Corcoran.

CAPTAIN.   A splendid fellow indeed, Sir Joseph.

SIR JOSEPH.   I hope you treat your crew kindly, Captain Corcoran.

CAPTAIN.   Indeed I hope so, Sir Joseph.

SIR JOSEPH.   Never forget that they are the bulwarks of England's greatness, Captain Corcoran.

CAPTAIN.   So I have always considered them, Sir Joseph.

SIR JOSEPH.   No bullying, I trust—no strong language of any kind, eh?

CAPTAIN.   Oh, never, Sir Joseph.

SIR JOSEPH.   What, *never?*

CAPTAIN.   Hardly ever, Sir Joseph. They are an excellent crew, and do their work thoroughly without it.

SIR JOSEPH (*reproving*).   Don't patronize them, sir—pray don't patronize them.

CAPTAIN.   Certainly not, Sir Joseph.

SIR JOSEPH.   That you are their Captain is an accident of birth. I cannot permit these noble fellows to be patronized because an accident of birth has placed you above them and them below you.

CAPTAIN.   I am the last person to insult a British sailor, Sir Joseph.

SIR JOSEPH.   You are the last person who did, Captain Corcoran. Desire that splendid seaman to step forward.

CAPTAIN.   Ralph Rackstraw, come here.

SIR JOSEPH (*sternly*).   If what?

CAPTAIN.   I beg your pardon—

SIR JOSEPH.   If you *please*.

CAPTAIN.   Oh, yes, of course. If you please. (RALPH *steps forward*).

SIR JOSEPH.   You're a remarkably fine fellow.

RALPH.   Yes, your honour.

SIR JOSEPH.   And a first-rate seaman, I'll be bound.

RALPH.   There's not a smarter topman in the navy, your honour, though I say it who shouldn't.

SIR JOSEPH.   Not at all. Proper self-respect, nothing more. Can you dance a hornpipe?

RALPH.   No, your honour.

SIR JOSEPH.   That's a pity: all sailors should dance hornpipes. I will teach you one this evening, after dinner. Now tell me—don't be afraid —how does your Captain treat you, eh?

RALPH.   A better captain don't walk the deck, your honour.

ALL.   Hear!

SIR JOSEPH.   Good. I like to hear you speak well of your commanding officer; I dare say he don't deserve it, but still it does you credit. Can you sing?

RALPH. I can hum a little, your honour.

SIR JOSEPH. Then hum this at your leisure (*giving him MS. music*). It is a song that I have composed for the use of the Royal Navy. It is designed to encourage independence of thought and action in the lower branches of the service, and to teach the principle that a British sailor is any man's equal, excepting mine. Now, Captain Corcoran, a word with you in your cabin, on a tender and sentimental subject.

CAPTAIN. Aye, aye, Sir Joseph. Boatswain, in commemoration of this joyous occasion, see that extra grog is served out to the ship's company at seven bells.

BOATSWAIN. Beg pardon. If what, your honour?

CAPTAIN. If what? I don't think I understand you.

BOATSWAIN. If you *please,* your honour.

CAPTAIN. What!

SIR JOSEPH. The gentleman is quite right. If you *please.*

CAPTAIN (*stamping his foot impatiently*). If you *please!*

SIR JOSEPH. For I hold that on the seas
        The expression, "if you please,"
    A particularly gentlemanly tone implants.

HEBE. And so do his sisters, and his cousins, and his aunts!

ALL. And so do his sisters, and his cousins, and his aunts!

(*Exeunt* CAPTAIN, SIR JOSEPH, *and* RELATIVES.)

BOATSWAIN. Ah! Sir Joseph's a true gentleman; courteous and considerate to the very humblest.

RALPH. True, Boatswain, but we are not the very humblest. Sir Joseph has explained our true posi-tion to us. As he says, a British seaman is any man's equal excepting his, and if Sir Joseph says that, is it not our duty to believe him?

ALL. Well spoke! well spoke!

DICK. You're on a wrong tack, and so is he. He means well, but he don't know. When people have to obey other people's orders, equality's out of the question.

ALL (*recoiling*). Horrible! horrible!

BOATSWAIN. Dick Deadeye, if you go for to infuriate this here ship's crew too far, I won't answer for being able to hold 'em in. I'm shocked! that's what I am—shocked!

RALPH. Messmates, my mind's made up. I'll speak to the Captain's daughter, and tell her, like an honest man, of the honest love I have for her.

ALL. Hurrah!

RALPH. Is not my love as good as another's? Is not my heart as true as another's? Have I not hands and eyes and ears and limbs like another?

ALL. Aye, aye!

RALPH. True, I lack birth—

BOATSWAIN. You've a berth on board this very ship.

RALPH. Well said—I had forgotten that. Messmates—what do you say? do you approve my determination?

ALL. We do.

DICK. *I* don't.

BOATSWAIN. What is to be done with this here hopeless chap? Let us sing him the song that Sir Joseph has kindly composed for us. Perhaps it will bring this here miserable creetur to a proper state of mind.

GLEE—RALPH, BOATSWAIN, BOATSWAIN'S MATE,
        and CHORUS.

    A British tar is a soaring soul,
        As free as a mountain bird,
    His energetic fist should be ready to resist
        A dictatorial word.
    His nose should pant and his lip should curl,
    His cheeks should flame and his brow should
        furl,
    His bosom should heave and his heart should
        glow,
    And his fist be ever ready for a knock-down
        blow.

CHORUS.   His nose should pant, &c.

    His eyes should flash with an inborn fire,
        His brow with scorn be wrung;
    He never should bow down to a domineering
        frown,
        Or the tang of a tyrant tongue.

His foot should stamp and his throat should
    growl,
His hair should twirl and his face should scowl;
His eyes should flash and his breast protrude,
And this should be his customary attitude!
                            (*Pose.*)

CHORUS.   His foot should stamp, &c.

*All strike attitude and then dance off to hornpipe
and down hatchway, excepting* RALPH, *who remains, leaning pensively against bulwark. Enter*
JOSEPHINE *from cabin.*

JOSEPHINE. It is useless—Sir Joseph's attentions
nauseate me. I know that he is a truly great and
good man, but to me he seems tedious, fretful, and
dictatorial. Yet his must be a mind of no common
order, or he would not dare to teach my dear father to dance a hornpipe on the cabin table. (*Sees*
RALPH.) Ralph Rackstraw! (*Overcome by emotion.*)

RALPH. Aye, lady—no other than poor Ralph
Rackstraw.

JOSEPHINE (*aside*). How my head beats!
(*Aloud.*) And why poor, Ralph?

RALPH. I am poor in the essence of happiness,
lady—rich only in never-ending unrest. In me
there meet a combination of antithetical elements
which are at eternal war with one another. Driven
hither by objective influences—thither by subjec-
tive emotions—wafted one moment into blazing
day by mocking hope—plunged the next into the
Cimmerian darkness of tangible despair, I am but
a living ganglion of irreconcilable antagonisms. I
hope I make myself clear, lady?

JOSEPHINE. Perfectly. (*Aside.*) His simple eloquence goes to my heart. Oh, if I dared—but no,
the thought is madness! (*Aloud.*) Dismiss these
foolish fancies, they torture you but needlessly.
Come, make one effort.

RALPH (*aside*). I will—one. (*Aloud.*) Josephine!

JOSEPHINE (*indignantly*). Sir!

RALPH. Aye, even though Jove's armoury were
launched at the head of the audacious mortal
whose lips, unhallowed by relationship, dared to
breathe that precious word, yet would I breathe it
once, and then perchance be silent evermore. Josephine, in one brief breath I will concentrate the
hopes, the doubts, the anxious fears of six weary
months. Josephine, I am a British sailor, and I
love you!

JOSEPHINE. Sir, this audacity! (*Aside.*) Oh, my
heart, my heart! (*Aloud.*) This unwarrantable
presumption on the part of a common sailor!
(*Aside.*) Common! oh, the irony of the word!
(*Aloud.*) Oh, sir, you forget the disparity in our
ranks.

RALPH. I forget nothing, haughty lady. I love
you desperately, my life is in thy hand—I lay it at
your feet! Give me hope, and what I lack in education and polite accomplishments, that I will endeavour to acquire. Drive me to despair, and in
death alone I shall look for consolation. I am
proud and cannot stoop to implore. I have spoken
and I wait your word.

JOSEPHINE. You shall not wait long. Your proffered love I haughtily reject. Go, sir, and learn to
cast your eyes on some village maiden in your
own poor rank—they should be lowered before
your captain's daughter!

DUET — JOSEPHINE *and* RALPH.

JOSEPHINE. Refrain, audacious tar,
      Your suit from pressing.
    Remember what you are,
      And whom addressing!
    Proud lords to seek my hand
      In throngs assemble,
    The loftiest in the land
      Bow down and tremble!
(*Aside.*) I'd laugh my rank to scorn
      In union holy,
    Were he more highly born
      Or I more lowly!

RALPH. Proud lady, have your way,
      Unfeeling beauty!
    You speak and I obey,
      It is my duty!
    I am the lowliest tar
      That sails the water,
    And you, proud maiden, are
      My captain's daughter!
(*Aside.*) My heart with anguish torn
      Bows down before her;
    She laughs my love to scorn,

Yet I adore her!

(*Exit* JOSEPHINE *into cabin.*)

RALPH (*recit.*).   Can I survive this overbearing
Or live a life of mad despairing,
My proffered love despised, rejected?
No, no, it's not to be expected!

(*Calling off.*)

Messmates, ahoy!
Come here! Come here!

Enter SAILORS, HEBE, *and* RELATIVES.

ALL.   Aye aye, my boy,
What cheer, what cheer?
Now tell us, pray,
Without delay
What does she say—
What cheer, what cheer?

RALPH (*to* HEBE).
The maiden treats my suit with scorn,
Rejects my humble love, my lady.
She says I am ignobly born,
And cuts my hopes adrift, my lady.

ALL.   Oh, cruel one.

DICK.   She spurns your suit? Oho! Oho!
I told you so, I told you so.

SAILORS *and* RELATIVES.

Shall $\begin{Bmatrix} we \\ they \end{Bmatrix}$ submit? Are $\begin{Bmatrix} we \\ they \end{Bmatrix}$ but slaves?
Love comes alike to high and low—
Britannia's sailors rule the waves,
And shall they stoop to insult? No!

DICK.   You must submit, you are but slaves;
A lady she! Oho! Oho!
You lowly toilers of the waves,
She spurns you all—I told you so!

(*Goes off.*)

RALPH (*drawing a pistol*).
My friends, my leave of life I'm taking,
For oh, for oh, my heart is breaking.
When I am gone, oh, prithee tell
The maid that, as I died, I loved her well!

(*Loading it.*)

ALL (*turning away, weeping*).
Of life, alas, his leave he's taking,
For ah! his faithful heart is breaking.
When he is gone we'll surely tell
The maid that, as he died, he loved her
well.

(*During Chorus he has loaded pistol.*)

RALPH.   Be warned, my messmates all,
Who love in rank above you—
For Josephine I fall!

(*Puts pistol to his head. All the sailors stop
their ears.*)

Enter JOSEPHINE.

JOSEPHINE.   Ah! stay your hand! I love you!
ALL.   Ah stay your hand—she loves you!
RALPH (*incredulously*).   Loves me?
JOSEPHINE.   Loves you!
ALL.   Yes, yes—ah, yes—she loves you!

ENSEMBLE.
SAILORS *and* RELATIVES, *and* JOSEPHINE.

Oh joy, oh rapture unforeseen,
For now the sky is all serene,
The God of day—the orb of love,
Has hung his ensign high above,
The sky is all ablaze.

With wooing words and loving song,
We'll chase the lagging hours along,
And if $\begin{Bmatrix} I\ find \\ we\ find \end{Bmatrix}$ the maiden coy,
$\begin{Bmatrix} I'll \\ We'll \end{Bmatrix}$ murmur forth decorous joy
In dreamy roundelays!

DICK DEADEYE.   He thinks he's won his Josephine,
But though the sky is now serene,
A frowning thunderbolt above
May end their ill-assorted love
Which now is all ablaze.

Our captain, ere the day is gone,
Will be extremely down upon
The wicked men who art employ
To make his Josephine less coy
In many various ways.

JOSEPHINE.   This very night,
HEBE.   With bated breath
RALPH.   And muffled oar—
JOSEPHINE.   Without a light,
HEBE.   As still as death
RALPH.   We'll steal ashore.
JOSEPHINE.   A clergyman
RALPH.   Shall make us one
BOATSWAIN.   At half-past ten,
JOSEPHINE.   And then we can
RALPH.   Return, for none
BOATSWAIN.   Can part us then!
ALL.   This very night, &c.

DICK *appears at hatchway.*

DICK.   Forbear, nor carry out the scheme you've
planned;
She is a lady—you a foremast hand!

Remember, she's your gallant captain's
    daughter,
And you the meanest slave that crawls the
    water!

ALL.   Back, vermin, back,
              Nor mock us!
           Back, vermin, back,
              You shock us!

Let's give three cheers for the sailor's bride
Who casts all thought of rank aside—
Who gives up house and fortune too
For the honest love of a sailor true!

For a British tar is a soaring soul
    As free as a mountain bird;
His energetic fist should be ready to resist
    A dictatorial word!

His foot should stamp and his throat should
    growl,
His hair should twirl and his face should scowl,
His eyes should flash and his breast protrude,
And this should be his customary attitude—
                       (*pose*).

GENERAL DANCE.

CURTAIN.

ACT II.

Same scene. Night. Moonlight. CAPTAIN *discovered singing on poop-deck and accompanying himself on a mandolin.* LITTLE BUTTERCUP *seated on quarter-deck, gazing sentimentally at him.*

SONG — CAPTAIN CORCORAN.

Fair moon, to thee I sing,
    Bright regent of the heavens,
Say, why is everything
    Either at sixes or at sevens?
I have lived, hitherto,
    Free from the breath of slander,
Beloved by all my crew—
    A really popular commander.
But now my kindly crew rebel,
    My daughter to a tar is partial,
Sir Joseph storms, and sad to tell,
    He threatens a court martial!
        Fair moon, to thee I sing,
           Bright regent of the heavens,
        Say, why is everything
           Either at sixes or at sevens?

BUTTERCUP. How sweetly he carols forth his melody to the unconscious moon! Of whom is he thinking? Of some high-born beauty? It may be! (*Sighing.*) Who is poor little Buttercup that she should expect his glance to fall on one so lowly! And yet if he knew—(CAPTAIN *has come down.*)

CAPTAIN. Ah! Little Buttercup, still on board? That is not quite right, little one. It would have been more respectable to have gone on shore at dusk.

BUTTERCUP. True, dear Captain—but the recollection of your sad pale face seemed to chain me to the ship. I would fain see you smile before I go.

CAPTAIN. Ah! Little Buttercup, I fear it will be long before I recover my accustomed cheerfulness, for misfortunes crowd upon me, and all my old friends seem to have turned against me!

BUTTERCUP. Oh no—do not say "all," dear Captain. That were unjust to one, at least.

CAPTAIN. True, for you are staunch to me. (*Aside.*) If ever I gave my heart again, methinks it would be to such an one as this! (*Aloud.*) I am touched to the heart by your innocent regard for me, and were we differently situated, I think I could have returned it. But as it is, I fear I can never be more to you than a friend.

BUTTERCUP (*change of manner*). I understand! You hold aloof from me because you are rich and lofty—and I, poor and lowly. But take care! The poor bumboat woman has gipsy blood in her veins, and she can read destinies. There is a change in store for you!

CAPTAIN. A change!

BUTTERCUP. Aye—be prepared!

DUET — LITTLE BUTTERCUP *and* CAPTAIN.

BUTTERCUP. Things are seldom what they seem:
           Skim milk masquerades as cream;
           Highlows pass as patent leathers;
           Jackdaws strut in peacock's feathers.

CAPTAIN (*puzzled*). Very true,
                So they do.

BUTTERCUP. Black sheep dwell in every fold;
           All that glitters is not gold;
           Storks turn out to be but logs;
           Bulls are but inflated frogs.

CAPTAIN (*puzzled*). So they be,

Frequentlee.

BUTTERCUP. Drops the wind and stops the mill;
    Turbot is ambitious brill;
    Gild the farthing if you will,
    But it is a farthing still.

CAPTAIN (*puzzled*). Yes, I know,
    That is so.
    Though to catch your drift I'm
     striving,
    It is shady—it is shady;
    I don't see at what you're driving,
    Mystic lady—mystic lady.
(*Aside.*) Stern conviction's o'er me stealing,
    That the mystic lady's dealing
    In oracular revealing.

BUTTERCUP (*aside*). Stern conviction's o'er him
     stealing,
    That the mystic lady's dealing
    In oracular revealing.

BOTH.   Yes, I know—
     That is so!

CAPTAIN. Though I'm anything but clever,
    I could talk like that for ever;
    Once a cat was killed by care,
    Only brave deserve the fair.

BUTTERCUP. Very true,
     So they do.

CAPTAIN. Wink is often good as nod;
    Spoils the child who spares the rod;
    Thirsty lambs run foxy dangers;
    Dogs are found in many mangers.

BUTTERCUP. Frequentlee,
     I agree.

CAPTAIN. Paw of cat the chestnut snatches,
    Worn-out garments show new patches;
    Only count the chick that hatches;
    Men are grown up catchy-catchies.

BUTTERCUP. Yes, I know,
     That is so.
(*Aside.*) Though to catch my drift he's striving,
    I'll dissemble—I'll dissemble;
    When he sees at what I'm driving,
    Let him tremble—let him tremble!

ENSEMBLE.

Though a mystic tone { I / you } borrow,

{ I shall / You will } learn the truth with sorrow,
Here to-day and gone to-morrow;
  Yes, I know—
  That is so!

(*At the end exit* LITTLE BUTTERCUP *melo-dramatically.*)

CAPTAIN. Incomprehensible as her utterances are, I nevertheless feel that they are dictated by a sincere regard for me. But to what new misery is she referring? Time alone can tell!

Enter SIR JOSEPH.

SIR JOSEPH. Captain Corcoran, I am much disappointed with your daughter. In fact, I don't think she will do.

CAPTAIN. She won't do, Sir Joseph!

SIR JOSEPH. I'm afraid not. The fact is, that although I have urged my suit with as much eloquence as is consistent with an official utterance, I have done so, hitherto, without success. How do you account for this?

CAPTAIN. Really, Sir Joseph, I hardly know. Josephine is of course sensible of your condescension.

SIR JOSEPH. She naturally would be.

CAPTAIN. But perhaps your exalted rank dazzles her.

SIR JOSEPH. You think it does?

CAPTAIN. I can hardly say; but she is a modest girl, and her social position is far below your own. It may be that she feels she is not worthy of you.

SIR JOSEPH. That is really a very sensible suggestion, and displays more knowledge of human nature than I had given you credit for.

CAPTAIN. See, she comes. If your lordship would kindly reason with her, and assure her officially that it is a standing rule at the Admiralty that love levels all ranks, her respect for an official utterance might induce her to look upon your offer in its proper light.

SIR JOSEPH. It is not unlikely. I will adopt your suggestion. But soft, she is here. Let us withdraw, and watch our opportunity.

Enter JOSEPHINE. SIR JOSEPH *retires up and watches her.*

SCENA — JOSEPHINE.

The hours creep on apace,
  My guilty heart is quaking!
Oh, that I might retrace
  The step that I am taking.
Its folly it were easy to be showing,
What I am giving up and whither going.

On the one hand, papa's luxurious home,
  Hung with ancestral armour and old brasses,
Carved oak and tapestry from distant Rome,
  Rare "blue and white" Venetian finger glasses.
Rich oriental rugs, luxurious sofa pillows,
And everything that isn't old, from Gillow's.

And on the other, a dark, dingy room
 In some back street, with stuffy children crying,
Where organs yell, and clacking housewives fume,
 And clothes are hanging out all day a-drying.
With one cracked looking-glass to see your face in,
And dinner served up in a pudding basin!

  A simple sailor, lowly born,
   Unlettered and unknown,
  Who toils for bread from early morn
   Till half the night has flown!
  No golden rank can he impart—
   No wealth of house or land—
  No fortune save his trusty heart
   And honest brown right hand!
  And yet he is so wondrous fair
  That love for one so passing rare,
  So peerless in his manly beauty,
  Were little else than solemn duty!

  Oh, god of love, and god of reason, say,
  Which of you twain shall my poor heart obey!

SIR JOSEPH (*coming forward*). Madam, it has been represented to me that you are appalled by my exalted rank. I desire to convey to you officially my assurance that if your hesitation is attributable to that circumstance, it is uncalled for.

JOSEPHINE. Oh! then your lordship is of opinion that married happiness is *not* inconsistent with discrepancy in rank?

SIR JOSEPH. I am officially of that opinion.

JOSEPHINE. That the high and the lowly may be truly happy together, provided that they truly love one another?

SIR JOSEPH. Madam, I desire to convey to you officially my opinion that love is a platform upon which all ranks meet.

JOSEPHINE. I thank you, Sir Joseph. I *did* hesitate, but I will hesitate no longer. (*Aside.*) He little thinks how eloquently he has pleaded his rival's cause!

CAPTAIN CORCORAN *has entered.*

TRIO.
SIR JOSEPH, CAPTAIN, *and* JOSEPHINE.

CAPTAIN. Never mind the why and wherefore,
  Love can level ranks, and therefore,
  Though his lordship's station's mighty,
   Though stupendous be his brain,
  Though your tastes are mean and flighty
  And your fortune poor and plain,

CAPTAIN *and* SIR JOSEPH. Ring the merry bells
  on board-ship,
  Rend the air with warbling wild,

For the union of $\left\{\begin{matrix} \text{my} \\ \text{his} \end{matrix}\right\}$ lordship
  With a humble captain's child!

CAPTAIN. For a humble captain's daughter—

JOSEPHINE (*aside*). For a gallant captain's daughter.

SIR JOSEPH. And a lord who rules the water—

JOSEPHINE (*aside*). And a *tar* who ploughs the water!

ALL. Let the air with joy be laden,
  Rend with songs the air above,
  For the union of a maiden
  With the man who owns her love!

SIR JOSEPH. Never mind the why and wherefore,
  Love can level ranks, and therefore,
  Though your nautical relation
     (*alluding to* CAPTAIN)
  In my set could scarcely pass—
  Though you occupy a station
  In the lower middle class—

CAPTAIN *and* SIR JOSEPH. Ring the merry bells
  on board-ship,
  Rend the air with warbling wild,

For the union of $\left\{\begin{matrix} \text{my} \\ \text{his} \end{matrix}\right\}$ lordship

With a humble captain's child!

SIR JOSEPH. For a humble captain's daughter—

JOSEPHINE (aside). For a gallant captain's daughter—

CAPTAIN. And a lord who rules the water—

JOSEPHINE (aside). And a tar who ploughs the water!

ALL.   Let the air with joy be laden,
         Fill with songs the air above,
       For the union of a maiden
         With the man who owns her love!

JOSEPHINE. Never mind the why and wherefore,
       Love can level ranks, and therefore
       I admit its jurisdiction;
         Ably have you played your part;
       You have carried firm conviction
         To my hesitating heart.

CAPTAIN and SIR JOSEPH. Ring the merry bells on board-ship,
       Rend the air with warbling wild,
       For the union of $\begin{Bmatrix} \text{my} \\ \text{his} \end{Bmatrix}$ lordship
       With a humble captain's child!

CAPTAIN. For a humble captain's daughter—

JOSEPHINE (aside). For a gallant captain's daughter—

CAPTAIN and SIR JOSEPH. And a lord who rules the water—

JOSEPHINE (aside). And a tar who ploughs the water!
     (Aloud.)   Let the air with joy be laden.

CAPTAIN and SIR JOSEPH. Ring the merry bells on board-ship—

JOSEPHINE. For the union of a maiden—

CAPTAIN and SIR JOSEPH. For her union with his lordship.

ALL.   Rend with songs the air above
           For the man who owns her love!
               (Exit JOSEPHINE.)

CAPTAIN. Sir Joseph, I cannot express to you my delight at the happy result of your eloquence. Your argument was unanswerable.

SIR JOSEPH. Captain Corcoran, it is one of the happiest characteristics of this happy country that official utterances are invariably regarded as unanswerable. (Exit.)

CAPTAIN. At last my fond hopes are to be crowned. My only daughter is to be the bride of a Cabinet Minister. The prospect is Elysian.

During this speech DICK DEADEYE *has entered.*

DICK. Captain!

CAPTAIN. Deadeye! You here? Don't! (Recoiling from him.)

DICK. Ah, don't shrink from me, Captain. I'm unpleasant to look at, and my name's agin me, but I ain't as bad as I seem.

CAPTAIN. What would you with me?

DICK (mysteriously). I'm come to give you warning.

CAPTAIN. Indeed! Do you propose to leave the Navy then?

DICK. No, no, you misunderstand me; listen!

DUET — CAPTAIN and DICK DEADEYE.

DICK. Kind Captain, I've important information,
         Sing hey, the kind commander that you are,
       About a certain intimate relation,
         Sing hey, the merry maiden and the tar.

BOTH.   The merry, merry maiden and the tar.

CAPTAIN. Good fellow, in conundrums you are speaking,
         Sing hey, the mystic sailor that you are,
       The answer to them vainly I am seeking;
         Sing hey, the merry maiden and the tar.

BOTH.   The merry, merry maiden and the tar.

DICK. Kind captain, your young lady is a sighing,
         Sing hey, the simple captain that you are,
       This very night with Rackstraw to be flying;
         Sing hey, the merry maiden and the tar.

BOTH.   The merry, merry maiden and the tar.

CAPTAIN. Good fellow, you have given timely warning,
         Sing hey, the thoughtful sailor that you are.
       I'll talk to Master Rackstraw in the morning:
         Sing hey, the cat-o'-nine-tails and the tar!
               (Producing a "cat.")

BOTH.   The merry cat-o'-nine-tails and the tar!

CAPTAIN. Dick Deadeye—I thank you for your warning—I will at once take means to arrest their flight. This boat cloak will afford me ample disguise— So! (*Envelops himself in a mysterious cloak, holding it before his face.*)

DICK. Ha, ha! They are foiled—foiled—foiled!

Enter CREW *on tiptoe, with* RALPH *and* BOATSWAIN, *meeting* JOSEPHINE, *who enters on tiptoe with bundle of necessaries and accompanied by* LITTLE BUTTERCUP. *The* CAPTAIN, *shrouded in his boat-cloak, takes stage, unnoticed.*

ENSEMBLE.

Carefully on tiptoe stealing,
Breathing gently as we may,
Every step with caution feeling,
We will softly steal away.
(CAPTAIN *stamps. Chord.*)

ALL (*much alarmed*). Goodness me—
Why, what was that?

DICK. Silent be,
It was the cat!

ALL (*reassured*). It was—it was the cat!

CAPTAIN (*producing cat-o'-nine-tails*).
They're right, it was the cat!

ALL. Pull ashore, in fashion steady,
Hymen will defray the fare,
For a clergyman is ready
To unite the happy pair!
(*Stamp as before, and Chord.*)

Goodness me,
Why, what was that?

DICK. Silent be,
Again the cat!

ALL. It was again that cat!

CAPTAIN (*aside*). They're right—it was the cat!
(*Throwing off cloak.*) Hold! (*All start.*)
Pretty daughter of mine,
I insist upon knowing
Where you may be going
With these sons of the brine;

For my excellent crew,
Though foes they could thump any
Are scarcely fit company,
My daughter, for you.

CREW. Now, hark at that, do!
Though foes we could thump any,
We are scarcely fit company
For a lady like you!

RALPH. Proud officer, that haughty lip uncurl!
Vain man, suppress that supercilious sneer,
For I have dared to love your matchless girl,
A fact well known to all my messmates here!

CAPTAIN. Oh, horror!

RALPH *and* JOSEPHINE. { I, / He, } humble, poor, and lowly born,
The meanest in the port division—
The butt of epauletted scorn—
The mark of quarter-deck derision—

{ Have / Has } dared to raise { my / his } wormy eyes

Above the dust to which you'd mould { me, / him, }
In manhood's glorious pride to rise.

{ I am / He is } an Englishman—behold { me! / him! }

ALL. He is an Englishman!

BOATSWAIN. He is an Englishman,
For he himself has said it,
And it's greatly to his credit,
That he is an Englishman!

ALL. That he is an Englishman!

BOATSWAIN. For he might have been a Roosian,
A French, or Turk, or Proosian,
Or perhaps Itali-an!

ALL. Or perhaps Itali-an!

BOATSWAIN. But in spite of all temptations
To belong to other nations,
He remains an Englishman!

ALL.   Hurrah!
For the true born Englishman!

CAPTAIN (*trying to repress his anger*). In uttering a reprobation
To any British Tar,
I try to speak with moderation,
But you have gone too far.
I'm very sorry to disparage
A humble foremast lad,
But to seek your captain's child in marriage,
Why, damme, it's too bad!

During this, COUSIN HEBE *and* FEMALE RELATIVES *have entered.*

ALL (*shocked*). Oh!

CAPTAIN. Yes, damme, it's too bad!

ALL.   Oh!

CAPTAIN *and* DICK DEADEYE. Yes, damme, it's
    too bad!

During this SIR JOSEPH *has appeared. He is horrified at the bad language.*

HEBE.   Did you hear him—did you hear him?
        Oh, the monster overbearing!
    Don't go near him—don't go near him—
        He is swearing—he is swearing—

SIR JOSEPH (*with impressive dignity*). My pain
        and my distress,
    I find it is not easy to express;
    My amazement—my surprise—
    You may learn from the expression of my eyes!

CAPTAIN. My lord—one word—the facts are not
        before you,
    The word was injudicious, I allow—
    But hear my explanation, I implore you,
    And you will be indignant, too, I vow!

SIR JOSEPH. I will hear of no defence;
        Attempt none if you're sensible.
    That word of evil sense
        Is wholly indefensible.
    Go, ribald, get you hence
        To your cabin with celerity.
    This is the consequence
        Of ill-advised asperity!
        (*Exit* CAPTAIN, *disgraced, followed by*
                    JOSEPHINE.)

ALL.   Behold the consequence,
        Of ill-advised asperity!

SIR JOSEPH. For I'll teach you all, ere long,
        To refrain from language strong
    For I haven't any sympathy for ill-bred
        taunts!

HEBE.   No more have his sisters, nor his cousins
        nor his aunts.

ALL.   For he is an Englishman, &c.

SIR JOSEPH. Now, tell me, my fine fellow—for
you *are* a fine fellow—

RALPH. Yes, your honour.

SIR JOSEPH. How came your captain so far to
forget himself? I am quite sure you had given him
no cause for annoyance.

RALPH. Please your honour, it was thus wise.
You see I'm only a top-man—a mere foremast
hand—

SIR JOSEPH. Don't be ashamed of that. Your position as a top-man is a very exalted one.

RALPH. Well, your honour, love burns as brightly
in the fo'c'sle as it does on the quarter-deck, and
Josephine is the fairest bud that ever blossomed
upon the tree of a poor fellow's wildest hopes.

Enter JOSEPHINE; *she rushes to* RALPH's *arms.*
        SIR JOSEPH *is horrified.*

RALPH. She's the figurehead of my ship of life—
the bright beacon that guides me into my port of
happiness—the rarest, the purest gem that ever
sparkled on a poor but worthy fellow's trusting
brow!

ALL. Very pretty.

SIR JOSEPH. Insolent sailor! you shall repent this
outrage. Seize him! (*Two marines seize him and
handcuff him.*)

JOSEPHINE. Oh, Sir Joseph, spare him, for I love
him tenderly.

SIR JOSEPH. Away with him! I will teach this
presumptuous mariner to discipline his affections.
Have you such a thing as a dungeon on board?

ALL. We have!

SIR JOSEPH. Then load him with chains and take
him there at once!

OCTETTE.

RALPH. Farewell, my own,
        Light of my life, farewell!
    For crime unknown
        I go to a dungeon cell.

ALL. For crime, &c.

JOSEPHINE. I will atone.
        In the meantime, farewell!
    And all alone
        Rejoice in your dungeon cell!

ALL. And all, &c.

SIR JOSEPH. A bone, a bone,
        I'll pick with this sailor fell;
    Let him be shown
        At once to his dungeon cell.

ALL. Let him, &c.

BOATSWAIN, DICK DEADEYE, *and* COUSIN HEBE.
        He'll hear no tone
        Of the maiden he loves so well!
    No telephone
        Communicates with his cell!

ALL. No telephone, &c.

BUTTERCUP (*mysteriously*). But when is known
        The secret I have to tell,
    Wide will be thrown
        The door of his dungeon cell.

ALL. Wide will be thrown

The door of his dungeon cell.
(RALPH *is led off in custody*.)

SIR JOSEPH.   Josephine, I cannot tell you the distress I feel at this most painful revelation. I desire to express to you, officially, that I am hurt. You whom I honoured by seeking in marriage—you, the daughter of a captain in the Royal Navy!

BUTTERCUP.   Hold! *I* have something to say to that!

SIR JOSEPH.   You?

BUTTERCUP.   Yes, I!

SONG — BUTTERCUP.

A many years ago,
When I was young and charming,
As some of you may know,
I practised baby-farming.

ALL.   Now this is most alarming!
When she was young and charming,
She practised baby-farming,
A many years ago.

BUTTERCUP.   Two tender babes I nussed;
One was of low condition,
The other, upper crust,
A regular patrician.

ALL (*explaining to each other*).   Now, this is the position:
One was of low condition,
The other a patrician,
A many years ago.

BUTTERCUP.   Oh, bitter is my cup!
However could I do it?
I mixed those children up,
And not a creature knew it!

ALL.   However could you do it?
Some day, no doubt, you'll rue it,
Although no creature knew it,
So many years ago.

BUTTERCUP.   In time each little waif
Forsook his foster-mother.
The well-born babe was Ralph—
Your captain was the other!!!

ALL.   They left their foster mother,
The one was Ralph, our brother,
Our captain was the other,
A many years ago.

SIR JOSEPH.   Then I am to understand that Captain Corcoran and Ralph were exchanged in childhood's happy hour—that Ralph is really the Captain, and the Captain is Ralph?

BUTTERCUP.   That is the idea I intended to convey!

SIR JOSEPH.   Dear me! Let them appear before me, at once!

RALPH *enters as* CAPTAIN, CAPTAIN *as a common sailor*. JOSEPHINE *rushes to his arms*.

JOSEPHINE.   My father—a common sailor!

CAPTAIN.   It is hard, is it not, my dear?

SIR JOSEPH.   This is a very singular occurrence; I congratulate you both. (*To* RALPH.) Desire that remarkably fine seaman to step forward.

RALPH.   Corcoran, come here!

CAPTAIN.   If what? If you *please*.

SIR JOSEPH.   Perfectly right. If you *please*.

RALPH.   Oh. If you *please*. (CAPTAIN *steps forward*.)

SIR JOSEPH (*to* CAPTAIN).   You are an extremely fine fellow.

CAPTAIN.   Yes, your honour.

SIR JOSEPH.   So it seems that you were Ralph, and Ralph was you.

CAPTAIN.   So it seems, your honour.

SIR JOSEPH.   Well, I need not tell you that after this change in your condition, a marriage with your daughter will be out of the question.

CAPTAIN.   Don't say that, your honour—love levels all ranks.

SIR JOSEPH.   It does to a considerable extent, but it does not level them as much as that.

SIR JOSEPH (*handing* JOSEPHINE *to* RALPH).   Here —take her, sir, and mind you treat her kindly.

RALPH *and* JOSEPHINE.   Oh bliss, oh rapture!

SIR JOSEPH.   Sad my lot, and sorry,
What shall I do? I cannot live alone!

ALL.   What will he do? He cannot live alone!

HEBE.   Fear nothing—while I live I'll not desert you.
I'll soothe and comfort your declining days.

SIR JOSEPH.   No, don't do that.

HEBE.   Yes, but indeed I'd rather—

SIR JOSEPH (*resigned*).   To-morrow morn our vows shall all be plighted,
Three loving pairs on the same day united!

DUET — RALPH *and* JOSEPHINE.

Oh joy, oh rapture unforeseen,
The clouded sky is now serene,
The god of day—the orb of love,
Has hung his ensign high above,
The sky is all ablaze.

With wooing words and loving song
We'll chase the lagging hours along,
And if $\left\{\begin{array}{l}\text{he finds}\\ \text{I find}\end{array}\right\}$ the maiden coy,

We'll murmur forth decorous joy,
In dreamy roundelay.

CAPTAIN. For he is the Captain of the *Pinafore*.
ALL. And a right good captain too!
CAPTAIN. And though before my fall
    I was captain of you all,
      I'm a member of the crew.
ALL. Although before his fall, &c.
CAPTAIN. I shall marry with a wife,
    In my humble rank of life!
          (*Turning to* BUTTERCUP.)
    And you, my own, are she—

I must wander to and fro,
    But wherever I may go,
      I shall never be untrue to thee!
ALL. What, never?
CAPTAIN. No, never!
ALL. What, *never?*
CAPTAIN. Hardly ever!
ALL. Hardly ever be untrue to thee.
    Then give three cheers, and one cheer more
    For the faithful seamen of the *Pinafore*.

BUTTERCUP. For he loves little Buttercup, dear
    little Buttercup,
    I'm sure I shall never know why;
  But still he loves Buttercup, poor little Butter-
    cup,
    Sweet little Buttercup, aye!
ALL. For he loves, &c.

SIR JOSEPH. I'm the monarch of the sea,
    And when I've married thee (*to* HEBE),
  I'll be true to the devotion that my love im-
    plants,
HEBE. Then good-bye to his sisters and his cous-
    ins and his aunts,
    Especially his cousins,
    Whom he reckons up by dozens,
    His sisters, and his cousins, and his aunts!

ALL. For he is an Englishman,
    And he himself hath said it,
    And it's greatly to his credit
    That he is an Englishman!

CURTAIN.

Postscript

"NEXT DAY, a Sunday [May 26, 1878], Gilbert went round in a hansom to call on Sullivan, they read the Sunday paper notices together, and decided to cut out a hornpipe in Act One and 'Barrington's Serenade, Act Two.'" From the foregoing quotation in Leslie Baily's *The Gilbert and Sullivan Book,* derived presumably from Gilbert's diary, one learns that the two collaborators must have planned to cut the opening solo in Act Two—"Fair moon, to thee I sing"—but fortunately the advice of others, undoubtedly including Barrington's, prevailed. Nothing of any consequence was altered in the first-night text.

The libretto of *H.M.S. Pinafore* in hand at the Opéra Comique on Saturday, May 25, 1878, differed from the second issue of the first edition only in bibliographic points that had little textual importance. Even the third and fourth editions present relatively few word changes and no major alterations. Thus, this landmark of English operetta appears to have satisfied its exacting and fastidious creators from the very beginning in the same measure that it has satisfied countless thousands of audience members over a period of eighty years.

THE PIRATES
OF PENZANCE

Introduction

IN THE RECORD of Gilbert and Sullivan first performances *The Pirates of Penzance* was not only uniquely triple, in that there were three premières to consider, but triply unique. First, this was the initial joint effort of the D'Oyly Carte Opera Company, the newly formed triumvirate of Gilbert, Sullivan, and D'Oyly Carte. Secondly, it was the only one of their operas to have its true world production première in America. And thirdly, alone among their fourteen collaborations, there was no published libretto for the first-night audience nor indeed for ten months thereafter.

The year 1879 was memorable for the *Pinafore* craze that seethed madly across the length and breadth of America. The plan to fight this piracy at its source was conceived by the three partners-to-be early in the year, and at the same time they must have hatched their joint business future. Gilbert wrote in his diary entry of April 24: ". . . called on Sullivan to meet Carte and arrange about America. We are to start on 7th of October. Shares one-third each of profits. . . ." By summer Gilbert was well into his work on the new libretto, which stemmed from a pirate theme in his 1870 *Our Island Home* and —according to George Bernard Shaw—from ideas he had evolved in his 1871 adaptation of Offenbach's *Les Brigands*. D'Oyly Carte had crossed the Atlantic in early July to reconnoitre the two-fold strategy of an authentic New York *Pinafore* and an American-born new opera. Sullivan—he had been suffering cruelly from kidney stones and was operated on late in the same month—had by early August received a progress report from Gilbert: "I've broken the neck of Act II and see my way clearly to the end. I think it comes out very well." Also in August had come the dissolution of the Comedy Opera Company, leaving the three partners free to proceed with their new business plans.

Gilbert and Sullivan, together with their musical director Alfred Cellier and their leading lady Blanche Roosevelt, arrived in New York on the *Bothnia* November 5. D'Oyly Carte and the balance of the company followed on the *Gallia* November 11. Early in December, while performing America's first authentic *Pinafore* nightly at Ford's Fifth Avenue Theatre, the company rehearsed the new opera, or at least its second act. As Sullivan said in a letter to his mother: "I am writing night and day at the first Act—the second is done and in rehearsal. . . . I fear I left all my sketches for the first Act at home, as I have searched everywhere for them. I would have telegraphed for them, but they could not have arrived in time. It is a great nuisance as I have to rewrite it all now, and can't recollect every number I did." Gilbert, in a letter he wrote to Percy de Strzelecki many years later (August 14, 1902), recalled Sullivan's dilemma over this missing music: ". . . his marvelous memory enabled him to reproduce a considerable part of it—almost note for note, as he subsequently discovered on comparing the new with the old score. Almost the only 'number' that he could not recall was the chorus that accompanies the entrance of the Major General's daughters in Act I, and as the situation was practically identical with the entrance of the troupe of Greek comedians in *Thespis,* I suggested that he should transfer the music and words, as they stood, from one piece to the other. This he did very successfully."

But the pace at which Sullivan had to drive himself to set the first act and then score this new opera remains unparalleled even in his hectic creative habit of working up to the last minute. The tag ends of his diary entries for that last fortnight of December tell the story: Dec. 10—"I wrote til 4:30." Dec. 13—"Came home and wrote. Had no dinner." Dec. 17—"Went to bed at 5 (a.m.)." Dec. 18—"Went to bed at 4." Dec. 19—"Wrote till 6 a.m." Dec. 20—"Wrote till 4 a.m." Sunday, Dec. 21—"Came home and worked till 5:30

(a.m.)." Dec. 25, Christmas Day—"Worked all day . . . till 5:30 (a.m.)." Dec. 27—"Finished full score at 7 a.m. on the morning of 28th Sunday." Dec. 29 (after a band rehearsal during the day followed by a full dress rehearsal of Act II at night)—"In despair because it went so badly. Finished at 1." And finally Dec. 30—"Full band rehearsal of 2nd Act at 10:30. . . . Full dress rehearsal at 8. . . . Over at 1. Came home with Cellier, Clay and Gilbert; all set to work at the Overture. Gilbert and Clay knocked off at 3 a.m. Cellier and I wrote till 5 and finished it." That was 5 o'clock on the morning of the New York world première. But some twenty hours earlier there had already been a "first performance" of *The Pirates of Penzance.*

THE PRE-PRODUCTION PREMIERE

THE TOWN OF PAIGNTON on the Devonshire coast, only a few miles southwest of Torquay along the shore of Tor Bay, was the setting for the first of the three "first performances" of *The Pirates of Penzance.* D'Oyly Carte had probably selected this obscure spot for three reasons. First and most important, he had his first-string touring *Pinafore* company at Torquay during this holiday season. Secondly, Paignton boasted a tiny, but better than average, theatre, the Royal Bijou. And thirdly, just as Hollywood studios often locate their "sneak previews" in isolated suburban theatres, Carte probably wished to avoid as much as possible the attention and attendance of the London press and theatregoers. The performance, at two p.m., Tuesday, December 30, was "For one day only" and for one purpose alone: to secure British copyright.

"The Bijou was quite a pretty little theatre," wrote Adair Fitz-Gerald of this occasion, "which was owned by Mr. William Dendy, a wealthy gentleman of some local eminence, of considerable artistic taste, and a great lover of music." With D'Oyly Carte, Gilbert, and Sullivan all in America the entire responsibility for this performance fell on Miss Helen Lenoir, Carte's able secretarial assistant, who was eight years later to become the second Mrs. Richard D'Oyly Carte. One can deduce that she had hoped to have the book and music in time for Sunday rehearsing, as the original scheduling of this performance, on evidence of the corrected playbill, was Monday, December 29. But according to the *New York Musical Review*'s London Correspondent despatch dated the 30th, "The score was expected to arrive only by the *Bothnia* yesterday, and the members of Mr. D'Oyly Carte's traveling company . . . can necessarily know nothing of the music until it is

placed in their hands shortly before they step upon the stage." This "score" was certainly not the full score, for Sullivan's diary is clear that he did not begin scoring the opera till December 17 and finished December 30, obviously too late to send to England. Leslie Baily cites Sullivan's diary as recording that the Act I music (i.e., the vocal setting) was sent from New York on the seventeenth, which must have been the shipment referred to by the *Musical Review* as expected to arrive on the twenty-ninth. It is probable that the Act II music had been in England some weeks in advance, although certainly not in its New York première form. So Helen Lenoir had to postpone this copyright performance by one day to await the all-important music aboard the *Bothnia.* She did not —as direly predicted by the *Musical Review*—let her *Pinafore* company perform the following day without rehearsal. According to Fitz-Gerald she "held the one and only full rehearsal the same evening Monday, December 29, on the stage of the Torquay theatre after the performance of *Pinafore.*"

In little more than twelve hours from this rehearsal in Torquay the tired *Pinafore* company were giving a strange rendering of the new opera —scarcely a performance in any accepted sense— dressed in their *Pinafore* costumes augmented by colored handkerchiefs, worn on the head, to indicate those who were pirates, and (understandably) carrying their parts on stage with them. Gilbert recalled in 1909 that "the performers read their parts from printed copies and the music of the songs was largely extemporized by them." No identifiable copy of this printed text has survived, but Gilbert was a long way from Paignton that afternoon and thirty years is a long way for memory. It is entirely possible no printed libretto existed. The scenery used was whatever odds and ends the little Bijou happened to have stored backstage. The audience numbered not more than fifty and, if Fitz-Gerald can be believed (difficult in this instance), "appeared perfectly satisfied [and] unaware that they were assisting at any unusual function."

"A new and original comic Opera by Messrs. W. S. Gilbert and A. Sullivan, entitled *The Pirates of Penzance,* or *Love and Duty,* was produced at this theatre yesterday (Tuesday)," wrote the local critic for the *Paignton and Newton Directory,* "and met with an enthusiastic reception. So far as we can judge from a first performance it bids fair to rival *H.M.S. Pinafore* in popularity." This reviewer found the story exceedingly funny, "and of the music we can speak in the highest praise. The airs are catching, and the concerted pieces are well worthy of our most popular English composer (Mr. Arthur Sullivan). We congratulate the talented author and composer on another brilliant success."

Another reporter at the Bijou that afternoon was the local correspondent for the *Theatre* who signed himself "A.L.L." at the end of an interesting three-page description of the occasion. (An explanatory note at the beginning of this review, initialed by Clement Scott, who was then the magazine's editor, has created the impression that Scott himself traveled down to Paignton to cover this performance, but there is no reason to believe he did.) Reporter A.L.L. made clear that what he heard that afternoon was probably the identical text filed for license at the Lord Chamberlain's office only forty-eight hours earlier: (*File No. 269. Theatre: Bijou, Paignton. Date of License: 27 December, 1879*—was the information on the official label.) He quoted a four-line Pirates' response from the second-act finale that is found in no other copy of the libretto except in this file copy, where it appears as a quartette sung by "Mabel, King, Fred, & Ruth, kneeling":

> To Queen Victoria's name we bow,
>   As free-born Britons should;
> We can resist no longer now,
>   And would not if we could.

Also, in addition to its specific reference to the Bijou, the Lord Chamberlain's is the only known version of *The Pirates of Penzance* in which the subtitle *Love and Duty* and the pirate character James are found, conforming with the modest leaflet playbill that served the Paignton performance as program.

It was a very different *Pirates* from that heard in New York the next evening. There was no "Poor wandering one" aria for Mabel, and the first act ended with a *Brindisi* sung by the King—

Paignton poster with postponement "snipe."

Comrades, let us join in plighting
These our honorary members . . .

In the second act there was no "Come friends who plough the sea," and the opera ended with a bitterly satiric thrust at the entailed peerage, a song with separate verses for the Major-General, the Sergeant, Ruth, and Mabel:

Hymn to the Nobility

GENERAL. Let foreigners look down with scorn
    On legislators heaven-born;
  We know what limpid wisdom runs
    From Peers and all their eldest Sons.
  Enrapt the true-born Briton hears
  The wisdom of his House of Peers.

SERGEANT.   And if a noble lord should die
    And leave no nearer progeny,
  His twentieth cousin takes his place
    And legislates with equal grace.

RUTH. But should a Son or Heir survive,
    Or other nearer relative,
  Then twentieth cousins get you hence—
    You're persons of no consequence.
  When issue male their chances bar,
  How paltry twentieth cousins are!

MABEL. How doubly blest that glorious land
    Where rank and brains go hand in hand,
  Where wisdom pure and virtue hale

Obey the law of strict entail.
No harm can touch a country when
It's ruled by British Noblemen.

The cast contained several names of later note. Fred Billington, as the Sergeant of Police, was to be acclaimed one of the most beloved of Savoyards. Mr. Federici, as the Pirate King, and Mr. Cadwalader, as Frederick, became well known in D'Oyly Carte Companies touring England and America, and the former carried the torch of Gilbert and Sullivan to Australia, where he was a great favorite. Heading the bill in the role of the Major-General was "Mr. R. Mansfield"—none other than Richard Mansfield, shortly to decorate the American Shakespearian stage, but in 1880 an ex-chorus member and Grossmith understudy who had joined the company on December 10. His later friend and press agent, Paul Wilstach, recalled the scene in his biography of Mansfield, a description so fancifully inaccurate as to trespass even beyond those broad limits granted theatrical press-agentry:

The *Pirates* had been produced in America [not yet] and this was an expedient to prevent its being pirated in England. The *Pinafore* company playing in Torquay drove over for the afternoon and sang and acted the parts. It was an amusing experience indeed. There could scarcely have been a numerous audience . . . but it included Mrs. D'Oyly Carte, Mr. Gilbert, and not-yet-Sir Arthur Sullivan. [Gilbert and Sullivan were in New York, and Helen Lenoir was not-yet-Mrs. D'Oyly Carte.] Mr. Gilbert had completed the book, but Arthur Sullivan had not yet written all the music to his own satisfaction. The Major-General's patter song balked his most ingenious effort. [There is no evidence that it did.] It was marked "to be recited" in the part given Mansfield, but he was so amused at the ingenuity of the rhyme and rhythm that he committed the song to memory on the instant, and insisted on being allowed to sing it. "But there is no music," protested the director of the orchestra. "Just give me sixteenth notes in the key of G, two beats to the measure, play soft and follow me," he replied, and began the song. . . . He chattered the words off at a furious rate, but with a crisp, distinct enunciation that gave every syllable its value—making the tune up as he went along. Everyone roared at the effect, and the composer [who at that moment was conducting a full band rehearsal in New York] was so amused that he never attempted to write any other music for this song . . . [It is quite possible that Sullivan's setting for this patter song was not ready in time for Paignton and that it was marked to be recited, but it was certainly sung to Sullivan's music at the New York dress rehearsal a few hours after Mr. Mansfield's extemporizing.]

Although acknowledging the sketchy quality of *The Pirates* matinee debut at the Bijou, the *Theatre* magazine's on-the-spot reporter heard and saw enough of both author and composer to give him a glimmer of the success that was to shine so brightly on the Fifth Avenue Theatre and Opéra Comique stages. "Impossible as it is to judge of the opera from its hasty and imperfect performance at Paignton," he wrote in summary, "and premature as it would be to pronounce any opinion on its merits or demerits, anyone acquainted with Mr. Gilbert's dry and peculiar humour . . . will see that such a plot . . . gives him plenty of scope for jesting, and we may prepare ourselves for a vast deal of amusement next season. If we add to this that Mr. Sullivan's music trips and sparkles as irresistibly as the pipe of the Pied Piper in its devil-may-care gaiety, there can be no doubt that, in spite of Frederick and duty, the *Pirates of Penzance* will worthily succeed that most absurd, most fascinating *Pinafore*."

THE WORLD PRODUCTION PREMIERE

THE BIG QUESTION in those last few weeks of *Pinafore*-plagued 1879, only the new year could answer: Would the new Gilbert and Sullivan opera be as good as *Pinafore*? If it had no other distinction, the world première at the Fifth Avenue Theatre, New York, on New Year's Eve, was the first of ten post-*Pinafore* Gilbert and Sullivan first nights to bear that unconstructive comparison. It can be assumed that every member of the gala audience felt this question; that every representative of the Press did, is a matter of record.

The Pirates of Penzance received what may be considered as essentially its first representation at the Fifth Avenue Theatre last evening [began the *Sun* in its lead sentence], for though it was played once on Monday afternoon [the *Sun* had not noted the Paignton postponement to Tuesday] of the present week at a little obscure theatre in an out-of-the-way English town, that was done simply to preserve to the authors an English copyright in their play, which would have been sacrificed by its prior performance in this country. . . . The two questions that would naturally be asked by those who were not present at the first representation would be, first, whether the piece was successful, and, secondly, is it as good as *Pinafore*? Both of these inquiries we should be inclined to answer affirmatively.

Its success with the audience was instantaneous . . . the performance was constantly stopped by the laughter and applause that attended the humorous parts. As for a comparison with "that infernal nonsense, *Pinafore*" . . . it can fairly be made. . . . Gilbert's share of the present work is even brighter than in the former opera. . . . As for Mr. Sullivan, he has evidently spared no pains to prevent himself from falling behind his previous reputation, and has given to *The Pirates* even a more elaborate and carefully written score, and a broader and more scholarly treatment, than he brought to the composition of the *Pinafore*.

The *New York Times*, although reporting that "an audience that completely filled the house" had received the performance "with the utmost enthusiasm," proclaimed: "It was evident that the new piece was a success." The *Times* then hedged the popular issue: "Whether it will be received with the same favor that [has] been accorded to *Pinafore* is very doubtful . . ." The *Tribune* also stated the problem clearly but had no answer: "The first question about the new operetta by Messrs. Sullivan and Gilbert will be how it compares with *Pinafore*. Of course every work ought to stand or fall on its own merits, but comparison in this case is unavoidable." And, as though to seek a silver lining in the inevitable gloomy negative, the *Tribune*'s reviewer mused: "Whether the principal airs are destined to be strummed in all our parlors and whistled in all our streets, remains to be seen. They will last longer if they escape such flattering hard usage."

The *Herald* declined the challenge: "The opera was received with marked approval and made a palpable hit last evening, though the question of its permanency in public favor [i.e., as compared with *Pinafore*] was not established." And then this reviewer showed his complete impartiality by

Fifth Avenue Theatre, Broadway and 28th Street, New York.

arguing both for and against: "It is a great improvement on *Pinafore* in the fineness of its texture; it is brighter, prettier and more artistic, and the quality of the work is of a much better standard than was the nautical opera we had from these gentlemen. [But on the other hand] the music of the *Pirates* . . . is hardly of that character which may be termed strikingly popular, and there are few bright, brisk airs or flowing melodies such as abound in *Pinafore* and which quickly took the popular ear . . . the opera has not the popular musical ring of *Pinafore* and (thank Heaven!) will not, in all probability, be whistled by every boy or ground out upon every organ in the land."

The *World* surrendered to the Jolly Roger rather than to the Union Jack of Captain Corcoran's saucy ship: "Compared with *Pinafore* it is infinitely superior in plot, language, and humor, while musically there can be no comparison, the airs and choruses of last year's wonderful success being mere trifles unworthy of critical attention while the music Mr. Sullivan has written for *The Pirates of Penzance* might have been written for grand opera. The humor of the music lies in fact in its serious imitation of grand opera . . ." But the *Dramatic Mirror,* although admitting *"The Pirates* is a very praiseworthy work, both musically and dramatically,"* and that it "will probably enjoy a long life of popular favor," still closed its review with the pro-*Pinafore* party-line prediction —"but it will not approach the success attained by its predecessor."

The audience at the Fifth Avenue Theatre that New Year's Eve was described by the *Herald* as "one of the largest and most fashionable of the season." In the chatty detail of the *Hour,* "All New York was there," and among those in the boxes were "Mrs. Schlesinger and Miss Jerome, both looking charming and showing the audience how to use the opera-glass, and how to look when stared at, . . . Mrs. Vanderbilt, without diamonds, and Mrs. J. J. Astor, in the seventeenth row of stalls."

The composer himself, of course, conducted, and the resulting "thorough harmony and evenness of execution on the part of the musicians," said the *Dramatic Mirror,* "showed conclusive evidence of the benefit of Sullivan's personal supervision." Sullivan later wrote: "When I went into the Orchestra at 8 I felt more dead than alive, and I looked so, everybody told me. . . . When the curtain went up after the Overture, I began to pull myself together and thought only of the piece." The *Dramatic Mirror*'s professional eye also praised the stage direction: "Gilbert's quaint creation is illustrated by the company just as Gilbert conceived it." And of the mounting, the *Herald* reported: "The opera is beautifully and richly costumed and set upon the stage. . . . The set in the second act is well worthy the prompt acknowledgment it received."

To forestall piracy there was no printed libretto for the public that night, nor for almost twelve months to come (see page 136). In addition to the usual near-tabloid-size Fifth Avenue Theatre program, on this special occasion the audience was treated to a choice of souvenir programs printed on either white or plum-colored silk. All three of these programs contained, for the second time at a Gilbert and Sullivan première, the line: *On the OPENING NIGHT the Orchestra will be conducted by Mr. ARTHUR SULLIVAN.*

The cast included a number of D'Oyly Carte's top principals, imported from England. J. H. Ryley, described by George Odell as a richly humorous comedian, came from Carte's touring *Pinafore* company. In the opinion of the *Dramatic Mirror* his Major-General Stanley was "the artistic success of the evening . . . an army counterpart of the famous Sir Joseph Porter. His performance was a very clever study, and though his singing qualities are not particularly good, this lack was lost sight of in the general excellence of his acting. [How often has this been said of the very model of a modern Major-General!] Bass-baritone Signor Brocolini (born John Clarke of Brooklyn, from which habitat the stage name was derived) was, to the *World*'s reviewer, "artistic in his delineation of the tender-hearted pirate chief and sang his music grandly." But the *Dramatic Mirror* found "the acting requirements of the character . . . beyond his grasp." Miss Alice Barnett, the Little Buttercup of the British touring *Pinafore,* "distinguished herself," raved the *World,* "by creating a character as distinct as any in the range of literature or the lyric stage." (!!!) "The remaining ladies," wrote the *Dramatic Mirror* in covering Rosina Brandram, Jessie Bond, and Miss Minnie Barlow (nicknamed "Billie" by Gilbert), all British imports, "did what little they might with the opportunities their minor parts afforded them, and shared in the effect of what was an exceptionally smooth rendition of a new opera."

The leading lady was twenty-three-year-old Miss Blanche Roosevelt, born in Sandusky, Ohio, the daughter of Wisconsin's first Senator, William H. Tucker. Like so many American opera singers, she had studied in France and Italy and had been launched on a European opera career using a latinized name, Madame Rosavella, contrived from her mother's maiden name, Roosevelt. She made her debut at Covent Garden as Violetta in *La Traviata.* Miss Roosevelt told an interviewer for *Frank Leslie's Illustrated* that she had met Sullivan in Paris in August, and had been engaged to sing Josephine at the Opéra Comique. And to the

Interior of the Fifth Avenue Theatre, at about the time of the PIRATES OF PENZANCE *world première.*

interviewer's question, had the new opera been written expressly for her, she gushed breathlessly: "It has; and, oh! the music suits my voice to perfection. It is a charming opera as a composition, while Mr. Gilbert is at his very best; indeed, both Mr. Sullivan and Mr. Gilbert are at their best in this opera. I have gotten all my dresses for it from Madame Latreille, of the Rue Lafitte, Paris."

Not to deflate beautiful Blanche, but for the record, a letter from D'Oyly Carte to Sullivan (in Switzerland), on August 26, scarcely substantiates her statement that the opera or even the part of Mabel was written especially for her: "I am inclined to think that Rosavella's voice may be too thin for America, however she is here and I am to hear her sing tomorrow. They are accustomed to hear big voices and fine singers. My particular fancy for America and who would I am certain make a success is Helene Crosmond. . . . Her voice is now superb and she is inclined to go. . . . I could perhaps take Rosavella at the [Opéra] Comique." The decision hinged on terms, Carte offering £20, Miss Crosmond asking £100. In

the face of this difference it is not surprising that Rosavella landed the job.

Of her performance that night creating the role of Mabel, the consensus of press comment favored her appearance over her voice and acting ability. "Miss Blanche Roosevelt was the heroine, than whom" in the *Sun*'s opinion "a prettier or more picturesque one could not be found. Her voice is fairly managed, but it is thin in texture and not always true." The *Tribune* wrote: "Miss Rosavella's Mabel was certainly a pretty object to look upon; she sang creditably; she acted with zeal and good sense." But the *World* thought "she was evidently suffering from a cold," and the *Dramatic Mirror* noted "a certain awkwardness of action that seems constantly present."

Blanche was shortly to apply her beauty and talents in pursuit of a literary career. It is provocative to recollect that, four years later, as Madame Macchetta—unencumbered by her husband, the Marchese d'Alligri, whom she had married in Milan—she became the first fair occupant of Guy de Maupassant's guest-room at his favorite home,

"La Guillette" at Etretat on the Normandy coast —a long way from Sandusky.

It remained for the tenor Hugh Talbot, who sang as Signor Talbo in Her Majesty's Opera, London, to perpetrate the worst individual first-night performance in all Gilbert and Sullivan history. It is hard to understand why he was not dismissed at the final curtain, but instead he stayed with the company for over four months. ("It is quite obvious why," was Miss Bridget D'Oyly Carte's comment, edged with bitter experience—"*no other tenor was available.* How constantly this seems to happen!") What might be termed Hugh Talbot's "press-book" for that first night has a certain morbid, and probably unique, fascination (see excerpts below).

Somehow, in spite of Mr. Talbot, the performance went sensationally well. Sullivan wrote, "There was no doubt about its success, we took *nine* encores, and might have had more if I liked." Among the numbers receiving most acclaim was the unaccompanied chorus, "Hail Poetry," (see page 123), which the *Times* described as having "the character of a serious prayer," and the Chorus of Policemen, which the same reviewer regarded as "the most musically-humorous number of the evening." The *Sun* even went so far as to venture that this chorus was "droller than anything in the *Pinafore.*" The first performance, before an audience, of "Come friends who plough the sea" was not singled out by the press for any special comment. Little did they suspect they were witnessing the birth of the American folk-song "Hail! Hail! The gang's all here."

"What do I think of the piece myself?" wrote Sullivan to his mother on January 2. "The li-

Excerpt from Gilbert's letter of February 12, 1880, to Marion Johnson Long ("Dear Johnnie"), a member of the Opéra Comique chorus.

bretto is ingenious, clever, wonderfully funny in parts, and sometimes brilliant in dialogue—beautifully written for music, as is all Gilbert does, and all the action and business perfect. The music is infinitely superior in every way to the *Pinafore* —'tunier' and more developed, of a higher class altogether. I think that in time it will be more popular. Then the *mise-en-scène* and the dresses are something to be dreamed about. I never saw such a beautiful combination of colour and form on any stage. All the girls dressed in the old-fashioned English style, every dress designed separately by Faustin, and some of the girls look as if they had stepped out of a Gainsborough picture. The New York ladies are raving about them. The 'Policemen's Chorus' is an enormous hit and they are cheered tremendously when they march on

---

MR. HUGH TALBOT

TIMES. The essential part of the young pirate apprentice received inadequate attention from the tenor. His make-up resulted in his appearing, in the first act, to be of advanced age; he was not, apparently, acquainted with his lines, and his singing was weak and tame. But the others were so spirited and generally enthusiastic that the effect of the opera was not materially injured by this weak spot in the cast.

SUN. Mr. Talbot, the tenor, had unfortunately apparently not thought it necessary to commit his lines, and made nonsense of much of his role, reflecting no credit upon himself, and nearly bringing the play at times into confusion.

WORLD. With the exception of Mr. Hugh Talbot, who may be taken as a fair illustration of George Eliot's statement that when Nature made a tenor she spoiled a man, too much praise cannot be given to the members of the company. Mr. Talbot sang some of the airs allotted to the tenor admirably, but he was utterly innocent of any appreciation whatever of the humor of the situations and shamefully ignorant of his lines.

MIRROR. Hugh Talbot . . . was not so successful. The gentleman has a weak, uncertain voice, of nasal quality and limited volume, and laboured under the disadvantage of not knowing his lines. Mr. Talbot, like a great many other tenors recalled to mind, has an effeminate bearing and a simpering manner, that no doubt would be charming in a young miss fresh from the confines of a select boarding-school, but on the stage they are loathsome and disgusting.

HERALD. The members of the company were not all perfect in their parts, Mr. Talbot seriously interfering with the full effect of some good points by groping after his cue in a most vague manner.

TRIBUNE. Mr. Talbot would perhaps have done better things with *Frederic* if he had taken the trouble to learn his part. He has a version of the text considerably different from Mr. Gilbert's, and such as it is, he stumbles over it in a most disquieting way. We shall suspend criticism upon his performance until he knows his lines.

THE HOUR. The actors and singers acquitted themselves with credit, with the exception of the tenor, to whom the lines of his part were a sad stumbling-block, and who consequently at times did inexcusable mischief.

SULLIVAN'S LETTER TO HIS MOTHER, JANUARY 2, 1880. Our Company and all the Chorus are charming people and devoted to us, and spared themselves no pains or trouble to do their work thoroughly well. All except the Tenor who is an idiot—vain and empty-headed. He very nearly upset the piece on the first night as he didn't know his words, and forgot his music. We shall, I think, have to get rid of him.

with their Bulls'-Eyes all alight, and are always encored. I am sanguine of its success in London, for there are local allusions, etc., which will have twice the force they have here. . . . The laughter and applause continued through the whole piece until the very end, and then there were thunder calls for Gilbert and myself. . . ." Indeed both Gilbert and Sullivan were called to the footlights at the end of each act; according to the *Times*,

"there was no lack of enthusiasm, and flowers were given in profusion to the actresses." The *Hour* recorded that "at the end of the piece Mr. Gilbert was called upon for a speech, but Mr. D'Oyly Carte had to apologize for him, as the witty librettist left the theatre the moment he heard his name called."

"So," in the words of Sullivan to his mother, "the New Year opens auspiciously for me."

DECEMBER 31, 1879 [*first night of* The Pirates of Penzance.] *No rehearsal, except Band at 11 for Overture. Home at 1:45 to breakfast. Too ill to eat. Went to bed to try and get sleep, but could not. Stayed in bed till 5:30. Gilbert came. Got up feeling miserably ill. Head on fire. Dressed slowly and got to New York club at 7:30. Had 12 oysters and a glass of champagne. Went to Theatre. House crammed with the elite of New York. Went into the orchestra, more dead than alive, but got better when I took the stick in my hand— fine reception. Grand success. Went to Grant's afterwards, driving Adele home. Mr. & Mrs. Woolsey there to see old year out. Went afterwards to Mrs. Murray's (72 Fifth Av:) to a reception. Then home—could not sleep, so did not go to bed till 3:30. Felt utterly worn out.*

ARTHUR SULLIVAN'S DIARY

THE LONDON PREMIERE

THREE MONTHS and three days after its New York opening, *The Pirates of Penzance* was presented to expectant Londoners at the Opéra Comique. In this interval Gilbert and Sullivan had rehearsed and launched three additional American companies to tour the eastern half of the country. In each instance—at Philadelphia, February 9; at Newark, N.J., February 16; and at Buffalo, February 21—Sullivan conducted the first performance. Then on March 3 both he and Gilbert sailed for England on the *Gallia*. D'Oyly Carte, who did not accompany them, and several members of the New York company were at the pier to wish them a prosperous voyage. The *Gallia* that bore them homeward had, on its west-bound crossing, brought Helen Lenoir to New York to help Carte with his four *Pirates* companies and to remain as his American representative for a greater part of the next six years.

"Mr. W. S. Gilbert and Mr. Arthur Sullivan have arrived in England, flushed with their American victory," wrote Clement Scott in "Our Omnibus Box" of the *Theatre*. . . . "On landing it was discovered that the score of the famous *Pirates of Penzance* was missing, and great was the consternation at the Opéra Comique Theatre, where George Grossmith and Rutland Barrington were awaiting a taste of the delectable music, and a read at the inimitable libretto. Luckily the missing

packet turned up, having travelled twice across the Atlantic, and the play which we all anticipate with so much eagerness has been for some time in active rehearsal." This fanciful little item must have been a figment of press-agentry. If it were taken literally and a round-trip of the *Gallia* had to intervene before the score was in London rehearsal, the month of March would have been wasted. As it was, once back in England both Gilbert and Sullivan were hard at work rehearsing the home company every day in the new opera, while every night it still performed *Pinafore*. And in three weeks' time, on Saturday evening, April 3, the third and last "first performance" of *The Pirates of Penzance* was unveiled. In the words of the *Daily News*, "The anticipation of the treat to be derived from Mr. Gilbert's rich vein of satirical humour and Mr. Sullivan's genial and tuneful music were fully realized . . . at the Opéra Comique in the Strand before an audience that crowded every portion of the building, and by whom the piece was received throughout with enthusiastic applause."

"To the inevitable question, Is it as good as *The Pinafore?*"—posed the *Standard*—"an affirmative answer may at once be given." But the *Times* held the opposite view: "Of invention there is little or no trace in the latest combined production of Mr. Gilbert and Mr. Sullivan. . . . The music to *The Pirates of Penzance* did not seem

Richard Temple as the Pirate King.

quite equal to that of the *Pinafore,* certainly not to that of *The Sorcerer,* in our opinion the master-piece of its joint authors." Yet the *Musical Times* "unhesitatingly" declared it to be a higher class of opera than any they had previously written.

The program that night bore no date; but the wording PRODUCTION OF, leading into the title on the cover page, was the then current theatrical designation of a first performance. In no place does this program specify that the composer conducted, though, in fact, he did. On its cover and in its dramatis personae Sullivan's name preceded Gilbert's. There was a curtain raiser—as noted by the *Daily News*—"the pleasant vaudeville *In the Sulks,* written by Mr. F. Desprez, with lively music by Mr. A. Cellier." (It had opened in the same theatre on February 21, sharing the bill in the closing weeks of the long *Pinafore* run.) Reasonable certainty that this otherwise undistinguished program was, indeed, that of the first night is clinched by the fortunate circumstance that the sole copy observed bears in contemporary ink handwriting the date and seat-location of its owner: *"3 April 1880 Amphitheatre."* This copy also contains an ephemeral but dramatic bit of evidence of the tragedy that according to Rutland Barrington very nearly caused the postponement of the first performance—an "indulgence slip"

telling the audience of Miss (Harriet) Everard's "sudden indisposition" in consequence of which "the part of Ruth has been undertaken at 24 hours notice by Miss Emily Cross, for whom the indulgence of the audience tonight is requested." Such information was no more and no less than D'Oyly Carte would have given out if his contralto had cancelled because of a severe cold. Both the *Times* and the *Daily News* used the same commonplace word "indisposition," but the *Standard* was more factual with "injured at rehearsal." The true seriousness of what had removed a star-principal from that first night's performance—and, indeed from a promising career with the D'Oyly Carte Opera Company—was so successfully played down that subsequent Gilbert and Sullivan literature has for seventy-five years completely overlooked the truth . . . save in one obscure instance afforded by the hand of Gilbert himself.

In the author's preface to the *Savoy Operas,* published by Bell in 1909, appears the following: "A tragic incident occurred at the last rehearsal but one. Miss Everard (the admirable Mrs. Partlet of *The Sorcerer* and Little Buttercup of *H.M.S. Pinafore*) was standing in the middle of the stage when a heavy 'set piece' which had been carelessly 'footed,' fell forward upon her and caused a fracture of the skull of which the poor lady died in a week. A telegram was immediately despatched to a very clever actress-contralto, Miss Emily Cross, who played the part, letter-perfect and note-perfect, two days later, with great success." In Rutland Barrington's description of this accident, published a year earlier than Gilbert's account, the actor took credit for the selection of Miss Cross. But, perhaps due to theatrical superstition, he gave no inkling of the grim fact that Miss Everard's accident had led to her death: "She was standing in the center of the stage at rehearsal one morning, when I noticed the front piece of a stock of scenery falling forward. I called to her to run, and got my back against the falling wing and broke its force to a great extent, but it nevertheless caught her on the head, taking off a square of hair as neatly as if done with a razor. The shock and injury combined laid her up for some time . . ."

Gilbert's recollection that she died in a week was faulty. The comment given in Dunn's *Gilbert & Sullivan Dictionary* (1936) on "Helen" (*sic*) Everard—"She did not create the part of Ruth . . . but she played it later on several occasions" —is more accurate. Advertisements in the *Times* indicate that she performed the role for ten days, June 19-30. Probably it was then clear she was not well enough to continue, for she was again replaced by Emily Cross on July 1. Her death from consumption on February 22, 1882, at the age of 38, was recorded by the *Era* two years after the accident, "from the effects of which," read the obituary, "she never entirely recovered." In a letter to Sullivan in August 1879, D'Oyly Carte indicated that he had offered her the part of Ruth in the New York Company but "Everard positively declines going." That fateful decision was to help shape Savoyard casting history; certainly the remarkable career of Rosina Brandram was to stem from it.

The performance that Saturday night went well and was particularly well received. In the *Standard*'s opinion "the excellent orchestra was heard at its best . . . under the guidance of Mr. Sullivan, whose appearance was the signal for hearty and long-continued cheers." The *Daily News,* in describing the physical production, thought: "The dresses are bright and well contrasted; and the two scenes painted by Mr. J. O'Connor . . . are beautiful." And the *Times,* in agreeing, found "the *mise en scène* did great credit to the establishment over which Mr. D'Oyly Carte presides" and added that "the admirable singing of the chorus testified to careful and conscientious rehearsing under the composer's direction." Gilbert's stage direction came in for its meed of praise in the *Standard:* "The 'business' of the scene and arrangement of the characters are invariably strong points in Mr. Gilbert's pieces, and the results of his careful superintendence are always visible."

For the composer the same reviewer was especially enthusiastic: "How completely Mr. Sullivan enters into the spirit of his companion's words has been acknowledged again and again; and here even the simplest airs are rescued from being commonplace by the piquant and skillful orchestration. . . . With the exceptions of three or four numbers, every song and concerted piece was encored, and the Policemen had to sing a supremely funny song and chorus . . . a third time." To this the *Daily News* added the ultimate commendation: "In the music of *The Pirates of Penzance* Mr. Sullivan has been even more successful than in either *The Sorcerer* or *H.M.S. Pinafore.* It abounds throughout in genuine comic humour, untinged by either coarseness or undue flippancy."

The *Times* carped analytically—as it had when reviewing *Pinafore*—on the sore point of Gilbert vs. Sullivan. It argued that although "lighted up with the incessant fireworks of Mr. Gilbert's wit" and containing "all the elements of popularity," Gilbert's text still did not form the proper basis of musical construction as a libretto. "Music is fully able to deal with broadly comic phases of human life," pontificated the *Times,* "but Mr. Gilbert's characters are not comic in themselves, but only in reference to other characters chiefly of the operatic type, whose exaggerated attitude and parlance they mimic. He writes in fact not comedies but parodies, and the music has accordingly to follow him to the sphere of all others most uncongenial to it—the mock-heroic. The skill and ingenuity evinced by Mr. Sullivan in such disadvantageous circumstances cannot be sufficiently admired. His tunes are always fresh and lively, and the few opportunities of genuine sentimental utterance offered to him are turned to excellent account." And the *Times* did not fail to toss to the composer that golden apple that was to tempt and harass him for his whole career: "Certain passages in the first duet between Frederic and Ruth and elsewhere, where the composer becomes serious in spite of himself, make one regret what might have been, or, perhaps, might still be if Mr. Sullivan would attempt a genuine dramatic effort."

For the cast that night there was uniform acclaim. The *Daily News* thought "Mr. G. Grossmith's makeup and demeanour as the Major-General were excellent; the mixture of dry, quaint humour and caricatured military sternness have been happily combined." Rutland Barrington, whose role on stage he recorded as only seventeen minutes, won highest praise from the *Times:* "Mr. Barrington was absolutely sublime in the small but by no means unimportant part of the Sergeant of Police." In contradistinction to the shambles created of the role of Frederic in the New York première, Mr. George Power's "sympathetic tenor voice," according to the *Times,* "was heard to great advantage in the sentimental music allotted to the dutiful Frederic." And the *Standard* critic wrote that "Mr. Power acts as Frederic just in that simple-minded way that brings out most strongly the absurdity of the character, and he sings exceedingly well." Mr. Richard Temple, in the opinion of the *Daily News,* "was a capital representative of the Pirate Chief of old-fashioned melodrama and gave his music with amusing exaggeration."

The leading lady was making her first appearance on the stage (according to the *Standard*) and for such a tense occasion fared splendidly. Wrote the *Times:* "Miss Marian Hood (Mabel) is in possession of a fine soprano voice of considerable compass, which, but for her habit of straining it, would be very sympathetic. The bravura passages . . . were attacked with considerable courage and success, and the pretty madrigal . . . was given with exquisite feeling. Further careful study may make an excellent singer of Miss Hood." Years later Barrington recalled her as "a perfect picture to look at and equally pleasant to listen to . . . tall, slight, and graceful, a typical English girl [and with a fond flight of memory to Mr. Goldbury's song in *Utopia, Limited*], with a wealth of fair hair which, I believe, was all her own."

In the role of Ruth, the emergency substitute, Miss Emily Cross, according to the *Daily News* "acted well and gave her declamatory music very effectively. Much credit is due to this lady for her efficiency in the performance of a character which she undertook at very short notice." The *Times* added that "with one trifling slip in a song, [she] was not only perfect in words and music, but played with admirable humour and appreciation." As to the other principals, in the words of the *Standard:* "Miss Gwynne as Edith shows graceful vivacity, and Misses LaRue and Bond lead the General's daughters." After the return of the veterans from the original New York company on July 29 Alice Barnett assumed the role of Ruth for the rest of the run; Jessie Bond replaced Julia Gwynne as Edith; and Miss Gwynne and Miss Barlow displaced Miss LaRue and Neva Bond in the parts of Kate and Isabel respectively.

The *Times,* looking down its critical nose at the divergence of its own reviewer's opinion with the undeniable enthusiasm of the Opéra Comique's customers, explained righteously: "The question of popular success is of course quite different from that of artistic merit. On the first night the satisfaction of the crowded audience was boundless, culminating in the call before the curtain of the performers (including the four-and-twenty maidens) and the authors." In fact, according to the *Musical Times:* "Messrs. Gilbert and Sullivan were called forward both at the end of the first act and at the conclusion of the work; and the delighted auditors, who had encored nearly every piece in the opera, seemed loath to allow them to retire."

François Cellier wrote of that evening: "All were now more readily able to appreciate the essence of the fun of our two humourists. The consequence was that the applause on the opening night of *The Pirates of Penzance* was more spontaneous than on any previous occasion. . . . The press, now quite assured that Gilbert and Sullivan had come to stay, and were more than likely to achieve further conquests, became less reserved and more generous in their critical reviews . . . the general verdict of the experts was that the last was the best production of Gilbert and Sullivan and D'Oyly Carte."

Cheered the *Standard:* "The success is in every way complete."

APRIL 3 (SATURDAY) 1880.

Rained.

ARTHUR SULLIVAN'S DIARY

A New and Original Melo-Dramatic Opera,

IN TWO ACTS,

THE PIRATES
OF PENZANCE

OR,

THE SLAVE OF DUTY.

Dramatis Personae.

RICHARD, *A Pirate Chief*	MR. BROCOLINI.
SAMUEL, *His Lieutenant*	MR. FURNEAUX COOK.
FREDERIC, *A Pirate Apprentice*	MR. HUGH TALBOT.
MAJOR-GENERAL STANLEY, *of the British Army*	MR. J. H. RYLEY.
EDWARD, *A Sergeant of Police*	MR. F. CLIFTON.
MABEL, *General Stanley's Youngest Daughter*	MISS BLANCHE ROOSEVELT.

KATE ⎫
EDITH ⎬ *General Stanley's Daughters* ⎫ MISS R. BRANDRAM.
ISABEL ⎭   MISS JESSIE BOND.
      MISS BARLOW.

RUTH, *A Piratical "Maid-of-All-Work"*	MISS ALICE BARNETT.

GENERAL STANLEY'S DAUGHTERS, PIRATES, POLICEMEN, &c.

ACT I. — A Rocky Seashore on the Coast of Cornwall, England.

ACT II. — A Ruined Chapel on General Stanley's Estate.

THE PIRATES OF PENZANCE

OR,

THE SLAVE OF DUTY.

———

ACT I.

SCENE. — *A rocky sea-shore on the coast of Cornwall. In the distance is a calm sea, on which a schooner is lying at anchor. As the curtain rises groups of* PIRATES *are discovered, some drinking, some playing cards.* SAMUEL, *the Pirate Lieutenant, is going from one group to another, filling the cups from a flask.* FREDERIC *is seated in a despondent attitude at the back of the scene.* RUTH *kneels at his feet.*

OPENING CHORUS.

Pour, oh, pour the pirate sherry!
    Fill, oh, fill the pirate glass!
And, to make us more than merry,
    Let the pirate bumper pass.

SOLO — SAMUEL.

For to-day our pirate 'prentice
    Rises from indentures freed.
Strong his arm and keen his scent is;
    He's a pirate now indeed!

ALL.

Here's good luck to Frederic's ventures!
Frederic's out of his indentures!

SOLO — SAMUEL.

Two-and-twenty, now he's rising,
    And alone he's fit to fly;
Which we're bent on signalizing
    With unusual revelry.

ALL.

Here's good luck to Frederic's ventures!
Frederic's out of his indentures!
    So pour, oh, pour the pirate sherry, &c.

FREDERIC *rises and comes forward with* PIRATE KING, *who enters.*

KING. Yes, Frederic, from to-day you rank as a full-blown member of our band.

ALL. Hurrah!

FREDERIC. My friends, I thank you all, from my heart, for your kindly wishes. Would that I could repay them as they deserve!

KING. What do you mean?

FREDERIC. To-day I am out of my indentures, and to-day I leave you for ever.

ALL. Leave us?

FREDERIC. For ever!

KING. But this is quite unaccountable. A keener hand at scuttling a Cunarder or cutting out a White Star never shipped a handspike.

FREDERIC. Yes, I have done my best for you. And why? It was my duty under my indentures, and I am the slave of duty. As a child I was regularly apprenticed to your band. It was through an error. No matter, the mistake was ours, not yours, and I was in honor bound by it.

SAMUEL. An error? What error?

FREDERIC. I may not tell you. It would reflect upon my well-loved Ruth.

[113]

RUTH *comes downstage.*

RUTH. Nay, dear master, my mind has long been gnawed by the cankering tooth of mystery. Better have it out at once.

SONG — RUTH.

When Frederic was a little lad he proved so
   brave and daring,
His father thought he'd 'prentice him to some
   career seafaring.
I was, alas! his nursery-maid, and so it fell to
   my lot
To take and bind this promising boy apprentice
   to a pilot.
    A life not bad for a hardy lad, though cer-
     tainly not a high lot;
    Though I'm a nurse, you might do worse
     than make your boy a pilot.

I was a stupid nursery-maid, on breakers always steering,
And I did not catch the word aright, through
   being hard of hearing.
Mistaking my instructions, which within my
   brain did *gyrate*,
I took and bound this promising boy apprentice
   to a pirate.
    A sad mistake it was to make, and doom him
     to a vile lot:
    I bound him to a pirate—you—instead of to
     a pilot!

I soon found out, beyond all doubt, the scope
   of this disaster;
But I hadn't the face to return to my place and
   break it to my master.
A nursery-maid is never afraid of what you people *call* work,

So I made up my mind to go as a kind of piratical maid-of-all-work;
    And that is how you find me now a member
     of your shy lot,
    Which you wouldn't have found had he been
     bound apprentice to a pilot.

RUTH (*kneeling at his feet*). Oh pardon, Frederic! pardon!

FREDERIC. Rise, sweet one; I have long pardoned you. (RUTH *rises.*)

RUTH. The two words were so much alike!

FREDERIC. They still are, though years have rolled over their heads! But this afternoon my obligation ceases. Individually, I love you all with affection unspeakable; but collectively, I look upon you with a disgust that amounts to absolute detestation. Oh pity me, my beloved friends, for such is my sense of duty that once out of my indentures I shall feel myself bound to devote myself, heart and soul, to your extermination.

ALL. Poor lad! poor lad! (*All weep.*)

KING. Well, Frederic, if you conscientiously feel that it is your duty to destroy us, we cannot blame you for acting on that conviction. Always act in accordance with the dictates of your conscience, my boy, and chance the consequences.

SAMUEL. Besides, we can offer you but little temptation to remain with us. We don't seem to make piracy pay. I'm sure I don't know why, but we don't.

FREDERIC. I know why, but, alas! I mustn't tell you; it wouldn't be right.

KING. Why not, my boy? It's only half-past eleven, and you are one of us until the clock strikes twelve.

SAMUEL. True, and until then you are bound to protect our interests.

ALL. Hear! hear!

FREDERIC. Well, then, it is my duty as a pirate to tell you that you are too tender-hearted. For instance, you make a point of never attacking a weaker party than yourselves, and when you attack a stronger party you invariably get thrashed.

KING. There is some truth in that.

FREDERIC. Then, again, you make a point of never molesting an orphan.

SAMUEL. Of course: we are orphans ourselves, and know what it is.

FREDERIC. Yes, but it has got about, and what is the consequence? Every one we capture says he's an orphan. The last three ships we took proved to be manned entirely by orphans, and so we had to let 'em go. One would think that Great Britain's mercantile navy was recruited solely from her orphan asylums, which we know is not the case.

SAMUEL. But, hang it all! you wouldn't have us absolutely merciless?

FREDERIC. There's my difficulty. Until twelve o'clock I would; after twelve o'clock I wouldn't. Was ever a man placed in so delicate a situation?

RUTH. And Ruth, your own Ruth, whom you love so well, and who has won her middle-aged way into your boyish heart—what is to become of her?

KING. Oh, he will take you with him.

FREDERIC. Well, Ruth, I feel some little difficulty about you. It is true that I admire you very much, but I have been constantly at sea since I was eight years old, and yours is the only woman's face I have seen during that time. I think it is a sweet face.

RUTH. It is—oh, it is!

FREDERIC. I say I *think* it is—that is my impression. But as I have never had an opportunity of comparing you with other women, it is just possible I may be mistaken.

KING. True.

FREDERIC. What a terrible thing it would be if I were to marry this innocent person, and then find out that she is, on the whole, plain!

KING. Oh, Ruth is very well—very well indeed.

SAMUEL. Yes, there are the remains of a fine woman about Ruth.

FREDERIC. Do you really think so? Then I will not be so selfish as to take her from you. In justice to her and in consideration for you I will leave her behind. (*Hands* RUTH *to* KING.)

KING. No, Frederic, this must not be. We are rough men, who lead a rough life, but we are not so utterly heartless as to deprive thee of thy love. I think I am right in saying that there is not one here who would deprive thee of this inestimable treasure for all the world holds dear.

ALL (*loudly*). Not one!

KING. No, I thought there wasn't. Keep thy love, Frederic—keep thy love! (*Hands her back to* FREDERIC.)

FREDERIC. You're very good, I'm sure.

KING. Well, it's the top of the tide, and we must be off. Farewell, Frederic. When your process of extermination begins, let our deaths be as swift and painless as you can conveniently make them.

FREDERIC. I will. By the love I have for you, I swear it. Would that you could render this extermination unnecessary by accompanying me back to civilization!

KING. No, Frederic, it cannot be. I don't think much of our profession, but, contrasted with respectability, it is comparatively honest. No, Frederic; I shall live and die a pirate king.

SONG — PIRATE KING.

Oh better far to live and die
Under the brave black flag I fly,
Than play a sanctimonious part
With a pirate head and a pirate heart.

Away to the cheating world go you,
Where pirates all are well-to-do;
But I'll be true to the song I sing,
And live and die a Pirate King!
  For I am a Pirate King!

ALL.   You are! Hurrah for our Pirate King!

KING.   And it is, it is a glorious thing
  To be a Pirate King!

ALL.   Hurrah, hurrah for our Pirate King!

KING.   When I sally forth to seek my prey
I help myself in a royal way.
I sink a few more ships, it's true,
Than a well-bred monarch ought to do;
But many a king on a first-class throne,
If he wants to call his crown his own,
Must manage somehow to get through
More dirty work than ever *I* do,
  Though I am a Pirate King.

ALL.   You are! Hurrah for our Pirate King!

KING.   And it is, it is a glorious thing
  To be a Pirate King!

ALL.   It is! Hurrah for our Pirate King!
  (*Exeunt all except* FREDERIC *and* RUTH.)

RUTH.   Oh take me with you! I cannot live if I am left behind.

FREDERIC.   Ruth, I will be quite candid with you. You are very dear to me, as you know, but I must be circumspect. You see, you are considerably older than I: a lad of twenty-one usually looks for a wife of seventeen.

RUTH.   A wife of seventeen! You will find me a wife of a thousand!

FREDERIC.   No, but I shall find you a wife of forty-seven, and that is quite enough now. Ruth, tell me candidly and without reserve: compared with other women, how are *you?*

RUTH.   I will answer you truthfully, master: I have a slight cold, but otherwise I am quite well.

FREDERIC.   I am sorry for your cold, but I was referring rather to your personal appearance. Compared with other women, are you beautiful?

RUTH (*bashfully*).   I have been told so, dear master.

FREDERIC.   Ah, but lately?

RUTH.   Oh, no; years and years ago.

FREDERIC.   But what do you think yourself?

RUTH.   It is a delicate question to answer, but I think I am a fine woman.

FREDERIC.   That is your candid opinion?

RUTH.   Yes: I should be deceiving you if I told you otherwise.

FREDERIC.   Thank you, Ruth, I believe you, for I am sure you would not practise on my inexperience. I wish to do the right thing, and if—I say, *if*—you are really a fine woman, your age shall be no obstacle to our union. (*Shakes hands with her.*)
(*Chorus of* GIRLS *heard in the extreme distance:* "Climbing over rocky mountains," &c.)

FREDERIC.   Hark! surely I hear voices. Who has ventured to approach our all but inaccessible lair? Can it be Custom House? No, it does not sound like Custom House.

RUTH (*aside*).   Confusion! It is the voices of young girls! If he should see them I am lost.

FREDERICK (*climbing rocky arch and looking off*). By all that's marvellous, a bevy of beautiful maidens!

RUTH (*aside*).   Lost! lost! lost!

FREDERIC.   How lovely, how surpassingly lovely, is the plainest of them! What grace! what delicacy! what refinement! and Ruth—Ruth told me she was beautiful!

RECITATIVE.

FREDERIC.   Oh false one, you have deceived me!
RUTH.   I have deceived you?
FREDERIC.   Yes, deceived me! (*Denouncing her.*)

DUET — FREDERIC *and* RUTH.

FREDERIC.   You told me you were fair as gold.
RUTH (*wildly*).   And, master, am I not so?
FREDERIC.   And now I see you're plain and old.
RUTH.   I am sure I am not a jot so.
FREDERIC.   Upon my ignorance you play.
RUTH.   I'm not the one to plot so.
FREDERIC.   Your face is lined, your hair is gray.
RUTH.   It's gradually got so.
FREDERIC.   Faithless woman, to deceive me!—I who trusted so!

RUTH.   Master, master, do not leave me; hear me ere you go!
  My love, without reflecting,
  Oh, do not be rejecting.
Take a maiden tender, her affection raw and green,
  At very highest rating
  Has been accumulating
Summers seventeen, summers seventeen.
  Don't, beloved master,
  Crush me with disaster!
What is such a dower to the dower I have here?
  My love, unabating,
  Has been accumulating
Forty-seven year, forty-seven year!

ENSEMBLE.

RUTH.	FREDERIC.
Don't, beloved master, Crush me with disaster! What is such a dower to the dower I have here? etc.	Yes, your former master Saves you from disaster. Your love would be uncomfortably fervid, it is clear, If, as you are stating, It's been accumulating Forty-seven year, for- ty-seven year!

(*He renounces her, and she goes off in despair.*)

RECITATIVE — FREDERIC.

What shall I do? Before these gentle maidens
I dare not show in this detested costume.
No, better far remain in close concealment
Until I can appear in decent clothing.
(*Hides in cave as they enter, climbing over the rocks.*)

GIRLS.   Climbing over rocky mountain,
    Skipping rivulet and fountain,
    Passing where the willows quiver
    By the ever-rolling river,
      Swollen with the summer rain;
    Threading long and leafy mazes,
    Dotted with unnumbered daisies,
    Scaling rough and rugged passes,
    Climb the hardy little lasses,
      Till the bright seashore they gain.

EDITH.   Let us gaily tread the measure,
    Make the most of fleeting leisure,
    Hail it as a true ally,
    Though it perish by and by.

ALL.   Hail it as a true ally,
Though it perish by and by.

EDITH.   Every moment brings a treasure
    Of its own especial pleasure:
    Though the moments quickly die,
    Greet them gaily as they fly.   (*Dance.*)

KATE.   Far away from toil and care,
    Revelling in fresh sea-air,
    Here we live and reign alone,
    In a world that's all our own.
    Here, in this our rocky den,
    Far away from mortal men,
    We'll be queens and make decrees:
    They may honor them who please.

ALL.   Let us gaily tread the measure, etc.

KATE.   What a picturesque spot! I wonder where we are?

EDITH.   And I wonder where papa is? We have left him ever so far behind.

ISABEL.   Oh, he will be here presently. Remember, poor papa is not as young as we are, and we came over a rather difficult country.

KATE.   But how thoroughly delightful it is to be so entirely alone! Why, in all probability we are the first human beings who ever set foot on this enchanting spot.

ISABEL.   Except the mermaids: it's the very place for mermaids—

KATE.   Who are only human beings down to the waist—

EDITH.   And who can't be said, strictly, to set *foot* anywhere. Tails they may, but feet they *cannot.*

KATE.   But what shall we do until papa and the servants arrive with the luncheon? (*All listen and come down.*)

EDITH.   We are quite alone, and the sea is as

smooth as glass. Suppose we take off our shoes and stockings and paddle?

ALL.   Yes, yes—the very thing!

They prepare to carry out the suggestion. They have all taken off one shoe, when FREDERIC *comes forward from cave.*

FREDERIC (*recitative*).   Stop, ladies, pray!

ALL (*hopping on one foot*).   A man!

FREDERIC.   I had intended
   Not to intrude myself upon your notice
   In this effective but alarming costume,
   But under these peculiar circumstances it is
     my bounden duty to inform you
   That your proceedings will not be unwit-
   nessed.

EDITH.   But who are you, sir? Speak!
                 (*All hopping.*)

FREDERIC.   I am a pirate!

ALL (*recoiling, hopping*).   A pirate! Horror!

FREDERIC.   Ladies, do not shudder.
   This evening I renounce my vile profession,
   And to that aid, O pure and peerless maidens,
   O blushing buds of ever-blooming beauty,
   I, sore of heart, implore your kind assistance.

EDITH.   How pitiful his tale!
KATE.   How rare his beauty!
ALL.   How pitiful his tale! how rare his beauty!
             (*Put on their shoes.*)

SONG — FREDERIC.

Oh, is there not one maiden breast
   Which does not feel the moral beauty
Of making worldly interest
   Subordinate to sense of duty?
Who would not give up willingly
   All matrimonial ambition
To rescue such an one as I
   From his unfortunate position?

ALL.   Alas! there's not one maiden breast
   Which seems to feel the moral beauty
Of making worldly interest
   Subordinate to sense of duty.

FREDERIC.   Oh, is there not one maiden here
   Whose homely face and bad complexion
Have caused all hope to disappear
   Of ever winning man's affection?
To such an one, if such there be,
   I swear, by heaven's arch above you,
If you will cast your eyes on me,
   However plain you be, I'll love you.

ALL.   Alas! there's not one maiden here

Whose homely face and bad complexion
Have caused all hope to disappear
   Of ever winning man's affection.

FREDERIC (*in despair*).   Not one?
ALL.   No, no, not one.
FREDERIC.   Not one?
ALL.   No, no!

      MABEL *enters through arch.*

MABEL.   Yes, one!
ALL.   'Tis Mabel!
MABEL.   Yes, 'tis Mabel!

RECITATIVE — MABEL.

O sisters, deaf to pity's name?
   For shame!
It's true that he has gone astray,
   But, pray,
Is that a reason good and true
   Why you
Should all be deaf to pity's name?
   For shame!

ALL (*aside*).   The question is, had he not been
     A thing of beauty,
Would she be swayed by quite as keen
     A sense of duty?

SOLO — MABEL.

Poor wandering one,
   Though thou hast surely strayed,
Take heart of grace,
Thy steps retrace.
   Be not afraid,
Poor wandering one.
If such poor love as mine
Can help thee find
True peace of mind,
Why, take it—it is thine,
   Poor wandering one!

Take heart; fair days will shine.
Take any heart—take mine!

ALL. Take heart! though danger lowers;
Take any heart—but ours!

MABEL *and* FREDERIC *go to mouth of cave and converse.* KATE *beckons her sisters, who form in a semicircle around her.*

EDITH. What ought we to do,
Gentle sisters, pray?
Propriety, we know,
Says we ought to stay,
While sympathy exclaims,
"Free them from your tether;
Play at other games;
Leave them here together."

KATE. Her case may any day
Be yours, my dear, or mine;
Let her make her hay
While the sun doth shine.
Let us compromise
(Our hearts are not of leather):
Let us shut our eyes
And talk about the weather.
(EDITH, KATE, *and* GIRLS *retire up, and sit two and two, facing each other, in a line across the stage.*)

CHATTERING CHORUS (*during which* FREDERIC *and* MABEL *fondle.*)

How beautifully blue the sky!
The glass is rising very high.
Continue fine I hope it may,

And yet it rained but yesterday.
To-morrow it may pour again
(I hear the country wants some rain);
Yet people say, I know not why,
That we shall have a warm July.

SOLO — MABEL.

(*During this the* GIRLS *continue their chatter* pianissimo, *but listening eagerly all the time.*)

Did ever maiden wake
From dream of homely duty,
To find her daylight break
With such exceeding beauty?
Did ever maiden close
Her eyes on wakening sadness,
To dream of, Goodness knows!
How much exceeding gladness?

FREDERIC. Ah yes, ah yes, this is exceeding gladness.
(FREDERIC *and* MABEL *turn and see that the* GIRLS *are listening; detected, they continue their chatter,* forte.)

GIRLS. How beautifully blue the sky! etc. etc.

SOLO — FREDERIC.

(*During this the* GIRLS *continue their chatter,* pianissimo, *as before, but listening intently all the time.*)

Did ever pirate roll
His soul in guilty dreaming,
And wake to find that soul

With peace and virtue beaming?
Did ever pirate loathed
    Forsake his hideous mission,
To find himself betrothed
    To a lady of position?

MABEL.   Ah yes, ah yes, I am a lady of position.
(MABEL *and* FREDERIC *turn as before.* GIRLS
    resume their chatter, forte.)

ENSEMBLE.

MABEL.	FREDERIC.	GIRLS.
Did ever maiden wake, etc.	Did ever pirate loathed, etc.	How beautifully blue the sky, etc.

RECITATIVE — FREDERIC.

Stay; we must not lose our senses;
Men who stick at no offences
    Will anon be here.
Piracy their dreadful trade is;
Pray you, get you hence, young ladies,
    While the coast is clear.

GIRLS.   No, we must not lose our senses;
    If they stick at no offences,
        We should not be here.
    Piracy their dreadful trade is—
    Nice associates for young ladies!
        Let us disappear.

(*During this Chorus the* PIRATES *enter stealthily
and form in a semicircle behind the* GIRLS. *As
the* GIRLS *move to go off, each* PIRATE *seizes
a* GIRL.)

ALL.   Too late!
PIRATES.   Ha! ha!
ALL.   Too late!
PIRATES.   Ha! ha!
    Ha! ha! ha! ha! Ha! ha! ha! ha!

ENSEMBLE.

PIRATES.	GIRLS.
Now here's a first-rate opportunity	We have missed our opportunity
To get married with impunity,	Of escaping with impunity;
And indulge in the felicity	So farewell to the felicity
Of unbounded domesticity.	Of our maiden domesticity.
You shall quickly be parsonified,	We shall quickly be parsonified,
Conjugally matrimonified,	Conjugally matrimonified,
By a doctor of divinity	By a doctor of divinity
Who resides in this vicinity.	Who resides in this vicinity.

RECITATIVE.

MABEL (*coming forward*).

Hold, monsters! ere your pirate caravanserai
Proceeds against our will to wed us all,
Just bear in mind that we are wards in chancery,
    And father is a Major-General!

SAMUEL.

We'd better pause, or dangers may befall;
    Their father is a Major-General.

GIRLS.

Yes, yes, he is a Major-General.

The MAJOR-GENERAL *has entered unnoticed,
    on rock.*

GENERAL.   Yes, I am a Major-General!

ALL.   You are! Hurrah for the Major-General!

GENERAL.   And it is a glorious thing to be a
    Major-General!

ALL.   It is! Hurrah for the Major-General!

SONG — MAJOR-GENERAL.

I am the very pattern of a modern major-gineral:
I've information vegetable, animal, and mineral;
I know the kings of England, and I quote the
    fights historical,
From Marathon to Waterloo, in order categorical;
I'm very well acquainted, too, with matters
    mathematical;
I understand equations, both the simple and
    quadratical;
About binomial theorem I'm teeming with a
    lot of news—
(*Bothered for next rhyme.*) Lot o' news—lot
    o' news—
(*Struck with an idea.*) With many cheerful facts
    about the square of the hypotenuse;
(*Joyfully.*) With many cheerful facts about the
    square of the hypotenuse!

ALL.

With many cheerful facts about the square of
    the hypotenuse!

GENERAL.

I'm very good at integral and differential calculus;
I know the scientific names of beings animalculous;
In short, in matters vegetable, animal, and mineral
I am the very model of a modern major-gineral!

ALL.

In short in matters vegetable, animal, and mineral
He is the very model of a modern major-gineral!

GENERAL.

I know our mythic history, King Arthur's and
Sir Caradoc's;
I answer hard acrostics; I've a pretty taste for
paradox—
I quote in elegiacs all the crimes of Heliogabalus;
In conics I can floor peculiarities parabolous;
I can tell undoubted Raphaels from Gerard
Dows and Zoffanies;
I know the croaking chorus from the *Frogs* of
Aristophanes;
Then I can hum a fugue of which I've heard the
music's din afore—
(*Bothered for next rhyme.*) Din afore? din
afore? din afore?—
(*Struck with an idea.*) And whistle all the airs
from that infernal nonsense, *Pinafore,*
(*Joyously.*) And whistle all the airs from that
infernal nonsense, *Pinafore.*

ALL.

And whistle all the airs from that infernal nonsense, *Pinafore.*

GENERAL.

Then I can write a washing-bill in Babylonic
cuneiform,
And tell you every detail of Caractacus's uniform.
In short, in matters vegetable, animal, and mineral
I am the very pattern of a modern major-gineral!

ALL.

In short, in matters vegetable, animal, and mineral
He is the very pattern of a modern major-gineral!

GENERAL.

In fact, when I know what is meant by "mamelon" and "ravelin"—
When I can tell at sight a chassepot rifle from
a javelin—
When such affairs as sorties and surprises I'm
more wary at,
And when I know precisely what is meant by
"commissariat"—
When I have learnt what progress has been
made in modern gunnery—
When I know more of tactics than a novice in
a nunnery,—

In short, when I've a smattering of elemental
strategy—
(*Bothered for the rhyme.*) Strategy! strategy!—
(*Struck with an idea.*)
(*Joyously.*) You'll say a better major-general
has never *sat* agee.

ALL.

We'll say a better major-general has never *sat*
agee.

GENERAL.

For my military knowledge, though I'm plucky
and adventury,
Has only been brought down to the beginning
of the century;
But still, in learning vegetable, animal, and mineral
I am the very model of a modern major-gineral.

ALL.

But still in learning vegetable, animal, and mineral
He is the very model of a modern major-gineral.

GENERAL.   And now that I've introduced myself,
I should like to have some idea of what's going on.

KATE.   Oh, papa! we—

SAMUEL.   Permit me; I'll explain it in two words:
we propose to marry your daughters.

GENERAL.   Dear me!

GIRLS.   Against our wills, papa—against our wills!

GENERAL.   Oh, but you mustn't do that. May I
ask—this is a picturesque uniform, but I'm not
familiar with it—what are you?

KING.   We are all single gentlemen.

GENERAL.   Yes, I gathered that. Anything else?

KING.   No, nothing else.

EDITH.   Papa, don't believe them. They are pirates
—the famous Pirates of Penzance!

GENERAL.   The Pirates of Penzance? I have often
heard of them.

MABEL.   Yes, all except this gentleman (*indicating* FREDERIC), who was a pirate once, but who
is out of his indentures to-day.

GENERAL.   But wait a bit. I object to pirates as
sons-in-law.

KING.   We object to major-generals as fathers-in-
law. But we waive that point; we do not press it,
we look over it.

GENERAL (*aside*).   Hah! an idea! (*Aloud.*) And
do you mean to say that you would deliberately
rob me of these the sole remaining props of my old
age, and leave me to go through the remainder of
life unfriended, unprotected, and alone?

KING.   Well, yes; that's the idea.

GENERAL.   Tell me, have you ever known what it
is to be an orphan?

ALL THE PIRATES (*disgusted*).   Oh, dash it all!

KING.   Here we are again!

GENERAL.   I ask you, have you ever known what
it is to be an orphan?

KING (*sighing*).   Often.

GENERAL.   Yes, orphan. Have you ever known
what it is to be one?

KING.   I say, often.

ALL (*disgusted*).   Often! often! often! (*Turning
away.*)

GENERAL.   I don't think we quite understand one
another. I ask you, have you ever known what it
is to be an orphan? and you say "Orphan." As I
understand you, you are merely repeating the
word "orphan" to show that you understand me.

KING.   I didn't repeat the word "often."

GENERAL.   Pardon me; you did indeed.

KING.   I only repeated it once.

GENERAL.   True, but you repeated it.

KING.   But not often.

GENERAL.   Stop! I think I see where we are getting confused. When you said "orphan" did you
mean "orphan," a person who has lost his parents,
or "often," frequently?

KING.   Oh, I beg your pardon! I see you mean
frequently.

GENERAL.   Ah, you said "often" frequently.

KING.   No, only once.

GENERAL.   Exactly, you said "often, frequently,"
only once.

FINALE.

RECITATIVE — GENERAL.

Oh, men of dark and dismal fate,
     Forego your cruel employ;
Have pity on my lonely state—
     I am an orphan boy!

KING.   An orphan boy?
GENERAL.   An orphan boy!
PIRATES.   How sad! an orphan boy!

SOLO — GENERAL.

These children whom you see
     Are all that I can call my own.

PIRATES.   Poor fellow!

GENERAL.   Take them away from me,
     And I shall be indeed alone.

PIRATES.   Poor fellow!

GENERAL. If pity you can feel,
    Leave me my sole remaining joy.
        See, at your feet they kneel;
        Your hearts you cannot steel
    Against the sad, sad tale of the lonely orphan
        boy.
PIRATES (*sobbing*). Poor fellow!
        See, at our feet they kneel;
        Our hearts we cannot steel
    Against the sad, sad tale of the lonely orphan
        boy.
KING.   The orphan boy!
SAMUEL.   The orphan boy!
ALL. The lonely orphan boy! Poor fellow!

ENSEMBLE.

GENERAL.	GIRLS (*aside*).
I'm telling a terrible story,	He's telling a terrible story,
But it doesn't diminish my glory;	Which will tend to diminish his glory,
For they would have taken my daughters	Though they would have taken his daughters
Over the billowy waters,	Over the billowy waters.
If I hadn't in elegant diction	It's easy in elegant diction
Indulged in an innocent fiction,	To call it an innocent fiction,
Which is not in the same category	But it comes in the same category
As a regular, terrible story.	As a regular, terrible story.

PIRATES (*aside*).

If he's telling a terrible story,
He shall die by a death that is gory—
One of the cruellest slaughters
That ever was known in these waters;
And we'll finish his moral affliction
By a very complete malediction,
As a compliment valedictory,
If he's telling a terrible story.

KING. Although our dark career
        Sometimes involves the crime of stealing,
    We rather think that we're
        Not altogether void of feeling.
    Although we live by strife,
        We're always sorry to begin it,
    And what, we ask, is life
        Without a touch of Poetry in it?

ALL (*kneeling*). Hail, Poetry, thou heaven-born
        maid!

Thou gildest e'en the pirate's trade.
Hail, flowing fount of sentiment!
All hail, divine emollient!

KING. You may go, for you're at liberty; our
        pirate rules protect you,
    And honorary members of our band we do elect
        you.

SAMUEL.   For he is an orphan boy!

ALL.   He is! Hurrah for the orphan boy!

GENERAL.   And it sometimes is a useful thing to
be an orphan boy.

ALL.   It is! Hurrah for the orphan boy!
Hurrah for the orphan—

MABEL *and* FREDERIC.   Oh, happy day! with joyous glee
We will away and married be!

GENERAL.   Oh, happy day! with joyous glee
They will away and married be!

MABEL.   Should it befall auspiciously,
My sisters all will bridesmaids be.

GENERAL.   Should it befall auspiciously,
Her sisters all will bridesmaids be.

ALL.   Oh, happy day! etc.

RECITATIVE.

RUTH.   Oh, master, hear one word, I do implore
you!
Remember Ruth, your Ruth, who kneels
before you!

PIRATES.   Yes, yes, remember Ruth who kneels
before you.

FREDERIC.   Away! you did deceive me!

PIRATES.   Away! you did deceive him.

RUTH.   Oh, do not leave me!

PIRATES.   Oh, do not leave her!

FREDERIC.   Away! you grieve me!

PIRATES.   Away! you grieve him!

FREDERIC.   I wish you'd leave me!

PIRATES.   We wish you'd leave him!

ENSEMBLE.

Pray observe the magnanimity
We ⎱
They ⎰ display to lace and dimity.
Never was such opportunity
To get married with impunity;
But ⎰we ⎱ give up the felicity
    ⎱they⎰
Of unbounded domesticity,
Though a doctor of divinity
Is located in this vicinity.

KING.   For we all are orphan boys!

ALL.   We are! Hurrah for the orphan boys!

GENERAL.   And it sometimes is a useful thing to
be an orphan boy.

ALL.   It is! Hurrah for the orphan boy!

GIRLS *and* GENERAL *go up rocks, while* PIRATES
indulge in a wild dance of delight. The GENERAL
produces a British flag, and the PIRATE KING *produces a black flag with skull and crossbones.*

END OF ACT I.

ACT II.

SCENE. — *A ruined chapel by moonlight. Aisles divided by pillars and arches; ruined Gothic windows at back.* GENERAL STANLEY *discovered seated pensively, surrounded by his daughters.*

CHORUS.

Oh dry the glistening tear
    That dews that martial cheek;
Thy loving children hear,
    In them thy comfort seek.
With sympathetic care
    Their arms around thee creep,
For, oh, they cannot bear
    To see their father weep.

Enter MABEL *and* FREDERIC.

SOLO — MABEL.

Dear father, why leave your bed
    At this untimely hour,
When happy daylight is dead
    And darksome dangers lower?
See, Heaven has lit her lamp,
    The midnight hour is past,
The chilly night-air is damp,
    And the dew is falling fast.
Dear father, why leave your bed
When happy daylight is dead?

Enter FREDERIC.

MABEL. Oh, Frederic, cannot you reconcile it with your conscience to say something that will relieve my father's sorrow?

FREDERIC. I will try, dear Mabel, but why does he sit, night after night, in this draughty old ruin?

GENERAL. Why do I sit here? To escape from the pirates' clutches I described myself as an orphan, and I am no orphan. I came here to humble myself before the tombs of my ancestors, and to implore their pardon for the disgrace I have brought upon them.

FREDERIC. But you forget, sir. You only bought the property a year ago, and the stucco on your baronial castle is scarcely dry.

GENERAL. Frederic, in this chapel are ancestors; you cannot deny that. I don't know whose ancestors they *were,* but I know whose ancestors they *are,* and I shudder to think that their descendant by purchase (if I may so describe myself) should have brought disgrace upon what I have no doubt was an unstained escutcheon.

FREDERIC. Be comforted. Had you not acted as you did, these reckless men would assuredly have called in the nearest clergyman, and have married your large family on the spot.

GENERAL. I thank you for your proffered solace, but it is unavailing. At what time does your expedition march against these scoundrels?

FREDERIC. At eleven, and before midnight I hope to have atoned for my involuntary association with these pestilent scourges by sweeping them from the face of the earth.—And then, my Mabel, you will be mine!

GENERAL. Are your devoted followers at hand?

FREDERIC. They are; they only wait my orders.

RECITATIVE — GENERAL.

Then, Frederic, let your escort lion-hearted
Be summoned to receive a general's blessing
Ere they depart upon their dread adventure.

FREDERIC. Dear sir, they come!

Enter POLICE, *marching in single file.*

ALL. Good luck! they bear them bravely!

(*The* POLICE *form in line, facing audience.*)

SONG — SERGEANT.

When the foeman bears his steel—
ALL (*using their clubs as trumpets*). Tarantara!
            tarantara!
SERGEANT. We uncomfortable feel;
ALL.   Tarantara!
SERGEANT. And we find the wisest thing—
ALL.   Tarantara! tarantara!
SERGEANT. Is to slap our chests and sing—
ALL.   Tarantara!
SERGEANT. For when threatened with *émeutes*—
ALL.   Tarantara! tarantara!
SERGEANT. And your heart is in your boots—
ALL.   Tarantara!
SERGEANT. There is nothing brings it round—
ALL.   Tarantara! tarantara!
SERGEANT. Like the trumpet's martial sound—
ALL.   Tarantara!
SERGEANT. Tarantara-ra-ra-ra-ra-ra! etc.
ALL.   Tarantara-ra-ra-ra-ra-ra!

MABEL (*addressing* SERGEANT).

Go, ye heroes, go to glory!
Though you die in combat gory,
Ye shall live in song and story—
      Go to immortality!
Go to death and go to slaughter;
Die, and every Cornish daughter
With her tears your graves shall water—
      Go, ye heroes, go and die!

ALL.   Go, ye heroes, go and die!
SERGEANT. Though to us it's evident—
ALL.   Tarantara! tarantara!
SERGEANT. These attentions are well meant—
ALL.   Tarantara!
SERGEANT. Such expressions don't appear—
ALL.   Tarantara! tarantara!
SERGEANT. Calculated men to cheer—
ALL.   Tarantara!
SERGEANT. Who are going to meet their fate—
ALL.   Tarantara! tarantara!
SERGEANT. In a highly nervous state—
ALL.   Tarantara!
SERGEANT. Still, to us it's evident—
ALL.   Tarantara! tarantara!
SERGEANT. These attentions are well meant—
ALL.   Tarantara!

ALL.   Yes, to them it's evident, etc. etc.

EDITH (*addressing* SERGEANT).

Go, and do your best endeavor.
And before all links we sever
We will say farewell for ever—
      Go to glory and the grave!
For your foes are fierce and ruthless,
False, unmerciful, and truthless;
Young and tender, old and toothless,
      All in vain their mercy crave.

ALL. Yes, your foes are fierce and ruthless, etc.

CHORUS OF POLICE.

We observe too great a stress—
      Tarantara! tarantara!
On the risks that on us press—
      Tarantara!
And of reference a lack—
      Tarantara! tarantara!
To our chance of coming back—
      Tarantara!

SERGEANT. Still, perhaps it would be wise—
POLICE.   Tarantara! tarantara!
SERGEANT. Not to carp or criticise—
ALL.   Tarantara!
SERGEANT. For it's very evident—
ALL.   Tarantara! tarantara!
SERGEANT. These attentions are well meant—
ALL.   Tarantara!
ALL. Yes, to us it's evident
      These attentions are well meant—
            Tarantara-ra-ra-ra-ra! etc. etc.
      Go, ye heroes, go to glory! etc. etc.
GENERAL. Away! away!
POLICE (*without moving*). Yes, yes, we go!
GENERAL. These pirates slay.
POLICE. Yes, yes, we go.
GENERAL. Then do not stay.
POLICE. We go, we go.
GENERAL. Then why all this delay?
POLICE. All right! We go, we go;
            Yes, forward on the foe!
               Ho! ho! ho! ho!
            We go, we go, we go!
               Tarantara-ra-ra-ra!
GENERAL. Then forward on the foe!
ALL. Yes! forward!
POLICE. Yes! forward!
GENERAL. Yes! but you *don't* go!
POLICE. We go, we go, we go!
ALL. At last they really go! Tarantara-ra-ra!

ENSEMBLE.

CHORUS OF ALL BUT POLICE.

Go, and do your best
    endeavor,
And before all links we
    sever
We will say farewell
    forever;
    Go to glory and the
    grave!
For your foes are fierce
    and ruthless,
False, unmerciful, and
    truthless;
Young and tender, old
    and toothless,
    All in vain their mer-
    cy crave, etc.

CHORUS OF POLICE.

Such expressions don't
    appear—
    Tarantara! tarantara!
Calculated men to
    cheer—
    Tarantara!
Who are going to their
    fate—
    Tarantara! tarantara!
In a highly nervous
    state—
    Tarantara!
We observe too great a
    stress—
    Tarantara! tarantara!
On the risks that on us
    press—
    Tarantara!
And of reference a
    lack—
    Tarantara! tarantara!
To our chance of com-
    ing back—
    Tarantara!

MABEL *tears herself from* FREDERIC *and exit, followed by her sisters, consoling her. The* GEN-ERAL *and others follow the* POLICE. FREDERIC *remains alone.*

RECITATIVE — FREDERIC.

Now for the pirates' lair! Oh, joy unbounded!
Oh, sweet relief! Oh, rapture unexampled!
At last I may atone, in some slight measure,
For the repeated acts of theft and pillage
Of which, at a sense of duty's stern dictation,
I, circumstances' victim, have been guilty.

The PIRATE KING *and* RUTH *appear at the window, armed.*

KING.   Young Frederic!
    (Covering him with pistol.)
FREDERIC.   Who calls?
KING.   Your late commander.   *(Coming down.)*
RUTH.   And I, your little Ruth!
    (Covering him with pistol.)
FREDERIC.   Oh, mad intruders!
    How dare ye face me? Know ye not, rash ones,
    That I have doomed you to extermination?
    *(*KING *and* RUTH *hold a pistol to each ear.)*

KING.   Have mercy on us! Hear us ere you slaugh-
    ter!

FREDERIC.   I do not think I ought to listen to you.
    Yet, mercy should alloy our stern resentment,
    And so I will be merciful. Say on.

TRIO — RUTH, KING, *and* FREDERIC.

When first you left our pirate fold
    We tried to cheer our spirits faint,
According to our customs old,
    With quips and quibbles quaint;
But all in vain the quips we heard;
    We lay and sobbed upon the rocks,
Until to somebody occurred
    A curious paradox.

FREDERIC.   A paradox?

KING *and* RUTH (*laughing*).   A paradox—
    A most ingenious paradox.
We've quips and quibbles heard in flocks,
But none to beat this paradox.
    Ha! ha! ha! ha! Ho! ho! ho! ho!

KING.   We knew your taste for curious quips,
    For cranks and contradictions queer,
And with the laughter on our lips
    We wished you there to hear.
We said, "If we could tell it him,
    How Frederic would the joke enjoy!"
And so we've risked both life and limb
    To tell it to our boy.

FREDERIC (*interested*).   That paradox.

KING *and* RUTH (*laughing*).   That paradox,
    That most ingenious paradox.
We've quips and quibbles heard in flocks,
But none to beat that paradox!
    Ha! ha! ha! ha! Ho! ho! ho! ho!

CHANT — KING.

For some ridiculous reason—to which, however,
    I've no desire to be disloyal—
Some person in authority—I don't know who;
    very likely the Astronomer-Royal—
Has decided that although for such a beastly
    month as February twenty-eight days as a
    general rule are plenty,
One year in every four his days shall be reckoned
    as nine-and-twenty.
Through some singular coincidence—I shouldn't
    be surprised if it were owing to the agency
    of an ill-natured fairy—
You are the victim of this clumsy arrangement,
    having been born in leap-year on the twenty-
    ninth of February;
And so, by a simple arithmetical process, you'll
    easily discover,
That though you've lived twenty-one years, yet,
    if we go by birthdays, you are only five and a
    little bit over!

RUTH *and* KING.   Ha! ha! ha! ha! Ho! ho! ho! ho!

FREDERIC.
    Dear me! Let's see (*counting on fingers*):

Yes, yes,—with yours my figures do agree.
Ha! ha! ha! ha! Ho! ho! ho! ho!
        (FREDERIC *more amused than any.*)
How quaint the ways of Paradox!
At common sense she gaily mocks.
Though, counting in the usual way,
    Years twenty-one I've been alive,
Yet, reckoning by my natal day,
    I am a little boy of five!

ALL.   He is a little boy of five, ha! ha!
    At common sense she gaily mocks,
    So quaint a way has Paradox!
    Ha! ha! ha! ha!

KING.   Ho! ho! ho! ho!

RUTH.   Ha! ha! ha! ha!

FREDERIC.   Ha! ha! ha! ha!

ALL.   Ho! ho! ho! ho!
    (*All throw themselves back on seats, exhausted
                with laughing.*)

FREDERIC.   Upon my word, this is most curious, most absurdly whimsical. Five and a quarter! No one would think it to look at me.

RUTH.   You are glad now, I'll be bound, that you spared us. You would never have forgiven yourself when you discovered that you had killed two of your comrades.

FREDERIC.   My comrades?

KING.   I'm afraid you don't appreciate the delicacy of your position. You were apprenticed to us—

FREDERIC.   Until I reached my twenty-first year.

KING.   No, until you reached your twenty-first birthday (*producing document*), and, going by birthdays, you are as yet only five and a quarter.

FREDERIC.   You don't mean to say you are going to hold me to that?

KING.   No, we merely remind you of the fact, and leave the rest to your sense of duty.

FREDERIC (*wildly*).   Don't put it on that footing. As I was merciful to you just now, be merciful to me. I implore you not to insist on the letter of your bond just as the cup of happiness is at my lips.

RUTH.   We insist on nothing. We content ourselves with pointing out to you your duty.

FREDERIC.   Well, you have appealed to my sense of duty, and my duty is only too clear. I abhor your infamous calling, I shudder at the thought that I have ever been mixed up with it, but duty is before all. At any cost, I will do my duty.

KING.   Bravely spoken! Come, you are one of us once more.

FREDERIC.   Lead on, I follow! (*Suddenly.*) Oh, horror!

KING *and* RUTH.   What is the matter?

FREDERIC.   Ought I to tell you? No! no! I cannot do it; and yet, as one of your band—

KING.   Speak out, I charge you, by that sense of conscientiousness to which we have never yet appealed in vain.

FREDERIC.   General Stanley, the father of my Mabel—

KING *and* RUTH.   Yes! yes!

FREDERIC.   He escaped from you on the plea that he was an orphan?

KING.   He did.

FREDERIC.   It breaks my heart to betray the honored father of the girl I adore, but as your apprentice I have no alternative. It is my duty to tell you that General Stanley is no orphan.

KING *and* RUTH.   What?

FREDERIC.   More than that, he never was one!

KING.   Am I to understand that to save his contemptible life he dared to practise on our credulous simplicity? (FREDERIC *nods as he weeps.*) Our revenge shall be swift and terrible. We will go and collect our band and attack Tremorden Castle this very night.

FREDERIC.   But—

KING.   Not a word! he is doomed!

TRIO.

KING *and* RUTH.	FREDERIC.
Away! away! my heart's on fire;	Away! away! ere I expire.
I burn, this base deception to repay;	I find my duty hard to do to-day.
This very day my vengeance dire	My heart is filled with anguish dire;
Shall glut itself in gore. Away! away!	It strikes me to the core. Away! away!

KING.   With falsehood foul
    He tricked us of our brides;
Let vengeance howl—
    The pirate so decides!
Our nature stern
    He softened with his lies,
And, in return,
    This night the traitor dies.

ALL.   Yes, yes, to-night the traitor dies!

RUTH.   To-night he dies.

KING.   Yes, or early to-morrow.

FREDERIC.   His girls likewise?

RUTH.   They will welter in sorrow!

KING.   The one soft spot—

FREDERIC.   In their natures they cherish;

RUTH.   And all who plot—

KING.   To abuse it shall perish.

ALL.   Yes, all who plot
    To abuse it shall perish!
    Away! away! etc.

Exeunt KING *and* RUTH. FREDERIC *throws himself on a stone in blank despair. Enter* MABEL.

RECITATIVE.

MABEL.   All is prepared; your gallant crew await you.
    My Frederic in tears? It cannot be
    That lion heart quails at the coming conflict?

FREDERIC.   No, Mabel, no. A terrible disclosure
    Has just been made.
    Mabel, my dearly-loved one,
    I bound myself to serve the pirate captain
    Until I reached my one-and-twentieth birthday.

MABEL.   But you *are* twenty-one?

FREDERIC.   I've just discovered
    That I was born in leap-year, and that birthday
    Will not be reached by me till 1940.

MABEL.   Oh horrible! catastrophe appalling!

FREDERIC.   And so, farewell!

MABEL.   No, no! Oh, Frederic, hear me!

DUET — MABEL *and* FREDERIC.

MABEL.   Stay, Frederic, stay!
    They have no legal claim.
    No shadow of a shame
    Will fall upon thy name.
    Stay, Frederic, stay!

FREDERIC.   Nay, Mabel, nay!
    To-night I quit these walls.
    The thought my soul appals,
    But when stern duty calls,
    I must obey!

MABEL.   Stay, Frederic, stay!

FREDERIC.   Nay, Mabel, nay!

MABEL.   They have no claim.

FREDERIC.   But duty's name!
    The thought my soul appals,
    But when stern duty calls,
    I must obey!

BALLAD — MABEL.

Oh leave me not to pine
    Alone and desolate!
No fate seemed fair as mine—

No happiness so great—
And Nature day by day
Has sung in accents clear
This joyous roundelay,
"He loves thee—he is here!
Fa la! fa la! fa la!
He loves thee—he is here!"

FREDERIC. Oh I must leave thee here,
In endless night to dream,
Where joy is dark and drear
And sorrow all supreme—
Where Nature day by day
Will sing in altered tone
This weary roundelay,
"He loves thee—he is gone!
Fa la! fa la! fa la!
He loves thee—he is gone!"

FREDERIC. In 1940 I of age shall be:
I'll then return and claim you, I declare it!

MABEL. It seems so long!

FREDERIC. Swear that till then you will be true
to me.

MABEL (*aside*). Yes, I'll be strong.
(*Aloud.*) By all the Stanleys dead and gone I
swear it!

ENSEMBLE.

Oh here is love, and here is truth,
And here is food for joyous laughter:
$\left.\begin{array}{l}\text{He}\\\text{She}\end{array}\right\}$ will be faithful to $\left\{\begin{array}{l}\text{his}\\\text{her}\end{array}\right.$ sooth
Till we are wed, and even after.

What joy to know that though $\left\{\begin{array}{l}\text{he}\\\text{I}\end{array}\right\}$ must

Embrace piratical adventures,
$\left.\begin{array}{l}\text{He}\\\text{She}\end{array}\right\}$ will be faithful to $\left\{\begin{array}{l}\text{his}\\\text{her}\end{array}\right\}$ trust
Till $\left\{\begin{array}{l}\text{he is}\\\text{I am}\end{array}\right\}$ out of $\left\{\begin{array}{l}\text{his}\\\text{my}\end{array}\right\}$ indentures!

FREDERIC. Farewell! Adieu!

MABEL. The same to you!

BOTH. Farewell! Adieu!
(FREDERIC *rushes to window and leaps out.*)

RECITATIVE — MABEL.

Distraction! Frederic! loved one! oh return!
With love I burn!
(*Recollecting.*) Stay! I'm a Stanley! Even to the
grave I will be brave.
His conscience bids him give up love and all
At duty's call;
Mine teaches me that though I love him so,
He is my foe.

(*Feeling pulse.*) Yes, I am brave! O family de-
scent!
How great thy charm! thy sway how excellent!
Come one and all, undaunted men in blue,
A crisis now affairs are coming to.

Enter POLICE, *marching in single file.*

SERGEANT. Though in body and in mind, taran-
tara! tarantara!
We are timidly inclined, tarantara!
And anything but blind, tarantara! tarantara!
To the danger that's behind, tarantara!
Yet, when the danger's near, tarantara! taran-
tara!
We manage to appear, tarantara!

As insensible to fear, tarantara! tarantara!
As anybody here, tarantara!
Tarantara! tarantara-ra-ra-ra-ra-ra!

MABEL.   Sergeant, approach. Young Frederic was to have led you to death and glory.

ALL.   That is not a pleasant way of putting it.

MABEL.   No matter. He will not so lead you, for he has allied himself once more with his old associates.

ALL.   He has acted shamefully!

MABEL.   You speak falsely; you know nothing about it. He has acted nobly!

ALL.   He has acted nobly!

MABEL.   Dearly as I loved him before, his heroic sacrifice to his sense of duty has endeared him to me tenfold; but if it was *his* duty to constitute himself my foe, it is likewise *my* duty to regard him in that light. He has done his duty; I will do mine. Go ye and do yours. (*Exit* MABEL.)

ALL.   Very well.

SERGEANT.   This is perplexing.

ALL.   We cannot understand it at all.

SERGEANT.   Still, if he is actuated by a sense of duty—

ALL.   That makes a difference, of course. At the same time, we repeat we cannot understand it.

SERGEANT.   No matter. Our course is clear; we must do our best to capture these pirates alone. It is most distressing to us to be the agents where-by your erring fellow-creatures are deprived of that liberty which is so dear to all, but we should have thought of that before we joined the force.

ALL.   We should.

SERGEANT.   It is too late now.

ALL.   It is.

SONG — SERGEANT.

When a felon's not engaged in his employment—

ALL.   His employment,

SERGEANT.   Or maturing his felonious little plans—

ALL.   Little plans,

SERGEANT.   His capacity for innocent enjoy-ment—

ALL.   -Cent enjoyment

SERGEANT.   Is just as great as any honest man's—

ALL.   Honest man's.

SERGEANT.   Our feelings we with difficulty smoth-er—

ALL.   -Culty smother,

SERGEANT.   When constabulary duty's to be done—

ALL.   To be done.

SERGEANT.   Ah, take one consideration with an-other—

ALL.   With another,

SERGEANT.   A policeman's lot is not a happy one—

ALL.   Happy one.
             When constabulary duty's to be done—
             To be done—
             The policeman's lot is not a happy one—
             Happy one!

SERGEANT.   When the enterprising burglar's not a-burgling—

ALL.   Not a-burgling,

SERGEANT.   When the cut-throat isn't occupied in crime—

ALL.   -Pied in crime,

SERGEANT.   He loves to hear the little brook a-gurgling—

ALL.   Brook a-gurgling,

SERGEANT.   And listen to the merry village chime—

ALL.   Village chime.

SERGEANT.   When the coster's finished jumping on his mother—

ALL.   On his mother,

SERGEANT.   He loves to lie a-basking in the sun—

ALL.   In the sun.

SERGEANT.   Ah, take one consideration with an-
              other—

ALL.   With another,

SERGEANT.   The policeman's lot is not a happy
              one—

ALL.   Happy one!
              When constabulary duty's to be
              done—
              To be done,
              The policeman's lot is not a happy
              one—
              Happy one!

CHORUS OF PIRATES (outside, in the distance).

          A rollicking band of pirates we,
          Who, tired of tossing on the sea,
          Are trying their hand at a burglaree
          With weapons grim and gory!

SERGEANT. Hush! hush! I hear them on the manor
              poaching;
     With stealthy step the pirates are approaching.

CHORUS OF PIRATES (resumed nearer).

     We are not coming for plate or gold—
     A story General Stanley told—
     We seek a penalty fifty-fold
          For General Stanley's story.

POLICE.   They seek a penalty.

PIRATES (without).   Fifty-fold!
              We seek a penalty—

POLICE.   Fifty-fold!

ALL.   We ⎫
       They ⎭ seek a penalty fifty-fold
       For General Stanley's story.

POLICE.   They come in force,
              The bold, burglarious elves;
          Our obvious course
              Is to conceal ourselves.

POLICE *conceal themselves in aisle. As they do so, the* PIRATES, *with* RUTH *and* FREDERIC, *are seen appearing at ruined window. They enter cautiously, and come downstage on tiptoe. The* KING *is laden with burglarious tools and pistols, etc. etc.*

CHORUS — PIRATES.

(Very loud.)   With cat-like tread
              Upon our prey we steal—
          In silence dread
              Our cautious way we feel.

POLICE (pianissimo).   Tarantara! tarantara!

PIRATES.   No sound at all:

          We never speak a word;
          A fly's footfall
          Would be distinctly heard.

POLICE.   Tarantara! tarantara!

PIRATES.   Ha! ha!
          Ho! ho!
     So stealthily the pirate creeps
     While all the household soundly sleeps.
          Gurr! gurr!
          Gurr! gurr! (Imitating snoring.)
          Ha! ha! Ho! ho!

POLICE (pianissimo).   Tarantara! Tarantara!
     (Forte.)   Tarantara!

PIRATES.   Come friends, who plough the sea,
              Truce to navigation;
              Take another station;
          Let us vary piracy
          With a little burglary!

SAMUEL.   Here's your crowbar
              And your centre-bit;
          Your life-preserver—
              You may want to hit!
          Your silent matches,
              Your dark-lantern seize;
              Take your file and your skeleton
              keys!

PIRATES.   With cat-like tread, etc.

POLICE.   Tarantara, tarantara, etc.

RECITATIVE — FREDERIC.

     Hush! not a word! I see a light inside.
              (Looks through keyhole.)
     The Major-General comes, so quickly hide.

MAJOR-GENERAL (without).   Yes, yes, the Ma-
              jor-General comes.

PIRATES.   He comes!

MAJOR-GENERAL (entering in dressing-gown, car-
     rying a light).   Yes, yes, I come!

POLICE.   He comes!

MAJOR-GENERAL.   Yes, yes, I come.

ALL.   The Major-General comes!

SOLO — GENERAL.

     Tormented with the anguish dread
          Of falsehood unatoned,
     I lay upon my sleepless bed,
          And tossed and turned and groaned.
     The man who finds his conscience ache
          No peace at all enjoys;
     And as I lay in bed awake
          I thought I heard a noise.

PIRATES.   He thought he heard a noise!
    Ha! ha! ha! ha! ha! ha!

POLICE.   He thought he heard a noise!
    Tarantara-ra-ra!

GENERAL.   No, all is still
    In dale, on hill;
    My mind is set at ease.
    So still the scene
    It might have been
    The sighing of the breeze.

BALLAD — GENERAL.

Sighing softly to the river
    Comes the lonely breeze,
Setting Nature all a-quiver,
    Rustling through the trees.

ALL.   Through the trees.

GENERAL.   And the brook in rippling measure
    Laughs for very love,
    While the poplars in their pleasure
    Wave their arms above.

POLICE and PIRATES.   Yes, the trees for very love
    Wave their leafy arms above.
    River, river, little river!
    May thy loving prosper ever!
    Heaven speed thee, poplar tree!
    May thy wooing happy be!

GENERAL.   Yes, the breeze is but a rover!
    When he wings away,
    Brook and poplar mourn a lover,
    Sighing "Well-a-day!"

ALL.   Well-a-day!

GENERAL.   Ah, the doing and undoing
    That the rogue could tell!
    When the breeze is out a-wooing,
    Who can woo so well?

POLICE and PIRATES.
    Shocking tales the rogue could tell;
    Nobody can woo so well!
    Pretty brook, thy dream is over,
    For thy love is but a rover.
    Sad the lot of poplar trees
    Courted by a fickle breeze!

Enter the GENERAL'S *daughters, led by* MABEL, *all in white peignoirs and nightcaps, and carrying candles.*

GIRLS.   Now, what is this? and what is that? and why does father leave his rest
At such a time of night as this, so very incompletely dressed?
Dear father is, and always was, the most methodical of men;
It's his invariable rule to go to bed at half-past ten.
What strange occurrence can it be that calls dear father from his rest
At such a time of night as this, so very, so very incompletely dressed?

KING (*springing up*).   Forward, my men, and
    seize that general there!
    His life is over.

GENERAL.   The pirates! Oh, despair!

MABEL and GIRLS.   The pirates! oh, the pirates!
    Oh, despair!

PIRATES.   Yes, yes, we are the pirates, so despair!
    (*They seize the* GENERAL.)

KING.   With base deceit
    You worked upon our feelings;
    Revenge is sweet,
    And flavors all our dealings.
    With courage rare,
    And resolution manly,
    For death prepare,
    Unhappy General Stanley!

FREDERIC (*coming forward*).   Alas! alas! unhappy General Stanley!

GENERAL.   Frederic here? Oh joy! oh rapture!—
    Summon your men and effect their capture.

MABEL.   Frederic, save us!

FREDERIC. Beautiful Mabel,
I would if I could, but I am not able.

PIRATES. He's telling the truth; he is not able.

POLICE (*pianissimo*). Tarantara! tarantara!
(*They bind the* GENERAL *to broken pillar.*)

MABEL (*wildly*). Is he to die, unshriven and un-
annealed?

GIRLS. Oh spare him!

MABEL. Will no one in his cause a weapon wield?

GIRLS. Oh spare him!

POLICE (*springing up*). Yes, we are here, though
hitherto concealed.

GIRLS. Oh, rapture!

POLICE. So to our powers, pirates, quickly yield!

GIRLS. Oh, rapture!

A struggle ensues between PIRATES *and* POLICE,
RUTH *tackling* SERGEANT. *Eventually the* POLICE
are overcome and fall prostrate, the PIRATES
standing over them with drawn swords.

ENSEMBLE.

PIRATES.	POLICE.
We triumph now, for well we trow	You triumph now, for well we trow
Your mortal career's cut short;	Our mortal career's cut short;
No pirate band will take its stand	No pirate band will take its stand
At the Central Criminal Court.	At the Central Criminal Court.

GENERAL. To gain a brief advantage you've contrived,
But your proud triumph will not be long-lived!

KING. Don't say you're orphans, for we know
that game.

SERGEANT. On your allegiance we've a stronger
claim:
We charge you yield, in Queen Victoria's name!

KING (*baffled*). You do?

POLICE. We do!
We charge you yield in Queen Victoria's name!
(PIRATES *kneel;* POLICE *stand over them
triumphantly.*)

KING. We yield at once with humbled mien,
Because, with all our faults, we love our queen.

POLICE. Yes, yes, with all their faults they love
their queen.
(POLICE, *holding* PIRATES *by the collar, take
out handkerchiefs and weep.*)

GENERAL. Away with them, and place them at
the bar!

RUTH. One moment; let me tell you who they
are.
They are no members of the common throng;
They are all noblemen who have gone wrong.

GENERAL, POLICE, *and* GIRLS. What! *All* noblemen?

KING *and* PIRATES. Yes, all noblemen!

GENERAL, POLICE, *and* GIRLS. What! All?

KING. Well, nearly all.

ALL. They are nearly all noblemen who have
gone wrong.
Then give three cheers, both loud and strong,
For the twenty noblemen who have gone wrong!
Then give three cheers, both loud and strong,
For the noblemen who have gone wrong!

GENERAL. No Englishman unmoved that statement hears,
Because, with all our faults, we love our House
of Peers! (*All kneel.*)

ALL. Hail, ever hail, O House of Peers!
To wisdom that mankind reveres
We listen with respectful ears,
For, oh! we love our House of Peers!
(*All rise. Each* PIRATE *takes a* GIRL.)

RECITATIVE — GENERAL.

I pray you pardon me, ex-pirate king;
Peers will be peers, and youth will have its fling.
Resume your ranks and legislative duties,
And take my daughters, all of whom are beau-
ties.

FINALE.

RUTH. At length we are provided, with unusual
facility,
To change piratic crime for dignified respectability.

KING. Combined, I needn't say, with the unparalleled felicity

Of what we have been longing for—unbounded domesticity.

MABEL. To-morrow morning early we will quickly be parsonified—
Hymeneally coupled, conjugally matrimonified.

SERGEANT. And this shall be accomplished by that doctor of divinity
Who happily resides in the immediate vicinity.

CHORUS. Who happily resides in the immediate vicinity.

GENERAL. My military knowledge, though I'm plucky and adventury,
Has only been brought down to the beginning of the century;
But still, in getting off my daughters—eight or nine or ten in all—
I've shown myself the model of a modern Major-General.

ALL.   His military knowledge, etc.

DANCE.

CURTAIN

Postscript

"RESPECTING THE PUBLICATION in advance of our New Opera," wrote Gilbert to the editor of *Scribner's Monthly,* June 11, 1879, "we have decided to keep both the score and the libretto in manuscript with the view of protecting, as effectually as possible, such rights as your Common Law may grant us. Under any circumstances we think the publication in advance would be an injudicious step, as calculated to deaden the interest that playgoers in the States may take in our work, when it comes to be placed upon the Stage."

A year later, in June 1880, as the first New York *Pirates* run ended, the *New York Times* accurately appraised the weakness of this strategy: "If the public had been afforded an opportunity to know something of the words and music of *The Pirates of Penzance,* and to become as familiar with it as was the case with *Pinafore,* the former opera would doubtless have met with more favor. It is undeniably a more amusing and meritorious work than *Pinafore,* but no one has ever read the words or learned the music, and the result has been that it has not become so popular as it deserved to be." But even when these observations were made, almost six months after the New York première, there was still no published libretto or vocal score on either side of the Atlantic. In fact there was none until—at the earliest—late October, ten months removed from the first "first night."

The full explanation of this unusual condition has never been made clear. Why did they wait so long? There seems little question that Gilbert, Sullivan, and D'Oyly Carte had entered into a seriously conceived and rigidly observed pact, probably on advice of their counsel. Even as late as April 16, 1880, almost two weeks after the first London performance, Gilbert wrote an unidentifiable journalist connected with the *World,* "I send you, herewith, a copy of *The Pirates.* I must ask you to let me have it back, at your convenience, as I am not allowed to give a copy away."

With manuscript librettos in existence at both J. M. Stoddart & Co. in Philadelphia, and Chappell & Co. in London—and with work-proofs being pulled for rehearsal purposes in both hemispheres for more than six months before publication—an accurate determination of the true first performance text must await evidence not yet uncovered. Certainly it was not the version heard at Paignton. Sullivan's own diary notation showed that this was shipped from New York to London on December 17 (fourteen days before the New York opening!), time enough for him and Gilbert to evolve quite a different libretto.

Part of the manuscript of one version of this New York libretto is now identifiable as the same from which Leslie Baily quoted and illustrated a few fragments in his *The Gilbert and Sullivan Book* (1952). His source could not be located four years later at the time *The First-Night Gilbert and Sullivan* was in preparation, but now has been rediscovered. It is of Act I alone, using the Paignton subtitle "Love and Duty," perhaps a clue in itself as this was the part of the new opera accidentally left behind in London and therefore needing to be rewritten in New York. Significantly, Gilbert had used the entire Fifth Avenue Theatre cast for his manuscript D.P. Secondly, his finale was almost verbatim that of the Act I finale of the first Stoddart libretto, which omits—whether deliberately or by oversight—the "Oh, happy day! with joyous glee" couplets for Mabel and the General, and the nine short lines that follow for Pirates, Frederic, and Ruth prior to the closing Ensemble. (See page 124.) Thirdly, Gilbert's autograph 5-line stage direction at End of Act I was used by Stoddart with but one word changed—"ecstasy" modified to "delight."

It is likely that this must have been very close to the Stoddart "original manuscripts"—in his files by his own admission (which was printed on the libretto jacket), and thus the basis for the New York première. Probably the twin of this manuscript accompanied Gilbert and Sullivan back to London in early March after two months of refinements, to become the basis for the Chappell edition, the first published work-book of the opera. This is the lone instance among Gilbert and Sullivan operas where the publication of the libretto was later than that of the first vocal score, a fact evidenced by the change in the corporate name of the printer. From the advertising can be deduced that neither vocal score nor libretto could have been published until after October 15, 1880. On that date Arthur Sullivan conducted the première of *The Martyr of Antioch* at the Leeds Festival (a portion of the text arranged by W. S. Gilbert!), and the music of this "Sacred Musical Drama" was advertised for sale in first editions of both these *Pirates* publications. To add confusion, both the vocal score and the British first libretto show casts on their D.P. pages (dated April 3, 1880) that are later than that of the first London performance.

It has already been established by the date of copyright that the first American libretto could not have been available for sale before December, eleven months from the New York first night. Most likely the British libretto was already out and copies in Stoddart's hands; for Stoddart released his own first edition with certain cuts that reflected the London version. For example, it lacked "Come, friends, who plough the sea!"—and carelessly omitted an important bit of the close of the first act. Both of these were quickly reinstated in a second American edition that immediately followed the first (but at the same time certain of the British textual refinements were made). The text that has been assembled in this first-night edition is, therefore, a hybrid that has never before appeared in print. It contains the Stoddart first American edition text, plus the portions shortly reinstated from the second edition but without the British refinements. In this way, it is hoped, the text is returned to an approximation of what the audience heard in New York on New Year's Eve, 1879.

It is interesting that for a time there were a British version and an American version of the opera libretto, both authorized by D'Oyly Carte. The American version certainly contained "Come, friends, who plough the sea!" The British libretto did not, through many issues and variants of two editions, *until the third edition* (after World War I), although this popular number had existed in the vocal score from its earliest publication. The American version had a completely different Finale to the second act that was probably never sung in London and was never published in England, although appearing in a prepublication proof copy. The American version contains the line, "A keener hand at scuttling a Cunarder or cutting out a White Star never shipped a handspike." But this was a change from the original Lord Chamberlain's and Gilbert's manuscript copies which had "P. & O." in place of "White Star." Undoubtedly and correctly Gilbert reasoned that Peninsula and Orient would not be as simple as ABC for the average American to recognize as a shipping line, while for any Britisher it was as simple as "P. &

O." So all the librettos on both sides of the Atlantic carried "White Star" for forty years, until the third British edition.

The minor differences between this first-night text and the libretto of current D'Oyly Carte production usage are too numerous to treat here. Ruth's solo verse, "Don't, beloved master" (page 116), has been cut, as has Frederic's solo, "Did ever pirate loathed" (page 120). In each instance, however, these lines are repeated in the immediately following ensembles. In the ensemble of "I'm telling a terrible story" (page 123) the last half of the pirates' portion is changed to conform to the part sung by the girls. And the verse, "For we all are orphan boys!," at the first-act curtain is dropped.

In the middle of the second act, after Mabel's ballad (which was misprinted "Oh leave me not to live" in the American first edition and so was even misquoted by some of the press), Mabel and Frederic have a second verse to their ensemble and Mabel has a recitative after Frederic's departure (see page 130). Both this second verse and recitative have been cut from later editions, along with the connecting lines that repeat "Farewell! Adieu!" Later, when the Police hear the Pirates approaching off-stage, their four-line verse about "burglarious elves"—a holdover from the Paignton text, occurring only in the American first edition and in the Lord Chamberlain's file copy—was immediately changed to the current well-known lines, "They come in force, with stealthy stride. . . ."

The "Ha! Ha! Ho! Ho!," the "Gurr! Gurr!" snoring noise, and the Policemen's "Tarantara's" are cut from between "A fly's footfall would be distinctly heard" and "Come, friends, who plough the sea!" There is a tightening-up of repetitious lines by Pirates and Police. The Pirate King's line, "His life is over," was only in the American first and second editions and then cut. When the Pirates surprise General Stanley and his daughters there is some rearrangement in order to cut Frederic's "Alas! alas! Unhappy General Stanley." And the battle cry of the Police was changed from "So to our powers . . ." to "So to our prowess" in the British first-edition libretto, and later to "So to constabulary" in the third and current editions.

The close of the opera, from Ruth's entrance—"One moment! Let me tell you who they are"—to the curtain, is so different in modern text and performance than in this first-night New York version that it is quoted below. This abbreviated ending, with a reprise of "Poor wand'ring one" in place of the patter-song type of Finale, is in current use and yet is almost identical with that of the first British edition:

Enter RUTH.

RUTH.   One moment! let me tell you who they are.
They are no members of the common
throng;
They are all noblemen who have gone
wrong!

GIRLS.   They are all noblemen, who have gone
wrong.

GEN.   No Englishman unmoved that statement
hears,
Because, with all our faults, we love our
House of Peers.

RECIT.—GENERAL

I pray you pardon me, ex-Pirate King,
Peers will be peers, and youth will have its fling.

Resume your ranks and legislative duties,
And take my daughters, all of whom are beauties.

FINALE.

Poor wandering ones!
Though ye have surely strayed,
Take heart of grace,
Your steps retrace,
Poor wandering ones!
Poor wandering ones!
If such poor love as ours
Can help you find
True peace of mind,
Why, take it, it is yours!

ALL.   Poor wandering ones! &c.

CURTAIN.

PATIENCE

Introduction

"I HAVE TO RE-WRITE the Sorcerer for early performance & I have to finish the new Libretto as soon as possible—& I have just had to begin it all over again after I had finished two-thirds of it."

Gilbert disclosed in this heretofore unpublished letter to his friend the critic Clement Scott, that at least at the date he wrote it—November 7, 1880—he considered the new opera on which he was working to be a rewrite of *The Sorcerer*. Bizarre as this might seem, it is believable and understandable. There is no question that *The Sorcerer* was originally inspired by his *Bab Ballad,* "The Rival Curates." It is also clear, from the outset of his work on the libretto that was to be *Patience,* that Gilbert was exploring the possibilities of expanding the theme of this same *Bab Ballad.* So, in the long summer of his indecision, 1880, it is entirely credible that his means of re-using "The Rival Curates" became, for a time, the rewriting and elaborating of *The Sorcerer.*

Isaac Goldberg gave a hint of this possibility (without knowing of the existence of the letter to Clement Scott) when he called attention to a comment about *The Sorcerer* in a *Punch* column entitled "Our Representative Man," March 16, 1878, in which the concept of amplifying the basic plot of *The Sorcerer* was comically envisaged. Goldberg wrote: "An early reviewer of *The Sorcerer,* commenting upon the boldness of placing a 'live burlesque Vicar on the stage,' was carried by his irreverent fancies to contemplate 'a Ballet of Bishops, or a Pastorale Symphony danced by Pew-openers to the accompaniment of Pan-Anglicans playing on pipes.' Perhaps had not Gilbert at the last moment changed his mind, we should have been treated to some such innovation . . . ." This passage from Goldberg's *The Story of Gilbert and Sullivan* occurs, not in the *Sorcerer* chapter, but significantly in the chapter he devotes to *Patience.*

There are other factors to be considered. Gil-

bert and D'Oyly Carte were fanatical in the lengths to which they would go to foil American pirates through confusion and secrecy. Two years later they permitted *Iolanthe* to be brought as far as final dress rehearsal under the pseudonym of *Perola* (see page 174) for no other reason than confusion to the enemy. So it may well be that Gilbert's reference to rewriting *The Sorcerer* was a deliberate red herring for Clement Scott to spread among the press. There is no evidence of any kind that the three partners had any concern with reviving *The Sorcerer* at this time, let alone rewriting it. Not until 1884 did Gilbert set about to alter a portion of its second act—in no sense a rewriting of the opera—for the first major Gilbert and Sullivan revival.

His reference to having finished two-thirds of the work and then having to begin it all over again jibes with a letter Gilbert wrote to Arthur Sullivan six days earlier, on November 1, 1880. "I want to see you particularly about the new piece. Although it is about two-thirds finished, I don't feel comfortable about it. I mistrust the clerical element. I feel hampered by the restrictions which the nature of the subject places upon my freedom of action, and I want to revert to my old idea of rivalry between two aesthetic fanatics, worshipped by a chorus of female aesthetics, instead of a couple of clergymen worshipped by a chorus of female devotees."

Twenty-one years later, for the introduction of a new American edition of *Patience,* Gilbert wrote: "The genesis of *Patience* is to be found in the *Bab Ballad* called 'The Rival Curates.' In the original draft of the MS. of my play, Reginald Bunthorne and Archibald Grosvenor were two clergymen belonging to adjoining parishes, as in the ballad [Gilbert had long forgotten any connection with *The Sorcerer*]. . . . While I was engaged upon the construction of this plot, I became uneasy at the thought of the danger I was incurring by dealing so freely with members of the clerical order, and I felt myself crippled at every turn by the necessity of protecting myself from a charge of irreverence." With this documented record of creative indecision there is no wonder the completion of the opera that was to follow *The Pirates* was so long delayed.

The new production was entitled *Patience,* and according to the *Era,* in a pun of the period, patience the first-nighters had to have in full measure, as Act I ran an hour and forty minutes. It might have added that the audience and D'Oyly Carte had to have ample patience long before that Saturday evening, April 23, through the many months of preparation. Indeed, D'Oyly Carte had expected Gilbert and Sullivan to have their next work ready for him in the autumn of 1880. But as is clear from Gilbert's correspondence, it was not till November that Gilbert had decided to focus his satire on the Aesthetic craze which had already been so admirably ridiculed editorially by *Punch* and caricatured in its illustrations by George du Maurier. This delay had permitted Francis Burnand to beat Gilbert to the boards with an extremely successful comedy, *The Colonel,* on this same theme of aestheticism.

Sullivan, on the other hand, after being deeply engrossed in his Sacred Musical Drama, *The Martyr of Antioch,* for the Leeds Festival in the autumn of 1880, had left for Nice, not to return until February. "The year 1881 opens while I am still at Nice," he wrote in his diary. "Having brought with me some numbers of the new opera Gilbert and I intend doing, I occasionally try to find a few ideas amongst them. . . . But my natural indolence, aided by the sunshine, prevents my doing any real work. I enjoy myself in the 'dolce far niente.' " A further distraction to both librettist and composer was inescapable when the trial of the case of D'Oyly Carte and Colleagues vs. the Comedy Opera Company began on March 10, 1881. So it is understandable why D'Oyly Carte felt it necessary to include in both the programs and the librettos of *Patience* in the hands of his opening-night audience the sentence—"The Management considers it advisable to state that the libretto of this opera was completed in November last."—And he could have added that it was not really begun till November, either.

"The new joint production of Mr. Arthur Sullivan and Mr. W. S. Gilbert was brought out here on Saturday evening," read the *Daily News* for Monday, April 25, 1881, and continued, "The great and prolonged success which has attended the previous instances of this collaboration . . . naturally led to a widespread public interest in the new effort of so distinguished a composer and so eminent a literary humorist; and, accordingly, the pretty theatre in the Strand was crowded in every part."

In the regular program that night, elaborately rubricated, it was noted that on Saturday, April 23, the forepiece *In the Sulks,* billed to precede *Patience* at eight o'clock on all other evenings, would be omitted. Although Arthur Sullivan conducted this first performance, the fact is not so stated in the program.

"Pending the arrival of Dr. Sullivan in the conductor's chair," wrote the sport reviewing for the *Sporting Times,* "I gazed with furtive curiosity on my neighbours, and confess that the presence of so many representatives of the Good, the Beautiful, and the True, filled me with surpassing awe. It was, indeed, a pretty sight to witness the enthusiasm with which Richard D'Oyly Carte greeted the advent of his friends and patrons," among whom he touched lightly on "Mr. George Lewis' pink rosebud," "the comfortable abandon of Mr. Stephen Coleman," "the severe but noble aspect of Mr. Alfred Watson," "Mr. Chappell, of the white whiskers, [who] furnishes the world with the book of *Patience,*" "the slate-coloured robe of Mrs. Arthur Lewis, erstwhile Kate Terry," "the charming combination of claret and yellow worn by Mrs. Marcus Stone."

Then, according to this same reporter, "a fierce clamour of screams, yells, and hisses, which descended from the Gallery," signaled the arrival of Oscar Wilde himself. "HIMSELF. . . . There with the sacred daffodil . . . stood the exponent of uncut hair . . . Ajax-like defying the gods!" Mention of his name was superfluous, for surely this description could hardly have referred to anyone else. Yet it is odd that no other reporter that night confirmed this newsworthy presence at the Opéra Comique, although his brother, William Wilde, was noted in the audience as a most presentable representative of the aristocracy.

The *Era* described the opera as "opening with a superb scene, the Exterior of Castle Bunthorne, painted by Mr. John O'Connor with remarkable skill and introducing some charming effects, one of those quaint medieval structures in which the modern aesthetic poet delights." Both the *Era* and the *Daily News* felt that the first act could stand a little cutting. Gilbert's own reaction was to cut out the second verse of the duet for Patience and Angela, beginning "Time fled, and one unhappy day," which was sung on opening night by Leonora Braham and Jessie Bond, but must have disappeared from performances early in the following week (see page 152).

At the close of Act I the principal performers took curtain calls while the effervescent gentleman from the *Sporting Times* recorded: "End of Act I. General enthusiasm for cigarettes and Chartreuse at the departure bar. Chorus of delight, accompanied by Frank Cellier, arises from the visitors . . . everyone goes about saying, 'Hey, willow waly, O.' Nobody knows what this means, but all say, 'Aesthetic, don't cher know.' "

"Nothing could be better than the song of Lady Jane at the opening of the second Act," was the *Era*'s appraisal of 'Silvered is the raven hair,' a sentiment shared by many. And in this act the critics also made special note of the trio for the Duke, the Colonel, and the Major, "who have doffed their uniforms and are dressed and made up in the aesthetic style, looking like figures cut out of a Pre-Raphaelite picture and vivified. The constrained attitudes, distorted positions, and grotesque gestures of the three, and the quaint music which they sing, produced a richly humorous effect." Thus the *Daily News*. Oddly enough, this trio does not appear to have been encored. But there were nine numbers which, according to the *Daily News,* were encored (Arthur Sullivan remembered only eight). In the first act these were "If you want a receipt for that popular mystery," "If you're anxious for to shine," "Prithee, pretty maiden," "I hear the soft note," and the ensemble *tutti* at its close. In the second act the encored numbers were "Silvered is the raven hair," "The magnet and the churn," "So go to him," and "When I go out of door." The *Daily News* reported that "applause and laughter were constantly alternated throughout the evening."

Mr. Gilbert's contribution, according to the *Era,* was "certainly very funny, and, although there will not be found, perhaps, such striking passages as in *Pinafore,* the current of drollery and whimsical illusion runs through the entire opera." The same critic thought Sullivan's music "just the kind

PUNCH *cartoon portrait of W. S. Gilbert on his yacht, "Chloris," by Linley Sambourne, August 6, 1881.*

we might expect from such a fluent and tuneful composer. The instrumentation is full of graceful passages, and conducted by the composer the band did ample justice to them."

The *Daily News* summed up the well-rounded success of the performance: "The composer's settings of the lyrical portions of Mr. Gilbert's witty satire are, in nearly every case, bright and melodious, and many of the numbers will undoubtedly be widely in request as soon as published. . . . The sentiment and grace of most of Mr. Sullivan's music give additional zest to the quaintness and humour of other portions, and there is little doubt that the combination of these qualities with the merits of Mr. Gilbert's book will secure a success as great as any that has hitherto resulted from the same cooperation."

The cast performed excellently. George Grossmith as Bunthorne "was quite in his element. He invested the character with a grotesque drollery, amusing in the extreme." So wrote the critic from the *Era,* who also found Rutland Barrington "well suited in the character of the Idyllic Poet" (Grosvenor). And the *Daily News* added in describing this pair that "the comic grimness of the first [had] been admirably contrasted by the mild simplicity of the other." The *Daily News* reported Richard Temple, the Colonel, "looked, sang, and acted well, as did the representatives of the other Dragoon Officers, Mr. F. Thornton as the Major, and Mr. D. Lely as the Lieutenant-Duke."

Miss Leonora Braham, in the title role, "appeared for the first time at this theatre, and rendered the pretty milkmaid uncommonly interesting," wrote the *Era,* and added: "Miss Braham may be warmly congratulated upon her success. She was quite an ideal milkmaid." The *Daily News* agreed that she "sang with brightness of voice and refinement of style, and acted with unaffected naïveté and grace." This same critic found Jessie Bond "a charming Lady Angela" who, together with Julia Gwynne (Lady Saphir) and Miss Fortescue (Lady Ella), "contributed much to the attractiveness of the principal group of 'rapturous maidens.' " Alice Barnett "sustained the character of the strong-minded Lady Jane with thorough appreciation of its musical and dramatic humour."

At the end of the opera, according to the *Era,* "the curtain fell amidst hearty applause, and Mr. Gilbert and Mr. Sullivan were called to the footlights and congratulated most emphatically upon their success. . . . Judging by the reception of the opera on the first night, we anticipate that no change will be required in the bill of the Opéra Comique during the present year." How right the gentleman from the *Era* was in this prediction!— and how wrong! In point of fact, the first run of *Patience* was for a total of 578 performances, but only the first 170 of these were destined to be on the stage of the Opéra Comique. For as these first-night reviews were being written, the opening of D'Oyly Carte's new Savoy Theatre was only thirty weeks removed.

APRIL 23 (SATURDAY) 1881. *Crammed house at Opéra Comique. Enthusiastic reception on entering the orchestra. New piece performed for first time. Went splendidly. Eight encores. Seemed a great success. Called at the Fielding* [Club] *for a lemon and soda.*

ARTHUR SULLIVAN'S DIARY

An Entirely New and Original Aesthetic Opera,

IN TWO ACTS,

ENTITLED

PATIENCE

OR,

BUNTHORNE'S BRIDE!

Dramatis Personae.

COLONEL CALVERLEY		MR. RICHARD TEMPLE.
MAJOR MURGATROYD	*Officers of Dragoon Guards*	MR. FRANK THORNTON.
LIEUT. THE DUKE OF DUNSTABLE		MR. DURWARD LELY.
REGINALD BUNTHORNE, *A Fleshly Poet*		MR. GEORGE GROSSMITH.
ARCHIBALD GROSVENOR, *An Idyllic Poet*		MR. RUTLAND BARRINGTON.
MR. BUNTHORNE'S SOLICITOR		MR. G. BOWLEY.

CHORUS OF OFFICERS OF DRAGOON GUARDS.

THE LADY ANGELA		MISS JESSIE BOND.
THE LADY SAPHIR	*Rapturous Maidens*	MISS JULIA GWYNNE.
THE LADY ELLA		MISS FORTESCUE.
THE LADY JANE		MISS ALICE BARNETT.

and

PATIENCE, *A Dairy Maid*   MISS LEONORA BRAHAM.

CHORUS OF RAPTUROUS MAIDENS.

ACT I. — Exterior of Castle Bunthorne.

ACT II. — A Glade.

PATIENCE

OR,

BUNTHORNE'S BRIDE!

ACT I.

SCENE. — *Exterior of Castle Bunthorne. Entrance to castle by draw-bridge over moat. Young ladies dressed in æsthetic draperies are grouped about the stage. They play on lutes, mandolins, &c., as they sing, and all are in the last stage of despair.* ANGELA, ELLA, *and* SAPHIR *lead them.*

CHORUS.

Twenty love-sick maidens we,
  Love-sick all against our will.
Twenty years hence we shall be,
  Twenty love-sick maidens still!

SOLO — ANGELA.

Love feeds on love, they say, or love will die—
ALL.   Ah, miserie!
  Yet my love lives, although no hope have I!
ALL.   Ah, miserie!
  Alas, poor heart, go hide thyself away—
ALL.   Ah, miserie!
  To weeping concords tune thy roundelay!
ALL.   Ah, miserie!

CHORUS.

All our love is all for one,
  Yet that love he heedeth not,
He is coy and cares for none,
  Sad and sorry is our lot!
      Ah, miserie!

SOLO — ELLA.

Go, breaking heart,
  Go, dream of love requited!
Go, foolish heart,
  Go, dream of lovers plighted;
Go, madcap heart,
  Go, dream of never waking;
And in thy dream
  Forget that thou art breaking!

ALL.   Ah, miserie!

ANGELA. There is a strange magic in this love of ours! Rivals as we all are in the affections of our Reginald, the very hopelessness of our love is a bond that binds us to one another!

SAPHIR. Jealousy is merged in misery. While he, the very cynosure of our eyes and hearts, remains icy insensible—what have we to strive for?

ELLA. The love of maidens is, to him, as interesting as the taxes!

SAPHIR. Would that it were! He pays his taxes.

ANGELA. And cherishes the receipts!

Enter LADY JANE.

JANE (*suddenly*). Fools!

ANGELA. I beg your pardon?

JANE. Fools and blind! The man loves—wildly loves!

ANGELA. But whom? None of us!

JANE. No, none of us. His weird fancy has lighted, for the nonce, on Patience—the village milkmaid!

SAPHIR. On Patience? Oh, it cannot be!

JANE. Bah! But yesterday I caught him in her dairy, eating fresh butter with a table-spoon. To-day he is not well!

SAPHIR. But Patience boasts that she has never loved—that love is, to her, a sealed book! Oh, he cannot be serious.

JANE. 'Tis but a passing fancy of the poet's— 'twill quickly pass away. (*Aside.*) Oh Reginald, if you but knew what a wealth of golden love is waiting for you, stored up in this rugged old bosom

of mine, the milkmaid's triumph would be short indeed! (*All sigh wearily.*)

PATIENCE *appears on an eminence. She looks down with pity on the despondent ladies.*

RECITATIVE — PATIENCE.

Still brooding on their mad infatuation!
    I thank thee, Love, thou comest not to me;
Far happier I, free from thy ministration,
    Than dukes or duchesses who love can be!

SAPHIR (*looking up*). 'Tis Patience—happy girl!
    Loved by a poet!

PATIENCE. Your pardon, ladies. I intrude upon you! (*Going.*)

ANGELA. Nay, pretty child, come hither.
        (PATIENCE *descends.*)   Is it true
That you have never loved?

PATIENCE.   Most true indeed.

SOPRANOS. Most marvellous!

CONTRALTOS.   And most deplorable!

SONG — PATIENCE.

I cannot tell what this love may be
That cometh to all but not to me.
It cannot be kind as they'd imply,
Or why do these gentle ladies sigh?
It cannot be joy and rapture deep,
Or why do these gentle ladies weep?
It cannot be blissful as 'tis said,
Or why are their eyes so wondrous red?

Though everywhere true love I see
A-coming to all, but not to me,
I cannot tell what this love may be!
    For I am blithe and I am gay,
    While they sit sighing all night, all day.
    Think of the gulf 'twixt them and me,
    "Fal la la la!"—and "Miserie!"

CHORUS.   Yes, she is blithe, &c.

PATIENCE.

If love is a thorn, they show no wit
Who foolishly hug and foster it.
If love is a weed, how simple they
Who gather and gather it, day by day!
If love is a nettle that makes you smart,
Why do you wear it next your heart?
And if it be none of these, say I,
Why do you sit and sob and sigh?
        Though everywhere, &c.

CHORUS.   For she is blithe, &c.

ANGELA. Ah, Patience, if you have never loved, you have never known true happiness! (*All sigh.*)

PATIENCE. But the truly happy seem to have so much on their minds. The truly happy never seem quite well.

JANE. There is a transcendentality of delirium—an acute accentuation of supremest ecstasy—which the earthy might easily mistake for indigestion. But it is *not* indigestion—it is æsthetic transfiguration! (*To the others.*) Enough of babble. Come!

PATIENCE. But I have some news for you. The 35th Dragoon Guards have halted in the village, and are even now on their way to this very spot.

ANGELA. The 35th Dragoon Guards!

SAPHIR. They are fleshly men, of full habit!

ELLA. We care nothing for Dragoon Guards!

PATIENCE. But, bless me, you were all in love with them a year ago!

SAPHIR. A year ago!

ANGELA. My poor child, you don't understand these things. A year ago they were very well in our eyes, but since then our tastes have been etherealized, our perceptions exalted. (*To others.*) Come! It is time to lift up our voices in morning carol to our Reginald. Let us to his door.

The ladies go off two and two into the Castle, singing refrain of "Twenty love-sick maidens we," and accompanying themselves on harps and mandolins.
PATIENCE *watches them in surprise, as she climbs the rock by which she entered.*

March.   Enter Officers of Dragoon Guards, led by MAJOR.

CHORUS OF DRAGOONS.

The soldiers of our Queen
   Are linked in friendly tether;
Upon the battle scene
   They fight the foe together.
There every mother's son
   Prepared to fight and fall is;
The enemy of one
   The enemy of all is!

Enter COLONEL.

SONG — COLONEL.

If you want a receipt for that popular mystery,
   Known to the world as a Heavy Dragoon,
Take all the remarkable people in history,
   Rattle them off to a popular tune.
The pluck of Lord Nelson on board of the Vic-
   tory—
   Genius of Bismarck devising a plan;
The humour of Fielding, (which sounds contra-
   dictory)—
   Coolness of Paget about to trepan—
The science of Jullien, the eminent musico—
   Wit of Macaulay, who wrote of Queen
   Anne—
The pathos of Paddy, as rendered by Bouci-
   cault—
   Style of the Bishop of Sodor and Man—
The dash of a D'Orsay, divested of quackery—
Narrative powers of Dickens and Thackeray—
Victor Emmanuel—peak-haunting Peveril—
Thomas Aquinas, and Doctor Sacheverell—
   Tupper and Tennyson—Daniel Defoe—
   Anthony Trollope and Mr. Guizot!
Take of these elements all that is fusible,
Melt them all down in a pipkin or crucible,
Set them to simmer and take off the scum,
And a Heavy Dragoon is the residuum!

CHORUS.   Yes! yes! yes! yes!
   A Heavy Dragoon is the residuum!

COLONEL.

If you want a receipt for this soldierlike paragon,
   Get at the wealth of the Czar (if you can)—
The family pride of a Spaniard from Aragon—
   Force of Mephisto pronouncing a ban—
A smack of Lord Waterford, reckless and rol-
   licky—
   Swagger of Roderick, heading his clan—
The keen penetration of Paddington Pollaky—
   Grace of an Odalisque on a divan,
The genius strategic of Cæsar or Hannibal—
Skill of Sir Garnet in thrashing a cannibal—
Flavour of Hamlet—the Stranger, a touch of
   him—
Little of Manfred (but not very much of him)—

Beadle of Burlington—Richardson's show—
Mr. Micawber and Madame Tussaud!
   Take of these elements all that is fusible—
   Melt 'em all down in a pipkin or crucible—
   Set 'em to simmer and take off the scum,
   And a Heavy Dragoon is the residuum!

ALL.   Yes! yes! yes! yes!
   A Heavy Dragoon is the residuum!

COLONEL.   Well, here we are again on the scene of our former triumphs. But where's the Duke?

Enter DUKE, *listlessly, and in low spirits.*

DUKE.   Here I am! (*Sighs.*)

COLONEL.   Come, cheer up, don't give way!

DUKE.   Oh, for that, I'm as cheerful as a poor devil can be expected to be, who has the misfortune to be a duke, with a thousand a day!

MAJOR.   Humph! Most men would envy you!

DUKE.   Envy *me?* Tell me, Major, are you fond of toffee?

MAJOR.   Very!

COLONEL.   We are all fond of toffee.

ALL.   We are!

DUKE.   Yes, and toffee in moderation is a capital thing. But to *live* on toffee—toffee for breakfast, toffee for dinner, toffee for tea—to have it supposed that you care for nothing *but* toffee, and that you would consider yourself insulted if anything but toffee were offered to you—how would you like *that?*

COLONEL.   I can believe that, under those circumstances, even toffee would become monotonous.

DUKE.   For "toffee" read flattery, adulation, and abject deference, carried to such a pitch that I began, at last, to think that man was born bent at an angle of forty-five degrees? Great heavens, what is there to adulate in me! Am I particularly intelligent, or remarkably studious, or excruciatingly witty, or unusually accomplished, or exceptionally virtuous?

COLONEL.   You're about as commonplace a young man as ever I saw.

ALL.   You are!

DUKE.   Exactly! That's it exactly! That describes me to a T! Thank you all very much! Well, I couldn't stand it any longer so I joined this regiment. In the army, thought I, I shall be occasionally snubbed, perhaps even bullied, who knows? The thought was rapture, and here I am.

COLONEL (*looking off*).   Yes, and here are the ladies!

DUKE.   But who is the gentleman with the long hair?

COLONEL.   I don't know.

DUKE. He seems popular!

COLONEL. He *does* seem popular!

BUNTHORNE *enters, followed by ladies, two and two, singing and playing on harps as before. He is composing a poem, and quite absorbed. He sees no one, but walks across stage, followed by ladies.*

COLONEL. Angela! (*Holding out his hands in greeting.*)

MAJOR. Saphir! (*Ditto.*)

They take no notice of Dragoons—to the surprise and indignation of those Officers.

CHORUS OF LADIES.

In a melancholy train
  Two and two we walk all day—
Pity those who love in vain
  None so sorrowful as they
    Who can only sigh and say,
    Woe is me, alackaday!

CHORUS OF DRAGOONS.

Now is not this ridiculous—and is not this pre-
  posterous?
  A thorough-paced absurdity—explain it if
    you can.
Instead of rushing eagerly to cherish us and fos-
  ter us,
  They all prefer this melancholy literary man.
    Instead of slyly peering at us,
    Casting looks endearing at us,
  Blushing at us, flushing at us—flirting with
    a fan;
  They're actually sneering at us, fleering at us,
    jeering at us!
Pretty sort of treatment for a military man!
Pretty sort of treatment for a military man!

ANGELA. Mystic poet, hear our prayer,
    Twenty love-sick maidens we—
    Young and wealthy, dark and fair—
    And we die for love of thee!

CHORUS. Yes, we die for love of thee—
    Twenty love-sick maidens we!

BUNTHORNE (*aside—slyly*). Though my book I
    seem to scan
    In a rapt ecstatic way,
    Like a literary man
    Who despises female clay,
    I hear plainly all they say,
    Twenty love-sick maidens they!

OFFICERS (*to each other*). He hears plainly, &c.

ELLA. Though so excellently wise,
    For a moment mortal be,

Deign to raise thy purple eyes
    From thy heart-drawn poesy.
  Twenty love-sick maidens see—
  Each is kneeling on her knee! (*All kneel.*)

CHORUS OF LADIES. Twenty love-sick, &c.

BUNTHORNE (*aside*). Though, as I remarked be-
  fore,
    Anyone convinced would be
  That some transcendental lore
    Is monopolizing me,
  Round the corner I can see
  Each is kneeling on her knee!

OFFICERS (*to each other*). Round the corner, &c.

ENSEMBLE.

OFFICERS. Now is not this ridiculous, &c.

LADIES. Mystic poet, hear our prayers, &c.

BUNTHORNE (*aside*). Though my book I seem
  to scan, &c.

COLONEL. Angela! what is the meaning of this?

ANGELA. Oh, sir, leave us; our minds are but ill-attuned to light love-talk.

MAJOR. But what in the world has come over you all?

JANE. Bunthorne! *He* has come over us. He has come among us, and he has idealized us.

DUKE. Has he succeeded in idealizing *you*?

JANE. He has!

DUKE. Bravo, Bunthorne!

JANE. My eyes are open; I despair droopingly; I am soulfully intense; I am limp and I cling!

During this BUNTHORNE *is seen in all the agonies of composition. The ladies are watching him intently as he writhes. At last, he hits on the word he wants and writes it down. A general sense of relief.*

BUNTHORNE. Finished! At last! Finished! (*He staggers, overcome with the mental strain, into arms of* COLONEL.)

COLONEL. Are you better now?

BUNTHORNE. Yes—oh, it's you—I beg your pardon—I am better now. The poem is finished, and my soul has gone out into it. That was all. It was nothing worth mentioning, it occurs three times a day. (*Sees* PATIENCE, *who has entered during this scene.*) Ah, Patience! Dear Patience! (*Holds her hand; she seems frightened.*)

ANGELA. Will it please you read it to us, sir?

SAPHIR. This we supplicate. (*All kneel.*)

BUNTHORNE. Shall I?

ALL THE DRAGOONS. No!

BUNTHORNE (*annoyed—to* PATIENCE). I will read it if *you* bid me!

PATIENCE (*much frightened*). You can if you like!

BUNTHORNE. It is a wild, weird, fleshly thing; yet very tender, very yearning, very precious. It is called, "Oh, Hollow! Hollow! Hollow!"

PATIENCE. Is it a hunting song?

BUNTHORNE. A hunting song? No, it is *not* a hunting song. It is the wail of the poet's heart on discovering that everything is commonplace. To understand it, cling passionately to one another

and think of faint lilies! (*They do so as he recites.*)

"OH, HOLLOW! HOLLOW! HOLLOW!"

What time the poet hath hymned
The writhing maid, lithe-limbed,
   Quivering on amaranthine asphodel,
How can he paint her woes,
Knowing, as well he knows,
   That all can be set right with calomel?

When from the poet's plinth
The amorous colocynth
   Yearns for the aloe, faint with rap-
      turous thrills,
How can he hymn their throes
Knowing as well he knows
   That they are only uncompounded pills?

Is it, and can it be,
Nature hath this decree,
   Nothing poetic in the world shall dwell?
Or that in all her works
Something poetic lurks,
   Even in colocynth and calomel?
               I cannot tell.

ANGELA. How purely fragrant!

SAPHIR. How earnestly precious!

DUKE. Well, it seems to me to be nonsense.

SAPHIR. Nonsense, yes, perhaps—but oh, what precious nonsense!

ALL. Ah!

COLONEL. This is all very well, but you seem to forget that you are engaged to us!

SAPHIR. It can never be. You are not Empyrean. You are not Della Cruscan. You are not even Early English. Oh, be Early English ere it is too late! (*Officers look at each other in astonishment.*)

JANE (*looking at uniform*). Red and yellow! Primary colours! Oh, South Kensington!

DUKE. We didn't design our uniforms, but we don't see how they could be improved.

JANE. No, you wouldn't. Still there *is* a cob-webby grey velvet, with a tender bloom like cold gravy, which, made Florentine fourteenth century, trimmed with Venetian leather and Spanish altar lace, and surmounted with something Japanese—it matters not what—would at least be Early English! Come, maidens.

Exeunt maidens, two and two, singing refrain of "Twenty love-sick maidens we." The Officers watch them off in astonishment.

DUKE. Gentlemen, this is an insult to the British uniform—

MAJOR. A uniform that is accustomed to carry everything before it!

COLONEL. A uniform that has been as successful in the courts of Venus as on the field of Mars!

SONG — COLONEL.

When I first put this uniform on,
    I said, as I looked in the glass,
        "It's one to a million
        That any civilian,
    My figure and form will surpass.
      Gold lace has a charm for the fair,
      And I've plenty of that, and to spare,
        While a lover's professions,
        When uttered in Hessians,
    Are eloquent everywhere!"
        A fact that I counted upon,
        When I first put this uniform on!

CHORUS OF DRAGOONS.

By a simple coincidence, few
    Could ever have reckoned upon,
The same thing occurred to me, too,
    When I first put this uniform on!

COLONEL.

I said, when I first put it on,
    "It is plain to the veriest dunce
        That every beauty
        Will feel it her duty
    To yield to its glamour at once.
      They will see that I'm freely gold-laced
      In a uniform handsome and chaste"—
        But the peripatetics
        Of long-haired æsthetics,
    Are very much more to their taste—
        Which I never counted upon
        When I first put this uniform on!

CHORUS.

By a simple coincidence few
    Could ever have counted upon,
I didn't anticipate that,
    When I first put this uniform on!
        (*The Dragoons go off angrily.*)

As soon as he is alone, BUNTHORNE *changes his manner and becomes intensely melodramatic.*

RECITATIVE AND SONG — BUNTHORNE.

Am I alone,
    And unobserved? I am!
Then let me own
    I'm an æsthetic sham!
This air severe
    Is but a mere
        Veneer!
This cynic smile
    Is but a wile
        Of guile!

This costume chaste
    Is but good taste
        Misplaced!

Let me confess!
A languid love for lilies does *not* blight me!
Lank limbs and haggard cheeks do *not* delight me!
    I do *not* care for dirty greens
        By any means.
    I do *not* long for all one sees
        That's Japanese.
    I am *not* fond of uttering platitudes
        In stained-glass attitudes.
    In short, my mediævalism 's affectation,
    Born of a morbid love of admiration!

SONG.

If you're anxious for to shine in the high æsthetic
    line as a man of culture rare,
You must get up all the germs of the transcenden-
    tal terms, and plant them everywhere.
You must lie upon the daisies and discourse in
    novel phrases of your complicated state of
    mind,
The meaning doesn't matter if it's only idle chatter
    of a transcendental kind.
        And every one will say,
        As you walk your mystic way,
"If this young man expresses himself in terms too
    deep for *me*,
Why, what a very singularly deep young man this
    deep young man must be!"

Be eloquent in praise of the very dull old days
    which have long since passed away,
And convince 'em, if you can, that the reign of
    good Queen Anne was Culture's palmiest
    day.
Of course you will pooh-pooh whatever's fresh
    and new, and declare it's crude and mean,
For Art stopped short in the cultivated court of the
    Empress Josephine.
        And every one will say,
        As you walk your mystic way,
"If that's not good enough for him which is good
    enough for *me*,
Why, what a very cultivated kind of youth this
    kind of youth must be!"

Then a sentimental passion of a vegetable fashion
    must excite your languid spleen,
An attachment *à la* Plato for a bashful young po-
    tato, or a not-too-French French bean!
Though the Philistines may jostle, you will rank
    as an apostle in the high æsthetic band,
If you walk down Piccadilly with a poppy or a lily
    in your mediæval hand.
        And every one will say,

As you walk your flowery way,
"If he's content with a vegetable love which would
    certainly not suit *me*,
Why, what a most particularly pure young man
    this pure young man must be!"

At the end of his song PATIENCE *enters.*
He sees her.

BUNTHORNE. Ah! Patience, come hither. I am pleased with thee. The bitter-hearted one, who finds all else hollow, is pleased with thee. For you are not hollow. *Are* you?

PATIENCE. I beg your pardon—I interrupt you.

BUNTHORNE. Life is made up of interruptions. The tortured soul, yearning for solitude, writhes under them. Oh, but my heart is a-weary! Oh, I am a cursed thing! Don't go.

PATIENCE. Really, I'm very sorry—

BUNTHORNE. Tell me, girl, do you ever yearn?

PATIENCE (*misunderstanding him*). I earn my living.

BUNTHORNE (*impatiently*). No, no! Do you know what it is to be heart-hungry? Do you know what it is to yearn for the Indefinable, and yet to be brought face to face, daily, with the Multiplication Table? Do you know what it is to seek oceans and to find puddles?—to long for whirlwinds and to have to do the best you can with the bellows? That's my case. Oh, I am a cursed thing!

PATIENCE. If you please, I don't understand you —you frighten me!

BUNTHORNE. Don't be frightened—it's only poetry.

PATIENCE. If that's poetry, I don't like poetry.

BUNTHORNE (*eagerly*). Don't you? (*Aside.*) Can I trust her? (*Aloud.*) Patience, you don't like poetry—well, between you and me, *I* don't like poetry. It's hollow, unsubstantial—unsatisfactory. What's the use of yearning for Elysian Fields when you know you can't get 'em, and would only let 'em out on building leases if you had 'em?

PATIENCE. Sir, I—

BUNTHORNE. Don't go. Patience, I have long loved you—let me tell you a secret. I am not as bilious as I look. If you like I will cut my hair. There is more innocent fun within me than a casual spectator would imagine. You have never seen me frolicsome. Be a good girl—a very good girl— and you shall.

PATIENCE. Sir, I will speak plainly. In the matter of love I am untaught, I have never loved but my great-aunt. But I am quite certain that, under any circumstances, I couldn't possibly love *you*.

BUNTHORNE. Oh, you think not?

PATIENCE. I'm quite sure of it. Quite sure. Quite.

BUNTHORNE. Very good. Life is henceforth a blank. I have only to ask that you will not abuse my confidence: though *you* despise me, I am extremely popular with the other young women.

PATIENCE. I only ask that you will leave me and never renew the subject.

BUNTHORNE. Certainly. Broken-hearted and desolate, I go. What is to become of me? (*Recites.*)

Oh, to be wafted away,
    From this black Aceldama of sorrow,
Where the dust of an earthy to-day
    Is the earth of a dusty to-morrow!

It is a little thing of my own. I call it "Heart Foam." I shall not publish it. Farewell!
                            (*Exit* BUNTHORNE.)

PATIENCE. What does it all mean? Why does he love me? Why does he expect me to love him? He's not a relation! It frightens me!

Enter ANGELA.

ANGELA. Why, Patience, what is the matter?

PATIENCE. Lady Angela, tell me two things. Firstly, what on earth is this love that upsets everybody; and secondly, how is it to be distinguished from insanity?

ANGELA. Poor blind child! Oh, forgive her, Eros! Why, love is of all passions the most essential! It is the embodiment of purity, the abstraction of refinement, the idealization of utter unselfishness!

PATIENCE. Love is?

ANGELA. Yes.

PATIENCE. Dear me. Go on.

ANGELA. True love refines, purifies, elevates, exalts, and chastens. It is the one romantic feature in this chaos of materialism; it is the one unselfish emotion in this whirlpool of grasping greed!

PATIENCE. Oh, dear! oh! (*Beginning to cry.*)

ANGELA. Why are you crying?

PATIENCE. To think that I have lived all these years without having experienced this ennobling and unselfish passion! Why, what a wicked girl I must be! For it *is* unselfish, isn't it?

ANGELA. Absolutely. Love that is tainted with selfishness is no love. Oh, try, try, try to love! It really isn't difficult if you give your whole mind to it.

PATIENCE. I'll set about it at once. I won't go to bed until I'm head over ears in love with somebody.

ANGELA. Noble girl. But is it possible that you have never loved anybody?

PATIENCE. Only my great-aunt.

ANGELA. Your great-aunt don't count.

PATIENCE. Then there's nobody. At least—no, nobody. Not since I was a baby. But *that* don't count.

ANGELA. I don't know—tell me all about it.

DUET — PATIENCE *and* ANGELA.

PATIENCE. Long years ago, fourteen, maybe,
     When but a tiny babe of four,
   Another baby played with me,
     My elder by a year or more.
   A little child of beauty rare,
   With marvellous eyes and wondrous hair,
   Who, in my child-eyes, seemed to me
   All that a little child should be!
       Ah, how we loved, that child and I,
         How pure our baby joy!
       How true our love—and, by the bye,
         He was a little boy!

ANGELA. Ah, old, old tale of Cupid's touch!
     I thought as much—I thought as much!
       He *was* a little boy!

PATIENCE (*shocked*). Pray don't misconstrue
       what I say—
     Remember, pray—remember, pray,
       He was a *little* boy!

ANGELA. No doubt, yet spite of all your pains,
     The interesting fact remains—
       He was a little *boy!*

ENSEMBLE.

{ Ah, yes / No doubt } in spite of all { my / her } pains, &c.

PATIENCE. Time fled, and one unhappy day—
     The first I'd ever known—
   They took my little friend away,
     And left me weeping all alone!
   Ah, how I sobbed, and how I cried,
   Then I fell ill and nearly died,
   And even now I weep apace
   When I recall that baby face!
       We had one hope—one heart—one
         will—
       One life, in one employ;
     And, though it's not material, still
       He was a little *boy!*

ANGELA. Ah, old, old tale of Cupid's touch, &c.

PATIENCE. Pray don't misconstrue what I say, &c.

ANGELA. No doubt, yet spite of all your pains, &c.

PATIENCE. Ah, yes, in spite of all my pains, &c.

     (*At end of Duet exit* ANGELA.)

PATIENCE. It's perfectly appalling to think of the dreadful state I must be in! I had no idea that love was a duty. No wonder they all look so unhappy. Upon my word, I hardly like to associate with myself. I don't think I'm respectable. I'll go at once and fall in love with—(*Enter* GROSVENOR.) A stranger!

DUET — PATIENCE *and* GROSVENOR.

GROSVENOR. Prithee, pretty maiden—prithee tell
       me true,
     (Hey, but I am doleful, willow willow waly!)
   Have you e'er a lover a-dangling after you?
       Hey willow waly O!
         I would fain discover
         If you have a lover?
       Hey willow waly O!

PATIENCE. Gentle sir, my heart is frolicsome and
       free—
     (Hey but he's doleful, willow willow waly!)
   Nobody I care for comes a-courting me—
       Hey willow waly O!
         Nobody I care for
         Comes a-courting—therefore,
       Hey willow waly O!

GROSVENOR. Prithee, pretty maiden, will you
       marry me?
     (Hey, but I'm hopeful, willow willow waly!)
   I may say, at once, I'm a man of propertee—
       Hey willow waly O!

> Money, I despise it,
> But many people prize it,
> Hey willow waly O!

PATIENCE.   Gentle sir, although to marry I design—
> (Hey, but he's hopeful—willow willow waly!)
> As yet I do not know you, and so I must decline.
> Hey willow waly O!
> To other maidens go you—
> As yet I do not know you,
> Hey willow waly O!

GROSVENOR.   Patience! Can it be that you don't recognize me?

PATIENCE.   Recognize you? No, indeed I don't!

GROSVENOR.   Have fifteen years so greatly changed me?

PATIENCE.   Fifteen years? What do you mean?

GROSVENOR.   Have you forgotten the friend of your youth, your Archibald?—your little play-fellow? Oh, Chronos, Chronos, this is too bad of you!

PATIENCE.   Archibald! Is it possible? Why, let me look! It is! It is! It must be! Oh, how happy I am! I thought we should never meet again! And how you've grown!

GROSVENOR.   Yes, Patience, I am much taller and much stouter than I was.

PATIENCE.   And how you've improved!

GROSVENOR.   Yes, Patience, I am very beautiful! (*Sighs.*)

PATIENCE.   But surely *that* don't make you un-happy?

GROSVENOR.   Yes, Patience. Gifted as I am with a beauty which probably has not its rival on earth —I am, nevertheless, utterly and completely mis-erable.

PATIENCE.   Oh—but why?

GROSVENOR.   My child-love for you has never faded. Conceive, then, the horror of my situation when I tell you that it is my hideous destiny to be madly loved by every woman who sets eyes on me!

PATIENCE.   Horrible indeed!

GROSVENOR.   Ah, Patience, you may thank your stars that *you* are not cursed with the fatal gift of beauty! It has been my bane through life!

PATIENCE.   But why do you make yourself so pic-turesque? Why not disguise yourself, disfigure yourself, anything to escape this persecution?

GROSVENOR.   No, Patience, that may not be. These gifts—irksome as they are—have been con-fided to me for the enjoyment and delectation of my fellow-creatures. I am a trustee for Beauty, and it is my duty to see that the conditions of my trust are faithfully discharged.

PATIENCE.   And you, too, are a Poet?

GROSVENOR.   Yes, I am the Apostle of Simplicity. I am called "Archibald the All-Right"—for I am infallible!

PATIENCE.   And is it possible that you conde-scend to love such a girl as I?

GROSVENOR.   Yes, Patience, is it not strange? I have loved you with a Florentine fourteenth-cen-tury frenzy for full fifteen years!

PATIENCE.   Oh, marvellous! I have hitherto been deaf to the voice of love—I seem now to know what love is! It has been revealed to me—it is Archibald Grosvenor!

GROSVENOR.   Yes, Patience, it is! (*Embrace.*)

PATIENCE (*as in a trance*).   The purifying gift— the ennobling influence has descended upon me, and I am inconceivably happy! We will never, never part!

GROSVENOR.   We will live and die together!

PATIENCE.   I swear it!

GROSVENOR.   We both swear it! (*Embrace.*)

PATIENCE (*recoiling from him*).   But—oh horror!

GROSVENOR.   What's the matter?

PATIENCE.   Why, you are perfection! Incompar-ably beautiful in body and in mind! A source of endless ecstasy to all who know you!

GROSVENOR.   I know I am—well?

PATIENCE.   Then, bless my heart, there can be nothing unselfish in loving *you!*

GROSVENOR.   Merciful powers, I never thought of that!

PATIENCE.   To monopolize those features on which all women love to linger; to keep to myself those attributes which were designed for the en-joyment and delectation of my fellow creatures? It would be unpardonable!

GROSVENOR.   Too true! Oh, fatal perfection, again you interpose between me and my happiness!

PATIENCE.   Oh, if you were but a thought less beautiful than you are!

GROSVENOR.   Would that I were; but candour compels me to admit that I'm not!

PATIENCE.   Our duty is clear; we must part, and for ever!

GROSVENOR.   Oh, misery! And yet I cannot ques-tion the propriety of your decision. Farewell, Pa-tience!

PATIENCE.   Farewell, Archibald! But stay!

GROSVENOR.   Yes, Patience?

PATIENCE.   Although I may not love *you*—for you are perfect—there is nothing to prevent your loving *me*. I am plain, homely, unattractive!

GROSVENOR.   Why, that's true!

PATIENCE. The love of such a man as you for such a girl as I must be unselfish!

GROSVENOR. Unselfishness itself!

DUET — PATIENCE and GROSVENOR.

PATIENCE. Though to marry you would very selfish be—

GROSVENOR. Hey, but I'm doleful—willow willow waly!

PATIENCE. You may all the same continue loving me—

GROSVENOR. Hey, but I'm doleful—willow willow waly!

BOTH.

All the world ignoring,
$\left\{\begin{array}{l}\text{You}\\\text{I'll}\end{array}\right\}$ go on adoring—
Hey willow waly O!

(*At the end, exeunt despairingly, in opposite directions.*)

Enter BUNTHORNE *crowned with roses and hung about with garlands, and looking very miserable. He is led by* ANGELA *and* SAPHIR (*each of whom holds an end of the rose-garland by which he is bound*), *and accompanied by procession of maidens. They are dancing classically, and playing on cymbals, double pipes, and other archaic instruments.*

CHORUS.

Let the merry cymbals sound,
    Gaily pipe Pandæan pleasure,
With a Daphnephoric bound
    Tread a gay but classic measure.

Every heart with hope is beating,
For at this exciting meeting
    Fickle Fortune will decide
    Who shall be our Bunthorne's bride!

Enter Dragoons, led by COLONEL, MAJOR, *and* DUKE. *They are surprised at proceedings.*

CHORUS OF DRAGOONS.

Now tell us, we pray you,
Why thus you array you—
Oh, poet, how say you—
    What is it you've done?

DUKE. Of rite sacrificial,
    By sentence judicial,
    This seems the initial,
        Then why don't you run?

COLONEL. They cannot have led you
    To hang or behead you,
    Nor may they *all* wed you,
        Unfortunate one!

CHORUS OF DRAGOONS.

Then tell us, we pray you,
Why thus they array you—
Oh, poet, how say you—
    What is it you've done?

RECITATIVE — BUNTHORNE.

Heart-broken at my Patience's barbarity,
    By the advice of my solicitor (*introducing his solicitor*),
In aid—in aid of a deserving charity,
    I've put myself up to be raffled for!

MAIDENS. By the advice of his solicitor
    He's put himself up to be raffled for!

DRAGOONS. Oh, horror! urged by his solicitor,
    He's put himself up to be raffled for!

MAIDENS. Oh, heaven's blessing on his solicitor!

DRAGOONS. A hideous curse on his solicitor!
    (*The Solicitor, horrified at the Dragoons' curse, rushes off.*)

COLONEL. Stay, we implore you,
    Before our hopes are blighted!
You see before you
    The men to whom you're plighted!

CHORUS OF DRAGOONS.

Stay, we implore you,
For we adore you;
To us you're plighted
To be united—
    Stay, we implore you!

SOLO — DUKE.

Your maiden hearts, ah, do not steel
To pity's eloquent appeal,
Such conduct British soldiers feel.
(*Aside to Dragoons.*)   Sigh, sigh, all sigh!
                    (*They all sigh.*)

To foeman's steel we rarely see
A British soldier bend the knee,
Yet, one and all, they kneel to ye—
(*Aside to Dragoons.*)   Kneel, kneel, all kneel!
                    (*They all kneel.*)

Our soldiers very seldom cry,
And yet—I need not tell you why—
A tear-drop dews each martial eye!
(*Aside to Dragoons.*)   Weep, weep, all weep!
                    (*They all weep.*)

ENSEMBLE.

Our soldiers very seldom cry
And yet—I need not tell you why—
A tear-drop dews each manly eye!
Weep, weep, all weep!

BUNTHORNE (*who has been impatient during this
    appeal*). Come walk up, and purchase
    with avidity,
Overcome your diffidence and natural timidity,
Tickets for the raffle should be purchased with
    avidity,
    Put in half a guinea and a husband you may
        gain—
Such a judge of blue-and-white, and other kinds
    of pottery—
From early Oriental, down to modern terra-cot-
    ta-ry—
Put in half a guinea—you may draw him in a
    lottery—

Such an opportunity may not occur again.

CHORUS.   Such a judge of blue and white, &c.

*Maidens crowd up to purchase tickets—during
this Dragoons dance in single file around stage—
to express their indifference.*

DRAGOONS.   We've been thrown over, we're aware,
        But we don't care—but we don't care!
        There's fish in the sea, no doubt of it,
        As good as ever came out of it,
        And some day we shall get our share,
        So we don't care—so we don't care!

*During this, the girls have been buying tickets. At
last,* JANE *presents herself.* BUNTHORNE *looks at
her with aversion.*

RECITATIVE.

BUNTHORNE.   And are *you* going a ticket for to
buy?

JANE (*surprised*).   Most certainly I am; why
should not I?

BUNTHORNE (*aside*).   Oh, Fortune, this is hard!
    (*Aloud.*) Blindfold your eyes;
Two minutes will decide who wins the prize!
                (*Girls blindfold themselves.*)

CHORUS OF MAIDENS.

Oh, Fortune, to my aching heart be kind;
Like us, thou art blindfolded, but not blind!
                (*Each uncovers one eye.*)
Just raise your bandage, thus, that you may see,
And give the prize, and give the prize to me!
                (*They cover their eyes again.*)

BUNTHORNE.   Come, Lady Jane, I pray you draw
the first!

JANE (*joyfully*). He loves me best!

BUNTHORNE (*aside*). I want to know the worst!

JANE *draws a paper, and is about to open it, when* PATIENCE *enters.* PATIENCE *snatches paper from* JANE *and tears it up.*

PATIENCE. Hold! Stay your hand!

ALL (*uncovering their eyes*). What means this interference?
  Of this bold girl I pray you make a clearance!

JANE. Away with you, and to your milk-pails go!

BUNTHORNE (*suddenly*). She wants a ticket! Take a dozen!!!

PATIENCE.   No!

SOLO — PATIENCE *kneeling to* BUNTHORNE.

If there be pardon in your breast
  For a poor penitent,
Who with remorseful thought opprest,
  Sincerely doth repent,
If you, with one so lowly, still
  Desire to be allied,
Then you may take me, if you will,
  For I will be your bride!

ALL.   Oh, shameless one!
        Oh, boldfaced thing!
      Away you run—
        Go, take you wing,
      You shameless one!
        You boldfaced thing!

BUNTHORNE. How strong is love! For many and many a week,
She's loved me fondly and has feared to speak,
But Nature, for restraint too mighty far,
Has burst the bonds of Art—and here we are!

PATIENCE. No, Mr. Bunthorne, no—you're wrong again,
Permit me—I'll endeavour to explain!

SONG — PATIENCE.

                True love must single-hearted be—
BUNTHORNE.   Exactly so!
PATIENCE. From every selfish fancy free—
BUNTHORNE.   Exactly so!
PATIENCE. No idle thought of gain or joy,
        A maiden's fancy should employ—
        True love must be without alloy.
ALL.   Exactly so!
PATIENCE. Imposture to contempt must lead—
COLONEL.   Exactly so—
PATIENCE. Blind vanity's dissension's seed—
MAJOR.   Exactly so—
PATIENCE. It follows then, a maiden who

Devotes herself to loving *you*
        (*indicating* BUNTHORNE)
  Is prompted by no selfish view!

ALL.   Exactly so—

SAPHIR (*taking* BUNTHORNE *aside*). Are you resolved to wed this shameless one?

ANGELA. Is there no chance for any other?

BUNTHORNE (*decisively*).   None!
                    (*Embraces* PATIENCE.)

ANGELA, SAPHIR, *and* ELLA *take* COLONEL, DUKE, *and* MAJOR *down, while girls gaze fondly at other Officers.*

SESTETTE.

I hear the soft note of the echoing voice
  Of an old old love, long dead—
It whispers my sorrowing heart "rejoice"—
  For the last sad tear is shed—
The pain that is all but a pleasure we'll change
  For the pleasure that's all but pain,
And never, oh, never, this heart will range
  From that old old love again!
                (*Girls embrace Officers.*)

CHORUS. Yes, the pain that is all, &c. (*Embrace.*)

As the Dragoons and Girls are embracing, enter GROSVENOR, *reading. He takes no notice of them but comes slowly down, still reading. The Girls are all strangely fascinated by him and gradually withdraw from Dragoons.*

ANGELA. But who is this, whose god-like grace
        Proclaims he comes of noble race;
        And who is this whose manly face
        Bears sorrow's interesting trace?

ENSEMBLE — TUTTI.

Yes, who is this, &c.

GROSVENOR. I am a broken-hearted troubadour,
        Whose mind's æsthetic and whose tastes are pure!

ANGELA. Æsthetic! He is æsthetic!

GROSVENOR. Yes, yes—I am æsthetic
        And poetic!

ALL THE LADIES. Then, we love you!

The Girls leave Dragoons and group, kneeling, around GROSVENOR. *Fury of* BUNTHORNE, *who recognizes a rival.*

DRAGOON. They love him! Horror!

BUNTHORNE *and* PATIENCE. They love him! Horror!

GROSVENOR. They love me! Horror! Horror! Horror!

ENSEMBLE — TUTTI.

GIRLS.

Oh, list while we a love confess
That words imperfectly express,
Those shell-like ears, ah, do not close
To blighted love's distracting woes!
Nor be distressed, nor scandalized
If what we do is ill-advised,
Or we shall seek within the tomb
Relief from our appalling doom!

PATIENCE.

List, Reginald, while I confess
A love that's all unselfishness;
That it's unselfish, goodness knows,
You won't dispute it, I suppose.
For you are hideous—undersized,
And everything that I've despised,
And I shall love you, I presume,
Until I sink into the tomb!

GROSVENOR.

Again my cursed comeliness
Spreads hopeless anguish and distress;
Thine ears, oh, Fortune, do not close
To my intolerable woes.
Let me be hideous, undersized,
Contemned, degraded, loathed, despised,
Or bid me seek within the tomb
Relief from my detested doom!

BUNTHORNE.

My jealousy I can't express,
Their love they openly confess,
His shell-like ear he does not close
To their recital of their woes—
I'm more than angry and surprised,
I'm pained, and shocked, and scandalized,
But he shall meet a hideous doom
Prepared for him by—I know whom!

ACT DROP

ACT II.

SCENE. — *A glade. In the centre a small sheet of water.* JANE *is discovered leaning on a violoncello, upon which she presently accompanies herself.*

JANE.   The fickle crew have deserted Reginald and transferred their allegiance to his rival, and all, forsooth, because he has glanced with passing favour on a puling milkmaid! Fools! of that fancy he will soon weary—and then I, who alone am faithful to him, shall reap my reward. But do not dally too long, Reginald, for I am ripe, Reginald, and already I am decaying. Better secure me ere I have gone too far!

RECITATIVE — JANE.

Sad is that woman's lot who, year by year,
Sees, one by one, her beauties disappear,
When Time, grown weary of her heart-drawn
     sighs,
Impatiently begins to "dim her eyes"!
Compelled, at last, in life's uncertain gloamings,
To wreathe her wrinkled brow with well saved
     "combings,"
Reduced, with rouge, lip-salve and pearly grey,
To "make up" for lost time as best she may!

SONG — JANE.

Silvered is the raven hair—
     Spreading is the parting straight,
Mottled the complexion fair,

Halting is the youthful gait.
  Hollow is the laughter free,
  Spectacled the limpid eye,
  Little will be left of me,
    In the coming bye and bye!

Fading is the taper waist—
  Shapeless grows the shapely limb,
And although securely laced,
  Spreading is the figure trim!
Stouter than I used to be,
  Still more corpulent grow I—
There will be too much of me
  In the coming bye and bye!   (*Exit.*)

Enter GROSVENOR *followed by maidens, two and two, each playing on an archaic instrument, as in Act I. He is reading abstractedly, as* BUNTHORNE *did in Act I, and pays no attention to them.*

CHORUS OF MAIDENS.

Turn, oh, turn in this direction,
  Shed, oh shed a gentle smile,
With a glance of sad perfection
  Our poor fainting hearts beguile!
On such eyes as maidens cherish
  Let thy fond adorers gaze,
Or incontinently perish,
  In their all-consuming rays!
      (*He sits—they group around him.*)

GROSVENOR (*aside*).   The old, old tale. How rapturously these maidens love me, and how hopelessly! Oh, Patience, Patience, with the love of thee in my heart, what have I for these poor mad maidens but an unvalued pity? Alas, they will die of hopeless love for me, as I shall die of hopeless love for thee!

ANGELA.   Sir, will it please you read to us?
      (*Kneels.*)

GROSVENOR (*sighing*).   Yes, child, if you will. What shall I read?

ANGELA.   One of your own poems.

GROSVENOR.   One of my own poems? Better not, my child. *They* will not cure thee of thy love.

ELLA.   Mr. Bunthorne used to read us a poem of his own every day.

SAPHIR.   And, to do him justice, he read them extremely well.

GROSVENOR.   Oh, did he so? Well, who am I that I should take upon myself to withhold my gifts from you? What am I but a trustee? Here is a decalet—a pure and simple thing, a very daisy—a babe might understand it. To appreciate it it is not necessary to think of anything at all.

ANGELA.   Let us think of nothing at all!

GROSVENOR *recites*.

Gentle Jane was as good as gold,
She always did as she was told.
She never spoke when her mouth was full,
Or caught blue-bottles their legs to pull;
Or spilt plum jam on her nice new frock,
Or put white mice in the eight-day clock,
Or vivisected her last new doll,
Or fostered a passion for alcohol.
And when she grew up she was given in marriage
To a first-class earl who keeps his carriage!

GROSVENOR.   I believe I am right in saying that there is not one word in that decalet which is calculated to bring the blush of shame to the cheek of modesty.

ANGELA.   Not one: it is purity itself.

GROSVENOR.   Here's another.

Teasing Tom was a very bad boy;
A great big squirt was his favourite toy;
He put live shrimps in his father's boots,
And sewed up the sleeves of his Sunday suits;
He punched his poor little sisters' heads,
And cayenne-peppered their four-post beds;
He plastered their hair with cobbler's wax,
And dropped hot halfpennies down their backs.
  The consequence was he was lost to*ta*lly,
  And married a girl in the *corps de bally!*

SAPHIR.   How simple—how earnest—how true!

ANGELA.   Marked you how grandly—how relentlessly—the damning catalogue of crime strode on, till Retribution, like a poisèd hawk, came swooping down upon the Wrong-Doer. Oh, it was terrible!

GROSVENOR (*aside*).   This is simply cloying. (*Aloud.*) Ladies, I am sorry to distress you, but you have been following me about ever since Monday, and this is Saturday. I should like the usual half-holiday, and if you will kindly allow me to close early to-day, I shall take it as a personal favour.

ELLA.   Oh, sir, do not send us from you, for our love leaps to our lips, and our hearts go out to you!

GROSVENOR.   Poor, poor girls! It is best to speak plainly. I know that I am loved by you, but I never can love you in return, for my heart is fixed elsewhere! Remember the fable of the Magnet and the Churn!

ANGELA (*wildly*).   But we don't know the fable of the Magnet and the Churn!

GROSVENOR.   Don't you? Then I will sing it to you.

SONG — GROSVENOR.

A magnet hung in a hardware shop,
And all around was a loving crop
Of scissors and needles, nails and knives,
Offering love for all their lives;
But for iron the magnet felt no whim,
Though he charmed iron, it charmed not him,
From needles and nails and knives he'd turn,
For he'd set his love on a Silver Churn!

ALL.   A Silver Churn?

GROSVENOR.   A Silver Churn!

> His most æsthetic,
> Very magnetic
> Fancy took this turn—
> "If I can wheedle
> A knife or needle,
> Why not a Silver Churn?

CHORUS.   His most æsthetic, &c.

GROSVENOR.   And Iron and Steel expressed sur-
prise,
The needles opened their well-drilled eyes,
The pen-knives felt "shut up," no doubt,
The scissors declared themselves "cut out,"
The kettles they boiled with rage, 'tis said,
While every nail went off its head,
And hither and thither began to roam,
Till a hammer came up—and drove them home.

ALL.   It drove them home?

GROSVENOR.   It drove them home!

> While this magnetic,
> Peripatetic
> Lover he lived to learn,
> By no endeavour
> Can magnet ever
> Attract a Silver Churn!

ALL.   While this magnetic, &c.

(*They go off in low spirits, gazing back at him
from time to time.*)

GROSVENOR.   At last they are gone! What *is* this
mysterious fascination that I seem to exercise over
all I come across? A curse on my fatal beauty, for
I am sick of conquests!

PATIENCE *appears.*

PATIENCE.   Archibald!

GROSVENOR (*turns and sees her*).   Patience!

PATIENCE.   I have escaped with difficulty from my
Reginald. I wanted to see you so much that I might
ask you if you still love me as fondly as ever?

GROSVENOR.   Love you? If the devotion of a lifetime— (*Seizes her hand.*)

PATIENCE (*indignantly*).   Hold! Unhand me, or I
scream. (*He releases her.*) If you are a gentleman,
pray remember that I am another's! (*Very tenderly.*) But you *do* love me, don't you?

GROSVENOR.   Madly, hopelessly, despairingly!

PATIENCE.   That's right! I never can be yours; but
that's right!

GROSVENOR.   And you love this Bunthorne?

PATIENCE.   With a heart-whole ecstasy that
withers, and scorches, and burns, and stings!
(*Sadly.*) It is my duty.

GROSVENOR.   Admirable girl! But you are not
happy with him?

PATIENCE.   Happy? I am miserable beyond description!

GROSVENOR.   That's right! I never can be yours;
but that's right!

PATIENCE.   But go now—I see dear Reginald approaching. Farewell, dear Archibald, I cannot tell
you how happy it has made me to know that you
still love me.

GROSVENOR.   Ah, if I only dared— (*Advances
towards her.*)

PATIENCE.   Sir! This language to one who is promised to another! (*Tenderly.*) Oh, Archibald, think
of me sometimes, for my heart is breaking! He is
so unkind to me, and you would be so loving!

GROSVENOR.   Loving! (*Advances towards her.*)

PATIENCE.   Advance one step, and as I am a good
and pure woman, I scream! (*Tenderly.*) Farewell,
Archibald! (*Sternly.*) Stop there! (*Tenderly.*)
Think of me sometimes! (*Angrily.*) Advance at
your peril! Once more, adieu!

(GROSVENOR *sighs, gazes sorrowfully at her,
sighs deeply, and exit. She bursts into tears.*)

Enter BUNTHORNE, *followed by* JANE. *He is moody
and preoccupied.*

JANE *sings.*

> In a melancholy train,
> One and one I walk all day;
> Pity those who love in vain—
> None so sorrowful as they,
> Who can only sigh and say,
> Woe is me, alack aday!

BUNTHORNE (*seeing* PATIENCE).   Crying, eh?
What are you crying about?

PATIENCE.   I've only been thinking how dearly I
love you!

BUNTHORNE.   Love me! Bah!

JANE.   Love him! Bah!

BUNTHORNE (*to* JANE).   Don't you interfere.

JANE.   He always crushes me!

PATIENCE (*going to him*). What is the matter, dear Reginald? If you have any sorrow, tell it to me, that I may share it with you. (*Sighing.*) It is my duty!

BUNTHORNE (*snappishly*). Whom were you talking with, just now?

PATIENCE. With dear Archibald.

BUNTHORNE (*furiously*). With dear Archibald! Upon my honour, this is too much!

JANE. A great deal too much!

BUNTHORNE (*angrily to* JANE). Do be quiet!

JANE. Crushed again!

PATIENCE. I think he is the noblest, purest, and most perfect being I have ever met. But I don't love him. It is true that he is devotedly attached to me, but indeed I don't love *him*. Whenever he gets affectionate, I scream. It is my duty! (*Sighing.*)

BUNTHORNE. I dare say!

JANE. So do I! *I* dare say!

PATIENCE. Why, how could I love him and love you too? You can't love two people at once!

BUNTHORNE. I don't believe you know what love is!

PATIENCE (*sighing*). Yes I do! There was a happy time when I didn't, but a bitter experience has taught me!

BALLAD — PATIENCE.

Love is a plaintive song,
    Sung by a suffering maid,
Telling a tale of wrong,
    Telling of hope betrayed.
Tuned to each changing note,
    Sorry when *he* is sad.
Blind to his every mote
    Merry when he is glad!

    Love that no wrong can cure,
        Love that is always new,
    That is the love that's pure,
        That is the love that's true!

Rendering good for ill,
    Smiling at every frown,
Yielding your own self-will,
    Laughing your tear-drops down,
Never a selfish whim,
    Trouble, or pain to stir;
Everything for him,
    Nothing at all for her!

    Love that will aye endure,
        Though the rewards be few,
    That is the love that's pure,
        That is the love that's true!

(*At the end of ballad, exit* PATIENCE *weeping.*)

BUNTHORNE. Everything has gone wrong with me since that idyllic idiot came here. Before that I was admired; I may say, loved.

JANE. Too mild. Adored!

BUNTHORNE. Do let a poet soliloquize! The damozels used to follow me wherever I went; now they all follow him!

JANE. Not all! *I* am still faithful to you.

BUNTHORNE. Yes, and a pretty damozel *you* are!

JANE. No, not pretty. Massive. Cheer up! I will never leave you, I swear it!

BUNTHORNE. Oh, thank you! I know what it is; it's his confounded mildness. They find me too highly spiced, if you please! And no doubt I *am* highly spiced.

JANE. Not for my taste!

BUNTHORNE (*savagely*). No, but I am for theirs. But I can be as mild as he. If they want insipidity, they shall have it. I'll meet this fellow on his own ground and beat him on it.

JANE. You shall. And I will help you.

BUNTHORNE. You will? Jane, there's a good deal of good in you after all!

DUET — BUNTHORNE *and* JANE.

JANE. So go to him and say to him, with compliment ironical—

BUNTHORNE.   Sing "Hey to you—
            Good day to you"—
        And that's what I shall say!

JANE. "Your style is much too sanctified—your cut is too canonical—"

BUNTHORNE.   Sing "Bah to you
            Ha! ha! to you"—
        And that's what I shall say!

JANE. "I was the beau ideal of the morbid young æsthetical—
        To doubt my inspiration was regarded as heretical—
        Until you cut me out with your placidity emetical."

BUNTHORNE.   Sing "Booh to you—
            Pooh, pooh, to you"—
        And that's what I shall say!

BOTH.   Sing "Hey to you, good day to you"—
        Sing "Bah to you, ha! ha! to you"
        Sing "Booh to you, pooh, pooh to you—"

        And that's what $\begin{Bmatrix} you \\ I \end{Bmatrix}$ shall say!

BUNTHORNE. I'll tell him that unless he will consent to be more jocular—

JANE. Say "Booh to you—

Pooh, pooh to you"—
And that's what you should say!

BUNTHORNE. To cut his curly hair and stick an
eye-glass in his ocular—

JANE. Sing "Bah to you—
Ha! ha! to you"—
And that's what you should say!

BUNTHORNE. To stuff his conversation full of
quibble and of quiddity,
To dine on chops and roly-poly
pudding with avidity—
He'd better clear away with all convenient rapidity.

JANE. Sing "Hey to you—
Good day to you"—
And that's what you should say.

BOTH. Sing "Booh to you—pooh, pooh to you,"
Sing "Bah to you—ha! ha! to you,"
Sing "Hey to you—good day to you—"

And that's what $\left\{ \begin{array}{c} \text{I} \\ \text{you} \end{array} \right\}$ shall say!

(*Exeunt* JANE *and* BUNTHORNE *together.*)

Enter DUKE, COLONEL, *and* MAJOR. *They have
abandoned their uniforms, and are dressed and
made up in imitation of Æsthetics. They have long
hair, and other outward signs of attachment to the
brotherhood. As they sing they walk in stiff, constrained, and angular attitudes—a grotesque exaggeration of the attitudes adopted by Bunthorne and
the Young Ladies in Act I.*

TRIO.

DUKE, COLONEL, *and* MAJOR.

It's clear that mediæval art alone retains its zest,
To charm and please its devotees we've done
our little best.
We're not quite sure if all we do has the Early
English ring;
But, as far as we can judge, it's something like
this sort of thing:
You hold yourself like this (*attitude*),
You hold yourself like that (*attitude*),
By hook and crook you try to look both angular
and flat (*attitude*).
We venture to expect
That what we recollect,
Though but a part of true High Art, will have
its due effect.

If this is not exactly right, we hope you won't
upbraid;
You can't get high Æsthetic tastes like trousers,
ready made.
True views on Mediævalism, Time alone will
bring,

But, as far as we can judge, it's something like
this sort of thing:
You hold yourself like this (*attitude*),
You hold yourself like that (*attitude*),
By hook and crook you try to look both angular
and flat (*attitude*).
To cultivate the trim,
Rigidity of limb,
You ought to get a Marionette, and form your
style on him (*attitude*).

COLONEL (*attitude*). Yes, it's quite clear that our
only chance of making a lasting impression on
these young ladies is to become as æsthetic as they
are.

MAJOR (*attitude*). No doubt. The only question
is how far we've succeeded in doing so. I don't
know why, but I've an idea that this is not quite
right.

DUKE (*attitude*). *I* don't like it. I never did. I
don't see what it means. I do it, but I don't like it.

COLONEL. My good friend, the question is not
whether we like it, but whether they do. They understand these things; we don't. Now I shouldn't
be surprised if this is effective enough—at a distance.

MAJOR. I can't help thinking we're a little stiff at
it. It would be extremely awkward if we were to be
"struck" so!

COLONEL. I don't think we shall be struck so.
Perhaps we're a little awkward at first—but every-
thing must have a beginning. Oh, here they come!
'Tention!

They strike fresh attitudes, as ANGELA *and*
SAPHIR *enter.*

ANGELA (*seeing them*). Oh, Saphir—see—see!
The immortal fire has descended on them, and they
are of the Inner Brotherhood—perceptively intense and consummately utter! (*The Officers have
some difficulty in maintaining their constrained attitudes.*)

SAPHIR (*in admiration*). How Botticellian! How
Fra Angelican! Oh, Art! I thank thee for this boon!

COLONEL (*apologetically*). I'm afraid we're not
quite right.

ANGELA. Not supremely, perhaps, but oh so all-
but! (*To* SAPHIR.) Oh, Saphir, are they not quite
too all-but?

SAPHIR. They are indeed jolly utter.

MAJOR (*in agony*). What do the Inner Brotherhood usually recommend for cramp?

COLONEL. Ladies, we will not deceive you. We
have done this with a view of expressing the ex-
tremity of our devotion to you. We trust that it is
not without its effect.

ANGELA. We will not deny that we are much moved by this proof of your attachment.

SAPHIR. Yes, your conversion to the principles of Æsthetic Art in its highest development has touched us deeply.

ANGELA. And if Mr. Grosvenor should remain obdurate—

SAPHIR. Which we have every reason to believe he will—

MAJOR (*aside, in agony*). I wish they'd make haste.

ANGELA. We are not prepared to say that our yearning hearts will not go out to you.

COLONEL (*as giving a word of command*). By sections of threes—Rapture! (*All strike a fresh attitude, expressive of æsthetic rapture.*)

SAPHIR. Oh, it's extremely good—for beginners it's admirable.

MAJOR. The only question is, who will take who?

SAPHIR. Oh, the Duke chooses first, as a matter of course.

DUKE. Oh, I couldn't think of it—you are really too good!

COLONEL. Nothing of the kind. You are a great matrimonial fish, and it's only fair that each of these ladies should have a chance of hooking you.

DUKE. Won't it be rather awkward?

COLONEL. Awkward, not at all. Observe, suppose you choose Angela, I take Saphir, Major takes nobody. Suppose you choose Saphir, Major takes Angela, I take nobody. Suppose you choose neither, I take Angela, Major takes Saphir. Clear as day!

ANGELA. Capital!

SAPHIR. The very thing!

QUINTETTE.
DUKE, COLONEL, MAJOR, ANGELA, *and* SAPHIR.

DUKE (*taking* SAPHIR).

If Saphir I choose to marry,
    I shall be fixed up for life;
Then the Colonel need not tarry,
    Angela can be his wife.
        (*Handing* ANGELA *to* COLONEL.)

(DUKE *dances with* SAPHIR, COLONEL *with* ANGELA, MAJOR *dances alone.*)

MAJOR (*dancing alone*).

In that case unprecedented
    Single I shall live and die—
I shall have to be contented
    With their heartfelt sympathy!

ALL (*dancing as before*).

He will have to be contented
    With our heartfelt sympathy!

DUKE (*taking* ANGELA).

If on Angy I determine,
    At my wedding she'll appear,
Decked in diamond and ermine,
    Major then can take Saphir!
        (*Handing* SAPHIR *to* MAJOR.)

(DUKE *dances with* ANGELA, MAJOR *with* SAPHIR. COLONEL *dances alone.*)

COLONEL (*dancing*).

In that case unprecedented,

Single I shall live and die,
I shall have to be contented
    With their heartfelt sympathy!

ALL (*dancing as before*).

He will have to be contented
    With our heartfelt sympathy!

DUKE (*taking both* ANGELA *and* SAPHIR).

After some debate internal,
    If on neither I decide,
Saphir then can take the Colonel
        (*Handing* SAPHIR *to* COLONEL),
    Angy be the Major's bride!
        (*Handing* ANGELA *to* MAJOR.)

(COLONEL *dances with* SAPHIR, MAJOR *with*
ANGELA, DUKE *dances alone.*)

DUKE (*dancing*).

In that case unprecedented,
    Single I must live and die,
I shall have to be contented
    With their heartfelt sympathy!

ALL (*dancing as before*).

He will have to live contented
    With our heartfelt sympathy!

(*At the end,* DUKE, COLONEL, *and* MAJOR,
and two girls dance off arm in arm.)

Enter GROSVENOR.

GROSVENOR. It is very pleasant to be alone. It is pleasant to be able to gaze at leisure upon those features which all others may gaze upon at their good will! (*Reclining on bank of lake, and looking at his reflection in the water.*) Ah! I am a very Narcissus!

Enter BUNTHORNE, *moodily.*

BUNTHORNE. It's no use, I can't live without admiration. Since Grosvenor came here, insipidity has been at a premium. Ah, he is there!

GROSVENOR. Ah, Bunthorne! come here—look! Is it not beautiful?

BUNTHORNE (*looking in lake*). Which?

GROSVENOR. Mine.

BUNTHORNE. Bah! I am in no mood for trifling.

GROSVENOR. And what is amiss?

BUNTHORNE. Ever since you came here, you have entirely monopolized the attentions of the young ladies. I don't like it, sir!

GROSVENOR. My dear sir, how can I help it? They are the plague of my life. My dear Mr. Bunthorne, with your personal disadvantages, you can have no idea of the inconvenience of being madly loved, at first sight, by every woman you meet. I assure you that when I see you wandering through the village, all by yourself, I feel that I would give everything I possess to be as universally unpopular as you are.

BUNTHORNE. Sir, until you came here I was adored!

GROSVENOR. Exactly—until I came here. That's my grievance. I cut everybody out! I assure you, if you could only suggest some means whereby, consistently with my duty to society, I could escape these inconvenient attentions, you would earn my everlasting gratitude.

BUNTHORNE. I will do so at once. You may be surprised to hear it, but, however popular it may be with the world at large, your personal appearance is highly objectionable to *me*.

GROSVENOR. It is? (*Shaking his hand.*) Oh thank you, thank you! Oh, if there were only a few more like you what a happy man I should be! How can I express my gratitude?

BUNTHORNE. By making a complete change at once. Your conversation must henceforth be perfectly matter-of-fact. You must cut your hair. In appearance and costume you must be absolutely commonplace.

GROSVENOR (*decidedly*). No. Pardon me, that's impossible.

BUNTHORNE. Take care. When I am thwarted I am very terrible.

GROSVENOR. I can't help that. I am a man with a mission. I am here to preach, in my own person, the Principles of Perfection. I am, as it were, a Banquet of Beauty upon which all who will may feast. It is most unpleasant to be a Banquet, but I must not shirk my responsibilities.

BUNTHORNE. I don't think you quite appreciate the consequences of thwarting me.

GROSVENOR. I don't care what they are.

BUNTHORNE. Suppose—I won't go so far as to say that I will do it—but suppose, for one moment, I were to curse you? (GROSVENOR *quails.*) Ah! Very well. Take care.

GROSVENOR. But surely you would never do that? (*In great alarm.*)

BUNTHORNE. I don't know. It would be an extreme measure, no doubt. Still—

GROSVENOR (*wildly*). But you would not do it— I am sure you would not (*throwing himself at* BUNTHORNE's *knees, and clinging to him*). Oh, reflect, reflect! You had a mother once.

BUNTHORNE. Never!

GROSVENOR. Then you had an aunt! (BUNTHORNE *affected.*) Ah! I see you had! By the memory of that aunt, I implore you to pause ere you resort to this last fearful expedient. Oh, Mr. Bunthorne, reflect, reflect! (*Weeping.*)

BUNTHORNE (*aside, after a struggle with himself*). I must not allow myself to be unmanned! (*Aloud.*) It is useless. Consent at once, or may a nephew's curse—

GROSVENOR. Hold. Are you absolutely resolved?

BUNTHORNE. Absolutely.

GROSVENOR. Will nothing shake you?

BUNTHORNE. Nothing. I am adamant.

GROSVENOR. Very good (*rising*). Then I yield. I will comply with your wishes.

BUNTHORNE. Ha! You swear it?

GROSVENOR. I do. Cheerfully. I have long wished for a reasonable pretext for such a change as you suggest. It has come at last. I do it on compulsion!

BUNTHORNE. Victory! I triumph!

DUET — BUNTHORNE *and* GROSVENOR.

BUNTHORNE. When I go out of door,
Of damozels a score,
    (All sighing and burning,
    And clinging and yearning)
Will follow me as before.
I shall, with cultured taste,
Distinguish gems from paste,
    And "High diddle diddle"
    Will rank as an idyll,
If I pronounce it chaste!
    A most intense young man,
    A soulful-eyed young man,
An ultra-poetical, super-æsthetical,
    Out-of-the-way young man,

BOTH.   A most intense young man, &c.

GROSVENOR. Conceive me, if you can,
An every-day young man:
    A commonplace type,
    With a stick and a pipe,
And a half-bred black-and-tan.
    Who thinks suburban "hops"
    More fun than "Monday Pops,"
Who's fond of his dinner,
And doesn't get thinner
    On bottled beer and chops.
    A commonplace young man—
    A matter-of-fact young man—
A steady-and-stolid-y, jolly bank-holiday
    Every-day young man!

BUNTHORNE. A Japanese young man—
    A blue-and-white young man—
Francesca-da-Rimini, miminy-piminy,
Je-ne-sais-quoi young man.

GROSVENOR. A Chancery Lane young man—

A Somerset House young man—
A very delectable, highly respectable,
    Threepenny-bus young man!

BUNTHORNE.   A pallid and thin young man—
    A haggard and lank young man—
A greenery-yallery, Grosvenor Gallery,
    Foot-in-the-grave young man!

GROSVENOR.   A Sewell & Cross young man—
    A Howell & James young man—
A pushing young particle—what's the next article—
    Waterloo House young man!

ENSEMBLE.

BUNTHORNE.	GROSVENOR.
Conceive me, if you can,	Conceive me, if you can,
A crotchetty, cracked young man,	A matter-of-fact young man,
An ultra-poetical, super-æsthetical,	An alphabetical, arith-metical,
Out-of-the-way young man!	Every-day young man!

(*At the end*, GROSVENOR *dances off.* BUNTHORNE *remains.*)

BUNTHORNE. It is all right! I have committed my last act of ill-nature, and henceforth I'm a reformed character. (*Dances about stage, humming refrain of last air.*)

Enter PATIENCE. *She gazes in astonishment at him.*

PATIENCE. Reginald! Dancing! And—what in the world have you done to yourself?

BUNTHORNE. Patience, I'm a changed man. Hitherto I've been gloomy, moody, fitful—uncertain in temper and selfish in disposition—

PATIENCE. You have indeed! (*Sighing.*)

BUNTHORNE. All that is changed. I have reformed. I have modelled myself upon Mr. Grosvenor. Henceforth I am mildly cheerful. My conversation will blend amusement with instruction. I shall still be æsthetic; but my æstheticism will be of the most pastoral kind.

PATIENCE. Oh, Reginald! Is all this true?

BUNTHORNE. Quite true. Observe how amiable I am. (*Assuming a fixed smile.*)

PATIENCE. But, Reginald, how long will this last?

BUNTHORNE. With occasional intervals for rest and refreshment, as long as I do.

PATIENCE. Oh, Reginald, I'm so happy! (*In his arms.*) Oh dear, dear Reginald, I cannot express

the joy I feel at this change. It will no longer be a duty to love you, but a pleasure—a rapture—an ecstasy!

BUNTHORNE.   My darling!

PATIENCE.   But—oh, horror! (*Recoiling from him.*)

BUNTHORNE.   What's the matter?

PATIENCE.   Is it quite certain that you have absolutely reformed—that you are henceforth a perfect being—utterly free from defect of any kind?

BUNTHORNE.   It is quite certain. I have sworn it!

PATIENCE.   Then I never can be yours!

BUNTHORNE.   Why not?

PATIENCE.   Love, to be pure, must be absolutely unselfish, and there can be nothing unselfish in loving so perfect a being as you have now become!

BUNTHORNE.   But—

PATIENCE.   It is useless, Reginald. When you were objectionable I could love you conscientiously, but now that you are endowed with every quality that can make a woman happy, it would be the height of selfishness even to think of such a thing.

BUNTHORNE.   But stop a bit, I don't want to reform—I'll relapse—I'll be as I was—

PATIENCE.   No; love should purify—it should never debase. Farewell, Reginald—think of me sometimes as one who did her duty to you at all cost—at all sacrifice.

BUNTHORNE.   But I assure you, I—interrupted!

Enter GROSVENOR, *followed by all the young ladies, who are followed by chorus of Dragoons. He has had his hair cut, and is dressed in an ordinary suit of dittos and a pot hat. They all dance cheerfully round the stage in marked contrast to their former languor.*

CHORUS — GROSVENOR *and* GIRLS.

GROSVENOR.	GIRLS.
I'm a Waterloo House young man, A Sewell & Cross young man, A steady and stolid-y, jolly bank-holiday, Every-day young man.	We're Swears & Wells young girls, We're Madame Louise young girls, We're prettily pattering, cheerily chattering, Every-day young girls.

GROSVENOR.   I'm a Waterloo House young man!

GIRLS.   We're Swears & Wells young girls!

GROSVENOR.   I'm a Sewell & Cross young man!

GIRLS.   We're Madame Louise young girls!

GROSVENOR.   } I'm a steady and stolid-y, jolly bank-holiday, Every-day young man!

LADIES.   } We're prettily pattering, cheerily chattering, Every-day young girls!

BUNTHORNE.   Angela — Ella — Saphir — what—what does this mean?

ANGELA.   It means that Archibald the All Right cannot be wrong; and if the All Right chooses to discard æstheticism, it proves that æstheticism ought to be discarded.

PATIENCE.   Oh, Archibald! Archibald! I'm shocked—surprised—horrified!

GROSVENOR.   I can't help it. I'm not a free agent. I do it on compulsion.

PATIENCE.   This is terrible. Go! I shall never set eyes on you again. But—oh joy!

GROSVENOR.   What is the matter?

PATIENCE.   Is it quite, quite certain that you will always be a commonplace young man?

GROSVENOR.   Always—I've sworn it.

ANGELA.   Why, then, there's nothing to prevent my loving you with all the fervour at my command!

GROSVENOR.   Why, that's true.

PATIENCE.   My Archibald!

GROSVENOR.   My Patience! (*They embrace.*)

BUNTHORNE.   Crushed again!

Enter JANE.

JANE (*who is still æsthetic*).   Cheer up! I am still here. I have never left you, and I never will!

BUNTHORNE.   Thank you, Jane. After all, there is no denying it, you're a fine figure of a woman!

JANE.   My Reginald!

BUNTHORNE.   My Jane!

Flourish. Enter COLONEL, DUKE, *and* MAJOR.

COLONEL. Ladies, the Duke has at length deter-mined to select a bride! (*General excitement.*)

DUKE. I have a great gift to bestow. Approach, such of you as are truly lovely. (*All come forward, bashfully, except* JANE *and* PATIENCE.) In per-sonal beauty you have all that is necessary to make a woman happy. In common fairness, I think I ought to choose the only one among you who has the misfortune to be distinctly plain. (*Girls retire disappointed.*) Jane!

JANE (*leaving* BUNTHORNE'S *arms*). Duke! (JANE *and* DUKE *embrace.* BUNTHORNE *is utterly dis-gusted.*)

BUNTHORNE. Crushed again!

FINALE.

DUKE.   After much debate internal,
    I on Lady Jane decide,

Saphir now may take the Colonel,
    Angy be the Major's bride!

(SAPHIR *pairs off with* COLONEL, ANGELA *with the* MAJOR, ELLA *with* SOLICITOR.)

BUNTHORNE.   In that case unprecedented
    Single I must live and die,
    I shall have to be contented
    With a tulip or li*ly*!

(*Takes a lily from button-hole and gazes affectionately at it.*)

ALL.   He will have to be contented
    With a tulip or li*ly*!

Greatly pleased with one another,
    To get married we decide,
    Each of us will wed the other,
    Nobody be Bunthorne's Bride!

DANCE.

CURTAIN.

Postscript

THE VERY FIRST solo line in the opera carries a variation in text between the first edition and subsequent editions. After the "Twenty love-sick maidens we" chorus, Angela sings "Love feeds on love, they say, or love will die—"; in the second edition and thereafter this line is changed to read "Love feeds on hope . . . ," but this is a relatively minor distinction. The one important difference between the first-night edition and all later editions is the presence of a second twelve-line verse to the Patience and Angela duet on page 152, "Time fled, and one unhappy day—." It was sung on the opening night but must have been removed very shortly thereafter, as it does not appear in the second edition which was in the public's hands by the end of the following week.

There are other alterations of lesser importance, most of them tending to shorten the text. The name "Algernon" (probably meaningfully directed at Swinburne) was erroneously used as Bun-thorne's first name in the stage direction on page 148, "Bunthorne enters, followed by ladies. . . ." This was corrected in the second edition. The name Algernon popped up, again erroneously, at the bot-tom of page 153 when Patience bids farewell to Grosvenor. The line read 'Farewell, Algernon! But stay!' This was not corrected to 'Farewell, Archibald!' until the fifth edition of the libretto, more than thirty years later. It was evidently an unnoticed holdover from one of the prepublication proof-issues of the text.

Even though one of the encored numbers on opening night was the Ensemble—Tutti at the close of Act I, its four eight-line verses of this were all reduced to four-line verses by deleting the last four lines of each. This change was not made until the fifth edition and it remains in its shortened form in the current official acting text.

It is amusing to note that, yielding to the prog-ress of transportation media, the "Threepenny-bus young man" (on page 164) became a "Twopenny-tube young man" in the fifth edition. But the line yielded again to progress, this time to the rise in prices in the London Underground, and reverted to the original "Threepenny-bus young man," where it remains today.

The Opening at the Savoy

"To the Public. Ladies and Gentlemen.
I beg leave to lay before you some details of a new theatre, which I have caused to be built, with the intention of devoting it to the representation of the Operas of Messrs. W. S. Gilbert and Arthur Sullivan, with whose joint productions I have, up to now, had the advantage of being associated." With these words Richard D'Oyly Carte began a long public letter, dated Thursday, October 6, 1881, describing the Savoy Theatre, newly built between the Strand and the Victoria Embankment. (The date was within two weeks of exactly three years since he had taken Messrs. G. and S. to view the site for a theatre he was already proposing to build for the presentation of operas.) And he concluded: "The theatre will be opened under my management on Monday next, October the 10th, and I have the satisfaction to be able to announce that the opening piece will be Messrs. W. S. Gilbert and Arthur Sullivan's Opera, *Patience,* which, produced at the Opéra Comique on April 23, is still running with a success beyond any precedent. The piece is mounted afresh with new scenery, costumes, and increased chorus. It is being again rehearsed under the personal direction of the author and composer, and on the opening night the Opera will be conducted by the composer.

"I am, ladies and gentlemen,
Your obedient servant,
R. D'Oyly Carte"

This letter was printed in a four-page folder, probably to be put in the hands of Carte's invited guests at the originally scheduled preview, Wednesday, October 5, as well as for press release the following day, Thursday the sixth, the day of his originally planned opening. But continuing delays caused by complications involving his "marvelous" new electric light system forced a change in schedule—and many more letters to the press. The postponed preview took place Saturday evening the eighth, before an array of guests including notables of the theatre and the press. On this same day the indefatigable Carte wrote still another letter to the press for release on Monday, October 10 (and probably given out that Saturday at the preview). In his letter he explained the nature, limitations, and difficulties of the electrical miracle he would unveil on his opening night:

"The arrangements for the application of the electric light to the Savoy Theatre are still not completed. The work is actively progressing, but may not be sufficiently advanced to be used on Monday evening. Under these circumstances the opening of the theatre will not be further post-

Cartoon of D'Oyly Carte opening his new Savoy Theatre, by Arthur Bryan in the ENTR'ACTE *of October 8, 1881.*

poned, but should the light not be ready the building will be illuminated by gas in the usual way. The contractors hope, however, to be able to light the auditorium on Monday, but the lighting of the stage by electricity will probably not be perfected for some days longer. I may explain that there are 1,200 lights in my theatre, that it has not before been attempted to light anything approaching this number of incandescent lamps as a single undertaking, and that the contractors find that the engines provided do not give sufficient power. An additional engine will be added immediately . . ."

But even with three years' planning, the night of Monday, October 10, 1881, must have cost D'Oyly Carte years of life. His concern was not the usual risk of the theatrical manager with a new show, but the all-out gamble of a businessman promoting an untried technical device. Characteristically, he had spared nothing in his efforts. And he had also hedged by equipping the Savoy Theatre with the best available gas lighting, the "Sunlight," which, in the judgment of the *Fan*'s reporter, "is at present the most reliable means of illumination, the arrangements for the electric

The Savoy Theatre façade.

light being as yet scarcely perfect." As though to bring him luck and to propitiate the great electrophysicist, Michael Faraday—dead fourteen years —Carte, according to *Penny Illustrated,* had engaged a Mr. Farady to superintend the installation of his theatre's lighting plant.

The press in its comments the next day made particular reference to the moment after Arthur Sullivan had made his entrance. Wrote the *Chronicle:*

A tap of Mr. Sullivan's baton on the desk, and the beautiful satin drapery constituting the curtain, was parted in the centre, and on being raised disclosed the whole of the company, in the dresses worn by them in *Patience,* gathered together to sing the National Anthem. The "love-sick maidens" of the aesthetic opera sang a couple of verses, first the soprani alone, then the contralti, and finally their companions, gave the

third verse in harmonized chorus. Up to this time the gas burner had been the only light before the curtain. . . . But ere the overture to *Patience* commenced, the curtain was again parted, and Mr. D'Oyly Carte stepped in front of the footlights to make a short explanation. He said for that night at least the front of the house only would be illuminated by the electric light, and that this was a mere experiment. . . . The experiment might fail, the lamps might go out, but one gas light would be left burning, and, if necessary, the theatre could be at once lighted. . . . Mr. Carte also begged the indulgence of the audience for Mr. Rutland Barrington, who was suffering from a severe sore throat, which, of course, interfered with his vocalisation, and the manager then retired amid encouraging applause, accompanied by a feeling of curiosity as to whether the electric light would really be found to "work." The Sun-burner was then lowered, and all eyes were turned towards the pear-shaped lamps beneath the centre of the gallery, the upper circle, and the balcony tiers. As if by the wave of a fairy's wand the theatre immediately became filled with a soft, soothing light, clearer and far more grateful than gas. . . . The audience gave a cheer at the commencement of what certainly marks a fresh chapter to the history of electric lighting. . . .

(In the words of his granddaughter, commenting seventy-six years later about this exciting moment: "D'Oyly was certainly a showman of the first order and no mistake! I bet he had them [the electric lights] turned on and off the whole day and was full of confidence in them by then.") Even though there were a few seconds halfway through the first act when the electric lights went out altogether, "only the most obstinate and objectionably precise individuals can assert," concluded the *Chronicle*, "that last night the electric light did not realise expectations."

It was not till two and a half months later that the Savoy stage itself was illuminated by electricity. The occasion was the matinee performance of Wednesday, December 28, fully reported by the *Times:* "The comparative safety of the new system was pointed out to the audience by Mr. D'Oyly Carte . . . who enveloped one of the

lamps in a piece of highly inflammable muslin. On the glass being broken and the vacuum destroyed, the flame was immediately extinguished without even singeing the muslin." The *Daily News* described this spectacular demonstration, presented at the close of the first act, in detail. Apparently it was "sufficiently alarming in appearance to cause a visible movement towards the exits on behalf of one or two nervous visitors," but "proved to be as completely innocuous as had been predicted."

(This bulb-smashing demonstration did not take place on the opening night of the Savoy, as has been recorded in book and film. The error—an understandable one—derived from the fact that the source of the story was an undated clipping from a trade weekly that had received its misinformation from the faulty recollection of George Grossmith twenty-five years after the event. Actually the item was from the *Electrical Times* of December 13, 1906. Thorough press coverage of the Savoy opening contained not a word about so spectacular an event. On the contrary, the date is given specifically by *Lloyds Weekly* in an article that described the bulb-smashing in detail and enthusiastically predicted: "Wednesday, December 28, 1881, will be a memorable day in the

The lobby of the Savoy Theatre.

history of electric light. . . . The example of the Savoy will, no doubt, soon be followed by other theatres.")

"A more brilliant audience than that which attended the opening night of the Savoy has seldom been seen in any theatre other than Covent Garden Opera House," wrote François Cellier in his published recollections. Their "ohs" and "ahs" as the splendor of the new theatre sparkled all around them lie between the lines of the press coverage accorded the occasion. "White, pale yellow, and gold are the colours chiefly employed"—thus the *Fan* reviewer described the décor of the auditorium—"the use of gold being singularly tasteful and judicious. With these colours the cinnamon silk of the box curtains, with its rich brocade, and the Venetian red of the background of the boxes, dress circle, and gallery, blend very harmoniously. Dark blue silk is used for the covering of the stall chairs, and forms the base of the colour as seen from the dress circle." And the curtain of the Savoy stage was described by some reporters not as rising or falling but as opening or closing. "Instead of the customary Act-drop, two curtains of yellow satin fall from the opposite sides of the stage, with happy effect."

The Savoy Theatre's opening-night program, a simple affair, mentioned that "On this occasion the Performance will be conducted by the Composer." (It was the first time such a notice had appeared in a Gilbert and Sullivan program except in America. From this night on, such mention became a standard element in the programs of all performances which Sullivan conducted.) The occasion might well have warranted a more elaborate program, as D'Oyly Carte was an advocate of lavish souvenirs, but probably the uncertainties created by his lighting system dissuaded him from planning one. Along with the program, according to the *Daily News,* "notices were distributed . . . that the arrangements for the lighting of the stage by electricity would not be perfected for a few days"—an "indulgence slip" for a particularly temperamental star making her debut!

Program and press noted that *Patience* would have "entirely new scenery, dresses, and increased chorus." It was natural and foresighted of Carte to recognize that a production mounted for the dim illumination of gaslight would need something quite different when exposed to the bright glare of electricity. Henry Emden designed the new sets. It is interesting to note the difference in the response of the press to the new *Patience* as compared with the original production. In the latter the first-act scene had drawn detailed rave-notices and the second-act scene the merest mention. For the new *Patience* it was the Forest Glade set of the second act that "revealed qualities far ex-

celling in beauty those in which the opera had been mounted at the old house." The *Chronicle*'s reviewer described "banks of ferns, with, in one corner, a stream of real water trickling over small boulders." This elaborately realistic touch must have replaced the painted lake of the Opéra Comique's Act II set, which the reporter from the *London Figaro* noted had been abolished, so that "Grosvenor and Bunthorne now admire themselves in a small hand-glass which the former carries, instead of in the glassy bosom of the somewhat conventional pool."

"From the moment when Mr. Sullivan, on taking his seat in front of the orchestra, was greeted with warm cheers, to the termination of the representation, the applause was almost continuous. Every movement of importance had to be repeated," wrote the *Fan* reviewer. The *Chronicle* counted eight encores. The *Illustrated London News* found that "without any apparent effort, Miss Alice Barnett, the massive Lady Jane, and Mr. Grossmith, the bilious and Fra Angelican Bunthorne, have worked up their scenes to exactly the proper concert pitch, and they were rewarded with a triple encore for their amusing duet ["So go to him and say to him"] in the second act." (The *Fan* had it a double encore.)

Apparently the entire company rose to the occasion, as the *Fan* continued: "It is in the nature of an important occasion to put actors on their metal. All, accordingly, acquitted themselves well; and the performance, in addition to the ensemble, which comes from long practice, had indescribable spirit." Only Rutland Barrington appears to have been out of sorts that night, but "indulgence" was enthusiastically accorded him. "An apology was offered for Mr. Barrington, whom a severe cold had almost deprived of voice. In so benignant a mood was the audience that a solo, which Mr. B. spoke rather than sang, obtained the customary encore." "I was almost voiceless," he wrote in his memoirs. "I had implored both Carte and Sullivan to excuse me from playing . . . but they declared they would rather have me with no voice than alter the cast on such an occasion. I was glad afterwards that they had been firm about it." Aside from the increased number of the chorus, the only difference in the cast from that of the original *Patience* company was the replacement of Richard Temple by Walter Browne in the role of Colonel Calverley.

Barrington had another good reason for remembering this Savoy opening night. It happened in the second act, and was mercifully not noted by the press. In his own words—"When I took my seat on a rustic tree-trunk preparatory to singing 'The Magnet and the Churn,' I heard an ominous kind of *r-r-r-i-p-p-p* and immediately felt conscious of a horrible draught on my right leg. . . . My beautiful velvet knee-breeches had gone crack. It was an awful moment. . . . Had they but been made of red velvet it would not have mattered so much, for I felt I was blushing all over and it might have escaped notice, though some of the aesthetic maidens were already choking with laughter."

Just as he had apparently attended the first night of *Patience* at the Opéra Comique, Oscar Wilde was in the audience at the Savoy on October 10. This information was handled irreverently by the *Penny Illustrated:* "The verse-spinner whose remunerative affectation is caricatured in *Patience* was among the aesthetes present at the opening of the Savoy. But Oscar didn't appear at all to mind the mild ridicule of the 'too-too' Grossmith and Barrington. Why should he? Poking fun at aestheticism by *Patience* and *The Colonel* has

but made him more notorious." It should be mentioned, as a parenthetical reminder, that astute D'Oyly Carte was manager for Oscar Wilde's lectures on aestheticism and poetry readings. The personal appearances at both these important *Patience* "first nights" were assuredly not by chance.

The *Chronicle*'s man was there for the final curtain: "The many encores prolonged the performance to a later hour than usual, but when the curtain fell there were calls for Messrs. Gilbert and Sullivan (who came on together), for Mr. Phipps [C. J. Phipps, architect of the Savoy, had also designed the Gaiety Theatre for John Hollingshead], and finally for Mr. Carte." Sullivan's nephew records that after the performance he took the Prince of Wales behind the scenes and presented every member of the company to him. The fact of the Prince's attendance is also con-

The Savoy Theatre—curtain down. Note the pear-shaped electric globes.

The Savoy Theatre, with curtain up on Act I of PATIENCE.

firmed by George Grossmith's reminiscences, but a competent authority at Windsor Castle denies that H.R.H. was at the Savoy on that occasion.

Apparently the inexhaustible Sullivan did not go to bed that night. On leaving the theatre he went to Gilbert's house for a late supper, then home to change his clothes; and he caught the early morning Great Eastern train to Norwich, where, according to his biographers, "he conducted a performance [or more likely it was a rehearsal] of *The Martyr of Antioch* at the Festival at ten o'clock next morning."

OCTOBER 10 (MONDAY) 1881. *Rehearsal at Savoy at 11. Lasted till 4.30. Lady K. Coke, Mrs. R. [Ronalds] etc. there. Came home L. W. ["Little Woman," but who?] tea. Dined at home with Smythe [Walter Smythe, his secretary]. Went to conduct first performance of Patience in the New Theatre. Great house—enthusiastic reception for all. Went back to sup at Gilberts—returned home 3 a.m. changed my clothes—had coffee and drove to Liverpool Street to take 5.10 a.m. train to Norwich.*

ARTHUR SULLIVAN'S DIARY

IOLANTHE

Introduction

IT WAS THE NIGHT of Saturday, November 25, 1882. "The Savoy Theatre, lighted like no other theatre in Europe, and looking exceptionally brilliant on this occasion, was crammed to its utmost capacity," recorded the *Era*. The very air on Savoy Hill must have seemed charged with D'Oyly Carte's surplus of electricity as he unveiled the Savoy's first world-première performance—*Iolanthe, or The Peer and the Peri*—"in the presence of," according to the *People,* "one of the most brilliant audiences ever attracted to the theatre."

A gossip reporter counted Lord and Lady Donoughmore, Lord Dunraven, Lord and Lady Londesborough, Lady Molesworth, Lady Augusta Fane, Sir George Wombwell, Sir Bruce Seton, Mrs. Ronalds, Mr. A. B. Coutts ("the Baroness was absent, her old friend and associate in many charitable schemes, Lord Harrowby, having been buried that day," as the reporter for the *World* carefully explained, and continued listing the assembled V.I.P.'s), Mr. Hamilton Aide, Dr. George Grove, Mr. J. R. Robinson, Mr. Hollingshead, Mr. Frederic Clay, and of course Captain Eyre Massey Shaw, seated in the middle of the stalls. "I think too I caught a momentary glimpse, emerging from a curtain, of G!—No, no! I don't mean the grand old man [Gladstone?], I mean a grand young woman." The society press clearly had caught the excitement of the occasion.

The audience that night was provided with both plain and souvenir programs. Appropriately enough the designer of this souvenir had worked into the decoration of its cover and inside spread that sensational Savoy theatrical novelty, the electric light bulb, in a motif suggesting the triple-bracket sconces that elaborated the fasciae of the balconies. A little later in its run *Iolanthe* had other newly designed souvenir programs in which this motif of the electric light bulbs was abandoned. Programs after the opening night included the forepiece *Mock Turtles,* which had shared the bill with *Patience* and was kept on at the Savoy except for the night of November 25.

Mr. Arthur Sullivan "received an ovation on taking his seat in the orchestra," observed the *Advertiser*. Few if any in that glittering audience on such an occasion of triumphant good will could know that within the hour, as he was leaving his house to go to the theatre, Sullivan had received word that his brokers had gone bankrupt and all his savings, £7,000, had been lost. Seldom have fortunes been repaired so rapidly; but then, there were fairy wands at work on the Savoy stage that night.

The overture, according to Sullivan himself in an interview in *Home News* seven years later, "was a quick bit of work" which he wrote without the assistance he sometimes enlisted in the last-minute preparation of these forepieces. "And there was a lot of fresh writing in it too. I daresay you will recollect the 'Captain Shaw' motive combined with those florid passages for the wood-wind." His diary makes clear that he started to "re-compose the Overture afresh" on November 21 and finished it between midnight and seven a.m. the morning of the 23rd, just forty-eight hours before the first night. He had, some weeks previously, October 29, written Alfred Cellier, who was in New York rehearsing the American company for a simultaneous première: ". . . Act I: Overture. Write one yourself." So on November 25 there were two different *Iolanthe* overtures heard by the two hemispheres.

"The scene of the First Act is a remarkably pretty rustic landscape with practicable bridge," as the *Advertiser* described it. Jessie Bond, playing the title role that night, has added a note on the "practicable" hazards of Gilbert's stagecraft realism: "The river from which Iolanthe emerges . . . was a shallow trough of real water, and I was always afraid of slipping into it when I rose through the trapdoor on my little platform, and crossed it on the lily-leaves which were my stepping stones."

The procession of Peers "gorgeously clad," according to the *Observer,* "in their robes and coronets, as Knights of the Garter, of the Thistle, and of St. Patrick, and K.C.B.'s," was an immediate success with press and public. Wrote the *Advertiser*'s critic, "The entrance of these noblemen, cloaked and gartered and coroneted, is the most absurd thing conceivable," and the *Era* added its own superlative: "Nothing could be better of its kind than the pompous blustering mock-heroic march that ushers in the procession. . . . The state costumes of Messrs. Ede & Son, court robe-makers to Her Majesty, are alone worth a visit to see." *Punch,* ever eager to sting Gilbert, commented with tongue in cheek that this "is excellent fooling which will probably tell well in America."

Of the finale to the first act Sullivan was later quoted as having said: "I think *Iolanthe* contained the longest finale I ever wrote. Goodness knows how many pages of the score it covered." (It runs to thirty-five pages of the vocal score; that of *The Grand Duke* is thirty-four pages.)

"The Second Act opens with a most beautiful and remarkable scene of Palace Yard, Westminster," said the *Era*'s most enthusiastic reviewer. "There was great applause at the rising of the curtain, as the scene realised the actual spot with a fidelity rare even in these realistic days."

Gilbert and D'Oyly Carte, bent on making the most of the new wonder, employed "self-lighting fairies with electricity stored somewhere about the small of their backs," as Beatty-Kingston in the *Theatre* referred to "the last thing in Savoy innovations." It was in the second act, a nighttime scene, that "the Fairy Queen and her three chief attendants wear each an electric star in their hair.

The effect of this brilliant spark of electricity is wonderful"—at least in the opinion of the *Advertiser*'s reviewer. According to *Lloyd's,* the effect was "too dazzling to be pleasant, and in a dark scene obscures the face."

The Savoy's primitive electric lighting system did not permit the full dimming down of the house lights even during the performance. So there was ample illumination for members of the audience to follow their libretto texts. Clement Scott, who reviewed the opening night for the *Illustrated London News,* described his own experience: "I was so interested in the book that I could scarcely attend to the stage, except with my ears, and this feeling was general, for the whole audience was plunged into the mysteries of the libretto, and when the time came for the turning over of the leaves of the book there was such a rustling as is only equalled when musicians are following a score at an Oratorio."

Certainly a high spot of entertainment for the first-nighters came in the second act when Alice Barnett, stretching her arms directly toward Eyre Massey Shaw, Captain of the London Fire Brigade, in the audience, sang the lines, "O Captain Shaw, type of true love kept under!" Gilbert may well have guessed that the popular goateed and mustachioed social lion would be in the house that night—but was it a miracle of good fortune or the genius of D'Oyly Carte that placed him in the center stalls clearly visible to Alice Barnett? The reviewer for the *Advertiser* in commenting on the occasion wrote: "This may not seem in the telling to suggest much of the facetious, but the effect of the fairies calling dolorously upon the gallant Captain is indescribably funny." And in the *Theatre* Beatty-Kingston wrote: "The boxes, stalls, and circles were chiefly occupied by his friends and acquaintances whose outburst of hilarity upon hearing Miss Barnett describe him as a 'type of true love kept under' was a memorable incident of the first night."

As for the cast, "The performance . . . was uniformly meritorious," in the opinion of the sports-minded gentleman of the *Weekly Times.* "The Savoy 'eleven' is a good one, and its members never miss a chance of backing one another up." It was a wonder all members of the company managed successfully to use the correct name for the title-character in song and dialogue that night. Right up to twelve days before production the opera had been named *Perola,* allegedly in order to confound the snooping press and American pirates. Gilbert had even gone to the trouble of having set in type on libretto-size pages a privately printed *Description of Stage Business* with *Perola* used throughout not only as the title but wherever the name Iolanthe occurred. The con-

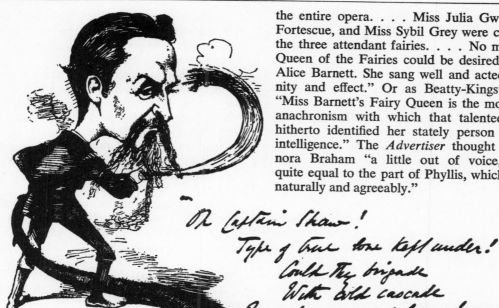

the entire opera. . . . Miss Julia Gwynne, Miss Fortescue, and Miss Sybil Grey were charming as the three attendant fairies. . . . No more stately Queen of the Fairies could be desired than Miss Alice Barnett. She sang well and acted with dignity and effect." Or as Beatty-Kingston put it, "Miss Barnett's Fairy Queen is the most startling anachronism with which that talented lady has hitherto identified her stately person and quick intelligence." The *Advertiser* thought Miss Leonora Braham "a little out of voice, but . . . quite equal to the part of Phyllis, which she plays naturally and agreeably."

Oh Captain Shaw!
Type of true love kept under!
Could thy brigade
With cold cascade
Quench my great love, I wonder!
"Iolanthe" Act 2.
W. S. Gilbert.

Captain Eyre Massey Shaw (with cold cascade), from a cartoon in ENTR'ACTE, *May 13, 1882.*

fusion has a more likely explanation, not publicized for obvious reasons. In using the title *Iolanthe* Gilbert and Carte ran afoul of Henry Irving's rights that stemmed from his one-act Idyll by that name staged in 1880. In a letter Gilbert wrote Carte on October 13, 1882, he suggests that Carte be the one to see Irving "as I have never disguised my opinion of his acting." Fortunately Carte was successful.

"Mr. George Grossmith, as the Lord Chancellor, brings all his comic talent and skill to bear upon one of the drollest impersonations imaginable," wrote the critic of the *Era,* who also found that "Mr. Rutland Barrington and Mr. Durward Lely acquitted themselves well. They had little to sing, but their delivery of the eccentric dialogue did it full justice and gained them frequent and hearty applause." He added that Richard Temple, "although at times it was felt that a tenor voice would have been best for the part, sang so well, and made so much of the comic lines given to his part, that he fully deserved the cordial reception he met with." Mr. Charles Manners, a newcomer, the *Weekly Times* reported as "splendidly stolid and dense as a Grenadier sentry."

On the distaff side, in the opinion of the *Era,* "Miss Jessie Bond, as Iolanthe, may . . . be credited with all the grace, delicacy, and fascination we should expect from a fairy mother, and her singing of the really exquisite melody in the last scene was one of the most successful items in

From reviewers' accounts it would appear that five numbers were encored on opening night, four of them involving George Grossmith: "The law is the true embodiment," "When I went to the bar," the nightmare song, and the Act II trio (in which the "wild dance" captured the fancy of the audience just as it has at all subsequent revivals). The quartette, "In friendship's name," the *Era* cited "as one of the gems of the opera. . . . We dislike encores but here there was really an excuse, for the quartette is elegant and tuneful in no ordinary degree."

"And the opera concludes"—again to quote Beatty-Kingston—"with a dance and chorus, professedly preparatory for a flight 'sky-high, sky-high,' where noble Lords are to 'exchange House of Peers for House of Peris.' It would not surprise me to learn that this *jeu de mots* suggested the fundamental paradox upon which the plot of *Iolanthe* has been most ingeniously built up."

It is interesting that alone among the major critics Beatty-Kingston chided Gilbert for bringing a serious note into his social satire (the reference was to the song "Fold your flapping wings," sung by Strephon in the second act): "The libretto of *Iolanthe* has been utilized by its author as the vehicle for conveying to society at large a feeling protest on behalf of the indigent, and a scathing satire upon the hereditary moiety of our Legislature. Advocacy and denunciation of this sort are all very well in melodrama, where telling 'points' may always be made with the unmerited wrongs of the poor and the reprehensible uselessness of the aristocracy. But they jar upon the ear and taste alike when brought to bear upon us through the medium of a song sung by half a fairy in a professedly comic opera."

And if Gilbert was gratified (as he must have been) by this rise to his bait, imagine his delight with the following charge of "injustice" made by the same critic: "No man living knows better than Mr. Gilbert that, in proportion to the total male adult population of this country, there are as many pompous asses out of the peerage as in it."

This second act many critics (and Sullivan himself) regarded as over-long on the opening night. It is significant that the song assailed by Beatty-Kingston was one of the two major cuts made by Gilbert to shorten the act for later performances.

The press in general applauded the new opera enthusiastically, although several felt it was not as good as *Patience*. "The composer has risen to his opportunity," wrote the *Daily Telegraph,* "and we are disposed to account *Iolanthe* his best effort in all the Gilbertian series." The *Era*'s reviewer drew attention to Gilbert and Sullivan's unfortunate fate of being required always to compete with their own past successes: "There is no necessity for comparisons between former Operas and the work which drew so large an audience to the Savoy Theatre last Saturday night. Enough to say that the visitors laughed and applauded as of old, and as they will probably laugh and applaud for a twelvemonth to come."

A number of critics found the libretto of *Iolanthe* repetitive of Gilbert's other operettas. Wrote the *Globe,* "If in the development of this plot, Mr. Gilbert has employed devices familiar—possibly too familiar—to his admirers, it may be pleaded on his behalf that 'nothing succeeds like success.' " And from the *Echo:* "Same set of puppets that Mr. Gilbert has dressed over and over before."

The *Times* pontificated in words as unlikely to promote a comic opera of the 1880's as they would a musical comedy of today: "The public once more were indebted to their favourites for an evening of genuine, healthy, albeit not supremely intellectual enjoyment."

At least one critic attending the Savoy that evening (for *Bell's Life*) was, to put it mildly, not amused: "It seems to me that he [Gilbert] starts primarily with the object of bringing Truth and Love and Friendship into contempt; just as we are taught the devil does. . . . I have much pleasure in bidding adieu to Mr. Gilbert's unwholesome feeling and in calling the attention of my readers to an interesting exhibition of pictures of Venice now on view at the rooms of the Fine Arts Society, New Bond Street."

NOVEMBER 25 (SATURDAY) 1882. *First performance of* Iolanthe *at the Savoy Theatre. House crammed. Awfully nervous; more so than usual on going into Orchestra. Tremendous reception. First Act went splendidly. The second dragged, and I was afraid it must be compressed. However it finished well, and Gilbert and myself were called and heartily cheered. Very low afterwards. Came home.*

ARTHUR SULLIVAN'S DIARY

An Entirely Original Fairy Opera,

IN TWO ACTS,

ENTITLED

IOLANTHE

OR,

THE PEER AND THE PERI.

Dramatis Personae.

THE LORD CHANCELLOR	MR. GEORGE GROSSMITH.
EARL OF MOUNTARARAT	MR. RUTLAND BARRINGTON.
EARL TOLLOLLER	MR. DURWARD LELY.
PRIVATE WILLIS, *of the Grenadier Guards*	MR. MANNERS.
STREPHON, *An Arcadian Shepherd*	MR. R. TEMPLE.
QUEEN OF THE FAIRIES	MISS ALICE BARNETT.
IOLANTHE, *A Fairy, Strephon's Mother*	MISS JESSIE BOND.

CELIA		MISS FORTESCUE.
LEILA	*Fairies*	MISS JULIA GWYNNE.
FLETA		MISS SYBIL GREY.

PHYLLIS, *An Arcadian Shepherdess and Ward in Chancery*	MISS LEONORA BRAHAM.

CHORUS OF DUKES, MARQUISES, EARLS, VISCOUNTS, BARONS, AND FAIRIES.

ACT I. — An Arcadian Landscape.

ACT II. — Palace Yard, Westminster.

DATE. — Between 1700 and 1882.

IOLANTHE

OR,

THE PEER AND THE PERI.

ACT I.

SCENE. — *An Arcadian landscape. A river runs around the back of the stage. A rustic bridge crosses the river.*

Enter Fairies, led by LEILA, CELIA, *and* FLETA. *They trip around the stage, singing as they dance.*

CHORUS.

Tripping hither, tripping thither,
Nobody knows why or whither;
We must dance and we must sing,
Round about our fairy ring!

SOLO — CELIA.

We are dainty little fairies,
   Ever singing, ever dancing;
We indulge in our vagaries
   In a fashion most entrancing.
If you ask the special function
   Of our never-ceasing motion,
We reply, without compunction,
   That we haven't any notion!

CHORUS.

No, we haven't any notion!
Tripping hither, &c.

SOLO — LEILA.

If you ask us how we live,
Lovers all essentials give—
   We can ride on lovers' sighs,
   Warm ourselves in lovers' eyes,
   Bathe ourselves in lovers' tears,
   Clothe ourselves in lovers' fears,
   Arm ourselves with lovers' darts,
   Hide ourselves in lovers' hearts.
When you know us, you'll discover
That we almost live on lover!

CHORUS.

Tripping hither, &c.

(*At the end of chorus, all sigh wearily.*)

CELIA. Ah, it's all very well, but since our Queen banished Iolanthe, fairy revels have not been what they were!

LEILA. Iolanthe was the life and soul of fairy land. Why, she wrote all our songs and arranged all our dances! We sing her songs and we trip her measures, but we don't enjoy ourselves!

FLETA. To think that five-and-twenty years have elapsed since she was banished! What could she have done to have deserved so terrible a punishment?

LEILA. Something awful! She married a mortal!

FLETA. Oh. Is it injudicious to marry a mortal?

LEILA. Injudicious? It strikes at the root of the whole fairy system! By our laws, the fairy who marries a mortal, dies!

CELIA. But Iolanthe didn't die!

Enter FAIRY QUEEN.

QUEEN. No, because your Queen, who loved her with a surpassing love, commuted her sentence to penal servitude for life, on condition that she left her husband and never communicated with him again!

LEILA (*aside to* CELIA). That sentence of penal servitude she is now working out, on her head, at the bottom of that stream!

QUEEN. Yes, but when I banished her, I gave her all the pleasant places of the earth to dwell in. I'm sure I never intended that she should go and live at the bottom of a stream! It makes me perfectly wretched to think of the discomfort she must have undergone!

[179]

LEILA. Think of the damp! And her chest was always delicate.

QUEEN. And the frogs! Ugh! I never shall enjoy any peace of mind until I know why Iolanthe went to live among the frogs!

FLETA. Then why not summon her and ask her?

QUEEN. Why? Because if I set eyes on her I should forgive her at once!

CELIA. Then why not forgive her? Twenty-five years—it's a long time!

LEILA. Think how we loved her!

QUEEN. Loved her? What was your love to mine? Why, she was invaluable to me! Who taught me to curl myself inside a buttercup? Iolanthe! Who taught me to swing upon a cobweb? Iolanthe! Who taught me to dive into a dewdrop—to nestle in a nutshell—to gambol upon gossamer? Iolanthe!

LEILA. She certainly did surprising things!

FLETA. Oh give her back to us, great Queen, for your sake if not for ours! (*All kneel in supplication.*)

QUEEN (*irresolute*). Oh, I should be strong, but I am weak! I should be marble, but I am clay! Her punishment has been heavier than I intended. I did not mean that she should live among the frogs—and—well, well, it shall be as you wish—it shall be as you wish!

INVOCATION — QUEEN.

Iolanthe!
From thy dark exile thou art summoned!

Come to our call—
Come, Iolanthe!

CELIA.   Iolanthe!

LEILA.   Iolanthe!

ALL.   Come to our call,
Come, Iolanthe!

IOLANTHE *rises from the water. She is clad in water-weeds. She approaches the* QUEEN *with head bent and arms crossed.*

IOLANTHE. With humbled breast
And every hope laid low,
To thy behest,
Offended queen, I bow!

QUEEN. For a dark sin against our fairy laws,
We sent thee into life-long banishment;
But mercy holds her sway within our hearts—
Rise—thou art pardoned!

IOLANTHE.   Pardoned!

ALL.   Pardoned!

IOLANTHE. Ah!

Her weeds fall from her, and she appears clothed as a fairy. The QUEEN *places a diamond coronet on her head, and embraces her. The others also embrace her.*

CHORUS.

Welcome to our hearts again,
Iolanthe! Iolanthe!
We have shared thy bitter pain,
Iolanthe! Iolanthe!
Every heart and every hand
In our loving little band
Welcome thee to fairy land,
Iolanthe!

QUEEN. And now, tell me, with all the world to choose from, why on earth did you decide to live at the bottom of that stream?

IOLANTHE. To be near my son, Strephon.

QUEEN. Bless my heart, I didn't know you had a son!

IOLANTHE. He was born soon after I left my husband by your royal command—but he does not even know of his father's existence.

FLETA. How old is he?

IOLANTHE. Twenty-four.

LEILA. Twenty-four! No one, to look at you, would think you had a son of twenty-four! But that's one of the advantages of being immortal. We never grow old! Is he pretty?

IOLANTHE. He's extremely pretty, but he's inclined to be stout.

ALL (disappointed). Oh!

QUEEN. I see no objection to stoutness, in moderation.

CELIA. And what is he?

IOLANTHE. He's an Arcadian shepherd—and he loves Phyllis, a Ward in Chancery.

CELIA. A mere shepherd! and he half a fairy!

IOLANTHE. He's a fairy down to the waist—but his legs are mortal.

ALL. Dear me!

QUEEN. I have no reason to suppose that I am more curious than other people, but I confess I should like to see a person who is a fairy down to the waist, but whose legs are mortal.

IOLANTHE. Nothing easier, for here he comes!

Enter STREPHON, *singing and dancing and playing on a flageolet. He does not see the fairies, who retire up stage as he enters.*

SONG — STREPHON.

Good morrow—good mother—
    Good mother—good morrow!
By some means or other,
    Pray banish your sorrow!
        With joy beyond telling
        My bosom is swelling,
        So join in a measure
        Expressive of pleasure.
For I'm to be married to-day—to-day—
    Yes, I'm to be married to-day!

CHORUS (aside). Yes, he's to be married to-day
        —to-day—
    Yes, he's to be married to-day!

IOLANTHE. Then the Lord Chancellor has at last given his consent to your marriage with his beautiful ward, Phyllis?

STREPHON. Not he, indeed. To all my tearful prayers he answers me, "A shepherd lad is no fit helpmate for a Ward of Chancery." I stood in court, and there I sang him songs of Arcadee, with flageolet accompaniment—in vain. At first he seemed amused, so did the bar; but quickly wearying of my song and pipe, bade me get out. A servile usher, then, in crumpled bands and rusty bombazine, led me, still singing, into Chancery Lane! I'll go no more: I'll marry her to-day, and brave the upshot, be it what it may! (*Sees* FAIRIES.) But who are these?

IOLANTHE. Oh Strephon! rejoice with me, my Queen has pardoned me!

STREPHON. Pardoned you, mother? This is good news indeed!

IOLANTHE. And these ladies are my beloved sisters.

STREPHON. Your sisters! Then they are—my aunts! (*Kneels.*)

QUEEN. A pleasant piece of news for your bride on her wedding day.

STREPHON. Hush! My bride knows nothing of my fairyhood. I dare not tell her, lest it frighten her. She thinks me mortal, and prefers me so.

LEILA. Your fairyhood doesn't seem to have done you much good.

STREPHON. Much good! It's the curse of my existence! What's the use of being half a fairy? My body can creep through a keyhole, but what's the good of that when my legs are left kicking behind? I can make myself invisible down to the waist,

but that's of no use when my legs remain exposed to view! My brain is a fairy brain, but from the waist downwards I'm a gibbering idiot. My upper half is immortal, but my lower half grows older every day, and some day or other must die of old age. What's to become of my upper half when I've buried my lower half I really don't know!

QUEEN. I see your difficulty, but with a fairy brain you should seek an intellectual sphere of action. Let me see. I've a borough or two at my disposal. Would you like to go into Parliament?

IOLANTHE. A fairy Member! That would be delightful!

STREPHON. I'm afraid I should do no good there —you see, down to the waist, I'm a Tory of the most determined description, but my legs are a couple of confounded Radicals, and, on a division, they'd be sure to take me into the wrong lobby. You see they're two to one, which is a strong working majority.

QUEEN. Don't let that distress you; you shall be returned as a Liberal-Conservative, and your legs shall be our peculiar care.

STREPHON (*bowing*). I see your Majesty does not do things by halves.

QUEEN. No, we are fairies down to the feet.

ENSEMBLE.

QUEEN. Fare thee well, attractive stranger.

FAIRIES. Fare thee well, attractive stranger.

QUEEN. Shouldst thou be in doubt or danger,
Peril or perplexitee,
Call us, and we'll come to thee!

FAIRIES. Call us, and we'll come to thee!

Tripping hither, tripping thither,
Nobody knows why or whither.
We must now be taking wing.
To another fairy ring!

(FAIRIES *and* QUEEN *trip off,* IOLANTHE, *who takes an affectionate farewell of her son, going off last.*)

Enter PHYLLIS, *singing and dancing, and accompanying herself on a flageolet.*

SONG — PHYLLIS.

Good morrow, good lover!
Good lover, good morrow!
I prithee discover,
Steal, purchase, or borrow,
Some means of concealing
The care you are feeling,
And join in a measure
Expressive of pleasure,
For we're to be married to-day—to-day,
For we're to be married to-day!

BOTH. Yes, we're to be married, &c.

STREPHON (*embracing her*). My Phyllis! And to-day we are to be made happy for ever!

PHYLLIS. Well, we're to be married.

STREPHON. It's the same thing.

PHYLLIS. I suppose it is. But, oh, Strephon, I tremble at the step I'm taking! I believe it's penal servitude for life to marry a Ward of Court without the Lord Chancellor's consent! I shall be of age in two years. Don't you think you could wait two years?

STREPHON. Two years! Why you can't have seen yourself! Here, look at that (*showing her a pocket mirror*), and tell me if you think it rational to expect me to wait two years?

PHYLLIS (*looking at herself*). No. You're quite right—it's asking too much. One must be reasonable.

STREPHON. Besides, who knows what will happen in two years? Why you might fall in love with the Lord Chancellor himself by that time!

PHYLLIS. Yes. He's a clean old gentleman.

STREPHON. As it is, half the House of Lords are sighing at your feet.

PHYLLIS. The House of Lords are certainly extremely attentive.

STREPHON. Attentive? I should think they were! Why did five-and-twenty Liberal Peers come down to shoot over your grass-plot last autumn? It couldn't have been the sparrows. Why did five-and-twenty Conservative Peers come down to fish your pond? Don't tell me it was the gold-fish! No, no—delays are dangerous, and if we are to marry, the sooner the better.

DUET — STREPHON *and* PHYLLIS.

None shall part us from each other,
    One in life and death are we:
All in all to one another—
    I to thee and thou to me!

Thou the tree and I the flower—
    Thou the idol, I the throng—
Thou the day and I the hour—
    Thou the singer, I the song!

All in all since that fond meeting
    When, in joy, I woke to find
Mine the heart within thee beating,
    Mine the love that heart enshrined!
Thou the stream and I the willow—
    Thou the sculptor; I the clay—
Thou the ocean; I the billow—
    Thou the sunrise; I the day!

(*Exeunt* STREPHON *and* PHYLLIS *together*.)

March. Enter Procession of Peers.

CHORUS.

Loudly let the trumpet bray!
        Tantantara!
    Gaily bang the sounding brasses!
        Tzing!
As upon its lordly way
    This unique procession passes,
        Tantantara! Tzing! Boom!
Bow, bow, ye lower middle classes!
Bow, ye tradesmen, bow, ye masses!
Blow the trumpets, bang the brasses!
        Tantantara! Tzing! Boom!
We are peers of highest station,
Paragons of legislation,
Pillars of the British nation!
        Tantantara! Tzing! Boom!

Enter the LORD CHANCELLOR, *followed by his trainbearer.*

SONG — LORD CHANCELLOR.

The Law is the true embodiment
Of everything that's excellent.
It has no kind of fault or flaw,

And I, my lords, embody the Law.
The constitutional guardian I
Of pretty young Wards in Chancery,
All very agreeable girls—and none
Are under the age of twenty-one.
　　A pleasant occupation for
　　A rather susceptible Chancellor!

ALL.　A pleasant, &c.

But though the compliment implied
Inflates me with legitimate pride,
It nevertheless can't be denied
That it has its inconvenient side.
For I'm not so old, and not so plain,
And I'm quite prepared to marry again,
But there'd be the deuce to pay in the Lords
If I fell in love with one of my Wards!
　　Which rather tries my temper, for
　　I'm *such* a susceptible Chancellor!

ALL.　Which rather, &c.

And everyone who'd marry a Ward
Must come to me for my accord,
And in my court I sit all day,
Giving agreeable girls away,
With one for him—and one for he—
And one for you—and one for ye—
And one for thou—and one for thee—
But never, oh never a one for me!
　　Which is exasperating, for
　　A highly susceptible Chancellor!

ALL.　Which is, &c.

Enter LORD TOLLOLLER.

TOLLOLLER.　And now, my Lords, to the business of the day.

CHANCELLOR.　By all means. Phyllis, who is a Ward of Court, has so powerfully affected your Lordships, that you have appealed to me in a body to give her to whichever one of you she may think proper to select, and a noble lord has just gone to her cottage to request her immediate attendance. It would be idle to deny that I, myself, have the misfortune to be singularly attracted by this young person. My regard for her is rapidly undermining my constitution. Three months ago I was a stout man. I need say no more. If I could reconcile it with my duty, I should unhesitatingly award her to myself, for I can conscientiously say that I know no man who is so well-fitted to render her exceptionally happy. But such an award would be open to misconstruction, and therefore, at whatever personal inconvenience, I waive my claim.

TOLLOLLER.　My Lord, I desire, on the part of this House, to express its sincere sympathy with your Lordship's most painful position.

CHANCELLOR.　I thank your Lordships. The feelings of a Lord Chancellor who is in love with a Ward of Court are not to be envied. What is his position? Can he give his own consent to his own marriage with his own Ward? Can he marry his own Ward without his own consent? And if he marries his own Ward without his own consent, can he commit himself for contempt of his own Court? And if he commit himself for contempt of his own Court, can he appear by counsel before himself, to move for arrest of his own judgment? Ah, my Lords, it is indeed painful to have to sit upon a woolsack which is stuffed with such thorns as these!

Enter LORD MOUNTARARAT.

MOUNTARARAT.　My Lords, I have much pleasure in announcing that I have succeeded in inducing the young person to present herself at the Bar of this House.

Enter PHYLLIS.

RECITATIVE — PHYLLIS.

My well-loved Lord and Guardian dear,
You summoned me, and I am here!

CHORUS OF PEERS.

Oh, rapture, how beautiful!
How gentle—how dutiful!

SOLO — LORD TOLLOLLER.

Of all the young ladies I know
　　This pretty young lady's the fairest;
Her lips have the rosiest show,
　　Her eyes are the richest and rarest.
Her origin's lowly, it's true,
　　But of birth and position we've plenty;
We've grammar and spelling for two,
　　And blood and behaviour for twenty!

CHORUS.　Her origin's lowly, it's true,
　　But we've grammar and spelling for two;
　　Of birth and position we've plenty,
　　With blood and behaviour for twenty!

SOLO — LORD MOUNTARARAT.

Though the views of the House have diverged
　　On every conceivable motion,
All questions of Party are merged
　　In a frenzy of love and devotion;
If you ask us distinctly to say
　　What Party we claim to belong to,
We reply without doubt or delay,
　　The Party I'm singing this song to!

CHORUS.　If you ask us distinctly to say,
　　We reply, without doubt or delay,
　　That the Party we claim to belong to

Is the Party we're singing this song to!

SOLO — PHYLLIS.

I'm very much pained to refuse,
    But I'll stick to my pipes and my tabors;
I can spell all the words that I use,
    And my grammar's as good as my neighbours'.
As for birth—I was born like the rest,
    My behaviour is rustic but hearty,
And I know where to turn for the best,
    When I want a particular Party!

CHORUS.   Though her station is none of the best,
    I suppose she was born like the rest;
    And she knows where to look for her hearty,
    When she wants a particular Party!

RECITATIVE — PHYLLIS.

Nay, tempt me not.
    To rank I'll not be bound:
In lowly cot
    Alone is virtue found!

CHORUS. Nay, do not shrink from us—we will
    not hurt you—
    The Peerage is not destitute of virtue.

BALLAD — LORD TOLLOLLER.

Spurn not the nobly born
    With love affected,
Nor treat with virtuous scorn
    The well-connected.
High rank involves no shame—
We boast an equal claim

With him of humble name
    To be respected!
Blue blood! blue blood!
        When virtuous love is sought
        Thy power is naught,
    Though dating from the flood,
        Blue blood!

CHORUS.   Blue blood! Blue blood! &c.

Spare us the bitter pain
    Of stern denials,
Nor with lowborn disdain
    Augment our trials.
Hearts just as pure and fair
May beat in Belgrave Square,
As in the lowly air
    Of Seven Dials!
Blue blood! blue blood!
    Of what avail art thou
    To serve us now?
Though dating from the flood,
    Blue blood!

CHORUS.   Blue blood! Blue blood! &c.

RECITATIVE — PHYLLIS.

My Lord, it may not be.
    With grief my heart is riven!
You waste your words on me,
    For ah! my heart is given!

ALL. Given!

PHYLLIS. Given!

ALL. Oh, horror!!!

RECITATIVE — LORD CHANCELLOR.

And who has dared to brave our high dis-
    pleasure,
    And thus defy our definite command?

Enter STREPHON. PHYLLIS *rushes to his arms.*

STREPHON. 'Tis I—young Strephon! mine this
    priceless treasure!
    Against the world I claim my darling's hand!
    A shepherd I—

ALL.   A shepherd he!
STREPHON. Of Arcady—
ALL.   Of Arcadee!
STREPHON. Betrothed are we!
ALL.   Betrothed are they—
STREPHON. And mean to be—
ALL.   Espoused to-day!

ENSEMBLE.

STREPHON.   THE OTHERS.

A shepherd I   A shepherd he
Of Arcady,   Of Arcadee,
Betrothed are we   Betrothed is he
And mean to be   And means to be
  Espoused to-day!   Espoused to-day!

DUET — LORD MOUNTARARAT *and* LORD
    TOLLOLLER (*aside to each other*).

'Neath this blow,
    Worse than stab of dagger—
Though we mo-
    Mentarily stagger,
In each heart
    Proud are we innately—
Let's depart,
    Dignified and stately!

ALL. Let's depart,
    Dignified and stately!

CHORUS OF PEERS.

Though our hearts she's badly bruising,
In another suitor choosing,
Let's pretend it's most amusing.
    Ha! ha! ha! ha! Tzing! Boom!

*Exeunt all the Peers marching round stage with
much dignity.* LORD CHANCELLOR *separates*
PHYLLIS *from* STREPHON *and orders her off. She
follows Peers. Manent* LORD CHANCELLOR *and*
    STREPHON.

LORD CHANCELLOR. Now, sir, what excuse have
you to offer for having disobeyed an order of the
Court of Chancery?

STREPHON. My Lord, I know no Courts of Chancery; I go by Nature's Acts of Parliament. The
bees—the breeze—the seas—the rooks—the
brooks—the gales—the vales—the fountains and
the mountains, cry, "You love this maiden—take
her, we command you!" 'Tis writ in heaven by the
bright barbëd dart that leaps forth into lurid light
from each grim thunder-cloud. The very rain pours
forth her sad and sodden sympathy! When chorused Nature bids me take my love, shall I reply,
"Nay, but a certain Chancellor forbids it?" Sir,
you are England's Lord High Chancellor, but are
you Chancellor of birds and trees, King of the
winds, and Prince of thunder-clouds?

LORD CHANCELLOR. No. It's a nice point. I don't
know that I ever met it before. But my difficulty
is that at present there's no evidence before the
Court that chorused Nature has interested herself
in the matter.

STREPHON. No evidence! You have my word for
it. I tell you that she bade me take my love.

LORD CHANCELLOR. Ah! but, my good sir, you
mustn't tell us what she told you—it's not evidence. Now an affidavit from a thunderstorm, or
a few words on oath from a heavy shower, would
meet with all the attention they deserve.

STREPHON. And have you the heart to apply the
prosaic rules of evidence to a case which bubbles
over with poetical emotion?

LORD CHANCELLOR. Distinctly. I have always
kept my duty strictly before my eyes, and it is to
that fact that I owe my advancement to my present distinguished position.

SONG — LORD CHANCELLOR.

When I went to the Bar as a very young man
    (Said I to myself—said I),
I'll work on a new and original plan
    (Said I to myself—said I):
I'll never assume that a rogue or a thief
Is a gentleman worthy implicit belief
Because his attorney has sent me a brief
    (Said I to myself—said I!).

I'll never throw dust in a juryman's eyes
    (Said I to myself—said I),
Or hoodwink a judge who is not over-wise
    (Said I to myself—said I),
Or assume that the witnesses summoned in force
In Exchequer, Queen's Bench, Common Pleas,
        or Divorce,
Have perjured themselves as a matter of course
    (Said I to myself—said I!).

Ere I go into court I will read my brief through
    (Said I to myself—said I),
And I'll never take work I'm unable to do
    (Said I to myself—said I).

My learned profession I'll never disgrace
By taking a fee with a grin on my face,
When I haven't been there to attend to the case
    (Said I to myself—said I!).

In other professions in which men engage
    (Said I to myself—said I),
The Army, the Navy, the Church, and the Stage
    (Said I to myself—said I),
Professional licence, if carried too far,
Your chance of promotion will certainly mar—
And I fancy the rule might apply to the Bar
    (Said I to myself—said I!).   (*Exit.*)

To STREPHON, *who is in tears, enter* IOLANTHE.

STREPHON. Oh, Phyllis, Phyllis! To be taken from you just as I was on the point of making you my own! Oh, it's too much—it is too much!

IOLANTHE. My son in tears—and on his wedding day!

STREPHON. My wedding day! Oh, mother, weep with me, for the law has interposed between us, and the Lord Chancellor has separated us for ever!

IOLANTHE. The Lord Chancellor! (*Aside.*) Oh, if he did but know!

STREPHON (*overhearing her*). If he did but know what?

IOLANTHE. No matter! The Lord Chancellor has no power over you. Remember you are half a fairy. You can defy him—down to the waist.

STREPHON. Yes, but from the waist downwards he can commit me to prison for years! Of what avail is it that my body is free, if my legs are working out seven years' penal servitude?

IOLANTHE. True. But take heart—our Queen has promised you her special protection. I'll go to her and lay your peculiar case before her.

STREPHON. My beloved mother! How can I repay the debt I owe you?

FINALE — QUARTETTE.

(*As it commences, the Peers appear at the back, advancing unseen and on tiptoe.* MOUNTARARAT *and* TOLLOLLER *lead* PHYLLIS, *between them, who listens in horror to what she hears.*)

STREPHON (*to* IOLANTHE). When darkly looms
        the day,
    And all is dull and grey,
    To chase the gloom away
        On thee I'll call!

PHYLLIS (*speaking aside to* MOUNTARARAT).
    What was that?

MOUNTARARAT (*aside to* PHYLLIS). I think I
    heard him say
        That on a rainy day,

To while the time away,
    On her he'd call!

CHORUS. We think we heard him say, &c.
(PHYLLIS *much agitated at her lover's supposed faithlessness.*)

IOLANTHE (*to* STREPHON). When tempests wreck
        thy bark,
    And all is drear and dark,
    If thou shouldst need an Ark,
        I'll give thee one!

PHYLLIS (*speaking aside to* TOLLOLLER). What was that?

TOLLOLLER (*aside to* PHYLLIS). I heard the
        minx remark,
    She'd meet him after dark
    Inside St. James's Park,
        And give him one!

ALL. The prospect's not so bad,
    {My / Thy} heart so sore and sad
    May very soon be glad
        As summer sun;
    But while the sky is dark,
    And tempests wreck {my / thy} bark,
    If {I should / thou shouldst} need an Ark,
    {Thou'lt / I'll} give {me / thee} one!

PHYLLIS (*revealing herself*). Ah!

(IOLANTHE *and* STREPHON *much confused.*)

PHYLLIS.   Oh, shameless one, tremble!
    Nay, do not endeavour
    Thy fault to dissemble,
      We part—and for ever!
    I worshipped him blindly,
    He worships another—

STREPHON.   Attend to me kindly,
    This lady's my mother!

PHYLLIS.   This lady's his *what?*
STREPHON.   This lady's my mother!
TENORS.   This lady's his *what?*
BASSES.   He says she's his mother!

They point derisively to IOLANTHE, *laughing heartily at her. She clings for protection to* STREPHON.

Enter LORD CHANCELLOR. IOLANTHE *veils herself.*

CHANCELLOR.   What means this mirth unseemly,
    That shakes the listening earth?

TOLLOLLER.   The joke is good extremely,
    And justifies our mirth.

MOUNTARARAT.   This gentleman is seen
    With a maid of seventeen,
    A-taking of his *dolce far niente;*
    And wonders he'd achieve,
    For he asks us to believe
She's his mother—and he's nearly five-and-twenty!

CHANCELLOR (*sternly*).   Recollect yourself, I
    pray,
    And be careful what you say—
As the ancient Romans said, *festina lente.*
    For I really do not see
    How so young a girl could be
The mother of a man of five-and-twenty.

ALL.   Ha! ha! ha! ha! ha!

STREPHON.   My Lord, of evidence I have no
    dearth—
She is—has been—my mother, from my birth!

BALLAD.

    In babyhood
    Upon her lap I lay,
      With infant food
    She moistened my clay:
      Had she withheld
    The succour she supplied,
      By hunger quelled,
    Your Strephon might have died!

CHANCELLOR (*much moved*).   Had that refresh-
    ment been denied,
    Indeed our Strephon might have died!

ALL (*much affected*).   Had that refreshment
    been denied,

    Indeed our Strephon might have died!

MOUNTARARAT.   But as she's not
    His mother, it appears,
    Why weep these hot
      Unnecessary tears?
    And by what laws
      Should we, so joyously,
    Rejoice, because
      Our Strephon didn't die?
    Oh rather let us pipe our eye,
    Because our Strephon didn't die!

ALL.   That's very true—let's pipe our eye
    Because our Strephon didn't die!

All weep. IOLANTHE, *who has succeeded in hiding
her face from* LORD CHANCELLOR, *escapes unnoticed.*

PHYLLIS. Go, traitorous one—for ever we must
    part:
    To one of you, my Lords, I give my heart!

ALL.   Oh rapture!
STREPHON. Hear me, Phyllis, ere you leave me!
PHYLLIS.   Not a word—you did deceive me!
ALL.   Not a word—you did deceive her!

BALLAD — PHYLLIS.

    For riches and rank I do not long—
      Their pleasures are false and vain:
    I gave up the love of a lordly throng
      For the love of a simple swain.
    But now that that simple swain's untrue,
    With sorrowful heart I turn to you—
      A heart that's aching,
      Quaking, breaking,
    As sorrowful hearts are wont to do!

    The riches and rank that you befall
      Are the only baits you use,
    So the richest and rankiest of you all
      My sorrowful heart shall choose.
    As none are so noble—none so rich
    As this couple of lords, I'll find a niche
      In my heart that's aching,
      Quaking, breaking,
    For one of you two—and I don't care
    which!

ENSEMBLE.

PHYLLIS (*to* MOUNTARARAT *and* TOLLOLLER).
    To you I give my heart so rich!
ALL (*puzzled*).   To which?
PHYLLIS.   I do not care!
    To you I yield—it is my doom!
ALL.   To whom?
PHYLLIS.   I'm not aware!

I'm yours for life if you but choose.

ALL.   She's whose?

PHYLLIS.   That's your affair;
I'll be a countess, shall I not?

ALL.   Of what?

PHYLLIS.   I do not care!

ALL.   Lucky little lady!
            Strephon's lot is shady;
            Rank, it seems, is vital,
            "Countess" is the title,
            But of what I'm not aware!

STREPHON.   Can I inactive see my fortune fade?
                    No, no!
            Mighty protectress, hasten to my aid!

Enter Fairies, tripping, headed by CELIA, LEILA,
and FLETA, *and followed by* QUEEN.

            CHORUS OF FAIRIES.

Tripping hither, tripping thither,
Nobody knows why or whither;
        Why you want us we don't know,
        But you've summoned us, and so
            Enter all the little fairies
            To their usual tripping measure!
        To oblige you all our care is—
            Tell us, pray, what is your pleasure!

STREPHON.   The lady of my love has caught me
            talking to another—

ALL.   Oh, fie! Strephon is a rogue!

STREPHON.   I tell her very plainly that the lady is
            my mother—

ALL.   Taradiddle, taradiddle, tol lol lay!

STREPHON.   She won't believe my statement, and
            declares we must be parted
    Because on a career of double-dealing I have
        started,
    Then gives her hand to one of these, and leaves
        me broken-hearted—

ALL.   Taradiddle, taradiddle, tol lol lay!

QUEEN. Ah cruel ones, to part two faithful lov-
        ers from each other!

ALL.   Oh, fie! Strephon is a rogue!

QUEEN. You've done him an injustice, for the
        lady *is* his mother!

ALL.   Taradiddle, taradiddle, tol lol lay!

CHANCELLOR (*aside*). That fable perhaps may
        serve his turn as well as any other.
    I didn't see her face, but if they fondled one
        another,
    And she's but seventeen—I don't believe it was
        his mother!

ALL.   Taraddidle, taradiddle, tol lol lay!

TOLLOLLER. I've often had a use
            For a thoroughbred excuse
    Of a sudden (which is English for "*repente*")
            But of all I ever heard
            This is much the most absurd,
    For she's seventeen and he is five-and-twenty!

ALL.   He says she is his mother, and he's four- or
        five-and-twenty!
                Oh, fie! Strephon is a rogue!

MOUNTARARAT. Now listen, pray, to me,
            For this paradox will be
    Carried nobody at all *contradicente*.
            Her age, upon the date
            Of his birth, was *minus* eight,
    If she's seventeen, and he is five-and-twenty!

ALL.   To say she is his mother is an utter bit of
        folly!
                Oh, fie! Strephon is a rogue!
    Perhaps his brain is addled, and it's very mel-
        ancholy!
                Taradiddle, taradiddle, tol lol lay!
    I wouldn't say a word that could be construed
        as injurious,
    But to find a mother younger than her son is
        very curious,
    And that's a kind of mother that is usually
        spurious.
                Taradiddle, taradiddle, tol lol lay!

CHANCELLOR.   Go away, madam,
　　　　　　I should say, madam,
　　　　　　You display, madam,
　　　　　　　Shocking taste.

　　　　　　It is rude, madam,
　　　　　　To intrude, madam,
　　　　　　With your brood, madam,
　　　　　　　Brazen-faced!

　　　　　　You come here, madam,
　　　　　　Interfere, madam,
　　　　　　With a peer, madam
　　　　　　　(I am one).

　　　　　　You're aware, madam,
　　　　　　What you dare, madam,
　　　　　　So take care, madam,
　　　　　　　And begone!

ENSEMBLE.

FAIRIES (*to* QUEEN).	PEERS.
Let us stay, madam,	Go away, madam,
I should say, madam,	I should say, madam,
They display, madam,	You display, madam,
Shocking taste.	Shocking taste.
It is rude, madam,	It is rude, madam,
To allude, madam,	To intrude, madam,
To your brood, madam,	With your brood,
Brazen-faced!	madam,
	Brazen-faced!
We don't fear, madam,	You come here, madam,
Any peer, madam,	Interfere, madam,
Though, my dear	With a peer, madam
madam,	(I am one).
This is one.	
They will stare, madam,	You're aware, madam,
When aware, madam,	What you dare, madam,
What they dare, madam,	So take care, madam,
What they've done!	And begone!

QUEEN (*furious*). Bearded by these puny mortals!
　　　　I will launch from fairy portals
　　　　All the most terrific thunders
　　　　In my armoury of wonders!

PHYLLIS (*aside*). Surely these must be immortals!
　　　　Should they launch from fairy portals

All their most terrific wonders,
We should then repent our blunders!

QUEEN.   Oh! Chancellor unwary,
　　　　It's highly necessary,
　　　　　Your tongue to teach
　　　　　Respectful speech—
　　　　Your attitude to vary!

　　　　Your badinage so airy,
　　　　Your manner arbitrary,
　　　　　Are out of place
　　　　　When face to face
　　　　With an influential Fairy!

ALL THE PEERS (*aside*).   I never knew
　　　　　We were speaking to
　　　　　An influential Fairy!

CHANCELLOR.   A plague on this vagary!
　　　　I'm in a nice quandary!
　　　　　Of hasty tone
　　　　　With dames unknown;
　　　　I ought to be more chary!

　　　　It seems that she's a fairy
　　　　From Andersen's library,
　　　　　And I took her for
　　　　　The proprietor
　　　　Of a Ladies' Seminary!

ALL.　　　$\begin{cases} He \\ We \end{cases}$ took her for
　　　　　The proprietor
　　　　Of a Ladies' Seminary!

QUEEN.   When next your Houses do assemble,
        You may tremble!

CELIA.   Our wrath, when gentlemen offend us
        Is tremendous!

LEILA.   They meet, who underrate our calling,
        Doom appalling!

QUEEN.   Take down our sentence as we speak it,
   And *he* shall wreak it! (*Indicating* STREPHON.)

QUEEN.   Henceforth, Strephon, cast away
    Crooks and pipes and ribbons so gay—
    Flocks and herds that bleat and low;
    Into Parliament you shall go!

FAIRIES.   Into Parliament he shall go!
    Backed by our supreme authority,
    He'll command a large majority:
    Into Parliament he shall go!

QUEEN.   In the Parliamentary hive,
    Liberal or Conservative—
    Whig or Tory—I don't know—
    But into Parliament you shall go!

FAIRIES.   Into Parliament, &c.

PEERS.   Ah, spare us!

    QUEEN (*speaking through music*).

Every bill and every measure
That may gratify his pleasure,
Though your fury it arouses,
Shall be passed by both your Houses!
You shall sit, if he sees reason,
Through the grouse and salmon season:
He shall end the cherished rights
You enjoy on Wednesday nights:
He shall prick that annual blister,
Marriage with deceased wife's sister:
Titles shall ennoble, then,
All the Common Councilmen:
  Peers shall teem in Christendom,
    And a Duke's exalted station
  Be attainable by Com-
    Petitive Examination!

      PEERS.

    Oh horror!
    But we'll dissemble
  The coward fear that makes us
    tremble!

    FAIRIES *and* PHYLLIS.

    Their horror!
  They can't dissemble
Nor hide the fear that makes
    them tremble!

ENSEMBLE.

PEERS.	FAIRIES, PHYLLIS, *and* STREPHON.
Young Strephon is the kind of lout	With Strephon for your foe, no doubt,
We do not care a fig about!	A fearful prospect opens out,
We cannot say	And who shall say
What evils may	What evils may
Result in consequence.	Result in consequence?
But lordly vengeance will pursue	A hideous vengeance will pursue
All kinds of common people who	All noblemen who venture to
Oppose our views,	Oppose his views,
Or boldly choose	Or boldly choose
To offer us offence.	To offer him offence.
He'd better fly at humbler game,	'Twill plunge them into grief and shame,
Or our forbearance he must claim	His kind forbearance they must claim,
If he'd escape	If they'd escape
In any shape	In any shape
A very painful wrench!	A very painful wrench.
Your powers we dauntlessly pooh-pooh:	Although our threats you now pooh-pooh,
A dire revenge will fall on you	A dire revenge will fall on you,
If you besiege	Should he besiege
Our high *prestige*	Your high *prestige*
(The word "*prestige*" is French).	(The word "*prestige*" is French.)

PEERS.   Our lordly style
        You shall not quench
      With base *canaille!*

FAIRIES.   (That word is French.)

PEERS.   Distinction ebbs
      Before a herd
      Of vulgar *plebs!*

FAIRIES.   (A Latin word.)

PEERS.   'Twould fill with joy,
      And madness stark
      The ὁι πολλοί!

FAIRIES.   (A Greek remark.)

PEERS.	FAIRIES.
You needn't wait:	We will not wait,
Away you fly!	We go sky-high!
Your threatened hate	Our threatened hate
We thus defy!	You won't defy!

FAIRIES.	Your lordly style We'll quickly quench With base *canaille*—	
PEERS.	(That word is French!)	
FAIRIES.	Distinction ebbs Before a herd Of vulgar *plebs!*	
PEERS.	(A Latin word.)	
FAIRIES.	'Twill fill with joy And madness stark The ὁι πολλοί!	
PEERS.	(A Greek remark.)	

PEERS.

You needn't wait:
   Away you fly—
Your threatened hate
   We won't defy!

FAIRIES.

We will not wait,
   We go, sky-high,
Our threatened hate
   You won't defy!

FAIRIES *threaten* PEERS *with their wands.* PEERS *kneel as begging for mercy.* PHYLLIS *implores* STREPHON *to relent. He casts her from him, and she falls fainting into the arms of* LORD MOUNT-ARARAT *and* LORD TOLLOLLER.

END OF ACT I.

ACT II.

SCENE. — *Palace Yard, Westminster.* PRIVATE WILLIS *discovered on sentry. Moonlight.*

SONG — PRIVATE WILLIS.

When all night long a chap remains
   On sentry-go, to chase monotony
He exercises of his brains,
   That is, assuming that he's got any.
Though never nurtured in the lap
   Of luxury, yet I admonish you,
I am an intellectual chap,
   And think of things that would astonish
      you.
      I often think it's comical—Fal, lal, la!
      How Nature always does contrive—
         Fal, lal, la!
        That every boy and every gal,
          That's born into the world alive,
        Is either a little Liberal,
          Or else a little Conservative!
          Fal, lal, la!

When in that house M.P.'s divide,
   If they've a brain and cerebellum, too,
They've got to leave that brain outside,
   And vote just as their leaders tell 'em to.
But then the prospect of a lot
   Of dull M.P.'s in close proximity,
All thinking for themselves, is what
   No man can face with equanimity.
      Then let's rejoice with loud Fal lal—
         Fal, lal, la!
      That Nature wisely does contrive—
         Fal, lal, la!
      That every boy and every gal
        That's born into the world alive,
      Is either a little Liberal,

Or else a little Conservative!
Fal, lal, la!

Enter FAIRIES, *with* CELIA, LEILA, *and* FLETA.
They trip round stage.

CHORUS OF FAIRIES.

Strephon's a Member of Parliament!
    And carries every Bill he chooses.
To his measures all assent;—
    Showing that fairies have their uses.
        Whigs and Tories
        Dim their glories,
Giving an ear to all his stories—
Lords and Commons are both in the blues:
Strephon makes them shake in their shoes!

ALL.   Shake in their shoes!
                Shake in their shoes!
Strephon makes them shake in their shoes!

Enter PEERS *from Westminster Hall.*

CHORUS OF PEERS.

Strephon's a Member of Parliament!
    Running amuck at all abuses.
His unqualified assent
    Somehow nobody now refuses.
        Whigs and Tories
        Dim their glories,
Giving an ear to all his stories—
Carrying every Bill he may wish:
Here's a pretty kettle of fish!
        Kettle of fish—
        Kettle of fish—
Here's a pretty kettle of fish!

Enter LORD MOUNTARARAT *and* LORD TOLLOLLER
from Westminster Hall.

CELIA.   You seem annoyed.

MOUNTARARAT.   Annoyed! I should think so!
Why this ridiculous *protégé* of yours is playing the
deuce with everything! To-night is the second reading of his Bill to throw the Peerage open to Com-
petitive Examination!

TOLLOLLER.   And he'll carry it, too!

MOUNTARARAT.   Carry it? Of course he will! He's
a Parliamentary Pickford—he carries everything!

LEILA.   Yes. If you please, that's our fault!

MOUNTARARAT.   The deuce it is!

CELIA.   Yes; we influence the members and compel them to vote just as he wishes them to.

LEILA.   It's our system. It shortens the debates.

TOLLOLLER.   Well, but think what it all means. I
don't so much mind for myself, but with a House

of Peers with no grandfathers worth mentioning,
the country must go to the dogs!

LEILA.   I suppose it must!

MOUNTARARAT.   I don't want to say a word
against brains—I've a great respect for brains—
I often wish I had some myself—but with a House
of Peers composed exclusively of people of intellect, what's to become of the House of Commons?

LEILA.   I never thought of that!

MOUNTARARAT.   This comes of women interfering
in politics. It so happens that if there is an institution in Great Britain which is not susceptible of
any improvement at all, it is the House of Peers!

SONG — LORD MOUNTARARAT.

When Britain really ruled the waves—
    (In good Queen Bess's time)
The House of Peers made no pretence
To intellectual eminence,
    Or scholarship sublime;
Yet Britain won her proudest bays
In good Queen Bess's glorious days!

CHORUS.   Yes, Britain won, &c.

When Wellington thrashed Bonaparte,
　　As every child can tell,
The House of Peers throughout the war,
Did nothing in particular,
　　And did it very well:
Yet Britain set the world a-blaze
In good King George's glorious days!

CHORUS.　Yes, Britain set, &c.

And while the House of Peers withholds
　　Its legislative hand,
And noble statesmen do not itch
To interfere with matters which
　　They do not understand,
As bright will shine Great Britain's rays,
As in King George's glorious days!

CHORUS.　As bright will shine, &c.

LEILA (*who has been much attracted by the Peers during this song*). Charming persons, are they not?

CELIA. Distinctly. For self-contained dignity, combined with airy condescension, give me a British Representative Peer!

TOLLOLLER. Then pray stop this *protégé* of yours before it's too late. Think of the mischief you're doing!

LEILA (*crying*). But we *can't* stop him now. (*Aside to* CELIA.) Aren't they lovely! (*Aloud.*) Oh why did you go and defy us, you great geese!

DUET — LEILA *and* CELIA.

LEILA.　　In vain to us you plead—
　　　　　　　Don't go;
　　　　　　Your prayers we do not heed—
　　　　　　　Don't go!
　　　　　　It's true we sigh,
　　　　　　　But don't suppose
　　　　　　A tearful eye
　　　　　　　Forgiveness shows.
　　　　　　　　Oh no!
　　　　　　We're very cross indeed—
　　　　　　　Don't go!

ALL.　　　It's true we sigh, &c.

CELIA.　　Your disrespectful sneers—
　　　　　　　Don't go!
　　　　　　Call forth indignant tears!
　　　　　　　Don't go!
　　　　　　You break our laws—
　　　　　　　You are our foe!
　　　　　　We cry because
　　　　　　　We hate you so!
　　　　　　　You know!
　　　　　　You very wicked Peers!
　　　　　　　Don't go!

FAIRIES.

You break our laws,
　　You are our foe:
We cry because
　　We hate you so!
　　You know!
You very wicked Peers!
　　Don't go!

MOUNTARARAT & TOLLOLLER.

We break their laws,
　　They are our foe:
They cry because
　　They hate us so!
　　Oh, ho!
If that's the case, my
　　dears,
We'll go!

Exeunt MOUNTARARAT, TOLLOLLER, *and Peers. Fairies gaze wistfully after them. Enter* FAIRY QUEEN.

QUEEN. Oh shame—shame upon you! Is this your fidelity to the laws you are bound to obey? Know ye not that it is death to marry a mortal?

LEILA. Yes, but it's not death to *wish* to marry a mortal!

FLETA. If it were, you'd have to execute us all!

QUEEN. Oh, this is weakness! Subdue it!

CELIA. We know it's weakness, but the weakness is so strong!

LEILA. We are not all as tough as you are!

QUEEN. Tough! Do you suppose that I am insensible to the effect of manly beauty? Look at that man (*referring to sentry*). A perfect picture! (*To sentry.*) Who are you, Sir?

WILLIS (*coming to "attention"*). Private Willis, B Company, 1st Grenadier Guards.

QUEEN. You're a very fine fellow, sir.

WILLIS. I am generally admired.

QUEEN. I can quite understand it. (*To Fairies.*) Now here is a man whose physical attributes are simply god-like. That man has a most extraordinary effect upon me. If I yielded to a natural impulse, I should fall down and worship that man. But I mortify this inclination: I wrestle with it, and it lies beneath my feet! That is how I treat my regard for that man!

SONG — FAIRY QUEEN.

Oh, foolish fay,
　　Think you, because
His brave array
　　My bosom thaws,
I'd disobey
　　Our fairy laws?
Because I fly
　　In realms above,
In tendency
　　To fall in love
Resemble I
　　The amorous dove?
(*Aside.*) Oh, amorous dove!

Type of Ovidius Naso!
This heart of mine
Is soft as thine,
Although I dare not say so!

CHORUS.   Oh, amorous dove, &c.

On fire that glows
With heat intense
I turn the hose
Of common sense,
And out it goes
At small expense!
We must maintain
Our fairy law;
That is the main
On which to draw—
In that we gain
A Captain Shaw!
(*Aside.*) Oh, Captain Shaw!
Type of true love kept under!
Could thy Brigade
With cold cascade
Quench my great love, I wonder!

CHORUS.   Oh, Captain Shaw! &c.
(*Exeunt Fairies and* FAIRY QUEEN, *sorrowfully.*)

Enter PHYLLIS.

PHYLLIS (*half crying*).   I can't think why I'm not
in better spirits! I'm engaged to two noblemen at
once. That ought to be enough to make any girl
happy. But I'm miserable! Don't suppose it's because I care for Strephon, for I hate him! No girl
could care for a man who goes about with a
mother considerably younger than himself!

Enter LORD MOUNTARARAT.

MOUNTARARAT.   Phyllis! My own! (*Embracing
her.*)
PHYLLIS.   Don't! How dare you! But perhaps you
are the nobleman I'm engaged to?
MOUNTARARAT.   I am one of them.
PHYLLIS.   Oh! But how come *you* to have a peer-
age?
MOUNTARARAT.   It's a prize for being born first.
PHYLLIS.   A kind of Derby Cup.
MOUNTARARAT.   Not at all! I come of a very old
and distinguished family.
PHYLLIS.   And you're proud of your race? But of
course you are—you won it! But why are people
made peers?
MOUNTARARAT.   The principle is not easy to ex-
plain. I'll give you an example.

De Belville was regarded as the Crichton of his
age:
His tragedies were reckoned much too thoughtful for the stage:

His poems held a noble rank—although it's very
true
That, being very proper, they were read by very
few.
He was a famous Painter, too, and shone upon
the Line,
And even Mister Ruskin came and worshipped
at his shrine:
But, alas, the school he followed was heroically
high—
The kind of Art men rave about, but very sel-
dom buy.
And everybody said,
"How can he be repaid—
This very great—this very good—this very
gifted man?"
But nobody could hit upon a practicable plan!

He was a great Inventor, and discovered, all
alone,
A plan for making everybody's fortune but his
own;
For in business an Inventor's little better than
a fool,
And my highly gifted friend was no exception to
the rule.
His poems—people read 'em in the sixpenny
Reviews;
His pictures—they engraved 'em in the *Illus-
trated News;*
His inventions—they perhaps might have en-
riched him by degrees,
But all his little income went in Patent Office
fees!
So everybody said
"How *can* he be repaid—
This *very* great—this *very* good—this *very*
gifted man?"
But nobody could hit upon a practicable plan!

At last the point was given up in absolute des-
pair,
When a distant cousin died, and he became a
millionaire!
With a county seat in Parliament, a moor or two
of grouse,
And a taste for making inconvenient speeches
in the House.
Then, Government conferred on him the high-
est of rewards—
They took him from the Commons and they put
him in the Lords!
And who so fit to sit in it, deny it if you can,
As this very great—this very good—this very
gifted man?
Though I'm more than half afraid
That it sometimes may be said
That we never should have revelled in that
source of proper pride—

However great his merits—if his cousin hadn't died!

Enter TOLLOLLER.

TOLLOLLER. Phyllis! My darling! (*Embraces her.*)

PHYLLIS. Here's the other! Well, have you settled which it's to be?

TOLLOLLER. Not altogether. It's a difficult position. It would be hardly delicate to toss up. On the whole we would rather leave it to you.

PHYLLIS. It can't possibly concern me. You are both Earls, and you are both rich, and you are both plain.

MOUNTARARAT. So we are. At least I am.

TOLLOLLER. So am I.

MOUNTARARAT. No, no!

TOLLOLLER. I am indeed. Very plain.

MOUNTARARAT. Well, well—perhaps you are.

PHYLLIS. There's really nothing to choose between you. If one of you would forgo his title, and distribute his estates among his Irish tenantry, why then I should then see a reason for accepting the other.

MOUNTARARAT. Tolloller, are you prepared to make this sacrifice?

TOLLOLLER. No!

MOUNTARARAT. Not even to oblige a lady?

TOLLOLLER. No!

MOUNTARARAT. Then the only question is, which of us shall give way to the other? Perhaps, on the whole, she would be happier with me. I don't know. I may be wrong.

TOLLOLLER. No. I don't know that you are. I really believe she would. But the painful part of the thing is that if you rob me of the girl of my heart, one of us must die. The Tollollers have invariably destroyed their successful rivals. It's a family tradition that I have sworn to respect.

MOUNTARARAT. Humph! Did you swear it before a Commissioner?

TOLLOLLER. I did. On affidavit!

MOUNTARARAT. Ha! Then I don't see how you can help yourself!

TOLLOLLER. It's a painful position, for I have a very strong regard for you, George.

MOUNTARARAT (*much affected*). My dear Thomas!

TOLLOLLER. You are very dear to me, George. We were boys together—at least *I* was. If I were to survive you, my existence would be hopelessly embittered.

MOUNTARARAT. Then, my dear Thomas, you must not do it. I say it again and again—if it will have this effect upon you, you must not do it. No, no. If one of us is to destroy the other, let it be me!

TOLLOLLER. No, no.

MOUNTARARAT. Ah, yes!—by our boyish friendship I implore you!

TOLLOLLER (*much moved*). Well, well, be it so. But, no—no—I cannot consent to an act which would crush you with unavailing remorse.

MOUNTARARAT. But it would not do so. I should be very sad at first—oh, who would not be?—but it would wear off. I like you *very much*—but not, perhaps, as much as you like me.

TOLLOLLER. George, you're a noble fellow, but that tell-tale tear betrays you. No, George; you are very fond of me, and I cannot consent to give you a week's uneasiness on my account.

MOUNTARARAT. But, dear Thomas, it would not last a week! Remember, you lead the House of Lords! on your demise I shall take your place! Oh, Thomas, it would not last a day!

PHYLLIS (*coming down*). Now I do hope you're not going to fight about me, because it's really not worth while.

TOLLOLLER (*looking at her*). Well, I don't believe it is!

MOUNTARARAT. Nor I. The sacred ties of Friendship are paramount. No consideration shall induce me to raise my hand against Thomas!

TOLLOLLER. And in my eyes the life of George is more sacred than love itself!

QUARTETTE.

MOUNTARARAT, TOLLOLLER, PHYLLIS, *and* WILLIS.

TOLLOLLER.   Though p'r'aps I may incur your blame,
          The things are few
          I would not do
     In Friendship's name!

MOUNTARARAT.   And I may say I think the same;
          Not even love
          Should rank above
     True Friendship's name!

PHYLLIS.   Then free me, pray; be mine the blame;
          Forget your craze
          And go your ways
     In Friendship's name!

WILLIS.   Accept, oh Friendship, all the same,
     This sacrifice to thy dear name!

ALL.   Oh, many a man, in Friendship's name,
     Has yielded fortune, rank, and fame!
     But no one yet, in the world so wide,
     Has yielded up a promised bride!

(*Exeunt* MOUNTARARAT *and* TOLLOLLER, *lovingly, in one direction, and* PHYLLIS *in another.*)

Enter LORD CHANCELLOR, *very miserable.*

RECITATIVE.

CHANCELLOR.   Love, unrequited, robs me of my rest:
     Love, hopeless love, my ardent soul encumbers:
     Love, nightmare-like, lies heavy on my chest,
     And weaves itself into my midnight slumbers!

SONG — LORD CHANCELLOR.

When you're lying awake with a dismal headache, and repose is taboo'd by anxiety,
I conceive you may use any language you choose to indulge in, without impropriety;
For your brain is on fire—the bedclothes conspire of usual slumber to plunder you:
First your counterpane goes, and uncovers your toes, and your sheet slips demurely from under you;
Then the blanketing tickles—you feel like mixed pickles—so terribly sharp is the pricking,
And you're hot, and you're cross, and you tumble and toss till there's nothing 'twixt you and the ticking.
Then the bedclothes all creep to the ground in a heap, and you pick 'em all up in a tangle;
Next your pillow resigns and politely declines to remain at its usual angle!

Well, you get some repose in the form of a doze, with hot eye-balls and head ever aching,
But your slumbering teems with such horrible dreams that you'd very much better be waking;
For you dream you are crossing the Channel, and tossing about in a steamer from Harwich—
Which is something between a large bathing machine and a very small second-class carriage—
And you're giving a treat (penny ice and cold meat) to a party of friends and relations—
They're a ravenous horde—and they all came on board at Sloane Square and South Kensington Stations.
And bound on that journey you find your attorney (who started that morning from Devon);
He's a bit undersized, and you don't feel surprised when he tells you he's only eleven.
Well, you're driving like mad with this singular lad (by-the-by, the ship's now a four-wheeler),
And you're playing round games, and he calls you bad names when you tell him that "ties pay the dealer";
But this you can't stand, so you throw up your hand, and you find you're as cold as an icicle,
In your shirt and your socks (the black silk with gold clocks), crossing Salisbury Plain on a bicycle:
And he and the crew are on bicycles, too—which they've somehow or other invested in—
And he's telling the tars, all the particulars of a company he's interested in—
It's a scheme of devices, to get at low prices, all goods from cough mixtures to cables
(Which tickled the sailors) by treating retailers, as though they were all vegetables—
You get a good spadesman to plant a small tradesman (first take off his boots with a boot-tree),
And his legs will take root, and his fingers will shoot, and they'll blossom and bud like a fruit-tree—
From the greengrocer tree you get grapes and green pea, cauliflower, pineapple, and cranberries,
While the pastry-cook plant, cherry brandy will grant, apple puffs, and three-corners, and banberries—
The shares are a penny, and ever so many are taken by Rothschild and Baring,
And just as a few are allotted to you, you awake with a shudder despairing—
You're a regular wreck, with a crick in your neck, and no wonder you snore, for your head's on the floor, and you've needles and pins from your soles to your shins, and your flesh is a-creep, for your left leg's asleep, and you've cramp in your toes, and a fly on your nose, and some fluff in your lung, and a feverish tongue, and a thirst that's intense, and a general sense that

you haven't been sleeping in clover;
But the darkness has passed, and it's daylight at last, and the night has been long—ditto ditto my song—and thank goodness they're both of them over!

(LORD CHANCELLOR *falls exhausted on a seat*.)

LORDS MOUNTARARAT *and* TOLLOLLER *come forward*.

MOUNTARARAT. I am much distressed to see your Lordship in this condition.

CHANCELLOR. Ah, my Lords, it is seldom that a Lord Chancellor has reason to envy the position of another, but I am free to confess that I would rather be two Earls engaged to Phyllis than any other half-dozen noblemen upon the face of the globe!

TOLLOLLER (*without enthusiasm*). Yes. It's an enviable position when you're the only one.

MOUNTARARAT. Oh yes, no doubt—most enviable. At the same time, seeing you thus, we naturally say to ourselves, "This is very sad. His Lordship is constitutionally as blithe as a bird—he trills upon the bench like a thing of song and gladness. His series of judgments in F sharp, given *andante* in six-eight time, are among the most remarkable effects ever produced in a Court of Chancery. He is, perhaps, the only living instance of a judge whose decrees have received the honour of a double *encore*. How can we bring ourselves to do that which will deprive the Court of Chancery of one of its most attractive features?"

CHANCELLOR. I feel the force of your remarks, but I am here in two capacities, and they clash, my Lord, they clash! I deeply grieve to say that in declining to entertain my last application, I presumed to address myself in terms which render it impossible for me ever to apply to myself again. It was a most painful scene, my Lord—most painful!

TOLLOLLER. This is what it is to have two capacities! Let us be thankful that we are persons of no capacity whatever.

MOUNTARARAT. Come, come. Remember you are a very just and kindly old gentleman, and you need have no hesitation in approaching yourself, so that you do so respectfully and with a proper show of deference.

CHANCELLOR. Do you really think so? Well, I will nerve myself to another effort, and, if that fails, I resign myself to my fate!

TRIO.

LORD CHANCELLOR, LORDS MOUNTARARAT *and* TOLLOLLER.

MOUNTARARAT. If you go in
You're sure to win—
Yours will be the charming maidie:
Be your law
The ancient saw,
"Faint heart never won fair lady!"

ALL. Faint heart never won fair lady!
Every journey has an end—
When at the worst affairs will mend—
Dark the dawn when day is nigh—
Hustle your horse and don't say die!

TOLLOLLER. He who shies
At such a prize
Is not worth a maravedi;
Be so kind
To bear in mind—
"Faint heart never won fair lady!"

ALL. Faint heart never won fair lady!
While the sun shines make your hay—
Where a will is, there's a way—
Beard the lion in his lair—
None but the brave deserve the fair!

CHANCELLOR. I'll take heart
And make a start—
Though I fear the prospect's shady—
Much I'd spend
To gain my end—
Faint heart never won fair lady!

ALL. Faint heart never won fair lady!
Nothing venture, nothing win—
Blood is thick, but water's thin—
In for a penny, in for a pound—
It's Love that makes the world go round!
(*Dance, and exeunt arm-in-arm together*.)

Enter STREPHON.

RECITATIVE.

My Bill has now been read a second time:
His ready vote no Member now refuses;

In verity I wield a power sublime,
    And one that I can turn to mighty uses!
What joy to carry, in the very teeth
    Of Ministry, Cross-Bench, and Opposition,
Some rather urgent measures—quite beneath
    The ken of patriot and politician!

SONG.

Fold your flapping wings,
    Soaring Legislature!
Stoop to little things—
    Stoop to Human Nature!
Never need to roam,
    Members patriotic,
Let's begin at home—
        Crime is no exotic!
            Bitter is your bane—
                Terrible your trials—
            Dingy Drury Lane!
                Soapless Seven Dials!

Take a tipsy lout
    Gathered from the gutter—
Hustle him about—
    Strap him to a shutter:
What am I but he,
    Washed at hours stated—
Fed on filagree—
        Clothed and educated?
            He's a mark of scorn—
                I might be another,
            If I had been born
                Of a tipsy mother!

Take a wretched thief
    Through the city sneaking,
Pocket handkerchief
    Ever, ever seeking:
What is he but I
    Robbed of all my chances—
Picking pockets by
        Force of circumstances?
            I might be as bad—
                As unlucky, rather—
            If I'd only had
                Fagin for a father!

Enter PHYLLIS.

PHYLLIS (*starting*). Strephon!

STREPHON (*starting*). Phyllis! But I suppose, I should say "My Lady." I have not yet been informed which title your ladyship has pleased to select?

PHYLLIS. I—I haven't quite decided. You see, *I* have no *mother* to advise *me!*

STREPHON. No. I have.

PHYLLIS. Yes; a *young* mother.

STREPHON. Not very—a couple of centuries or so.

PHYLLIS. Oh! She wears well.

STREPHON. She does. She's a fairy.

PHYLLIS. I beg your pardon—a what?

STREPHON. Oh, I've no longer any reason to conceal the fact—she's a fairy.

PHYLLIS. A fairy! Well, but—that would account for a good many things! Then—I suppose *you're* a fairy?

STREPHON. I'm half a fairy.

PHYLLIS. Which half?

STREPHON. The upper half—down to the waistcoat.

PHYLLIS. Dear me (*prodding him with her fingers*). There is nothing to show it! But why didn't you tell me this before?

STREPHON. I thought you would take a dislike to me. But as it's all off, you may as well know the truth—I'm only half a mortal!

PHYLLIS (*crying*). But I'd rather have half a mortal I do love, than half a dozen I don't!

STREPHON. Oh, I think not—go to your half dozen.

PHYLLIS (*crying*). It's only two! and I hate 'em! Please forgive me!

STREPHON. I don't think I ought to. Besides, all sorts of difficulties will arise. You know, my grandmother looks quite as young as my mother. So do all my aunts.

PHYLLIS. I quite understand. Whenever I see you kissing a very young lady, I shall know it's an elderly relative.

STREPHON. You will? Then, Phyllis, I think we shall be very happy! (*Embracing her.*)

PHYLLIS. We won't wait long.

STREPHON. No—we might change our minds. We'll get married first.

PHYLLIS. And change our minds afterwards?

STREPHON. That's the usual course.

DUET — STREPHON *and* PHYLLIS.

STREPHON. If we're weak enough to tarry
                Ere we marry,
                    You and I,
            Of the feeling I inspire
                You may tire
                    By and by.
            For Peers with flowing coffers
                Press their offers—
                    That is why
            I think we will not tarry
                Ere we marry,
                    You and I!

PHYLLIS.   If we're weak enough to tarry
        Ere we marry,
           You and I,
  With some more attractive maiden,
        Jewel-laden,
           You may fly.
If by chance we should be parted,
        Broken hearted
           I should die—
So I think we will not tarry
        Ere we marry,
           You and I!

PHYLLIS.   But does your mother know you're— I mean, is she aware of an engagement?

Enter IOLANTHE.

IOLANTHE.   She is—and thus she welcomes her daughter-in-law! (*Kisses her.*)

PHYLLIS.   She kisses just like other people! But the Lord Chancellor!

STREPHON.   I forgot him! Mother, none can resist your fairy eloquence: you will go to him, and plead for us?

IOLANTHE (*much agitated*).   No, no, impossible!

STREPHON.   But our happiness—our very lives, depend upon our obtaining his consent!

PHYLLIS.   Oh, madam, you cannot refuse to do this!

IOLANTHE.   You know not what you ask! The Lord Chancellor is—my husband!

STREPHON *and* PHYLLIS.   Your husband!

IOLANTHE.   My husband and your father! (*Addressing* STREPHON, *who is much moved.*)

PHYLLIS.   Then our course is plain: on his learning that Strephon is his son, all objection to our marriage will be at once removed!

IOLANTHE.   No, he must never know! He believes me to have died childless, and dearly as I love him, I am bound, under penalty of death, not to undeceive him. But see—he comes! Quick—my veil! (*They retire up as* IOLANTHE *veils herself.*)

Enter LORD CHANCELLOR.

CHANCELLOR.   Victory! Victory! Success has crowned my efforts, and I may consider myself engaged to Phyllis! At first I wouldn't hear of it— it was out of the question. But I took heart. I pointed out to myself that I was no stranger to myself—that, in point of fact, I had been personally acquainted with myself for some years. This had its effect. I admitted that I had watched my professional advancement with considerable interest, and I handsomely added that I yielded to no one in admiration for my private and professional virtues. This was a great point gained. I then en-

deavoured to work upon my feelings. Conceive my joy when I distinctly perceived a tear glistening in my own eye! Eventually, after a severe struggle with myself, I reluctantly—most reluctantly— consented!

IOLANTHE *comes down veiled*—STREPHON *and* PHYLLIS *go off on tiptoe.*

RECITATIVE.

IOLANTHE.   My Lord, a suppliant at your feet I kneel.
  Oh, listen to a mother's fond appeal!
  Hear me to-night! I come in urgent need—
  'Tis for my son, young Strephon, that I plead!

BALLAD — IOLANTHE.

  He loves! If in the bygone years
    Thine eyes have ever shed
  Tears—bitter, unavailing tears,
    For one untimely dead—
  If in the eventide of life
    Sad thoughts of her arise,
  Then let the memory of thy wife
    Plead for my boy—he dies!

  He dies! If fondly laid aside
    In some old cabinet,
  Memorials of thy long-dead bride
    Lie, dearly treasured yet,
  Then let her hallowed bridal dress—
    Her little dainty gloves—
  Her withered flowers—her faded tress—
    Plead for my boy—he loves!
(*The* LORD CHANCELLOR *is moved by this appeal. After a pause:*)

CHANCELLOR.   It may not be—for so the fates decide!
  Learn thou that Phyllis is my promised bride!

IOLANTHE (*in horror*).   Thy bride! No! No!

CHANCELLOR.   It shall be so!
  Those who would separate us woe betide!

IOLANTHE.   My doom thy lips have spoken—
    I plead in vain!

CHORUS OF FAIRIES (*without*).   Forbear! forbear!

IOLANTHE.   A vow already broken
    I break again!

CHORUS OF FAIRIES (*without*).   Forbear! forbear!

IOLANTHE.   For him—for her—for thee
    I yield my life.
    Behold—it may not be!
    I am thy wife.

CHORUS OF FAIRIES (*without*).   Aiaiah! Aiaiah! Willaloo!

CHANCELLOR (*recognizing her*). Iolanthe! thou livest?

IOLANTHE. Aye!
I live! Now let me die!

Enter FAIRY QUEEN *and* FAIRIES. IOLANTHE *kneels to her.*

QUEEN. Once again thy vows are broken:
Thou thyself thy doom hath spoken!

CHORUS OF FAIRIES. Aiaiah! Aiaiah!
Willahalah! Willaloo!
Laloiah! Laloiah!
Willahalah! Willaloo!

QUEEN. Bow thy head to Destiny:
Death thy doom, and thou shalt die!

CHORUS OF FAIRIES. Aiaiah! Aiaiah! &c.

The PEERS *and* STREPHON *enter. The* QUEEN *raises her spear.*

LEILA. Hold! If Iolanthe must die, so must we all; for, as she has sinned, so have we!

QUEEN. What!

PEERS *and* FAIRIES *kneel to her*—LORD MOUNT-ARARAT *with* CELIA; LORD TOLLOLLER *with* LEILA.

CELIA. We are all fairy duchesses, marchionesses, countesses, viscountesses, and baronesses.

MOUNTARARAT. It's our fault. They couldn't help themselves.

QUEEN. It seems they *have* helped themselves, and pretty freely, too! (*After a pause.*) You have all incurred death; but I can't slaughter the whole company! And yet (*unfolding a scroll*) the law is clear—every fairy must die who marries a mortal!

CHANCELLOR. Allow me, as an old equity draughtsman, to make a suggestion. The subtleties of the legal mind are equal to the emergency. The thing is really quite simple—the insertion of a single word will do it. Let it stand that every fairy shall die who *don't* marry a mortal, and there you are, out of your difficulty at once!

QUEEN. We like your humour. Very well! (*Altering the MS. in pencil.*) Private Willis!

SENTRY (*coming forward*). Ma'am!

QUEEN. To save my life, it is necessary that I marry at once. How should you like to be a fairy guardsman?

SENTRY. Well, ma'am, I don't think much of the British soldier who wouldn't ill-conwenience himself to save a female in distress.

QUEEN. You are a brave fellow. You're a fairy from this moment. (*Wings spring from Sentry's shoulders.*) And you, my Lords, how say you? Will you join our ranks? (FAIRIES *kneel to* PEERS *and implore them to do so.*)

MOUNTARARAT (*to* TOLLOLLER). Well, now that the Peers are to be recruited entirely from persons of intelligence, I really don't see what use *we* are, down here.

TOLLOLLER. None whatever.

QUEEN. Good! (*Wings spring from shoulders of Peers.*) Then away we go to Fairyland.

FINALE.

PHYLLIS. Soon as we may,
Off and away!
We'll commence our journey airy—
Happy are we—
As you can see,
Every one is now a fairy!

ALL. Every one is now a fairy!

IOLANTHE, QUEEN, & PHYLLIS. Though as a general rule we know
Two strings go to every bow,
Make up your minds that grief 'twill bring,
If you've two beaux to every string.

ALL. Though as a general rule, &c.

CHANCELLOR. Up in the sky,
Ever so high,
Pleasures come in endless series;
We will arrange
Happy exchange—
House of Peers for House of Peris!

ALL. House of Peers for House of Peris!

CHANCELLOR, MOUNTARARAT, & TOLLOLLER.
Up in the air, sky-high, sky-high,
Free from Wards in Chancery,

$\left\{ \begin{array}{c} \text{I} \\ \text{He} \end{array} \right\}$ will be surely happier, for

$\left\{ \begin{array}{c} \text{I'm} \\ \text{He's} \end{array} \right\}$ such a susceptible Chancellor!

ALL. Up in the air, &c.

CURTAIN.

Postscript

THE CHIEF CHANGE in Iolanthe was the deletion, soon after the opening, of two songs in Act II: the De Belville song for Mountararat and Strephon's "Fold your flapping wings." "De Belville was regarded as the Crichton of his age" appeared in Act II after the final chorus of "Oh Captain Shaw!" and the exit of the Fairy Queen.

In the first edition of the libretto used by the audience in the Savoy Theatre November 25, 1882, and in the performance that night, following Phyllis's entrance and soliloquy (page 195) Lord Mountararat entered alone, embraced Phyllis, had a short passage of dialog with her, and then delivered the De Belville song, before the entrance of Lord Tolloller. The word "delivered" is deliberate, for this number apparently was recited rather than sung by Rutland Barrington. Furthermore, on that occasion he appears to have omitted the second verse.

Previous students of Gilbert & Sullivan opera have maintained that the De Belville song was cut out in rehearsal and was never used in an actual performance except in the United States. This has led to the conclusion that the libretto text reprinted here for the first time since 1882 was a pre-first-night edition, a bibliographic curiosity, and not the libretto of the actual opening night performance. Indisputable proof, heretofore overlooked, lies in the review of the first-night performance by the *Advertiser*, November 27, 1882.

> The opera contains surprises in plenty, and one that came with singular effect on Saturday night. Those who had books of the words came in due course to a kind of Bab Ballad, and in Mr. Gilbert's best vein, "De Belville was regarded as the Crichton of his age." It fell to the lot of Lord Mountararat, and everyone of course thought Mr. Barrington would sing it. To the intense surprise, however, of the audience, the facetious ballad was recited. It should have made a stronger mark than it did for it is very cleverly written. The middle verse was omitted, which was a pity, for not a line of so good a thing should be lost.

Gilbert must have shared this reviewer's feeling about his lyric for he printed the De Belville song in *Songs of a Savoyard* in 1890, indexing it as "omitted in representation" and titling it "The Reward of Merit," an ironic name for a lyric whose merit has been largely overlooked.

It is likely that the cloud of error that has obscured the facts regarding this song grew from within the D'Oyly Carte organization itself, climaxed by a seemingly official nod of approval from Rupert D'Oyly Carte in an explanatory note to "Mountararat's Lost Lyric" in the *Gilbert & Sullivan Journal*, June 1929:

> Mountararat's song (which was set to music by Sullivan) was cut out at rehearsal before the first production. The dialogue was altered to meet this cut. The same applies to the other *Iolanthe* lyric [i.e. 'Fold your flapping wings']. As the operas were printed in the United States after their first production without reference to the author and composer, they never had an opportunity to correct the scores or libretti.

The foregoing indicates that Rupert D'Oyly Carte maintained erroneously that both these songs were cut out before opening night. He also implied, in the words "without reference to the author and composer," that the American libretto and vocal score were piracies beyond the control of Gilbert, Sullivan, and his father Richard D'Oyly Carte. This was not the case. Both the first American libretto and vocal score were copyrighted by J. M. Stoddart & Co. by arrangement with D'Oyly Carte (the former in November, the latter in December 1882) and carry an "Authorized Copyright Editions" notice over the names of Gilbert and Sullivan. The early American librettos, like the British first edition, printed both the songs in question. The first American vocal score printed only "Fold your flapping wings" and omitted the De Belville song as did the British second-edition libretto. The first British edition of the vocal score omitted both songs as did the third-edition libretto.

It is difficult to understand why the music for the De Belville song was not used on opening night as it certainly was performed some five hours later when *Iolanthe* received its American première at the Standard Theatre in New York. The review of this occasion in *Music and Drama*, December 2, 1882, makes this indisputable: "The song, 'De Belville was regarded' (for Mountararat) is another capital number, although not altogether free from the influence of Mozart. There is, however, a vigor and spontaneity about it, allied with genial good nature, that cannot fail to render it popular."

"Fold your flapping wings, soaring Legislature" (page 199) appeared immediately after the Lord Chancellor, Lord Tolloller, and Lord Mountararat danced off the stage arm-in-arm, having sung the last encored verse of their ever popular Trio, "Faint heart never won fair lady!" In the first and second editions of the libretto and at least in the opening-night performance at the Savoy, Strephon entered (with no libretto comment as to his low spirits) and delivered himself of a recitative of eight lines commencing "My bill has now been read a second time," from which he launched into the song, "Fold your flapping wings." At the conclusion of this song Phyllis entered. In all editions of the libretto after the second, Strephon enters "in very low spirits" with a three-line soliloquy, "I suppose one ought to enjoy oneself in Parliament . . . ," which is interrupted by the entrance of Phyllis.

From the fact that this song was not removed from the second edition at the same time the De Belville song was dropped, it can be surmised that it was sung in more London performances than merely on the opening night. The *Daily News* in its review of November 27, 1882, mentioned this as a "declamatory song." Yet, Beatty-Kingston, writing for the *Theatre,* January 1, 1883, referred to it as a "song" and as "sung" on opening night, when he took Gilbert to task in his review for moral preachment in this lyric (see pages 175-6).

Again, it is from the review of the American first-performance in *Music and Drama* that one learns how the music was first received: "An exquisite song for Strephon in A Minor, *'Fold your flapping wings,'* is quite classical in its way, accompanied by strings only, except in the last verse, when the scoring was most picturesque, the word-music being adroitly employed in most artistic fashion." In America the music of this song was included in the first edition of the vocal score, and so, fortunately, has survived, whereas that of the De Belville song has disappeared altogether.

Princess Ida

Introduction

IF IT IS TRUE—as it probably is—that Arthur Sullivan was the only person in the world who attended the first nights of all fourteen Gilbert and Sullivan operas, from overture to final curtain, then it was the first night of *Princess Ida* that came closest to breaking this unique attendance record. Even D'Oyly Carte did not expect his composer-colleague to be on hand at the Savoy the night of Saturday, January 5, 1884. In fact, Carte had set aside the programs already printed for the first performance because they included the line, "The Opera will be conducted on this occasion by the Composer," and had ordered a rerun which substituted the line, "Musical Conductor, Mr. Frank Cellier." As far as Carte was aware, Sullivan lay, painfully ill and mercifully drugged, in his Queen's Mansions flat.

Excess of work, the paralytic stroke of his close friend and fellow-conductor Frederic Clay, and the emotional strain of the departure of his brother's widow to permanent residence in California—all had worn Sullivan's slim thread of physical resistance to the breaking-point. The scoring and rehearsing of his new opera had him working round the clock. He had completed the score of *Princess Ida* on January 1. On January 2, after a morning of rehearsal, he composed two more of its songs. On Friday, January 4, the day before the production, "he attended a full-dress rehearsal that lasted till 2:30 a.m. He went home and got into bed, but before daylight he was attacked by violent pain and a doctor was summoned. Morphia was injected. It might have been water, for it was of no avail. Saturday dawned. That night the crowds would be hustling at the Savoy for admission to the first performance. He lay in bed, inert and helpless, seeing these things happening in some panorama that swept across his mind. Happening without him. The doctor departed knowing full well that his patient was too ill to get up, therefore his warnings against so doing were unnecessary. But towards the afternoon Sullivan crawled out of bed, dropped to the floor, then struggled to a chair. He had made up his mind."

A combination of more morphine and black coffee enabled him to dress and leave for the Savoy Theatre. The performance was billed to start at eight p.m. Sullivan did not arrive till after that time, when, of course, the audience was already seated and the second-run programs distributed. So the surprised D'Oyly Carte had no opportunity to change back to the correct first-run copies that announced the composer as conducting. But he evidently used these January 5, "composer-conducting" programs to fill in at performances early the following week when considerations of thrift prevailed over those of accuracy. (Sullivan could not have conducted them, as he was flat on his back.) Two members of the audience on Monday and Wednesday thoughtfully wrote the dates "January 7" and "January 9" on their copies of this first-run program. A member of the first-night audience had written "January 5 Amphitheatre" on his copy of the second-run program, helpfully completing this chain of evidence.

If there was a souvenir program that night, it is either not identifiable or remains to be located. A four-page, gold-decorated program appeared early in the *Princess Ida* run. The much-used eight-page, full-color souvenir designed by Miss Alice Havers (Mrs. Morgan) was not circulated until the very end of June or early July (according to an article printed in the *World,* on June 25, 1884).

One reviewer in the theatre that evening recorded 8:25 as the time the performance got under way. This lateness gave unusual opportunity for the first-nighters of the pit to ogle and discuss the first-nighters of the stalls and boxes. Wallis Mackay, "Our Captious Critic" in the *Illustrated Sporting and Dramatic News,* on that occasion described the scene:

> I was curious to investigate the young people, who usually, indeed invariably, occupy the front rows of the pit and volubly give their comments on the play, players, and audience. I, therefore, betook me to the pit, which in the Savoy Theatre is as comfortable and more roomy than the stalls of many of our houses. The young men were all there, and eager for the fray. There had been some rumour of one of those "organized oppositions" that are so frequent and unfair, but it did not come off to any great extent. The young men were all excitement, and greedily looked out at the arrivals in the stalls, "There, that's so-and-so," and "There's Lord Thingamy," with loud comments. . . . Each young man was armed with a large pair of opera-glasses, in some cases rising to the proportions of telescopes lashed together. These were levelled all round with eager competition to criticise the defenseless wretches in the stalls; and certainly where the young men gain their various and curious experiences and information from is a mystery to me, but they gabbled away until Sir Arthur [he had been knighted in May 1883] took his seat in the orchestra, and then they settled down for the night's business, where we will leave them.

Among the targets for these young men of the Savoy pit on January 5 were the Baroness Burdett-Coutts, philanthropist and patroness of the arts, and her American husband Mr. William Burdett-Coutts; Baron Rothschild; Sir Albert Sassoon, the Anglo-Indian merchant; Sir George Arthur, the Earl of Dunraven, and the beautiful Miss Fortescue (she had graced the original casts of both *Patience* and *Iolanthe*) on the arm of her fiancé Lord Garmoyle. (Before the year was out she was to collect £10,000 heart balm from him . . . "though but a simple chorus maiden," as Percy Fitzgerald's period prose described her.) The reviewer for *England* exuberantly reported Lord Tennyson in the audience, but the presence of his Laureateship was refuted by another journal. Edmund Yates, Archibald Forbes, and Bronson Howard were there, as well as Arthur Pinero

with his recent bride, the actress Myra Holme. All in all, it was, as headlined by the *Sportsman,* a "Brilliant Night at the Savoy."

The performance began with a short musical prelude instead of the usual overture, and then the curtains parted on the first of three sets described by Beatty-Kingston in the *Theatre* as "amongst the most beautiful pictures ever exhibited on any stage." The Prologue and Act II were by Henry Emden. The set for Act I, which Beatty-Kingston preferred of the three, was by Hawes Craven. Of the costumes in this act, the *Sportsman* bantered: "The girls were dressed with a quaint richness, suggesting Portia after a visit to Swan & Edgar's."

The critic for the *Observer,* who thought the opera was too long, wrote: "The Prologue, however, which is brief and to the point, is full of spirit. . . . [It] ends as brightly as it began, and the verdict so far upon *Princess Ida* is wholly favourable."

After the Prologue, at the climax of Act I, occurred the only stage-effect mishap ever recorded to have marred a Gilbert-trained and -stage-managed opening night. In the confusion attendant on Princess Ida's discovery that her Castle Adamant girls' college had been penetrated by Nature's sole mistake, Man, Leonora Braham playing the title role is supposed to fall into a stream from which she is promptly rescued by Hilarion. The sight-lines for this effect had not been checked properly. As the *Sportsman* put it: "The plunge and Hilarion's jump into the water were badly managed on Saturday night, and evoked the derisive laughter of 'the gods,' the simple facts of the case evidently being that the scene had not been studied from the theatrical Olympian heights."

The finale of Act I, "To yield at once to such a foe," apparently "was not heard to advantage on the first night . . . and a little more rehearsal" was recommended as "evidently desirable" by the *Saturday Review,* even though it "nevertheless was encored. . . ."

Faced with two intermissions for his first three-act opera, "Mr. D'Oyly Carte, a careful, clever manager," wrote *Sporting Life,* "has issued intimation that the entr'actes will be lengthy and asking indulgence." So it would appear that "indulgence slips" that evening must have been contained in each program or circulated separately, but no surviving copy has yet come to light. Carte was right to have been concerned with his scene changes. The *Referee* reported that it was nearly eleven o'clock before the curtain rose on the last act. It was this last act, Act II, that by press consensus was the least successful. The *Figaro* wrote that it "drags and is from every point of view the weakest."

At 8.0 p.m.,

A respectful operatic perversion of Tennyson's "PRINCESS," in a Prologue and
Two Acts, entitled

❋ PRINCESS IDA; ❋

Or, CASTLE ADAMANT.

Written by W. S. GILBERT, Composed by ARTHUR SULLIVAN.

PROLOGUE	...	Pavilion in King Hildebrand's Palace	...	Emden.
ACT I....	...	Gardens of Castle Adamant	..	Hawes Craven.
ACT II.	...	Courtyard of Castle Adamant	...	Emden.

Musical Conductor, Mr. FRANK CELLIER.   Stage Manager. Mr. W. H. SEYMOUR.

The Opera produced under the personal direction of the Author and Composer.

The Dresses by Madame AUGUSTE and Miss FISHER. The Armour by M. LEBLANC
GRANGER, of Paris. The entire Theatre, Stage, and Auditorium is lighted by Electricity.
The arrangements for this lighting are carried out by Messrs. SIEMENS BROS. & Co.,
Limited; the Lamps used being Swan's Incandescent Lamps. The Telephones used
on the Stage are lent by the UNITED TELEPHONE Co.

No Fees of any kind.

❖ DRAMATIS PERSONÆ. ❖

King Hildebrand	...	...	...	Mr. RUTLAND BARRINGTON.
Hilarion, *his Son*	...	...	...	...	Mr. BRACY.
Cyril				
Florian	*Hilarion's Friends*	...	...	Mr. DURWARD LELY.
King Gama	...	...	...	Mr. GEORGE GROSSMITH.
Arac	...	...		...	Mr. R. TEMPLE.
Guron	...	...	*his Sons*	...	Mr. W. GREY.
Scynthius	...			...	... Mr. LUGG.
Princess Ida, *Gama's Daughter*	...	Miss LEONORA BRAHAM.
Lady Blanche	...	*Professors at Prin-*	Miss BRANDRAM.
Lady Psyche	...	*cess Ida's College*	... Miss KATE CHARD.
Melissa, *Lady Blanche's Daughter*	...	...	... Miss JESSIE BOND.
Sacharissa	...		...	Miss SYBIL GREY.
Chloe	...	...	*Girl Graduates*	... Miss HEATHCOTE.
Ada	...	...		... Miss TWYMAN.

Soldiers, Courtiers, "Girl Graduates," "Daughters of the Plough," etc.

*Inside spread of the gold-decorated souvenir program of an early performance, with Durward
Lely unaccountably listed as both Cyril and Florian.*

A summary of critical opinion evoked by this performance indicated that Sullivan had fared very much better than his collaborator. W. S. Gilbert had used for his libretto his own "Whimsical Allegory, *The Princess,* Being a respectful perversion of Mr. Tennyson's Poem." This was a burlesque in blank verse (with incidental music borrowed from several then-popular French operettas), which had played the Olympic Theatre just fourteen years earlier, in 1870. Perhaps it was the essential seriousness, purity, and dignity of the original poem; perhaps the respect with which the public instinctively held their knighted Poet Laureate, the aging Tennyson . . . whatever the basic cause, Gilbert's humorous invention did not win its usual jocular victory that night.

The press very nearly unanimously found the one-and-only three-act Gilbert and Sullivan opera too long. The ominous word "dull" was used by many critics and such ugly adjectives as "clumsy," "tedious," and "tiresome" appeared, probably for the first time in a Gilbert and Sullivan first-night review. But despite these clear evidences of a negative reaction, so strong was the hold of this librettist-composer team over the London theatre-going public and critics, so solidly were their opera offerings associated in the public mind with success, that many in the audience that night probably did not fully realize they had not witnessed the anticipated smash-hit till a day or so later. Certainly the reviews of the following two days, Sunday and Monday, were a mixed lot. Undoubtedly the word-of-mouth must have been equally indecisive, a condition not calculated to promote a long theatrical run.

An amusing illustration of this lack of unanimity appeared in the *World* and was seized upon gleefully by its sister-publication, the *Sporting Times:*

The great and grand jest of the week has been afforded by Edmund at the expense of that erudite gentleman, Mr. Engel, the harmonist, the subject being the *Princess Ida.* Just compare these clippings from the same number of the *World* and see if you don't agree with us:

From an article signed E.Y. [drama critic Edmund Yates]—"It was a desperately dull performance . . . there were not three and a half jokes worth remembering throughout three and a half hours' misery. . . . We are always hearing of Mr. Gilbert's wonderful stage management but the tumble of the Princess and her rescue from drowning were so ludicrously mismanaged as to evoke hisses and laughter."

And from an article signed L.E. [music critic

Louis Engel]—"Mr. Gilbert has rendered this piece as amusing as his immense talent so many times proved was safe to do . . . the opera itself from beginning to end, more or less applauded by a public d'élite . . . the performance going as smoothly as in the whole world, first evenings go only at this theatre. . . . The rehearsing at this theatre is so conscientious that there is never a hitch in the performance."

Musically the première of *Princess Ida* had been undeniably effective. Wrote the *Observer*, "The success of the opera was never for a moment in doubt last night, and Sir Arthur Sullivan's music, whilst more ambitious in many of its elements than in his other comic operas, seems sure of gaining speedy popularity. . . . The composer himself conducted the singularly smooth performance, and at its close acknowledged with Mr. Gilbert the unanimously favourable verdict of the audience." It was after this curtain call that his superhuman control over illness and pain simply let go. The *Globe* mentioned that Sullivan fainted after "presenting himself with Mr. Gilbert on the stage to receive the congratulations of the audience." And the *Illustrated Sporting and Dramatic News* recorded, "It was distressing to learn that Sir Arthur, after the exertions and anxieties of his evening's work, should have been taken ill."

It is possible that the uncertainty of his collaborator's health that evening prompted Gilbert to remain in the theatre, contrary to his usual first-night routine of absenting himself until curtain-call time. This may be deduced from an anecdote he recounted many years later: "In the last act the principal ladies were dressed in very imposing armour which was supplied by a Paris *armurier*. On the first night I was sitting in the green-room during the progress of the last act, reading a newspaper, when this gentleman, who had come over from Paris to enjoy the effect of his armour upon the stage, broke in upon me in a wild state of delight, '*Mais savez-vous, monsieur,*' said he, '*que vous avez là un succès solide?*' I replied to the effect that the piece seemed to be going very well. '*Mais vous êtes si calme!*' he exclaimed with a look of unbounded astonishment. I suppose he expected to see me kissing all the carpenters."

Oblivious of the composer's physical failure, most of the press lauded his artistic triumph. The instrumentation, in particular, provoked great admiration from those sufficiently musical. On this point Beatty-Kingston in the *Theatre* rhapsodized: "[It] abounds in novel treatments and subtle devices, bearing witness, times without number, to Arthur Sullivan's inexhaustible fertility of invention in such matters. . . . From beginning to end the instrumental parts of *Princess Ida* are fraught with enchanting combinations and joyful sur-

prises." And he added for good measure, "As a writer of apt and beautiful accompaniments to the voice, he is unrivalled by any living composer."

Herman Klein, music critic of the *Sunday Times,* really outdid himself and his professional colleagues in adulation: "The score of the new opera at the Savoy may be summed up in a sentence— it is the best in every way that Sir Arthur Sullivan has produced, apart from his serious works. . . . In *Princess Ida* I cannot detect a single piece that does not bear obvious traces of artistic thought and elaboration. . . . To the orchestra, indeed, the composer has given an importance and connection with the dramatic action which not only exceeds what he has done in this respect in his preceding operas, but in doing so far surpasses in beauty and musicianly resource the instrumentation of any of the modern French productions that form the nearest approach to this class of composition. . . . Besides its exquisite orchestration *Princess Ida* is rich in vocal concerted music—much more so, in fact, than in solos. . . . Humour is almost as strong a point with Sir Arthur Sullivan as with his clever collaborator, and when attained by such legitimate means it is simply irresistible."

Of the cast that night Mr. Durward Lely, as Cyril, seems to have scored the chief vocal success among the men. Both the popular George Grossmith and Rutland Barrington had smaller parts in this opera than was their usual lot. Said the *Observer,* "The ponderous Hildebrand of Mr. Barrington contrasts most effectively with the malignant impishness of Mr. Grossmith's Gama, and neither actor misses a point that is to be made." Indeed, added the *Saturday Review* of Grossmith, "His songs and dialogue are . . . so well given that one greatly wishes for more of them."

Both Leonora Braham and Rosina Brandram, as Princess Ida and Lady Blanche, had their usual critical approval, although neither appears to have been regarded as cast in a particularly sympathetic or appropriate part. Jessie Bond drew the special admiration of Beatty-Kingston, who described her as making "the distinct hit of the evening . . . in the small part of Melissa, which she invested with captivating interest." Beatty-Kingston also liked the chorus that night, writing that "such chorus singing as that of the Savoy Company cannot be heard in any continental opera house with which I am acquainted." But the *Saturday Review* dissented—"The choristers want more drilling yet."

Probably most of the first-night audience were aware of the fact—amply treated by theatrical gossip writers of the press for weeks in advance— that Gilbert and D'Oyly Carte had tried to get Lillian Russell for the role of Princess Ida. A contract had been signed, but later canceled by mutual consent. The *Saturday Review*'s critic reopened this delicate subject in describing Miss Braham's performance as Princess Ida, carefully avoiding the naming of names: "An American actress who was engaged for the character is reported to have differed with the management as to the necessity for rehearsals, and the engagement was broken off."

Perhaps there were admirers in the house that night who felt that Miss Braham, since she had been cast in a part originally offered to an American actress, should be treated as an American. The journal *Truth* found space for this illuminating and descriptive passage: "One of the most amusing incidents of the evening was the outburst of indignation which greeted two or three bouquets that were thrown to Miss Braham. In America an actress often finds herself knee-deep in flowers. Here it would seem that the popular voice is against her being given a bouquet—why, I do not know. Certainly a man who arrives with a huge nosegay, puts it under his seat, and at a given moment rises to hurl it onto the stage, looks a fool, and seems to be aware of the fact. But if this amuses him and pleases the actress who is the recipient of the floral tribute, it harms no-one else, and is a very innocent form of folly."

Two brave critics, already much quoted, were so well impressed with the performance that in spite of adverse opinion they must have heard around them at the theatre, they both recklessly predicted success and a long run. Declared Herman Klein in the *Sunday Times:* "I have only space to add that the Savoy performance is very nearly, if not absolutely, perfect. . . . A long and prosperous run in the case of *Princess Ida* may, I think, be confidently foretold." And Beatty-Kingston closed his review in the *Theatre* with these lines: "The first performance was an ideal one. Everybody was letter-perfect in his or her words, and note-perfect in the music; the stage management was a miracle of efficiency, and the piece went as faultlessly as if it had been running the three hundred or so nights that are before it in what metaphysical Lady Blanche calls 'The Inevitable Must.' "—Alas, for *Princess Ida* to reach even the minimum three hundred performances of this forecast, Londoners had to wait thirty-five years until its 1919 revival.

JANUARY 5 (SATURDAY) 1884. *Resolved to conduct the first performance of the new opera* Princess Ida *at night, but from the state I was in it seemed hopeless. At 7 p.m. had another strong hypodermic injection to ease the pain, and a strong cup of black coffee to keep me awake. Managed to get up and dress, and drove to the theatre more dead than alive—went into the Orchestra at 8.10. Tremendous house—usual reception. Very fine performance—not a hitch. Brilliant success. After the performance I turned very faint and could not stand.*

ARTHUR SULLIVAN'S DIARY

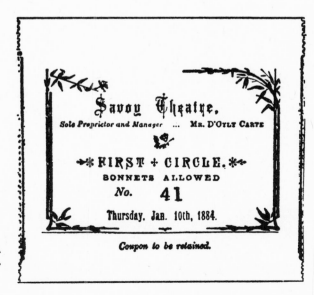

A ticket to PRINCESS IDA *during its first performance week.*

A Respectful Operatic Per-Version
of Tennyson's "Princess"

IN A PROLOGUE AND TWO ACTS,

ENTITLED

OR,

CASTLE ADAMANT.

Dramatis Personae.

KING HILDEBRAND		MR. RUTLAND BARRINGTON.
HILARION, *His Son*		MR. H. BRACY.
CYRIL	} *Hilarion's Friends*	MR. DURWARD LELY.
FLORIAN		MR. RYLEY.
KING GAMA		MR. GEORGE GROSSMITH.
ARAC		MR. RICHARD TEMPLE.
GURON	} *His Sons*	MR. LUGG.
SCYNTHIUS		MR. W. GREY.
PRINCESS IDA, *Gama's Daughter*		MISS LEONORA BRAHAM.
LADY BLANCHE, *Professor of Abstract Science*		MISS BRANDRAM.
LADY PSYCHE, *Professor of Humanities*		MISS CHARD.
MELISSA, *Lady Blanche's Daughter*		MISS JESSIE BOND.
SACHARISSA		MISS SYBIL GREY.
CHLOE	} *Girl Graduates*	MISS HEATHCOTE.
ADA		MISS TWYMAN.

SOLDIERS, COURTIERS, "GIRL GRADUATES," "DAUGHTERS OF THE PLOUGH," &c.

PROLOGUE. — Pavilion in King Hildebrand's Palace.

ACT I. — Gardens of Castle Adamant.

ACT II. — Courtyard of Castle Adamant.

Princess Ida

OR,

CASTLE ADAMANT

——————

PROLOGUE.

SCENE. — *Pavilion attached to* KING HILDEBRAND'S *Palace. Soldiers and Courtiers discovered looking out through opera glasses, telescopes, etc.,* FLORIAN *leading.*

CHORUS.

Search throughout the panorama
For a sign of royal Gama,
    Who to-day should cross the water
    With his fascinating daughter—
        Ida is her name.

Some misfortune evidently
Has detained them—consequently
    Search throughout the panorama
    For the daughter of King Gama,
        Prince Hilarion's flame!

SOLO.

FLORIAN. Will Prince Hilarion's hopes be sadly
    blighted?

ALL. Who can tell?

FLORIAN. Will Ida break the vows that she has
    plighted?

ALL. Who can tell?

FLORIAN. Will she back out, and say she did not
    mean them?

ALL. Who can tell?

FLORIAN. If so, there'll be the deuce to pay between them!

ALL.   No, no—we'll not despair,
        For Gama would not dare
        To make a deadly foe
        Of Hildebrand, and so,
           Search throughout, &c.

Enter KING HILDEBRAND, *with* CYRIL.

HILDEBRAND. See you no sign of Gama?

FLORIAN.   None, my liege!

HILDEBRAND. It's very odd, indeed. If Gama fail
    To put in an appearance at our Court
    Before the sun has set in yonder west,
    And fail to bring the Princess Ida here
    To whom our son Hilarion was betrothed
    At the extremely early age of one,
    There's war between King Gama and ourselves!
    (*Aside to* CYRIL.) Oh, Cyril, how I dread
    this interview!
    It's twenty years since he and I have met.
    He was a twisted monster—all awry—
    As though dame Nature, angry with her work,
    Had crumpled it in fitful petulance!

CYRIL. But, sir, a twisted and ungainly trunk
    Often bears goodly fruit. Perhaps he was
    A kind, well-spoken gentleman?

HILDEBRAND.   Oh, no!
    For, adder-like, his sting lay in his tongue.
    (His "sting" is present, though his "stung"
    is past.)

FLORIAN (*looking through glass*). But stay, my
    liege; o'er yonder mountain's brow
    Comes a small body, bearing Gama's arms;
    And now I look more closely at it, sir,
    I see attached to it King Gama's legs;
    From which I gather this corollary
    That that small body must be Gama's own!

HILDEBRAND. Ha! Is the Princess with him?

FLORIAN.   Well, my liege,
    Unless her highness is full six feet high,
    And wears mustachios too—and smokes
    cigars—

And rides *en cavalier* in coat of steel—
I do not think she is.

HILDEBRAND.   One never knows.
      She's a strange girl, I've heard, and does odd
         things!
      Come, bustle there!
      For Gama place the richest robes we own—
      For Gama place the coarsest prison dress—
      For Gama let our best spare bed be aired—
      For Gama let our deepest dungeon yawn—
      For Gama lay the costliest banquet out—
      For Gama place cold water and dry bread!
      For as King Gama brings the Princess here,
      Or brings her not, so shall King Gama have
      Much more than everything—much less than
         nothing!

SONG AND CHORUS.

HILDEBRAND. Now hearken to my strict com-
      mand
On every hand, on every hand—

CHORUS.

      To your command,
      On every hand,
      We dutifully bow!

HILDEBRAND. If Gama bring the Princess here,
      Give him good cheer, give him good cheer.

CHORUS.

      If she come here
      We'll give him a cheer,
      And we will show you how.
Hip, hip, hurrah! hip, hip, hurrah!
Hip, hip, hurrah! hip, hip, hurrah!
      We'll shout and sing
      Long live the King,
      And his daughter, too, I trow!
Then shout ha! ha! hip, hip, hurrah!
For the fair Princess and her good papa,
      Hip, hip, hurrah!
      Hip, hip, hurrah!
      Hip, hip, hurrah! hurrah!

HILDEBRAND. But if he fail to keep his troth,
      Upon our oath, we'll trounce them both!

CHORUS.

      He'll trounce them both,
      Upon his oath.
      As sure as quarter-day!

HILDEBRAND. We'll shut him up in a dungeon
      cell,
And toll his knell on a funeral bell.

CHORUS.

From dungeon cell

      His funeral knell
      Shall strike him with dismay!
And we'll shout ha! ha! hip, hip, hurrah!
Hip, hip, hurrah! hip, hip, hurrah!
      As up we string,
      The faithless King,
      In the old familiar way!
We'll shout ha! ha! hip, hip, hurrah!
As we make an end of her false papa.
      Hip, hip, hurrah!
      Hip, hip, hurrah!
      Hip, hip, hurrah! hurrah!

                              (*Exeunt all.*)

Enter HILARION.

RECITATIVE — HILARION.

To-day we meet, my baby bride and I—
   But ah, my hopes are balanced by my fears!
What transmutations have been conjured by
   The silent alchemy of twenty years!

BALLAD — HILARION.

      Ida was a twelvemonth old,
         Twenty years ago!
      I was twice her age, I'm told,
         Twenty years ago!
      Husband twice as old as wife
      Argues ill for married life.
      Baleful prophecies were rife,
         Twenty years ago!

      Still, I was a tiny prince
         Twenty years ago.
      She has gained upon me, since
         Twenty years ago.
      Though she's twenty-one, it's true,
      I am barely twenty-two—
      False and foolish prophets you,
         Twenty years ago!

Enter HILDEBRAND.

HILARION. Well, father, is there news for me at
      last?

HILDEBRAND. King Gama is in sight, but much I
      fear
With no Princess!

HILARION.   Alas, my liege, I've heard
      That Princess Ida has forsworn the world,
      And, with a band of women, shut herself
      Within a lonely country house, and there
      Devotes herself to stern philosophies!

HILDEBRAND. Then I should say the loss of such
      a wife
Is one to which a reasonable man
Would easily be reconciled.

HILARION.   Oh, no!

Or I am not a reasonable man.
She *is* my wife—has been for twenty years!
(*Looking through glass.*) I think I see her
now!

HILDEBRAND.   Ha! let me look!

HILARION.   In my mind's eye, I mean—a blushing
    bride,
All bib and tucker, frill and furbelow!
How exquisite she looked, as she was borne,
Recumbent, in her foster-mother's arms!
How the bride wept—nor would be com-
    forted
Until the hireling mother-for-the-nonce,
Administered refreshment in the vestry.
And I remember feeling much annoyed
That she should weep at marrying with me.
But then I thought, "These brides are all
    alike.
You cry at marrying me? How much more
    cause
You'd have to cry if it were broken off!"
These were my thoughts; I kept them to my-
    self,
For at that age I had not learnt to speak.

Enter Courtiers, with CYRIL *and* FLORIAN.

CHORUS.   From the distant panorama
        Come the sons of royal Gama.
            Who, to-day, should cross the water
            With his fascinating daughter—
                Ida is her name!

Enter ARAC, GURON, *and* SCYNTHIUS.

            SONG.

ARAC.   We are warriors three,
        Sons of Gama, Rex.

        Like most sons are we,
            Masculine in sex.

ALL THREE.   Yes, yes,
            Masculine in sex.

ARAC.   Politics we bar,
            They are not our bent;
        On the whole we are
            Not intelligent.

ALL THREE.   No, no,
            Not intelligent.

ARAC.   But with doughty heart,
            And with trusty blade,
        We can play our part—
            Fighting is our trade.

ALL THREE.   Yes, yes,
            Fighting is our trade.

        Bold, and fierce, and strong, ha! ha!
            For a war we burn.
        With its right or wrong, ha! ha!
            We have no concern.
        Order comes to fight, ha! ha!
            Order is obeyed.
        We are men of might, ha! ha!
            Fighting is our trade.
                Yes—yes,
        Fighting is our trade, ha! ha!
            Fighting is our trade.

CHORUS.   They are men of might, ha! ha!
        Order comes to fight, ha! ha!
        Order is obeyed, ha! ha!
            Fighting is their trade!

            Enter KING GAMA.

            SONG — GAMA.

If you give me your attention, I will tell you
    what I am:
I'm a genuine philanthropist—all other kinds
    are sham.
Each little fault of temper and each social defect
In my erring fellow creatures, I endeavour to
    correct.
To all their little weaknesses I open people's
    eyes;
And little plans to snub the self-sufficient I de-
    vise;
I love my fellow creatures—I do all the good I
    can—
Yet everybody says I'm such a disagreeable
    man!
            And I can't think why!

To compliments inflated I've a withering reply,
And vanity I always do my best to mortify;
A charitable action I can skilfully dissect;

And interested motives I'm delighted to detect;
I know everybody's income and what everybody
    earns;
And I carefully compare it with the income-tax
    returns;
But to benefit humanity however much I plan,
Yet everybody says I'm such a disagreeable
    man!
        And I can't think why!

I'm sure I'm no ascetic; I'm as pleasant as can
    be;
You'll always find me ready with a crushing
    repartee,
I've an irritating chuckle, I've a celebrated
    sneer,
I've an entertaining snigger, I've a fascinating
    leer.
To everybody's prejudice I know a thing or
    two;
I can tell a woman's age in half a minute—and
    I do.
But although I try to make myself as pleasant
    as I can,
Yet everybody says I'm such a disagreeable
    man!
        And I can't think why!

GAMA. So this is Castle Hildebrand? Well, well!
    Dame Rumour whispered that the place was
      grand;
    She told me that your taste was exquisite,
    Superb, unparalleled!

HILDEBRAND (*gratified*). Oh, really, king!

GAMA. But she's a liar! Why, how old you've
    grown!
    Is this Hilarion? Why, you've changed too—
    You were a singularly handsome child!
    (*To* FLORIAN.) Are you a courtier? Come
      then, ply your trade,
    Tell me some lies. How do you like your
      king?
    Vile rumour says he's all but imbecile.
    Now, that's not true?

FLORIAN.   My lord, we love our king.
    His wise remarks are valued by his court
    As precious stones.

GAMA.   And for the self-same cause,
    Like precious stones, his sensible remarks
    Derive their value from their scarcity!
    Come, now, be honest, tell the truth for once!
    Tell it of me. Come, come, I'll harm you not.
    This leg is crooked—this foot is ill-designed—
    This shoulder wears a hump! Come, out with
      it!
    Look, here's my face! Now, am I not the
      worst

Of Nature's blunders?

CYRIL.   Nature never errs.
    To those who know the workings of your
      mind,
    Your face and figure, sir, suggest a book
    Appropriately bound.

GAMA (*enraged*).   Why, harkye, sir,
    How dare you bandy words with me?

CYRIL.   No need
    To bandy aught that appertains to you.

GAMA (*furiously*). Do you permit this, king?

HILDEBRAND.   We are in doubt
    Whether to treat you as an honoured guest,
    Or as a traitor knave who plights his word
    And breaks it.

GAMA (*quickly*). If the casting vote's with me,
    I give it for the former!

HILDEBRAND.   We shall see.
    By the terms of our contract, signed and
      sealed,
    You're bound to bring the Princess here to-
      day:
    Why is she not with you?

GAMA.   Answer me this;
    What think you of a wealthy purse-proud
      man,
    Who, when he calls upon a starving friend,
    Pulls out his gold and flourishes his notes,
    And flashes diamonds in the pauper's eyes?
    What name have you for such an one?

HILDEBRAND.   A snob.

GAMA. Just so. The girl has beauty, virtue, wit,
    Grace, humour, wisdom, charity, and pluck.
    Would it be kindly, think you, to parade
    These brilliant qualities before *your* eyes?
    Oh no, King Hildebrand, I am no snob!

HILDEBRAND (*furiously*). Stop that tongue,
    Or you shall lose the monkey head that holds
      it!

GAMA. Bravo! your king deprives me of my head,
    That he and I may meet on equal terms!

HILDEBRAND. Where is she now?

GAMA.   In Castle Adamant,
    One of my many country houses. There
    She rules a woman's University,
    With full a hundred girls, who learn of her.

CYRIL. A hundred girls! A hundred ecstasies!

GAMA. But no mere girls, my good young gentle-
    man:

With all the college learning that you boast,
The youngest there will prove a match for
you.

CYRIL.   With all my heart, if she's the prettiest!
(*To* FLORIAN.) Fancy, a hundred matches—
all alight!—
That's if I strike them as I hope to do!

GAMA.   Despair your hope; their hearts are dead
to men.
He who desires to gain their favour must
Be qualified to strike their teeming brains,
And not their hearts. They're safety matches,
sir,
And they light only on the knowledge box—
So *you've* no chance!

FLORIAN.   Are there no males whatever in those
walls?

GAMA.   None, gentlemen, excepting letter mails—
And they are driven (as males often are
In other large communities) by women.
Why, bless my heart, she's so particular
She'll scarcely suffer Dr. Watts's hymns—
And all the animals she owns are "hers"!
The ladies rise at cockcrow every morn—

CYRIL.   Ah, then they have male poultry?

GAMA.   Not at all,
(*Confidentially*.) The crowing's done by an
accomplished hen!

DUET — GAMA *and* HILDEBRAND.

GAMA.   Perhaps if you address the lady
Most politely, most politely—
Flatter and impress the lady,
Most politely, most politely—
Humbly beg and humbly sue—
She may deign to look on you,
But your doing you must do
Most politely, most politely!

ALL.   Humbly beg and humbly sue, &c.

HILDEBRAND.   Go you, and inform the lady,
Most politely, most politely,
If she don't, we'll storm the lady,
Most politely, most politely!
(*To* GAMA.) You'll remain as hostage
here;
Should Hilarion disappear,
We will hang you, never fear,
Most politely, most politely!

ALL.   { He'll
        { I'll } remain as hostage here, &c.
        { You'll }

(GAMA, ARAC, GURON, *and* SCYNTHIUS *are
marched off in custody*, HILDEBRAND *following*.)

RECITATIVE — HILARION.

Come, Cyril, Florian, our course is plain,
To-morrow morn fair Ida we'll engage;
But we will use no force her love to gain,
Nature has armed us for the war we wage!

TRIO — HILARION, CYRIL, *and* FLORIAN.

HILARION.   Expressive glances
Shall be our lances,
And pops of Sillery
Our light artillery.
We'll storm their bowers
With scented showers
Of fairest flowers
That we can buy!

CHORUS.   Oh dainty triolet!
Oh fragrant violet!
Oh gentle heigho-let
(Or little sigh)!
On sweet urbanity,
Though mere inanity,
To touch their vanity
We will rely!

CYRIL.   When day is fading,
With serenading
And such frivolity
We'll prove our quality.
A sweet profusion
Of soft allusion
This bold intrusion
Shall justify.

CHORUS.   Oh dainty triolet, &c.

FLORIAN.   We'll charm their senses
With verbal fences,
With ballads amatory
And declamatory.

And little heeding
Their pretty pleading,
Our love exceeding
We'll justify!

CHORUS.   Oh dainty triolet, &c.

Re-enter GAMA, ARAC, GURON, *and* SCYNTHIUS
heavily ironed.

RECITATIVE.

GAMA.   Must we, till then, in prison cell be thrust?

HILDEBRAND.   You must!

GAMA.   This seems unnecessarily severe!

ARAC, GURON, *and* SCYNTHIUS.   Hear, hear!

TRIO — ARAC, GURON, *and* SCYNTHIUS.

For a month to dwell
In a dungeon cell,
    Growing thin and wizen
    In a solitary prison,
Is a poor lookout
For a soldier stout
    Who is longing for the rattle
    Of a complicated battle—
For the rum-tum-tum
Of the military drum,
    And the guns that go boom! boom!

ALL.   Boom! boom! boom! boom!
        Rum-tummy-tummy-tum!
        Boom! boom!

HILDEBRAND.   When Hilarion's bride
        Has at length complied
            With the just conditions
            Of our requisitions,
        You may go in haste
        And indulge your taste
            For the fascinating rattle
            Of a complicated battle.
        For the rum-tum-tum,
        Of the military drum,
            And the guns that go boom! boom!

ALL.   Boom-boom, &c.

ALL.   But till that time { we'll / you'll } here remain,

        And bail { they / we } will not entertain.

        Should she { his / our } mandate disobey,

        { Our / Your } lives the penalty will pay!

(GAMA, ARAC, GURON, *and* SCYNTHIUS *are
marched off.*)

END OF PROLOGUE.

ACT I.

SCENE. — *Gardens in Castle Adamant. A river runs across the back of the stage, crossed by a rustic bridge. Castle Adamant in the distance. Girl graduates discovered seated at the feet of* LADY PSYCHE.

CHORUS.

Towards the empyrean heights
    Of every kind of lore,
We've taken several easy flights,
    And mean to take some more.
In trying to achieve success
    No envy racks our heart,
And all the knowledge we possess,
    We mutually impart.

SOLO — MELISSA.

Pray, what authors should she read
Who in Classics would succeed?

PSYCHE.   If you'd cross the Helicon,
You should read Anacreon,
Ovid's Metamorphoses,
Likewise Aristophanes,
And the works of Juvenal:
These are worth attention, all;
But, if you will be advised,
You will get them Bowdlerized!

CHORUS.   Yes, we'll do as we're advised,
We will get them Bowdlerized!

SOLO — SACHARISSA.

Pray you, tell us, if you can,
What's the thing that's known as Man?

PSYCHE.   Man will swear and Man will storm—
Man is not at all good form—
Man is of no kind of use—
Man's a donkey—Man's a goose—
Man is coarse and Man is plain—
Man is more or less insane—
Man's a ribald—Man's a rake,

Man is Nature's sole mistake!

CHORUS.   We'll a memorandum make—
Man is Nature's sole mistake!

And thus to empyrean heights
Of every kind of lore,
In search of wisdom's pure delight,
Ambitiously we soar.
In trying to achieve success
No envy racks our heart,
For all we know and all we guess,
We mutually impart!

Enter LADY BLANCHE. *All stand up demurely.*

BLANCHE.   Attention, ladies, while I read to you
The Princess Ida's list of punishments.
The first is Sacharissa. She's expelled!

ALL.   Expelled!

BLANCHE.   Expelled, because although she knew
No man of any kind may pass our walls,
She dared to bring a set of chessmen here!

SACHARISSA (*crying*).   I meant no harm; they're
only men of wood!

BLANCHE.   They're men with whom you give each
other mate,
And that's enough! The next is Chloe.

CHLOE.   Ah!

BLANCHE.   Chloe will lose three terms; for yesterday,
When looking through her drawing-book, I
found
A sketch of a perambulator!

ALL (*horrified*).   Oh!

BLANCHE.   *Double* perambulator, shameless girl!
That's all at present. Now, attention, pray:
Your Principal the Princess comes to give
Her usual inaugural address
To those young ladies who joined yesterday.

Enter the PRINCESS.

CHORUS.

Mighty maiden with a mission,
        Paragon of common sense,
Running fount of erudition,
        Miracle of eloquence,
    We are blind, and we would see;
    We are bound, and would be free;
    We are dumb, and we would talk;
    We are lame, and we would walk.
Mighty maiden with a mission—
        Paragon of common sense;
Running fount of erudition—
        Miracle of eloquence!

PRINCESS (*recit.*).   Minerva! hear me:

ARIA.

At this my call,
        A fervent few
        Have come to woo
The rays that from thee fall.

Oh, goddess wise
        That lovest light,
        Endow with sight
Their unillumined eyes.
Let fervent words and fervent thoughts be
mine,
That I may lead them to thy sacred shrine!

Women of Adamant, fair Neophytes—
Who thirst for such instruction as we give,
Attend, while I unfold a parable.
The elephant is mightier than Man,
Yet Man subdues him. Why? The elephant
Is elephantine everywhere but here (*tapping
her forehead*),
And Man, whose brain is to the elephant's
As Woman's brain to Man's—(that's rule of
three)—
Conquers the foolish giant of the woods,

As Woman, in her turn, shall conquer Man!
In Mathematics, Woman leads the way—
The narrow-minded pedant still believes
That two and two make four! Why, we can
    prove,
We women—household drudges as we are—
That two and two make five—or three—or
    seven;
Or five-and-twenty, if the case demands!
Diplomacy? The wiliest diplomate
Is absolutely helpless in our hands:
He wheedles monarchs—woman wheedles
    him!
Logic? Why, tyrant Man himself admits
It's waste of time to argue with a woman!
Then we excel in social qualities:
Though Man professes that he holds our sex
In utter scorn, I venture to believe
He'd rather spend the day with one of you,
Than with five hundred of his fellow men!
In all things we excel. Believing this,
A hundred maidens here have sworn to place
Their feet upon his neck. If we succeed,
We'll treat him better than he treated us:
But if we fail, why then let hope fail too!
Let no one care a penny how she looks—
Let red be worn with yellow—blue with
    green—
Crimson with scarlet—violet with blue!
Let all your things misfit, and you yourselves
At inconvenient moments come undone!
Let hair-pins lose their virtue: let the hook
Disdain the fascination of the eye—
The bashful button modestly evade
The soft embraces of the button-hole!
Let old associations all dissolve,
Let Swan secede from Edgar—Gask from
    Gask,
Sewell from Cross—Lewis from Allenby!
In other words—let Chaos come again!
(*Coming down.*) Who lectures in the Hall of
    Arts to-day?

BLANCHE.   I, madam, on Abstract Philosophy.
There I propose considering, at length,
Three points—the Is, the Might Be, and the
    Must.
Whether the Is, from being actual fact,
Is more important than the vague Might Be,
Or the Might Be, from taking wider scope,
Is for that reason greater than the Is:
And lastly, how the Is and Might Be stand
Compared with the inevitable Must!

PRINCESS.   The subject's deep—how do you treat
    it, pray?

BLANCHE.   Madam, I take three possibilities,
And strike a balance, then, between the three:

As thus: The Princess Ida Is our head,
The Lady Psyche Might Be—Lady Blanche,
Neglected Blanche, inevitably Must.
Given these three hypotheses—to find
The actual betting against each of them!

PRINCESS.   Your theme's ambitious: pray you
    bear in mind
Who highest soar fall farthest. Fare you well,
You and your pupils! Maidens, follow me.
(*Exeunt* PRINCESS *and* MAIDENS *singing refrain
of chorus, "And thus to empyrean heights," &c.
    Manet* LADY BLANCHE.)

BLANCHE.   I should command here—I was born
    to rule,
But do I rule? I don't. Why? I don't know.
I shall some day. Not yet. I bide my time.
I once was Some One—and the Was Will Be.
The Present as we speak becomes the Past,
The Past repeats itself, and so is Future!
This sounds involved. It's not. It's right
    enough.

SONG — LADY BLANCHE.

Come, mighty Must!
    Inevitable Shall!
In thee I trust.
    Time weaves my coronal!
Go, mocking Is!
    Go, disappointing Was!
That I am this
    Ye are the cursed cause!
Yet humble second shall be first,
    I ween;
And dead and buried be the curst
    Has Been!

Oh, weak Might Be!
    Oh, May, Might, Could, Would, Should!
How powerless ye
    For evil or for good!
In every sense
    Your moods I cheerless call,
Whate'er your tense
    Ye are Imperfect, all!
Ye have deceived the trust that I've shown
    In ye!
Away! The Mighty Must alone
    Shall be!   (*Exit* LADY BLANCHE.)

Enter HILARION, CYRIL, *and* FLORIAN, *climbing
over wall, and creeping cautiously among the trees
    and rocks at the back of the stage.*

TRIO — HILARION, CYRIL, FLORIAN.

Gently, gently,
Evidently
    We are safe so far,
After scaling

Fence and paling,
   Here, at last, we are!
In this college
Useful knowledge
   Everywhere one finds,
And already
Growing steady,
   We've enlarged our minds.

CYRIL. We've learnt that prickly cactus
   Has the power to attract us
              When we fall.

ALL.   When we fall!

HILARION. That nothing man unsettles
   Like a bed of stinging nettles,
              Short or tall.

ALL.   Short or tall!

FLORIAN. That bull-dogs feed on throttles—
   That we don't like broken bottles
              On a wall—

ALL.   On a wall.

HILARION. That spring-guns breathe defiance!
   And that burglary's a science
              After all!

ALL.   After all.

RECITATIVE.

FLORIAN. A Woman's college! maddest folly going!
  What can girls learn within its walls worth knowing?
  I'll lay a crown (the Princess shall decide it)
  I'll teach them twice as much in half-an-hour outside it!

HILARION. Hush, scoffer; ere you sound your puny thunder,
  List to their aims, and bow your head in wonder!

     They intend to send a wire
        To the moon—to the moon;
     And they'll set the Thames on fire
        Very soon—very soon;
     Then they learn to make silk purses
        With their rigs—with their rigs,
     From the ears of Lady Circe's
        Piggy-wigs—piggy-wigs.
     And weasels at their slumbers
        They trepan—they trepan;
     To get sunbeams from cucumbers,
        They've a plan—they've a plan.
     They've a firmly rooted notion
     They can cross the Polar Ocean,
     And they'll find Perpetual Motion,

        If they can—if they can.

     These are the phenomena
     That every pretty domina
        Hopes that we shall see
        At this Universitee.

ALL. These are the phenomena
     That every pretty domina
        Hopes that we shall see
        At this Universitee!

CYRIL. As for fashion, they forswear it,
     So they say—so they say—
  And the circle—they will square it
     Some fine day—some fine day—
  Then the little pigs they're teaching
     For to fly—for to fly;
  And the niggers they'll be bleaching,
     By and by—by and by!
  Each newly joined aspirant
     To the clan—to the clan—
  Must repudiate the tyrant
     Known as Man—known as Man—
  They mock at him and flout him,
  For they do not care about him,
  And they're "going to do without him"
     If they can—if they can!

     These are the phenomena
     That every pretty domina
        Hopes that we shall see
        At this Universitee.

ALL. These are the phenomena, &c.

HILARION. So that's the Princess Ida's castle! Well,
  They must be lovely girls, indeed, if it requires
  Such walls as those to keep intruders off!

CYRIL. To keep men off is only half their charge,
  And that the easier half. I much suspect
  The object of these walls is not so much
  To keep men off as keep the maidens in!

FLORIAN. But what are these? (*Examining some Collegiate robes.*)

HILARION (*looking at them*). Why, Academic robes,
  Worn by the lady undergraduates,
  When they matriculate. Let's try them on. (*They do so.*)
  Why, see,—we're covered to the very toes.
  Three lovely lady undergraduates
  Who, weary of the world and all its wooing—

FLORIAN. And penitent for deeds there's no undoing—

CYRIL. Looked at askance by well-conducted maids—

ALL.   Seek sanctuary in these classic shades!

TRIO — HILARION, CYRIL, FLORIAN.

HILARION.   I am a maiden, cold and stately,
    Heartless, I, with a face divine.
    What do I want with a heart, innately?
    Every heart I meet is mine!

ALL.   Haughty, humble, coy, or free,
        Little care I what maid may be.
    So that a maid is fair to see,
        Every maid is the maid for me!
                                    (*Dance.*)

CYRIL.   I am a maiden frank and simple,
    Brimming with joyous roguery;
    Merriment lurks in every dimple,
    Nobody breaks more hearts than I!

ALL.   Haughty, humble, coy, or free,
        Little care I what maid may be.
    So that a maid is fair to see,
        Every maid is the maid for me!
                                    (*Dance.*)

FLORIAN.   I am a maiden coyly blushing,
    Timid I as a startled hind;
    Every suitor sets me flushing:
    I am the maid that wins mankind!

ALL.   Haughty, humble, coy, or free,

    Little care I what maid may be.
    So that a maid is fair to see,
        Every maid is the maid for me!

Enter the PRINCESS, *reading. She does not
    see them.*

FLORIAN.   But who comes here? The Princess, as
        I live!
    What shall we do?

HILARION (*aside*).   Why, we must brave it out!
    (*Aloud.*) Madam, accept our humblest rever-
    ence.

    (*They bow, then suddenly recollecting them-
                        selves, curtsey.*)

PRINCESS (*surprised*).   We greet you, ladies. What
    would you with us?

HILARION (*aside*).   What shall I say? (*Aloud.*)
    We are three students, ma'am,
    Three well-born maids of liberal estate,
    Who wish to join this University.

(HILARION *and* FLORIAN *curtsey again.* CYRIL
*bows extravagantly, then, being recalled to him-
self by* FLORIAN, *curtseys.*)

PRINCESS.   If, as you say, you wish to join our
    ranks
    And will subscribe to all our rules, 'tis well.

FLORIAN. To all your rules we cheerfully subscribe.

PRINCESS. You say you're noblewomen. Well,
you'll find
No sham degrees for noblewomen here.
You'll find no sizars here, or servitors,
Or other cruel distinctions, meant to draw
A line 'twixt rich and poor: you'll find no
tufts
To mark nobility, except such tufts
As indicate nobility of brain.
As for your fellow-students, mark me well:
There are a hundred maids within these walls,
All good, all learned, and all beautiful:
They are prepared to love you: will you swear
To give the fulness of your love to them?

HILARION. Upon our words and honours, ma'am,
we will!

PRINCESS. But we go further: will you undertake
That you will never marry any man?

FLORIAN. Indeed we never will!

PRINCESS.   Consider well,
You must prefer our maids to all mankind!

HILARION. To all mankind we much prefer your
maids!

CYRIL. We should be dolts indeed, if we did not,
Seeing how fair—

HILARION (*aside to* CYRIL). Take care—that's
rather strong!

PRINCESS. But have you left no lovers at your
home
Who may pursue you here?

HILARION.   No, madam, none.
We're homely ladies, as no doubt you see,
And we have never fished for lover's love.
We smile at girls who deck themselves with
gems,
False hair, and meretricious ornament,
To chain the fleeting fancy of a man,
But do not imitate them. What we have
Of hair, is all our own. Our colour, too,
Unladylike, but not unwomanly,
Is Nature's handiwork, and man has learnt
To reckon Nature an impertinence.

PRINCESS. Well, beauty counts for naught within
these walls;
If all you say is true, you'll spend with us
A happy, happy time!

CYRIL.   If, as you say,
A hundred lovely maidens wait within,
To welcome us with smiles and open arms,

I think there's very little doubt we shall!

QUARTETTE.

PRINCESS, HILARION, CYRIL, FLORIAN.

PRINCESS.   The world is but a broken toy,
Its pleasure hollow—false its joy,
Unreal its loveliest hue,
Alas!
Its pains alone are true,
Alas!
Its pains alone are true.

HILARION.   The world is everything you say,
The world we think has had its day,
Its merriment is slow,
Alas!
We've tried it, and we know,
Alas!
We've tried it and we know.

TUTTI.

PRINCESS.	HILARION, CYRIL, FLORIAN.
The world is but a broken toy,	The world is but a broken toy,
Its pleasures hollow—false its joy,	We freely give it up with joy,
Unreal its loveliest hue,	Unreal its loveliest hue,
Alas!	Alas!
Its pains alone are true,	We quite agree with you,
Alas!	Alas!
Its pains alone are true!	We quite agree with you!

Exit PRINCESS. *The three gentlemen watch her off.*
LADY PSYCHE *enters, and regards them with
amazement.*

HILARION. I' faith, the plunge is taken, gentle-
men!
For, willy-nilly, we are maidens now,
And maids against our will we must remain!
(*All laugh heartily.*)

PSYCHE (*aside*). These ladies are unseemly in
their mirth.
(*The gentlemen see her, and, in confusion, resume their modest demeanour.*)

FLORIAN (*aside*). Here's a catastrophe, Hilarion!
This is my sister! She'll remember me,
Though years have passed since she and I
have met!

HILARION (*aside to* FLORIAN). Then make a virtue of necessity,
And trust our secret to her gentle care.

FLORIAN (to PSYCHE, *who has watched* CYRIL *in amazement*). Psyche,
Why, don't you know me? Florian!

PSYCHE (*amazed*).   Why, Florian!

FLORIAN.   My sister! (*Embraces her.*)

PSYCHE.   Oh, my dear!
What are you doing here—and who are these?

HILARION.   I am that Prince Hilarion to whom
Your Princess is betrothed. I come to claim
Her plighted love. Your brother Florian
And Cyril, come to see me safely through.

PSYCHE. The Prince Hilarion? Cyril too? How strange!
My earliest playfellows!

HILARION.   Why, let me look!
Are you that learned little Psyche who
At school alarmed her mates because she called
A buttercup "ranunculus bulbosus"?

CYRIL.   Are you indeed that Lady Psyche who
At children's parties drove the conjuror wild,
Explaining all his tricks before he did them?

HILARION. Are you that learned little Psyche, who
At dinner parties, brought into dessert,
Would tackle visitors with "You don't know
Who first determined longitude—I do—
Hipparchus 'twas—B.C. one sixty-three!"?
Are you indeed that small phenomenon?

PSYCHE.   That small phenomenon indeed am I!
But gentlemen, 'tis death to enter here:
We have all promised to renounce mankind!

FLORIAN. Renounce mankind? On what ground do you base
This senseless resolution?

PSYCHE.   Senseless? No.
We are all taught, and, being taught, believe
That Man, sprung from an Ape, is Ape at heart.

CYRIL. That's rather strong.

PSYCHE.   The truth is always strong.

SONG — LADY PSYCHE.

The Ape and the Lady.

A Lady fair, of lineage high,
Was loved by an Ape, in the days gone by—
The Maid was radiant as the sun,
The Ape was a most unsightly one—
   So it would not do—

His scheme fell through,
For the Maid, when his love took formal shape,
   Expressed such terror
   At his monstrous error,
That he stammered an apology and made his 'scape,
The picture of a disconcerted Ape.

With a view to rise in the social scale,
He shaved his bristles, and he docked his tail,
He grew moustachios, and he took his tub,
And he paid a guinea to a toilet club—
   But it would not do,
   The scheme fell through—
For the Maid was Beauty's fairest Queen,
   With golden tresses,
   Like a real princess's,
While the Ape, despite his razor keen,
Was the apiest Ape that ever was seen!

He bought white ties, and he bought dress suits,
He crammed his feet into bright tight boots—
And to start in life on a bran-new plan,
He christened himself Darwinian Man!
   But it would not do,
   The scheme fell through—
For the Maiden fair, whom the monkey craved,
   Was a radiant Being,
   With a brain far-seeing—
While a Man, however well-behaved,
At best is only a monkey shaved!
(*During this* MELISSA *has entered unobserved: she looks on in amazement.*)

MELISSA (*coming down*). Oh, Lady Psyche!

PSYCHE (*terrified*).   What! you heard us, then?
Oh, all is lost!

MELISSA.   Not so! I'll breathe no word!
(*Advancing in astonishment to* FLORIAN.)
How marvellously strange! and are you then
Indeed young men?

FLORIAN.   Well, yes, just now we are—
But hope by dint of study to become,
In course of time, young women.

MELISSA (*eagerly*).   No, no, no—
Oh don't do that! Is this indeed a man?
I've often heard of them, but, till to-day,
Never set eyes on one. They told me men
Were hideous, idiotic, and deformed!
They're quite as beautiful as women are!
As beautiful—they're infinitely more so!
Their cheeks have not that pulpy softness which
One gets so weary of in womankind:
Their features are more marked—and—oh their chins!
How curious!   (*Feeling his chin.*)

FLORIAN.   I fear it's rather rough.

MELISSA (*eagerly*). Oh don't apologize—I like it so!

QUINTETTE.

PSYCHE, MELISSA, HILARION, CYRIL, FLORIAN.

PSYCHE. The woman of the wisest wit
        May sometimes be mistaken, O!
        In Ida's views, I must admit,
        My faith is somewhat shaken, O!

CYRIL. On every other point than this,
        Her learning is unshaken, O!
        But Man's a theme with which she is
        Entirely unacquainted, O!
            —acquainted, O!
            —acquainted, O!
        Entirely unacquainted, O!

ALL. Then jump for joy and gaily bound,
      The truth is found—the truth is found!
      Set bells a-ringing through the air—
      Ring here and there and everywhere—
      And echo forth the joyous sound,
      The truth is found—the truth is found!
                                    (*Dance.*)

MELISSA. My natural instinct teaches me
          (And instinct is important, O!)
          You're everything you ought to be,
          And nothing that you oughtn't, O!

HILARION. That fact was seen at once by you
           In casual conversation, O!
           Which is most creditable to
           Your powers of observation, O!
               —servation, O!
               —servation, O!
           Your powers of observation, O!

ALL. Then jump for joy, &c.

Exeunt PSYCHE, HILARION, CYRIL, *and* FLORIAN.
MELISSA *going. Enter* LADY BLANCHE.

BLANCHE. Melissa!

MELISSA (*returning*). Mother!

BLANCHE.   Here—a word with you.
            Those are the three new students?

MELISSA (*confused*).   Yes, they are.
          They're charming girls.

BLANCHE.   Particularly so.
            So graceful, and so very womanly!
            So skilled in all a girl's accomplishments!

MELISSA (*confused*). Yes—very skilled.

BLANCHE.   They sing so nicely too!

MELISSA. They *do* sing nicely!

BLANCHE.   Humph! It's very odd.
            One is a tenor, two are baritones!

MELISSA (*much agitated*). They've all got colds!

BLANCHE.   Colds! Bah! D'ye think I'm blind?
            These "girls" are men disguised!

MELISSA.   Oh no—indeed!
          You wrong these gentlemen—I mean—why
            see,
          Here is an *étui* dropped by one of them (*picking up an étui*)
          Containing scissors, needles, and—

BLANCHE (*opening it*).   Cigars!
          Why these *are* men! And you knew this, you
            minx!

MELISSA. Oh, spare them—they are gentlemen
            indeed!
          The Prince Hilarion (married years ago
          To Princess Ida) with two trusted friends!
          Consider, mother, he's her husband now,
          And has been, twenty years! Consider too,
          You're only second here—you should be first.
          Assist the Prince's plan, and when he gains
          The Princess Ida, why, you *will* be first.
          You will design the fashions—think of that—
          And always serve out all the punishments!
          The scheme is harmless, mother—wink at it!

BLANCHE (*aside*). The prospect's tempting! Well,
            well, well, I'll try—
          Though I've not winked at anything for years!
          'Tis but one step towards my destiny—
          The mighty Must! the inevitable Shall!

DUET — MELISSA *and* LADY BLANCHE.

MELISSA. Now wouldn't you like to rule the roast,
            And guide this University?

BLANCHE.   I must agree
            'Twould pleasant be.
              (Sing hey, a Proper Pride!)

MELISSA. And wouldn't you like to clear the coast
            Of malice and perversity?

BLANCHE.   Without a doubt
            I'll bundle 'em out,
              Sing hey, when I preside!

BOTH. Sing, hoity-toity! Sorry for some!

Marry come up and $\begin{Bmatrix} \text{my} \\ \text{her} \end{Bmatrix}$ day will come!
              Sing Proper Pride
              Is the horse to ride,
          And Happy-go-lucky, my Lady, O!

BLANCHE. For years I've writhed beneath her
            sneers,

Although a born Plantagenet!

MELISSA.   You're much too meek,
Or you would speak.
(Sing hey, I'll say no more!)

BLANCHE.   Her elder I, by several years,
Although you'd never imagine it.

MELISSA.   Sing, so I've heard
But never a word
Have I ever believed before!

BOTH.   Sing, hoity-toity! Sorry for some!

Marry come up, $\begin{Bmatrix} my \\ her \end{Bmatrix}$ day will come!
Sing, she shall learn
That a worm will turn.
Sing Happy-go-lucky, my Lady, O!
(*Exit* LADY BLANCHE.)

MELISSA.   Saved for a time, at least!

Enter FLORIAN, *on tiptoe.*

FLORIAN (*whispering*).   Melissa—come!

MELISSA.   Oh, sir! you must away from this at
once—
My mother guessed your sex! It was my
fault—
I blushed and stammered so that she ex-
claimed,
"Can these be men?" Then, seeing this, "Why
these—"
"*Are men,*" she would have added, but "*are
men*"
Stuck in her throat! She keeps your secret, sir,
For reasons of her own—but fly from this

And take me with you—that is—no—not
that!

FLORIAN.   I'll go, but not without you! (*Bell.*)
Why, what's that?

MELISSA.   The luncheon bell.

FLORIAN.   I'll wait for luncheon then!

Enter HILARION *with* PRINCESS, CYRIL *with*
PSYCHE, LADY BLANCHE *and* LADIES. *Also "Daughters of the Plough" bearing luncheon, which they
spread on the rocks.*

CHORUS.

Merrily ring the luncheon bell!
Here in meadow of asphodel,
Feast we body and mind as well,
So merrily ring the luncheon bell!

SOLO — BLANCHE.

Hunger, I beg to state,
Is highly indelicate,
This is a fact profoundly true
So learn your appetites to subdue.

ALL.   Yes, yes,
We'll learn our appetites to subdue!

SOLO — CYRIL (*eating*).

Madam, your words so wise,
Nobody should despise,
Cursed with an appetite keen I am
And I'll subdue it—
And I'll subdue it—
And I'll subdue it with cold roast lamb!

ALL.   Yes—yes—
We'll subdue it with cold roast lamb!

CHORUS.   Merrily ring, &c.

PRINCESS.   You say you know the court of Hildebrand?
There is a Prince there—I forget his name—

HILARION.   Hilarion?

PRINCESS.   Exactly—is he well?

HILARION.   If it be well to droop and pine and
mope,
To sigh "Oh, Ida! Ida!" all day long,
"Ida! my love! my life! Oh come to me!"
If it be well, I say, to do all this,
Then Prince Hilarion is very well.

PRINCESS.   He breathes *our* name? Well, it's a
common one!
And is the booby comely?

HILARION.   Pretty well.
I've heard it said that if I dressed myself

In Prince Hilarion's clothes (supposing this
Consisted with my maiden modesty),
I might be taken for Hilarion's self.
But what is this to you or me, who think
Of all mankind with undisguised contempt?

PRINCESS.   Contempt? Why, damsel, when I think of man,
Contempt is not the word.

CYRIL (getting tipsy).   I'm sure of that,
Or if it is, it surely should not be!

HILARION (aside to CYRIL). Be quiet, idiot, or
they'll find us out!

CYRIL.   The Prince Hilarion's a goodly lad!

PRINCESS.   You know him then?

CYRIL (tipsily).   I rather think I do!
We are inseparables!

PRINCESS.   Why, what's this?
You love him then?

CYRIL.   We do indeed—all three!

HILARION. Madam, she jests! (Aside to CYRIL.)
Remember where you are!

CYRIL. Jests? Not at all! Why, bless my heart alive,
You and Hilarion, when at the Court,
Rode the same horse!

PRINCESS (horrified).   Astride?

CYRIL.   Of course! Why not?
Wore the same clothes—and once or twice, I think,
Got tipsy in the same good company!

PRINCESS. Well, these are nice young ladies, on my word!

CYRIL (tipsy). Don't you remember that old kissing-song
He'd sing to blushing Mistress Lalage,
The hostess of the Pigeons? Thus it ran:

SONG — CYRIL.

(During symphony HILARION and FLORIAN try
to stop CYRIL. He shakes them off angrily.)

Would you know the kind of maid
Sets my heart a flame-a?
Eyes must be downcast and staid,
Cheeks must flush for shame-a!
She may neither dance nor sing,
But, demure in everything,
Hang her head in modest way,
With pouting lips that seem to say:
"Kiss me, kiss me, kiss me, kiss me,
Though I die of shame-a."
Please you, that's the kind of maid
Sets my heart a flame-a!

When a maid is bold and gay
With a tongue goes clang-a,
Flaunting it in brave array,
Maiden may go hang-a!
Sunflower gay and hollyhock
Never shall my garden stock;
Mine the blushing rose of May,
With pouting lips that seem to say,
"Oh, kiss me, kiss me, kiss me, kiss me,
Though I die for shame-a!"
Please you that's the kind of maid
Sets my heart a flame-a!

PRINCESS. Infamous creature, get you hence away!
(HILARION, who has been with difficulty restrained by FLORIAN during this song, breaks from him and strikes CYRIL furiously on the breast.)

HILARION. Dog! there is something more to sing about!

CYRIL (sobered). Hilarion, are you mad?

PRINCESS (horrified).   Hilarion? Help!
Why these are men! Lost! lost! betrayed! undone!   (Running on to bridge.)
Girls, get you hence! Man-monsters, if you dare
Approach one step, I—— Ah!
(Loses her balance, and falls into the stream.)

PSYCHE.   Oh! save her, sir!

BLANCHE. It's useless, sir,—you'll only catch your death! (HILARION springs in.)

SACHARISSA. He catches her!

MELISSA.   And now he lets her go!
Again she's in his grasp——

PSYCHE.   And now she's not.
He seizes her back hair!

BLANCHE (not looking).   And it comes off!

PSYCHE. No, no! She's saved!—she's saved!—she's saved!—she's saved!
(HILARION is seen swimming with PRINCESS in one arm. The PRINCESS and he are brought to land.)

FINALE.

CHORUS OF LADIES.

Oh! joy, our chief is saved,
And by Hilarion's hand;
The torrent fierce he braved,

And brought her safe to land!
   For his intrusion we must own
   This doughty deed may well atone!

PRINCESS.   Stand forth, ye three,
         Whoe'er ye be,
   And hearken to our stern decree!

HILARION, CYRIL, *and* FLORIAN. Have mercy,
   lady—disregard your oaths!

PRINCESS. I know not mercy, men in women's
   clothes!
   The man whose sacrilegious eyes
   Invade our strict seclusion, dies.
   Arrest these coarse intruding spies!
      (*They are arrested by the "Daughters of the
         Plough."*)

FLORIAN, CYRIL, *and* LADIES. Have mercy, lady
   —disregard your oaths!

PRINCESS. I know not mercy, men in women's
   clothes!
         (CYRIL *and* FLORIAN *are bound.*)

SONG — HILARION.

   Whom thou hast chained must wear his
      chain,
      Thou canst not set him free,
   He wrestles with his bonds in vain
      Who lives by loving thee!
   If heart of stone for heart of fire,
      Be all thou hast to give,
   If dead to me my heart's desire,
      Why should I wish to live?

   No word of thine—no stern command
      Can teach my heart to rove.
   Then rather perish by thy hand,
      Than live without thy love!
   A loveless life apart from thee
      Were hopeless slavery,
   If kindly death will set me free,
      Why should I fear to die?
(*He is bound by two of the attendants, and the
      three gentlemen are marched off.*)

Enter MELISSA.

MELISSA. Madam, without the castle walls
         An armed band
   Demand admittance to our halls
         For Hildebrand!

ALL.   Oh horror!

PRINCESS.   Deny them!
   We will defy them!

ALL.   Too late—too late!
         The castle gate
      Is battered by them!

The gate yields. HILDEBRAND *and* SOLDIERS *rush
in.* ARAC, GURON, *and* SCYNTHIUS *are with them,
but with their hands handcuffed.*

ALL (SOLDIERS *and* LADIES). Too late—too late!
         The castle gate
      Is battered by them!

ENSEMBLE.

GIRLS.

Rend the air with
      wailing,
   Shed the shameful
      tear!
Walls are unavailing,
   Man has entered
      here!
Shame and desecration
   Are his staunch
      allies.
Let your lamentation
   Echo to the skies!

MEN.

Walls and fences
      scaling,
   Promptly we appear;
Walls are unavailing,
   We have entered
      here.
Female execration
   Stifle if you're wise.
Stop your lamentation,
   Dry your pretty eyes!

RECITATIVE.

PRINCESS. Audacious tyrant, do you dare
      To beard a maiden in her lair?

HILDEBRAND. Since you enquire,
         We've no desire
      To beard a maiden here, or anywhere!

SOLDIERS.   No, no—we've no desire
  To beard a maiden here, or anywhere!

   SOLO — HILDEBRAND.

   Some years ago,
   No doubt you know
  (And if you don't I'll tell you so),
   You gave your troth
   Upon your oath
  To Hilarion my son.
   A vow you make
   You must not break
  (If you think you may, it's a great mis-
    take),
   For a bride's a bride
   Though the knot were tied
    At the early age of one!
    And I'm a peppery kind of King,
    Who's indisposed for parleying
    To fit the wit of a bit of a chit,
    And that's the long and the short
     of it!

ALL.   For he's a peppery kind of King, &c.

HILDEBRAND.   If you decide
   To pocket your pride
  And let Hilarion claim his bride,
   Why, well and good,
   It's understood
  We'll let bygones go by—
   But if you choose
   To sulk in the blues,
  I'll make the whole of you shake in your
    shoes.
   I'll storm your walls,
   And level your halls,
    In the twinkling of an eye!

  For I'm a peppery Potentate,
  Who's little inclined his claim
   to bate,
  To fit the wit of a bit of a chit,
  And that's the long and the
   short of it.

  TRIO — ARAC, GURON, and SCYNTHIUS.

  We may remark, though nothing can
     Dismay us,
  That if you thwart this gentleman,
     He'll slay us.
  We don't fear death, of course—we're taught
     To shame it;
  But still upon the whole we thought
     We'd name it.
(*To each other.*)   Yes, yes, better perhaps to
  name it.

  Our interests we would not press
     With chatter,
  Three hulking brothers more or less
     Don't matter;
  If you'd pooh-pooh this monarch's plan,
     Pooh-pooh it,
  But when he says he'll hang a man,
     He'll do it.
(*To each other.*)   Yes, yes, devil doubt he'll do it.

PRINCESS (*recit.*).   Be reassured, nor fear his
  anger blind,
  His menaces are idle as the wind.
  He dares not kill you—vengeance lurks behind!

  ARAC, GURON, and SCYNTHIUS.

We rather think he dares, but never mind;
   No, no,—never, never mind!

HILDEBRAND.   Enough of parley—as a special
  boon,
  We give you till to-morrow afternoon:
  Release Hilarion, then, and be his bride,
  Or you'll incur the guilt of fratricide!

    ENSEMBLE.

PRINCESS.	THE OTHERS.
To yield at once to such a foe	Oh! yield at once, 'twere better so,
With shame were rife;	Than risk a strife!
So quick! away with him, although	And let the Prince Hilarion go—
He saved my life!	He saved thy life!
That he is fair, and strong, and tall,	Hilarion's fair, and strong, and tall:
Is very evident to all,	A worse misfortune might befall—
Yet I will die before I call	It's not so dreadful, after all,
Myself his wife!	To be his wife!

SOLO — PRINCESS.

Though I am but a girl,
Defiance thus I hurl;
    Our banners all
    On outer wall
We fearlessly unfurl.

ALL.   Though she is but a girl, &c.

PRINCESS.	THE OTHERS.
That he is fair, &c.	Hilarion's fair, &c.

The PRINCESS *stands, surrounded by girls kneeling.* KING HILDEBRAND *and soldiers stand on built rocks at back and sides of stage. Picture.*

CURTAIN.

ACT II.

SCENE. — *Outer walls and courtyard of Castle Adamant.* MELISSA, SACHARISSA, *and ladies discovered, armed with battle axes.*

CHORUS.

Death to the invader!
    Strike a deadly blow,
As an old Crusader
    Struck his Paynim foe!
Let our martial thunder
Fill his soul with wonder.
Tear his ranks asunder,
    Lay the tyrant low!

SOLO — MELISSA.

Thus our courage, all untarnished,
    We're instructed to display:
But to tell the truth unvarnished,
    We are more inclined to say,
"Please you, do not hurt us."

ALL.   "Do not hurt us, if it please you!"

MELISSA.   "Please you let us be."

ALL.   "Let us be—let us be!"

MELISSA.   "Soldiers disconcert us."

ALL.   "Disconcert us, if it please you!"

MELISSA.   "Frightened maids are we."

ALL.   "Maids are we—maids are we!"

MELISSA.   But 'twould be an error
    To confess our terror,
    So, in Ida's name,
    Boldly we exclaim:

CHORUS.   Death to the invader!
    Strike a deadly blow—
As an old Crusader
    Struck his Paynim foe!
    Let our martial thunder
    Fill his soul with wonder—
    Tear his ranks asunder—
    Lay the tyrant low!

Flourish. Enter PRINCESS, *armed, attended by* BLANCHE *and* PSYCHE.

PRINCESS.   I like your spirit, girls! We have to meet
Stern bearded warriors in fight to-day:
Wear naught but what is necessary to
Preserve your dignity before their eyes,
And give your limbs full play.

BLANCHE.   One moment, ma'am.
Here is a paradox we should not pass
Without enquiry. We are prone to say,
"This thing is Needful—that, Superfluous"—
Yet they invariably co-exist!
We find the Needful comprehended in
The circle of the grand Superfluous,
Yet the Superfluous cannot be bought
Unless you're amply furnished with the Needful.
These singular considerations are—

PRINCESS.   Superfluous, yet not Needful—so you see
The terms may independently exist.
(*To Ladies.*)   Women of Adamant, we have to show
That Woman, educated to the task,
Can meet Man, face to face, on his own ground,
And beat him there. Now let us set to work:
Where is our lady surgeon?

SACHARISSA.   Madam, here!

PRINCESS.   We shall require your skill to heal the wounds
Of those that fall.

SACHARISSA (*alarmed*).   What, heal the wounded?

PRINCESS.   Yes!

SACHARISSA.   And cut off real live legs and arms?

PRINCESS.   Of course!

SACHARISSA. I wouldn't do it for a thousand
    pounds!

PRINCESS. Why, how is this? Are you faint-
    hearted, girl?
    You've often cut them off in theory!

SACHARISSA. In theory I'll cut them off again
    With pleasure, and as often as you like,
    But not in practice.

PRINCESS.   Coward! get you hence,
    I've craft enough for that, and courage too,
    I'll do your work! My fusiliers, advance!
    Why, you are armed with axes! Gilded toys!
    Where are your rifles, pray?

CHLOE.   Why, please you, ma'am,
    We left them in the armoury, for fear
    That in the heat and turmoil of the fight,
    They might go off!

PRINCESS.   "They might!" Oh, craven souls!
    Go off, yourselves! Thank heaven, I have a
      heart
    That quails not at the thought of meeting
      men;
    I will discharge your rifles! Off with you!
    Where's my bandmistress?

ADA.   Please you, ma'am, the band
    Do not feel well, and can't come out to-day!

PRINCESS. Why this is flat rebellion! I've no time
    To talk to them just now. But, happily,
    I can play several instruments at once,
    And I will drown the shrieks of those that
      fall
    With trumpet music, such as soldiers love!
    How stand we with respect to gunpowder?
    My Lady Psyche—you who superintend
    Our lab'ratory—are you well prepared
    To blow these bearded rascals into shreds?

PSYCHE. Why, madam—

PRINCESS.   Well?

PSYCHE.   Let us try gentler means.
    We can dispense with fulminating grains
    While we have eyes with which to flash our
      rage!
    We can dispense with villainous saltpetre
    While we have tongues with which to blow
      them up!
    We can dispense, in short, with all the arts
    That brutalize the practical polemist!

PRINCESS (*contemptuously*). I never knew a
    more dispensing chemist!
    Away, away—I'll meet these men alone,
    Since all my women have deserted me!

(*Exeunt all but* PRINCESS, *singing refrain of
    "Death to the Invader," pianissimo.*)

PRINCESS. So fail my cherished plans—so fails
    my faith—
    And with it hope, and all that comes of hope!

SONG — PRINCESS.

I built upon a rock,
    But ere Destruction's hand
      Dealt equal lot
      To Court and cot,
    My rock had turned to sand!
      Ah, faithless rock,
      My simple faith to mock!

I leant upon an oak.
    But in the hour of need,
      Alack-a-day,
      My trusted stay
    Was but a bruisèd reed!
      Ah, trait'rous oak
      Thy worthlessness to cloak!

I drew a sword of steel,
    But when to home and hearth
      The battle's breath
      Bore fire and death,
    My sword was but a lath!
      Ah, coward steel,
      That fear can unanneal!

She sinks on a bank. Enter CHLOE *and all
    the ladies.*

CHLOE. Madam, your father and your brothers
    claim
    An audience!

PRINCESS.   What do they do here?

CHLOE.   They come
    To fight for you!

PRINCESS.   Admit them!

BLANCHE.   Infamous!
    One's brothers, ma'am, are men!

PRINCESS.   So I have heard.
    But all my women seem to fail me when
    I need them most. In this emergency,
    Even one's brothers may be turned to use.

Enter GAMA, *quite pale and unnerved.*

GAMA. My daughter!

PRINCESS.   Father! thou art free!

GAMA.   Aye, free!
    Free as a tethered ass! I come to thee
    With words from Hildebrand. Those duly
    given,

I must return to black captivity.
I'm free so far.

PRINCESS.   Your message.

GAMA.   Hildebrand
Is loth to war with women. Pit my sons,
My three brave sons, against these popinjays,
These tufted jack-a-dandy featherheads,
And on the issue let thy hand depend!

PRINCESS.   Insult on insult's head! Are we a stake
For fighting men? What fiend possesses thee,
That thou hast come with offers such as these
From such as he to such an one as I?

GAMA.   I am possessed
By the pale devil of a shaking heart!
My stubborn will is bent. I dare not face
That devilish monarch's black malignity!
He tortures me with torments worse than
     death,
I haven't anything to grumble at!
He finds out what particular meats I love,
And gives me them. The very choicest wines,
The costliest robes—the richest rooms are
     mine:
He suffers none to thwart my simplest plan,
And gives strict orders none should contradict
     me!
He's made my life a curse!   (*Weeps.*)

PRINCESS.   My tortured father!

SONG — GAMA.

Whene'er I spoke
Sarcastic joke
     Replete with malice spiteful,
This people mild

Politely smiled,
     And voted me delightful!
Now when a wight
Sits up all night
     Ill-natured jokes devising,
And all his wiles
Are met with smiles,
     It's hard, there's no disguising!

Oh, don't the days seem lank and long
When all goes right and nothing goes wrong,
And isn't your life extremely flat
With nothing whatever to grumble at!

     When German bands
     From music stands
Played Wagner imper*fectly*—
     I bade them go—
     They didn't say no,
But off they went directly!
     The organ boys
     They stopped their noise
With readiness surprising,
     And grinning herds
     Of hurdy-gurds
Retired apologizing!

Oh, don't the days seem lank and long, &c.

     I offered gold
     In sums untold
To all who'd contradict me—
     I said I'd pay
     A pound a day
To any one who kicked me—
     I bribed with toys
     Great vulgar boys
To utter something spiteful,
     But, bless you, no!
     They *would* be so
Confoundedly politeful!

In short, these aggravating lads
They tickle my tastes, they feed my fads,
They give me this and they give me that,
And I've nothing whatever to grumble at!
     (*He bursts into tears, and falls sobbing on
                              a bank.*)

PRINCESS.   My poor old father! How he must have
     suffered!
Well, well, I yield!

GAMA (*hysterically*).   She yields! I'm saved, I'm
     saved!

PRINCESS.   Open the gates—admit these warriors,
Then get you all within the castle walls.

*The gates are opened, and the Girls mount the
battlements as* HILDEBRAND *enters with Soldiers.
Also* ARAC, GURON, *and* SCYNTHIUS.

CHORUS OF SOLDIERS.

> When anger spreads his wing,
>   And all seems dark as night for it,
>   There's nothing but to fight for it.
> But ere you pitch your ring,
>   Select a pretty site for it
>   (This spot is suited quite for it).
> And then you gaily sing,
>
> "Oh, I love the jolly rattle
> Of an ordeal by battle;
> There's an end of tittle, tattle,
>   When your enemy is dead.
> It's an arrant molly-coddle
> Fears a crack upon the noddle,
> And he's only fit to swaddle
>   In a downy feather-bed!"

ALL.   For a fight's a kind of thing
>   That I love to look upon,
>   So let us sing,
>   Long live the King,
>   And his son Hilarion!

During this, HILARION, FLORIAN, *and* CYRIL *are brought out by the "Daughters of the Plough." They are still bound and wear the robes.*

GAMA.   Hilarion! Cyril! Florian! dressed as women!
>   Is this indeed Hilarion?

HILARION.   Yes it is!

GAMA.   Why, you look handsome in your women's clothes!
>   Stick to 'em! men's attire becomes you not!
>   (*To* CYRIL *and* FLORIAN.)   And you, young ladies, will you please to pray
>   King Hildebrand to set me free again?
>   Hang on his neck and gaze into his eyes,
>   He never could resist a pretty face!

HILARION.   You dog, you'll find though I wear woman's garb,
>   My sword is long and sharp!

GAMA.   Hush, pretty one!
>   Here's a virago! Here's a termagant!
>   If length and sharpness go for anything,
>   You'll want no sword while you can wag your tongue!

CYRIL.   What need to waste your words on such as he?
>   He's old and crippled.

GAMA.   Aye, but I've three sons,
>   Fine fellows, young, and muscular, and brave,
>   *They're* well worth talking to! Come, what d'ye say?

ARAC.   Aye, pretty ones, engage yourselves with us,
>   If three rude warriors affright you not!

HILARION.   Old as you are, I'd wring your shrivelled neck
>   If you were not the Princess Ida's father.

GAMA.   If I were not the Princess Ida's father,
>   And so had not her brothers for my sons,
>   No doubt you'd wring my neck—in safety, too!
>   Come, come, Hilarion, begin, begin!
>   Give them no quarter—they will give you none.
>   You've this advantage over warriors,
>   Who kill their country's enemies for pay,—
>   *You* know what you are fighting for—look there!
>   (*Pointing to Ladies on the battlements.*)

SONG — ARAC.

> This helmet, I suppose,
> Was meant to ward off blows;
>   It's very hot,
>   And weighs a lot,
> As many a guardsman knows,
> So off that helmet goes.

THE THREE KNIGHTS.   Yes, yes,
>   So off that helmet goes!
>   (*Giving their helmets to attendants.*)

ARAC.   This tight-fitting cuirass
>   Is but a useless mass;
>   It's made of steel,
>   And weighs a deal.

A man is but an ass
Who fights in a cuirass,
So off goes that cuirass.

ALL THREE.   Yes, yes,
So off goes that cuirass!
            (*Removing cuirasses.*)

ARAC. These brassets, truth to tell,
May look uncommon well,
But in a fight
They're much too tight,
They're like a lobster shell!

ALL THREE.   Yes, yes,
They're like a lobster shell.
            (*Removing their brassets.*)

ARAC. These things I treat the same
                        (*indicating leg pieces*).
(I quite forget their name.)
They turn one's legs
To cribbage pegs—
Their aid I thus disclaim,
Though I forget their name!

ALL THREE.   Yes, yes,
Though we forget their name,
Their aid we thus disclaim!
(*They remove their leg pieces and wear close-
fitting shape suits.*)

*Desperate fight between the three Princes and the
three Knights, during which the Ladies on the
battlements and the Soldiers on the stage sing
the following*

CHORUS.

This is our duty plain towards
Our Princess all immaculate:
We ought to bless her brothers' swords
And piously ejaculate:
Oh, Hungary!
Oh, Hungary!
Oh, doughty sons of Hungary!
May all success
Attend and bless
Your warlike ironmongery!

By this time, ARAC, GURON, *and* SCYNTHIUS *are
on the ground, wounded—*HILARION, CYRIL *and*
FLORIAN *stand over them.*

PRINCESS (*entering through gate and followed by
Ladies*). Hold! stay your hands!—we
yield ourselves to you!
Ladies, my brothers all lie bleeding there!
Bind up their wounds—but look the other
way.
(*Coming down.*) Is this the end? (*Bitterly,*

to LADY BLANCHE.) How say you, Lady
Blanche—
Can I with dignity my post resign?
And if I do, will you then take my place?

BLANCHE. To answer this, it's meet that we con-
sult
The great Potential Mysteries; I mean
The five Subjunctive Possibilities—
The May, the Might, the Would, the Could,
the Should.
Can you resign? The prince Might claim you;
if
He Might, you Could—and if you Should, I
Would!

PRINCESS. I thought as much! Then, to my fate
I yield—
So ends my cherished scheme! Oh, I had
hoped
To band all women with my maiden throng,
And make them all abjure tyrannic Man!

HILDEBRAND. A noble aim!

PRINCESS.   You ridicule it now;
But if I carried out this glorious scheme,
At my exalted name Posterity
Would bow in gratitude!

HILDEBRAND.   But pray reflect—
If you enlist all women in your cause,
And make them all abjure tyrannic Man,
The obvious question then arises, "How
Is this Posterity to be provided?"

PRINCESS. I never thought of that! My Lady
Blanche,
How do you solve the riddle?

BLANCHE.   Don't ask me—
Abstract Philosophy won't answer it.
Take him—he is your Shall. Give in to Fate!

PRINCESS. And you desert me. I alone am
staunch!

HILARION. Madam, you placed your trust in
Woman—well,
Woman has failed you utterly—try Man,
Give him one chance, it's only fair—besides,
Women are far too precious, too divine
To try unproven theories upon.
Experiments, the proverb says, are made
On humble subjects—try our grosser clay,
And mould it as you will!

CYRIL.   Remember, too,
Dear Madam, if at any time you feel,
A-weary of the Prince, you can return
To Castle Adamant, and rule your girls
As heretofore, you know.

PRINCESS.   And shall I find
        The Lady Psyche here?

PSYCHE.   If Cyril, ma'am,
        Does not behave himself, I think you will.

PRINCESS. And you, Melissa, shall I find *you*
        here?

MELISSA. Madam, however Florian turns out,
        Unhesitatingly I answer, No!

GAMA. Consider this, my love, if your mama
        Had looked on matters from your point of
                view
        (I wish she had), why, where would you have
                been?

BLANCHE. There's an unbounded field of specu-
        lation,
        On which I could discourse for hours!

PRINCESS.   No doubt!
        We will not trouble you. Hilarion,
        I have been wrong—I see my error now.
        Take me, Hilarion—"We will walk the world
        Yoked in all exercise of noble end!
        And so through those dark gates across the
                wild
        That no man knows! Indeed, I love thee—
                Come!"

FINALE.

PRINCESS.
                With joy abiding,
                Together gliding
                    Through life's variety,
                    In sweet society,
                And thus enthroning
                The love I'm owning,
                On this atoning
                    I will rely!

CHORUS.
                It were profanity
                For poor humanity
                To treat as vanity
                    The sway of Love,
                In no locality
                Or principality
                Is our mortality
                    Its sway above!

HILARION.
                When day is fading,
                With serenading
                    And such frivolity
                    Of tender quality—
                With scented showers
                Of fairest flowers,
                The happy hours
                    Will gaily fly!

CHORUS.
                It were profanity, &c.

CURTAIN.

Postscript

GILBERT'S PREVIOUS BURLESQUE on Tennyson's poem, "The Princess," produced in 1870, had already received the librettist's careful revisions from actual stage performance. It is understandable, therefore, that when he based his opera libretto, *Princess Ida,* on this work much of the blank-verse dialog required little or no change after he was once satisfied with its revised form. Naturally the same lyrics had not appeared earlier. But even his alterations of these lyrics seem to have been satisfactorily resolved before publication of the libretto in England.

Thus, the libretto of *Princess Ida,* beginning with the first issue of the first edition, underwent no important textual changes and in fact very few changes of any kind up to the present day, though some can be found after 1911 when Chappell conformed the libretto lyrics to the vocal score.

In the first edition *Princess Ida* was divided into a Prologue and two Acts. Even though this was the libretto at the Savoy Theatre on opening night, most of the critics and probably all of the public persisted in referring to all three of the divisions of the opera as "Acts." It is not surprising, therefore, that in the second edition, and from then on, the libretto was printed in three Acts.

In the 1954 revival the only casualty among the lyrics in the official cuts was Lady Blanche's song in two stanzas, "Come, mighty Must!" (page 220).

Shortly before the preparation of this revised edition, Miss D'Oyly Carte called attention to a hitherto unnoticed discrepancy between the dramatis personae page of the libretto and the first-night program. The libretto listed Mr. Lugg as Guron and Mr. W. Grey [sic] as Scynthius. The first-night program gave the role of Guron to Warwick Gray and that of Scynthius to Mr. Lugg. As both the libretto and program were available at the Savoy Theatre on January 5, 1884, the Press could take its choice—and did, with misleading and confusing results.

Of ten daily newspapers and periodicals examined in which the *Princess Ida* notices specifically mentioned Guron and Scynthius, eight* were guided by the libretto—interesting assurance that it was in their hands for the performance. Their choice was unfortunate. The first edition of the libretto was wrong, and the vocal score followed its error. On the other hand, the first night program and subsequent programs were correct with respect to these two roles. They served to guide the reviewers of two January 7th journals, the *Morning Advertiser* and the *Weekly Times,* as well as the cast-listing that headed the long review in the *Sunday Times* of January 6th, even though the balance of the *Sunday Times* article, signed "Lorgnette," followed the libretto casting. All ten of the Press misspelled the name Gray, but at least the two who used the program, cast Guron and Scynthius correctly. Later, by the end of January, when the second edition of the libretto reset the opera in three acts, Guron and Scynthius were made right for the casts of posterity—from the *Original Plays, Third Series* of 1895 to *The D'Oyly Carte Opera Company—A Record of Productions* of 1962.

A further discrepancy came to light when this Pandora's box of bibliography was opened. In the true first edition of the libretto the name of the actress who played Ada was misspelled Miss Twynam, an error followed by the only three journals of those eight who, guided by the libretto, had mentioned this role, and also by the Chappell vocal score. The first-night program spelled Ada's name correctly as Twyman. So did the *Sunday Times* of January 6th in its cast listing (but this role was not mentioned in the reviews of the *Morning Advertiser* or the *Weekly Times*). But to compound confusion, the faulty spelling Twynam which *should* have been in the d.p. page of the libretto as reproduced on page 212 of the original edition of *The First-Night Gilbert and Sullivan* was corrected inadvertently by the editor, with no mention of such a change. It should *not* have been so corrected; and in this revised edition it has been returned to its proper improper state, an appropriate application of Gilbertian topsy-turvydom to bibliography.

* Note: 6 January 1884: *Sunday Times* (review); 7 January 1884: *Daily Telegraph, Standard, Sporting Life, Freeman Journal*—Dublin and *The Figaro, The Globe* and *The Theatre* magazine, 1 February.

THE MIKADO

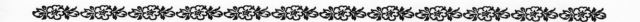

Introduction

"MESSRS. GILBERT AND SULLIVAN must be familiar with success by this time, but never in their brilliant partnership of sprightly music and fantastic fun has a more unanimous verdict of approval been passed upon their labours than when the curtain fell on Saturday last."

Press, public and performers joined with the critic of the *Era* to hail the birth of *The Mikado,* which posterity for more than seventy years thereafter was to make the most valuable stage property in the world.

Saturday evening, March 14, 1885, at the Savoy Theatre, provided one of the most electrifying experiences in all stage history and reached the high-water mark of first-night excitement and acclaim for Gilbert and Sullivan operas. Against this wave of enthusiasm for *The Mikado* the few small dissenting voices were then inconspicuous and seem today ridiculous. The *Evening News* held "it was not likely to add very much to the reputation of either author or composer." And the *Whitehall Review* would "scarcely augur for it a lasting or a popular success." But—

"Never during the whole of my experience have I assisted at such an enthusiastic first night as greeted this delightful work," wrote Rutland Barrington (creator of Pooh-Bah that evening) in his memoirs. "From the moment the curtain rose on the Court swells in Japanese plate attitudes to its final fall it was one long succession of uproarious laughter at the libretto and overwhelming applause for the music."

The gilded audience included several members of the royal family: the Duke and Duchess of Edinburgh, Princess Louise and Prince Louis of Battenberg. In fact, while Victoria's musician son was enjoying himself in the private box he was unaware of newsboys outside the Savoy Theatre shouting the completely unfounded report of "SERIOUS ACCIDENT TO THE DUKE OF EDINBURGH!" All that befell him and his Duchess that night was Her Royal Highness' complete captivation, which prompted her return visit to the following Tuesday's performance. Among others mentioned by the reporter for the *Watch* were James McNeill Whistler, Henry Labouchere (well-known editor and liberal), Mr. & Mrs. (Kate Terry) Arthur Lewis, Comyns Carr (who was to collaborate with Sullivan in *The Beauty Stone* in 1898), Charles Edward Perugini (artist-husband of Kate Macready Dickens, the novelist's second daughter), Mr. Inderwick, Q.C. (ardent first-nighting Queen's Counsel, who evidently on this occasion wore an unexpected "backwoodsman's beard"—see page 272), actor Corney Grain, actor-manager's wife Mrs. John Hare, and *Punch* editor and pre-Gilbert collaborator with Sullivan—Frank Burnand.

The regular programs for this distinguished gathering resembled those of *Princess Ida*—a format which was to be standard at the Savoy Theatre until *The Grand Duke.* D'Oyly Carte also provided two souvenir programs, one glossy blue,

Sullivan at the harmonium accompanying H.R.H. the Duke of Edinburgh's violin—after an original wash drawing by Arthur Bryan.

the other buff. Both carried the special line: *"On This Occasion* the Opera will be conducted by the *Composer."*

Two tensions were in delicate balance across the Savoy footlights that night: that of the pleasure-poised, success-expectant audience, and that of a company suffering—in plain language—first-night jitters. Final rehearsals had not gone well. Gilbert was in a particularly peckish mood and made the more irritable by the harassment of his own uncertainty. Grossmith was having trouble with his Ko-Ko lines. Barrington has written that Gilbert was not quite satisfied with his rendering of Pooh-Bah. And even Richard Temple, who turned out to be a superlative Mikado, very nearly lost his best song, "My object all sublime," when (in the words of Barrington) "for some reason Gilbert decided at the dress rehearsal that it would not go, and had better be cut. Cut it was, there and then, much to Temple's chagrin; but when the choristers heard the news they went in a body to Gilbert and implored him to reinstate it. This was done, with what success we know." As Barrington put it, "This must have been an anxious first night for Gilbert." But the *Figaro* reported that, as usual on his first nights, "Mr. Gilbert was not in the house till shortly before the fall of the curtain, when he came to the footlights, hand in hand with Sir Arthur Sullivan."

So it was the musical member of the partnership who, as usual, was at the helm during the perils of a first-night passage. Sullivan conducted a performance, which, according to the *Standard,* "except for an occasional lapse of memory on the part of the players—doubtless the result of nervousness—went, in all essentials, as smoothly as if the work had been given a hundred times." The *Morning Post* was rather more critical: "So soon as the strangeness of the first night is passed and the actors can speak their words without prompting, much better effects will doubtless follow. . . . A want of familiarity with the work they had to do was observed in more than one of the actors, and the usual brilliancy of a first-night's performance of a Gilbert and Sullivan piece was, therefore, lacking."

Poor George Grossmith seems to have been the principal offender. He later admitted: "The first night of *The Mikado* I shall never forget the longest day I live. It must have appeared to all that I was doing my best to spoil the piece. But what with my own want of physical strength, prostration through the numerous and very long rehearsals, my anxiety to satisfy the author, and the long rows of critics rendered *blasé* by the modern custom of half-a-dozen matinees a week, I lost my voice, the little there is of it, my confidence, and—what I maintain is most valuable to me—my own individuality. In fact I plead guilty to what Richard Barker [the stage manager] declared me to be . . . 'a lamentable spectacle!' " *Punch* possibly oversimplified hapless Grossmith's dilemma by assuring its readers: "It broke upon many of us there, as quite a revelation, that our George Grossmith's real humour had hitherto been less in his face and voice than in his legs. Throughout the First Act his legs were invisible, and the audience felt that something was wanting; they didn't know exactly what it was, but their favourite was not being funny. He didn't even look funny. He had a good song; he got flustered in the words; was nervous; but all this could have been forgiven him if he had only been funny—just once. . . . Suddenly in the Second Act, he gave a kick-up, and showed a pair of white stocking'd legs under the Japanese dress. It was an inspiration. Forthwith, the house felt a strong sense of relief—it had got what it wanted . . . what it had really missed, and at the first glimpse of George Grossmith's legs there arose a shout of long pent-up laughter. . . . From that time to the end of the piece there wasn't a dull minute."

But except for Ko-Ko, the other principal roles received uniformly favorable commendation. The *Daily News* found Richard Temple "excellent as the Mikado—his senile grin and waddling walk were extremely comic . . ." and it printed the entirety of his nearly-deleted "My object all sublime" in the first-night review. Beatty-Kingston in the *Theatre* observed: "The Pooh-Bah of Mr. Barrington is a masterpiece of pompous stolidity —nothing could possibly be better of its kind— and this popular comedian provided his many admirers with an agreeable surprise by singing every note of the music allotted to him perfectly in tune." Barrington recalled later that Gilbert "at the end of the performance . . . came to my dressing-room and thanked me for 'my invaluable aid to the success of the piece.'" And of the tenor lead, the *Standard* had appropriate praise: "Mr. Lely is the Nanki-Poo, and it naturally follows that the hero's music is given with taste, while Mr. Lely is known as one of the few tenors who can act. His first song, 'A wandering minstrel, I,' is one of the successes of the Opera." As "the 'general utility' noble lord, Pish-Tush," Beatty-Kingston found the Savoy Theatre newcomer, Frederick Bovill, possessor of "a fine mellow voice, which he produces very agreeably, and . . . in all respects an acquisition to the Savoy Company." However fine Mr. Bovill's baritone was, he evidently could not reach, to Sullivan's satisfaction, the bass depths required in the madrigal; for Gilbert later created a new character, Go-To, simply to take over the Pish-Tush part in that number.

"A word of cordial praise must be bestowed on Miss Rosina Brandram, the Katisha," commented the *Standard*'s reviewer: "Miss Brandram is known as an accomplished vocalist, and she amply justified her reputation." According to the *Theatre*, Leonora Braham, as Yum-Yum, "sang and acted to perfection. . . . She was more fascinating than ever, and more than once saved the action from dragging by her unaffected vivacity and winsome playfulness." The same review praised Miss Sybil Grey, as though new to the Savoy, for her Peep-Bo: "She has a pretty voice, her intonation is correct and her appearance attractive." Jessie Bond, as usual, according to the *Daily News,* "gave all possible charm and vivacity to the character and the music of Pitti-Sing." Diminutive Jessie divulged part of her success-secret in her memoirs: "There was nothing much to single me out from the Three Little Maids from School, so I persuaded the wardrobe mistress to give me a big obi, twice as big as any of the others. She did . . . and I made the most of my big, big bow, turning my back to the audience whenever I got a chance, and waggling it. The gallery was delighted, but *I* nearly got the sack for that prank! However, I did get noticed, which was what I wanted."

Hawes Craven's two sets received admiring comment from the press: "Japanese towns must be delightful places to live in if they resemble their counterfeit presentments at the Savoy." The "splendour" of the costumes, "rich and varied," "closely studied from Japanese fashions," received an ample share of notice. They, as well as the stage business, had been supervised by the directors of the Japanese Village that had been erected at Knightsbridge and was currently introducing London to the Oriental mode of life. In fact the programs carried a special acknowledgment to "the Directors and Native Inhabitants" of this village for valuable assistance. From such expert technical advice stemmed the marvelous use of fans by the whole company, especially noticed by the *Pall Mall Gazette*.

The costumes themselves found some unbelievers in this as yet not too orientally indoctrinated press. Beatty-Kingston grumbled: "They are unbecoming to men and women alike—especially to the latter . . . in fact, they obliterate the natural distinctions between the sexes, imparting to the prettiest girl's figure the seeming of a bolster loosely wrapped up in a dressing-gown." But the gentleman from the *Daily News* viewed these costumes, particularly the ladies', with an eye that had been east of Suez: "The Japanese gowns, with their delicate tints, their richly embroidered conceits and fantasies, and their ample sashes, lent not a little aid to the oddly pleasing effect. If the enthusiasm of the ladies among the audience may afford a token, sashes rising halfway from the waist to the shoulders and tied in huge double bows upon the backs of the wearers, may find a place ere long among the fashions of the day, unless Mr. Burnand, whose satirical eye was ob-

Cartoon in PUNCH, *March 28, 1885.*

served to be very busy on the occasion, should be disposed to bring the deterrent influences of the verse writers and draughtsmen of *Punch* to bear upon the threatened rage for Japanese eccentricities."

The overture was completed by Hamilton Clarke, who—according to a chatty interview Sullivan gave *Home News* four years later—"used to help me with them [his overtures] very often when I was pressed for time. Do you remember the Mikado overture? He did that for me. I just arranged the order of the piece—the 'Mikado's March,' then 'The sun whose rays,' first for the oboe and then for violins and 'cellos, two octaves apart, and finally the allegro. He wrote the whole thing in a few hours: in fact he made it almost too elaborate, for I had to cut it down a little."

From the rise of the curtain on Act I, it was clear that this joint effort found the collaborators in magnificently equal balance. "The text of *The Mikado* sparkles with countless gems of wit . . . and its author's rhyming and rhythmic gifts have never been more splendidly displayed," wrote Beatty-Kingston in the *Theatre;* "as for the dialogue, it is positively so full of points and hits as to keep the wits of the audience constantly on the strain." And of the music, the same critic effused: "What a graphic and fertile melodist is Sullivan! What an accomplished orchestrator! . . . Beyond a doubt *The Mikado* is as good as any of its forerunners. It contains half a dozen numbers, each of which is sufficiently attractive to ensure the opera's popularity; musical jewels of great price, all aglow with the lustre of a pure and luminous genius."

The author of these verbal ecstasies on *The Mikado* as dramatic entertainment, is said to have brought Gilbert close to apoplexy with a pedantic, humorless dissection of *The Mikado* as an abstract social document. Isaac Goldberg, writing about this review, observes: "One critic regarded this work as a subtle menace to society. Beatty-Kingston's description of *The Mikado* is a classic of temperamental incomprehension, written as Katisha herself might have reviewed it for the Titipu *Times.*" Another Savoy Opera historian, S. J. Adair Fitz-Gerald, who knew personally all the principal figures associated with their initial productions, has quoted a portion of this same review, ending: "All these people, Gilbert's Dramatis Personae and their 'principals' to boot, are carefully shown to be unsusceptible of a single kindly feeling or wholesome impulse." He comments: "Did I not know from personal knowledge that Beatty-Kingston was absolutely devoid of the right sense of humour, I should have imagined that he was trying to pull the leg of the whole of the universe."

The text of the performance heard on March 14, 1885—and the first edition of the libretto in the hands of the audience that evening—differed in several important respects from the later standardized performances and from succeeding editions of the libretto. The most spectacular difference was the presence of Yum-Yum's beautiful solo, "The sun whose rays," in the first act instead of its later position at the opening of Act II. "Exquisitely pretty is the trio of the three little maids," wrote the *Graphic,* "and the succeeding three-part song, solo, and chorus, which serves to carry off the stage all the party save Yum-Yum. Her song, 'The sun whose rays,' apart from the delicately-veiled irony, is a facile piece of versification, allied with a melody one phrase of which seems to suggest that the lovely 'Song of the Bird' in Wagner's *Siegfried* haunts the memory of Sir Arthur Sullivan, as it previously had affected the recollection of M. Gounod."

In an early issue of the *Gilbert and Sullivan Journal,* forty-one years after the event, Leonora Braham recalled the background of this important shift: "The morning after the production of *The Mikado* at a rehearsal just to pick up some loose ends in the last night's performance [Such alterations were radical. Loose ends, indeed!] I told Sir Arthur Sullivan that I had found much difficulty in giving a good interpretation of my song, 'The Moon and I' (it then came immediately after the 'Three Little Maids' trio and the quintette [*sic*] 'So please you, Sir,' with just a few lines spoken before it, which left me breathless)." Sullivan apparently recognized the validity of his leading lady's complaint and moved this prominent and exposed aria to its position at the opening of Act II, after the "Braid the raven hair" chorus.

Of the seven encores Sullivan recalled that night, the first received perhaps the most exciting reception ever accorded any comic opera lyric. In the words of Beatty-Kingston, "The greatest success of the evening, as far as reiterate and rapturous recalls were concerned, at least, was the Trio and chorus, 'Three Little Maids from School,' which the first-nighters insisted upon hearing three times, and would gladly have listened to a fourth, had not their request been steadfastly declined. Nothing fresher, gayer, or more captivating has ever bid for public favour than this delightful composition." And on the acting side of the footlights, Rutland Barrington had the last word: "The Trio and Chorus, 'Three Little Maids from School' . . . was received with such enthusiasm and insistent encores as no musical number in my experience, or I believe in any one's else, has ever equalled. It seemed as if we should never get on with the piece."

George Grossmith's "I've got a little list" song,

also in Act I, won this award from the *Daily News:* "Among the noteworthy incidents of the evening was the sudden hush of expectancy when Mr. Grossmith, in singing Ko-Ko's song in the first act, appeared to be about to name the distinguished statesmen who, without any irreparable damage to the interests of their country, might be offered up as victims. . . . The outburst of merriment which followed on the conclusion of the lyric showed that the audience greatly enjoyed the joke of this evasion." Frederick Halton, in his Gilbert and Sullivan *Concordance,* suggests that Grossmith and—through him—Gilbert were not altogether as lacking in specific political bias as "The task of filling up the blanks I'd rather leave to you" might indicate. Although Gilbert's lyric stopped short of naming names, it seems likely that Gilbert's stage direction did not. "Gee-Gee" was a skillful pantomimist. It was known to any Londoner able to buy his way in to a Savoy Theatre first night, that Gladstone wore abnormally large collars and frequently showed his profile, that Lord Salisbury wore a large, bushy beard, that the Marquis of Hartington wore a longer and less-bushy beard, and that Joseph Chamberlain was addicted to a monocle and a flower in his lapel. So with such material in the hands of pantomimist Grossmith, it is likely that Gilbert helped his audience in their task of filling up the blanks.

In the second act, both the madrigal, "Brightly dawns our wedding day," and the Mikado's "My object all sublime," which Gilbert so nearly cut from the production, were encored. The ebullient "Flowers that bloom in the spring" was accorded a triple encore, and has been stopping the show ever since.

As the *Daily News* summed up: "The production of the opera on Saturday night was conducted by the composer, who was enthusiastically received, he, Mr. Gilbert, Mr. D'Oyly Carte, and the principal performers having been called before the curtain. The house was crowded in every part . . . and the genuine applause which prevailed throughout the evening promises a long and successful run for *The Mikado.*"

Thomas F. Dunhill, musicianly defender of Arthur Sullivan, has written: "If a man's masterpiece is the work which appeals to the largest number of people of all nationalities and shades of thought, then it must be said that *The Mikado* was Sullivan's *chef d'œuvre.*" Some masterpieces take years to attain their majority in terms of popular recognition; but this masterpiece was born in electrifying applause that has persisted for over threescore years and ten in very nearly every civilized part of the world.

MARCH 14 (SATURDAY) 1885. *New Opera, "The Mikado" or "The Town of Titipu," produced at the Savoy Theatre with every sign of real success. A most brilliant house. Tremendous reception. All went very well except Grossmith, whose nervousness nearly upset the piece. A* treble *encore for "Three Little Maids" and for "The Flowers that Bloom in the Spring." Seven encores taken—might have taken twelve.*

ARTHUR SULLIVAN'S DIARY

An Entirely New and Original Japanese Opera,

IN TWO ACTS,

ENTITLED

THE MIKADO

OR,

THE TOWN OF TITIPU.

Dramatis Personae.

THE MIKADO OF JAPAN	MR. R. TEMPLE.
NANKI-POO, *His Son, Disguised as a Wandering Minstrel, and in Love with Yum-Yum*	MR. DURWARD LELY.
KO-KO, *Lord High Executioner of Titipu*	MR. GEORGE GROSSMITH.
POOH-BAH, *Lord High Everything Else*	MR. RUTLAND BARRINGTON.
PISH-TUSH, *A Noble Lord*	MR. FREDERICK BOVILL.

YUM-YUM ⎞
PITTI-SING ⎬ *Three Sisters—Wards of Ko-Ko*
PEEP-BO ⎠

MISS LEONORA BRAHAM.
MISS JESSIE BOND.
MISS SYBIL GREY.

KATISHA, *An Elderly Lady, in Love with Nanki-Poo*   MISS ROSINA BRANDRAM.

CHORUS OF SCHOOL-GIRLS, NOBLES, GUARDS, AND COOLIES.

ACT I. — Court-yard of Ko-Ko's Official Residence.

ACT II. — Ko-Ko's Garden.

THE MIKADO

OR,

THE TOWN OF TITIPU.

ACT I.

SCENE. — *Court-yard of* KO-KO's *Palace in Titipu. Japanese nobles discovered standing and sitting in attitudes suggested by native drawings.*

CHORUS.

If you want to know who we are,
    We are gentlemen of Japan:
On many a vase and jar—
    On many a screen and fan,
        We figure in lively paint:
        Our attitudes queer and quaint—
        You're wrong if you think it ain't.

If you think we are worked by strings,
    Like a Japanese marionette,
You don't understand these things:
    It is simply Court etiquette.
        Perhaps you suppose this throng
        Can't keep it up all day long?
        If that's your idea, you're wrong.

Enter NANKI-POO *in great excitement. He carries a native guitar on his back, and a bundle of ballads in his hand.*

RECITATIVE — NANKI-POO.

Gentlemen, I pray you tell me,
Where a lovely maiden dwelleth,
Named Yum-Yum, the ward of Ko-Ko?
In pity speak—oh speak, I pray you!

A NOBLE. Why, who are you who ask this question?

NANKI-POO. Come gather round me, and I'll tell you.

SONG — NANKI-POO.

A wandering minstrel I—
    A thing of shreds and patches,
    Of ballads, songs, and snatches,
And dreamy lullaby!

My catalogue is long,

Through every passion ranging,
And to your humours changing
I tune my supple song!

Are you in sentimental mood?
    I'll sigh with you,
        Oh, willow, willow!
On maiden's coldness do you brood?
    I'll do so, too—
        Oh, willow, willow!
I'll charm your willing ears
With songs of lover's fears,
While sympathetic tears
    My cheeks bedew—
        Oh, willow, willow!

But if patriotic sentiment is wanted,
    I've patriotic ballads cut and dried;
For where'er our country's banner may be
            planted,
    All other local banners are defied!
Our warriors, in serried ranks assembled,
    Never quail—or they conceal it if they
            do—
And I shouldn't be surprised if nations
            trembled
    Before the mighty troops of Titipu!

And if you call for a song of the sea,
    We'll heave the capstan round,
With a yeo heave ho, for the wind is free,
Her anchor's a-trip and her helm's a-lee,
    Hurrah for the homeward bound!
        Yeo-ho—heave ho—
    Hurrah for the homeward bound!

To lay aloft in a howling breeze
    May tickle a landsman's taste,
But the happiest hours a sailor sees
    Is when he's down

At an inland town,
With his Nancy on his knees, yeo ho!
And his arm around her waist!

Then man the capstan—off we go,
    As the fiddler swings us round,
With a yeo heave ho,
And a rumbelow,
    Hurrah for the homeward bound!

A wandering minstrel I, &c.

Enter PISH-TUSH.

PISH-TUSH.   And what may be your business with Yum-Yum?

NANKI-POO.   I'll tell you. A year ago I was a member of the Titipu town band. It was my duty to take the cap round for contributions. While discharging this delicate office, I saw Yum-Yum. We loved each other at once, but she was betrothed to her guardian Ko-Ko, a cheap tailor, and I saw that my suit was hopeless. Overwhelmed with despair, I quitted the town. Judge of my delight when I heard, a month ago, that Ko-Ko had been condemned to death for flirting! I hurried back at once, in the hope of finding Yum-Yum at liberty to listen to my protestations.

PISH-TUSH.   It is true that Ko-Ko was condemned to death for flirting, but he was reprieved at the last moment, and raised to the exalted rank of Lord High Executioner under the following remarkable circumstances:—

SONG — PISH-TUSH.

Our great Mikado, virtuous man,
When he to rule our land began,
    Resolved to try
    A plan whereby

Young men might best be steadied.
So he decreed, in words succinct,
That all who flirted, leered, or winked
(Unless connubially linked),
    Should forthwith be beheaded.

    And I expect you'll all agree
    That he was right to so decree.
        And I am right,
        And you are right,
    And all is right as right can be!

CHORUS.   And I expect, &c.

This stern decree, you'll understand,
Caused great dismay throughout the land;
    For young and old
    And shy and bold
    Were equally affected.
The youth who winked a roving eye,
Or breathed a non-connubial sigh,
Was thereupon condemned to die—
    He usually objected.

    And you'll allow, as I expect,
    That he was right to so object.
        And I am right,
        And you are right,
    And everything is quite correct!

CHORUS.   And you'll allow, as I expect, &c.

And so we straight let out on bail
A convict from the county jail,
    Whose head was next
    On some pretext
    Condemnèd to be mown off,
And made *him* Headsman, for we said,
"Who's next to be decapited
Cannot cut off another's head
    Until he's cut his own off."

    And we are right, I think you'll say,
    To argue in this kind of way.
        And I am right,
        And you are right,
    And all is right—too-looral-lay!

CHORUS.   And they were right, &c.

(*Exeunt* CHORUS.)

Enter POOH-BAH.

NANKI-POO.   Ko-Ko, the cheap tailor, Lord High Executioner of Titipu! Why, that's the highest rank a citizen can attain!

POOH-BAH.   It is. Our logical Mikado, seeing no moral difference between the dignified judge who condemns a criminal to die, and the industrious mechanic who carries out the sentence, has rolled the two offices into one, and every judge is now his own executioner.

NANKI-POO. But how good of you (for I see that you are a nobleman of the highest rank) to condescend to tell all this to me, a mere strolling minstrel!

POOH-BAH. Don't mention it. I am, in point of fact, a particularly haughty and exclusive person, of pre-Adamite ancestral descent. You will understand this when I tell you that I can trace my ancestry back to a protoplasmal primordial atomic globule. Consequently, my family pride is something inconceivable. I can't help it. I was born sneering. But I struggle hard to overcome this defect. I mortify my pride continually. When all the great officers of State resigned in a body, because they were too proud to serve under an ex-tailor, did I not unhesitatingly accept all their posts at once?

PISH-TUSH. And the salaries attached to them? You did.

POOH-BAH. It is consequently my degrading duty to serve this upstart as First Lord of the Treasury, Lord Chief Justice, Commander-in-Chief, Lord High Admiral, Master of the Buckhounds, Groom of the Back Stairs, Archbishop of Titipu, and Lord Mayor, both acting and elect, all rolled into one. And at a salary! A Pooh-Bah paid for his services! I a salaried minion! But I do it! It revolts me, but I do it.

NANKI-POO. And it does you credit.

POOH-BAH. But I don't stop at that. I go and dine with middle-class people on reasonable terms. I dance at cheap suburban parties for a moderate fee. I accept refreshment at any hands, however lowly. I also retail State secrets at a very low figure. For instance, any further information about Yum-Yum would come under the head of a State secret. (NANKI-POO *takes the hint, and gives him money*.) (*Aside.*) Another insult, and I think a light one!

SONG — POOH-BAH.

Young man, despair,
    Likewise go to;
Yum-Yum the fair
    You must not woo.
    It will not do:
    I'm sorry for you,
You very imperfect ablutioner!
    This very day
        From school Yum-Yum
    Will wend her way,
        And homeward come
        With beat of drum
        And a rum-tum-tum,
To wed the Lord High Executioner!
    And the brass will crash,
        And the trumpets bray,

And they'll cut a dash
    On their wedding day.
From what I say, you may infer
It's as good as a play for him and her,
She'll toddle away, as all aver,
With the Lord High Executioner!

    It's a hopeless case
        As you may see,
    And in your place
        Away I'd flee;
        But don't blame me—
        I'm sorry to be
Of your pleasure a diminutioner.
        They'll vow their pact
        Extremely soon,
            In point of fact
        This afternoon.
        Her honeymoon
        With that buffoon
At seven, commences, so *you* shun her!

ALL. The brass will crash, &c.

RECITATIVE.

NANKI-POO. And have I journeyed for a month, or nearly,
    To learn that Yum-Yum, whom I love so dearly,
    This day to Ko-Ko is to be united!

POOH-BAH. The fact appears to be as you've recited:
    But here he comes, equipped as suits his station;
    He'll give you any further information.

Enter KO-KO, attended.

CHORUS.

Behold the Lord High Executioner!
    A personage of noble rank and title—
A dignified and potent officer,
    Whose functions are particularly vital.
    Defer, defer,
To the noble Lord High Executioner!

SOLO — KO-KO.

Taken from the county jail
    By a set of curious chances;
Liberated then on bail,
    On my own recognizances;
Wafted by a favouring gale
    As one sometimes is in trances,
To a height that few can scale,
    Save by long and weary dances;
Surely, never had a male
    Under such like circumstances
So adventurous a tale,
    Which may rank with most romances.

CHORUS. Behold the Lord High Executioner, &c.

KO-KO. Gentlemen—I'm much touched by this reception. I can only trust that by strict attention to duty I shall ensure a continuance of those favours which it will ever be my study to deserve. Gentlemen, I expect my three beautiful wards, Yum-Yum, Peep-Bo, and Pitti-Sing, in a few minutes. If you will kindly receive them with a show of abject deference, I shall feel obliged to you. I know how painful it must be to noblemen of your rank to have to humiliate yourselves before a person of my antecedents, but discipline must be observed. (CHORUS *bow and exeunt*.) Pooh-Bah, it seems that the festivities in connection with my approaching marriage must last a week. I should like to do it handsomely, and I want to consult you as to the amount I ought to spend upon them.

POOH-BAH. Certainly. In which of my capacities? As First Lord of the Treasury, Lord Chamberlain, Attorney-General, Chancellor of the Exchequer, Privy Purse, or Private Secretary?

KO-KO. Suppose we say as Private Secretary.

POOH-BAH. Speaking as your Private Secretary, I should say that as the city will have to pay for it, don't stint yourself, do it well.

KO-KO. Exactly—as the city will have to pay for it. That is your advice.

POOH-BAH. As Private Secretary. Of course you will understand that, as Chancellor of the Exchequer, I am bound to see that due economy is observed.

KO-KO. Oh. But you said just now, "Don't stint yourself, do it well."

POOH-BAH. As Private Secretary.

KO-KO. And now you say that due economy must be observed.

POOH-BAH. As Chancellor of the Exchequer.

KO-KO. I see. Come over here, where the Chancellor can't hear us. (*They cross stage.*) Now, as my Solicitor, how do you advise me to deal with this difficulty?

POOH-BAH. Oh, as your Solicitor, I should have no hesitation in saying, "Chance it——"

KO-KO. Thank you (*shaking his hand*). I will.

POOH-BAH. If it were not that, as Lord Chief Justice, I am bound to see that the law isn't violated.

KO-KO. I see. Come over here where the Chief Justice can't hear us. (*They cross the stage.*) Now, then, as First Lord of the Treasury?

POOH-BAH. Of course, as First Lord of the Treasury, I could propose a special vote that would cover all expenses, if it were not that, as leader of the Opposition, it would be my duty to resist it, tooth and nail. Or, as Paymaster-General, I could so cook the accounts, that as Lord High Auditor I should never discover the fraud. But then, as Archbishop of Titipu, it would be my duty to denounce my dishonesty and give myself into my own custody as First Commissioner of Police.

KO-KO. That's extremely awkward.

POOH-BAH. I don't say that all these people couldn't be squared; but it is right to tell you that I shouldn't be sufficiently degraded in my own estimation unless I was insulted with a very considerable bribe.

KO-KO. The matter shall have my careful consideration. But my bride and her sisters approach, and any little compliment on your part, such as an abject grovel in a characteristic Japanese attitude, would be esteemed a favour.

Enter procession of YUM-YUM'S *schoolfellows, heralding* YUM-YUM, PEEP-BO, *and* PITTI-SING.

CHORUS.

Comes a train of little ladies
    From scholastic trammels free;
Each a little bit afraid is,
    Wondering what the world can be!

    Is it but a world of trouble—
        Sadness set to song?
    Is its beauty but a bubble
        Bound to break ere long?

    Are its palaces and pleasures
        Fantasies that fade?
    And the glory of its treasures

Shadow of a shade?

Schoolgirls we, eighteen and under,
From scholastic trammels free,
And we wonder—how we wonder!—
What on earth the world can be!

TRIO.

YUM-YUM, PEEP-BO, *and* PITTI-SING.

THE THREE.
Three little maids from school are we,
Pert as a school girl well can be,
Filled to the brim with girlish glee,
Three little maids from school!

YUM-YUM.
Everything is a source of fun.   (*Chuckle.*)

PEEP-BO.
Nobody's safe, for we care for none!
(*Chuckle.*)

PITTI-SING.
Life is a joke that's just begun! (*Chuckle.*)

THE THREE.
Three little maids from school!

ALL (*dancing*).
Three little maids who, all unwary,
Come from a ladies' seminary,
Freed from its genius tutelary—

THE THREE (*suddenly demure*).
Three little maids from school!

YUM-YUM.
One little maid is a bride, Yum-Yum—

PEEP-BO.
Two little maids in attendance come—

PITTI-SING.
Three little maids is the total sum.

THE THREE.
Three little maids from school!

YUM-YUM.
From three little maids take one away—

PEEP-BO.
Two little maids remain, and they—

PITTI-SING.
Won't have to wait very long, they say—

THE THREE.
Three little maids from school!

ALL (*dancing*).
Three little maids who, all unwary,
Come from a ladies' seminary,
Freed from its genius tutelary—

THE THREE (*suddenly demure*).
Three little maids from school!

KO-KO. At last, my bride that is to be! (*About to embrace her.*)

YUM-YUM. You're not going to kiss me before all these people?

KO-KO. Well, that was the idea.

YUM-YUM (*aside to* PEEP-BO). It seems odd, don't it?

PEEP-BO. It's rather peculiar.

PITTI-SING. Oh, I expect it's all right. Must have a beginning, you know.

YUM-YUM. Well, of course I know nothing about these things; but I've no objection if it's usual.

KO-KO. Oh, it's quite usual, I think. Eh, Lord Chamberlain? (*Appealing to* POOH-BAH.)

POOH-BAH. I have known it done. (KO-KO *embraces her.*)

YUM-YUM. That's over! (*Sees* NANKI-POO, *and rushes to him.*) Why, that's never you? (*The Three Girls rush to him and shake his hands, all speaking at once.*)

YUM-YUM. Oh, I'm so glad! I haven't seen you for ever so long, and I'm right at the top of the school, and I've got three prizes, and I've come home for good, and I'm not going back any more!

PEEP-BO. And have you got an engagement? —Yum-Yum's got one, but she don't like it, and she'd ever so much rather it was you. I've come home for good, and I'm not going back any more!

PITTI-SING. Now tell us all the news, because you go about everywhere, and we've been at school, but thank goodness that's all over now, and we've come home for good, and we're not going back any more!

(*These three speeches are spoken together in one breath.*)

KO-KO. I beg your pardon. Will you present me?

YUM-YUM. Oh, this is the musician who used—
PEEP-BO. Oh, this is the gentleman who used—
PITTI-SING. Oh, it is only Nanki-Poo who used—

KO-KO. One at a time, if you please.

YUM-YUM. He's the gentleman who used to play so beautifully on the—on the—

PITTI-SING. On the Marine Parade.

YUM-YUM. Yes, I think that was the name of the instrument.

NANKI-POO. Sir, I have the misfortune to love your ward, Yum-Yum—oh, I know I deserve your anger!

KO-KO. Anger! not a bit, my boy. Why, I love her myself. Charming little girl, isn't she? Pretty eyes, nice hair. Taking little thing, altogether. Very glad to hear my opinion backed by a competent authority. Thank you very much. Good-bye. (*To* PISH-TUSH.) Take him away. (PISH-TUSH *removes him.*)

PITTI-SING (*who has been examining* POOH-BAH). I beg your pardon, but what is this? Customer come to try on?

KO-KO. That is a Tremendous Swell. (*She starts back in alarm.*)

POOH-BAH. Go away, little girls. Can't talk to little girls like you. Go away, there's dears.

KO-KO. Allow me to present you, Pooh-Bah. These are my three wards. The one in the middle is my bride elect.

POOH-BAH. What do you want me to do to them? Mind, I *will not* kiss them.

KO-KO. No, no, you sha'n't kiss them: a little bow—a mere nothing—you needn't mean it, you know.

POOH-BAH. It goes against the grain. They are not young ladies, they are young persons.

KO-KO. Come, come, make an effort, there's a good nobleman.

POOH-BAH (*aside to* KO-KO). Well, I sha'n't mean it. (*With a great effort.*) How de do, how de do, little girls! (*Aside.*) Oh my protoplasmal ancestor!

KO-KO. That's very good. (*Girls indulge in suppressed laughter.*)

POOH-BAH. I see nothing to laugh at. It is very painful to me to have to say "How de do, how de do, little girls," to young persons. I'm not in the habit of saying "How de do, how de do, little girls" to anybody under the rank of a Stockbroker.

KO-KO (*aside to girls*). Don't laugh at him—he's under treatment for it. (*Aside to* POOH-BAH.) Never mind them, they don't understand the delicacy of your position.

POOH-BAH. We know how delicate it is, don't we?

KO-KO. I should think we did! How a nobleman of your importance can do it at all is a thing I never can, never shall understand.

(KO-KO *retires up and goes off.*)

QUARTETTE AND CHORUS.

YUM-YUM, PEEP-BO, *and* PITTI-SING.

So please you, Sir, we much regret
If we have failed in etiquette
Towards a man of rank so high—
We shall know better by and by.
But youth, of course, must have its fling,
    So pardon us,
    So pardon us,
And don't in girlhood's happy spring,
    Be hard on us,
    Be hard on us,
If we're disposed to dance and sing,
    Tra la la, &c. (*dancing*).

CHORUS OF GIRLS. But youth, of course, &c.

POOH-BAH. I think you ought to recollect
    You cannot show too much respect
    Towards the highly-titled few;
    But nobody does, and why should you?
That youth at us should have its fling
    Is hard on us,
    Is hard on us;
To our prerogative we cling—
    So pardon us,
    So pardon us,
If we decline to dance and sing—
    Tra la la, &c. (*dancing*).

CHORUS OF GIRLS. But youth, of course, must have its fling, &c.

(*Exeunt all but* YUM-YUM.)

YUM-YUM. How pitiable is the condition of a young and innocent child brought from the gloom of a ladies' academy into the full-blown blaze of her own marriage ceremony; and with a man for whom I care nothing! True, he loves me, but everybody does that. Sometimes I sit and wonder, in my artless Japanese way, why it is that I am so much more attractive than anybody else in the whole world? Can this be vanity? No! Nature is lovely and rejoices in her loveliness. I am a child of Nature, and take after my mother.

SONG — YUM-YUM.

The sun, whose rays
Are all ablaze
   With ever-living glory,
Does not deny
His majesty—
   He scorns to tell a story!
He don't exclaim,
"I blush for shame,
   So kindly be indulgent."
But, fierce and bold,
In fiery gold,
   He glories all effulgent!

    I mean to rule the earth,
      As he the sky—
    We really know our worth,
      The sun and I!

Observe his flame,
That placid dame,
   The moon's Celestial Highness;
There's not a trace
Upon her face
   Of diffidence or shyness:
She borrows light
That, through the night,
   Mankind may all acclaim her!
And, truth to tell,
She lights up well,
   So I, for one, don't blame her!

    Ah, pray make no mistake,
      We are not shy;
    We're very wide awake,
      The moon and I!

Enter NANKI-POO.

NANKI-POO. Yum-Yum, at last we are alone! I have sought you night and day for three weeks, in the belief that your guardian was beheaded, and I find that you are about to be married to him this afternoon!

YUM-YUM. Alas, yes!

NANKI-POO. But you do not love him?

YUM-YUM. Alas, no!

NANKI-POO. Modified rapture! But why do you not refuse him?

YUM-YUM. What good would that do? He's my guardian, and he wouldn't let me marry you!

NANKI-POO. But I would wait until you were of age!

YUM-YUM. You forget that in Japan girls do not arrive at years of discretion until they are fifty.

NANKI-POO. True; from seventeen to forty-nine are considered years of indiscretion.

YUM-YUM. Besides—a wandering minstrel, who plays a wind instrument outside tea-houses, is hardly a fitting husband for the ward of a Lord High Executioner.

NANKI-POO. But— (*Aside.*) Shall I tell her? Yes! She will not betray me! (*Aloud.*) What if it should prove that, after all, I am no musician!

YUM-YUM. There! I was certain of it, directly I heard you play!

NANKI-POO. What if it should prove that I am no other than the son of His Majesty the Mikado?

YUM-YUM. The son of the Mikado! But why is your Highness disguised? And what has your Highness done? And will your Highness promise never to do it again?

NANKI-POO. Some years ago I had the misfortune to captivate Katisha, an elderly lady of my father's court. She misconstrued my customary affability into expressions of affection, and claimed me in marriage, under my father's law. My father, the Lucius Junius Brutus of his race, ordered me to marry her within a week, or perish ignominiously on the scaffold. That night I fled his court, and, assuming the disguise of a Second Trombone, I joined the band in which you found me when I had the happiness of seeing you! (*Approaching her.*)

YUM-YUM (*retreating*). If you please, I think your Highness had better not come too near. The laws against flirting are excessively severe.

NANKI-POO. But we are quite alone, and nobody can see us.

YUM-YUM. Still that don't make it right. To flirt is illegal, and we must obey the law.

NANKI-POO. Deuce take the law!

YUM-YUM. I wish it would, but it won't!

NANKI-POO. If it were not for that, how happy we might be!

YUM-YUM. Happy indeed!

NANKI-POO. If it were not for the law, we should now be sitting side by side, like that. (*Sits by her.*)

YUM-YUM. Instead of being obliged to sit half a mile off, like that. (*Crosses and sits at other side of stage.*)

NANKI-POO. We should be gazing into each other's eyes, like that (*approaching and gazing at her sentimentally*).

YUM-YUM. Breathing vows of unutterable love
—like that (*sighing and gazing lovingly at him*).

NANKI-POO. With our arms round each other's
waists like that (*embracing her*).

YUM-YUM. Yes, if it wasn't for the law.

NANKI-POO. If it wasn't for the law.

YUM-YUM. As it is, of course, we couldn't do
anything of the kind.

NANKI-POO. Not for worlds!

YUM-YUM. Being engaged to Ko-Ko, you know!

NANKI-POO. Being engaged to Ko-Ko!

DUET — YUM-YUM *and* NANKI-POO.

YUM-YUM. Were I not to Ko-Ko plighted,
    I would say in tender tone,
"Loved one, let us be united—
    Let us be each other's own!"
I would say "Oh, gentle stranger,
    Press me closely to thy heart,
Sharing every joy and danger,
    We will never part!"

BOTH.   We will never part!
           We will never part!

YUM-YUM. But, as I'm to marry Ko-Ko,
    To express my love *"con fuoco"*
Would distinctly be no *gioco*,
    And for yam I should get toco!

BOTH. Toco, toco, toco, toco!

YUM-YUM. So I will not say, "Oh, stranger,
    Press me closely to thy heart,
Sharing every joy and danger,
    We will never, never part!"
Clearly understand, I pray,
This is what I never say—
    This — oh, this — oh, this — oh,
    this —
    This is what I'll never say.

NANKI-POO. Were you not to Ko-Ko plighted
    I should thrill at words like those.
Joy of joys is love requited,
    Love despised is woe of woes.
I would merge all rank and station—
    Worldly sneers are nought to us—
And, to mark my admiration,
    I would kiss you fondly thus—
                  (*Kisses her.*)

BOTH. $\begin{Bmatrix} I \\ He \end{Bmatrix}$ would kiss $\begin{Bmatrix} you \\ me \end{Bmatrix}$ fondly thus—
                                (*kiss*).
      $\begin{Bmatrix} I \\ He \end{Bmatrix}$ would kiss $\begin{Bmatrix} you \\ me \end{Bmatrix}$ fondly thus—
                                (*kiss*).

NANKI-POO. But as you're engaged to Ko-Ko,
    To embrace you thus, *con fuoco*,

Would distinctly be no *gioco*,
    And for yam I should get toco—

BOTH. Toco, toco, toco, toco!

NANKI-POO. So in spite of all temptation,
    Such a theme I'll not discuss,
And on no consideration
    Will I kiss you fondly thus—
                  (*kissing her*).
Let me make it clear to you,
    This, oh this, oh this, oh this
                  (*kissing her*),
    This is what I'll never do!
      (*Exeunt in opposite directions.*)

Enter KO-KO.

KO-KO (*looking after* YUM-YUM). There she
goes! To think how entirely my future happiness
is wrapped up in that little parcel! Really, it hardly
seems worth while! Oh, matrimony!— (*Enter*
PISH-TUSH.) Now then, what is it? Can't you see
I'm soliloquizing? You have interrupted an apos-
trophe, sir!

PISH-TUSH. I am the bearer of a letter from His
Majesty the Mikado.

KO-KO (*taking it from him reverentially*). A letter from the Mikado! What in the world can he
have to say to me? (*Reads letter.*) Ah, here it is
at last! I thought it would come! The Mikado is
struck by the fact that no executions have taken
place in Titipu for a year, and decrees that unless
somebody is beheaded within one month, the post
of Lord High Executioner shall be abolished, and
the city reduced to the rank of a village!

PISH-TUSH. But that will involve us all in irretrievable ruin!

KO-KO. Yes—somebody will have to suffer.
Send the Recorder to me. (*Exit* PISH-TUSH.) I
expected something of this sort! I knew it couldn't
go on! Well, they've brought it on themselves, and
the only question is, Who shall it be? Fortunately,
there will be no difficulty in pitching upon somebody whose death will be a distinct gain to society.

SONG — KO-KO.

As it seems to be essential that a victim should
be found,
 I've got a little list—I've got a little list
Of social offenders who might well be underground,
 And who never would be missed—who never
would be missed!
There's the pestilential nuisances who write for
autographs—
All people who have flabby hands and irritating
laughs—
All children who are up in dates and floor you
with 'em flat—
All persons who in shaking hands, shake hands
with you like *that*—
And all third persons who on spoiling *tête-à-
têtes* insist—
 They'd none of 'em be missed—they'd none
of 'em be missed!

   As a victim must be found,
   If you'll only look around,
   There are criminals at large
   (And enough to fill a barge),
    Whose swift decapitation
    Would be hailed with acclamation,
    If accomplished by the nation
   At a reasonable charge.

There's the nigger serenader, and the others of
his race,
 And the piano organist—I've got him on the
list!
And the people who eat peppermint and puff it
in your face,
 They never would be missed—they never
would be missed!
Then the idiot who praises, with enthusiastic
tone,
All centuries but this, and every country but
his own;
And the lady from the provinces, who dresses
like a guy,
And "who doesn't think she waltzes, but would
rather like to try";
And that singular anomaly, the lady novelist—
 I don't think she'd be missed—I'm *sure* she'd
not be missed!

   If a victim must be found, &c.

And that *nisi prius* nuisance, who just now is
rather rife,
 The Judicial humorist—I've got him on the
list!
All funny fellows, comic men, and clowns of
private life—
 They'd none of 'em be missed—they'd none
of 'em be missed!

And apologetic statesmen of a compromising
kind,
Such as—what d'ye call him—Thing 'em bob,
and likewise Never Mind,
And 'St—'st—'st—and What's-his-name, and
also You-know-who—
The task of filling up the blanks I'd rather leave
to *you.*
But it really doesn't matter whom you put upon
the list,
 For they'd none of 'em be missed—they'd
none of 'em be missed!

   If a victim must be found, &c.

   Enter POOH-BAH *and* PISH-TUSH.

POOH-BAH. This is very uncomfortable news.

KO-KO. Yes. There's no help for it, I shall have
to execute somebody. The only question is, who
shall it be?

POOH-BAH. Well, it seems unkind to say so, but
as you're already under sentence of death for
flirting, everything seems to point to *you.*

KO-KO. To me? What are you talking about? I
can't execute myself, Recorder!

POOH-BAH. Why not?

KO-KO. Why not? Because, in the first place,
self-decapitation is an extremely difficult, not to
say dangerous, thing to attempt; and, in the second, it's suicide, and suicide is a capital offence.

POOH-BAH. That is so, no doubt.

PISH-TUSH. We might reserve that point.

POOH-BAH. True, it could be argued six months
hence, before the full Court.

KO-KO. Besides, I don't see how a man *can* cut
off his own head.

POOH-BAH. A man might try.

PISH-TUSH. Even if you only succeeded in cutting it half off, that would be something.

POOH-BAH. It would be taken as an earnest of
your desire to comply with the Imperial will.

KO-KO. No. Pardon me, but there I am adamant.
As official Headsman, my reputation is at stake,
and I can't consent to embark on a professional
operation unless I see my way to a successful result.

POOH-BAH. This professional conscientiousness
is highly creditable to *you,* but it places us in a
very awkward position.

KO-KO. My good sir, the awkwardness of your
position is grace itself compared with that of a
man engaged in the act of cutting off his own
head.

PISH-TUSH. I am afraid that, unless you can ob-
tain a substitute———

KO-KO. A substitute? Oh, certainly—nothing

easier. (*To* Pooh-Bah.) Pooh-Bah, I appoint you my substitute.

Pooh-Bah. I should like it above all things. Such an appointment would realize my fondest dreams. But no, at any sacrifice, I must set bounds to my insatiable ambition!

TRIO.

KO-KO.	POOH-BAH.	PISH-TUSH.
My brain it teems	I am so proud,	I heard one day,
With endless schemes	If I allowed	A gentleman say
Both good and new	My family pride	That criminals who
For Titipu;	To be my guide,	Are cut in two
But if I flit,	I'd volunteer	Can hardly feel
The benefit	To quit this sphere	The fatal steel,
That I'd diffuse	Instead of you,	And so are slain
The town would lose!	In a minute or two,	Without much pain.
Now every man	But family pride	If this is true
To aid his clan	Must be denied,	It's jolly for you;
Should plot and plan	And set aside,	Your courage screw
As well as he can,	And mortified,	To bid us adieu,
And so,	And so,	And go
Although	Although	And show
I'm ready to go,	I wish to go,	Both friend and foe
Yet recollect	And greatly pine	How much you dare.
'Twere dis-respect	To brightly shine,	I'm quite aware
Did I neglect	And take the line	It's your affair,
To thus effect	Of a hero fine,	Yet I declare
This aim direct,	With grief con-dign	I'd take your share,
So I object—	I must decline–	But I don't much care—
So I object—	I must decline–	I don't much care—
So I object—	I must decline–	I don't much care—

All. To sit in solemn silence in a dull, dark dock,
  In a pestilential prison, with a life-long lock,
  Awaiting the sensation of a short, sharp shock,
  From a cheap and chippy chopper on a big
    black block!   (*Exeunt all but* Ko-Ko.)

Ko-Ko. This is simply appalling! I, who allowed myself to be respited at the last moment, simply in order to benefit my native town, am now required to die within a month, and that by a man whom I have loaded with honours! Is this public gratitude? Is this—(*Enter* Nanki-Poo *with a rope in his hands*.) Go away, sir! how dare you? Am I never to be permitted to soliloquize?

Nanki-Poo. Oh, go on—don't mind me.

Ko-Ko. What are you going to do with that rope?

Nanki-Poo. I am about to terminate an unendurable existence.

Ko-Ko. Terminate your existence? Oh, nonsense! What for?

Nanki-Poo. Because you are going to marry the girl I adore.

Ko-Ko. And do you suppose that I am likely to stand quietly by while you deliberately take your life?

Nanki-Poo. Please yourself: you can withdraw if you prefer it.

Ko-Ko. Withdraw if I prefer it! Are you aware, sir, that I am Lord High Executioner of this city, and that in that capacity, it is my duty to prevent unnecessary bloodshed?

Nanki-Poo. I know nothing about your capacity. I only know that I die to-day.

Ko-Ko. Nonsense, sir. I won't permit it. I am a humane man, and if you attempt anything of the kind I shall order your instant arrest. Come, sir, desist at once, or I summon my guard.

Nanki-Poo. That's absurd. If you attempt to raise an alarm, I instantly perform the Happy Despatch with this dagger.

Ko-Ko. No, no, don't do that. This is horrible! (*Suddenly.*) Why you cold-blooded scoundrel, are you aware that, in taking your life, you are committing a crime from which civilization recoils in horror?—a crime which is, in its essence, unmanly, cowardly, and impious? Are you aware that in depriving yourself of an existence which—which—which is—Oh! (*Struck by an idea.*)

Nanki-Poo. What's the matter?

Ko-Ko. Is it *absolutely certain* that you are resolved to die?

Nanki-Poo. Absolutely!

Ko-Ko. Will *nothing* shake your resolution?

Nanki-Poo. Nothing.

Ko-Ko. Threats, entreaties, prayers—all useless?

Nanki-Poo. All! My mind is made up.

Ko-Ko. Then, if you really mean what you say, and if you are absolutely resolved to die, and if nothing whatever will shake your determination—don't spoil yourself by committing suicide, but be beheaded handsomely at the hands of the Public Executioner!

Nanki-Poo. I don't see how that would benefit me.

Ko-Ko. You don't? Observe: you'll have a month to live, and you'll live like a fighting cock at my expense. When the day comes there'll be a grand public ceremonial—you'll be the central figure—no one will attempt to deprive you of that distinction. There'll be a procession—bands—dead march—bells tolling—all the girls in tears—Yum-Yum distracted—then, when it's all over, general rejoicings, and a display of fireworks in the evening. *You* won't see them, but they'll be there all the same.

NANKI-POO. Do you think Yum-Yum would really be distracted at my death?

KO-KO. I am convinced of it. Bless you, she's the most tender-hearted little creature alive.

NANKI-POO. I should be sorry to cause her pain. Perhaps, after all, if I were to withdraw from Japan and travel in Europe for a couple of years, I might contrive to forget her.

KO-KO. Oh, I don't think you could forget Yum-Yum so easily, and, after all, what is more miserable than a love-blighted life?

NANKI-POO. True.

KO-KO. Life without Yum-Yum—why it seems absurd!

NANKI-POO. And yet there are a good many people in the world who have to endure it.

KO-KO. Poor devils, yes! You are quite right not to be of their number.

NANKI-POO (*suddenly*). I *won't* be of their number!

KO-KO. Noble fellow!

NANKI-POO. I'll tell you how we'll manage it. Let me marry Yum-Yum to-morrow, and in a month you may behead me.

KO-KO. No, no. I draw the line at Yum-Yum.

NANKI-POO. Very good. If you can draw the line, so can I (*preparing rope*).

KO-KO. Stop, stop—listen one moment—be reasonable. How can I consent to your marrying Yum-Yum if I'm going to marry her myself?

NANKI-POO. My good friend, she'll be a widow in a month, and you can marry her then.

KO-KO. That's true, of course. I quite see that, but, dear me, my position during the next month will be most unpleasant—most unpleasant!

NANKI-POO. Not half so unpleasant as my position at the end of it.

KO-KO. But—dear me—well—I agree—after all, it's only putting off my wedding for a month. But you won't prejudice her against me, will you? You see, I've educated her to be my wife; she's been taught to regard me as a wise and good man. Now I shouldn't like her views on that point disturbed.

NANKI-POO. Trust me, she shall never learn the truth from me.

FINALE.

Enter CHORUS, POOH-BAH, *and* PISH-TUSH.

CHORUS.

With aspect stern
    And gloomy stride,
We come to learn
    How you decide.

Don't hesitate
    Your choice to name;
A dreadful fate
    You'll suffer all the same.

POOH-BAH. To ask you what you mean to do we punctually appear.

KO-KO. Congratulate me, gentlemen, I've found a Volunteer!

ALL. The Japanese equivalent for Hear, Hear, Hear!

KO-KO (*presenting him*).   'Tis Nanki-Poo!

ALL.   Hail, Nanki-Poo!

KO-KO.   I think he'll do?

ALL.   Yes, yes, he'll do!

KO-KO. He yields his life if I'll Yum-Yum surrender;
    Now I adore that girl with passion tender,
    And could not yield her with a ready will,
        Or her allot,
        If I did not
    Adore myself with passion tenderer still!

ALL.   Ah, yes!
    He loves himself with passion tenderer still!

KO-KO (*to* NANKI-POO). Take her—she's yours!

Enter YUM-YUM, PEEP-BO, *and* PITTI-SING.

NANKI-POO *and* YUM-YUM.   Oh, rapture!

ENSEMBLE.

YUM-YUM *and* NANKI-POO.   The threatened cloud has passed away,
    And brightly shines the dawning day;
    What though the night may come too soon,
    There's yet a month of afternoon!
        Then let the throng
        Our joy advance,
        With laughing song,
        And merry dance,
    With joyous shout and ringing cheer,
    Inaugurate our brief career!

CHORUS. Then let the throng, &c.

PITTI-SING. A day, a week, a month, a year—
　　　　Or be it far, or be it near,
　　　　Life's eventime comes much too soon,
　　　　You'll live at least a honeymoon!

ALL.　　　Then let the throng, &c.

SOLO — POOH-BAH.

As in three weeks you've got to die,
　　If Ko-Ko tells us true,
'Twere empty compliment to cry
　　Long life to Nanki-Poo!
But as you've got three weeks to live
　　As fellow citizen,
This toast with three times three we'll give—
　　"Long life to you—till then!"

CHORUS. May all good fortune prosper you,
　　　　May you have health and riches too,
　　　　May you succeed in all you do!
　　　　Long life to you—till then!

DANCE.

Enter KATISHA *melodramatically.*

KATISHA. Your revels cease—assist me, all of
　　　　you!

CHORUS. Why who is this whose evil eyes
　　　　Rain blight on our festivities?

KATISHA. I claim my perjured lover, Nanki-Poo!
　　Oh, fool! to shun delights that never cloy!
　　Come back, oh, shallow fool! come back to joy!

CHORUS. Go, leave thy deadly work undone;
　　　　Away, away! ill-favoured one!

NANKI-POO (*aside to* YUM-YUM). Ah!
　　　　'Tis Katisha!
　　　　The maid of whom I told you.
　　　　　　　　　　(*About to go.*)

KATISHA (*detaining him*). No!
　　　　You shall not go,
　　　　These arms shall thus enfold you!

SONG — KATISHA.

(*Addressing* NANKI-POO.) Oh fool that fleest
　　　　My hallowed joys!
　　Oh blind, that seest
　　　　No equipoise!
　　Oh rash, that judgest
　　　　From half, the whole!
　　Oh base, that grudgest
　　　　Love's lightest dole!
　　　　Thy heart unbind,
　　　　Oh fool, oh blind!
　　　　Give me my place,
　　　　Oh rash, oh base!

CHORUS. If she's thy bride, restore her place,

Oh fool, oh blind, oh rash, oh base!

KATISHA (*addressing* YUM-YUM). Pink cheek,
　　　　that rulest
　　Where wisdom serves!
　　Bright eye, that foolest
　　　　Steel-tempered nerves;
　　Rose-lip, that scornest
　　　　Lore-laden years—
　　Sweet tongue, that warnest
　　　　Who rightly hears—
　　　　Thy doom is nigh,
　　　　Pink cheek, bright eye!
　　　　Thy knell is rung,
　　　　Rose-lip, sweet tongue!

CHORUS. If true her tale, thy knell is rung,
　　　　Pink cheek, bright eye, rose-lip, sweet
　　　　tongue!

PITTI-SING. Away, nor prosecute your quest—
　　　　From our intention well expressed,
　　　　You cannot turn us!
　　　The state of your connubial views
　　　Towards the person you accuse
　　　　Does not concern us!
　　For he's going to marry Yum-Yum—

ALL.　　　　　　　　　　Yum-Yum!

PITTI-SING. Your anger pray bury,
　　　　For all will be merry,
　　　I think you had better succumb—

ALL.　　　　　　　　　Cumb—cumb!

PITTI-SING. And join our expressions of glee,
　　　On this subject I pray you be dumb—

ALL.　　　　　　　　　Dumb—dumb.

PITTI-SING. You'll find there are many
　　　　Who'll wed for a penny—
　　The word for your guidance is, "Mum"—

ALL.　　　　　　　　　Mum—mum!

PITTI-SING. There's lots of good fish in the sea!

ALL. There's lots of good fish in the sea!
　　　　And you'll find there are many, &c.

SOLO — KATISHA.

The hour of gladness
　　Is dead and gone;
In silent sadness
　　I live alone!
The hope I cherished
　　All lifeless lies,
And all has perished
　　Save love, which never dies!

Oh, faithless one, this insult you shall rue!
In vain for mercy on your knees you'll sue.

I'll tear the mask from you disguising!

NANKI-POO (*aside*).   Now comes the blow!

KATISHA. Prepare yourself for news surprising!

NANKI-POO (*aside*).   How foil my foe?

KATISHA.   No minstrel he, despite bravado!

YUM-YUM (*aside, struck by an idea*).
                    Ha! ha! I know!

KATISHA.   He is the son of your—

(NANKI-POO *and* YUM-YUM, *interrupting,* **sing**
Japanese words, to drown her voice.)
          O ni! bikkuri shakkuri to!
          O sa! bikkuri shakkuri to!

KATISHA.   In vain you interrupt with this tor-
          nado:
          He is the only son of your——

ALL.   O ni! bikkuri shakkuri to!

KATISHA.   I'll spoil——

ALL.   O ni! bikkuri shakkuri to!

KATISHA.   Your gay gambado!
          He is the son——

ALL.   O ni! bikkuri shakkuri to!

KATISHA.   Of your——

ALL.   O ni! bikkuri shakkuri to!

ENSEMBLE.

KATISHA.	THE OTHERS.

Ye torrents roar!
    Ye tempests howl!
Your wrath outpour
    With angry growl!
De ye your worst, my
    vengeance
    call
Shall rise triumphant
    over all!
    Prepare for woe,
    Ye haughty
    lords,
    At once I go
    Mikado-wards,
And when he learns his
    son is found,
My wrongs with venge-
    ance will be
    crowned!
	We'll hear no more
	    Ill-omened owl,
	To joy we soar,
	    Despite your
	    scowl.
	The echoes of our
	    festival
	Shall rise triumphant
	    over all!
	    Away you go,
	    Collect your
	    hordes;
	    Proclaim your woe
	    In dismal
	    chords!
	We do not heed their
	    dismal sound,
	For joy reigns every-
	    where
	    around!

KATISHA *rushes furiously up stage, clearing the
crowd away right and left, finishing on steps at
the back of stage.*

END OF ACT I.

ACT II.

SCENE. — KO-KO's *garden.* YUM-YUM *discovered seated at her bridal toilet, surrounded by maidens, who are dressing her hair and painting her face and lips, as she judges of the effect in a mirror.*

CHORUS.

Braid the raven hair—
   Weave the supple tress—
Deck the maiden fair
   In her loveliness—
Paint the pretty face—
   Dye the coral lip—
Emphasize the grace
   Of her ladyship!
Art and nature, thus allied,
Go to make a pretty bride!

SOLO — PITTI-SING.

Sit with downcast eye—
   Let it brim with dew—
Try if you can cry—
   We will do so, too.
When you're summoned, start
   Like a frightened roe—
Flutter, little heart,
   Colour, come and go!
Modesty at marriage tide
Well becomes a pretty bride!

CHORUS.   Braid the raven hair, &c.

YUM-YUM. Yes, everything seems to smile upon me. I am to be married to-day to the man I love best, and I believe I am the very happiest girl in Japan!

PEEP-BO. The happiest girl indeed, for she is indeed to be envied who has attained happiness in all but perfection.

YUM-YUM. In "all but" perfection?

PEEP-BO. Well, dear, it can't be denied that the fact that your husband is to be beheaded in a month is, in its way, a drawback.

PITTI-SING. I don't know about that. It all depends!

PEEP-BO. At all events, *he* will find it a drawback.

PITTI-SING. Not necessarily. Bless you, it all depends!

YUM-YUM (*in tears*). I think it very indelicate of you to refer to such a subject on such a day. If my married happiness *is* to be—to be—

PEEP-BO. Cut short.

YUM-YUM. Well, cut short—in a month, can't you let me forget it? (*Weeping.*)

Enter NANKI-POO *followed by* PISH-TUSH.

NANKI-POO. Yum-Yum in tears—and on her wedding morn!

YUM-YUM (*sobbing*). They've been reminding me that in a month you're to be beheaded! (*Bursts into tears.*)

PITTI-SING. Yes, we've been reminding her that you're to be beheaded! (*Bursts into tears.*)

PEEP-BO. It's quite true, you know, you *are* to be beheaded! (*Bursts into tears.*)

NANKI-POO (*aside*). Humph! How some bridegrooms would be depressed by this sort of thing! (*Aloud.*) A month? Well, what's a month? Bah! These divisions of time are purely arbitrary. Who says twenty-four hours make a day?

PITTI-SING. There's a popular impression to that effect.

NANKI-POO. Then we'll efface it. We'll call each second a minute—each minute an hour—each hour a day—and each day a year. At that rate we've about thirty years of married happiness before us!

PEEP-BO. And at that rate, this interview has already lasted four hours and three quarters! (*Exit.*)

YUM-YUM (*still sobbing*). Yes. How time flies when one is thoroughly enjoying oneself!

NANKI-POO. That's the way to look at it! Don't let's be downhearted! There's a silver lining to every cloud.

YUM-YUM. Certainly. Let's—let's be perfectly happy! (*Almost in tears.*)

PISH-TUSH. By all means. Let's—let's thoroughly enjoy ourselves.

PITTI-SING. It's—it's absurd to cry! (*Trying to force a laugh.*)

YUM-YUM. Quite ridiculous! (*Trying to laugh.*)
(*All break into a forced and melancholy laugh.*)

QUARTETTE.

YUM-YUM, PITTI-SING, NANKI-POO, *and* PISH-TUSH.

Brightly dawns our wedding day;
   Joyous hour, we give thee greeting!
   Whither, whither art thou fleeting?
Fickle moment, prithee stay!

What though mortal joys be hollow?
Pleasures come, if sorrows follow:
Though the tocsin sound, ere long,
 Ding dong! Ding dong!
Yet until the shadows fall
Over one and over all,
Sing a merry madrigal—
   A madrigal!

Fal-la—fal-la! &c. (*ending in tears*).

Let us dry the ready tear,
 Though the hours are surely creeping;
 Little need for woeful weeping,
Till the sad sundown is near.
 All must sip the cup of sorrow—
 I to-day and thou to-morrow:
This the close of every song—
 Ding dong! Ding dong!
What, though solemn shadows fall,
Sooner, later, over all?
Sing a merry madrigal—
   A madrigal!
Fal-la—fal-la! &c. (*ending in tears*).
   (*Exeunt* PITTI-SING *and* PISH-TUSH.)

NANKI-POO *embraces* YUM-YUM. *Enter* KO-KO.
NANKI-POO *releases* YUM-YUM.

KO-KO. Go on—don't mind me.

NANKI-POO. I'm afraid we're distressing you.

KO-KO. Never mind, I must get used to it. Only please do it by degrees. Begin by putting your arm round her waist. (NANKI-POO *does so.*) There; let me get used to that first.

YUM-YUM. Oh, wouldn't you like to retire? It must pain you to see us so affectionate together!

KO-KO. No, I must learn to bear it! Now oblige me by allowing her head to rest on your shoulder. (*He does so*—KO-KO *much affected.*) I am much obliged to you. Now—kiss her! (*He does so*— KO-KO *writhes with anguish.*) Thank you—it's simple torture!

YUM-YUM. Come, come, bear up. After all, it's only for a month.

KO-KO. No. It's no use deluding oneself with false hopes.

NANKI-POO. }
YUM-YUM. } What do you mean?

KO-KO (*to* YUM-YUM). My child—my poor child. (*Aside.*) How shall I break it to her? (*Aloud.*) My little bride that was to have been—

YUM-YUM (*delighted*). *Was* to have been!

KO-KO. Yes, you never can be mine!.

YUM-YUM (*in ecstasy*). What!!!

KO-KO. I've just ascertained that, by the Mika-

do's law, when a married man is beheaded his wife is buried alive.

NANKI-POO. }
YUM-YUM. } Buried alive!

KO-KO. Buried alive. It's a most unpleasant death.

NANKI-POO. But whom did you get that from?

KO-KO. Oh, from Pooh-Bah. He's my solicitor.

YUM-YUM. But he may be mistaken!

KO-KO. So I thought, so I consulted the Attorney-General, the Lord Chief Justice, the Master of the Rolls, the Judge Ordinary, and the Lord Chancellor. They're all of the same opinion. Never knew such unanimity on a point of law in my life!

NANKI-POO. But stop a bit! This law has never been put in force?

KO-KO. Not yet. You see, flirting is the only crime punishable with decapitation, and married men never flirt.

NANKI-POO. Of course they don't. I quite forgot that! Well, I suppose I may take it that my dream of happiness is at an end!

YUM-YUM. Darling—I don't want to appear selfish, and I love you with all my heart—I don't suppose I shall ever love anybody else half as much—but when I agreed to marry you—my own—I had no idea—pet—that I should have to be buried alive in a month!

NANKI-POO. Nor I! It's the very first I've heard of it!

YUM-YUM. It—it makes a difference, don't it?

NANKI-POO. It *does* make a difference, of course!

YUM-YUM. You see—burial alive—it's such a stuffy death! You see my difficulty, don't you?

NANKI-POO. Yes, and I see my own. If I insist on your carrying out your promise, I doom you to a hideous death; if I release you, you marry Ko-Ko at once!

TRIO.

YUM-YUM, NANKI-POO, *and* KO-KO.

YUM-YUM. Here's a how-de-do!
 If I marry you,
 When your time has come to perish,
 Then the maiden whom you cherish
  Must be slaughtered too!
  Here's a how-de-do!

NANKI-POO. Here's a pretty mess!
 In a month or less,
 I must die without a wedding!
 Let the bitter tears I'm shedding
  Witness my distress,
  Here's a pretty mess!

KO-KO. Here's a state of things!
To her life she clings!
Matrimonial devotion
Doesn't seem to suit her notion—
Burial it brings!
Here's a state of things!

ENSEMBLE.

YUM-YUM and NANKI-POO	KO-KO.
With a passion that's intense I worship and adore, But the laws of common sense We oughtn't to ignore. If what he says is true, It is death to marry you! Here's a pretty state of things! Here's a pretty how-de-do!	With a passion that's intense You worship and adore, But the laws of common sense You oughtn't to ignore. If what I say is true, It is death to marry you! Here's a pretty state of things! Here's a pretty how-de-do! (*Exit* YUM-YUM.)

KO-KO (*going up to* NANKI-POO). My poor boy, I'm really very sorry for you.

NANKI-POO. Thanks, old fellow. I'm sure you are.

KO-KO. You see I'm quite helpless.

NANKI-POO. I quite see that.

KO-KO. I can't conceive anything more distressing than to have one's marriage broken off at the last moment. But you shan't be disappointed of a wedding—you shall come to mine.

NANKI-POO. It's awfully kind of you, but that's impossible.

KO-KO. Why so?

NANKI-POO. To-day I die.

KO-KO. What do you mean?

NANKI-POO. I can't live without Yum-Yum. This afternoon I perform the Happy Despatch.

KO-KO. No, no—pardon me—I can't allow that.

NANKI-POO. Why not?

KO-KO. Why, hang it all, you're under contract to die by the hand of the Public Executioner in a month's time! If you kill yourself, what's to become of me? Why, I shall have to be executed in your place!

NANKI-POO. It would certainly seem so!

Enter POOH-BAH.

KO-KO. Now then, Lord Mayor, what is it?

POOH-BAH. The Mikado and his suite are approaching the city, and will be here in ten minutes.

KO-KO. The Mikado! He's coming to see whether his orders have been carried out! (*To* NANKI-POO.) Now look here, you know—this is getting serious—a bargain's a bargain, and you really mustn't frustrate the ends of justice by committing suicide. As a man of honour and a gentleman, you are bound to die ignominiously by the hands of the Public Executioner.

NANKI-POO. Very well, then—behead me.

KO-KO. What, now?

NANKI-POO. Certainly; at once.

KO-KO. My good sir, I don't go about prepared to execute gentlemen at a moment's notice. Why, I never even killed a blue-bottle!

POOH-BAH. Still, as Lord High Executioner,——

KO-KO. My good sir, as Lord High Executioner I've got to behead him in a month. I'm not ready yet. I don't know how it's done. I'm going to take lessons. I mean to begin with a guinea pig, and work my way through the animal kingdom till I come to a second trombone. Why, you don't suppose that, as a humane man, I'd have accepted the post of Lord High Executioner if I hadn't thought the duties were purely nominal? I *can't* kill you— I can't kill anything! (*Weeps.*)

NANKI-POO. Come, my poor fellow, your feelings do you credit, but you must nerve yourself to this —you must, indeed. We all have unpleasant duties to discharge at times; and when these duties present themselves we must nerve ourselves to an effort. Come, now—after all, what is it? If I don't mind, why should you? Remember, sooner or later it must be done.

KO-KO (*springing up suddenly*). *Must it?* I'm not so sure about that!

NANKI-POO. What do you mean?

KO-KO. Why should I kill you when making an affidavit that you've been executed will do just as well? Here are plenty of witnesses—the Lord Chief Justice and Lord High Admiral, Commander-in-Chief, Secretary of State for the Home Department, First Lord of the Treasury, and Chief Commissioner of Police. They'll all swear to it— won't you? (*To* POOH-BAH.)

POOH-BAH. Am I to understand that all of us high Officers of State are required to perjure ourselves to ensure your safety?

KO-KO. Why not? You'll be grossly insulted, as usual.

POOH-BAH. Will the insult be cash down, or at a date?

KO-KO. It will be a ready-money transaction.

POOH-BAH (*aside*). Well, it will be a useful discipline. (*Aloud.*) Very good. Choose your fiction, and I'll endorse it! (*Aside.*) Ha! ha! Family Pride, how do you like *that,* my buck?

NANKI-POO. But I tell you that life without Yum-Yum—

KO-KO. Oh, Yum-Yum, Yum-Yum! Bother Yum-Yum! Here, Commissionaire (*to* POOH-BAH), go and fetch Yum-Yum. (*Exit* POOH-BAH.) Take Yum-Yum and marry Yum-Yum, only go away and never come back again. (*Enter* POOH-BAH *with* YUM-YUM *and* PITTI-SING.) Here she is. Yum-Yum, are you particularly busy?

YUM-YUM. Not particularly.

KO-KO. You've five minutes to spare?

YUM-YUM. Yes.

KO-KO. Then go along with his Grace the Archbishop of Titipu; he'll marry you at once.

YUM-YUM. But if I'm to be buried alive?

KO-KO. Now don't ask any questions, but do as I tell you, and Nanki-Poo will explain all.

NANKI-POO. But one moment—

KO-KO. Not for worlds. Here comes the Mikado, no doubt to ascertain whether I've obeyed his decree, and if he finds you alive, I shall have the greatest difficulty in persuading him that I've beheaded you. (*Exeunt* NANKI-POO *and* YUM-YUM, *followed by* POOH-BAH.) Close thing that, for here he comes!

March.—Enter procession, heralding
MIKADO, *with* KATISHA.

CHORUS.

"March of the Mikado's Troops."

> Miya sama, miya sama,
> On ma no mayé ni
> Pira-Pira suru no wa
> Nan gia na
> Toko tonyaré tonyaré na!

DUET — MIKADO *and* KATISHA.

MIKADO.   From every kind of man
   Obedience I expect;
   I'm the Emperor of Japan—

KATISHA.   And I'm his daughter-in-law elect!
   He'll marry his son
   (He has only got one)
   To his daughter-in-law elect.

MIKADO.   My morals have been declared
   Particularly correct;

KATISHA.   But they're nothing at all, compared
   With those of his daughter-in-law elect!
    Bow—Bow—
   To his daughter-in-law elect!

ALL.   Bow—Bow—
   To his daughter-in-law elect.

MIKADO.   In a fatherly kind of way
   I govern each tribe and sect,
   All cheerfully own my sway—

KATISHA.   Except his daughter-in-law elect!
   As tough as a bone,
   With a will of her own,
   Is his daughter-in-law elect!

MIKADO.   My nature is love and light—
   My freedom from all defect—

KATISHA.   Is insignificant quite,
   Compared with his daughter-in-law
    elect!
   Bow! Bow!
   To his daughter-in-law elect!

ALL.   Bow! Bow!
   To his daughter-in-law elect.

SONG — MIKADO.

A more humane Mikado never
 Did in Japan exist,
  To nobody second,

I'm certainly reckoned
A true philanthropist.
It is my very humane endeavour
To make, to some extent,
Each evil liver
A running river
Of harmless merriment.

    My object all sublime
    I shall achieve in time—
To let the punishment fit the crime,
    The punishment fit the crime;
    And make each prisoner pent
    Unwillingly represent
A source of innocent merriment,
    Of innocent merriment!

All prosy dull society sinners,
    Who chatter and bleat and bore,
    Are sent to hear sermons
    From mystical Germans
Who preach from ten to four.
The amateur tenor, whose vocal vil-
        lainies
    All desire to shirk,
    Shall, during off-hours,
    Exhibit his powers
To Madame Tussaud's waxwork.

    My object all sublime, &c.

The lady who dyes a chemical yellow,
    Or stains her grey hair puce,
    Or pinches her figger,
    Is blacked like a nigger
With permanent walnut juice.
The idiot who, in railway carriages,
    Scribbles on window panes,
    We only suffer
    To ride on a buffer
In Parliamentary trains.

The advertising quack who wearies
    With tales of countless cures,
    His teeth, I've enacted,
    Shall all be extracted
By terrified amateurs.
The music-hall singer attends a series
    Of masses and fugues and "ops"
    By Bach, interwoven
    With Spohr and Beethoven,
At classical Monday Pops.

The billiard sharp whom any one
        catches,
    His doom's extremely hard—
    He's made to dwell
    In a dungeon cell
On a spot that's always barred.
And there he plays extravagant matches
    In fitless finger-stalls

    On a cloth untrue
    With a twisted cue,
And elliptical billiard balls!

    My object all sublime, &c.

Enter POOH-BAH, *who hands a paper to* KO-KO.

KO-KO. I am honoured in being permitted to welcome your Majesty. I guess the object of your Majesty's visit—your wishes have been attended to. The execution has taken place.

MIKADO. Oh, you've had an execution, have you?

KO-KO. Yes. The Coroner has just handed me his certificate.

POOH-BAH. I am the Coroner. (KO-KO *hands certificate to* MIKADO.)

MIKADO (*reads*). "At Titipu, in the presence of the Lord Chancellor, Lord Chief Justice, Attorney-General, Secretary of State for the Home Department, Lord Mayor and Groom of the Second Floor Front."

POOH-BAH. They were all present, your Majesty. I counted them myself.

MIKADO. Very good house. I wish I'd been in time for the performance.

KO-KO. A tough fellow he was, too—a man of gigantic strength. His struggles were terrific. It was really a remarkable scene.

TRIO.

KO-KO, PITTI-SING, *and* POOH-BAH.

KO-KO. The criminal cried, as he dropped him
                down,
        In a state of wild alarm—
    With a frightful, frantic, fearful frown
        I bared my big right arm.
    I seized him by his little pig-tail,
        And on his knees fell he,
            As he squirmed and struggled
            And gurgled and guggled,
        I drew my snickersnee!
            Oh never shall I
            Forget the cry,
        Or the shriek that shriekèd he,
            As I gnashed my teeth,
            When from its sheath
        I drew my snickersnee!

CHORUS.   We know him well,
                He cannot tell
            Untrue or groundless tales—
                He always tries
                To utter lies,
            And every time he fails.

PITTI-SING. He shivered and shook as he gave
                the sign
        For the stroke he didn't deserve;
    When all of a sudden his eye met mine,
        And it seemed to brace his nerve,
    For he nodded his head and kissed his
                hand,
        And he whistled an air, did he,
            As the sabre true
            Cut cleanly through
        His cervical vertebræ!
            When a man's afraid,
            A beautiful maid
        Is a cheering sight to see;
            And it's oh, I'm glad,
            That moment sad
        Was soothed by sight of me!

CHORUS.   Her terrible tale
                You can't assail,
            With truth it quite agrees;
                Her taste exact
                For faultless fact
            Amounts to a disease.

POOH-BAH. Now though you'd have said that
                head was dead
        (For its owner dead was he),
    It stood on its neck with a smile well-bred,
        And bowed three times to me!
    It was none of your impudent off-hand
                nods,
        But as humble as could be.
            For it clearly knew
            The deference due
        To a man of pedigree!
            And it's oh, I vow,
            This deathly bow
        Was a touching sight to see;
            Though trunkless, yet
            It couldn't forget
        The deference due to me!

CHORUS.   This haughty youth
                He speaks the truth
            Whenever he finds it pays,
                And in this case
                It all took place
            Exactly as he says!   (*Exeunt* CHORUS.)

MIKADO. All this is very interesting, and I should like to have seen it. But we came about a totally different matter. A year ago my son, the heir to the throne of Japan, bolted from our imperial court.

KO-KO. Indeed? Had he any reason to be dissatisfied with his position?

KATISHA. None whatever. On the contrary, I was going to marry him—yet he fled!

POOH-BAH. I am surprised that he should have fled from one so lovely!

KATISHA. That's not true. You hold that I am not beautiful because my face is plain. But you know nothing; you are still unenlightened. Learn, then, that it is not in the face alone that beauty is to be sought. But I have a left shoulder-blade that is a miracle of loveliness. People come miles to see it. My right elbow has a fascination that few can resist. It is on view Tuesdays and Fridays, on presentation of visiting card. As for my circulation, it is the largest in the world. Observe this ear.

KO-KO. Large.

KATISHA. Large? Enormous! But think of its delicate internal mechanism. It is fraught with beauty! As for this tooth, it almost stands alone. Many have tried to draw it, but in vain.

KO-KO. And yet he fled!

MIKADO. And is now masquerading in this town, disguised as a second trombone.

KO-KO. ⎫
POOH-BAH. ⎬ A second trombone!
PITTI-SING. ⎭

MIKADO. Yes; would it be troubling you too much if I asked you to produce him? He goes by the name of Nanki-Poo.

KO-KO. Oh, no; not at all—only—

MIKADO. Yes?

KO-KO. It's rather awkward, but in point of fact, he's gone abroad!

MIKADO.   Gone abroad? His address!

KO-KO.   Knightsbridge!

KATISHA (*who is reading certificate of death*). Ha!

MIKADO.   What's the matter?

KATISHA.   See here—his name—Nanki-Poo—beheaded this morning! Oh where shall I find another! Where shall I find another!

(KO-KO, POOH-BAH, *and* PITTI-SING *fall on their knees.*)

MIKADO (*looking at paper*). Dear, dear, dear; this is very tiresome. (*To* KO-KO.) My poor fellow, in your anxiety to carry out my wishes, you have beheaded the heir to the throne of Japan!

(*Together.*) {
KO-KO. But I assure you we had no idea—
POOH-BAH. But, indeed, we didn't know—
PITTI-SING. We really hadn't the least notion—
}

MIKADO.   Of course you hadn't. How could you? Come, come, my good fellow, don't distress your-self—it was no fault of yours. If a man of exalted rank chooses to disguise himself as a second trombone, he must take the consequences. It really distresses me to see you take on so. I've no doubt he thoroughly deserved all he got. (*They rise.*)

KO-KO.   We are infinitely obliged to your Majesty—

MIKADO.   Obliged? not a bit. Don't mention it. How *could* you tell?

POOH-BAH.   No, of course we couldn't know that he was the Heir Apparent.

PITTI-SING.   It wasn't written on his forehead, you know.

KO-KO.   It might have been on his pocket-handkerchief, but Japanese don't use pocket-handkerchiefs! Ha! ha! ha!

MIKADO. Ha! ha! ha! (*To* KATISHA.) I forget the punishment for compassing the death of the Heir Apparent.

KO-KO.
POOH-BAH. } Punishment! (*They drop down on their knees again.*)
PITTI-SING.

MIKADO.   Yes. Something lingering, with boiling oil in it, I fancy. Something of that sort. I think boiling oil occurs in it, but I'm not sure. I know it's something humorous, but lingering, with either boiling oil or melted lead. Come, come, don't fret —I'm not a bit angry.

KO-KO (*in abject terror*). If your Majesty will accept our assurance, we had no idea—

MIKADO. Of course you hadn't. That's the pathetic part of it. Unfortunately the fool of an act says "compassing the death of the Heir Apparent." There's not a word about a mistake, or not knowing, or having no notion. There should be, of course, but there isn't. That's the slovenly way in which these Acts are drawn. However, cheer up, it'll be all right. I'll have it altered next session.

KO-KO. What's the good of that?

MIKADO. Now let's see—will after luncheon suit you? Can you wait till then?

KO-KO, PITTI-SING, *and* POOH-BAH. Oh yes—we can wait till then!

MIKADO. Then we'll make it after luncheon. I'm really very sorry for you all, but it's an unjust world, and virtue is triumphant only in theatrical performances.

GLEE.

MIKADO, KATISHA, KO-KO, POOH-BAH, *and* PITTI-SING.

MIKADO *and* KATISHA. See how the Fates their gifts allot,
> For A is happy—B is not.
> Yet B is worthy, I dare say,
> Of more prosperity than A!

KO-KO, POOH-BAH, *and* PITTI-SING. *Is* B more worthy?

MIKADO *and* KATISHA.   I should say
> He's worth a great deal more than A.

ENSEMBLE.   Yet A is happy!
> Oh so happy!
> Laughing, Ha! ha!
> Chaffing, Ha! ha!
> Nectar quaffing, Ha! ha! ha! ha!
> Ever joyous, ever gay,
> Happy, undeserving A!

KO-KO, POOH-BAH, *and* PITTI-SING. If I were Fortune—which I'm not—
> B should enjoy A's happy lot,
> And A should die in miserie,
> That is, assuming I am B.

MIKADO *and* KATISHA. But *should* A perish?

KO-KO, POOH-BAH, *and* PITTI-SING. That should he,
> (Of course, assuming I am B).

> B should be happy!
> Oh so happy!
> Laughing, Ha! ha!
> Chaffing, Ha! ha!
> Nectar quaffing, Ha! ha! ha! ha!
> But condemned to die is he,
> Wretched, meritorious B!

(*Exeunt* MIKADO *and* KATISHA.)

KO-KO. Well! a nice mess you've got us into, with your nodding head and the deference due to a man of pedigree!

POOH-BAH. Merely corroborative detail, intended to give artistic verisimilitude to a bald and unconvincing narrative.

PITTI-SING. Corroborative detail indeed! Corroborative fiddlestick!

KO-KO. And you're just as bad as he is with your cock-and-a-bull stories, about catching his eye, and his whistling an air. But that's so like you! You must put in your oar!

POOH-BAH. But how about your big right arm?

PITTI-SING. Yes, and your snickersnee!

KO-KO. Well, well, never mind that now. There's only one thing to be done. Nanki-Poo hasn't started yet—he must come to life again at once —(*Enter* NANKI-POO *and* YUM-YUM *prepared for journey.*) Here he comes. Here, Nanki-Poo, I've good news for you—you're reprieved.

NANKI-POO. Oh, but it's too late. I'm a dead man, and I'm off for my honeymoon.

KO-KO. Nonsense. A terrible thing has just happened. It seems you're the son of the Mikado.

NANKI-POO. Yes, but that happened some time ago.

KO-KO. Is this a time for airy persiflage? Your father is here, and with Katisha!

NANKI-POO. My father! And with Katisha!

KO-KO. Yes, he wants you particularly.

POOH-BAH. So does she.

YUM-YUM. Oh, but he's married now.

KO-KO. But, bless my heart, what has that to do with it.

NANKI-POO. Katisha claims me in marriage, but I can't marry her because I'm married already— consequently she will insist on my execution, and if I'm executed, my wife will have to be buried alive.

YUM-YUM. You see our difficulty.

KO-KO. Yes, I don't know what's to be done.

NANKI-POO. There's one chance for you. If you could persuade Katisha to marry you, she would have no further claim on me, and in that case I could come to life without any fear of being put to death.

KO-KO. I marry Katisha!

YUM-YUM. I really think it's the only course.

KO-KO. But, my good girl, have you seen her? She's something appalling!

PITTI-SING. Ah, that's only her face. She has a left elbow which people come miles to see!

POOH-BAH. I am told that her right heel is much admired by connoisseurs.

KO-KO. My good sir, I decline to pin my heart upon any lady's right heel.

NANKI-POO. It comes to this: While Katisha is single, I prefer to be a disembodied spirit. When Katisha is married, existence will be as welcome as the flowers in spring.

DUET — NANKI-POO *and* KO-KO.

NANKI-POO. The flowers that bloom in the spring,
　　　Tra la,
　　Breath promise of merry sunshine—
　As we merrily dance and we sing,
　　　Tra la,
　We welcome the hope that they bring,
　　　Tra la,
　　Of a summer of roses and wine;
　　　And that's what we mean when we say
　　　　that a thing
　　　Is welcome as flowers that bloom in the
　　　　spring.
　　　Tra la la la la la, &c.

ALL. And that's what we mean, &c.

KO-KO. The flowers that bloom in the spring,
　　　Tra la,
　　Have nothing to do with the case.
　I've got to take under my wing,
　　　Tra la,
　A most unattractive old thing,
　　　Tra la,
　　With a caricature of a face;
　　　And that's what I mean when I say, or
　　　　I sing,
　　　"Oh bother the flowers that bloom in
　　　　the spring!"
　　　Tra la la la la la, &c.

ALL. And that's what he means when he ventures to sing, &c.
(*Dance, and exeunt* NANKI-POO, YUM-YUM, POOH-BAH, *and* PITTI-SING.)

Enter KATISHA.

RECITATIVE — KATISHA.

Alone, and yet alive! Oh, sepulchre!
My soul is still my body's prisoner!
Remote the peace that Death alone can give—
My doom, to wait! my punishment, to live!

SONG — KATISHA.

Hearts do not break!
They sting and ache
For old sake's sake,
　　But do not die!
Though with each breath
They long for death,
As witnesseth
　　The living I!
　　　Oh, living I!
　　　Come, tell me why,
　　　When hope is gone
　　　Dost thou stay on?
　　　Why linger here,
　　　Where all is drear?
May not a cheated maiden die?

KO-KO (*approaching her timidly*). Katisha!

KATISHA. The miscreant who robbed me of my love! But vengeance pursues—they are heating the cauldron!

KO-KO. Katisha—behold a suppliant at your feet! Katisha—mercy!

KATISHA. Mercy? Had you mercy on him? See here, you! You have slain my love. He did not love *me,* but he would have loved me in time. I am an acquired taste—only the educated palate can appreciate *me.* I was educating *his* palate when he left me. Well, he is dead, and where shall I find another? It takes years to train a man to love me—am I to go through the weary round again, and, at the same time, implore mercy for you who robbed me of my prey—I mean my pupil—just as his education was on the point of completion? Oh, where shall I find another!

KO-KO (*suddenly, and with great vehemence*). Here!—Here!

KATISHA. What!!!

KO-KO (*with intense passion*). Katisha, for years

I have loved you with a white-hot passion that is slowly but surely consuming my very vitals! Ah, shrink not from me! If there is aught of woman's mercy in your heart, turn not away from a love-sick suppliant whose every fibre thrills at your tiniest touch! True it is that, under a poor mask of disgust, I have endeavoured to conceal a passion whose inner fires are broiling the soul within me. But the fire will not be smothered—it defies all attempts at extinction, and, breaking forth, all the more eagerly for its long restraint, it declares it-self in words that will not be weighed—that can-not be schooled—that should not be too severely criticised. Katisha, I dare not hope for your love—but I will not live without it!

KATISHA.   You, whose hands still reek with the blood of my betrothed, dare to address words of passion to the woman you have so foully wronged!

KO-KO.   I do—accept my love, or I perish on the spot!

KATISHA.   Go to! Who knows so well as I that no one ever yet died of a broken heart!

KO-KO.   You know not what you say. Listen!

SONG — KO-KO.

On a tree by a river a little tom-tit
    Sang "Willow, titwillow, titwillow!"
And I said to him, "Dicky-bird, why do you sit
    Singing 'Willow, titwillow, titwillow'?
Is it weakness of intellect, birdie?" I cried,
"Or a rather tough worm in your little inside?"
With a shake of his poor little head he replied,
    "Oh willow, titwillow, titwillow!"

He slapped at his chest, as he sat on that bough,
    Singing "Willow, titwillow, titwillow!"
And a cold perspiration bespangled his brow,
    Oh willow, titwillow, titwillow!
He sobbed and he sighed, and a gurgle he gave,
Then he threw himself into the billowy wave,
And an echo arose from the suicide's grave—
    "Oh willow, titwillow, titwillow!"

Now I feel just as sure as I'm sure that my name
    Isn't Willow, titwillow, titwillow,
That 'twas blighted affection that made him ex-
    claim,
    "Oh willow, titwillow, titwillow!"
And if you remain callous and obdurate, I
Shall perish as he did, and you will know why,
Though I probably shall not exclaim as I die,
    "Oh willow, titwillow, titwillow!"

(*During this song* KATISHA *has been greatly af-fected, and at the end is almost in tears.*)

KATISHA (*whimpering*). Did he really die of love?

KO-KO.   He really did.

KATISHA.   All on account of a cruel little hen?

KO-KO.   Yes.

KATISHA.   Poor little chap!

KO-KO.   It's an affecting tale, and quite true. I knew the bird intimately.

KATISHA.   Did you? He must have been very fond of her!

KO-KO.   His devotion was something extraordi-nary.

KATISHA (*still whimpering*). Poor little chap! And—if I refuse you, will you go and do the same?

KO-KO.   At once.

KATISHA.   No, no—you mustn't! Anything but that! (*Falls on his breast.*) Oh, I'm a silly little goose!

KO-KO (*making a wry face*). You are!

KATISHA.   And you won't hate me because I'm just a little teeny weeny wee bit blood-thirsty, will you?

KO-KO.   Hate you? Oh Katisha! is there not beauty even in blood-thirstiness?

KATISHA.   My idea exactly!

DUET — KO-KO *and* KATISHA.

KATISHA.   There is beauty in the bellow of the
        blast,
    There is grandeur in the growling of the gale,
      There is eloquent outpouring
      When the lion is a-roaring,
    And the tiger is a-lashing of his tail!

KO-KO.   Yes, I like to see a tiger
      From the Congo or the Niger,
    And especially when lashing of his tail!

KATISHA.   Volcanos have a splendour that is
        grim,
    And earthquakes only terrify the dolts,
      But to him who's scientific
      There's nothing that's terrific
    In the falling of a flight of thunderbolts!

KO-KO.   Yes, in spite of all my meekness,
      If I have a little weakness,
    It's a passion for a flight of thunderbolts.

BOTH.   If that is so,
      Sing derry down derry!
      It's evident, very,
        Our tastes are one.
    Away we'll go,
      And merrily marry,
      Nor tardily tarry,
        'Till day is done!

KO-KO.   There is beauty in extreme old age—
    Do you fancy you are elderly enough?
        Information I'm requesting
        On a subject interesting:
    Is a maiden all the better when she's tough?

KATISHA.   Throughout this wide dominion
        It's the general opinion
    That she'll last a good deal longer when she's
        tough.

KO-KO.   Are you old enough to marry, do you
        think?
    Won't you wait till you are eighty in the
        shade?
        There's a fascination frantic
        In a ruin that's romantic;
    Do you think you are sufficiently decayed?

KATISHA.   To the matter that you mention
        I have given some attention,
    And I think I am sufficiently decayed.

BOTH.   If that is so,
        Sing derry down derry!
        It's evident, very,
            Our tastes are one!
      Away we'll go,
        And merrily marry,
        Nor tardily tarry
            Till day is done!
                (*Exeunt together.*)

Flourish. Enter the MIKADO, *attended by* PISH-
TUSH *and Court.*

MIKADO.   Now, then, we've had a capital lunch, and we're quite ready. Have all the painful preparations been made?

PISH-TUSH.   Your Majesty, all is prepared.

MIKADO.   Then produce the unfortunate gentleman and his two well-meaning but misguided accomplices.

Enter KO-KO, KATISHA, POOH-BAH, *and* PITTI-
SING. *They throw themselves at the* MIKADO'S *feet.*

KATISHA.   Mercy! Mercy for Ko-Ko! Mercy for Pitti-Sing! Mercy even for Pooh-Bah!

MIKADO.   I beg your pardon, I don't think I quite caught that remark.

KATISHA.   Mercy! My husband that was to have

been is dead, and I have just married this miserable object.

MIKADO.   Oh! You've not been long about it!

KO-KO.   We were married before the Registrar.

POOH-BAH.   *I* am the Registrar.

MIKADO.   I see. But my difficulty is that, as you have slain the Heir-Apparent——

Enter NANKI-POO *and* YUM-YUM. *They kneel.*

NANKI-POO.   The Heir-Apparent is *not* slain.

MIKADO.   Bless my heart, my son!

YUM-YUM.   And your daughter-in-law elected!

KATISHA (*seizing* KO-KO).   Traitor, you have deceived me!

MIKADO.   Yes, you are entitled to a little explanation, but I think he will give it better whole than in pieces.

KO-KO.   Your Majesty, it's like this. It is true that I stated that I had killed Nanki-Poo—

MIKADO.   Yes, with most affecting particulars.

POOH-BAH.   Merely corroborative detail intended to give verisimilitude to a bald and—

KO-KO.   *Will* you refrain from putting in your oar? (*To* MIKADO.) It's like this: When your Majesty says, "Let a thing be done," it's as good as done—practically, it *is* done—because your Majesty's will is law. Your Majesty says, "Kill a gentleman," and a gentleman is told off to be killed. Consequently, that gentleman is as good as dead—practically, he *is* dead—and if he is dead, why not say so?

MIKADO.   I see. Nothing could possibly be more satisfactory!

FINALE.

YUM-YUM *and* NANKI-POO.   The threatened cloud
        has passed away,
    And brightly shines the dawning day;
    What though the night may come too soon,
    We've years and years of afternoon!

ALL.   Then let the throng
        Our joy advance,
      With laughing song
        And merry dance,
    With joyous shout and ringing cheer,
    Inaugurate our new career!
        Then let the throng, &c.

CURTAIN.

Postscript

THE FIRST EDITION of the *Mikado* libretto, representing the text as performed on March 14, 1885, had 48 pages. The second and subsequent editions standardized the text at 47 pages for many years until the present 46-page version.

The *Sunday Times* of March 22, 1885, commented: *"The Mikado* now goes much more briskly than it did on the first night. . . . It has not been found necessary to make any important cuts in the dialog, but the transposition of one or two of the songs has brought about a considerable improvement. Ko-Ko now sings his patter song, 'They'd none of them be missed,' almost immediately after his first entry, and Yum-Yum's air, 'The sun whose rays,' is given in the second instead of the first act." From this reporting it is clear that Gilbert and Sullivan wasted no time. What with a Sunday morning rehearsal after the first night (if Leonora Braham's recollection is accurate), it is unlikely that the original first-edition text was performed more than two or three times at the most. The transpositions noted by the *Sunday Times* left the libretto in substantially the form that is known today.

There is no question that the first-edition version of Ko-Ko's "List" song was sung on the first night, as the *Daily News* review quotes the chorus, "As a victim must be found. . . ." The modern Savoyard, however, will wish to note how the transposition was made. Ko-Ko's speech immediately after the last chorus of his opening solo on page 248 is revised:

Ko-Ko. Gentlemen, I'm much touched by this reception. I can only trust that by strict attention to duty I shall ensure a continuance of those favours which it will ever be my study to deserve. If I should ever be called upon to act professionally, I am happy to think that there will be no difficulty in finding plenty of people whose loss will be a distinct gain to society at large.

Then follows the "List" song, but with the first line altered to: "As some day it may happen that a victim must be found," and with a new chorus replacing "As a victim must be found, if you'll only look around . . ." at the end of each verse:

He's got 'em on the list—he's got 'em on the list;
And they'll none of 'em be missed—they'll none of
  'em be missed.

A corresponding adjustment must be made on pages 252-3: Ko-Ko's speech immediately following Pish-Tush's statement, "But that will involve us all in irretrievable ruin!" is cut out, as is the short line given to Poo-Bah ("This is very uncomfortable news") that followed the original "List" song.

A deletion, rather than a transposition, was made in the "Kissing Duet" (see page 252) after the first edition. The original four-verse duet was reduced to two by cutting out the second and third verses. Thus in all later versions the second, and final, verse begins "So in spite of all temptation. . . ."

The major shift of Yum-Yum's song, "The sun whose rays," from its first-act position on page 251 immediately after the "So pardon us" Quartette to the opening of the second act, immediately following the "Braid the raven hair" chorus, naturally caused the deletion of her speech beginning "How pitiable is the condition of a young and innocent child. . . ." In other words, Nanki-Poo enters at the close of the Quartette. The adjustment in the second act is a matter of adding the following speech by Yum-Yum after the opening chorus on page 258:

YUM-YUM. Yes, I am indeed beautiful! Sometimes I sit and wonder, in my artless Japanese way, why it is that I am so much more attractive than anybody else in the whole world. Can this be vanity? No! Nature is lovely and rejoices in her loveliness. I am a child of Nature, and take after my mother.

This is followed by the singing of "The sun whose rays," after which Pitti-Sing and Peep-Bo enter, and Yum-Yum returns to the original first-night text with her lines beginning: "Yes, everything seems to smile upon me."

It is a matter of more than bibliographic interest to note that a hybrid, freak issue of the libretto exists that has "The sun whose rays" in both first and second acts. This error would be of little consequence were it not for the fact that a copy (or copies) of this hybrid appears to have been the source of the American early *Mikado* librettos which blindly followed the duplication of Yum-Yum's aria.

There are numerous minor alterations and cuts in which later editions vary from the first-night text, among them the shortening of Ko-Ko's lines on page 248, of Ko-Ko's and Nanki-Poo's dialog on pages 254-5, and of Nanki-Poo's speech, page

260. But the only other change of consequence is in the second-act Finale, which in modern performance incorporates fourteen lines of reprise adapted from Pitti-Sing's interruption of Katisha at the close of the first act. Thus, between the Mikado's line, "I see. Nothing could possibly be more satisfactory!" and the Yum-Yum and Nanki-Poo Finale, "The threatened cloud has passed away . . . ," the modern libretto has:

FINALE.

PITTI-SING. For he's gone and married Yum-Yum—
ALL.   Yum-Yum!
PITTI-SING.   Your anger pray bury,
            For all will be merry,
        I think you had better succumb—

ALL.   Cumb—cumb!
PITTI-SING. And join our expressions of glee!
KO-KO. On this subject I pray you be dumb—
ALL.   Dumb—dumb!
KO-KO.   Your notions, though many,
        Are not worth a penny,
        The word for your guidance is "Mum"—
ALL.   Mum—mum!
KO-KO. You've a very good bargain in me.
ALL.   On this subject we pray you be dumb—
                  Dumb—Dumb!
    We think you had better succumb—
                  Cumb—cumb!
       You'll find there are many
       Who'll wed for a penny,
    There are lots of good fish in the sea.

RUDDYGORE

Introduction

HISSES AT A Gilbert and Sullivan opening! That was news indeed for Londoners reading their Monday morning *Times* on January 24, 1887: "The production of Gilbert and Sullivan's new operetta, *Ruddygore* . . . (a most unfortunate name, by-the-by), was on Saturday evening accompanied by a phenomenon never before experienced at the Savoy Theatre. With the rapturous applause of a more than sympathetic first-night audience, which called composer and author, Mr. D'Oyly Carte, the manager, and all the principal performers before the curtain, a small but very determined minority mingled its hisses . . . We have no hesitation in attributing them to the feebleness of the second act and the downright stupidity of its dénouement."

Across the Atlantic, under the headlined exaggeration—

THE FIRST FLAT FAILURE;
THE GILBERT AND SULLIVAN
OPERA NOT A SUCCESS

the *New York Times* in its Sunday edition, January 23, reported: "When the curtain finally fell there was hissing—the first ever heard in the Savoy Theatre. The audience even voiced sentiments in words and there were shouts and cries such as these: 'Take off this rot!' 'Give us *The Mikado!*' "

"Give us *The Mikado!*" indeed. One reporter at the Savoy the night of Saturday, January 22, wrote: "It is the misfortune of Messrs. Gilbert and Sullivan that they are their own rivals, and every new work makes their task harder" (*Pall Mall Budget*). With the enormous and unprecedented popularity of *The Mikado,* ninth collaboration of the author and the composer, an almost insuperable obstacle to their unbroken success rhythm had been laid athwart the course of their next venture. *The Mikado* had been taken off the Savoy stage on January 19, after a record run of 672 performances. It was withdrawn, not because it was no longer attracting good houses but in order to make way for the new opera. To *Mikado*-mad London theatregoers it was unlikely that any new opera in early 1887 could replace their established favorite. Gilbert and Sullivan had temporarily met their match—in Gilbert and Sullivan. And they were, in a sense, also the victims of their own superabundance of publicity. If newspaper lineage is an accurate measure of public interest, then the indications were that the magnitude of anticipation focused on *The Mikado*'s successor was overwhelming. The *Daily News* alone ran three separate articles on the *Ruddygore* first night in its issue of Monday, January 24, and closed the lead-sentence of one of these with the opinion: "It was universally believed that the presentation of Sullivan and Gilbert's new comic opera of *Ruddygore* on Saturday night would be, par excellence, the first night of the season."

"Everybody who was anybody prided himself

MR RICHARD TEMPLE · AS
SIR RODERICK MURGATROYD

on being at the Savoy Theatre tonight," bubbled the *World:* "The place was simply packed with celebrities." It was, ruled the *Umpire,* "one of the most brilliant audiences to be found in London —representative of all the elements that go to make up what is termed as 'Society.' " The *Daily News* reported, name by name, the presence of scores of these elite, with vintage commentary to match:

In the absence of Royalty, the Lord Mayor [Sir Reginald Hanson, looking "rubicund and jolly"] and the Lady Mayoress occupied the principal box on the left-hand side of the house. Lady Hanson wore an exquisite toilette and some remarkably fine diamonds; she was, naturally, vastly amused at the reference, from the lips of Miss Braham, to her book of etiquette, "composed, if I may believe the title-page, by no less an authority than the wife of a Lord Mayor." The pair who attracted perhaps the largest share of public attention were Lord and Lady Randolph Churchill [father and mother of Sir Winston; she was the beautiful American, Jenny Jerome], sitting in the very centre of the stalls. . . . Lord Dunraven, Mr. Henry Manners, and . . . the Earl and Countess of Onslow were also present. The lawyers were in great force. . . . Mr. Inderwick, who had long ago got rid of the backwoodsman's beard which he first displayed to an admiring world on the first night of *The Mikado,* was in the stalls. . . . Artists abounded. Sir John Millais, who assiduously cultivates a squirearchical aspect, and Mr. Frank Holl could hardly fail to be entertained at Mr. Gilbert's pleasantry in regard of their craft. [Millais' portrait of Sullivan and Holl's of Gilbert now hang in the National Portrait Gallery.] Mr. Whistler [was] among the company . . . so were Mr. and Mrs. Perugini (she is the daughter, it will be remembered, of Charles Dickens, who sat

as the model for the lady in the 'Black Brunswicker'). . . . Stagecraft was not greatly in evidence [but was represented by Mr. and Mrs. Pinero (Miss Myra Holme) and, as usual at these first nights, by Mrs. Arthur Lewis (Miss Kate Terry). Journalism was, of course, well represented, including] Mr. Frank Burnand, Mr. William Archer, Mr. Clement Scott, Mr. Wilde . . . [and] Mr. Moy Thomas, who has been called the doyen of dramatic critics. . . .

The title of any dramatic work engages the public in critical skirmish even before the curtain rises. So it was that night at the Savoy, and one and all, press and public, fell on the title *Ruddygore* with critical vehemence. In retrospect it is interesting to speculate on how two craftsmen so experienced at appealing to public taste could have made such a blunder. For it was clearly a carefully selected title, chosen by both collaborators. As Gilbert explained: "We have a sort of superstition about never fixing our titles until just before the opera is produced. It is not easy to get a good title; I dare say I had half a dozen for this, printing them in block letters to see the effect on the eye. We finally fixed on 'Ruddygore.' We only changed 'Titipoo' [sic] to 'The Mikado' at the last moment."

This statement was published in the *Pall Mall Budget* on January 27. By February 2 Gilbert and Sullivan had yielded to unanimous disapproval and had revised the title by substituting "I" for "Y," thereby, to Victorian British tastes, removing the unfortunate connotation educed by "ruddy." But of course the libretto available to the audience on January 22 carried the *y* spelling, as did both the regular and the souvenir programs.

The first act, by unanimous verdict, was a delight: "Everything sparkles with the flashes of Mr. Gilbert's wit and the graces of Sir Arthur Sullivan's melodiousness," wrote the *Times* reviewer; "one is almost at a loss what to select for quotation from an embarrassment of humorous riches." According to the *St. James Gazette:* "Number after number was rapturously encored, and every droll sally of dialogue was received with a shout of appreciative mirth." And the *Illustrated Sporting and Dramatic News:* "One of Mr. Gilbert's happiest efforts."

Perhaps the best-received number in this act— and hence of the whole night—was Richard Dauntless' ballad, "I shipped, d'ye see, in a revenue sloop." The last-named paper reported it "capitally sung by Mr. Lely, who immediately afterwards danced a hornpipe so skillfully that he was compelled to repeat it, on the second occasion introducing fresh steps. The greedy gods demanded another repetition, but in vain." One reporter, who must have been sitting down front, caught more intimate overtones: "The enthusi-

astically-demanded encore was somewhat marred
by the inability of the orchestra to pick up the
time, whereat Sir Arthur was obviously and audibly irate. . . ."

Another obviously and "audibly" irate reaction
to this "Parlez-vous" Song, as it was dubbed, was
as topsy-turvy as anything in its Gilbertian source.
In the house that night was one "T. Johnson,"
correspondent for the Paris *Figaro*. Having a
limited appreciation of British humor, and still
more limited nautical understanding, the Gallic
gentleman blasted at Gilbert and Sullivan as having insulted France and the French navy. So, at
a time when they must have been working madly
on changes to *Ruddygore*, Gilbert and Sullivan
had to create a joint explanation in French to still
this international teapot tempest.

The first act also contained a "delightfully
melodious" duet for Richard and Rose, "The
battle's roar is over," which one first-night reviewer prophesied would be "popular all over the
world." But, although this number still remains in
the latest editions of the libretto, it has been cut
from the D'Oyly Carte Opera Company's current
productions.

Act I finished as well as it began. Again to
quote the *Illustrated Sporting and Dramatic News*,
"The concluding portion of the finale was encored, all the leading artists were called before
the curtain and heartily applauded, and the favourable verdict on Act I was unanimous."

MISS LEONORA BRAHAM AS ROSE MAYBUD.

Anticipating the delay in setting up the elaborate Picture Gallery scene for the second act,
D'Oyly Carte had indulgence slips on hand for his
first-night patrons. Apparently during the half-
hour intermission there was a noisy demonstration
from the gallery when they spotted Sir Randolph
Churchill; but someone, evidently with the voice
and assurance of a sergeant-major, called out "NO
POLITICS!" and the dissidents subsided.

When the curtain went up on the second act,
D'Oyly Carte had every reason to believe he had
another gigantic success. "Then," according to
the *St. James Gazette*, "gradually the enthusiasm
faded away and was hardly to be revived. . . .
Shortly after the beginning of the second act the
interest of the story had begun to flag, until at last
the plot had seemed within an ace of collapsing altogether." The *Pall Mall Budget* was more lenient:
"Mr. Gilbert has scarcely shown his usual skill in
securing a good 'curtain,' but the players seemed
to be nervous from the first. Miss Braham forgot
her lines, and was not in voice; Mr. Grossmith was
in the same plight, and did not do justice to what
is, at present, certainly not too good a part. But
first-night nervousness must be condoned, however much it mars the effect of the play."

All seemed to go well until after the "Happily
coupled are we" duet. Then, apparently, the heavy
burlesque in action and dialog involving the device
"Foiled—and by a Union Jack!" did not get over.
Rose's ballad immediately following must have
slowed up the show, for Gilbert cut it in half the
next week. There were complications with the
operation of stage equipment in the descent of the
Ancestors from their frames. And Sir Roderic's
song, "The Ghosts' high noon," even though
praised as one of the high spots of the opera by
many critics (and sung "splendidly" by Richard
Temple), was held by some to be couched musi-

MISS JESSIE BOND AS MAD MARGARET AND MR. RUTLAND BARRINGTON AS SIR DESPARD MURGATROYD.

cally in a style that savored too much of Grand Opera.

The *Times* expounded in some detail:

> The ghost scene of the second act, representing the descent of the Murgatroyd ancestry from their picture frames, of which preliminary notices and hints of the initiated had led one to expect much, was a very tame affair. In the first instance, the stage management was not here equal to Savoy level. A set of very ugly daubs . . . pulled up as you might a patent iron shutter to reveal a figure in the recess behind, can scarcely be called a good example of modern stage contrivance, especially when, as on Saturday night, one of these blinds or shutters comes down at an odd moment, while another refuses to move in time. . . . The musical treatment of these scenes appears to us pitched in the wrong key. Sir Arthur Sullivan, in a parallel situation of *The Sorcerer,* has shown that the mock-ghastly as well as the mock-heroic is quite within his reach. . . . But the present ghost-scene has evidently not found him in a happy mood. He treats Mr. Gilbert's grotesque spectres as if they were a dread reality coming straight from the charnel house.
>
> We miss in the instrumentation those touches of exaggerated horror which in *The Sorcerer* always remind one of the real purport of the scene, and the song sung by Mr. Temple, who himself has not humour in his anatomy, with a powerful voice, might well find its place in a tragic opera of a somewhat conventional type. The innate seriousness of the music, the sincerest of all arts, has evidently been too much for the composer, and the result is one evidently quite different from that which he and the dramatist intended.

The *Daily News,* on the other side of the fence, enjoyed both the visual effect and the music:

> The stage is darkened, and Sir Arthur Sullivan conducts with a baton tipped with a tiny incandescent lamp. The expedient is new to London, and it was, we believe, first used after the recent manoeuvres of the Germany army, when a military band of 1,200 performers serenaded the Kaiser in the dark. The whole of the music of the picture scene is far removed above the ordinary level of comic opera, and is among the best things of this sort that Sir Arthur Sullivan has ever written. It is almost serious in aim, but although somewhat after the style of grand opera, there is many a whimsical touch of burlesque in the orchestra.

"Almost necessarily all that followed appeared to be anti-climactic," commented one reviewer.

But—all that followed could not be so readily disposed of by the majority of the Press, even though including the rollickingly successful triple patter-song and the sensationally applauded duet, "I once was a very abandoned person." Between these two numbers, Robin's solo patter-song, "For thirty-five years I've been sober and wary," although sung on January 22 and in the performances of the following week, was replaced by Gilbert with a completely different patter-song on February 2. (See page 304-5 for details.)

An enthusiast in the first-night audience, who signed himself "A Savoyard" in a lengthy analytical letter to the editor of the *St. James Gazette,* felt that "the love-scene between Hannah and the ghost of a man who has been ten years dead produced an uncomfortable impression. . . . It is a grisly idea; it is not funny; and it is in doubtful taste." Gilbert made radical cuts in this love-scene, immediately following Hannah's ballad, "There grew a little flower"; and he altered the technical arrangements so that Roderic, shortly after the first night, did not make his reappearance, accompanied by red flames, via a trap. The much-criticized conclusion was drastically changed: the Ancestors were not brought back to life a second time, the dialog was reduced, and the four solo verses of the Finale were cut. The effect, according to the press of the following week, was to make "the second act proceed with greater briskness."

As usual the opera was magnificently mounted, in fact more expensively than any of its predeces-

MR DURWARD LELY AS
RICHARD DAUNTLESS.

sors. Gilbert had disclosed, stated the *Era,* that the total cost would be six or seven thousand pounds. Hawes Craven designed the sets. The military costumes worn by the men reproduced with exact and costly fidelity some twenty regimental uniforms of about the Waterloo year. And the company itself received high praise from many reviewers. The *Theatre*'s representative wrote: "The performance of *Ruddygore,* on the night of its production, was from first to last unexceptionable. All the old Savoy favourites of the metropolitan public were fitted with parts affording to them ample opportunities for the advantageous display of their respective humorous specialties, and each one of them, from a theatrical point of view, covered himself or herself with glory." To Rutland Barrington he paid specific praise: "Better comic acting than his, or more highly finished, I have never seen and never wish to see."

Leonora Braham did not fare so well. In the *Times* it was reported that her Rose Maybud was "acted most charmingly, but [she] sang persistently out of tune, probably on account of nervousness or indisposition." Jessie Bond made a decided hit: so true to life was her portrayal of Mad Margaret that Forbes Winslow, a famous authority on mental disorders, wrote Miss Bond a congratulatory letter and inquired "where she had found the model from which she had studied, and so faithfully copied the phases of insanity."

Of the two collaborators, the composer received the greater journalistic acclaim: "Sir Arthur Sullivan's music, taken all for all," wrote the *Daily Telegraph,* is "the best he has yet contributed to the stage of comic opera." The reviewer for the *Theatre,* signing himself "Clavichord," pulled out all the stops:

The music of *Ruddygore* is so melodious and graceful throughout that it may be accepted as a supreme illustration of the principle—or is it instinct?—that has guided Arthur Sullivan during his brilliant career as an operatic composer, viz., that beauty is the soul of Art. Whilst Wagner, Berlioz, Brahms, Saint Saëns, and other modern composers of indisputable genius have strenuously endeavoured to prove that ugliness is artistic, our leading English musician has stuck to beauty, and has been amply rewarded for his unswerving constancy. Unless I be much mistaken, *Ruddygore* will rank amongst his *chefs d'oeuvre.*

"When the curtain fell," the *Daily News* reported, "all the artists, the author, the conductor, and the manager were called to the front, and hearty cheering announced another Savoy success."

As for those "sibilant sounds," an elaborate—though certainly not particularly credible—explanation was devised by Helen Lenoir, then rep-

resenting D'Oyly Carte in America (the following year she was to become the second Mrs. Richard D'Oyly Carte). Interviewed by the New York *Tribune* on February 20, she said: "One curious thing happened on the first night. There was a line in which one of the characters spoke of an appeal to the Supreme Court. [See page 303.] Some oversensitive people construed this as an appeal to the Supreme Being and promptly hissed at what they considered irreverence on Mr. Gilbert's part. Of course the line was cut out the next night. But it was curious, wasn't it?"

The same first-nighter's account quoted previously from the *St. James Gazette,* seems to give an accurate appraisal:

During the second act I was painfully conscious that the author had gotten out of touch with his audience. . . . One gentleman, writing to a morning paper, asserts that the disaffected were not hooting the play at all, but were expressing their sentiments regarding Lord Randolph Churchill, who was at that moment leaving the theatre. But this theory will not stand examination. The hissing, or rather the hooting, commenced as the curtain fell on the last act; it entirely ceased while the performers were called before the curtain; it recommenced immediately

MR. GEORGE GROSSMITH. AS ROBIN OAKAPPLE.

The title problem—cartoon by Arthur Bryan in the ILLUSTRATED SPORTING & DRAMATIC NEWS *of February 5, 1887.*

the call for 'authors' began, and was at its height while the author and composer were visible. The expressions of displeasure . . . were distinctly evoked by the play, and are intelligible to anyone who closely watched the audience on Saturday night during the second act of *Ruddygore*.

One clue to the disparity in newspaper accounts can be found in the simple matter of deadline. The *Sunday Times* and the *Sunday Express* obviously had deadlines to meet that did not apply to the Monday morning dailies. It seems likely that their reviewers left the Savoy either before or at the moment of the final curtain. This can explain the unqualified character of their praise. Wrote the *Sunday Times:* "Another brilliant success has attended the latest joint effort of Mr. W. S. Gilbert and Sir Arthur Sullivan. Their new and original 'supernatural' opera, entitled *Ruddygore* . . . received with every demonstration of delight by a distinguished and representative audience. . . . Sir Arthur Sullivan conducted, as is his wont on first nights. He was enthusiastically applauded, both on taking his place and at the end of the opera. . . . On the whole, *Ruddygore* with its quaint cynical humour and clever dialogue, its fanciful, melodious and picturesque music, and its superb *mise-en-scène,* cannot be considered inferior to any of its predecessors." And under the headline, "ANOTHER BRILLIANT SUCCESS," the *Sunday Express* heartily agreed: "As far as we can judge from a first performance it appears to be likely to achieve a popularity which out-Gilberts Gilbert. From the raising of the first curtain to the close of the last act the piece runs merrily."

The fact remains that "it was, for the Savoy, a very stormy first night," recalled Rutland Barrington, and ". . . responsible for what had been hitherto an unheard-of occurrence with us, a rehearsal the morning after the production, for cuts." (Leonora Braham recollected a Sunday morning rehearsal after the first night of *The Mikado,* but it could quite possibly have been for a limited group of performers and not a general rehearsal.)

For all this mixed reception, it must be remembered that *Ruddygore* ran for 288 performances. As Gilbert said to Barrington: "I could do with a few more such failures."

JANUARY 22. *Production of* Ruddygore *at Savoy. Very enthusiastic up to the last 20 minutes, then the audience showed dissatisfaction. Revivication* [sic] *of ghosts, etc., very weak. Enthusiastic reception.*

ARTHUR SULLIVAN'S DIARY

An Entirely Original Supernatural Opera,

IN TWO ACTS,

ENTITLED

RUDDYGORE

OR,

THE WITCH'S CURSE!

Dramatis Personae.

MORTALS.

ROBIN OAKAPPLE, *A Young Farmer*	MR. GEORGE GROSSMITH.
RICHARD DAUNTLESS, *His Foster-Brother— a Man-o'-War's-Man*	MR. DURWARD LELY.
SIR DESPARD MURGATROYD, *of Ruddygore— a Wicked Baronet*	MR. RUTLAND BARRINGTON.
OLD ADAM GOODHEART, *Robin's Faithful Servant*	MR. RUDOLPH LEWIS.
ROSE MAYBUD, *A Village Maiden*	MISS LEONORA BRAHAM.
MAD MARGARET	MISS JESSIE BOND.
DAME HANNAH, *Rose's Aunt*	MISS ROSINA BRANDRAM.
ZORAH } *Professional Bridesmaids*	MISS JOSEPHINE FINDLAY.
RUTH }	MISS LINDSAY.

GHOSTS.

SIR RUPERT MURGATROYD, *The First Baronet*	MR. PRICE.
SIR JASPER MURGATROYD, *The Third Baronet*	MR. CHARLES.
SIR LIONEL MURGATROYD, *The Sixth Baronet*	MR. TREVOR.
SIR CONRAD MURGATROYD, *The Twelfth Baronet*	MR. BURBANK.
SIR DESMOND MURGATROYD, *The Sixteenth Baronet*	MR. TUER.
SIR GILBERT MURGATROYD, *The Eighteenth Baronet*	MR. WILBRAHAM.
SIR MERVYN MURGATROYD, *The Twentieth Baronet*	MR. COX.

and

SIR RODERIC MURGATROYD, *The Twenty-first Baronet*	MR. RICHARD TEMPLE.

CHORUS OF OFFICERS, ANCESTORS, AND PROFESSIONAL BRIDESMAIDS.

ACT I. — The Fishing Village of Rederring, in Cornwall.

ACT II. — Picture Gallery in Ruddygore Castle.

TIME. — Early in the Present Century.

RUDDYGORE

OR,

THE WITCH'S CURSE.

___

ACT I.

SCENE. — *The fishing village of Rederring (in Cornwall).* ROSE MAYBUD'S *cottage is seen at left.*

Enter Chorus of Bridesmaids. They range themselves in front of ROSE'S *cottage.*

CHORUS OF BRIDESMAIDS.

Fair is Rose as the bright May-day;
   Soft is Rose as the warm west-wind;
Sweet is Rose as the new-mown hay—
   Rose is the queen of maiden-kind!
     Rose, all glowing
       With virgin blushes, say—
     Is anybody going
       To marry you to-day?

SOLO — ZORAH.

Every day, as the days roll on,
Bridesmaids' garb we gaily don,
Sure that a maid so fairly famed
Won't very long remain unclaimed.
Hour by hour and day by day
Several months have passed away,
And though she's the fairest flower that blows,
Nobody yet has married Rose!

CHORUS.   Rose, all glowing
       With virgin blushes, say—
     Is anybody going
       To marry you to-day?

Enter OLD HANNAH, *from cottage.*

HANNAH. Nay, gentle maidens, you sing well but vainly, for Rose is still heart-free, and looks but coldly upon her many suitors.

ZORAH. It's very disappointing. Every young man in the village is in love with her, but they are appalled by her beauty and modesty, and won't declare themselves; so, until she makes her own choice, there's no chance for anybody else.

RUTH. This is, perhaps, the only village in the world that possesses an endowed corps of professional bridesmaids who are bound to be on duty every day from ten to four—and it is at least six months since our services were required. The pious charity by which we exist is practically wasted!

ZORAH. We shall be disendowed—that will be the end of it! Dame Hannah—you're a nice old person—*you* could marry if you liked. There's old Adam—Robin's faithful servant—he loves you with all the frenzy of a boy of fourteen.

HANNAH. Nay—that may never be, for I am pledged!

ALL. To whom?

HANNAH. To an eternal maidenhood! Many years ago I was betrothed to a god-like youth who wooed me under an assumed name. But on the very day upon which our wedding was to have been celebrated, I discovered that he was no other than Sir Roderic Murgatroyd, one of the bad Baronets of Ruddygore, and the uncle of the man who now bears that title. As a son of that accursed race he was no husband for an honest girl, so, madly as I loved him, I left him then and there. He died but ten years since, but I never saw him again.

ZORAH. But why should you not marry a bad Baronet of Ruddygore?

RUTH. All baronets are bad; but was he worse than other baronets?

HANNAH. My child, he was accursed!

ZORAH. But who cursed him? Not you, I trust!

HANNAH. The curse is on all his line and has been, ever since the time of Sir Rupert, the first Baronet. Listen, and you shall hear the legend.

LEGEND — HANNAH.

Sir Rupert Murgatroyd
    His leisure and his riches
He ruthlessly employed
    In persecuting witches.
With fear he'd make them quake—
He'd duck them in his lake—
    He'd break their bones
    With sticks and stones,
And burn them at the stake!

CHORUS.   This sport he much enjoyed,
             Did Rupert Murgatroyd—
                 No sense of shame
                 Or pity came
             To Rupert Murgatroyd!

Once, on the village green,
    A palsied hag he roasted,
And what took place, I ween,
    Shook his composure boasted,
For, as the torture grim
Seized on each withered limb,
    The writhing dame
    'Mid fire and flame
Yelled forth this curse on him:

"Each lord of Ruddygore,
    Despite his best endeavour,
Shall do one crime, or more,
    Once, every day, for ever!
This doom he can't defy

However he may try,
    For should he stay
    His hand, that day
In torture he shall die!"

The prophecy came true:
    Each heir who held the title
Had, every day, to do
    Some crime of import vital;
Until, with guilt o'erplied,
"I'll sin no more!" he cried,
    And on the day
    He said that say,
In agony he died!

CHORUS.   And thus, with sinning cloyed,
             Has died each Murgatroyd,
                 And so shall fall,
                 Both one and all,
             Each coming Murgatroyd!
                 (*Exeunt Chorus of Bridesmaids.*)

Enter ROSE MAYBUD *from cottage, with small basket on her arm.*

HANNAH. Whither away, dear Rose? On some errand of charity, as is thy wont?

ROSE. A few gifts, dear aunt, for deserving villagers. Lo, here is some peppermint rock for old gaffer Gadderby, a set of false teeth for pretty little Ruth Rowbottom, and a pound of snuff for the poor orphan girl on the hill.

HANNAH. Ah, Rose, pity that so much goodness should not help to make some gallant youth happy for life! Rose, why dost thou harden that little heart of thine? Is there none hereaway whom thou couldst love?

ROSE. And if there were such an one, verily it would ill become me to tell him so.

HANNAH. Nay, dear one, where true love is, there is little need of prim formality.

ROSE. Hush, dear aunt, for thy words pain me sorely. Hung in a plated dish-cover to the knocker of the workhouse door, with nought that I could call mine own, save a change of baby-linen and a book of etiquette, little wonder if I have always regarded that work as a voice from a parent's tomb. This hallowed volume (*producing a book of etiquette*), composed, if I may believe the title-page, by no less an authority than the wife of a Lord Mayor, has been, through life, my guide and monitor. By its solemn precepts I have learnt to test the moral worth of all who approach me. The man who bites his bread, or eats peas with a knife, I look upon as a lost creature, and he who has not acquired the proper way of entering and leaving a room, is the object of my pitying horror. There are those in this village who bite their nails, dear aunt, and nearly all are wont to use their pocket combs in public places. In truth, I could pursue this painful theme much further, but behold, I have said enough.

HANNAH. But is there not one among them who is faultless, in thine eyes? For example—young

Robin. He combines the manners of a Marquis with the morals of a Methodist. Couldst thou not love *him*?

ROSE. And even if I could, how should I confess it unto him? For lo, he is shy, and sayeth nought!

BALLAD — ROSE.

If somebody there chanced to be
   Who loved me in a manner true,
My heart would point him out to me,
   And I would point him out to you.
(*Referring to book.*)
   But here it says of those who point,
   Their manners must be out of joint—
     You *may* not point—
     You *must* not point—
   It's manners out of joint, to point!
Had I the love of such as he,
   Some quiet spot he'd take me to,
Then he could whisper it to me,
   And I could whisper it to you.
(*Referring to book.*)
   But whispering, I've somewhere met,
   Is contrary to etiquette:
     Where can it be? (*Searching book.*)
     Now let me see—
         (*Finding reference.*)
     Yes, Yes!
It's contrary to etiquette!
        (*Showing it to* HANNAH.)

If any well-bred youth I knew,
   Polite and gentle, neat and trim,
Then I would hint as much to you,
   And you could hint as much to him.
(*Referring to book.*)
   But here it says, in plainest print,
   "It's most unladylike to hint"—

You *may* not hint,
You *must* not hint—
It says you mustn't hint, in print!
And if I loved him through and through—
   (True love and not a passing whim),
Then I could speak of it to you,
   And you could speak of it to him.
(*Referring to book.*)
   But here I find it doesn't do
   To speak until you're spoken to.
     Where can it be? (*Searching book.*)
     Now let me see—
         (*Finding reference.*)
"Don't speak until you're spoken to"!
        (*Exit* HANNAH.)

ROSE. Poor Aunt! Little did the good soul think, when she breathed the hallowed name of Robin, that he would do even as well as another. But he resembleth all the youths in this village, in that he is unduly bashful in my presence, and lo, it is hard to bring him to the point. But soft, he is here!

ROSE *is about to go when* ROBIN *enters and calls her.*

ROBIN. Mistress Rose!

ROSE (*surprised*). Master Robin!

ROBIN. I wished to say that—it is fine.

ROSE. It is passing fine.

ROBIN. But we do want rain.

ROSE. Aye, sorely! Is that all?

ROBIN (*sighing*). That is all.

ROSE. Good day, Master Robin!

ROBIN. Good day, Mistress Rose! (*Both going —both stop.*)

ROSE. ⎱ I crave pardon, I—
ROBIN. ⎰ I beg pardon, I—

ROSE. You were about to say?—

ROBIN. I would fain consult you—

ROSE. Truly?

ROBIN. It is about a friend.

ROSE. In truth I have a friend myself.

ROBIN. Indeed? I mean, of course—

ROSE. And I would fain consult you—

ROBIN (*anxiously*). About him?

ROSE (*prudishly*). About *her*.

ROBIN (*relieved*). Let us consult one another.

DUET — ROBIN *and* ROSE.

ROBIN. I know a youth who loves a little maid—
   (Hey, but his face is a sight for to see!)
Silent is he, for he's modest and afraid—
   (Hey, but he's timid as a youth can be!)

ROSE. I know a maid who loves a gallant youth—

(Hey, but she sickens as the days go by!)
She cannot tell him all the sad, sad truth—
(Hey, but I think that little maid will die!)

ROBIN. Poor little man!

ROSE. Poor little maid!

ROBIN. Poor little man!

ROSE. Poor little maid!

BOTH. Now tell me pray, and tell me true,

What in the world should the $\begin{cases} \text{young man} \\ \text{maiden} \end{cases}$ do?

ROBIN. He cannot eat and he cannot sleep—
(Hey, but his face is a sight for to see!)
Daily he goes for to wail—for to weep—
(Hey, but he's wretched as a youth can be!)

ROSE. She's very thin and she's very pale—
(Hey, but she sickens as the days go by!)
Daily she goes for to weep—for to wail—
(Hey, but I think that little maid will die!)

ROBIN. Poor little maid!

ROSE. Poor little man!

ROBIN. Poor little maid!

ROSE. Poor little man!

BOTH. Now tell me pray, and tell me true,

What in the world should the $\begin{cases} \text{young man} \\ \text{maiden} \end{cases}$ do?

ROSE. If I were the youth I should offer her my
name—
(Hey, but her face is a sight for to see!)

ROBIN. If I were the maid I should feed his honest flame—
(Hey, but he's bashful as a youth can be!)

ROSE. If I were the youth I should speak to her
to-day—
(Hey, but she sickens as the days go by!)

ROBIN. If I were the maid I should meet the lad
half way—
(For I really do believe that timid youth will
die!)

ROSE. Poor little man!

ROBIN. Poor little maid!

ROSE. Poor little man!

ROBIN. Poor little maid!

BOTH. I thank you, $\begin{cases} \text{miss,} \\ \text{sir,} \end{cases}$ for your counsel true;

I'll tell that $\begin{cases} \text{youth} \\ \text{maid} \end{cases}$ what $\begin{cases} \text{he} \\ \text{she} \end{cases}$ ought to do!

(Exit ROSE.)

ROBIN. Poor child! I sometimes think that if she wasn't quite so particular I might venture—but no, no—even then I should be unworthy of her!

He sits desponding. Enter OLD ADAM.

ADAM. My kind master is sad! Dear Sir Ruthven Murgatroyd—

ROBIN. Hush! As you love me, breathe not that hated name. Twenty years ago, in horror at the prospect of inheriting that hideous title and, with it, the ban that compels all who succeed to the baronetcy to commit at least one deadly crime per day, for life, I fled my home and concealed myself in this innocent village under the name of Robin Oakapple. My younger brother, Despard, believing me to be dead, succeeded to the title and its attendant curse. For twenty years I have been dead and buried. Don't dig me up now.

ADAM. Dear master, it shall be as you wish, for have I not sworn to obey you for ever in all things? Yet, as we are here alone, and as I belong to that particular description of good old man to whom the truth is a refreshing novelty, let me call you by your own right title once more! (ROBIN *assents.*) Sir Ruthven Murgatroyd! Baronet! Of Ruddygore! Whew! It's like eight hours at the seaside!

ROBIN. My poor old friend! Would there were more like you!

ADAM. Would there were indeed! But I bring you good tidings. Your foster-brother, Richard, has returned from sea—his ship the *Tom-Tit* rides yonder at anchor, and he himself is even now in this very village!

ROBIN. My beloved foster-brother? No, no—it cannot be!

ADAM. It is even so—and see, he comes this way!

Enter Chorus of Bridesmaids.

CHORUS.

From the briny sea
    Comes young Richard, all victorious!
Valorous is he—
    His achievements all are glorious!
Let the welkin ring
With the news we bring
    Sing it—shout it—
    Tell about it—
Safe and sound returneth he,
All victorious from the sea!

Enter RICHARD. *The girls welcome him as he greets old acquaintances.*

BALLAD — RICHARD.

I shipped, d'ye see, in a Revenue sloop,
    And, off Cape Finistere,
        A merchantman we see,
        A Frenchman, going free,
    So we made for the bold Mounseer,
        D'ye see?
    We made for the bold Mounseer.
But she proved to be a Frigate—and she up
        with her ports,
    And fires with a thirty-two!
        It come uncommon near,
        But we answered with a cheer,
    Which paralysed the Parley-voo,
        D'ye see?
    Which paralysed the Parley-voo!

Then our Captain he up and he says, says he,
    "That chap we need not fear,—
        We can take her, if we like,
        She is sartin for to strike,
    For she's only a darned Mounseer,
        D'ye see?
    She's only a darned Mounseer!
But to fight a French fal-lal—it's like hittin'
        of a gal—
    It's a lubberly thing for to do;
        For we, with all our faults,
        Why we're sturdy British salts,
    While she's only a Parley-voo,
        D'ye see?
    A miserable Parley-voo!"

So we up with our helm, and we scuds before
        the breeze
    As we gives a compassionating cheer;
        Froggee answers with a shout
        As he sees us go about,
    Which was grateful of the poor Mounseer,
        D'ye see?
    Which was grateful of the poor Mounseer!

And I'll wager in their joy they kissed each
        other's cheek
    (Which is what them furriners do),
        And they blessed their lucky stars
        We were hardy British tars
    Who had pity on a poor Parley-voo,
        D'ye see?
    Who had pity on a poor Parley-voo!
(*Exeunt* CHORUS, *as* ROBIN *comes forward.*)

ROBIN. Richard!

RICHARD. Robin!

ROBIN. My beloved foster-brother, and very dearest friend, welcome home again after ten long years at sea! It is such deeds as you have just described that cause our flag to be loved and dreaded throughout the civilized world!

RICHARD. Why, lord love ye, Rob, that's but a trifle to what we *have* done in the way of sparing life! I believe I may say, without exaggeration, that the marciful little *Tom-Tit* has spared more French frigates than any craft afloat! But 'tain't for a British seaman to brag, so I'll just stow my jawin' tackle and belay. (ROBIN *sighs.*) But 'vast heavin', messmate, what's brought *you* all a-cock-bill?

ROBIN. Alas, Dick, I love Rose Maybud, and love in vain!

RICHARD. *You* love in vain? Come, that's too good! Why you're a fine strapping muscular young fellow—tall and strong as a to'-gall'n-m'st—taut as a fore-stay—aye, and a barrowknight to boot, if all had their rights!

ROBIN. Hush, Richard—not a word about my true rank, which none here suspect. Yes, I know well enough that few men are better calculated to win a woman's heart than I. I'm a fine fellow, Dick, and worthy any woman's love—happy the girl who gets me, say I. But I'm timid, Dick; shy—nervous—modest—retiring—diffident—and I cannot tell her, Dick, I cannot tell her! Ah, you've no idea what a poor opinion I have of myself, and how little I deserve it.

RICHARD. Robin, do you call to mind how, years ago, we swore that, come what might, we would always act upon our hearts' dictates?

ROBIN. Aye, Dick, and I've always kept that oath. In doubt, difficulty, and danger, I've always asked my heart what I should do, and it has never failed me.

RICHARD. Right! Let your heart be your compass, with a clear conscience for your binnacle light, and you'll sail ten knots on a bowline, clear of shoals, rocks, and quicksands! Well, now, what does my heart say in this here difficult situation? Why it says, "Dick," it says—(it calls me "Dick" acos it's known me from a babby)—"Dick," it says, "*you* ain't shy—*you* ain't modest—speak you up for him as is!" Robin, my lad, just you lay me alongside, and when she's becalmed under my lee, I'll spin her a yarn that shall sarve to fish you two together for life!

ROBIN. Will you do this thing for me? Can you, do you think? Yes (*feeling his pulse*). There's no false modesty about *you*. Your—what I would call bumptious self-assertiveness (I mean the expression in its complimentary sense) has already made you a bos'n's mate, and it will make an admiral of you in time, if you work it properly, you dear, incompetent old impostor! My dear fellow, I'd give my right arm for one tenth of your modest assurance!

SONG — ROBIN.

My boy, you may take it from me,
　　That of all the afflictions accurst
　　　　With which a man's saddled
　　　　And hampered and addled,
　　A diffident nature's the worst.
Though clever as clever can be—
　　A Crichton of early romance—
　　　　You must stir it and stump it,
　　　　And blow your own trumpet,
　　Or, trust me, you haven't a chance.
　　　　If you wish in the world to advance,
　　　　Your merits you're bound to en-
　　　　　　hance,
　　　　　　You must stir it and stump it,
　　　　　　And blow your own trumpet,
　　　　Or, trust me, you haven't a chance!

Now take, for example, *my* case:
　　I've a bright intellectual brain—
　　　　In all London city
　　　　There's no one so witty—
　　I've thought so again and again.
I've a highly intelligent face—
　　My features cannot be denied—
　　　　But, whatever I try, sir,
　　　　I fail in—and why, sir?
　　I'm modesty personified!
　　　　If you wish in the world to advance,
　　　　　　&c.

As a poet, I'm tender and quaint—
　　I've passion and fervour and grace—
　　　　From Ovid and Horace
　　　　To Swinburne and Morris,
　　They all of them take a back place.
Then I sing and I play and I paint:
　　Though none are accomplished as I,
　　　　To say so were treason:
　　　　You ask me the reason?
　　I'm diffident, modest, and shy!
　　　　If you wish in the world to advance,
　　　　　　&c.　　　　　(*Exit* ROBIN.)

RICHARD (*looking after him*). Ah, it's a thousand pities he's such a poor opinion of himself, for a finer fellow don't walk! Well, I'll do my best for him. "Plead for him as though it was for your own father"—that's what my heart's a-remarkin' to me just now. But here she comes! Steady! Steady it is! (*Enter* ROSE—*he is much struck by her.*) By the Port Admiral but she's a tight little craft! Come, come, she's not for you, Dick, and yet—she's fit to marry Lord Nelson! By the Flag of Old England, I can't look at her unmoved.

ROSE. Sir, you are agitated—

RICHARD. Aye, aye, my lass, well said! I am agitated, true enough!—took flat aback, my girl, but 'tis naught—'twill pass. (*Aside.*) This here heart of mine's a-dictatin' to me like anythink. Question is, have I a right to disregard its promptings?

ROSE. Can I do ought to relieve thine anguish, for it seemeth to me that thou art in sore trouble? This apple—(*offering a damaged apple*).

RICHARD (*looking at it and returning it*). No, my lass, 'tain't that: I'm—I'm took flat aback—I never see anything like you in all my born days. Parbuckle me, if you ain't the loveliest gal I've ever set eyes on. There—I can't say fairer than that, can I?

ROSE. No. (*Aside.*) The question is, is it meet that an utter stranger should thus express himself? (*Refers to book.*) Yes—"Always speak the truth."

RICHARD. I'd no thoughts of sayin' this here to you on my own account, for, truth to tell, I was chartered by another; but when I see you my heart it up and it says, says it, "This is the very lass for *you,* Dick"—"Speak up to her, Dick," it says—(it calls me Dick acos we was at school together)—"Tell her all, Dick," it says, "never sail under false colours—it's mean!" *That's* what my heart tells me to say, and in my rough, common-sailor fashion, I've said it, and I'm a-waitin' for your reply. I'm a-tremblin', miss. Lookye here—(*holding out his hand*). That's narvousness!

ROSE (*aside*). Now, how should a maiden deal with such an one? (*Consults book.*) "Keep no one in unnecessary suspense." (*Aloud.*) Behold, I will not keep you in unnecessary suspense. (*Refers to book.*) "In accepting an offer of marriage, do so with apparent hesitation." (*Aloud.*) I take you, but with a certain show of reluctance. (*Refers to book.*) "Avoid any appearance of eagerness." (*Aloud.*) Though you will bear in mind that I am far from anxious to do so. (*Refers to book.*) "A little show of emotion will not be misplaced!" (*Aloud.*) Pardon this tear! (*Wipes her eye.*)

RICHARD. Rose, you've made me the happiest blue-jacket in England! I wouldn't change places with the Admiral of the Fleet, no matter who he's a-huggin' of at this present moment! But, axin' your pardon, miss (*wiping his lips with his hand*), might I be permitted to salute the flag I'm a-goin' to sail under?

ROSE (*referring to book*). "An engaged young lady should not permit too many familiarities." (*Aloud.*) Once! (*Richard kisses her.*)

DUET — RICHARD *and* ROSE.

RICHARD. The battle's roar is over,
O my love!
Embrace thy tender lover,
O my love!
From tempests' welter,
From war's alarms,
O give me shelter
Within those arms!
Thy smile alluring,
All heart-ache curing,
Gives peace enduring,
O my love!

ROSE. If heart both true and tender,
O my love!
A life-love can engender,
O my love!
A truce to sighing
And tears of brine,
For joy undying
Shall aye be mine,
And thou and I, love,
Shall live and die, love,
Without a sigh, love—
My own, my love!

Enter ROBIN, *with Chorus of Bridesmaids.*

CHORUS. If well his suit has sped,
Oh, may they soon be wed!
Oh, tell us, tell us, pray,
What doth the maiden say?
In singing are we justified,
"Hail the Bridegroom—hail the Bride"?

ROBIN. Well—what news? Have you spoken to her?

RICHARD. Aye, my lad, I have—so to speak—spoke her.

ROBIN. And she refuses?

RICHARD. Why, no, I can't truly say she do.

ROBIN. Then she accepts! My darling! (*Embraces her.*)

BRIDESMAIDS. Hail the Bridegroom—hail the Bride!
Let the nuptial knot be tied:
In fair phrases
Hymn their praises,
Hail the Bridegroom—hail the Bride!

ROSE (*aside, referring to her book*). Now, what should a maiden do when she is embraced by the wrong gentleman?

RICHARD. Belay, my lad, belay. You don't understand.

ROSE. Oh, sir, belay, I beseech you!

RICHARD. You see, it's like this: she accepts—but it's *me!*

ROBIN. You! (RICHARD *embraces* ROSE.)

BRIDESMAIDS. Hail the Bridegroom—hail the Bride!

When the nuptial knot is tied—

ROBIN (*interrupting angrily*). Hold your tongues, will you! Now then, what does this mean?

RICHARD. My poor lad, my heart grieves for thee, but it's like this: The moment I see her, and just as I was a-goin' to mention your name, my heart it up and it says, says it—"Dick, you've fell in love with her yourself," it says; "Be honest and sailor-like—don't skulk under false colours—speak up," it says, "take her, you dog, and with her my blessin'!"

BRIDESMAIDS. "Hail the Bridegroom—hail the Bride!"—

ROBIN. Will you be quiet! Go away! (*Chorus make faces at him and exeunt.*) Vulgar girls!

RICHARD. What could I do? I'm bound to obey my heart's dictates.

ROBIN. Of course—no doubt. It's quite right—I don't mind—that is, not particularly—only it's—it *is* disappointing, you know.

ROSE (*to* ROBIN). Oh, but, sir, I knew not that thou didst seek me in wedlock, or in very truth I should not have hearkened unto this man, for behold, he is but a lowly mariner, and very poor withal, whereas thou art a tiller of the land, and thou hast fat oxen, and many sheep and swine, a considerable dairy farm, and much corn and oil!

RICHARD. That's true, my lass, but it's done now, ain't it, Rob?

ROSE. Still, it may be that I should not be happy in thy love. I am passing young and little able to judge. Moreover, as to thy character I know naught!

ROBIN. Nay, Rose, I'll answer for that. Dick has won thy love fairly. Broken-hearted as I am, I'll stand up for Dick through thick and thin!

RICHARD (*with emotion*). Thankye, messmate! that's well said. That's spoken honest. Thankye, Rob! (*Grasps his hand.*)

ROSE. Yet methinks I have heard that sailors are but worldly men, and little prone to lead serious and thoughtful lives!

ROBIN. And what then? Admit that Dick is *not* a steady character, and that when he's excited he uses language that would make your hair curl.—Grant that—he does. It's the truth, and I'm not going to deny it. But look at his *good* qualities. He's as nimble as a pony, and his hornpipe is the talk of the fleet!

RICHARD. Thankye Rob! That's well spoken. Thankye Rob!

ROSE. But it may be that he drinketh strong waters which do bemuse a man, and make him even as the wild beasts of the desert!

ROBIN. Well, suppose he does, and I don't say he don't, for rum's his bane, and ever has been. He *does* drink—I won't deny it. But what of that? Look at his arms—tattooed to the shoulder! (*Dick rolls up his sleeves.*) No, no—I won't hear a word against Dick!

ROSE. But they say that mariners are but rarely true to those whom they profess to love!

ROBIN. Granted—granted—and I don't say that Dick isn't as bad as any of 'em. (*Dick chuckles.*) You are, you know you are, you dog! a devil of a fellow—a regular out-and-out Lothario! But what then? You can't have everything, and a better hand at turning-in a dead-eye don't walk a deck! And what an accomplishment *that* is in a family man! No, no—not a word against Dick. I'll stick up for him through thick and thin!

RICHARD. Thankye, Rob, thankye. You're a true friend. I've acted accordin' to my heart's dictates, and such orders as them no man should disobey.

ENSEMBLE — RICHARD, ROBIN, ROSE.

In sailing o'er life's ocean wide
Your heart should be your only guide;
With summer sea and favouring wind
Yourself in port you'll surely find.

SOLO — RICHARD.

My heart says, "To this maiden strike—
    She's captured you.
She's just the sort of girl you like—
    You know you do.
If other man her heart should gain,
    I shall resign."
That's what it says to me quite plain,
    This heart of mine.

SOLO — ROBIN.

My heart says, "You've a prosperous lot,
    With acres wide;
You mean to settle all you've got
    Upon your bride.
It don't pretend to shape my acts
    By word or sign;

It merely states these simple facts,
    This heart of mine!

SOLO — ROSE.

Ten minutes since my heart said "white"—
    It now says "black."
It then said "left"—it now says "right"—
    Hearts often tack.
I must obey its latest strain—
    You tell me so.   (*To* RICHARD.)
But should it change its mind again,
    I'll let you know.
    (*Turning from* RICHARD *to* ROBIN, *who
                embraces her.*)

ENSEMBLE.

In sailing o'er life's ocean wide
No doubt the heart should be your guide,
But it is awkward when you find
A heart that does not know its mind!
(*Exeunt* ROBIN *with* ROSE L., *and* RICHARD,
                weeping, R.)

Enter MAD MARGARET. *She is wildly dressed in
picturesque tatters, and is an obvious caricature
of theatrical madness.*

SCENA — MARGARET.

Cheerily carols the lark
    Over the cot.
Merrily whistles the clerk
    Scratching a blot.
        But the lark
        And the clerk,
        I remark,
Comfort me not!

Over the ripening peach
    Buzzes the bee.
Splash on the billowy beach
    Tumbles the sea.
        But the peach
        And the beach

They are each
Nothing to me!

    And why?
    Who am I?
Daft Madge! Crazy Meg!
Mad Margaret! Poor Peg!
    He! he! he! he! he! (*Chuckling.*)
    Mad, I?
        Yes, very!
    But why?
        Mystery!
            Don't call!
                Whisht! whisht!

No crime—
    'Tis only
That I'm
    Love-lonely!
        That's all!
            Whisht! whisht!

BALLAD.

To a garden full of posies
    Cometh one to gather flowers,
    And he wanders through its bowers
Toying with the wanton roses,
    Who, uprising from their beds,
    Hold on high their shameless heads
With their pretty lips a-pouting,
Never doubting—never doubting
    That for Cytherean posies
    He would gather aught but roses!

In a nest of weeds and nettles,
    Lay a violet, half-hidden,
    Hoping that his glance unbidden
Yet might fall upon her petals.
    Though she lived alone, apart,
    Hope lay nestling at her heart,
But, alas, the cruel awaking
Set her little heart a-breaking,
    For he gathered for his posies
    Only roses—only roses!
                (*Bursts into tears.*)

Enter ROSE.

ROSE. A maiden, and in tears? Can I do aught
to soften thy sorrow? This apple—(*offering apple*).

MARGARET (*examines it and rejects it*). No!
(*Mysteriously.*) Tell me, are you mad?

ROSE. I? No! That is, I think not.

MARGARET. That's well! Then you don't love Sir
Despard Murgatroyd? All mad girls love him. *I*
love him. I'm poor Mad Margaret—Crazy Meg—
Poor Peg! He! he! he! he! (*Chuckling.*)

ROSE. Thou lovest the bad Baronet of Ruddygore? Oh, horrible—too horrible!

MARGARET. You pity me? Then be my mother! The squirrel had a mother, but she drank and the squirrel fled! Hush! They sing a brave song in our parts—it runs somewhat thus: (*Sings.*)

> "The cat and the dog and the little puppee
> Sat down in a—down in a—in a—"

I forget what they sat down in, but so the song goes! Listen—I've come to pinch her!

ROSE. Mercy, whom?

MARGARET. You mean "who."

ROSE. Nay! it is the accusative after the verb.

MARGARET. True. (*Whispers melodramatically.*) I have come to pinch Rose Maybud!

ROSE (*aside, alarmed*). Rose Maybud!

MARGARET. Aye! I love him—he loved me once. But that's all gone, Fisht! He gave me an Italian glance—thus—(*business*)—and made me his. He will give *her* an Italian glance, and make *her* his. But it shall not be, for I'll stamp on her—stamp on her—stamp on her! Did you ever kill anybody? No? Why not? Listen—I killed a fly this morning! It buzzed, and I wouldn't have it! So it died— pop! So shall she!

ROSE. But behold, *I* am Rose Maybud, and I would fain not die "pop."

MARGARET. You are Rose Maybud!

ROSE. Yes, sweet Rose Maybud!

MARGARET. Strange! They told me she was beautiful! And *he* loves *you!* No, no! If I thought that, I would treat you as the auctioneer and land-agent treated the lady-bird—I would rend you asunder!

ROSE. Nay, be pacified, for behold I am pledged to another, and lo, we are to be wedded this very day!

MARGARET. Swear me that! Come to a Commissioner and let me have it on affidavit! *I* once made an affidavit—but it died—it died—it died! But see, they come—Sir Despard and his evil crew! Hide, hide—they are all mad—quite mad!

ROSE. What makes you think that?

MARGARET. Hush! They sing choruses in public. That's mad enough, I think! Go—hide away, or they will seize you. Hush! Quite softly—quite, quite softly! (*Exeunt together, on tiptoe.*)

Enter Chorus of Bucks and Blades, heralded by Chorus of Bridesmaids.

CHORUS OF BRIDESMAIDS.

> Welcome, gentry,
> For your entry
> Sets our tender hearts a-beating.
> Men of station,
> Admiration
> Prompts this unaffected greeting.

> Hearty greeting offer we!
> Your exceeding
> Easy breeding—
> Just the thing our hearts to pillage—
> Cheers us, charms us,
> Quite disarms us:
> Welcome, welcome, to our village;
> To our village welcome be!

CHORUS OF BUCKS AND BLADES.

> When thoroughly tired
> Of being admired
> By ladies of gentle degree—degree,
> With flattery sated,
> High-flown and inflated,
> Away from the city we flee—we flee!
> From charms intramural
> To prettiness rural
> The sudden transition
> Is simply Elysian.
> So come, Amaryllis,
> Come, Chloe and Phyllis,
> Your slaves, for the moment, are we!

ALL. From charms intramural, &c.

CHORUS OF BRIDESMAIDS.

> The sons of the tillage
> Who dwell in this village
> Are people of lowly degree—degree.
> Though honest and active
> They're most unattractive
> And awkward as awkward can be—can be.
> They're clumsy clodhoppers
> With axes and choppers,
> And shepherds and ploughmen
> And drovers and cowmen
> And hedgers and reapers
> And carters and keepers,
> But never a lover for me!

ALL. They're clumsy clodhoppers, &c.

ALL. So welcome, gentry,

> For { your / our } entry
>
> Sets { our / their } tender hearts a-beating, &c.

Enter SIR DESPARD MURGATROYD.

SONG *and* CHORUS — SIR DESPARD.

SIR DESPARD. Oh why am I moody and sad?
CHORUS.   Can't guess!
SIR DESPARD. And why am I guiltily mad?
CHORUS.   Confess!
SIR DESPARD. Because I am thoroughly bad!
CHORUS.   Oh yes—

SIR DESPARD.	You'll see it at once in my face. Oh why am I husky and hoarse?
CHORUS.	Ah, why?
SIR DESPARD.	It's the workings of conscience, of course.
CHORUS.	Fie, fie!
SIR DESPARD.	And huskiness stands for remorse,
CHORUS.	Oh my!
SIR DESPARD.	At least it does so in my case!
SIR DESPARD.	When in crime one is fully employed—
CHORUS.	Like you—
SIR DESPARD.	Your expression gets warped and destroyed:
CHORUS.	It do.
SIR DESPARD.	It's a penalty none can avoid;
CHORUS.	How true!
SIR DESPARD.	I once was a nice-looking youth; But like stone from a strong catapult—
CHORUS (explaining to each other).	A trice—
SIR DESPARD.	I rushed at my terrible cult—
CHORUS (explaining to each other).	That's vice—
SIR DESPARD.	Observe the unpleasant result!
CHORUS.	Not nice.
SIR DESPARD.	Indeed I am telling the truth!
SIR DESPARD.	Oh innocent, happy though poor!
CHORUS.	That's we—
SIR DESPARD.	If I had been virtuous, I'm sure—
CHORUS.	Like me—
SIR DESPARD.	I should be as nice-looking as you're!
CHORUS.	May be.
SIR DESPARD.	You are very nice-looking indeed! Oh innocents, listen in time—
CHORUS.	We *doe.*
SIR DESPARD.	Avoid an existence of crime—
CHORUS.	Just so—
SIR DESPARD.	Or you'll be as ugly as I'm—
CHORUS (loudly).	No! No!
SIR DESPARD.	And now, if you please, we'll proceed.

All the girls express their horror of SIR DESPARD. *As he approaches them they fly from him, terror-stricken, leaving him alone on the stage.*

SIR DESPARD. Poor children, how they loathe me —me whose hands are certainly steeped in infamy, but whose heart is as the heart of a little child! But what *is* a poor baronet to do, when a whole picture-gallery of ancestors step down from their frames and threaten him with an excruciat-

ing death, if he hesitate to commit his daily crime? But, ha! ha! I am even with them! (*Mysteriously.*) I get my crime over the first thing in the morning and then, ha! ha! for the rest of the day I do good —I do good—I do good! (*Melodramatically.*) Two days since, I stole a child and built an orphan asylum. Yesterday I robbed a bank and endowed a bishopric. To-day I carry off Rose Maybud, and atone with a cathedral! This is what it is to be the sport and toy of a Picture Gallery! But I will be bitterly revenged upon them! I will give them all to the Nation, and nobody shall ever look upon their faces again!

Enter RICHARD.

RICHARD. Ax your honour's pardon, but—

SIR DESPARD. Ha! observed! And by a mariner! What would you with me, fellow?

RICHARD. Your honour, I'm a poor man-o'-war's man, becalmed in the doldrums—

SIR DESPARD. I don't know them.

RICHARD. And I make bold to ax your honour's advice. Does your honour know what it is to have a heart?

SIR DESPARD. My honour knows what it is to have a complete apparatus for conducting the circulation of the blood through the veins and arteries of the human body.

RICHARD. Aye, but has your honour a heart that ups and looks you in the face, and gives you quarter-deck orders that it's life and death to disobey?

SIR DESPARD. I have not a heart of that description, but I have a Picture Gallery that presumes to take that liberty.

RICHARD. Well, your honour, it's like this—Your honour had an elder brother—

SIR DESPARD. It had.

RICHARD. Who should have inherited your title and, with it, its cuss.

SIR DESPARD. Aye, but he died. Oh, Ruthven!—

RICHARD. He didn't.

SIR DESPARD. He did *not?*

RICHARD. He didn't. On the contrary, he lives in this here very village, under the name of Robin Oakapple, and he's a-going to marry Rose Maybud this very day.

SIR DESPARD. Ruthven alive, and going to marry Rose Maybud! Can this be possible?

RICHARD. Now the question I was going to ask your honour is—ought I to tell your honour this?

SIR DESPARD. I don't know. It's a delicate point. I think you ought. Mind, I'm not sure, but I think so.

RICHARD. That's what my heart says. It says, "Dick," it says (it calls me Dick acos it's entitled to take that liberty). "That there young gal would recoil from him if she knowed what he really were. Ought you to stand off and on, and let this young gal take this false step and never fire a shot across her bows to bring her to? No," it says, "you did *not* ought." And I won't ought, accordin'.

SIR DESPARD. Then you really feel yourself at liberty to tell me that my elder brother lives—that I may charge him with his cruel deceit, and transfer to his shoulders the hideous thraldom under which I have laboured for so many years! Free—free at last! Free to live a blameless life, and to die beloved and regretted by all who knew me!

DUET — SIR DESPARD *and* RICHARD.

RICHARD. You understand?

SIR DESPARD. I think I do.
   With vigour unshaken
   This step shall be taken.
  It's neatly planned.

RICHARD.   I think so too;
   I'll readily bet it
   You'll never regret it!

BOTH. For duty, duty must be done;
  The rule applies to every one,
  And painful though that duty be,
  To shirk the task were fiddle-de-dee!

SIR DESPARD. The bridegroom comes—

RICHARD.   Likewise the bride—
  The maidens are very
  Elated and merry;
   They are her chums.

SIR DESPARD. To lash their pride
  Were almost a pity,
  The pretty committee!

BOTH. But duty, duty must be done;
  The rule applies to every one,
  And painful though that duty be,
  To shirk the task were fiddle-de-dee!
   (*Exeunt* RICHARD *and* SIR DESPARD.)

Enter Chorus of Bridesmaids and Bucks.

CHORUS OF BRIDESMAIDS.

Hail the bride of seventeen summers:
  In fair phrases
  Hymn her praises;
Lift your song on high, all comers.
  She rejoices
  In your voices.
Smiling summer beams upon her,
Shedding every blessing on her:
  Maidens, greet her—
  Kindly treat her—
You may all be brides some day!

CHORUS OF BUCKS.

Hail the bridegroom who advances,
  Agitated,
  Yet elated.
He's in easy circumstances,
  Young and lusty,
  True and trusty:
Happiness untold awaits them
When the parson consecrates them;
  People near them,

Loudly cheer them—
You'll be bridegrooms some fine day!

Enter ROBIN, *attended by* RICHARD *and* OLD
ADAM, *meeting* ROSE, *attended by* ZORAH *and*
DAME HANNAH. ROSE *and* ROBIN *embrace.*

MADRIGAL.

ROSE. Where the buds are blossoming,
    Smiling welcome to the spring,
    Lovers choose a wedding day—
    Life is love in merry May!

GIRLS. Spring is green—Fal lal la!
    Summer's rose—Fal lal la!

ALL. It is sad when summer goes,
    Fal la!

MEN. Autumn's gold—Fal lal la!
    Winter's grey—Fal lal la!

ALL. Winter still is far away—
    Fal la!

    Leaves in autumn fade and fall.
    Winter is the end of all.
    Spring and summer teem with glee:
    Spring and summer, then, for me!
    Fal la!

HANNAH. In the spring-time seed is sown:
    In the summer grass is mown:
    In the autumn you may reap:
    Winter is the time for sleep.

GIRLS. Spring is hope—Fal lal la!
    Summer's joy—Fal lal la!

ALL. Spring and summer never cloy—
    Fal la!

MEN. Autumn, toil—Fal lal la!
    Winter, rest—Fal lal la!

ALL. Winter, after all, is best—
    Fal la!

ALL. Spring and summer pleasure you,
    Autumn, aye, and winter too—
    Every season has its cheer
    Life is lovely all the year!
    Fal la!

                                (*Gavotte.*)

After Gavotte, enter SIR DESPARD.

SIR DESPARD. Hold, bride and bridegroom, ere
    you wed each other,
    I claim young Robin as my elder brother!

ROBIN (*aside*). Ah, lost one!

SIR DESPARD. His rightful title I have long en-
    joyed:
    I claim him as Sir Ruthven Murgatroyd!

ROSE (*wildly*). Deny the falsehood, Robin, as
    you should;
        It is a plot!

ROBIN. I would, if conscientiously I could,
        But I cannot!

ALL. Ah, base one!

SOLO — ROBIN.

    As pure and blameless peasant,
        I cannot, I regret,
    Deny a truth unpleasant:
        I am that Baronet!

ALL.   He is that Baronet!

ROBIN.   But when completely rated
        Bad baronet am I,
    That I am what he's stated
        I'll recklessly deny!

ALL.   He'll recklessly deny!

ROBIN. When I'm a bad Bart. I will tell tara-
    diddles!

ALL. He'll tell taradiddles when he's a bad Bart.!

ROBIN. I'll play a bad part on the falsest of
    fiddles.

ALL. On very false fiddles he'll play a bad part!

ROBIN. But until that takes place I must be con-
    scientious—

ALL. He'll be conscientious until that takes place.

ROBIN. Then adieu with good grace to my morals
    sententious!

ALL. To morals sententious adieu with good
    grace!

ZORAH. Who is the wretch who hath betrayed
    thee?
        Let him stand forth!

RICHARD (*coming forward*). 'Twas I!

ALL.   Die, traitor!

RICHARD. Hold, my conscience made me!
        Withhold your wrath!

SOLO — RICHARD.

    Within this breast there beats a heart
        Whose voice can't be gainsaid.
    It bade me thy true rank impart,
        And I at once obeyed.
    I knew 'twould blight thy budding fate—
    I knew 'twould cause thee anguish great—
    But did I therefore hesitate?
        No! I at once obeyed!

ALL. Acclaim him who, when his true heart
    Bade him young Robin's rank impart,
        Immediately obeyed!

SOLO — ROSE (*addressing* ROBIN).

Farewell!
Thou hadst my heart—
    'Twas quickly won!
But now we part—
    Thy face I shun!
    Farewell!

Go bend the knee
    At Vice's shrine;
Of life with me
    All hope resign.
    Farewell!

(*To* SIR DESPARD.) Take me—I am thy bride!

ALL.   Hurrah!

BRIDESMAIDS.

Hail the Bridegroom—hail the Bride!
When the nuptial knot is tied;
Every day will bring some joy
That can never, never cloy!

Enter MARGARET, *who listens.*

SIR DESPARD. Excuse me, I'm a virtuous person
        now—
ROSE. That's why I wed you!
SIR DESPARD. And I to Margaret must keep my
        vow!
MARGARET. Have I misread you?
    Oh joy! with newly kindled rapture warmed,
        I kneel before you!   (*Kneels.*)
SIR DESPARD. I once disliked you; now that I've
        reformed,
        How I adore you!   (*They embrace.*)

BRIDESMAIDS.

Hail the Bridegroom—hail the Bride!
When the nuptial knot is tied,
Every day will bring some joy
That can never, never cloy!

ROSE. Richard, of him I love bereft,
        Through thy design,
Thou art the only one that's left,
        So I am thine!   (*They embrace.*)

BRIDESMAIDS.

Hail the Bridegroom—hail the Bride!
Let the nuptial knot be tied!

DUET — ROSE *and* RICHARD.

Oh, happy the lily
    When kissed by the bee;
And, sipping tranquilly,
    Quite happy is he;
And happy the filly
    That neighs in her pride;
But happier than any
A pound to a penny,
A lover is, when he
    Embraces his bride!

DUET — SIR DESPARD *and* MARGARET.

Oh, happy the flowers
    That blossom in June,
And happy the bowers
    That gain by the boon,
But happier by hours
    The man of descent,
Who, folly regretting,
Is bent on forgetting
His bad baronetting,
    And means to repent!

TRIO — HANNAH, ADAM, *and* ZORAH.

Oh, happy the blossom
    That blooms on the lea,
Likewise the opossum
    That sits on a tree,
But when you come across 'em,
    They cannot compare
With those who are treading
The dance at a wedding,
While people are spreading
    The best of good fare!

SOLO — ROBIN.

Oh, wretched the debtor
    Who's signing a deed!
And wretched the letter
    That no one can read!
But very much better
    Their lot it must be,
Than that of the person
I'm making this verse on,
Whose head there's a curse on—
    Alluding to me!

(*Repeat ensemble with chorus.*)

DANCE.

At the end of the dance, ROBIN *falls senseless on
    the stage. Picture.*

ACT DROP.

ACT II.

SCENE. — *Picture Gallery in Ruddygore Castle. The walls are covered with full-length portraits of the Baronets of Ruddygore from the time of* JAMES I.—*the first being that of* SIR RUPERT, *alluded to in the legend; the last, that of the last deceased Baronet,* SIR RODERIC.

Enter ROBIN *and* ADAM *melodramatically. They are greatly altered in appearance,* ROBIN *wearing the haggard aspect of a guilty roué;* ADAM, *that of the wicked steward to such a man.*

DUET — ROBIN *and* ADAM.

ROBIN.   I once was as meek as a new-born lamb,
    I'm now Sir Murgatroyd—ha! ha!
      With greater precision
      (Without the elision),
    Sir Ruthven Murgatroyd—ha! ha!

ADAM.   And I, who was once his *valley-de-sham,*
    As steward I'm now employed—ha! ha!
      The dickens may take him—
      I'll never forsake him!
    As steward I'm now employed—ha! ha!

BOTH.   How dreadful when an innocent heart
    Becomes, perforce, a bad young Bart.,
    And still more hard on old Adam
    His former faithful *valley-de-sham!*

ROBIN.   My face is the index to my mind,
    All venom and spleen and gall—ha! ha!
      Or, properly speaking,
      It soon will be reeking
    With venom and spleen and gall—ha! ha!

ADAM.   My name from Adam Goodheart you'll
    find
    I've changed to Gideon Crawle—ha! ha!
      For a bad Bart.'s steward
      Whose heart is much *too* hard,
    Is always Gideon Crawle—ha! ha!

BOTH.   How providential when you find
    The face an index to the mind,
    And evil men compelled to call
    Themselves by names like Gideon Crawle!

ROBIN.   This is a painful state of things, Gideon Crawle!

ADAM.   Painful, indeed! Ah, my poor master, when I swore that come what would, I would serve you in all things for ever, I little thought to what a pass it would bring me! The confidential adviser to the greatest villain unhung! It's a dreadful position for a good old man!

ROBIN.   Very likely, but don't be gratuitously offensive, Gideon Crawle.

ADAM.   Sir, I am the ready instrument of your abominable misdeeds because I have sworn to obey you in all things, but I have *not* sworn to allow deliberate and systematic villainy to pass unreproved. If you insist upon it I will swear that, too, but I have not sworn it yet. Now, sir, to business. What crime do you propose to commit to-day?

ROBIN.   How should I know? As my confidential adviser, it's your duty to suggest something.

ADAM.   Sir, I loathe the life you are leading, but a good old man's oath is paramount, and I obey. Richard Dauntless is here with pretty Rose Maybud, to ask your consent to their marriage. Poison their beer.

ROBIN.   No—not that—I know I'm a bad Bart., but I'm not as bad a Bart. as all that.

ADAM.   Well, there you are, you see! It's no use my making suggestions if you don't adopt them.

ROBIN (*melodramatically*).   How would it be, do you think, were I to lure him here with cunning wile—bind him with good stout rope to yonder post—and then, by making hideous faces at him, curdle the heart-blood in his arteries, and freeze the very marrow in his bones? How say you, Gideon, is not the scheme well planned?

ADAM.   It would be simply rude—nothing more. But soft—they come!

ADAM *and* ROBIN *retire up as* RICHARD *and* ROSE *enter, preceded by Chorus of Bridesmaids.*

DUET — RICHARD *and* ROSE.

RICHARD.   Happily coupled are we,
      You see—
    I am a jolly Jack Tar,
      My star,
    And you are the fairest,
    The richest and rarest
    Of innocent lasses you are,
      By far—
    Of innocent lasses you are!
    Fanned by a favouring gale,
      You'll sail
    Over life's treacherous sea
      With me,
    And as for bad weather
    We'll brave it together,
    And you shall creep under my lee,
      My wee!
    And you shall creep under my lee!

    For you are such a smart little craft—

Such a neat little, sweet little craft.
  Such a bright little, tight little,
    Slight little, light little,
Trim little, prim little craft!

CHORUS.   For she is such, &c.

ROSE.   My hopes will be blighted, I fear,
    My dear;
  In a month you'll be going to sea,
    Quite free,
  And all of my wishes
  You'll throw to the fishes
As though they were never to be;
    Poor me!
As though they were never to be,
And I shall be left all alone
    To moan,
And weep at your cruel deceit,
    Complete;
  While you'll be asserting
  Your freedom by flirting
With every woman you meet,
    You cheat—
With every woman you meet!

Though I am such a smart little craft—
Such a neat little, sweet little craft.
  Such a bright little, tight little,

    Slight little, light little,
Trim little, prim little craft!

CHORUS.   Though she is such, &c.

Enter ROBIN.

ROBIN.   Soho! pretty one—in my power at last, eh? Know ye not that I have those within my call who, at my lightest bidding, would immure ye in an uncomfortable dungeon where ye would linger out a lonesome lifetime, in sad and silent solitude? (*Calling.*) What ho! within there!

RICHARD.   Hold—we are prepared for this (*producing a Union Jack*). Here is a flag that none dare defy (*all kneel*), and while this glorious rag floats over Rose Maybud's head, the man does not live who would dare to lay unlicensed hand upon her!

ROBIN.   Foiled—and by a Union Jack! But a time will come, and then—

ROSE.   Nay, let me plead with him. (*To* ROBIN.) Sir Ruthven, have pity. In my book of etiquette the case of a maiden about to be wedded to one who unexpectedly turns out to be a baronet with a curse on him, is not considered. It is a comprehensive work, but it is not as comprehensive as that. Time was when you loved me madly. Prove that this was no selfish love by according your

consent to my marriage with one who, if he be not you yourself, is the next best thing—your dearest friend!

BALLAD — ROSE.

In bygone days I had thy love—
   Thou hadst my heart.
But Fate, all human vows above,
   Our lives did part!
By the old love thou hadst for me
By the fond heart that beat for thee—
By joys that never now can be,
   Grant thou my prayer!

ALL (*kneeling*).   Grant thou her prayer!

My heart that once in truth was thine,
   Another claims—
Ah, who can laws to love assign,
   Or rule its flames?
Our plighted heart-bond gently bless,
The seal of thy consent impress
Upon our promised happiness—
   Grant thou our prayer!

ALL (*kneeling*).   Grant thou her prayer!

ROBIN (*recit.*).   Take her—I yield!

ALL (*recit.*).   Oh rapture!

CHORUS.   Away to the parson we go—
         Say we're solicitous very
   That he will turn two into one—
         Singing hey, derry down derry!

RICHARD.   For she *is* such a smart little craft—

ROSE.   Such a neat little, sweet little craft—

RICHARD.   Such a bright little—

ROSE.   Tight little—

RICHARD.   Slight little—

ROSE.   Light little—

BOTH.   Trim little, slim little craft!

CHORUS.   For she *is* such a smart little craft, &c.
                  (*Exeunt all but* ROBIN.)

ROBIN.   For a week I have fulfilled my accursed doom! I have duly committed a crime a day! Not a great crime, I trust, but still in the eyes of one as strictly regulated as I used to be, a crime. But will my ghostly ancestors be satisfied with what I have done, or will they regard it as an unworthy subterfuge? (*Addressing Pictures.*) Oh, my fore-fathers, wallowers in blood, there came at last a day when, sick of crime, you, each and every, vowed to sin no more, and so, in agony, called welcome Death to free you from your cloying guiltiness. Let the sweet psalm of that repentant hour soften your long-dead hearts, and tune your

souls to mercy on your poor posterity! (*Kneeling.*)

The stage darkens for a moment. It becomes light again, and the Pictures are seen to have become animated.

CHORUS OF FAMILY PORTRAITS.

Painted emblems of a race,
   All accurst in days of yore,
Each from his accustomed place
   Steps into the world once more!

(*The Pictures step from their frames and march round the stage.*)

Baronet of Ruddygore,
   Last of our accursèd line,
Down upon the oaken floor—
   Down upon those knees of thine!
      Coward, poltroon, shaker, squeamer,
      Blockhead, sluggard, dullard, dreamer,
      Shirker, shuffler, crawler, creeper,
      Sniffler, snuffler, wailer, weeper,
      Earthworm, maggot, tadpole, weevil!
      Set upon thy course of evil
      Lest the King of Spectre-Land
      Set on thee his grisly hand!

(*The spectre of* SIR RODERIC *descends from his frame.*)

SIR RODERIC.   By the curse upon our race—
CHORUS.   Dead and hearsèd
         All accursèd!
SIR RODERIC.   Each inheriting this place—
CHORUS.   Sorrows shake it!
         Devil take it!
SIR RODERIC.   Must, perforce, or yea or nay—
CHORUS.   Yea or naying
         Be obeying!
SIR RODERIC.   Do a deadly crime each day!

CHORUS.   Fire and thunder,
         We knocked under—
   Some atrocious crime committed
   Daily ere the world we quitted!

SIR RODERIC.   Beware! beware! beware!

ROBIN.   Gaunt vision, who art thou
         That thus, with icy glare
            And stern relentless brow,
            Appearest, who knows how?

SIR RODERIC.   I am the spectre of the late
         Sir Roderic Murgatroyd,
      Who comes to warn thee that thy fate
         Thou cans't not now avoid.

ROBIN.   Alas, poor ghost!

SIR RODERIC.   The pity you
          Express, for nothing goes:
          We spectres are a jollier crew
          Than you, perhaps, suppose!

CHORUS.   Yes! yes!
          We spectres are a jollier crew
          Than you, perhaps, suppose!
          Ha! ha!

SONG — SIR RODERIC.

When the night wind howls in the chimney cowls,
     and the bat in the moonlight flies,
And inky clouds, like funeral shrouds, sail over
     the midnight skies—
When the footpads quail at the night-bird's wail,
     and black dogs bay the moon,
Then is the spectres' holiday—then is the ghosts'
     high-noon!

CHORUS.   Ha! ha!
          Then is the ghosts' high-noon!

As the sob of the breeze sweeps over the trees and
     the mists lie low on the fen,
From grey tomb-stones are gathered the bones
     that once were women and men,
And away they go, with a mop and a mow, to the
     revel that ends too soon,
For cockcrow limits our holiday—the dead of the
     night's high-noon!

CHORUS.   Ha! ha!
          The dead of the night's high-noon!

And then each ghost with his ladye-toast to their
     churchyard beds takes flight.
With a kiss, perhaps, on her lantern chaps, and
     a grisly grim, "good-night";
Till the welcome knell of the midnight bell rings
     forth its jolliest tune,
And ushers our next high holiday—the dead of
     the night's high-noon!

CHORUS.   Ha! ha!
          The dead of the night's high-noon!

ROBIN.   I recognize you now—you are the Picture that hangs at the end of the gallery.

SIR RODERIC.   In a bad light. I am.

ROBIN.   Are you considered a good likeness?

SIR RODERIC.   Pretty well. Flattering.

ROBIN.   Because as a work of art you are poor.

1ST GHOST.   That's true.

2ND GHOST.   No doubt.

3RD GHOST.   Wants tone.

4TH GHOST.   Not mellow enough.

SIR RODERIC.   I am crude in colour, but I have only been painted ten years. In a couple of centuries I shall be an Old Master, and then you will be sorry you spoke lightly of me.

ROBIN.   And may I ask why you have left your frames?

SIR RODERIC.   It is our duty to see that our successors commit their daily crimes in a conscientious and workmanlike fashion. It is our duty to remind you that you are evading the conditions under which you are permitted to exist.

ROBIN.   Really I don't know what you'd have. I've only been a bad baronet a week, and I've committed a crime punctually every day.

SIR RODERIC.   Let us enquire into this. Monday?

ROBIN.   Monday was a Bank Holiday.

SIR RODERIC.   True. Tuesday?

ROBIN.   On Tuesday I made a false income tax return.

ALL.   Ha! ha!

1ST GHOST.   That's nothing.

2ND GHOST.   Nothing at all.

3RD GHOST.   Everybody does that.

4TH GHOST.   It's expected of you.

SIR RODERIC.   Wednesday?

ROBIN (*melodramatically*).   On Wednesday, I forged a will.

SIR RODERIC.   Whose will?

ROBIN.   My own.

SIR RODERIC.   My good sir, you can't forge your own will!

ROBIN.   Can't I though! I like that! I *did!* Besides, if a man can't forge his own will, whose will can he forge?

1ST GHOST.   There's something in that.

2ND GHOST.   Yes, it seems reasonable.

3RD GHOST.   At first sight it does.

4TH GHOST.   Fallacy somewhere, I fancy!

ROBIN.   A man can do what he likes with his own?

SIR RODERIC.   I suppose he can.

ROBIN.   Well then, he can forge his own will, stoopid! On Thursday I shot a fox.

1ST GHOST.   Hear, hear!

SIR RODERIC.   That's better (*addressing Ghosts*). Pass the fox, I think? (*They assent.*) Yes, pass the fox. Friday?

ROBIN.   On Friday I forged a cheque.

SIR RODERIC.   Whose cheque?

ROBIN.   Gideon Crawle's.

SIR RODERIC.   But Gideon Crawle hasn't a banker.

ROBIN.   I didn't say I forged his banker—I said I forged his cheque.

1ST GHOST.   That's true.

2ND GHOST.   Yes, it seems reasonable.

3RD GHOST.   At first glance it does.

4TH GHOST.   Fallacy somewhere!

ROBIN.   On Saturday I disinherited my only son.

SIR RODERIC.   But you haven't got a son.

ROBIN.   No—not yet. I disinherited him in advance, to save time. You see—by this arrangement—he'll be born ready disinherited.

SIR RODERIC.   I see. But I don't think you can do that.

ROBIN.   My good sir, if I can't disinherit my own unborn son, whose unborn son can I disinherit?

1ST GHOST.   That's right enough.

2ND GHOST.   Yes, it seems reasonable.

3RD GHOST.   At first sight it does.

4TH GHOST.   Fallacy somewhere!

SIR RODERIC.   Yes, these arguments sound very well, but I can't help thinking that, if they were reduced to syllogistic form, they wouldn't hold water. Now quite understand us. We are foggy, but we don't permit our fogginess to be presumed upon. Unless you undertake to—well, suppose we say, carry off a lady? (*Addressing Ghosts.*) Those who are in favour of his carrying off a lady—(*all hold up their hands except a Bishop*). Those of the contrary opinion? (*Bishop holds up his hands.*) Oh, you're never satisfied! Yes, unless you undertake to carry off a lady at once—I don't care what lady—any lady—choose your lady—you perish in inconceivable agonies.

ROBIN.   Carry off a lady? Certainly not, on any account. I've the greatest respect for ladies, and I wouldn't do anything of the kind for worlds! No, no. I'm not that kind of baronet, I assure you! If that's all you've got to say, you'd better go back to your frames.

SIR RODERIC.   Very good—then let the agonies commence.

(GHOSTS *make passes.* ROBIN *begins to writhe in agony.*)

ROBIN.   Oh! Oh! Don't do that! I can't stand it!

SIR RODERIC.   Painful, isn't it? It gets worse by degrees.

ROBIN.   Oh—oh! Stop a bit! Stop it, will you? I want to speak.

(SIR RODERIC *makes signs to Ghosts, who resume their attitudes.*)

SIR RODERIC.   Better?

ROBIN.   Yes—better now! Whew!

SIR RODERIC.   Well, do you consent?

ROBIN.   But it's such an ungentlemanly thing to do!

SIR RODERIC.   As you please. (*To Ghosts.*) Carry on!

ROBIN.   Stop—I can't stand it! I agree! I promise! It shall be done!

SIR RODERIC.   To-day?

ROBIN.   To-day!

SIR RODERIC.   At once?

ROBIN.   At once! I retract! I apologize! I had no idea it was anything like that!

CHORUS.

He yields! He answers to our call!
        We do not ask for more.
A sturdy fellow, after all,
        This latest Ruddygore!
All perish in unheard-of woe
        Who dare our wills defy;
We want your pardon, ere we go,
For having agonized you so—
        So pardon us—
        So pardon us—
        So pardon us—
                Or die!

ROBIN.   I pardon you!
                I pardon you!

ALL.   He pardons us—
                        Hurrah!
(*The Ghosts return to their frames.*)

CHORUS.   Painted emblems of a race,
        All accurst in days of yore
Each to his accustomed place
        Steps unwillingly, once more!
(*By this time the Ghosts have changed to pictures again.* ROBIN *is overcome by emotion.*)

Enter ADAM.

ADAM.   My poor master, you are not well—

ROBIN.   Gideon Crawle, it won't do—I've seen 'em—all my ancestors—they're just gone. They say that I must do something desperate at once, or perish in horrible agonies. Go—go to yonder village—carry off a maiden—bring her here at once—anyone—I don't care which—

ADAM.   But—

ROBIN.   Not a word, but obey! Fly! (*Exit* ADAM.)

RECITATIVE AND SONG — ROBIN.

Away, Remorse!
        Compunction, hence!
Go, Moral Force!
        Go, Penitence!
To Virtue's plea
        A long farewell—
Propriety,
        I ring your knell!

Come guiltiness of deadliest hue,
Come desperate deeds of derring-do!

For thirty-five years I've been sober and wary—
My favourite tipple came straight from a dairy—
I kept guinea-pigs and a Belgian canary—
    A squirrel, white mice, and a small black-
       and-tan.
I played on the flute, and I drank lemon squashes—
I wore chamois leather, thick boots, and macin-
       toshes,
And things that will some day be known as ga-
       loshes,
    The type of a highly respectable man!

For the rest of my life I abandon propriety—
Visit the haunts of Bohemian society,
Wax-works, and other resorts of impiety,
    Placed by the moralist under a ban.
My ways must be those of a regular satyr,
At carryings-on I must be a first-rater—
Go night after night to a wicked theayter—
    It's hard on a highly respectable man!

Well, the man who has spent the first half of his
       tether,
On all the bad deeds you can bracket together,
Then goes and repents—in his cap it's a feather—
    Society pets him as much as it can.
It's a comfort to think, if I now go a cropper,
I sha'n't, on the whole, have done more that's im-
       proper
Than he who was once an abandoned tip-topper,
    But now is a highly respectable man!
                                   (*Exit* ROBIN.)

Enter SIR DESPARD *and* MARGARET. *They are both
dressed in sober black of formal cut, and present
a strong contrast to their appearance in Act I.*

DUET.

SIR DESPARD. I once was a very abandoned per-
    son—
MARGARET. Making the most of evil chances.
SIR DESPARD. Nobody could conceive a worse
    'un—
MARGARET. Even in all the old romances.
SIR DESPARD. I blush for my wild extravagances,
          But be so kind
          To bear in mind,
MARGARET. We were the victims of circum-
    stances!   (*Dance.*)
    That is one of our blameless dances.

MARGARET. I was an exceedingly odd young
    lady—
SIR DESPARD. Suffering much from spleen and
    vapours.

MARGARET. Clergymen thought my conduct
    shady—
SIR DESPARD. She didn't spend much upon linen-
    drapers.
MARGARET. It certainly entertained the gapers.
          My ways were strange
          Beyond all range—
SIR DESPARD. And paragraphs got into all the
    papers.   (*Dance.*)

SIR DESPARD. We only cut respectable capers.

SIR DESPARD. I've given up all my wild pro-
    ceedings.
MARGARET. My taste for a wandering life is
    waning.
SIR DESPARD. Now I'm a dab at penny readings.
MARGARET. They are not remarkably entertaining.
SIR DESPARD. A moderate livelihood we're
    gaining.
MARGARET.   In fact we rule
          A Sunday School.
SIR DESPARD. The duties are dull, but I'm not
    complaining,   (*Dance.*)

    This sort of thing takes a deal of training!

SIR DESPARD. We have been married a week.
MARGARET. One happy, happy week!
SIR DESPARD. Our new life—
MARGARET. Is delightful indeed!
SIR DESPARD. So calm!
MARGARET. So pure!
SIR DESPARD. So peaceful!
MARGARET. So unimpassioned! (*Wildly.*) Master,
all this I owe to you! See, I am no longer wild and
untidy. My hair is combed. My face is washed. My
boots fit!
SIR DESPARD. Margaret, don't. Pray restrain
yourself. Be demure, I beg.
MARGARET. Demure it is. (*Resumes her quiet
manner.*)
SIR DESPARD. Then make it so. Remember, you
are now a district visitor.
MARGARET. A gentle district visitor!
SIR DESPARD. You are orderly, methodical, neat;
you have your emotions well under control.
MARGARET. I have! (*Wildly.*) Master, when I
think of all you have done for me, I fall at your
feet. I embrace your ankles. I hug your knees!
(*Doing so.*)
SIR DESPARD. Hush. This is not well. This is cal-
culated to provoke remark. Be composed, I beg!
MARGARET. Ah! you are angry with poor little
Mad Margaret!

SIR DESPARD.   No, not angry; but a district visitor should learn to eschew melodrama. Visit the poor, by all means, and give them tea and barley-water, but don't do it as if you were administering a bowl of deadly nightshade. It upsets them. Then when you nurse sick people, and find them not as well as could be expected, why go into hysterics?

MARGARET.   Why not?

SIR DESPARD.   Because it's too jumpy for a sick room. Then again, as I've frequently told you, it is quite possible to take too much medicine.

MARGARET.   What, when you're ill?

SIR DESPARD.   Certainly. These are valuable remedies but they should be administered with discretion.

MARGARET.   How strange! Oh, Master! Master! —how shall I express the all-absorbing gratitude that—(*about to throw herself at his feet*).

SIR DESPARD.   Now! (*Warningly.*)

MARGARET.   Yes, I know, dear—it sha'n't occur again. (*He is seated—she sits on the ground by him.*) Shall I tell you one of poor Mad Margaret's odd thoughts? Well, then, when I am lying awake at night, and the pale moonlight streams through the latticed casement, strange fancies crowd upon my poor mad brain, and I sometimes think that if we could hit upon some word for you to use whenever I am about to relapse—some word that teems with hidden meaning—like "Basingstoke" —it might recall me to my saner self. For, after all, I am only Mad Margaret! Daft Meg! Poor Peg! He! he! he!

SIR DESPARD.   Poor child, she wanders! But soft— someone comes—Margaret—pray recollect yourself—Basingstoke, I beg! Margaret, if you don't Basingstoke at once, I shall be seriously angry.

MARGARET (*recovering herself*).   Basingstoke it is!

SIR DESPARD.   Then make it so.

Enter ROBIN. *He starts on seeing them.*

ROBIN.   Despard! And his young wife! This visit is unexpected.

MARGARET.   Shall I fly at him? Shall I tear him limb from limb? Shall I render him asunder? Say but the word and—

SIR DESPARD.   Basingstoke!

MARGARET (*suddenly demure*).   Basingstoke it is!

SIR DESPARD (*aside*).   Then make it so. (*Aloud.*) My brother—I call you brother, still, despite your horrible profligacy—we have come to urge you to abandon the evil courses to which you have committed yourself, and at any cost to become a pure and blameless ratepayer.

ROBIN.   That's all very well, but you seem to forget that on the day I reform I perish in excruciating torment.

SIR DESPARD.   Oh, better that than pursue a course of life-long villainy. Oh, seek refuge in death, I implore you!

MARGARET.   Why not die? Others have died and no one has cared. You will not be mourned.

SIR DESPARD.   True—you could die so well!

ROBIN.   You didn't seem to be of this opinion when *you* were a bad baronet.

SIR DESPARD.   No, because *I* had no good brother at *my* elbow to check *me* when about to do wrong.

ROBIN.   A home-thrust indeed! (*Aloud.*) But I've done no wrong yet.

MARGARET (*wildly*).   No wrong! He has done no wrong! Did you hear that!

SIR DESPARD.   Basingstoke.

MARGARET (*recovering herself*).   Basingstoke it is.

SIR DESPARD.   My brother—I still call you brother, you observe—you forget that you have been, in the eye of the law, a Bad Baronet of Ruddygore for ten years—and you are therefore responsible—in the eye of the law—for all the misdeeds committed by the unhappy gentleman who occupied your place.

ROBIN.   Meaning you?

SIR DESPARD.   Meaning me.

ROBIN.   I see! Bless my heart, I never thought of that! Was he—was I very bad?

SIR DESPARD.   Awful. Wasn't he? (*To* MARGARET.)

MARGARET.   Desperate! Oh, you were a flirt!

ROBIN.   And I've been going on like this for how long?

SIR DESPARD.   Ten years! Think of all the atrocities you have committed—by attorney, as it were —during that period. Remember how you trifled with this poor child's affections—how you raised her hopes on high (don't cry, my love—Basingstoke, you know), only to trample them in the dust when they were at the very zenith of their fulness. Oh fie, sir, fie—she trusted you!

ROBIN.   Meaning *you?*

SIR DESPARD.   Nothing of the kind, sir. I was simply your representative.

ROBIN.   Well, meaning *us,* then. What a scoundrel we must have been! There, there—don't cry, my dear (*to* MARGARET, *who is sobbing on* ROBIN'S *breast*), it's all right now. Birmingham you know—Birmingham—

MARGARET (*sobbing*). It's Ba—Ba—Basingstoke!

ROBIN.   Basingstoke! of course it is—Basingstoke.

MARGARET.   Then make it so!

ROBIN.   There, there—it's all right—he's married you now—that is, *I've* married you (*turning to* DESPARD)—I say, which of us has married her?

SIR DESPARD.   Oh, *I've* married her.

ROBIN (*aside*). Oh, I'm glad of that. (*To* MARGARET.) Yes, *he's* married you now (*passing her over to* DESPARD), and anything more disreputable than my conduct seems to have been I've never even heard of. But my mind is made up—I *will* defy my ancestors. I *will* refuse to obey their behests—thus, by courting death, atone in some degree for the infamy of my career!

MARGARET.   I knew it—I knew it—God bless you—(*hysterically*).

SIR DESPARD.   Basingstoke!

MARGARET.   Basingstoke it is! (*Recovers herself.*)

PATTER-TRIO.
ROBIN, DESPARD, *and* MARGARET.

ROBIN.   My eyes are fully open to my awful situation—
  I shall go at once to Roderic and make him an oration.
  I shall tell him I've recovered my forgotten moral senses,
  And I don't care two-pence halfpenny for any consequences.
  Now I do not want to perish by the sword or by the dagger,
  But a martyr may indulge a little pardonable swagger,
  And a word or two of compliment my vanity would flatter,
  But I've got to die to-morrow, so it really doesn't matter!

SIR DESPARD.   So it really doesn't matter—

MARGARET.   So it really doesn't matter—

ALL.   So it really doesn't matter, matter, matter, matter, matter!

MARGARET.   If it were not a little mad and generally silly,
  I should give you my advice upon the subject, willy-nilly;
  I should show you in a moment how to grapple with the question,
  And you'd really be astonished at the force of my suggestion.
  On the subject I shall write you a most valuable letter,
  Full of excellent suggestions, when I feel a little better;
  But at present I'm afraid I am as mad as any hatter,
  So I'll keep 'em to myself, for my opinion doesn't matter!

SIR DESPARD.   Her opinion doesn't matter—

ROBIN.   Her opinion doesn't matter—

ALL.   Her opinion doesn't matter, matter, matter, matter, matter!

SIR DESPARD.   If I had been so lucky as to have a steady brother
  Who could talk to me as we are talking now to one another—
  Who could give me good advice when he discovered I was erring
  (Which is just the very favour which on you I am conferring),
  My story would have made a rather interesting idyll,
  And I might have lived and died a very decent indiwiddle.
  This particularly rapid, unintelligible patter
  Isn't generally heard, and if it is it doesn't matter!

ROBIN.   If it is it doesn't matter—

MARGARET.   If it ain't it doesn't matter—

ALL.   If it is it doesn't matter, matter, matter, matter, matter!
        (*Exeunt* SIR DESPARD *and* MARGARET.)

Enter ADAM.

ADAM (*guiltily*).   Master—the deed is done!
ROBIN.   What deed?
ADAM.   She is here—alone, unprotected—
ROBIN.   Who?
ADAM.   The maiden. I've carried her off—I had a hard task, for she fought like a tiger-cat!
ROBIN.   Great heaven, I had forgotten her! I had

hoped to have died unspotted by crime, but I am foiled again—and by a tiger-cat! Produce her—and leave us!

ADAM *introduces* OLD HANNAH, *very much excited, and exits.*

ROBIN. Dame Hannah! This is—this is not what I expected.

HANNAH. Well sir, and what would you with me? Oh, you have begun bravely—bravely indeed! Unappalled by the calm dignity of blameless womanhood, your minion has torn me from my spotless home, and dragged me, blindfold and shrieking, through hedges, over stiles, and across a very difficult country, and left me, helpless and trembling, at your mercy! Yet not helpless, coward sir, for approach one step—nay, but the twentieth part of one poor inch—and this poniard (*produces a very small dagger*) shall teach ye what it is to lay unholy hands on old Stephen Trusty's daughter!

ROBIN. Madam, I am extremely sorry for this. It is not at all what I intended. Circumstances of a delicate nature compelled me to request your presence in this confounded castle for a brief period—but anything more correct—more deeply respectful than my intentions towards you, it would be impossible for anyone—however particular—to desire.

HANNAH (*wildly*). Am I a toy—a bauble—a pretty plaything—to grace your roystering banquets and amuse your ribald friends? Am I a gewgaw to wile away an idle hour withal, and then be cast aside like some old glove, when the whim quits you? Harkye, sir, do you take me for a gewgaw of this description?

ROBIN (*appalled*). Certainly not—nothing of the kind—anything more profoundly respectful—

HANNAH. Bah, I am not to be tricked by smooth

words, hypocrite! But be warned in time, for there are, without, a hundred gallant hearts whose trusty blades would hack him limb from limb who dared to lay unholy hands on old Stephen Trusty's daughter!

ROBIN. And this is what it is to embark upon a career of unlicensed pleasure!

(HANNAH, *who has taken a formidable dagger from one of the armed figures, throws her small dagger to* ROBIN.)

HANNAH. Harkye, miscreant, you have secured me, and I am your poor prisoner; but if you think I cannot take care of myself you are very much mistaken. Now then, it's one to one, and let the best man win! (*Making for him.*)

ROBIN (*in an agony of terror*). Don't! don't look at me like that! I can't bear it! Roderic! Uncle! Save me!

RODERIC *appears, rising through trap as far as his waist. Red flames accompany him.*

SIR RODERIC. What is the matter? Have you carried her off?

ROBIN. I have—she is there—look at her—she terrifies me! Come quite up and save me!

SIR RODERIC (*looking at* HANNAH). Little Nannikin!

HANNAH (*amazed*). Roddy-doddy!

SIR RODERIC. My own old love! Why how came *you* here?

HANNAH. This brute—he carried me off! Bodily! But I'll show him! (*About to rush at* ROBIN.)

SIR RODERIC. Stop! (*To* ROBIN.) What do you mean by carrying off this lady? Are you aware that, once upon a time she was engaged to be married to me? I'm very angry—very angry indeed.

ROBIN. Now I hope this will be a lesson to you in future, not to—

SIR RODERIC. Hold your tongue, sir.

ROBIN. Yes, uncle.

SIR RODERIC. Has he treated you with proper re-

spect since you've been here, Nannikin?

HANNAH. Pretty well, Roddy. Come quite up, dear!

SIR RODERIC. No, I don't think I shall.

ROBIN. No, I don't think I should.

SIR RODERIC. Hold your tongue, sir.

ROBIN. Yes, uncle.

SIR RODERIC. I'm very much annoyed. Have you given him any encouragement?

HANNAH (to ROBIN). Have I given you any encouragement? Frankly, now, have I?

ROBIN. No. Frankly, you have not. Anything more scrupulously correct than your conduct, it would be impossible to desire.

HANNAH. There now—come up, dear!

SIR RODERIC (reluctantly). Very well, but you don't deserve it, you know. (Comes up.)

ROBIN. Before we go any further, I am anxious to assure you on my honour as a gentleman, and with all the emphasis at my command, that anything more profoundly respectful—

SIR RODERIC. You go away.

ROBIN. Yes, uncle. (Exit ROBIN.)

SIR RODERIC. Little Nannikin!

HANNAH. Roddy-doddy!

SIR RODERIC. This is a strange meeting after so many years!

HANNAH. Very. I thought you were dead.

SIR RODERIC. I am. I died ten years ago.

HANNAH. And are you pretty comfortable?

ROBIN. Pretty well—that is—yes, pretty well.

HANNAH. You don't deserve to be, you bad, bad boy, for you behaved very shabbily to poor old Stephen Trusty's daughter. For I loved you all the while, dear; and it made me dreadfully unhappy to hear of all your goings-on, you bad, bad boy!

BALLAD — HANNAH.

There grew a little flower
    'Neath a great oak tree:
When the tempest 'gan to lower,
    Little heeded she:
No need had she to cower,
For she dreaded not its power—
She was happy in the bower
    Of her great oak tree!
      Sing hey,
      Lackaday!
Let the tears fall free
For the pretty little flower and the great
    oak tree!

BOTH.   Sing hey,
        Lackaday, &c.

When she found that he was fickle,
    Was that great oak tree,
She was in a pretty pickle,
    As she well might be—
But his gallantries were mickle,
For Death followed with his sickle,
And her tears began to trickle
    For her great oak tree!
      Sing hey,
      Lackaday! &c.

Said she, "He loved me never,
    Did that great oak tree,
But I'm neither rich nor clever,
    And so why should he?
But though fate our fortunes sever,
To be constant I'll endeavour,
Aye, for ever and for ever,
    To my great oak tree!"
      Sing hey,
      Lackaday! &c.
    (Falls weeping on RODERIC's bosom.)

SIR RODERIC. Little Nannikin!

HANNAH. Roddy-doddy!

SIR RODERIC. It's not too late, is it?

HANNAH. Oh Roddy! (Bashfully.)

SIR RODERIC. I'm quite respectable now, you know.

HANNAH. But you're a ghost, ain't you?

SIR RODERIC. Well, yes—a kind of ghost.

HANNAH. But what would be my legal status as a ghost's wife?

SIR RODERIC. It would be a very respectable position.

HANNAH. But I should be the wife of a dead husband, Roddy!

SIR RODERIC. No doubt.

HANNAH. But the wife of a dead husband is a widow, Roddy!

SIR RODERIC. I suppose she is.

HANNAH. And a widow is at liberty to marry again, Roddy!

SIR RODERIC. Dear me, yes—that's awkward. I never thought of that.

HANNAH. No, Roddy—I thought you hadn't.

SIR RODERIC. When you've been a ghost for a considerable time it's astonishing how foggy you become!

Enter ROBIN, excitedly, followed by Chorus of Bridesmaids.

ROBIN. Stop a bit—both of you.

SIR RODERIC. This intrusion is unmannerly.

HANNAH. I'm surprised at you.

ROBIN. I can't stop to apologize—an idea has

just occurred to me. A Baronet of Ruddygore can only die through refusing to commit his daily crime.

SIR RODERIC. No doubt.

ROBIN. Therefore, to refuse to commit a daily crime is tantamount to suicide!

SIR RODERIC. It would seem so.

ROBIN. But suicide is, itself, a crime—and so, by your own showing, you ought none of you to have ever died at all!

SIR RODERIC. I see—I understand! We are all practically alive!

ROBIN. Every man jack of you!

SIR RODERIC. My brother ancestors! Down from your frames! (*The Ancestors descend.*) You believe yourselves to be dead—you may take it from me that you're not, and an application to the Supreme Court is all that is necessary to prove that you never ought to have died at all!

(*The Ancestors embrace the Bridesmaids.*)

Enter RICHARD *and* ROSE, *also* SIR DESPARD *and* MARGARET.

ROBIN. Rose, when you believed that I was a simple farmer, I believe you loved me?

ROSE. Madly, passionately!

ROBIN. But when I became a bad baronet, you very properly loved Richard instead?

ROSE. Passionately, madly!

ROBIN. But if I should turn out *not* to be a bad baronet after all, how would you love me then?

ROSE. Madly, passionately!

ROBIN. As before?

ROSE. Why, of course!

ROBIN. My darling! (*They embrace.*)

CHORUS.

Hail the Bridegroom—hail the Bride!—

RICHARD (*interrupting them*). Will you be quiet? (*To* ROBIN.) Belay, my lad, belay, you don't understand!

ROSE. Oh sir, belay, if it's absolutely necessary.

ROBIN. Belay? Certainly not. (*To* RICHARD.) You see, it's like this—as all my ancestors are alive, it follows, as a matter of course, that the eldest of them is the family baronet, and I revert to my former condition.

RICHARD (*going to* ZORAH). Well, I think it's exceedingly unfair!

ROBIN (*To* FIRST GHOST). Here, great uncle, allow me to present you. (*To the others.*) Sir Ruthven Murgatroyd, Baronet, of Ruddygore!

ALL. Hurrah!

FIRST GHOST. Fallacy somewhere!

FINALE.

ROBIN. Having been a wicked baronet a week,
  Once again a modest livelihood I seek;
    Agricultural employment
    Is to me a keen enjoyment,
  For I'm naturally diffident and meek!

ROSE. When a man has been a naughty baronet,
  And expresses his repentance and regret,
    You should help him, if you're able,
    Like the mousie in the fable,
  That's the teaching of my Book of Etiquette.

RICHARD. If you ask me why I do not pipe my eye,
  Like an honest British sailor, I reply,
    That with Zorah for my missis,
    There'll be bread and cheese and kisses,
  Which is just the sort of ration I enjye!

SIR DESPARD *and* MARGARET. Prompted by a keen desire to evoke,
  All the blessed calm of matrimony's yoke,
    We shall toddle off to-morrow,
    From this scene of sin and sorrow,
  For to settle in the town of Basingstoke!

ALL.   For happy the lily
              That's kissed by the bee;
            And, sipping tranquilly,
              Quite happy is he;
            And happy the filly
              That neighs in her pride;
            But happier than any,
            A pound to a penny,
            A lover is, when he
              Embraces his bride!

CURTAIN.

Postscript

THE OFFENDING "Y" in Ruddygore was changed to "I" in the third edition of the libretto and in all newspaper advertising beginning February 2, 1887, eleven days after the opening.

The first act of *Ruddygore* remained unscathed through the spate of textual alterations that followed immediately the opera's first night. In fact, it has not varied appreciably in any later editions of the libretto. But in current D'Oyly Carte production practice the duet for Richard and Rose, "The battle's roar is over, O my love!", is omitted from performance, even though still retained in the libretto. The second-act text, on the other hand, underwent extensive changes in the first ten days of performance; most of these concerned dialog rather than lyrics.

At the beginning of Act II the duet between Robin and Old Adam was cut from six to three verses, losing the last three that were sung at the initial performance. One reason for this change was Gilbert's decision to have Robin's faithful servant keep the name Adam throughout the opera, instead of assuming the name Gideon Crawle as he did in the second act as originally performed. This change was made in the second edition of the libretto in all but one instance. That one (page 297), "Gideon Crawle, it won't do— I've seen 'em . . . ," was overlooked and retained through all editions of the libretto and even in the *Complete Operas* as published by Macmillan (1926) and Random House (1932). In the latest Chappell libretto it has at long last been corrected.

The duet for Richard and Rose, "Happily coupled are we, You see," is confined by current production practice solely to Richard's verse, omitting Rose's second verse rejoinder.

Only ten performances after the first night, Gilbert made two important changes in lyrics. He cut out entirely the second verse to Rose Maybud's ballad, "In bygone days I had thy love" (page 295), and he substituted a completely different three-verse patter-song to take the place of Robin's "For thirty-five years I've been sober and wary" (page 298). Between these he had trimmed away the lines for Sir Roderic and spectral chorus immediately following his descent from his frame.

It is likely that the substitution of the patter-song was the outcome of Gilbert's dissatisfaction at first leveled at the ten-line recitative preceding Robin's song. He had written Sullivan a letter on January 23, the day after the first night, in which he stated: "I can't help thinking that the second act would be greatly improved if the recitation [*sic*] before Grossmith's song were omitted, and the song reset to an air that would admit of his singing it desperately—almost in a passion—the torrent of which would take him off the stage at the end. . . . I feel this so strongly that I send this by hand, so that if you are of my opinion the matter could be put in hand at once, and perhaps sung on Wednesday next."

Sullivan must have disagreed, for no changes were made in either recitative or song in the three issues of the second edition that the busy publishers, Chappell & Co., turned out in what can be estimated to have been the five-performance-night interval from Thursday, January 27, through Tuesday, February 1. But in the third edition, February 2, and doubtless at that night's performance, the substitute song—"Henceforth all the crimes that I find in the *Times*"—was sung by Robin, following the same recitative as in the original edition that had provoked the author's initial displeasure.

The brunt of this important change was not borne by Grossmith but by his understudy, the till-then-unknown Henry Lytton, as an acute attack of peritonitis had suddenly forced the withdrawal of Grossmith after the opera had run only one week. Lytton performed the role of Robin from Monday, January 31, till mid-February.

The latest published text and recent performance usage pass directly from Robin's line, "Not a word, but obey! Fly!" to the entrance of Despard and Margaret. Even so, as a matter of interest and completeness, the substituted patter-song is here reproduced:

Henceforth all the crimes that I find in the *Times*,
    I've promised to perpetrate daily;
To-morrow I start, with a petrified heart,
    On a regular course of Old Bailey.
There's confidence tricking, bad coin, pocket-picking,
    And several other disgraces—
There's postage-stamp prigging, and then thimble-rigging,
    The three-card delusion at races!
Oh! a baronet's rank is exceedingly nice,
But the title's uncommonly dear at the price!

Ye well-to-do squires, who live in the shires,

Where petty distinctions are vital,
Who found Athenaeums and local museums,
    With views to a baronet's title—
Ye butchers and bakers and candlestick makers
    Who sneer at all things that are tradey—
Whose middle-class lives are embarrassed by wives
    Who long to parade as "My Lady,"
Oh! allow me to offer a word of advice,
The title's uncommonly dear at the price!

Ye supple M.P.'s, who go down on your knees,
    Your precious identity sinking,
And vote black or white as your leaders indite
    (Which saves you the trouble of thinking),
For your country's good fame, her repute, or her
        shame,
    You don't care the snuff of a candle—
But you're paid for your game when you're told
        that your name
    Will be graced by a baronet's handle—
Oh! allow me to give *you* a word of advice—
The title's uncommonly dear at the price!

                                    (*Exit* ROBIN.)

The duet for Despard and Margaret, "I once was a very abandoned person" (page 298), suffered a small alteration after the first night, which appears in the second and subsequent editions of the libretto. The reviewer for the *Weekly Dispatch,* who attended the opera during its first week (evidently armed with a first-edition libretto), noted in his January 31 issue: "Mr. Gilbert is very respectful to the susceptibilities of the religious public. When Miss Jessie Bond, attired in Methodistical garments, dances her grotesque dance with Mr. Barrington, she ought to sing, according to the book: 'And now we rule A Sunday school.' But she sings 'A national school' instead. No doubt the change was made at the last moment in deference to the feelings of Sunday-school teachers, who are sure to be present in great numbers at the first morning performance [i.e., matinee] of *Ruddygore.*"

A few dialog cuts follow, up to the ballad by Dame Hannah; and Sir Roderic's entrance, when summoned by his terrified nephew, is not made through a trap, but by stepping down from his portrait. After this ballad there are many changes in the first-night libretto. Without further dialog between Hannah and Roderic, Sir Ruthven enters, followed by all the characters and the chorus. His subsequent argument, couched in Gilbertian logic, is directed solely at his uncle Roderic, and not at the entire group of Ancestors who have not been brought back to life this second time. The Finale loses its four five-line solo verses, and the opera ends with the original closing chorus, which has itself undergone a few minor word-changes.

This drastic cutting of the whole last half of the second act succeeded in reducing the original 48-page libretto to 46 pages in the editions that paralleled the 1887 run. The most recent text is of 47 pages; and in the second act all references to "Robin," both in stage-directions and in dialog, are changed to "Sir Ruthven."

THE YEOMEN OF THE GUARD

Introduction

BOTH D'OYLY CARTE and Arthur Sullivan got what each most wanted for Christmas 1887, and Gilbert starred in the role of Santa Claus. The occasion was no holiday panto-mime but a Christmas morning meeting of the three partners at Sullivan's Queen's Mansions flat. For Carte, Gilbert had a libretto idea acceptable to Sullivan; for Sullivan he had a plot that was "an entirely new departure," close to the grand opera format so long the composer's goal. A few cheerful words in Sullivan's diary for Christmas day describe the incident:

Gilbert read plot of new piece (Tower of London); immensely pleased with it. Pretty story, no topsy-turvydom, very human and funny also.

There was no question that D'Oyly Carte badly needed this assurance of further continuity in his Gilbert and Sullivan collaboration. *Ruddigore* had not lived up to initial hopes and had been withdrawn after its 288th performance, November 5. A revived *H.M.S. Pinafore* launched its Savoy debut a week later with Sir Arthur in the pit. It was warmly welcomed but still could not be expected to enjoy the run of a new opera. That there was no ground for renewed creative agreement between librettist and composer had been repeatedly and depressingly manifest throughout the summer of 1887 and, in fact, right down to mid-October, when rehearsals for the stopgap revival of *Pinafore* were already under way. As usual Gilbert had been trying stubbornly to get Sullivan to accept a variant of his "lozenge plot." Sullivan, in resisting this formula, was more than ever insistent that he did not wish to set "the old story over again. . . . It is a 'puppet show,' and not human" he wrote in his diary, as late as September 4. "It is impossible to feel any sympathy with a single person."

At this critical moment in Savoy opera history —which might well have seen the skein break at ten collaborations, with the final four operas never to be written—it was Gilbert whose creative perseverance broke the deadlock. In a manner of speaking he swallowed his own "lozenge plot." "Gilbert told me that he had *given up* [the italics are Sullivan's, in his diary entry of mid-October] the subject over which there had been so much difficulty and dispute . . . and had found another about The Tower of London, an entirely new departure. Much relieved."

Gilbert's initial story was titled *The Tower of London.* Later it became *The Tower Warder;* and in September Gilbert wrote Sullivan: "The more I think of it, the more convinced I am that *The Beefeaters* is the name for the new piece. It is a good, sturdy, solid name. . . . *The Tower Warder* is nothing. No one knows (but the few) that Beefeaters are called Tower Warders." Sullivan, probably still smarting from the public reaction against the title *Ruddygore,* shied away from this suggestion. Many years later Gilbert explained the fate of his sturdy, solid name: "I had christened the piece *The Beefeaters,* but Sir Arthur Sullivan considered *The Beefeaters* to be an ugly word; so at his urgent instance the title was altered to *The Yeomen of the Guard.*"

"Judging by the crisp and epigrammatic title, *The Yeomen of the Guard; or, The Merryman and his Maid,*" jeered *Punch,* reviewing with heavy sarcasm the first-night performance, Wednesday, October 3, 1888, "the librettist seems, up to the last moment, to have been undecided as to what he should call his new and original infant." This keynote of uncertainty suggested by *Punch* appears to have been a prime factor throughout the gestation period and on the very day of delivery. It seems abundantly clear that Gilbert himself was feverishly uncertain of his departure from the tried and true formulas of topsy-turvydom. For once his Savoy opera libretto involved the behavior of real people in well-known surroundings, rather than the antics of comic caricatures in wholly fanciful or burlesqued settings. It follows logically that both cast and audience must have shared to some extent this unsettled state of mind. As *Punch* argued—"The fault of the representation is that . . . none of the actors play with conviction. They seem uncertain as to the character of the piece— is it serious, or isn't it?"

Even as late as that Wednesday, Gilbert was concerned that the comic features of his plot were too little and too late. It is extraordinary that the following letter could have passed between librettist and composer on the very morning of their production's debut:

Dear Sullivan,—

I desire before the production of our piece to place upon record the conviction that I have so frequently expressed to you in the course of rehearsal, that unless Meryll's introduced and wholly irrelevant song is withdrawn, the success of the first act will be most seriously imperilled.

Let me recapitulate:

The Act commences with Phoebe's song— *tearful in character.* This is followed by entrance of wardens—*serious and martial in character.* This is followed by Dame Carruthers' "Tower" song—*grim in character.* This is followed by trio for Meryll, Phoebe and Leonard—*sentimental in character.*

Thus it is that a professedly Comic Opera commences.

I wish moreover to accentuate the hint I gave you on Friday that the Wardens' couplets in the finale are too long, and should be reduced by one half. This, you will observe is not "cutting out your music," but cutting

Cartoon of D'Oyly Carte as a Tower Warder.

out a *repeat* of your music. And I may remind you that I am proposing to cut, not only your music, but my words.

It was actually a few minutes before curtain time that Sullivan met Gilbert at the Savoy and resolved these important production problems. Small wonder that there were uncertainties to be felt that night on both sides of the footlights.

Every Gilbert and Sullivan opera till that night had opened with a chorus number. As part of the "entirely new departure" *The Yeomen of the Guard* was to begin with the company's smallest principal—tiny Jessie Bond—alone on the stage. So it was Jessie Bond who bore the brunt of Gilbert's first-night jitters. In her own words, "I remember the first night of *The Yeomen* very well. Gilbert was always dreadfully overwrought on these occasions, but this time he was almost beside himself with nervousness and excitement. . . . I am afraid he made himself a perfect nuisance behind the scenes, and did his best, poor fellow, to upset us all. . . . It will be remembered that the curtain rises on Phoebe alone at her spinning-wheel; and Gilbert kept fussing about, 'Oh, Jessie, are you sure you're all right?'—Jessie this—Jessie that—until I was almost as demented as he was. At last I turned on him savagely. 'For Heaven's sake, Mr. Gilbert, go away and leave me alone, or I sha'n't be able to sing a note!' He gave me a final frenzied hug, and vanished."

The rest of the Gilbert story that night, after he had "vanished" from the Savoy stage, was told by the *Sunday Times:* "It is well known that nervousness prevents Mr. Gilbert ever sitting through one of his own works. . . . Consequently on Wednesday night, during the progress of *The Yeomen of the Guard,* he might have been seen in the stalls at Drury Lane, watching *The Armada.* . . . He turned up in time for his 'call' though."

In the front of the house before curtain time all was very much like the former magnificent Savoy first nights. As described in the *Sunday Times*— "What a brilliant night it was at the Savoy on Wednesday, when the proverbial 'all the world and his wife'—by the way, is marriage a failure with him?—flocked to hear Gilbert and Sullivan's new opera. A small crowd began to assemble outside the entrance to the unreserved parts of the house about three o'clock in the afternoon, and by the time the doors opened this had swelled to such an extent that hundreds must have gone away disappointed." And for the lucky faithful who gained admittance the votive rites of the true Savoyard were taken seriously, very much as they are today, according to an unregenerate observer from the *Sporting Times:*

> The First Night at the Savoy is apt to be a solemn function. Many of the merry deadheads one ordinarily chats with are conspicuous by their absence, and their places are occupied by long-haired musical critics who glare at you, if you move half an inch, and who exclaim 'Ssh' on the slightest provocation. Last Wednesday was no exception to the rule: and as the show was not over till 11:30, and there was but one interval for dr— —I mean stretching one's legs—it may be imagined that the occasion was somewhat of an ordeal. So it was, no doubt to a certain extent; but it must be owned that the excellence of the latest Gilbert and Sullivan opera prevented anything like boredom.

To any sharp-eyed member of the audience, a clue to the more serious nature of the evening was available in the title page of the libretto. In eight of the ten librettos that had preceded (and, indeed, in the three that were to follow) the word "Opera" is introduced by a qualifying word or phrase. These eight operas are Grotesque, Modern Comic, Nautical Comic, Melo-dramatic, Aesthetic, Fairy, Japanese, or Supernatural. (*Trial by Jury* is styled a Dramatic Cantata, and *Princess Ida* a Respectful Operatic Perversion.) But the eleventh Gilbert and Sullivan collaboration is described simply as "A New and Original Opera." The same designation appears in both the programs distributed at the Savoy that night, the usual regular program and the souvenir which made use of the Alice Haver color-lithographs of *Princess Ida.* With these programs the first-night audience received the inevitable indulgence slip, this time apologizing "on behalf of Mr. Pounds, who is suffering from a severe cold."

"It must be distinctly understood by visitors to the Savoy Theatre that in their new opera, *The Yeomen of the Guard,* Mr. Gilbert and Sir Arthur Sullivan have taken an entirely new departure." With these words the critic for the *Standard* began his column-long review. And, as though to emphasize this fact in advance for the musical sophisticates in the house that night, the novelty of things to come was apparent even before the curtain went up. For when the cheers heralding the composer's entrance to an augmented orchestra in the pit had subsided, the audience was treated to an overture in strict symphonic form for the first and only time in the Gilbert and Sullivan repertoire—"an excellent specimen of the composer's fancy," according to the critic for the *Standard*. Arthur Lawrence, Sullivan's friend and first biographer, has written that this overture was composed and scored in twelve hours; but this does not jibe with Sullivan's own work schedule as entered in his diary, which indicates that he sketched it on September 23, started the scoring the next day, and finished it at three thirty a.m. the morning of the twenty-sixth.

With the rise of the curtain "the one set in the opera elicited the first round of applause," reported the *Daily Telegraph,* in praising the scenery designed by Hawes Craven. "It shows the Tower as solidly built, to all appearance, as the original edifice a little lower down the river." It also disclosed Jessie Bond, at her spinning wheel alone on the stage, instead of the usual ensemble.

The seasoned Savoyards out front must have wondered what librettist and composer were really up to when they beheld and heard their perennial little soubrette sing what Thomas Dunhill has characterized as "an exquisite piece of lyrical music . . . tinged with a mood of quiet regret, halting here and there that the singer may breathe the most musical of sighs." Was this quite serious, or should they be ready for a comic twist, carefully disguised? But Jessie's Phoebe is weeping after her last "Ah me!" So—"There was but one doubt about last night's performance," commented the *Standard*. "It was not certain that spectators so used to finding fantastic drolleries hidden beneath apparently grave speeches would accept seriously what was meant to be serious, that, in fact, they would not laugh in the wrong place. The skill of the performers prevented any such mishap." And Jessie Bond didn't get the "bad laugh" that must have been ready, trembling on many lips. But the very fact that this atmosphere was in the air must, at least at the outset of the performance, have contributed a tension unique at Gilbert and Sullivan first nights.

For Gilbert this tension, as already noted, was particularly directed at the succession of non-comic songs at the opening of the first act. One of these —Sergeant Meryll's "A laughing boy but yesterday"—was heard by the Savoy audience on October 3 for the first and last time in performance. Just before curtain-time Gilbert and Sullivan had agreed to cut it. But because it was the one good solo opportunity the opera afforded Richard Temple, probably in deference to him, they decided to leave it in for the first night only. It is not a provocative or distinguished song; but Temple, with the knowledge that it was his first and last time to deliver it in performance, gave it his all with the result that it received special mention in several reviews. The *Era,* for example, reported— "The genial song of the Yeoman Meryll, 'A laughing boy but yesterday,' admirably suits Mr. Temple's hearty style."

Another "first" early in the opera—and, most fortunately for lovers of beautiful songs the world over, not a last performance—was the debut of D'Oyly Carte's new tenor, Courtice Pounds, in the ballad, "Is life a boon?" The severe cold advertised by Pounds' indulgence slips did not seem to hamper him in any way; or at least, there was nothing but praise for his performance—"a young tenor with a pure and sympathetic voice, a good singer, and a graceful actor," said the *Daily Telegraph* . . . "a decided acquisition" (the *Times*) . . . "the possessor of a charming voice and cultivated style. . . . He acts in a spirited and unaffected fashion, which is very rarely found in tenors, and did much for the general success" (the *Standard*). And for his opening ballad there was the universal agreement that it was the peer of the Elizabethan lyric poets it imitated.

But it remained for the duet between Geraldine Ulmar and George Grossmith to score the greatest hit of the evening. According to the *Daily Telegraph:* "Perhaps Mr. Gilbert's most successful lyric . . . "the 'singing farce of the Merryman and his Maid,' . . . made doubly attractive by Sir Arthur Sullivan's quaintly beautiful music . . . may take rank in popular esteem as the gem of the work. It was doubly encored last night amid great applause." The *Morning Advertiser* went all the way in its praise: "Sir Arthur Sullivan has never written anything more delicately melodious and elegant than this, in fact, of its kind he has never equalled it and probably never will, for it is not given to any composer to match such an exquisite thing." And of Miss Ulmar, the *Daily Telegraph* said the best in only six words: she "looked well, acted well, sang well." The *Standard* embellished this: "Miss Ulmar has, perhaps, never been seen

George Grossmith and Geraldine Ulmar, lampooned as the Merryman and his Maid.

and heard to such complete advantage. She adopts the various moods of the character of Elsie with excellent appreciation, and, it need hardly be said, sings delightfully."

Later in the first act warm acclaim was won by "Were I thy bride," intriguingly sung by Jessie Bond, "singularly bright and winsome" as Phœbe. Her acting as well as her singing of this role "contributed greatly to the life and charm of the stage" for most of the audience, including the critic of the *Daily Telegraph.* Many years later she confessed: "My share in the most beautiful of all the Gilbert and Sullivan operas was delightfully easy and natural. When Gilbert gave it [the part of Phœbe] to me at the first reading he said, 'Here you are, Jessie, you needn't act this, it's you.' "

The first-night production (and the first edition of the libretto then in hand) did not contain the chorus of Yeomen—"Oh, Sergeant Meryll, is it true"—later associated with the beginning of the finale to Act I. It did, however, include couplets for the Third and Fourth Yeomen, and the choruses that followed them. These Gilbert considered expendable, and so wrote Sullivan on the very morning of the opening. But in their eleventh-hour conference they must have agreed to leave them in at least for the first night. Within a week the Third and Fourth Yeomen were no longer listed by name in the program, so it can be assumed their solo Couplets were already cut.

In the second act the most notable numbers, in the estimate of the *Standard*'s reviewer, included "Point's capital song, 'Oh! a private buffoon is a light-hearted lover.' " (He meant "loon," but perhaps was a cynical bachelor.) The *Daily Telegraph* found the song had "the old ring" in it, and quoted the entire last verse. This critic wrote of George Grossmith that "it may be [his] warmest admirers were surprised at the merits of his Jester—an assumption of very considerable subtlety, and one in which no ordinary difficulties are surmounted. Whether giving expression to poor Jack's professional wit, or hiding a sorry heart behind light words . . . Mr. Grossmith was the master of the part he assumed." The *Times* gave the impression that the audience, uncertain of whether Gilbert was being truly serious, seized on Grossmith, their popular funny-man, with such relief that their ringing applause and roars of laughter might at times have been not quite to Gilbert's liking. Certainly the duet, "Hereupon we're both agreed," appears to have produced the same comic sensation on this first night's performance as it does regularly in current production.

The collaborator with Grossmith in this tale of cock and bull was Mr. H. W. Denny, making his Savoy debut in the role that would have been Rutland Barrington's had the perennial Pooh-Bah not chosen to leave the company for a fling at theatre management. "That the new actor was quite equal to his inimitable prototype cannot be said, but he showed considerable humour of the dry kind nevertheless," was the *Times'* characteristic contribution to a professional scrapbook. But the press generally hailed Denny as an important acquisition to the Savoy company. Of his performance in the role of Wilfred Shadbolt, the *Daily Telegraph* wrote without invidious comparison: "His jailer is a genuine character, full of strength, but never overdone."

After "a tuneful and tender ballad for Fairfax, 'Free from his fetters grim,'" reported the *Standard,* came what, for many, was one of the musical hits of the evening, "Strange adventure!"—"beau-

Gilbert as Jack Point, and Sullivan as Wilfred Shadbolt, "tell a tale of cock and bull."

tifully harmonized, and certain to be long remembered as one of the most delightful numbers of the opera." Even the *Times* conceded this to be "a perfect gem of its kind," and the *Daily Telegraph* saw fit to quote the complete second verse. In addition to Courtice Pounds and Richard Temple, this unaccompanied quartette comprised on the distaff side Miss Rose Hervey and the veteran Miss Rosina Brandram, whom the *Daily Telegraph* found "excellent as ever . . . a capital Dame Carruthers" and who had earlier in the performance (according to the *Standard*) "won one of the many encores of the evening for her fine song, 'When our gallant Norman foes.'"

How well the librettist and composer knew their audience, and how sure they were of their art even in the uncertainties of this so different collaboration, must have been dramatically clear to all at the Savoy that night when the final curtain turned out to be a reprise of the opera's hit-song. With the tragedy of the jilted jester at center-stage as the curtain came down, *The Yeomen of the Guard* maintained to the end the principle, established in the overture, of an "entirely new departure" in Gilbert and Sullivan joint creation. If at the outset there may have been an underlying atmosphere of uncertainty out front, at the close of the opera there was only vociferous appreciation as, reported by the *Daily Telegraph,* "the author and composer appeared before the curtain to receive well-earned congratulations from a unanimous audience." As encores had been demanded almost continually, it was after eleven thirty. But "when it finally descended," according to the *Standard,* "everyone concerned was called before the curtain . . . and there was not a single dissentient voice to mar the hearty cordiality with which the piece was received."

Gilbert did not fair as well as Sullivan in the morning-after press. Virtually every critic mentioned the similarity of the plot to that of Wallace's opera *Maritana,* which, in turn, had been based on *Don César de Bazan,* a French play by d'Ennery. Some made nothing of this, while others dwelt on the prototype at some length. *Punch,* in particular, reveled in such a fat opportunity to attack Gilbert. It hypothesized "an original opera, *The Beefeater's Bride; or, The Merryman and his Maritana*" by the unknown team of Sulbert and Gillivan, and then proceeded to play the role of the critical press:

The stern critics would promptly have pointed out that in good old Fitzball-and-Wallace, *Maritana,* Don César is in prison and condemned to die, and so is Colonel Fairfax in *The Beefeater's Bride;* that the Don is married in prison to a veiled gypsy dancer, Maritana, and the Colonel is married in prison to a veiled gypsy dancer, Elsie

Maynard; "Maynard," the critics would have bitterly exclaimed, "is but a poor English rendering of *Maritana!*" With scathing irony they would have shown how in the old opera, Don César escapes being shot, and returns "all alive-O"; while in the new and original work Colonel Fairfax escapes being decapitated, and also reappears on the scene. Don César enters disguised as a monk; Colonel Fairfax comes in as a Beefeater. Don César and Maritana subsequently fall in love with each other; so do Colonel Fairfax and Elsie Maynard. Don César is pardoned by the King for a very good reason; the Colonel is reprieved for no reason at all, except to finish the opera, "a reason" the satirical critic would have added, "sufficiently satisfactory to the audience." . . . Beyond the above points, there is absolutely no resemblance between the two plots, and though poor Sulbert (without Gillivan) would thus have suffered at the hands of the critical faculty for daring to claim novelty and originality for his story, yet for Mr. Gilbert, of the firm of Gilbert and Sullivan, the critics have nothing but obsequious compliments and good-natured excuses. As to the music, even the sharpest and most hostile ear could not detect a trace of Wallace in the latest composition of Sir Arthur Sullivan. He, at all events, is guiltless of any intrigue with Maritana. . . .

One can well imagine that the Gilbert hypertension at this point made him anything but a merryman with or without his Maritana.

The *Times* covered the *Maritana* subject in two sentences, the last being: "So obvious, indeed, is the resemblance that one would be inclined to suspect some subtle attempt at parody, did not the serious tone of Mr. Gilbert's work preclude any such thought." But regardless of a Wallace and *Maritana* issue, there were those who felt that without his topsy-turvydom Gilbert had fallen short of the mark. The *Times* concluded its review with the following observation:

Of the weakness of the plot no one seemed to take notice in the excitement of the general success. Upon the whole we can agree with the popular verdict—Mr. Gilbert is in his way a man of genius, and even at his worst is a head and

shoulders above the ordinary librettist. In the present instance he has not written a good play, but his lyrics are suave and good to sing, and, wedded to Sir Arthur Sullivan's melodies, they will no doubt find their way to many a home where English song is appreciated. . . .

To sum up, Sir Arthur Sullivan's score is fully equal to previous achievements, and the success of the piece will no doubt be largely due to it.

Wrote the critic of the *Standard:* "To the music it is impossible to give much higher praise than to say that Sir Arthur Sullivan's warmest admirers will be completely satisfied." The *Daily Telegraph* was more detailed in its praise:

The accompaniments . . . are delightful to hear, and especially does the treatment of the woodwind compel admiring attention. Schubert himself could hardly have handled those instruments more deftly, written for them more lovingly. . . . We place the songs and choruses in *The Yeomen of the Guard* before all his previous efforts of this particular kind. Thus the music follows the book to a higher plane, and we have a genuine English opera, forerunner of many others, let us hope, and possibly significant of an advance towards a national lyric stage.

This latter point was also made by the *Daily News,* which found the opera "a work of which lovers of true English music have good reason to be proud. . . . There appears to be a prospect of a genuine school of English opera . . . and this fact was clearly understood by the audience."

This opera, regarded by the *Daily News* and others as "more or less in the nature of an experiment," was predicted in a review of the first night of *Ruddygore* by the *Sporting Times* more than a year-and-a-half earlier. Their critic, with a crystal ball and with the first hisses of a Gilbert and Sullivan opening still in his ears, wrote: "A real comic opera, dealing with neither topsy-turveydom nor fairies, but a genuine dramatic story, written with all Mr. W. S. Gilbert's masterly power, and set to such music as Sir Arthur Sullivan alone can compose, would be a greater novelty and a more splendid success than anything we are at all likely to see during the present dramatic season."

OCTOBER 3. *Tired and nervous. Drove to the theatre at 8 to meet Gilbert and settle one or two points—arr. to cut down 2nd verse of couplet in Finale; to leave in Temple's song for the first night. Crammed house—usual enthusiastic reception. I was awfully nervous and continued so until the duet 'Heighday' which settled the fate of the Opera. Its success was tremendous; 3 times encored! After that everything went on wheels, and I think its success is even greater than the "Mikado." 9 encores.*

ARTHUR SULLIVAN'S DIARY

A New and Original Opera,

IN TWO ACTS,

ENTITLED

THE YEOMEN OF THE GUARD

OR,

THE MERRYMAN AND HIS MAID.

Dramatis Personae.

Sir Richard Cholmondeley, *Lieutenant of the Tower*	MR. W. BROWNLOW.
Colonel Fairfax, *under Sentence of Death*	MR. COURTICE POUNDS.
Sergeant Meryll, *of the Yeomen of the Guard*	MR. RICHARD TEMPLE.
Leonard Meryll, *His Son*	MR. W. R. SHIRLEY.
Jack Point, *A Strolling Jester*	MR. GEORGE GROSSMITH.
Wilfred Shadbolt, *Head Jailor and Assistant Tormentor*	MR. W. H. DENNY.
The Headsman	MR. RICHARDS.
First Yeoman	MR. WILBRAHAM.
Second Yeoman	MR. MEDCALF.
Third Yeoman	MR. MERTON.
Fourth Yeoman	MR. RUDOLPH LEWIS.
First Citizen	MR. REDMOND.
Second Citizen	MR. BOYD.
Elsie Maynard, *A Strolling Singer*	MISS GERALDINE ULMAR.
Phœbe Meryll, *Sergeant Meryll's Daughter*	MISS JESSIE BOND.
Dame Carruthers, *Housekeeper to the Tower*	MISS ROSINA BRANDRAM.
Kate, *Her Niece*	MISS ROSE HERVEY.

Chorus of Yeomen of the Guard, Gentlemen, Citizens, &c.

Scene. — Tower Green.   Date. — 16th Century.

THE YEOMEN OF THE GUARD

OR,

THE MERRYMAN AND HIS MAID.

ACT I.

SCENE. — *Tower Green.* PHŒBE *discovered spinning.*

SONG — PHŒBE.

When maiden loves, she sits and sighs,
    She wanders to and fro;
Unbidden tear-drops fill her eyes,
And to all questions she replies
    With a sad heigho!
    'Tis but a little word—"heigho!"
    So soft, 'tis scarcely heard—"heigho!"
      An idle breath—
      Yet life and death
    May hang upon a maid's "heigho!"

When maiden loves, she mopes apart,
    As owl mopes on a tree;
Although she keenly feels the smart,
She cannot tell what ails her heart,
    With its sad "Ah me!"
    'Tis but a foolish sigh—"Ah me!"
    Born but to droop and die—"Ah me!"
      Yet all the sense
      Of eloquence
    Lies hidden in a maid's "Ah me!"

                (*Weeps.*)

Enter WILFRED.

WILFRED. Mistress Meryll!

PHŒBE (*looking up*). Eh! Oh! it's you, is it? You may go away, if you like. Because I don't want you, you know.

WILFRED. Haven't you anything to say to me?

PHŒBE. Oh yes! Are the birds all caged? The wild beasts all littered down? All the locks, chains, bolts, and bars in good order? Is the Little Ease sufficiently uncomfortable? The racks, pincers, and thumbscrews all ready for work? Ugh! you brute!

WILFRED. These allusions to my professional duties are in doubtful taste. I didn't become a head-jailor because I like head-jailing. I didn't become an assistant-tormentor because I like assistant-tormenting. We can't *all* be sorcerers, you know. (PHŒBE *annoyed.*) Ah! you brought that upon yourself.

PHŒBE. Colonel Fairfax is *not* a sorcerer. He's a man of science and an alchemist.

WILFRED. Well, whatever he is, he won't be one long, for he's to be beheaded to-day for dealings with the devil. His master nearly had him last night, when the fire broke out in the Beauchamp Tower.

PHŒBE. Oh! how I wish he had escaped in the confusion! But take care; there's still time for a reply to his petition for mercy.

WILFRED. Ah! I'm content to chance that. This evening at half-past-seven—ah!

PHŒBE. You're a cruel monster to speak so unfeelingly of the death of a young and handsome soldier.

WILFRED. Young and handsome! How do *you* know he's young and handsome?

PHŒBE. Because I've seen him every day for weeks past taking his exercise on the Beauchamp Tower. (WILFRED *utters a cry of agony.*) There, I believe you're jealous of *him,* now. Jealous of a man I've never spoken to! Jealous of a poor soul who's to die in an hour!

WILFRED. I am! I'm jealous of everybody and

[315]

everything. I'm jealous of the very words I speak to you—because they reach your ears—and I mustn't go near 'em!

PHŒBE. How unjust you are! Jealous of the words you speak to me! Why, you know as well as I do, that I don't even like them.

WILFRED. You used to like 'em.

PHŒBE. I used to *pretend* I liked them. It was mere politeness to comparative strangers. (*Exit* PHŒBE, *with spinning wheel.*)

WILFRED. I don't believe you know what jealousy is! I don't believe you know how it eats into a man's heart—and disorders his digestion—and turns his interior into boiling lead. Oh, you are a heartless jade to trifle with the delicate organization of the human interior!

Enter crowd of Men and Women, followed by Yeomen of the Guard, led by SERGEANT MERYLL.

CHORUS (*as Yeomen march on*).

> Tower Warders,
> Under orders,
> Gallant pikemen, valiant sworders!
> Brave in bearing,
> Foeman scaring,
> In their bygone days of daring!
> Ne'er a stranger
> There to danger—
> Each was o'er the world a ranger:
> To the story
> Of our glory
> Each a bold contributory!

CHORUS OF YEOMEN.

> In the autumn of our life,
> Here at rest in ample clover,
> We rejoice in telling over
> Our impetuous May and June.
> In the evening of our day,
> With the sun of life declining,
> We recall without repining
> All the heat of bygone noon.

SOLO — SERGEANT MERYLL.

> This the autumn of our life,
> This the evening of our day;
> Weary we of battle strife,
> Weary we of mortal fray.
> But our year is not so spent,
> And our days are not so faded,
> But that we with one consent,
> Were our lovèd land invaded,
> Still would face a foreign foe,
> As in days of long ago.

PEOPLE.	YEOMEN.
Tower Warders, Under orders, &c.	In the autumn time of life, &c.

(*Exeunt Crowd. Manent Warders.*)

Enter DAME CARRUTHERS.

DAME. A good-day to you, Sergeant.

MERYLL. Good-day, Dame Carruthers. Busy to-day?

DAME. Busy, aye! the fire in the Beauchamp last night has given me work enough. A dozen poor prisoners—Richard Colfax, Sir Martin Byfleet, Colonel Fairfax, Warren the preacher-poet, and half-a-score others—all packed into one small cell, not six feet square. Poor Colonel Fairfax, who's to die to-day, is to be removed to No. 14 in the Cold Harbour Tower that he may have his last hour alone with his confessor; and I've to see to that.

MERYLL. Poor gentleman! He'll die bravely. I fought under him two years since, and he valued his life as it were a feather!

PHŒBE. He's the bravest, the handsomest, and the best young gentleman in England! He twice saved my father's life; and it's a cruel thing, a wicked thing, and a barbarous thing that so gallant a hero should lose his head—for it's the handsomest head in England!

DAME. For dealings with the devil. Aye! if all were beheaded who dealt with *him,* there'd be busy doings on Tower Green.

PHŒBE. You know very well that Colonel Fairfax is a student of alchemy—nothing more, and nothing less; but this wicked Tower, like a cruel giant in a fairy-tale, must be fed with blood, and that blood must be the best and bravest in England, or it's not good enough for the old Blunderbore. Ugh!

DAME. Silence, you silly girl; you know not what you say. I was born in the old keep, and I've grown grey in it, and, please God, I shall die and be buried in it; and there's not a stone in its walls that is not as dear to me as my own right hand.

SONG — DAME CARRUTHERS.

When our gallant Norman foes
  Made our merry land their own,
    And the Saxons from the Conqueror
      were flying,
At his bidding it arose,
  In its panoply of stone,
    A sentinel unliving and undying.
Insensible, I trow,
  As a sentinel should be,
    Though a queen to save her head should
      come a-suing,
There's a legend on its brow
  That is eloquent to me,
    And it tells of duty done and duty do-
      ing.

"The screw may twist and the rack may turn,
And men may bleed and men may burn,
On London town and all its hoard
I keep my solemn watch and ward!"

CHORUS.   The screw may twist, &c.

Within its wall of rock
  The flower of the brave
    Have perished with a constancy un-
      shaken.
From the dungeon to the block,
  From the scaffold to the grave,
    Is a journey many gallant hearts have
      taken.
And the wicked flames may hiss
  Round the heroes who have fought
    For conscience and for home in all its
      beauty;

But the grim old fortalice
  Takes little heed of aught
    That comes not in the measure of its
      duty.

"The screw may twist and the rack may turn,
And men may bleed and men may burn,
On London town and all its hoard
It keeps its silent watch and ward!"

(Exeunt all but PHŒBE *and* SERGEANT MERYLL.)

PHŒBE. Father! No reprieve for the poor gentleman?

MERYLL. No, my lass; but there's one hope yet. Thy brother Leonard, who, as a reward for his valour in saving his standard and cutting his way through fifty foes who would have hanged him, has been appointed a Yeoman of the Guard, will arrive this morning; and as he comes straight from Windsor, where the Court is, it may be—it *may* be—that he will bring the expected reprieve with him.

PHŒBE. Oh, that he may!

MERYLL. Amen! For the Colonel twice saved my life, and I'd give the rest of my life to save his! And wilt thou not be glad to welcome thy brave brother, with the fame of whose exploits all England is a-ringing?

PHŒBE. Aye, truly, if he brings the reprieve.

MERYLL. And not otherwise?

PHŒBE. Well, he's a brave fellow indeed, and I love brave men!

MERYLL. *All* brave men?

PHŒBE. Most of them, I verily believe! But I hope Leonard will not be too strict with me—they say he is a very dragon of virtue and circumspection! Now, my dear old father is kindness itself, and—

MERYLL. And leaves thee pretty well to thine own ways, eh? Well, I've no fears for thee; thou hast a feather-brain, but thou'rt a good lass.

PHŒBE. Yes, that's all very true, but if Leonard is going to tell me that I may not do this and I may not do that, and I must not talk to this one, or walk with that one, but go through the world with my lips pursed up and my eyes cast down, like a poor nun who has renounced mankind—why, as I have *not* renounced mankind, and don't mean to renounce mankind, I won't have it—there!

MERYLL. Nay, he'll not check thee more than is good for thee, Phœbe! He's a brave fellow, and bravest among brave fellows; and yet it seems but yesterday that he robbed the Lieutenant's orchard.

SONG — MERYLL.

A laughing boy but yesterday,
A merry urchin, blithe and gay!
　　Whose joyous shout
　　Came ringing out,
　Unchecked by care or sorrow—
To-day, a warrior, all sun-brown,
Whose deeds of soldierly renown
Are all the boast of London Town:
　　A veteran, to-morrow!

When at my Leonard's deeds sublime
A soldier's pulse beats double time,
　　And brave hearts thrill,
　　As brave hearts will,
　At tales of martial glory,
I burn with flush of pride and joy,
A pride unbittered by alloy,
To find my boy—my darling boy—
　　The theme of song and story!

Enter LEONARD MERYLL.

LEONARD. Father!

MERYLL. Leonard! my brave boy! I'm right glad to see thee, and so is Phœbe!

PHŒBE. Aye—hast thou brought Colonel Fairfax's reprieve?

LEONARD. Nay, I have here a despatch for the Lieutenant, but no reprieve for the Colonel!

PHŒBE. Poor gentleman! poor gentleman!

LEONARD. Aye, I would I had brought better news. I'd give my right hand—nay, my body—my life, to save his!

MERYLL. Dost thou speak in earnest, my lad?

LEONARD. Aye—I'm no braggart. Did he not save thy life? and am I not his foster-brother?

MERYLL. Then hearken to me. Thou hast come to join the Yeomen of the Guard.

LEONARD. Well?

MERYLL. None has seen thee but ourselves?

LEONARD. And a sentry, who took but scant notice of me.

MERYLL. Now to prove thy words. Give me the despatch, and get thee hence at once! Here is money, and I'll send thee more. Lie hidden for a space, and let no one know. I'll convey a suit of Yeoman's uniform to the Colonel's cell—he shall shave off his beard so that none shall know him, and I'll own him as my son, the brave Leonard Meryll, who saved his flag and cut his way through fifty foes who thirsted for his life. He will be welcomed without question by my brother-Yeomen, I'll warrant that. Now, how to get access to his cell? (*To* PHŒBE.) The key is with thy sour-faced admirer, Wilfred Shadbolt.

PHŒBE (*demurely*). I think—I say, I *think*—I

can get anything I want from Wilfred. I think—I say, I *think*—you may leave that to me.

MERYLL. Then get thee hence at once, lad—and bless thee for this sacrifice.

PHŒBE. And take my blessing too, dear, dear Leonard!

LEONARD. And thine, eh? Humph! Thy love is new-born; wrap it up, lest it take cold and die.

TRIO.
LEONARD, PHŒBE, MERYLL.

PHŒBE. Alas! I waver to and fro—
　　Dark danger hangs upon the deed!

ALL. Dark danger hangs upon the deed!

LEONARD. The scheme is rash and well may fail;
　　But ours are not the hearts that quail—
　　The hands that shrink—the cheeks that pale
　　　In hours of need!

ALL. No, ours are not the hearts that quail,
　　The hands that shrink, the cheeks that pale
　　　In hours of need!

MERYLL. The air I breathe, to him I owe:
　　My life is his—I count it naught!

PHŒBE *and* LEONARD. That life is his—so count it naught!

LEONARD.　　And shall I reckon risks I run
　　　　When services are to be done
　　　　To save the life of such an one?
　　　　Unworthy thought!

ALL.　　And shall we reckon risks we run
　　　　To save the life of such an one?
　　　　Unworthy thought!

PHŒBE. We may succeed—who can foretell—
　　May heaven help our hope—farewell!

ALL. We may succeed—who can foretell?
　　May heaven help our hope—farewell!

(LEONARD *embraces* MERYLL *and* PHŒBE, *and then exit*. PHŒBE *weeping*.)

MERYLL. Nay, lass, be of good cheer, we may save him yet.

PHŒBE. Oh! see, father—they bring the poor gentleman from the Beauchamp! Oh, father! his hour is not yet come?

MERYLL. No, no—they lead him to the Cold Harbour Tower to await his end in solitude. But softly—the Lieutenant approaches! He should not see thee weep.

Enter FAIRFAX, *guarded. The* LIEUTENANT *enters, meeting him.*

LIEUTENANT. Halt! Colonel Fairfax, my old friend, we meet but sadly.

FAIRFAX. Sir, I greet you with all good-will; and I thank you for the zealous care with which you have guarded me from the pestilent dangers which threaten human life outside. In this happy little community, Death, when he comes, doth so in punctual and business-like fashion; and, like a courtly gentleman, giveth due notice of his advent, that one may not be taken unawares.

LIEUTENANT. Sir, you bear this bravely, as a brave man should.

FAIRFAX. Why, sir, it is no light boon to die swiftly and surely at a given hour and in a given fashion! Truth to tell, I would gladly have my life; but if that may not be, I have the next best thing to it, which is death. Believe me, sir, my lot is not so much amiss!

PHŒBE (aside to MERYLL). Oh, father, father, I cannot bear it!

MERYLL. My poor lass!

FAIRFAX. Nay, pretty one, why weepest thou? Come, be comforted. Such a life as mine is not worth weeping for. (Sees MERYLL.) Sergeant Meryll, is it not? (To LIEUTENANT.) May I greet my old friend? (Shakes MERYLL'S hand.) Why, man, what's all this? Thou and I have faced the grim old king a dozen times, and never has his majesty come to me in such goodly fashion. Keep a stout heart, good fellow—we are soldiers, and we know how to die, thou and I. Take my word for it, it is easier to die well than to live well—for, in sooth, I have tried both.

BALLAD — FAIRFAX.

Is life a boon?
　　If so, it must befall
　　That Death, whene'er he call,
Must call too soon.
　　Though fourscore years he give,
　　Yet one would pray to live
Another moon!
　　What kind of plaint have I,
　　Who perish in July?
　　I might have had to die,
Perchance, in June!

Is life a thorn?
　　Then count it not a whit!
　　Man is well done with it;
Soon as he's born
　　He should all means essay
　　To put the plague away;
And I, war-worn,
　　Poor captured fugitive,
　　My life most gladly give—
　　I might have had to live
Another morn!

(At the end, PHŒBE is led off, weeping, by MERYLL.)

FAIRFAX. And now, Sir Richard, I have a boon to beg. I am in this strait for no better reason than because my kinsman, Sir Clarence Poltwhistle, one of the Secretaries of State, has charged me with sorcery, in order that he may succeed to my estate, which devolves to him provided I die unmarried.

LIEUTENANT. As thou wilt most surely do.

FAIRFAX. Nay, as I will most surely not do, by your worship's grace! I have a mind to thwart this good cousin of mine.

LIEUTENANT. How?

FAIRFAX. By marrying forthwith, to be sure!

LIEUTENANT. But heaven ha' mercy, whom wouldst thou marry?

FAIRFAX. Nay, I am indifferent on that score. Coming Death hath made of me a true and chivalrous knight, who holds all womankind in such esteem that the oldest, and the meanest, and the worst-favoured of them is good enough for him. So, my good Lieutenant, if thou wouldst serve a poor soldier who has but an hour to live, find me the first that comes—my confessor shall marry us, and her dower shall be my dishonoured name and a hundred crowns to boot. No such poor dower for an hour of matrimony!

LIEUTENANT. A strange request. I doubt that I should be warranted in granting it.

FAIRFAX. Tut tut! There never was a marriage fraught with so little of evil to the contracting parties. In an hour she'll be a widow, and I—a bachelor again, for aught I know!

LIEUTENANT. Well, I will see what can be done, for I hold thy kinsman in abhorrence for the scurvy trick he has played thee.

FAIRFAX. A thousand thanks, good sir; we meet again on this spot in an hour or so. I shall be a bridegroom then, and your worship will wish me joy. Till then, farewell. (*To Guard.*) I am ready, good fellows.

(*Exit with Guard into Cold Harbour Tower.*)

LIEUTENANT. He is a brave fellow, and it is a pity that he should die. Now, how to find him a bride at such short notice? Well, the task should be easy! (*Exit.*)

Enter JACK POINT *and* ELSIE MAYNARD, *pursued by a crowd of men and women.* POINT *and* ELSIE *are much terrified;* POINT, *however, assuming an appearance of self-possession.*

CHORUS.

Here's a man of jollity;
Jibe, joke, jollify!
Give us of your quality;
Come, fool, follify!

If you vapour vapidly,
River runneth rapidly;
Into it we fling
Bird who doesn't sing!

Give us an experiment
In the art of merriment;
Into it we throw
Cock who doesn't crow!

Banish your timidity,
And with all rapidity
Give us quip and quiddity—
Willy-nilly, O!

River none can mollify;
Into it we throw
Fool who doesn't follify,
Cock who doesn't crow!

POINT (*alarmed*). My masters, I pray you bear with us, and we will satisfy you, for we are merry folk who would make all merry as ourselves. For, look you, there is humour in all things, and the truest philosophy is that which teaches us to find it and to make the most of it.

ELSIE (*struggling with one of the crowd*). Hands off, I say, unmannerly fellow! (*Pushing him away.*)

POINT (*to First Citizen*). Ha! Didst thou hear her say, "Hands off"?

FIRST CITIZEN. Aye, I heard her say it, and I felt her do it! What then?

POINT. Thou dost not see the humour of that?

FIRST CITIZEN. Nay, if I do, hang me!

POINT. Thou dost not? Now observe. She said, "Hands off!" Whose hands? Thine. Off what? Off *her.* Why? Because she is a woman. Now had she *not* been a woman, thine hands had not been set upon her at all. So the reason for the laying on of hands is the reason for the taking off of hands, and herein is contradiction contradicted! It is the very marriage of *pro* with *con;* and no such lopsided union either, as times go, for *pro* is not more unlike *con* than man is unlike woman—yet men and women marry every day with none to say, "Oh, the pity of it" but I and fools like me! Now wherewithal shall we please you? We can rhyme you couplet, triolet, quatrain, sonnet, rondolet, ballade, what you will. Or we can dance you saraband, gondolet, carole, pimpernel, or Jumping Joan.

ELSIE. Let us give them the singing farce of the Merryman and his Maid—therein is song and dance too.

ALL. Aye, the Merryman and his Maid!

DUET — POINT *and* ELSIE.

POINT. I have a song to sing, O!

ELSIE.   Sing me your song, O!

POINT.   It is sung to the moon
               By a love-lorn loon,
         Who fled from the mocking throng, O!
      It's the song of a merryman, moping mum,
      Whose soul was sad, and whose glance was glum,
      Who sipped no sup, and who craved no crumb,
         As he sighed for the love of a ladye.
               Heighdy! heighdy!
               Misery me, lackadaydee!
      He sipped no sup, and he craved no crumb,
         As he sighed for the love of a ladye.

ELSIE. I have a song to sing, O!

POINT.   Sing me your song, O!

ELSIE.   It is sung with the ring
               Of the songs maids sing
         Who love with a love life-long, O!
      It's the song of a merrymaid, peerly proud,
      Who loved a lord, and who laughed aloud
      At the moan of the merryman, moping mum,
      Whose soul was sore, and whose glance was glum,
      Who sipped no sup, and who craved no crumb,

As he sighed for the love of a ladye!
 Heighdy! heighdy!
 Misery me, lackadaydee!
He sipped no sup, &c.

POINT.   I have a song to sing, O!

ELSIE.   Sing me your song, O!

POINT.   It is sung to the knell
            Of a churchyard bell,
    And a doleful dirge, ding dong, O!
It's a song of a popinjay, bravely born,
Who turned up his noble nose with scorn
At the humble merrymaid, peerly proud,
Who loved that lord, and who laughed aloud
At the moan of the merryman, moping mum,
Whose soul was sad, and whose glance was
    glum,
Who sipped no sup, and who craved no crumb,
    As he sighed for the love of a ladye!

BOTH.   Heighdy! heighdy!
            Misery me, lackadaydee!
    He sipped no sup, &c.

ELSIE.   I have a song to sing, O!

POINT.   Sing me your song, O!

ELSIE.   It is sung with a sigh
                And a tear in the eye,
        For it tells of a righted wrong, O!
It's a song of a merrymaid, once so gay,
Who turned on her heel and tripped away
From the peacock popinjay, bravely born,
Who turned up his noble nose with scorn

At the humble heart that he did not prize:
So she begged on her knees, with downcast eyes,
For the love of the merryman, moping mum,
Whose soul was sad and whose glance was
    glum,
Who sipped no sup, and who craved no crumb,
    As he sighed for the love of a ladye!

BOTH.   Heighdy! heighdy!
            Misery me, lackadaydee!
    His pains were o'er, and he sighed no more,
        For he lived in the love of a ladye!

FIRST CITIZEN.   Well sung and well danced!

SECOND CITIZEN.   A kiss for that, pretty maid!

ALL.   Aye, a kiss all round.

ELSIE (*drawing dagger*).   Best beware! I am
armed!

POINT.   Back, sirs—back! This is going too far.

SECOND CITIZEN.   Thou dost not see the humour
of it, eh? Yet there is humour in all things—even
in this (*trying to kiss her*).

ELSIE.   Help! help!

Enter LIEUTENANT *with guard. Crowd falls back.*

LIEUTENANT.   What is this pother?

ELSIE.   Sir, I sang to these folk, and they would
have repaid me with gross courtesy, but for your
honour's coming.

LIEUTENANT (*to mob*).   Away with ye! Clear the
rabble. (*Guards push crowd off, and go off with
them.*) Now, my girl, who are you, and what do
you here?

ELSIE.   May it please you, sir, we are two strolling players, Jack Point and I, Elsie Maynard, at
your worship's service. We go from fair to fair,

singing, and dancing, and playing brief interludes; and so we make a poor living.

LIEUTENANT. You two, eh? Are ye man and wife?

POINT. No, sir; for though I'm a fool, there is a limit to my folly. Her mother, old Bridget Maynard travels with us (for Elsie is a good girl), but the old woman is a-bed with fever, and we have come here to pick up some silver, to buy an electuary for her.

LIEUTENANT. Hark ye, my girl! Your mother is ill?

ELSIE. Sorely ill, sir.

LIEUTENANT. And needs good food, and many things that thou canst not buy?

ELSIE. Alas! sir, it is too true.

LIEUTENANT. Wouldst thou earn an hundred crowns?

ELSIE. An hundred crowns! They might save her life!

LIEUTENANT. Then listen! A worthy but unhappy gentleman is to be beheaded in an hour on this very spot. For sufficient reasons, he desires to marry before he dies, and he hath asked me to find him a wife. Wilt thou be that wife?

ELSIE. The wife of a man I have never seen!

POINT. Why sir, look you, I am concerned in this; for though I am not yet wedded to Elsie Maynard, time works wonders, and there's no knowing what may be in store for us. Have we your worship's word for it that this gentleman will die to-day?

LIEUTENANT. Nothing is more certain, I grieve to say.

POINT. And that the maiden will be allowed to depart the very instant the ceremony is at an end?

LIEUTENANT. The very instant. I pledge my honour that it shall be so.

POINT. An hundred crowns?

LIEUTENANT. An hundred crowns!

POINT. For my part, I consent. It is for Elsie to speak.

TRIO.

ELSIE, POINT, LIEUTENANT.

LIEUTENANT. How say you, maiden, will you wed
A man about to lose his head?
No harm to you can thence arise,
In half an hour, poor soul, he dies.
For half an hour
You'll be a wife,
And then the dower
Is yours for life.
This tempting offer why refuse?
If truth the poets tell,
Most men, before they marry, lose

Both head and heart as well!

ALL. Temptation, oh temptation,
Were we, in truth, intended
To shun, whate'er our station,
Your fascinations splendid;
Or fall, whene'er we view you,
Head over heels into you!

ELSIE. A strange proposal you reveal,
It almost makes my senses reel.
Alas! I'm very poor indeed,
And such a sum I sorely need.
Unfortunately,
Life and death
Have hung till lately
On a breath.
My mother, sir, is like to die;
This money life may bring.
Bear this in mind, I pray, if I
Consent to do this thing!

ALL. Temptation, oh temptation, &c.

POINT. Though as a general rule of life
I don't allow my promised wife,
My lovely bride that is to be,
To marry anyone but me,
The circumstances
Of this case
May set such fancies
Out of place;

So, if the fee is duly paid,
And he, in well-earned grave,
Within the hour is duly laid,
Objection I will waive!

ALL. Temptation, oh temptation, &c.

During this, the LIEUTENANT *has whispered to* WILFRED (*who has entered*). WILFRED *binds* ELSIE's *eyes with a kerchief, and leads her into the Cold Harbour Tower.*

LIEUTENANT. And so, good fellow, you are a jester?

POINT. Aye, sir, and, like some of my jests, out of place.

LIEUTENANT. I have a vacancy for such an one. Tell me, what are your qualifications for such a post?

POINT. Marry, sir, I have a pretty wit. I can rhyme you extempore; I can convulse you with quip and conundrum; I have the lighter philosophies at my tongue's tip; I can be merry, wise, quaint, grim, and sardonic, one by one, or all at once; I have a pretty turn for anecdote; I know all the jests—ancient and modern—past, present, and to come; I can riddle you from dawn of day to set of sun, and, if that content you not, well on to midnight and the small hours. Oh, sir, a pretty wit, I warrant you—a pretty, pretty wit!

RECITATIVE AND SONG — POINT.

I've jest and joke
    And quip and crank,
For lowly folk
    And men of rank.
I ply my craft
    And know no fear,
I aim my shaft
    At prince or peer.
At peer or prince—at prince or peer,
I aim my shaft and know no fear!

I've wisdom from the East and from the West,
    That's subject to no academic rule;
You may find it in the jeering of a jest,
    Or distil it from the folly of a fool.
I can teach you with a quip, if I've a mind;
    I can trick you into learning with a laugh;
Oh winnow all my folly, and you'll find
    A grain or two of truth among the chaff!

I can set a braggart quailing with a quip,
    The upstart I can wither with a whim;
He may wear a merry laugh upon his lip,
    But his laughter has an echo that is grim!
When they're offered to the world in merry
    guise,
    Unpleasant truths are swallowed with a
    will—
For he who'd make his fellow creatures wise
    Should always gild the philosophic pill!

LIEUTENANT. And how come you to leave your last employ?

POINT. Why sir, it was in this wise. My Lord was the Archbishop of Canterbury, and it was considered that one of my jokes was unsuited to His Grace's family circle. In truth I ventured to ask a poor riddle, sir—Wherein lay the difference between His Grace and poor Jack Point? His Grace was pleased to give it up, sir. And thereupon I told him that whereas His Grace was paid £10,000 a year for being good, poor Jack Point was good—for nothing. 'Twas but a harmless jest, but it offended His Grace, who whipped me and set me in the stocks for a scurril rogue, and so we parted. I had as lief not take post again with the dignified clergy.

LIEUTENANT. But I trust you are very careful not to give offence. I have daughters.

POINT. Sir, my jests are most carefully selected, and anything objectionable is expunged. If your honour pleases, I will try them first on your honour's chaplain.

LIEUTENANT. Can you give me an example? Say that I had sat me down hurriedly on something sharp?

POINT. Sir, I should say that you had sat down on the spur of the moment.

LIEUTENANT. Humph. I don't think much of that. Is that the best you can do?

POINT. It has always been much admired, sir, but we will try again.

LIEUTENANT. Well then, I am at dinner, and the joint of meat is but half cooked.

POINT. Why then, sir, I should say—that what is *under*done cannot be helped.

LIEUTENANT. I see. I think that manner of thing would be somewhat irritating.

POINT. At first, sir, perhaps; but use is everything, and you would come in time to like it.

LIEUTENANT. We will suppose that I caught you kissing the kitchen wench under my very nose.

POINT. Under *her* very nose, good sir—not under yours! *That* is where *I* would kiss her. Do you take me? Oh, sir, a pretty wit—a pretty, pretty wit!

LIEUTENANT. The maiden comes. Follow me, friend, and we will discuss this matter at length in my library.

POINT. I am your worship's servant. That is to say, I trust I soon shall be. But, before proceeding to a more serious topic, can you tell me, sir, why a cook's brain-pan is like an overwound clock?

LIEUTENANT. A truce to this fooling—follow me.

POINT. Just my luck; my best conundrum wasted! (*Exeunt.*)

Enter ELSIE *from Tower, followed by* WILFRED, *who removes the bandage from her eyes.*

RECITATIVE *and* BALLAD — ELSIE.

'Tis done! I am a bride! Oh, little ring,
    That bearest in thy circlet all the gladness
That lovers hope for, and that poets sing,
    What bringest thou to me but gold and sadness?
A bridegroom all unknown, save in this wise,
To-day he dies! To-day, alas, he dies!

    Though tear and long-drawn sigh
        Ill fit a bride,
    No sadder wife than I
        The whole world wide!
        Ah me! Ah me!
        Yet maids there be
    Who would consent to lose
        The very rose of youth,
        The flower of life,
    To be, in honest truth,
        A wedded wife,
        No matter whose!

Ere half an hour has rung,
    A widow I!
Ah! heaven, he is too young,
    Too brave to die!
      Ah me! Ah me!
        Yet wives there be
So weary worn, I trow,
That they would scarce complain,
    So that they could
    In half an hour attain
      To widowhood,
        No matter how!

(Exit ELSIE *as* WILFRED *comes down.)*

WILFRED *(looking after* ELSIE). 'Tis an odd freak, for a dying man and his confessor to be closeted alone with a strange singing girl. I would fain have espied them, but they stopped up the keyhole. *My* keyhole!

Enter PHŒBE *with* MERYLL, *who carries a bundle.* MERYLL *remains in the background, unobserved by* WILFRED.

PHŒBE *(aside).* Wilfred—and alone! Now to get the keys from him. *(Aloud.)* Wilfred—has no reprieve arrived?

WILFRED. None. Thine adored Fairfax is to die.

PHŒBE. Nay, thou knowest that I have naught but pity for the poor condemned gentleman.

WILFRED. I know that he who is about to die is more to thee than I, who am alive and well.

PHŒBE. Why, that were out of reason, dear Wilfred. Do they not say that a live ass is better than a dead lion? No, I don't mean that!

WILFRED. They say that, do they?

PHŒBE. It's unpardonably rude of them, but I believe they put it in that way. Not that it applies to thee, who art clever beyond all telling!

WILFRED. Oh, yes; as an assistant tormentor.

PHŒBE. As a wit, as a humorist, as a most philosophic commentator on the vanity of human resolution.

PHŒBE *slyly takes bunch of keys from* WILFRED'S *waistband, and hands them to* MERYLL, *who enters the Tower, unnoticed by* WILFRED.

WILFRED. Truly, I have seen great resolution give way under my persuasive methods *(working a small thumbscrew).* In the nice regulation of a screw—in the hundredth part of a single revolution lieth all the difference between stony reticence and a torrent of impulsive unbosoming that the pen can scarcely follow. Ha! ha! I am a mad wag.

PHŒBE *(with a grimace).* Thou art a most light-hearted and delightful companion, Master Wil-

fred. Thine anecdotes of the torture-chamber are the prettiest hearing.

WILFRED. I'm a pleasant fellow an I choose. I believe I am the merriest dog that barks. Ah, we might be passing happy together—

PHŒBE. Perhaps. I do not know.

WILFRED. For thou wouldst make a most tender and loving wife.

PHŒBE. Aye, to one whom I really loved. For there is a wealth of love within this little heart—saving up for—I wonder whom? Now, of all the world of men, I wonder whom? To think that he whom I am to wed is now alive and somewhere! Perhaps far away, perhaps close at hand! And I know him not! It seemeth that I am wasting time in not knowing him.

WILFRED. Now say that it is I—nay! suppose it for the nonce. Say that we are wed—suppose it only—say that thou art my very bride, and I thy cheery, joyous, bright, frolicsome husband—and that the day's work being done, and the prisoners stowed away for the night, thou and I are alone together—with a long, long evening before us!

PHŒBE *(with a grimace).* It is a pretty picture—but I scarcely know. It cometh so unexpectedly—and yet—and yet—*were* I thy bride—

WILFRED. Aye!—wert thou my bride—?

PHŒBE. Oh, how I would love thee!

BALLAD — PHŒBE.

Were I thy bride,
Then the whole world beside
    Were not too wide
      To hold my wealth of love—
    Were I thy bride!

Upon thy breast
My loving head would rest,
    As on her nest
      The tender turtle dove—
    Were I thy bride!

This heart of mine
Would be one heart with thine,
    And in that shrine
      Our happiness would dwell—
    Were I thy bride!

And all day long
Our lives should be a song:
    No grief, no wrong
      Should make my heart rebel—
    Were I thy bride!

The silvery flute,
The melancholy lute,
    Were night-owl's hoot
      To my love-whispered coo—

Were I thy bride!

The skylark's trill
Were but discordance shrill
To the soft thrill
    Of wooing as I'd woo—
Were I thy bride!

MERYLL *re-enters; gives keys to* PHŒBE *who replaces them at* WILFRED'S *girdle, unnoticed by him.*

The rose's sigh
Were as a carrion's cry
To lullaby
    Such as I'd sing to thee,
Were I thy bride!

A feather's press
Were leaden heaviness
To my caress.
    But then, of course, you see
    I'm not thy bride!
                    (*Exit* PHŒBE.)

WILFRED. No, thou'rt not—not yet! But, Lord, how she woo'd! I should be no mean judge of wooing, seeing that I have been more hotly woo'd than most men. I have been woo'd by maid, widow, and wife. I have been woo'd boldly, timidly, tearfully, shyly—by direct assault, by suggestion, by implication, by inference, and by innuendo. But this wooing is not of the common order: it is the wooing of one who must needs woo me, if she die for it! (*Exit* WILFRED.)

Enter MERYLL, *cautiously, from Tower.*

MERYLL (*looking after them*). The deed is, so far, safely accomplished. The slyboots, how she wheedled him! What a helpless ninny is a love-sick man! He is but as a lute in a woman's hands—she plays upon him whatever tune she will. But the Colonel comes. I' faith he's just in time, for the Yeomen parade here for his execution in two minutes!

Enter FAIRFAX, *without beard and moustache, and dressed in Yeoman's uniform.*

FAIRFAX. My good and kind friend, thou runnest a grave risk for me!

MERYLL. Tut, sir, no risk. I'll warrant none here will recognize you. You make a brave Yeoman, sir! So—this ruff is too high; so—and the sword should hang thus. Here is your halbert, sir; carry it thus. The Yeomen come. Now remember, you are my brave son, Leonard Meryll.

FAIRFAX. If I may not bear mine own name, there is none other I would bear so readily.

MERYLL. Now, sir, put a bold face on it; for they come.

Enter Yeomen of the Guard.

RECITATIVE — SERGEANT MERYLL.

Ye Tower Yeomen, nursed in war's alarms,
    Suckled on gunpowder, and weaned on glory,
Behold my son, whose all-subduing arms
    Have formed the theme of many a song and
        story!
        Forgive his aged father's pride; nor jeer
        His aged father's sympathetic tear!
                    (*Pretending to weep.*)

CHORUS.

Leonard Meryll!
Leonard Meryll!
Dauntless he in time of peril!
    Man of power,
    Knighthood's flower,
Welcome to the grim old Tower,
To the Tower, welcome thou!

RECITATIVE — FAIRFAX.

Forbear, my friends, and spare me this ovation;
I have small claim to such consideration:
The tales that of my prowess have been stated
Are all prodigiously exaggerated!

CHORUS.

'Tis ever thus!
Wherever valour true is found,
True modesty will there abound.
'Tis ever thus!

Wherever valour true is found,
True modesty will there abound.

COUPLETS.

FIRST YEOMAN. Didst thou not, oh, Leonard
Meryll!
Standard lost in last campaign,
Rescue it at deadly peril—
Bear it bravely back again?

CHORUS. Leonard Meryll, at his peril,
Bore it bravely back again!

SECOND YEOMAN. Didst thou not, when prisoner
taken,
And debarred from all escape,
Face, with gallant heart unshaken,
Death in most appalling shape?

CHORUS. Leonard Meryll faced his peril,
Death in most appalling shape!

FAIRFAX. Truly I was to be pitied,
Having but an hour to live;
I reluctantly submitted,
I had no alternative!
Oh, the facts that have been stated
Of my deeds of derring-do,
Have been much exaggerated,
Very much exaggerated,
Monstrously exaggerated!
Scarce a word of them is true!

THIRD YEOMAN. You, when brought to execu-
tion,
Like a demigod of yore,
With heroic resolution
Snatched a sword and killed a score!

CHORUS. Leonard Meryll, Leonard Meryll
Snatched a sword and killed a score!

FOURTH YEOMAN. Then escaping from the foe-
men,
Boltered with the blood you shed,
You, defiant, fearing no men,
Saved your honour and your head!

CHORUS. Leonard Meryll, Leonard Meryll
Saved his honour and his head!

FAIRFAX. True, my course with judgment shap-
ing,
Favoured, too, by lucky star,
I succeeded in escaping
Prison bolt and prison bar!
Oh! the tales that have been stated
Of my deeds of derring-do,
Have been much exaggerated, &c.

CHORUS. They are not exaggerated, &c.

Enter PHŒBE. *She rushes to* FAIRFAX *and
embraces him.*

RECITATIVE.

PHŒBE. Leonard!
FAIRFAX (*puzzled*). I beg your pardon?
PHŒBE.   Don't you know me?
I'm little Phœbe!
FAIRFAX (*still puzzled*). Phœbe? Is this Phœbe?
My little Phœbe? (*Aside.*) Who the deuce
may *she* be?
It can't be Phœbe, surely?
WILFRED.   Yes, 'tis Phœbe—
Thy sister Phœbe!
ALL.   Aye, he speaks the truth;
'Tis Phœbe!
FAIRFAX (*pretending to recognize her*). Sister
Phœbe!
PHŒBE.   Oh, my brother! (*Embrace.*)
FAIRFAX. Why, how you've grown! I did not
recognize you!
PHŒBE. So many years! Oh, brother! (*Embrace.*)
FAIRFAX.   Oh, my sister!
WILFRED. Aye, hug him, girl! There are three
thou mayst hug—
Thy father and thy brother and—myself!
FAIRFAX. Thyself, forsooth? And who art thou
thyself?
WILFRED. Good sir, we are betrothed. (FAIRFAX
turns enquiringly to PHŒBE.)
PHŒBE.   Or more or less—
But rather less than more!
WILFRED.   To thy fond care
I do commend thy sister. Be to her
An ever-watchful guardian—eagle-eyed!
And when she feels (as sometimes she does
feel)
Disposed to indiscriminate caress,
Be thou at hand to take those favours from
her!
ALL.   Yes, yes,
Be thou at hand to take those favours from
her!
PHŒBE (*in* FAIRFAX'S *arms*). Yes, yes,
Be thou at hand to take those favours from
me!

TRIO.
WILFRED, FAIRFAX, *and* PHŒBE.

WILFRED. To thy fraternal care
Thy sister I commend;
From every lurking snare
Thy lovely charge defend:
And to achieve this end,
Oh! grant, I pray, this boon—

She shall not quit thy sight:
From morn to afternoon—
From afternoon to night—
From seven o'clock to two—
From two to eventide—
From dim twilight to 'leven at night
She shall not quit thy side!

ALL.   Oh! grant, I pray, this boon, &c.

PHŒBE.   So amiable I've grown,
    So innocent as well,
That if I'm left alone,
    The consequences fell
    No mortal can foretell.
So grant, I pray, this boon—
    I shall not quit thy sight:
From morn to afternoon—
From afternoon to night—
From seven o'clock till two—
From two till day is done—
From dim twilight to 'leven at night
    All kinds of risk I run!

ALL.   So grant, I pray, this boon, &c.

FAIRFAX.   With brotherly readiness,
    For my fair sister's sake,
At once I answer "Yes"—
    That task I undertake—
    My word I never break.
I freely grant that boon,
    And I'll repeat my plight.
From morn to afternoon—   (Kiss.)
    From afternoon to night—   (Kiss.)
    From seven o'clock to two—   (Kiss.)
    From two to evening meal—   (Kiss.)
From dim twilight to 'leven at night
    That compact I will seal.   (Kiss.)

ALL.   He freely grants that boon, &c.

The Bell of St. Peter's begins to toll. The crowd enters; the block is brought on to the stage, and the headsman takes his place. The Yeomen of the Guard form up. FAIRFAX and two others entering the White Tower, to bring the prisoner to execution. The LIEUTENANT enters and takes his place, and tells off FAIRFAX and two others to bring the prisoner to execution.

CHORUS (*to tolling accompaniment*).

The prisoner comes to meet his doom:
The block, the headsman, and the tomb.
The funeral bell begins to toll—
May Heaven have mercy on his soul!

SOLO — ELSIE.

Oh, Mercy, thou whose smile has shone
    So many a captive on;

Of all immured within these walls,
    The very worthiest falls!

REPRISE OF CHORUS.

The prisoner comes to meet his doom—
The block, the headsman, and the tomb.
The funeral bell begins to toll—
May Heaven have mercy on his soul!

Enter FAIRFAX *and two other Yeomen from Tower in great excitement.*

FAIRFAX.   My lord! my lord! I know not how to tell
    The news I bear!
I and my comrades sought the prisoner's cell—
    He is not there!

ALL.   He is not there!
They sought the prisoner's cell—he is not there!

TRIO — FAIRFAX *and* TWO YEOMEN.

As escort for the prisoner
    We sought his cell, in duty bound;
The double gratings open were,
    No prisoner at all we found!
We hunted high, we hunted low,
    We hunted here, we hunted there—
The man we sought, as truth will show,
    Had vanished into empty air!

ALL.   Had vanished into empty air!
The man they sought with anxious care
Had vanished into empty air!

GIRLS.   Now, by our troth, the news is fair,
The man hath vanished into air!

ALL.   As escort for the prisoner
    They sought his cell in duty bound, &c.

LIEUTENANT.   Astounding news! The prisoner fled.
    (*To* WILFRED.) Thy life shall forfeit be instead!
            (WILFRED *is arrested.*)

WILFRED.   My lord, I did not set him free,
    I hate the man—my rival he!
            (WILFRED *is taken away.*)

MERYLL.   The prisoner gone—I'm all agape!
    Who could have helped him to escape?

PHŒBE.   Indeed I can't imagine who!
    I've no idea at all—have you?

DAME.   Of his escape no traces lurk—
    Enchantment must have been at work!

ELSIE (*aside to* POINT).   What have I done! Oh, woe is me!

I am his wife, and he is free!

Whate'er betide
You are his bride,
And I am left
Alone—bereft!
Yes, woe is *me*, I rather think!
Yes, woe is *me*, I rather think!

POINT. Oh, woe is *you?* Your anguish sink!
Oh, woe is *me*, I rather think!
Oh, woe is *me*, I rather think!
Yes, woe is *me*, I rather think!

ENSEMBLE.

LIEUTENANT.	ELSIE.	POINT.
All frenzied with despair I rave, The grave is cheated of its due. Who is the misbegotten knave Who hath contrived this deed to do? Let search be made throughout the land, Or my vindictive anger dread— A thousand marks to him I hand Who brings him here, alive or dead.	All frenzied with despair I rave, My anguish rends my heart in two. Unloved, to him my hand I gave; To him, unloved, bound to be true! Unloved, unknown, unseen—the brand Of infamy upon his head: A bride that's husbandless, I stand To all mankind for ever dead!	All frenzied with despair I rave, My anguish rends my heart in two. Your hand to him you freely gave; It's woe to *me*, not woe to you! My laugh is dead, my heart unmanned, A jester with a soul of lead! A lover loverless I stand, To womankind for ever dead!

The others sing the LIEUTENANT'S *verse, with altered pronouns. At the end,* ELSIE *faints in* FAIRFAX'S *arms; all the Yeomen and populace rush off the stage in different directions, to hunt for the fugitive, leaving only the Headsman on the stage, and* ELSIE *insensible in* FAIRFAX'S *arms.*

ACT DROP.

ACT II.

SCENE. — *Tower Green by Moonlight. Two days have elapsed. Women and Yeomen of the Guard discovered.*

CHORUS OF WOMEN.

Night has spread her pall once more,
And the prisoner still is free:
Open is his dungeon door,
Useless now his dungeon key!
He has shaken off his yoke—
How, no mortal man can tell!
Shame on loutish jailor-folk—
Shame on sleepy sentinel!

ALL.   He has shaken off his yoke, &c.

SOLO — DAME CARRUTHERS.

Warders are ye?
Whom do ye ward?
Bolt, bar, and key,
Shackle and cord,
Fetter and chain,
Dungeon of stone,
All are in vain—
Prisoner's flown!
Spite of ye all, he is free—he is free!
Whom do ye ward? Pretty warders are ye!

CHORUS OF YEOMEN.

Up and down, and in and out,
Here and there, and round about;
Every chamber, every house,
Every chink that holds a mouse,
Every crevice in the keep,
Where a beetle black could creep,
Every outlet, every drain,
Have we searched, but all in vain!

YEOMEN.	WOMEN.
Warders are we:	Warders are ye?
Whom do we	Whom do ye
ward?	ward?
Bolt, bar, and key,	Bolt, bar, and key;
Shackle and cord,	Shackle and cord,
Fetter and chain,	Fetter and chain,
Dungeon of stone,	Dungeon of stone,
All are in vain.	All are in vain.
Prisoner's flown!	Prisoner's flown!
Spite of us all, he is	Spite of ye all, he is
free! he is free!	free! he is free!
Whom do we ward?	Whom do ye ward?
Pretty warders	Pretty warders
are we!	are ye!
	(*Exeunt all.*)

Enter JACK POINT, *in low spirits, reading from a huge volume.*

POINT (*reads*). "The Merrie Jestes of Hugh Ambrose. No. 7863. The Poor Wit and the Rich Councillor. A certayne poor wit, being an-hungered, did meet a well-fed councillor. 'Marry, fool,' quoth the councillor, 'whither away?' 'In truth,' said the poor wag, 'in that I have eaten naught these two dayes, I do wither away, and that right rapidly!' The councillor laughed hugely, and gave him a sausage." Humph! The councillor was easier to please than my new master the Lieutenant. I would like to take post under that councillor. Ah! 'tis but melancholy mumming when poor, heartbroken, jilted Jack Point must needs turn to Hugh Ambrose for original light humour!

Enter WILFRED, *also in low spirits.*

WILFRED (*sighing*).   Ah, Master Point!

POINT (*changing his manner*).   Ha! friend jailor! Jailor that wast—jailor that never shalt be more! Jailor that jailed not, or that jailed, if jail he did, so unjailorly that 'twas but jerry-jailing, or jailing in joke—though no joke to him who, by unjailorlike jailing, did so jeopardize his jailorship. Come, take heart, smile, laugh, wink, twinkle, thou tormentor that tormentest none—thou racker that rackest not—thou pincher out of place—come, take heart, and be merry, as I am!—(*aside, dolefully*)—as I am!

WILFRED.   Aye, it's well for thee to laugh. Thou hast a good post, and hast cause to be merry.

POINT (*bitterly*).   Cause? Have we not all cause? Is not the world a big butt of humour, into which all who will may drive a gimlet? See, I am a salaried wit; and is there aught in nature more ridiculous? A poor, dull, heartbroken man, who must needs be merry, or he will be whipped; who must rejoice, lest he starve; who must jest you, jibe you, quip you, crank you, wrack you, riddle you, from hour to hour, from day to day, from year to year, lest he dwindle, perish, starve, pine, and die! Why, when there's naught else to laugh at, I laugh at myself till I ache for it!

WILFRED.   Yet I have often thought that a jester's calling would suit me to a hair.

POINT.   Thee? Would suit *thee,* thou death's-head and cross-bones?

WILFRED.   Aye, I have a pretty wit—a light, airy, joysome wit, spiced with anecdotes of prison cells and the torture chamber. Oh, a very delicate wit! I have tried it on many a prisoner, and there have been some who smiled. Now it is not easy to make a prisoner smile. And it should not be difficult to be a good jester, seeing that thou art one.

POINT.   Difficult? Nothing easier. Nothing easier. Attend, and I will prove it to thee!

SONG — POINT.

Oh! a private buffoon is a light-hearted loon,
    If you listen to popular rumour;
From morning to night he's so joyous and
        bright,
    And he bubbles with wit and good humour!
He's so quaint and so terse, both in prose and
        in verse;
    Yet though people forgive his transgression,
There are one or two rules that all family fools
    Must observe, if they love their profession.
        There are one or two rules,
            Half a dozen, maybe,
        That all family fools,
            Of whatever degree,
        Must observe, if they love their profession.

If you wish to succeed as a jester, you'll need
    To consider each person's auricular:
What is all right for B would quite scandalize C
    (For C is so very particular);
And D may be dull, and E's very thick skull
    Is as empty of brains as a ladle;
While F is F sharp, and will cry with a carp,
    That he's known your best joke from his
        cradle!
        When your humour they flout,
            You can't let yourself go;
        And it *does* put you out
            When a person says, "Oh,
    I have known that old joke from my
        cradle!"

If your master is surly, from getting up early
    (And tempers are short in the morning),
An inopportune joke is enough to provoke
    Him, to give you, at once, a month's warning.
Then if you refrain, he is at you again,
    For he likes to get value for money.
He'll ask then and there, with an insolent stare,

"If you know that you're paid to be funny?"
　　It adds to the task
　　　Of a merryman's place,
　　When your principal asks,
　　　With a scowl on his face,
　If you know that you're paid to be funny?

Comes a Bishop, maybe, or a solemn D.D.—
　Oh, beware of his anger provoking!
Better not pull his hair—don't stick pins in his
　　chair:
　He don't understand practical joking.
If the jests that you crack have an orthodox
　　smack,
　You may get a bland smile from these sages;
But should it, by chance, be imported from
　　France,
　Half-a-crown is stopped out of your wages!
　　　It's a general rule,
　　　　Though your zeal it may quench,
　　　If the family fool
　　　　Tells a joke that's too French,
　Half-a-crown is stopped out of his wages!

Though your head it may rack with a bilious
　　attack,
　And your senses with toothache you're los-
　　ing,
Don't be mopy and flat—they don't fine you
　　for that,
　If you're properly quaint and amusing!
Though your wife ran away with a soldier that
　　day,
　And took with her your trifle of money;
Bless your heart, they don't mind—they're ex-
　　ceedingly kind—
　They don't blame you—as long as you're
　　funny!
　　　It's a comfort to feel
　　　　If your partner should flit,
　　　Though *you* suffer a deal,
　　　　They don't mind it a bit—
　They don't blame you—so long as you're
　　funny!

POINT. And so thou wouldst be a jester, eh?
Now, listen! My sweetheart, Elsie Maynard, was
secretly wed to this Fairfax half an hour ere he
escaped.

WILFRED. She did well.

POINT. She did nothing of the kind, so hold thy
peace and perpend. Now, while he liveth she is
dead to me and I to her, and so, my jibes and
jokes notwithstanding, I am the saddest and the
sorriest dog in England!

WILFRED. Thou art a very dull dog indeed.

POINT. Now, if thou wilt swear that thou didst
shoot this Fairfax while he was trying to swim
across the river—it needs but the discharge of an
arquebus on a dark night—and that he sank and
was seen no more, I'll make thee the very Archbishop of jesters, and that in two days' time! Now,
what sayest thou?

WILFRED. I am to lie?

POINT. Heartily. But thy lie must be a lie of circumstance, which I will support with the testimony of eyes, ears, and tongue.

WILFRED. And thou wilt qualify me as a jester?

POINT. As a jester among jesters. I will teach
thee all my original songs, my self-constructed
riddles, my own ingenious paradoxes; nay, more,
I will reveal to thee the source whence I get them.
Now, what sayest thou?

WILFRED. Why, if it be but a lie thou wantest of
me, I hold it cheap enough, and I say yes, it is a
bargain!

ENSEMBLE — POINT *and* WILFRED.

BOTH.　Hereupon we're both agreed,
　　　　And all that we two
　　　　Do agree to
　　We'll secure by solemn deed,
　　　　To prevent all
　　　　Error mental.
　{ I / You } on Elsie { am / are } to call
　　　With a story
　　　Grim and gory;
　How this Fairfax died, and all
　{ I / You } declare to
　{ You're / I'm } to swear to!
　Tell a tale of cock and bull,
　Of convincing detail full:
　　　Tale tremendous,
　　　Heaven defend us!
　What a tale of cock and bull!

In return for { your / my } own part
{ You are / I am } making,
　Undertaking,
To instruct { me / you } in the art
　　(Art amazing,
　　Wonder raising)
Of a jester, jesting free.
　　Proud position—
　　High ambition!
And a lively one { I'll / you'll } be,
　　Wag-a-wagging,

Never flagging!
    Tell a tale of cock and bull,
        &c.   (*Exeunt together.*)

Enter FAIRFAX.

FAIRFAX.   A day and a half gone, and no news of poor Fairfax! The dolts! They seek him everywhere save within a dozen yards of his dungeon. So I am free! Free, but for the cursed haste with which I hurried headlong into the bonds of matrimony with—Heaven knows whom! As far as I remember, she should have been young; but even had not her face been concealed by her kerchief, I doubt whether, in my then plight, I should have taken much note of her. Free? Bah! The Tower bonds were but a thread of silk compared with these conjugal fetters which I, fool that I was, placed upon mine own hands. From the one I broke readily enough—how to break the other!

SONG — FAIRFAX.

Free from his fetters grim—
    Free to depart;
Free both in life and limb—
    In all but heart!
Bound to an unknown bride
    For good and ill;
Ah, is not one so tied
    A prisoner still?

Free, yet in fetters held
    Till his last hour,
Gyves that no smith can weld,
    No rust devour!
Although a monarch's hand
    Had set him free,
Of all the captive band
    The saddest he!

Enter MERYLL.

FAIRFAX.   Well, Sergeant Meryll, and how fares thy pretty charge, Elsie Maynard?

MERYLL.   Well enough, sir. She is quite strong again, and leaves us to-night.

FAIRFAX.   Thanks to Dame Carruthers' kind nursing, eh?

MERYLL.   Aye, deuce take the old witch! Ah, 'twas but a sorry trick you played me, sir, to bring the fainting girl to me. It gave the old lady an excuse for taking up her quarters in my house, and for the last two years I've shunned her like the plague. Another day of it and she would have married me! Good Lord, here she is again! I'll e'en go——(*going*).

Enter DAME CARRUTHERS *and* KATE, *her niece.*

DAME.   Nay, Sergeant Meryll, don't go. I have something of grave import to say to thee.

MERYLL (*aside*).   It's coming.

FAIRFAX (*laughing*).   I' faith, I think I'm not wanted here (*going*).

DAME.   Nay, Master Leonard, I've naught to say to thy father that his son may not hear.

FAIRFAX (*aside*).   True. I'm one of the family; I had forgotten!

DAME.   'Tis about this Elsie Maynard. A pretty girl, Master Leonard.

FAIRFAX.   Ay, fair as a peach blossom—what then?

DAME.   She hath a liking for thee, or I mistake not.

FAIRFAX.   With all my heart. She's as dainty a little maid as you'll find in a midsummer day's march.

DAME.   Then be warned in time, and give not thy heart to her. Oh, *I* know what it is to give my heart to one who will have none of it!

MERYLL (*aside*).   Ay, *she* knows all about that. (*Aloud.*) And why is my boy to take heed of her? She's a good girl, Dame Carruthers.

DAME.   Good enough, for aught I know. But she's no girl. She's a married woman.

MERYLL.   A married woman! Tush, old lady— she's promised to Jack Point, the Lieutenant's new jester.

DAME.   Tush in thy teeth, old man! As my niece Kate sat by her bedside to-day, this Elsie slept, and as she slept she moaned and groaned, and turned this way and that way—and, "How shall I marry one I have never seen?" quoth she—then, "An hundred crowns!" quoth she—then, "Is it certain he will die in an hour?" quoth she—then, "I love him not, and yet I am his wife," quoth she! Is it not so, Kate?

KATE. Aye, mother, 'tis even so.

FAIRFAX. Art thou sure of all this?

KATE. Aye, sir, for I wrote it all down on my tablets.

DAME. Now, mark my words: it was of this Fairfax she spake, and he is her husband, or I'll swallow my kirtle!

MERYLL (*aside*). Is this true, sir?

FAIRFAX. True? Why, the girl was raving! Why should she marry a man who had but an hour to live?

DAME. Marry? There be those who would marry but for a minute, rather than die old maids!

MERYLL (*aside*). Aye, I know one of them!

QUARTETTE.

KATE, FAIRFAX, DAME CARRUTHERS, *and* MERYLL.

Strange adventure! Maiden wedded
    To a groom she's never seen—
        Never, never, never seen!
Groom about to be beheaded,
    In an hour on Tower Green!
        Tower, Tower, Tower Green!
Groom in dreary dungeon lying,
Groom as good as dead, or dying,
For a pretty maiden sighing—
    Pretty maid of seventeen!
        Seven—seven—seventeen!

Strange adventure that we're trolling:
    Modest maid and gallant groom—
        Gallant, gallant, gallant groom!—
While the funeral bell is tolling,
    Holling, tolling, Bim-a-boom!
        Bim-a, Bim-a, Bim-a-boom!
Modest maiden will not tarry;
Though but sixteen year she carry,
She must marry, she must marry,
    Though the altar be a tomb—
        Tower—Tower—Tower tomb!

(*Exeunt* DAME CARRUTHERS, MERYLL, *and*
KATE.)

FAIRFAX. So my mysterious bride is no other than this winsome Elsie! By my hand, 'tis no such ill-plunge in Fortune's lucky bag! I might have fared worse with my eyes open! But she comes. Now to test her principles. 'Tis not every husband who has a chance of wooing his own wife!

Enter ELSIE.

FAIRFAX. Mistress Elsie!

ELSIE. Master Leonard!

FAIRFAX. So thou leavest us to-night?

ELSIE. Yes, Master Leonard. I have been kindly tended, and I almost fear I am loth to go.

FAIRFAX. And this Fairfax. Wast thou glad when he escaped?

ELSIE. Why, truly, Master Leonard, it is a sad thing that a young and gallant gentleman should die in the very fullness of his life.

FAIRFAX. Then, when thou didst faint in my arms, it was for joy at his safety?

ELSIE. It may be so. I was highly wrought, Master Leonard, and I am but a girl, and so, when I am highly wrought, I faint.

FAIRFAX. Now, dost thou know, I am consumed with a parlous jealousy?

ELSIE. Thou? And of whom?

FAIRFAX. Why, of this Fairfax, surely!

ELSIE. Of Colonel Fairfax!

FAIRFAX. Aye. Shall I be frank with thee? Elsie —I love thee, ardently, passionately! (ELSIE *alarmed and surprised.*) Elsie, I have loved thee these two days—which is a long time—and I would fain join my life to thine!

ELSIE. Master Leonard! Thou art jesting!

FAIRFAX. Jesting? May I shrivel into raisins if I jest! I love thee with a love that is a fever—with a love that is a frenzy—with a love that eateth up my heart! What sayest thou? Thou wilt not let my heart be eaten up?

ELSIE (*aside*). Oh, mercy! What am I to say?

FAIRFAX. Dost thou love me, or hast thou been insensible these two days?

ELSIE. I love all brave men.

FAIRFAX. Nay, there is love in excess. I thank heaven, there are many brave men in England; but if thou lovest them all, I withdraw my thanks.

ELSIE. I love the bravest best. But, sir, I may not listen—I am not free—I—I am a wife!

FAIRFAX. Thou a wife? Whose? His name? His hours are numbered—nay, his grave is dug, and his epitaph set up! Come, his name?

ELSIE. Oh, sir! keep my secret—it is the only barrier that Fate could set up between us. My husband is none other than Colonel Fairfax!

FAIRFAX. The greatest villain unhung! The most ill-begotten, ill-favoured, ill-mannered, ill-natured, ill-omened, ill-tempered dog in Christendom!

ELSIE. It is very like. He is naught to me—for I never saw him. I was blindfolded, and he was to have died within the hour; and he did not die— and I am wedded to him, and my heart is broken!

FAIRFAX. He was to have died, and he did *not* die? The scoundrel! The perjured, traitorous villain! Thou shouldst have insisted on his dying first, to make sure. 'Tis the only way with these Fairfaxes.

ELSIE.   I now wish I had!

FAIRFAX (*aside*). Bloodthirsty little maiden! (*Aloud.*) A fig for this Fairfax! Be mine—he will never know—he dares not show himself; and if he dare, what art thou to him? Fly with me, Elsie— we will be married to-morrow, and thou shalt be the happiest wife in England!

ELSIE. Master Leonard! I am amazed! Is it thus that brave soldiers speak to poor girls? Oh! for shame, for shame! I am wed—not the less because I love not my husband. I am a wife, sir, and I have a duty, and—oh, sir! thy words terrify me—they are not honest—they are wicked words, and un- worthy thy great and brave heart! Oh, shame upon thee! shame upon thee!

FAIRFAX. Nay, Elsie, I did but jest. I spake but to try thee—

Shot heard. Enter MERYLL, *hastily.*

MERYLL (*recit.*). Hark! What was that, sir?

FAIRFAX.   Why, an arquebus—
    Fired from the wharf, unless I much mistake.

MERYLL. Strange—and at such an hour! What can it mean?
(*In the meantime, the Chorus have entered.*)

CHORUS.

Now what can that have been—
    A shot so late at night,
    Enough to cause affright!
What can the portent mean?

Are foemen in the land?
    Is London to be wrecked?
    What are we to expect?
What danger is at hand?
    Yes, let us understand
    What danger is at hand!

LIEUTENANT *enters, also* POINT *and* WILFRED.

LIEUTENANT. Who fired that shot? At once the truth declare!

WILFRED. My lord, 'twas I—to rashly judge for- bear!

POINT. My lord, 'twas he—to rashly judge for- bear!

DUET AND CHORUS — WILFRED *and* POINT.

WILFRED. Like a ghost his vigil keeping—
POINT. Or a spectre all-appalling—
WILFRED. I beheld a figure creeping—
POINT. I should rather call it crawling—
WILFRED. He was creeping—
POINT.   He was crawling—
WILFRED. He was creeping, creeping—
POINT.   Crawling!

WILFRED. Not a moment's hesitation—
    I myself upon him flung,
With a hurried exclamation
    To his draperies I hung;
Then we closed with one another
In a rough-and-tumble smother;
Colonel Fairfax and no other
    Was the man to whom I clung!

FAIRFAX. Colonel Fairfax and no other
    Was the man to whom he clung!

ALL. Colonel Fairfax and no other
    Was the man to whom he clung!
Yes—they closed with one another
In a rough-and-tumble smother;
Colonel Fairfax and no other
    Was the man to whom he clung!

WILFRED. After mighty tug and tussle—
POINT. It resembled more a struggle—
WILFRED. He, by dint of stronger muscle—
POINT. Or by some infernal juggle—
WILFRED. From my clutches quickly sliding—
POINT. I should rather call it slipping—
WILFRED. With the view, no doubt, of hiding—
POINT. Or escaping to the shipping—
WILFRED. With a gasp, and with a quiver—
POINT. I'd describe it as a shiver—
WILFRED. He plunged headlong in the river
    And, alas, I cannot swim!

ALL. It's enough to make one shiver,
    With a gasp and with a quiver,
    He plunged headlong in the river,
    It was very brave of him!

WILFRED. Ingenuity is catching;
    With the view my king of pleasing,
    Arquebus from sentry snatching—
POINT. I should rather call it seizing—
WILFRED. With an ounce or two of lead
    I despatched him through the head!

ALL. He despatched him through the head!

WILFRED. I discharged it without winking,
    Little time he lost in thinking,
    Like a stone I saw him sinking—
POINT. I should say a lump of lead.
WILFRED. Like a stone, my boy, I said—
POINT. Like a heavy lump of lead.
WILFRED. Anyhow, the man is dead.

ALL. Whether stone or lump of lead,
    Arquebus from sentry seizing,
    With the view his king of pleasing,
        Wilfred shot him through the head,
        And he's very, very dead.

And it matters very little whether stone or lump
  of lead,
It is very, very certain that he's very, very dead!

CHORUS.

Hail! the valiant fellow who
Did this deed of derring-do;
Honours wait on such an one;
By my head, 'twas bravely done!

RECITATIVE — LIEUTENANT.

The river must be dragged—no time be lost;
The body must be found, at any cost.
To this attend without undue delay;
So set to work with what despatch ye may!
(*Exit.*)

ALL.   Yes, yes,
We'll set to work with what despatch we may!
(*Four men raise* WILFRED, *and carry him off on
                              their shoulders.*)

CHORUS. Hail the valiant fellow who
Did this deed of derring-do!
Honours wait on such an one;
By my head, 'twas bravely done!
(*Exeunt all but* ELSIE, POINT, FAIRFAX, *and
                              PHŒBE.*)

POINT (*to* ELSIE, *who is weeping*). Nay, sweetheart, be comforted. This Fairfax was but a pestilent fellow, and, as he had to die, he might as well die thus as any other way. 'Twas a good death.

ELSIE. Still, he was my husband, and had he not been, he was nevertheless a living man, and now he is dead; and so, by your leave, my tears may flow unchidden, Master Point.

FAIRFAX. And thou didst see all this?

POINT. Aye, with both eyes at once—this and that. The testimony of one eye is naught—he may lie. But when it is corroborated by the other, it is good evidence that none may gainsay. Here are both present in court, ready to swear to him!

PHŒBE. But art thou sure it was Colonel Fairfax? Saw you his face?

POINT. Aye, and a plaguey ill-favoured face too. A very hang-dog face—a felon face—a face to fright the headsman himself, and make him strike awry. Oh, a plaguey bad face, take my word for 't. (PHŒBE *and* FAIRFAX *laugh.*) How they laugh! 'Tis ever thus with simple folk—an accepted wit has but to say, "Pass the mustard," and they roar their ribs out!

FAIRFAX (*aside*). If ever I come to life again, thou shalt pay for this, Master Point!

POINT. Now, Elsie, thou art free to choose again, so behold me: I am young and well-favoured. I have a pretty wit. I can jest you, jibe you, quip you, crank you, wrack you, riddle you—

FAIRFAX. Tush, man, thou knowest not how to woo. 'Tis not to be done with time-worn jests and threadbare sophistries, with quips, conundrums, rhymes, and paradoxes. 'Tis an art in itself, and must be studied gravely and conscientiously.

TRIO.
FAIRFAX, ELSIE, *and* PHŒBE.

FAIRFAX. A man who would woo a fair maid,
  Should 'prentice himself to the trade;
    And study all day,
    In methodical way,
  How to flatter, cajole, and persuade.
  He should 'prentice himself at fourteen,
  And practice from morning to e'en;
    And when he's of age,
    If he will, I'll engage,
  He may capture the heart of a queen!

ALL. It is purely a matter of skill,
    Which all may attain if they will:
      But every Jack,
      He must study the knack
    If he wants to make sure of his Jill!

ELSIE. If he's made the best use of his time,
  His twig he'll so carefully lime
    That every bird
    Will come down at his word,
  Whatever its plumage and clime.
  He must learn that the thrill of a touch
  May mean little, or nothing, or much;
    It's an instrument rare,
    To be handled with care,
  And ought to be treated as such.

ALL. It is purely a matter of skill, &c.

PHŒBE. Then a glance may be timid or free,
  It will vary in mighty degree,
    From an impudent stare
    To a look of despair
  That no maid without pity can see;
  And a glance of despair is no guide—
  It may have its ridiculous side;
    It may draw you a tear
    Or a box on the ear;
  You can never be sure till you've tried!

ALL. It is purely a matter of skill, &c.

FAIRFAX (*aside to* POINT). Now listen to me—'tis done thus— (*Aloud.*) Mistress Elsie, there is one here who, as thou knowest, loves thee right well!

POINT (*aside*). That he does—right well!

FAIRFAX. He is but a man of poor estate, but he hath a loving, honest heart. He will be a true and trusty husband to thee, and if thou wilt be his

wife, thou shalt lie curled up in his heart, like a little squirrel in its nest!

POINT (*aside*). 'Tis a pretty figure. A maggot in a nut lies closer, but a squirrel will do.

FAIRFAX. He knoweth that thou wast a wife—an unloved and unloving wife, and his poor heart was near to breaking. But now that thine unloving husband is dead, and thou art free, he would fain pray that thou wouldst hearken unto him, and give him hope that thou wouldst be his!

PHŒBE (*alarmed*). He presses her hands—and he whispers in her ear! Ods boddikins, what does it mean?

FAIRFAX. Now, sweetheart, tell me—wilt thou be this poor good fellow's wife?

ELSIE. If the good, brave man—*is* he a brave man?

FAIRFAX. So men say.

POINT (*aside*). That's not true, but let it pass this once.

ELSIE. If this brave man will be content with a poor, penniless, untaught maid—

POINT (*aside*). Widow—but let *that* pass.

ELSIE. I will be his true and loving wife, and that with my heart of hearts!

FAIRFAX. My own dear love! (*Embracing her.*)

PHŒBE (*in great agitation*). Why, what's all this? Brother—brother—it is not seemly!

POINT (*also alarmed, aside*). Oh, I can't let *that* pass! (*Aloud.*) Hold, enough, Master Leonard! An advocate should have his fee, but methinks thou art over-paying thyself!

FAIRFAX. Nay, that is for Elsie to say. I promised thee I would show thee how to woo, and herein is the proof of the virtue of my teaching. Go, thou, and apply it elsewhere! (PHŒBE *bursts into tears.*)

QUARTETTE.

ELSIE, FAIRFAX, PHŒBE, *and* POINT.

ELSIE *and*
FAIRFAX.

When a wooer
    Goes a-wooing,
Naught is truer
    Than his joy.
Maiden hushing
    All his suing—
Boldly blushing—
    Bravely coy!

ALL.   Oh, the happy days of doing!
Oh, the sighing and the suing!
When a wooer goes a-wooing,
    Oh, the sweets that never cloy!

PHŒBE
(*weeping*).

When a brother
    Leaves his sister
For another,
    Sister weeps.
Tears that trickle,
    Tears that blister—
'Tis but mickle
    Sister reaps!

ALL.   Oh, the doing and undoing,
Oh, the sighing and the suing,
When a brother goes a-wooing,
    And a sobbing sister weeps!

POINT.   When a jester
    Is outwitted,
    Feelings fester,

Heart is lead!
Food for fishes
Only fitted,
Jester wishes
He was dead!

ALL.   Oh, the doing and undoing,
Oh, the sighing and the suing,
When a jester goes a-wooing,
And he wishes he was dead!
(*Exeunt all but* PHŒBE, *who remains weeping.*)

PHŒBE.   And I helped that man to escape, and I've kept his secret, and pretended that I was his dearly loving sister, and done everything I could think of to make folk believe I *was* his loving sister, and this is his gratitude! Before I pretend to be sister to anybody again, I'll turn nun, and be sister to everybody—one as much as another!

Enter WILFRED.

WILFRED.   In tears, eh? What a plague art thou grizzling for now?

PHŒBE.   Why am I grizzling? Thou hast often wept for jealousy—well, 'tis for jealousy I weep now. Aye, yellow, bilious, jaundiced jealousy. So make the most of that, Master Wilfred.

WILFRED.   But I have never given thee cause for jealousy. The Lieutenant's cook-maid and I are but the merest gossips!

PHŒBE.   Jealous of thee! Bah! I'm jealous of no craven cock-on-a-hill, who crows about what he'd do an he dared! I am jealous of another and a better man than thou—set that down, Master Wilfred. And he is to marry Elsie Maynard, the little pale fool, set that down, Master Wilfred, and my heart is well-nigh broken! There, thou hast it all! Make the most of it!

WILFRED.   The man thou lovest is to marry Elsie Maynard? Why, that is no other than thy brother, Leonard Meryll!

PHŒBE (*aside*).   Oh, mercy! what have I said?

WILFRED.   Why, what manner of brother is this, thou lying little jade? Speak! Who is this man whom thou hast called brother, and fondled, and coddled, and kissed—with my connivance, too! Oh! Lord, with my connivance! Ha! should it be this Fairfax! (PHŒBE *starts.*) It is! It is this accursed Fairfax! It's Fairfax! Fairfax, who—

PHŒBE.   Whom thou hast just shot through the head, and who lies at the bottom of the river!

WILFRED.   A—I—I may have been mistaken. We are but fallible mortals, the best of us. But I'll make sure—I'll make sure (*going*).

PHŒBE.   Stay—one word. I think it cannot be Fairfax—mind, I say I *think*—because thou hast just slain Fairfax. But whether he be Fairfax or no Fairfax, he is to marry Elsie—and—and—as thou hast shot him through the head, and he is dead, be content with that, and I will be thy wife!

WILFRED.   Is that sure?

PHŒBE.   Aye, sure enough, for there's no help for it! Thou art a very brute—but even brutes must marry, I suppose.

WILFRED.   My beloved! (*Embraces her.*)

PHŒBE (*aside*).   Ugh!

Enter LEONARD, *hastily.*

LEONARD.   Phœbe, rejoice, for I bring glad tidings. Colonel Fairfax's reprieve was signed two days since, but it was foully and maliciously kept back by Secretary Poltwhistle, who designed that it should arrive after the Colonel's death. It hath just come to hand, and it is now in the Lieutenant's possession!

PHŒBE.   Then the Colonel is free? Oh kiss me, kiss me, my dear! Kiss me, again, and again!

WILFRED (*dancing with fury*).   Ods bobs, death o' my life! Art thou mad? Am *I* mad? Are we *all* mad?

PHŒBE.   Oh my dear—my dear, I'm well-nigh crazed with joy! (*Kissing* LEONARD.)

WILFRED.   Come away from him, thou hussy—thou jade—thou kissing, clinging cockatrice! And as for thee, sir, I'll rip thee like a herring for this! I'll skin thee for it! I'll cleave thee to the chine! I'll—Oh! Phœbe! Phœbe! Phœbe! Who is this man?

PHŒBE.   Peace, fool. He is my brother!

WILFRED.   Another brother! Are there any more of them? Produce them all at once, and let me know the worst!

PHŒBE.   This is the real Leonard, dolt; the other was but his substitute. The *real* Leonard, I say—my father's own son.

WILFRED.   How do I know this? Has he "brother" writ large on his brow? I mistrust thy brothers! Thou art but a false jade! (*Exit* LEONARD.)

PHŒBE.   Now, Wilfred, be just. Truly I did deceive thee before—but it was to save a precious life—and to save it, not for me, but for another. They are to be wed this very day. Is not this enough for thee? Come—I am thy Phœbe—thy very own—and we will be wed in a year—or two—or three, at the most. Is not that enough for thee?

Enter MERYLL, *excitedly, followed by* DAME CARRUTHERS (*who listens, unobserved*).

MERYLL.   Phœbe, hast thou heard the brave news?

PHŒBE (*still in* WILFRED'S *arms*).   Aye, father.

MERYLL. I'm nigh mad with joy! (*Seeing* WIL-FRED.) Why, what's all this?

PHŒBE. Oh, father, he discovered our secret through my folly, and the price of his silence is—

WILFRED. Phœbe's heart.

PHŒBE. Oh, dear no—Phœbe's hand.

WILFRED. It's the same thing!

PHŒBE. *Is* it! (*Exeunt* WILFRED *and* PHŒBE.)

MERYLL (*looking after them*). 'Tis pity, but the Colonel had to be saved at any cost, and as thy folly revealed our secret, thy folly must e'en suffer for it! (DAME CARRUTHERS *comes down*.) Dame Carruthers!

DAME. So this is a plot to shield this arch-fiend, and I have detected it. A word from me, and three heads besides his would roll from their shoulders!

MERYLL. Nay, Colonel Fairfax is reprieved. (*Aside*.) Yet if my complicity in his escape were known! Plague on the old meddler! There's nothing for it!—(*Aloud*.) Hush, pretty one! Such bloodthirsty words ill become those cherry lips! (*Aside*.) Ugh!

DAME (*bashfully*). Sergeant Meryll!

MERYLL. Why look ye, chuck—for many a month I've—I've thought to myself—"There's snug love saving up in that middle-aged bosom for someone, and why not for thee—that's me—so take heart and tell her—that's thee—that thou—that's me—lovest her—thee—and—and" Well, I'm a miserable old man, and I've done it—and that's me! But not a word about Fairfax! The price of thy silence is—

DAME. Meryll's heart?

MERYLL. No, Meryll's *hand*.

DAME. It's the same thing!

MERYLL. *Is* it!

DUET — MERYLL *and* DAME CARRUTHERS.

DAME.   Rapture, rapture!
              When love's votary,
          Flushed with capture,
              Seeks the notary,
                  Joy and jollity
                  Then is polity;
                  Reigns frivolity!
          Rapture, rapture!

MERYLL.   Doleful, doleful!
              When humanity,
          With its soul full
              Of satanity,
                  Courting privity,
                  Down declivity
                  Seeks captivity!
          Doleful, doleful!

DAME.   Joyful, joyful!
              When virginity
          Seeks, all coyful,
              Man's affinity;
                  Fate all flowery,
                  Bright and bowery
                  Is her dowery!
          Joyful, joyful!

MERYLL.   Ghastly, ghastly!
              When man, sorrowful,
          Firstly, lastly,
              Of to-morrow full,
                  After tarrying,
                  Yields to harrying—
                  Goes a-marrying.
          Ghastly, ghastly!

FINALE.

Enter Yeomen, Women, and ELSIE *as Bride.*

CHORUS OF WOMEN.
(ELEGIACS.)

Comes the pretty young bride, a-blushing, timidly shrinking—
    Set all thy fears aside—cheerily, pretty young bride!
Brave is the youth to whom thy lot thou art willingly linking!

Flower of valour is he—loving as loving can be!
Brightly thy summer is shining,
Fair is the dawn of the day;
Take him, be true to him—
Tender his due to him—
Honour him, love and obey!

TRIO.

PHŒBE, ELSIE, *and* DAME CARRUTHERS.

'Tis said that joy in full perfection
Comes only once to womankind—
That, other times, on close inspection,
Some lurking bitter we shall find.
If this be so, and men say truly,
My day of joy has broken duly.
With happiness my soul is cloyed—
This is my joy-day unalloyed!

ALL.   Yes, yes,
This is her joy-day unalloyed!

Flourish. Enter LIEUTENANT.

LIEUTENANT.   Hold, pretty one! I bring to thee
News—good or ill, it is for thee to say.
Thy husband lives—and he is free,
And comes to claim his bride this very
day!

ELSIE.   No! no! recall those words—it cannot be!
Leonard, my Leonard, come, oh, come to me!
Leonard, my own—my loved one—where art
thou?
I knew not how I loved thine heart till now!

ENSEMBLE.

ELSIE *and* PHŒBE.	CHORUS *and* OTHERS.
Oh, day of terror! day of tears!	Oh, day of terror! day of tears!
What fearful tidings greet mine ears?	What words are these that greet our ears?
Oh, Leonard, come thou to my side,	Who is the man who, in his pride,
And claim me as thy loving bride.	So boldly claims thee as his bride?

LIEUTENANT *and* POINT.

Come, dry these unbecoming tears,
Most joyful tidings greet thine ears.
The man to whom thou art allied
Appears to claim thee as his bride.

Flourish. Enter COLONEL FAIRFAX, *handsomely
dressed, and attended by other Gentlemen.*

FAIRFAX (*sternly*).   All thought of Leonard Meryll
set aside.

Thou art mine own! I claim thee as my bride.

ELSIE.   A suppliant at thy feet I fall:
Thine heart will yield to pity's call!

FAIRFAX.   Mine is a heart of massive rock,
Unmoved by sentimental shock!

ALL.   Thy husband he!

ELSIE.   Leonard my loved one—come to me.
They bear me hence away!
But though they take me far from thee,
My heart is thine for aye!
My bruisèd heart,
My broken heart,
Is thine, my own, for aye!

(*To* FAIRFAX.) Sir, I obey,
I am thy bride;
But ere the fatal hour
I said the say
That placed me in thy power,
Would I had died!
Sir, I obey!
I am thy bride!
            (*Looks up and recognizes* FAIRFAX.)
Leonard!

FAIRFAX.   My own!

ELSIE.   Ah! (*Embrace.*)

ELSIE *and* { With happiness my soul is cloyed,
FAIRFAX. { This is my joy-day unalloyed!

ALL.   Yes! yes!
With happiness their souls are cloyed,
This is their joy-day unalloyed!

POINT.   Oh thoughtless crew!
Ye know not what ye do!
Attend to me, and shed a tear or two—
For I have a song to sing, O!

ALL.   Sing me your song, O! &c.

POINT.   It is sung to the moon
By a love-lorn loon,
Who fled from the mocking throng, O!
It's the song of a merryman moping mum,
Whose soul was sad and whose glance was
glum,
Who sipped no sup and who craved no
crumb,
As he sighed for the love of a ladye!

ALL.   Heighdy! Heighdy!
Misery me, lackadaydee!
He sipped no sup and he craved no crumb,
As he sighed for the love of a ladye!

ELSIE.   I have a song to sing, O!

ALL.   Sing me your song, O!

ELSIE.   It is sung with the ring
               Of the songs maids sing
             Who love with a love life-long, O!
           It's the song of a merrymaid, peerly proud,
           Who loved a lord, and who laughed aloud
           At the moan of the merryman moping mum,
           Whose soul was sad and whose glance was
               glum,

Who sipped no sup and who craved no
    crumb,
  As he sighed for the love of a ladye!

ALL.   Heighdy! Heighdy!
           Misery me, lackadaydee!
         He sipped no sup and he craved no crumb,
           As he sighed for the love of a ladye!

FAIRFAX *embraces* ELSIE *as* POINT *falls insensible
at their feet.*

CURTAIN.

Postscript

MANY ALTERATIONS—in some instances actually new writing—stand between what the Savoy audience heard on October 3, 1888, and current staged or recorded performances. Whereas the changes made in Gilbert and Sullivan's preceding opera, *Ruddygore*, were largely concerned with dialog, the changes in *The Yeomen of the Guard* in great part involved the lyrics, as will be observed from the following résumé:

The solo, "This the autumn of our life," following the Chorus of Yeomen on page 316, is in current performance given to the Second Yeoman rather than to Sergeant Meryll. The second verse of Dame Carruther's Tower song repeats "I keep my silent watch and ward!" instead of using "It keeps its silent. . . ." On page 318, the two-verse song for Sergeant Meryll, "A laughing boy but yesterday," appears only in the first edition and indeed was probably sung only on the first night (page 310). (Its music still exists in the score used by the Rudolph Aaronson first American production, in the possession of the New York Public Library.)

In the Trio of Phœbe, Leonard, and Meryll on page 318, the second half is rearranged and shortened in the third edition as follows:

MERYLL.	And shall I reckon risks I run When services are to be done To save the life of such an one? Unworthy thought!
PHŒBE *and* LEONARD.	And shall we reckon risks we run To save the life of such an one?
ALL.	Unworthy thought! We may succeed—who can foretell? May heaven help our hope—farewell!

In the second verse of the well-loved Duet for Jack Point and Elsie—"I have a song to sing, O!" (page 320)—the line "Whose soul was sore . . ." was changed in the third edition to "Whose soul was sad" to conform to the other three verses. At the same time Jack Point's "Sing me your song, O" at the beginning of the second verse, which originally had an interrogation mark, became "What is your song, O?" which of course it should be in order to justify the interrogation mark.

The Trio for Elsie Maynard, Jack Point, and the Lieutenant (page 322) in the first edition has three verses of twelve lines each, with a statement of the Chorus after each verse. This was considerably altered in the second edition so that the verses for Elsie, Point and the Lieutenant have ten, eight, and nine lines respectively, and the chorus comes in only once at the conclusion of the third verse. Here is the rewritten version as used in current production:

TRIO—ELSIE, POINT, *and* LIEUTENANT.

LIEUT. How say you, maiden, will you wed
    A man about to lose his head?
      For half an hour
        You'll be a wife,
      And then the dower
        Is yours for life.
    A headless bridegroom why refuse?
    If truth the poets tell,
    Most bridegrooms, ere they marry, lose
    Both head and heart as well!

ELSIE. A strange proposal you reveal,
    It almost makes my senses reel.
    Alas! I'm very poor indeed,
    And such a sum I sorely need.
      My mother, sir, is like to die,
        This money life may bring,
      Bear this in mind, I pray, if I
        Consent to do this thing!

POINT. Though as a general rule of life
    I don't allow my promised wife,
    My lovely bride that is to be,
    To marry anyone but me,
      Yet if the fee is promptly paid,
        And he, in well-earned grave,
      Within the hour is duly laid,
      Objection I will waive!
      Yes, objection I will waive!

ALL. Temptation, oh, temptation,
      Were we, I pray, intended
    To shun, whate'er our station,
      Your fascinations splendid;
    Or fall, whene'er we view you,
    Head over heels into you!

In current texts and performances the first line of Jack Point's Recitative on page 323 is "I've jibe and joke." Beginning with the third edition, Elsie Maynard's song following the Recitative, " 'Tis done! I am a bride! . . . ," has an additional four lines added to each verse. After the first verse:

    Ah me! What profit we,
      O maids that sigh,
    Though gold, though gold should live
      If wedded love must die?

After the second verse:

    O weary wives

Who widowhood would win,
Rejoice that ye have time
To weary in.

The entrance of the Yeomen at the beginning of the Act I Finale (page 325) is heralded by a new ten-line chorus added in the third edition of the libretto (although this had been in the earliest vocal score):

Oh, Sergeant Meryll, is it true—
    The welcome news we read in orders?
Thy son, whose deeds of derring-do
Are echoed all the country through,
    Has come to join the Tower Warders?
If so, we come to meet him,
That we may fitly greet him,
And welcome his arrival here
With shout on shout and cheer on cheer.
    Hurrah! Hurrah! Hurrah!

This is followed by Sergeant Meryll's Recitative, of which the opening line was changed to start, "Ye Tower Warders." In Fairfax's Recitative the last line becomes, "Have been prodigiously exaggerated!" The couplets for the 3rd and 4th Yeomen, together with the chorus lines for each, are cut from all texts after the first edition, as is Fairfax's second verse, "True, my course with judgment shaping. . . ." This shortened version, therefore, closes with Fairfax's first verse from which the line "Monstrously exaggerated!" has been cut; and the Chorus chimes in with

They are not exaggerated,
Not at all exaggerated,
Could not be exaggerated!
    Every word of them is true!

The chorus following each of the three verses to the Trio of Wilfred, Fairfax, and Phœbe (page 327) is changed in the third edition to start with "From morn to afternoon," &c. And the reprise of the subsequent four-line chorus, "The prisoner comes to meet his doom . . ." is omitted after the first edition.

At the end of the opening chorus of the second act, the reprised portion beginning "He has shaken off his yoke" is cut; and after Dame Carruthers' solo, the Chorus of Women adds "Pretty warders are ye!" &c. On page 331 Fairfax's speech beginning "A day and a half gone . . ." is corrected to conform with the stage direction ("Two days have elapsed") at the start of the act.

In the patter-duet between Point and Wilfred (page 333) the two lines given to Fairfax—"Colonel Fairfax and no other was the man to whom he clung!"—are cut, and although the following Chorus keeps its reprise of these two lines, the remaining four lines of its commentary are also cut. Later Wilfred's line is changed to "Down he dived

into the river" (instead of "He plunged headlong in the river") and the same change is made by the chorus. His final line in the first-edition duet is increased in the second edition to two lines— "Anyhow the man is dead. Whether stone or lump of lead"—which are both repeated by the closing chorus before proceeding with their "Arquebus from sentry seizing. . . ." Then the immediately following Chorus, "Hail! the valiant fellow who . . ." is cut out after the first edition so that in all later librettos and productions these four lines of chorus appear only once, after the Recitative of the Lieutenant, and not before it as well. (And a fifth line is added, "By my head, 'twas bravely done!" thereby conforming with the vocal score.)

The Duet, "Rapture, Rapture!" for Sergeant Meryll and Dame Carruthers (page 337), although still in the most recent published libretto, is no longer included in the official production. In the Finale—following the Trio of Phœbe, Elsie and Dame Carruthers—the Chorus in the third edition becomes "Yes, yes, With happiness her soul is cloyed! This is her joy-day unalloyed!" and Elsie's subsequent four-line plea is reduced to its first line only, "No! no! recall those words—it cannot be!"

The important change in the Finale reprise of "I have a song to sing, O!" leads one inevitably to that perennial focus of Savoyard disagreement: Does Jack Point die or merely swoon at the closing curtain? There is not space in these pages to permit airing all the pros and cons to this question, and like the answer to Point's "best conundrum" —Why is a cook's brain-pan like an overwound clock?—it will remain forever unresolved. But if the facts (as opposed to the hearsay) are considered in the light of Gilbert's dominant uncertainty, one is led to the following conclusions:

Gilbert meant what he wrote when he used the stage-direction: "Fairfax embraces Elsie as Point falls insensible at their feet." He did not write "dead" or "lifeless"; nor, in the course of a half-dozen opportunities to change this direction in proof-sheets of five issues of the second edition and the subsequent third edition current at the time of Gilbert's death, did he move to do so. This is all the more significant in the light of the controversial interest in the differing interpretations given the role of Point within a few weeks of the first-night performance. Gilbert was not one to leave anything on which he himself had strong feelings to an actor's personal discretion. That he did not instantly and with characteristic Gilbertian vigor *disapprove* a touring-company Jack Point who chose to play dead, may be due to his basic uncertainty of the impact of this real-life plot on his audiences, and to his showman's realization that the effect of a stage direction (in Miss Audrey Williamson's words) can "only depend on the imagination of player and audience." But the simple boy-meets-girl-boy-gets-girl formula inherent in the plots of both *The Mikado* and *The Yeomen* plays so differently! Nanki-Poo gets Yum-Yum just as Colonel Fairfax gets Elsie Maynard; but there are no tears for a *Bab Ballad* Ko-Ko as there are for a flesh-and-blood Jack Point.

One must agree with Thomas F. Dunhill: It is impossible to believe that Gilbert ever gave Sir Henry Lytton the sweeping approval for the death-ending contained in Lytton's recollection more than thirty years later: "It is just what I want. Jack Point should die and the end of the opera should be a tragedy." Perhaps it is significant that Lytton did not in Gilbert's lifetime play Jack Point at the Savoy. If the imaginations of Lytton and his provincial audiences saw *The Yeomen* as featuring the death of Point at the final curtain, it is entirely reconcilable that Gilbert, in London, did not *disapprove*. Let the distant customer always be right. After all—Frank Stockton never had to choose between the lady or the tiger.

It is most interesting that one of Gilbert's many alterations in *The Yeomen*'s lyrics from the first-night text lies in the finale reprise of "I have a song to sing, O!" and shows a softening of Elsie's feelings toward the rejected Point. Instead of singing heartlessly as "a merrymaid, peerly proud, who loved a lord, and who laughed aloud at the moan of the merryman . . ." Elsie now sings:

> It's the song of a merrymaid, nestling near,
> Who loved her lord—but who dropped a tear
> At the moan of the merryman, moping mum . . .

This change was first made in the libretto contemporary with the May 5, 1897, revival, as its Dramatis Personae page lists both the 1888 and the 1897 casts.

Leslie Baily writes that Rupert D'Oyly Carte confirmed this date for the change in Elsie's lyric, but that he (D'Oyly Carte) attributed it to the fact that Gilbert had been impressed by Lytton's interpretation of Jack Point. There is really no justification for this reasoning. George Grossmith and John Wilkinson had shared the Point role throughout the 1888-9 original run, and Walter Passmore played Point to Lytton's Shadbolt in the 1897 revival. Gilbert's motivation stemmed more likely from nothing more complicated than the making of an improvement that enabled the singing farce of "The Merryman and his Maid" more nearly to parallel the living triangle of his plot.

THE GONDOLIERS

Introduction

"THE GONDOLIERS A GREAT SUCCESS" headlined the *Sunday Times* of December 8, 1889. "A verdict of emphatic and unanimous approval was passed last night by a brilliant house upon Mr. W. S. Gilbert and Sir Arthur Sullivan's new comic opera. . . . That verdict was never for a moment in doubt. From the time the curtain rose . . . there reigned in the Savoy Theatre but one steady, undisturbed atmosphere of contentment—contentment with the music, the dances, the piece, the scenery, the dresses, and not the least of all, with the talented and loyal members of Mr. D'Oyly Carte's company. Once more, therefore, may it go forth to the world that the distinguished collaborators to whom the present generation is indebted for some of its most delightful entertainment have scored a great triumph—the greatest, beyond doubt, that has fallen to their lot since *The Mikado*."

"After a successful run of well nigh a year and a quarter, *The Yeomen of the Guard* has been withdrawn from the Savoy, and"—cheered the *Daily News* leader—"on Saturday night, in the presence of an audience who almost from first to last received the new work with unbounded enthusiasm, it was replaced by *The Gondoliers*. . . ."

The verdict was, indeed, very nearly unanimous: "*The Gondoliers* is one of the best, if not the best, of the Gilbert-Sullivan operas" (the *Globe*). "Mr. Gilbert and Sir Arthur Sullivan have scored again, and more heavily this time than with any other opera since they produced *The Mikado*" (the *Citizen*). "The success of *The Gondoliers* was complete from the opening chorus until the final dance" (*St. James Gazette*). "It is not opera or play; it is simply an entertainment—the most exquisite, the daintiest entertainment we have ever seen" (the *Echo*). And across the Atlantic, the New York *Herald*'s London reviewer wired—"The popular composer surpasses all his previous efforts, and W. S. Gilbert proves that he has lost none of his pleasing talent."

"*The Gondoliers,*" Leslie Baily has written in *The Gilbert & Sullivan Book*, "is a joyous opera, happy, kindly, exuberant, the sweet fruit of reconciliation . . ." The reconciliation had been, in a manner of speaking, a double one. The two collaborators had made up with each other after a quarrel over relative importance of librettist and composer, and they had made up with their public in reverting to the gay topsy-turvydom of their great previous successes. As the *Illustrated London News'* column, "The Playhouses," put it: "Mr. W. S. Gilbert has returned to the Gilbert of the past, and everyone is delighted. He is himself again . . . the Gilbert who on Saturday night was cheered till the audience was weary of cheering any more." Even anti-Gilbert *Punch* confessed: "Messrs. Gilbert and Sullivan's *Gondoliers* deserves to rank immediately after *The Mikado* and *Pinafore* bracketed. The *mise-en-scène* is in every way about as perfect as it is possible to be. . . . There are ever so many good things in the Opera. . . . The piece is so brilliant to the eye and ear, that there is never a dull moment on the stage or off it. It is just one of those simple *Bab-Ballady* stories which . . . may, especially on account of the music, be safely put down on the playgoer's list for 'a second hearing.' "

A detailed account in the *Daily News* fully recorded the social as well as the dramatic and musical values of the occasion: "The last great event of the theatrical year came off on Saturday night, when Sullivan and Gilbert's new comic opera was produced amid a scene of excitement, culminating in enthusiasm, which may almost be described as unprecedented. A good quarter of an hour before the overture commenced the favoured occupants of the reserved seats began to stream into the theatre, to find every other part of it crammed to the utmost limits of its capacity, and full of that hum and buzz with which the British public always signalises its expectation of an event of unusual interest. Mr. D'Oyly Carte was even then flitting about 'in front,' bearing the assured air of coming triumph, and warmly greeting his many friends.

"Among the occupants of private boxes earliest to arrive were Lord and Lady Londesborough, accompanied by Lord and Lady Raincliffe. Then came Mr. Reuben Sassoon, with Colonel Fitz-George and other friends. To the next box came Lady Randolph Churchill and two others; these were soon afterwards joined by Lord Dunraven. Facing each other in the opposite stage boxes were Mrs. Mackay and Mrs. Ronalds, each with a large party. [Both were American beauties of international *réclame:* one, wife of Comstock Lode millionaire John Mackay, grandmother of Ellin (Mrs. Irving) Berlin; the other, estranged wife of Pierre Lorillard Ronalds, Boston-born "permanent ambassadress to the Court of St. James," an amateur singer of great talent and lifelong intimate of Arthur Sullivan.] Mr. Alfred de Rothschild had another box, and yet another was allotted to Mr. Frederick Lehmann, who brought his daughter, Lady [Guy] Campbell. . . . Nearly every occupant of the stalls had some claim or other upon popular recognition"—including Captain Shaw, of the Fire Brigade—"once so melodiously apostrophised from the Savoy boards," as the *Sunday Times* recalled; and near him was Mr. Moffat, of the United States Consulate. Incidental Intelligence: The *Man of the World*'s reviewer reported, "The Americans are always conspicuous at a first night at the Savoy." And he added cryptically, "I can tell an American citizen (before he opens his mouth) by his shirt-cuffs."

The theatrical profession was well represented in Augustus Harris, John Hollingshead, John Hare (producers all), and Miss Florence St. John, in addition to a contingent of "old Savoyards who came to see the success of their former comrades": Miss Julia Gwynne, Miss Sybil Grey, Mr. J. G. Robertson, and Mr. Richard Temple. But the theatre could contain only a fraction—a fifth, the *Sunday Chronicle* estimated—of the hundreds who clamored for admission.

The regular program in the house that night resembled in general the regular first-night programs of the previous four operas, but in one respect it differed markedly: Astute Helen Lenoir, formerly assistant to and now wife of Manager Carte, had sold advertising space on the front cover as well as at the top and bottom and down the center of the inside spread. The souvenir program of the occasion featured classical allegorical figures devised by Alice Havers for the *Yeomen* late in 1889. Both these programs had in tiny numerals at the bottom of one page the quantity and date. Oddly, there seem to have been as many souvenir programs printed that night as regular programs, fifteen hundred of each, thereby insuring that every member of the audience had both of them. Perhaps this prodigality was dictated by the new advertisers. In both programs appeared the line: "On this occasion the Opera will be conducted by the Composer."

Again, as he had done for the first nights of *Ruddygore* and *Yeomen of the Guard*, D'Oyly Carte warned his audience that the intermission would be over-long and apologized in small gray paper leaflets that "in consequence of the complicated scenery . . . the kind indulgence of the audience is requested."

"And now for the story of last night"—as the enthusiastic *Sunday Times* reviewer began his detailed description of the event: "Sir Arthur, as is his wont on first performances, himself takes the baton in hand, and he is received on entering the orchestra with a prolonged round of applause. *The Gondoliers* does not, like *The Yeomen of the Guard*, boast a regular overture in classical form; simply the old style of introduction, bringing in two or three tunes to be heard later on, that is all. But the tunes serve their purpose." (Sullivan had explained his return to the old style of overture, when interviewed a week before by *Home News*. In reply to the question whether the overture would be in strict form, he said: "No. As you know, I took the trouble to do that in the case of *The Yeomen of the Guard*, but it went for nothing after the first night . . . Naturally I should prefer to please serious musicians in such a matter, but one must consider the general public.") "When the curtain rises," continued the *Sunday Times*, "it reveals the Piazzetta at Venice as it might have looked somewhere about the middle of last century. It is a glorious picture—one of Mr. Hawes Craven's masterpieces of colour and perspective."

After the opening chorus, when the two Palmieri brothers arrive upstage on their gondola, the audience stopped the performance with a welcoming demonstration for Giuseppe, Rutland Barrington, newly returned to the Savoy fold after his ill-fated try at theatre management. In his own words, "That was a very memorable first night for me. . . . I still feel very proud of the justification realized by the warmth of my reception that night, and I also remember it as giving an opportunity to a brother artist to display a consideration and tact for which one might often look in vain. Courtice Pounds and myself, as the two gondoliers, had to enter together in a boat, and we had hardly stepped out on to the stage and our greeting commenced, when he carefully hid behind some choristers until my welcome was ended. The public is always quick to recognize a graceful action, and his own reception was no less hearty on this account."

The entrance of Gianetta and Tessa evoked from the *Sunday Times* reviewer: "Miss Geraldine Ulmar and Miss Jessie Bond have never looked more charming than in these Venetian costumes, designed, like all the others, by that skillful genius, Mr. Percy Anderson." The arrival of His Grace the Duke of Plaza-Toro, with Duchess, daughter, and Private Drum, marked the company debuts of Mr. Frank Wyatt (the Duke) and Miss Decima Moore (Casilda). Their entrance number was encored as was the Duke's song, "In enterprise of martial kind." After Casilda and Luiz's recitative, on the first night and for an indeterminate period thereafter, Luiz (Mr. Brownlow) sang a ballad of two verses—"Thy wintry scorn I dearly prize"—which was specifically noted by the *Sunday Times* and is even found in Arthur Lawrence's biography of Sullivan, published the year before he died. This ballad appeared in the first edition of the libretto in the audience's hands December 7, 1889, but was replaced in the second edition, as in subsequent performances, by a duet for Casilda and Luiz. (See page 376.)

The *Daily News* commented that "both the ballad of Luiz and the paradoxical dialogue in which the lady confesses how much she loved him 'a quarter of an hour ago' somehow missed their point." This feeling, undoubtedly noted by Gilbert, must have led him to replace the ballad. "A pretty duet, with delicious little touches for muted violins, went better," continued the *Daily News*, referring to "There was a time—a time forever gone"; "and matters began to be still more lively with the entry of the Grand Inquisitor, a part played with rich humour by Mr. Denny. His song, in which he discloses the fact that he had entrusted

the babe to 'a highly respectable gondolier' . . . is so thoroughly English in style that the demand for an encore was uproarious."

After the quintet, and Tessa's and Gianetta's solos, came the finale with its rollicking quartette and its refrain, "A right down reg'lar Royal Queen," which, the *Daily News* reported, "the excited house at once encored, the pit emphatically demanding 'All of it,' a request laughingly granted by Sir A. Sullivan." This number made such a hit that, a few minutes later during the entr'acte, the gallery began whistling it, thereby helping the audience to endure with good humor the delay predicted by the management. The *Man of the World* commented facetiously, "The half-hour's interval was passed very pleasantly; but if the elaborate change of scenery cannot be effected more rapidly in future, I advise the ladies to take their needlework with them. The gentlemen will find the Savoy Hotel handy. . . ."

According to the *Morning Advertiser*, the first act had been prolonged "beyond the ordinary limit of time" by the encoring of almost everything sung. D'Oyly Carte and Sullivan must have conferred on this subject during the intermission, for the same reviewer noted that in the second act "frequent demands for repetitions were made, but a sensible opposition mercifully interposed." When the curtain rose on this act, the audience was treated to the characteristically lavish Savoy set-

"Monarchs of all they Savoy"
—from a PUNCH *cartoon of January 4, 1890, entitled "Once upon a time there were two kings."*

ting—"a Moorish pavilion at Barataria, with silver hanging lamps and a real water fountain splashing in the foreground." After Rutland Barrington had scored capitally with the patter-song, "Rising early in the morning," his brother monarch, Courtice Pounds, sang "Take a pair of sparkling eyes" to the delight of those privileged to hear the first public singing of this melodious favorite, described by the *Sunday Times* on that occasion as "one of Sir Arthur Sullivan's inspirations—a strain of purest melody, exquisitely accompanied by divided strings *pizzicati,* in imitation of a guitar." The arrival of the two girls, and their lively alternate-line song, set the stage for what the *Sunday Times* termed "the climax of energy and gaiety in this brightest of operas"—the cachucha. "The theme, which recalls the real Spanish *Cachucha,* is inspiriting beyond measure; the dance, in itself a treat to witness, is executed with a precision and *élan* that a troupe of terpsichorean professionals might envy. Nothing in its way to equal this has ever been done at the Savoy. We predict that all London will want to see the Cachucha danced by Geraldine Ulmar, Jessie Bond, Courtice Pounds, Rutland Barrington, and the incomparable Savoy chorus." It must have been these incomparables in their terpsichorean abandon that stimulated the *Topical Times* to note: "The attractions of *The Gondoliers* are numerous. To begin with, the chorus wore comparatively short skirts for the first time, and the gratifying fact is revealed to a curious world that the Savoy chorus are a very well-legged lot."

"But the musical gem of the opera has yet to come," bubbled the *Sunday Times.* "It is a quartet, 'In contemplative fashion' . . . a marvel of contrapuntal ingenuity, as mirth-provoking as it is clever, and notwithstanding its great difficulty, rendered with an ease and humour that fairly astound the musical listener. After this masterly piece of work, which the house would fain encore half a dozen times, the *dénouement* approaches. . . . The composer's inventive genius does not desert him as the end draws near. The concerted music is to the last a marvel of melodic grace and technical skill combined, while the closing finale furnishes welcome *reprises* of the barcarolle and the cachucha." The curtain fell at 11:30.

The *Daily News* held: "The performance was from first to last so thoroughly admirable as practically to be beyond criticism." The *Sunday Times* added that it "fully sustained the reputation of the Savoy for smoothness and efficiency of working on first nights. It went throughout 'with a snap,' as our American cousins would put it." The entire company was uproariously cheered when called before the curtain. "Sir Arthur Sullivan, who conducted with admirable coolness and judgment, came forward at the close with Mr.

Gilbert in response to one of the most enthusiastic 'calls' we ever remember witnessing at this theatre, Mr. D'Oyly Carte being similarly honoured." But, according to the *Sunday Chronicle,* "the demands for a speech were very sensibly refused." Cecil Howard, writing for the *Theatre,* praised the cast as "so truly excellent that had the opera been bad instead of so exceptionally clever, they would have almost certainly made of it a success."

The *Birmingham Post* noted "the fact that this was the first of the series which did not include Mr. Grossmith in the cast [he had been in every original cast since *The Sorcerer*], was present to the minds of all the audience." But the *Times* reported that his absence was not too noticeable; and the *Academy* stated somewhat unkindly: "That estimable, though limited, comedian and admirable social favourite must after all needs be reckoned as no exception to the rule '*Il n'y a pas d'homme nécessaire.*' " (Mrs. Grossmith was in the audience, however, and, according to the *Liverpool Post,* would "be able to tell 'Gee Gee,' toiling at Torquay, how the Savoy gets on without him.") The same Liverpool correspondent remarked: "Perhaps the only notable man in London absent through the play was Mr. Gilbert. Some say he was walking the streets, but he came back in time to share the ovation. . . . It was in accordance with his usual habitude that Mr. Gilbert abstained from sitting through the piece on the first night."

Exactly one week later Gilbert wrote his friend (later the Poet Laureate), Alfred Austin, an extraordinary (for him) belittling of his own work, undoubtedly stemming from the bitterness he still held for the critical denunciation of his play, *Brantingham Hall:* "Many thanks for your kind congratulations. The piece is ridiculous rubbish and is, accordingly, hailed as a masterpiece. If it had deserved one half of the encomiums passed upon it, it would have been howled off the stage."

Thomas F. Dunhill, in his *Sullivan's Comic Operas,* has stated: "Sullivan in *The Gondoliers* gave us what is perhaps the gayest music England has ever produced, and who shall say that . . . it is not a finely characteristic example of our national art?" In its opening-night review the *Daily Telegraph* mused: "We cannot tell whether or no Sir Arthur Sullivan went reluctantly from the melodrama of *The Yeomen of the Guard* to the rollicking comedy of its successor. Possibly the musician within him rebelled somewhat against a retrograde step . . . but, anyhow, the music of *The Gondoliers* conveys an impression of having been written *con amore.*" The *Evening News* revealed: "Sir Arthur Sullivan makes no secret of the fact that *The Gondoliers* has given him more trouble to compose than any of his previous works. The cause of this was his very natural anxiety to keep the work strung up to a prescribed pitch of brilliancy." Sir Arthur himself, in his previously quoted interview for *Home News* prior to the first night, explained: "There is a good deal more work in it than there was in the *Yeomen,* for nearly all the numbers are rapid. You will hear very little slow music in it. Of course the result is that there are more pages in the score. Two minutes' allegro means perhaps twenty pages, but with an andanted movement you would only use about six." The truth of this was noted, somewhat obliquely, by the sharp eyes of the *Hawk:* "There can be no doubt that Sir Arthur Sullivan has pulled *The Gondoliers* out of the Grand Canal. There are 47 pages in the libretto, and of these only 14 are dialogue." It is a fact that of the thirteen Gilbert and Sullivan operas with available vocal scores, *The Gondoliers*—with its 188 pages —is outstandingly the longest, sixty pages longer than that of *Pinafore.*

It seems likely that sincerity rather than any other motive prompted Gilbert to write his collaborator on the day after launching *The Gondoliers:* "I must thank you again for the magnificent work you have put into the piece. It gives one the chance of shining right through the twentieth century with a reflected light."

And Sullivan's reply surely bespoke that "sweet fruit of reconciliation" which, alas, was destined to fall from the tree before the summer of 1890: "Don't talk of reflected light. In such a perfect book as *The Gondoliers* you shine with an individual brilliancy which no other writer can hope to attain. If any thanks are due anywhere, they should be from me to you for the patience, willingness, and unfailing good nature with which you have received my suggestions, and your readiness to help me by according to them."

DECEMBER 7. *Quiet all day. Went to the theatre at 8. Began at 8:35. Of course crammed house—a great reception. Everything went splendidly with immense "go" and spirit, right up to the end. Gilbert and I got a tremendous ovation—we have never had such a brilliant first night. It looks as if the Opera were going to have a long run, and be a great success.*

ARTHUR SULLIVAN'S DIARY

An Entirely Original Comic Opera,

IN TWO ACTS,

ENTITLED

THE GONDOLIERS

OR,

THE KING OF BARATARIA.

Dramatis Personae.

THE DUKE OF PLAZA-TORO, *A Grandee of Spain*		MR. FRANK WYATT.
LUIZ, *His Attendant*		MR. BROWNLOW.
DON ALHAMBRA DEL BOLERO, *the Grand Inquisitor*		MR. DENNY.
MARCO PALMIERI		MR. COURTICE POUNDS.
GIUSEPPE PALMIERI		MR. RUTLAND BARRINGTON.
ANTONIO		MR. METCALF.
FRANCESCO	*Venetian Gondoliers*	MR. ROSE.
GIORGIO		MR. DE PLEDGE.
ANNIBALE		MR. WILBRAHAM.
OTTAVIO		MR. C. GILBERT.
THE DUCHESS OF PLAZA-TORO		MISS ROSINA BRANDRAM.
CASILDA, *Her Daughter*		MISS DECIMA MOORE.
GIANETTA		MISS GERALDINE ULMAR.
TESSA		MISS JESSIE BOND.
FIAMETTA	*Contadine*	MISS LAWRENCE.
VITTORIA		MISS COLE.
GIULIA		MISS PHYLLIS.
INEZ, *The King's Foster-Mother*		MISS BERNARD.

CHORUS OF GONDOLIERS AND CONTADINE, MEN-AT-ARMS, HERALDS, AND PAGES.

ACT I. — The Piazzetta, Venice.

ACT II. — Pavilion in the Palace of Barataria.

(An interval of three months is supposed to elapse between Acts I. and II.)

DATE. — 1750.

THE GONDOLIERS

OR,

THE KING OF BARATARIA.

___

ACT I.

SCENE. — THE PIAZZETTA, VENICE. *The Ducal Palace on the right.* FIAMETTA, GIULIA, VITTORIA, *and other Contadine discovered, each tying a bouquet of roses.*

CHORUS OF CONTADINE.

List and learn, ye dainty roses,
    Roses white and roses red,
Why we bind you into posies
    Ere your morning bloom has fled.
By a law of maiden's making
Accents of a heart that's aching,
Even though that heart be breaking,
    Should by maiden be unsaid:
Though they love with love exceeding,
They must seem to be unheeding—
Go ye then and do their pleading,
    Roses white and roses red!

FIAMETTA.

Two there are for whom, in duty,
    Every maid in Venice sighs—
Two so peerless in their beauty
    That they shame the summer skies.
We have hearts for them, in plenty,
We, alas, are four-and-twenty!
    They have hearts, but all too few,
    They, alas, are only two!

CHORUS.

Now ye know, ye dainty roses,
Why we bind you into posies
    Ere your morning bloom has fled,
    Roses white and roses red!

During this chorus ANTONIO, FRANCESCO, GIORGIO, *and other Gondoliers have entered unobserved by the Girls—at first two, then two more, then four, then half-a-dozen, then the remainder of the Chorus.*

RECITATIVE.

FRANCESCO. Good morrow, pretty maids; for whom prepare ye
    These floral tributes extraordinary?

FIAMETTA. For Marco and Giuseppe Palmieri,
    The pink and flower of all the Gondolieri.

GIULIA. They're coming here, as we have heard but lately,
    To choose two brides from us who sit sedately.

ANTONIO. Do all you maidens love them?

ALL.   Passionately!

ANTONIO. These gondoliers are to be envied greatly!

GIORGIO. But what of us, who one and all adore you?
    Have pity on our passion, I implore you!

FIAMETTA. These gentlemen must make their choice before you;

VITTORIA. In the meantime we tacitly ignore you.

GIULIA. When they have chosen two, that leaves you plenty—
    Two dozen we, and ye are four-and-twenty.

[351]

FIAMETTA *and* VITTORIA. Till then, enjoy your
  dolce far niente.

ANTONIO. With pleasure, nobody *contradicente!*

SONG — ANTONIO *and* CHORUS.

For the merriest fellows are we, tra la,
That ply on the emerald sea, tra la;
  With loving and laughing,
  And quipping and quaffing,
We're happy as happy can be, tra la—
  As happy as happy can be!

With sorrow we've nothing to do, tra la,
And care is a thing to pooh-pooh, tra la;
  And Jealousy yellow,
  Unfortunate fellow,
We drown in the shimmering blue, tra la,—
  We drown in the shimmering blue!

FIAMETTA (*looking off*). See, see, at last they
  come to make their choice—
  Let us acclaim them with united voice.
(MARCO *and* GIUSEPPE *appear in gondola at
  back.*)

ALL THE GIRLS. Hail, gallant gondolieri, ben'
  venuti!
  Accept our love, our homage, and our duty.
(MARCO *and* GIUSEPPE *jump ashore—the Girls
  salute them.*)

DUET — GIUSEPPE *and* MARCO,
  with CHORUS OF GIRLS.

GIUSEPPE *and* MARCO. Buon' giorno, signorine!
GIRLS.   Gondolieri carissimi!
          Siamo contadine!
GIUSEPPE *and* MARCO (*bowing*).
          Servitori umilissimi!
          Per chi questi fiori—
          Questi fiori bellis-
          simi?
GIRLS.   Per voi, bell' signori
          O eccellentissimi!
(*The Girls present their bouquets to* GIUSEPPE
and MARCO, *who are overwhelmed with them,
  and carry them with difficulty.*)
GIUSEPPE *and* MARCO (*their arms full of flowers*).
          O ciel'!
GIRLS.   Buon' giorno, cavalieri!
GIUSEPPE *and* MARCO (*deprecatingly*).
          Siamo gondolieri.
(*To* FIAMETTA *and* VITTORIA.)
          Signorina, io t'amo!
GIRLS (*deprecatingly*). Contadine siamo.
GIUSEPPE *and* MARCO. Signorine!
GIRLS (*deprecatingly*). Contadine!
(*Curtseying to* GIUSEPPE *and* MARCO).

          Cavalieri.
GIUSEPPE *and* MARCO (*deprecatingly*).
          Gondolieri! Poveri gon-
          dolieri!
CHORUS.   Buon' giorno, signorine,
          &c.

DUET — MARCO *and* GIUSEPPE.

We're called *gondolieri,*
But that's a vagary,
It's quite honorary
  The trade that we ply.

For gallantry noted
Since we were short-coated,
To ladies devoted,
  My brother and I!

When morning is breaking,
Our couches forsaking,
To greet their awaking
  With carols we come.

At summer day's nooning,
When weary lagooning,
Our mandolins tuning,
  We lazily thrum.

When vespers are ringing,
To hope ever clinging,
With songs of our singing
  A vigil we keep.

When daylight is fading,
Enwrapt in night's shading,
With soft serenading
  We lull them to sleep.

We're called *gondolieri,* &c.

RECITATIVE — MARCO *and* GIUSEPPE.

And now to choose our brides!
  As all are young and fair,
And amiable besides,
  We really do not care
  A preference to declare.
A bias to disclose
  Would be indelicate—
And therefore we propose
  To let impartial Fate
  Select for us a mate!

ALL.   Viva!
A bias to disclose
  Would be indelicate—
But how do they propose
  To let impartial Fate
  Select for them a mate?

MARCO. These handkerchiefs upon our eyes be
  good enough to bind,

GIUSEPPE. And take good care that both of us are absolutely blind;

BOTH. Then turn us round—and we, with all convenient despatch,
Will undertake to marry any two of you we catch!

ALL.   Viva!
They undertake to marry any two of us they catch!
(*The girls prepare to bind their eyes as directed.*)

FIAMETTA (*to* MARCO). Are you peeping?
Can you see me?

MARCO. Dark I'm keeping,
Dark and dreamy!
           (MARCO *slyly lifts bandage.*)

VITTORIA (*to* GIUSEPPE). If you're blinded
Truly say so.

GIUSEPPE. All right-minded
Players play so!   (*Slyly lifts bandage.*)

FIAMETTA (*detecting* MARCO). Conduct shady!
They are cheating!
Surely they de-
Serve a beating!   (*Replaces bandage.*)

VITTORIA (*detecting* GIUSEPPE).

This too much is;
  Maidens mocking—
Conduct such is
  Truly shocking!   (*Replaces bandages.*)

ALL.   You can spy, sir!
          Shut your eye, sir!
You may use it by-and-by, sir!
          You can see, sir!
          Don't tell me, sir!
That will do—now let it be, sir!

ALL THE GIRLS. My papa he keeps three horses,
          Black, and white, and dapple grey, sir;
Turn three times, then take your courses,
          Catch whichever girl you may, sir!

GIUSEPPE *and* MARCO *turn round, as directed, and try to catch the girls. Business of blind-man's buff. Eventually* MARCO *catches* GIANETTA, *and* GIUSEPPE *catches* TESSA. *The two girls try to escape, but in vain. The two men pass their hands over the girls' faces to discover their identity.*

GIUSEPPE. I've at length achieved a capture!
(*Guessing.*) This is Tessa! (*Removes bandage.*)
          Rapture, rapture!

MARCO (*guessing*). Gianetta fate has granted!
          (*Removes bandage.*)
Just the very girl I wanted!

GIUSEPPE (*politely to* MARCO). If you'd rather change—

TESSA.   My goodness! This indeed is simple rudeness.

MARCO (*politely to* GIUSEPPE). I've no preference whatever—

GIANETTA.   Listen to him! Well, I never!
                    (*Each man kisses each girl.*)
       Thank you, gallant *gondolieri*:
            In a set and formal measure
       It is scarcely necessary
            To express our pride and pleasure.
       Each of us to prove a treasure,
       Conjugal and monetary,
            Gladly will devote our leisure,
       Gay and gallant *gondolieri*.
            La, la, la, la, la! &c.

TESSA.   Gay and gallant *gondolieri*,
            Take us both and hold us tightly,
       You have luck extraordinary;
            We might both have been unsightly!
       If we judge your conduct rightly,
            'Twas a choice involuntary;
            Still we thank you most politely,
       Gay and gallant *gondolieri*!
            La, la, la, la, la! &c.

ALL THE GIRLS.   To these gallant *gondolieri*
            In a set and formal measure,
       It is scarcely necessary
            To express their pride and pleasure.
       Each of us to prove a treasure,
       Conjugal and monetary,
            Gladly will devote her leisure
       To the other *gondolieri*!
            La! la! la! la! la! &c.

ALL.   Fate in this has put his finger—
            Let us bow to Fate's decree,
       Then no longer let us linger,
            To the altar hurry we!
(*They all dance off two and two*—GIANETTA *with* MARCO, TESSA *with* GIUSEPPE.)

Flourish. A gondola arrives at the Piazzetta steps, from which enter the DUKE OF PLAZA-TORO, *the* DUCHESS, *their daughter* CASILDA, *and their attendant* LUIZ, *who carries a drum. All are dressed in pompous but old and faded clothes.*

ENTRÉE.

DUKE.   From the sunny Spanish shore,
            His Grace of Plaza-Tor'—

DUCHESS.   And His Grace's Duchess true—

CASILDA.   And His Grace's daughter, too—

LUIZ.   And His Grace's private drum

            To Venetia's shores have come:

ALL.   And if ever, ever, ever
            They get back to Spain,
       They will never, never, never
            Cross the sea again—

DUKE.   Neither that Grandee from the Spanish shore,
            The noble Duke of Plaza-Tor'—

DUCHESS.   Nor His Grace's Duchess, staunch and true—

CASILDA.   You may add, His Grace's daughter, too—

LUIZ.   And His Grace's own particular drum
            To Venetia's shore any more will come.

ALL.   And if ever, ever, ever
            They get back to Spain,
       They will never, never, never
            Cross the sea again!

DUKE. At last we have arrived at our destination. This is the Ducal Palace, and it is here that the Grand Inquisitor resides. As a Castilian hidalgo of ninety-five quarterings, I regret that I am unable to pay my state visit on a horse. As a Castilian hidalgo of that description, I should have preferred to ride through the streets of Venice; but owing, I presume, to an unusually wet season, the streets are in such a condition that equestrian exercise is impracticable. No matter. Where is our suite?

LUIZ (*coming forward*). Your Grace, I am here.

DUCHESS. Why do you not do yourself the honour to kneel when you address His Grace?

DUKE. My love, it is so small a matter! (*To* LUIZ.) Still, you may as well do it. (LUIZ *kneels.*)

CASILDA. The young man seems to entertain but an imperfect appreciation of the respect due from a menial to a Castilian hidalgo.

DUKE. My child, you are hard upon our suite. Still, he ought to have known better.

CASILDA. Papa, I've no patience with the presumption of persons in his plebeian position. If he does not appreciate that position, let him be whipped until he does.

DUKE. Let us hope the omission was not intended as a slight. I should be much hurt if I thought it was. So would he. (*To* LUIZ.) Where are the halberdiers who were to have had the honour of meeting us here, that our visit to the Grand Inquisitor might be made in becoming state?

LUIZ. Your Grace, the halberdiers are mercenary people who stipulated for a trifle on account.

DUKE. How tiresome! Well, let us hope the

Grand Inquisitor is a blind gentleman. And the band who were to have had the honour of escorting us? I see no band!

LUIZ. Your Grace, the band are sordid persons who required to be paid in advance.

DUCHESS. That's so like a band!

DUKE (annoyed). Insuperable difficulties meet me at every turn!

DUCHESS. But surely they know His Grace?

LUIZ. Exactly—they know His Grace.

DUKE. Well, let us hope that the Grand Inquisitor is a deaf gentleman. A cornet-à-piston would be something. You do not happen to possess the accomplishment of tootling like a cornet-à-piston?

LUIZ. Alas no, Your Grace! But I can imitate a farmyard.

DUKE (doubtfully). I don't see how that would help us. I don't see how we could bring it in.

CASILDA. It would not help us in the least. We are not a parcel of graziers come to market, dolt!

DUKE. My love, our suite's feelings! Still, we certainly are not graziers. (To LUIZ.) Be so good as to ring the bell and inform the Grand Inquisitor that His Grace the Duke of Plaza-Toro, Count Matadoro, Baron Picadoro—

DUCHESS. And suite—

DUKE. Have arrived at Venice, and seek—

CASILDA. Desire—

DUCHESS. Demand!

DUKE. And demand an audience.

LUIZ. Your Grace has but to command (rising).

DUKE (much moved). I felt sure of it—I felt sure of it! (Exit LUIZ into Ducal Palace.) And now, my love—(Aside to DUCHESS.) Shall we tell her? I think so—(Aloud to CASILDA.) And now, my love, prepare for a magnificent surprise. It is my agreeable duty to reveal to you a secret which should make you the happiest young lady in Venice!

CASILDA. A secret?

DUCHESS. A secret which, for State reasons, it has been necessary to preserve for twenty years.

DUKE. When you were a prattling babe of six months old you were married by proxy to no less a personage than the infant son and heir of His Majesty the immeasurably wealthy King of Barataria!

CASILDA. Married to the infant son of the King of Barataria? It was a most unpardonable liberty!

DUKE. Consider his extreme youth and forgive him. Shortly after the ceremony, that misguided monarch abandoned the creed of his forefathers, and became a Wesleyan Methodist of the most bigoted and persecuting type. The Grand Inquisi-

tor, determined that the innovation should not be perpetuated in Barataria, caused your smiling and unconscious husband to be stolen and conveyed to Venice. A fortnight since the Methodist Monarch and all his Wesleyan Court were killed in an insurrection, and we are here to ascertain the whereabouts of your husband, and to hail you, our daughter, as Her Majesty, the reigning Queen of Barataria! (Kneels.)

DUCHESS. Your Majesty! (Kneels.)

DUKE. It is at such moments as these that one feels how necessary it is to travel with a full band.

CASILDA. I, the Queen of Barataria! But I've nothing to wear! We are practically penniless!

DUKE. That point has not escaped me. Although I am unhappily in straitened circumstances at present, my social influence is something enormous; and a Company, to be called the Duke of Plaza-Toro, Limited, is in course of formation to work me. An influential directorate has been secured, and I shall myself join the Board after allotment.

CASILDA. Am I to understand that the Queen of Barataria may be called upon at any time to witness her honoured sire in process of liquidation?

DUCHESS. The speculation is not exempt from that drawback. If your father should stop, it will, of course, be necessary to wind him up.

CASILDA. But it's so undignified—it's so degrading! A Grandee of Spain turned into a public company! Such a thing was never heard of!

DUKE. My child, the Duke of Plaza-Toro does not follow fashions—he leads them. He always leads everybody. When he was in the army he led his regiment. He occasionally led them into action. He invariably led them out of it.

SONG — DUKE OF PLAZA-TORO.

In enterprise of martial kind,
    When there was any fighting,
He led his regiment from behind—
    He found it less exciting.
But when away his regiment ran,
    His place was at the fore, O—
        That celebrated,
        Cultivated,
        Underrated,
            Nobleman,
The Duke of Plaza-Toro!

ALL. In the first and foremost flight, ha, ha!
    You always found that knight, ha, ha!
        That celebrated,
        Cultivated,
        Underrated
            Nobleman,
    The Duke of Plaza-Toro!

DUKE. When to evade Destruction's hand
　　　To hide they all proceeded,
　　No soldier in that gallant band
　　　Hid half as well as he did.
　　He lay concealed throughout the war.
　　　And so preserved his gore, O!
　　　　That unaffected,
　　　　Undetected,
　　　　Well-connected
　　　　Warrior,
　　　The Duke of Plaza-Toro!

ALL.　In every doughty deed, ha, ha!
　　　He always took the lead, ha, ha!
　　　　That unaffected,
　　　　Undetected,
　　　　Well-connected
　　　　Warrior,
　　　The Duke of Plaza-Toro!

DUKE. When told that they would all be shot
　　　Unless they left the service,
　　That hero hesitated not,
　　　So marvellous his nerve is.
　　He sent his resignation in,
　　　The first of all his corps, O!
　　　　That very knowing,
　　　　Overflowing,
　　　　Easy-going,
　　　　Paladin,
　　　The Duke of Plaza-Toro!

ALL.　To men of grosser clay, ha, ha!
　　　He always showed the way, ha, ha!
　　　　That very knowing,
　　　　Overflowing,
　　　　Easy-going,
　　　　Paladin,
　　　The Duke of Plaza-Toro!

Exeunt DUKE *and* DUCHESS *into Grand Ducal Palace. As soon as they have disappeared,* LUIZ *and* CASILDA *rush to each other's arms.*

RECITATIVE — CASILDA *and* LUIZ.

O rapture, when alone together
　　Two loving hearts and those that bear them
May join in temporary tether,
　　Though Fate apart should rudely tear them!
Necessity, Invention's mother,

Compelled $\begin{Bmatrix} me \\ thee \end{Bmatrix}$ to a course of feigning—

But, left alone with one another,

$\begin{Bmatrix} \text{I will} \\ \text{Thou shalt} \end{Bmatrix}$ atone for $\begin{Bmatrix} my \\ thy \end{Bmatrix}$ disdaining!

BALLAD — LUIZ.

Thy wintry scorn I dearly prize,
　　Thy mocking pride I bless;

Thy scorn is love in deep disguise,
　　Thy pride is lowliness.
　　　Thy cold disdain,
　　　It gives no pain—
　　　'Tis mercy, played
　　　In masquerade.
　　　Thine angry frown
　　　Is but a gown
　　　That serves to dress
　　　Thy gentleness!

If angry frown and deep disdain
　　Be love in masked array,
So much the bitterer their arraign,
　　So much the sweeter they!
　　　With mocking smile
　　　My love beguile;
　　　With idle jest
　　　Appease my breast;
　　　With angry voice
　　　My soul rejoice;
　　　Beguile with scorn
　　　My heart forlorn!

Oh, happy he who is content to gain
　　Thy scorn, thine angry frown, thy deep disdain!

CASILDA. O Luiz, Luiz—what have you said! What have I done! What have I allowed you to do!

LUIZ. Nothing, I trust, that you will ever have reason to repent (*offering to embrace her*).

CASILDA (*withdrawing from him*). Nay, Luiz, it may not be. I have embraced you for the last time.

LUIZ (*amazed*). Casilda!

CASILDA. I have just learnt, to my surprise and indignation, that I was wed in babyhood to the infant son of the King of Barataria.

LUIZ. The son of the King of Barataria? The child who was stolen in infancy by the Inquisition?

CASILDA. The same. But, of course, you know his story.

LUIZ. Know his story? Why, I have often told you that my mother was the nurse to whose charge he was entrusted!

CASILDA. True. I had forgotten. Well, he has been discovered, and my father has brought me here to claim his hand.

LUIZ. But you will not recognize this marriage? It took place when you were too young to understand its import.

CASILDA. Nay, Luiz, respect my principles and cease to torture me with vain entreaties. Henceforth my life is another's.

LUIZ. But stay—the present and the future—

they are another's; but the past—that at least is ours, and none can take it from us. As we may revel in naught else, let us revel in that!

CASILDA. I don't think I grasp your meaning.

LUIZ. Yet it is logical enough. You say you cease to love me?

CASILDA (*demurely*). I say I *may* not love you.

LUIZ. But you do not say you *did* not love me?

CASILDA. I loved you with a frenzy that words are powerless to express—and that but ten brief minutes since!

LUIZ. Exactly. My own—that is, until ten minutes since, my own—my lately loved, my recently adored—tell me that until, say a quarter of an hour ago, I was all in all to thee! (*Embracing her.*)

CASILDA. I see your idea. It's ingenious, but don't do that (*releasing herself*).

LUIZ. There can be no harm in revelling in the past.

CASILDA. None whatever, but an embrace cannot be taken to act retrospectively.

LUIZ. Perhaps not!

CASILDA. We may recollect an embrace—I recollect many—but we must not repeat them.

LUIZ. Then let us recollect a few!

(*A moment's pause, as they recollect, then both heave a deep sigh.*)

LUIZ. Ah, Casilda, you were to me as the sun is to the earth!

CASILDA. A quarter of an hour ago?

LUIZ. About that.

CASILDA. And to think that, but for this miserable discovery, you would have been my own for life!

LUIZ. Through life to death—a quarter of an hour ago!

CASILDA. How greedily my thirsty ears would have drunk the golden melody of those sweet words a quarter—well it's now about twenty minutes since (*looking at her watch*).

LUIZ. About that. In such a matter one cannot be too precise.

DUET — CASILDA *and* LUIZ.

LUIZ. There was a time—
　　A time for ever gone—ah, woe is me!
　It was no crime
　　To love but thee alone—ah, woe is me!
　One heart, one life, one soul,
　　One aim, one goal—
　Each in the other's thrall,
　　Each all in all, ah, woe is me!

ENSEMBLE. Oh, bury, bury—let the grave close o'er
　The days that were—that never will be more!
　Oh, bury, bury love that all condemn,
　And let the whirlwind mourn its requiem!

CASILDA. Dead as the last year's leaves—
　　As gathered flowers—ah, woe is me!
　Dead as the garnered sheaves,
　　That love of ours—ah, woe is me!
　Born but to fade and die
　　When hope was high,
　Dead and as far away
　　As yesterday!—ah, woe is me!

ENSEMBLE. Oh, bury, bury—let the grave close o'er, &c.

Re-enter from the Ducal Palace the DUKE *and* DUCHESS, *followed by* DON ALHAMBRA BOLERO, *the Grand Inquisitor.*

DUKE. My child, allow me to present to you His Distinction Don Alhambra Bolero, the Grand Inquisitor of Spain. It was His Distinction who so thoughtfully abstracted your infant husband and brought him to Venice.

DON ALHAMBRA. So this is the little lady who is so unexpectedly called upon to assume the functions of Royalty! And a very nice little lady too!

DUKE. Jimp, isn't she?

DON ALHAMBRA. Distinctly jimp. Allow me (*proceeds to inspect her—she turns away scornfully*). Naughty temper!

DUKE. You must make some allowance. Her Majesty's head is a little turned by her access of dignity.

DON ALHAMBRA. I could have wished that Her Majesty's access of dignity had turned it in this direction. (*Aside.*) Prettily put!

DUCHESS. Unfortunately, if I am not mistaken, there appears to be some little doubt as to His Majesty's whereabouts.

CASILDA. A doubt as to his whereabouts? Then I may yet be saved!

DON ALHAMBRA. A doubt? Oh dear no—no doubt at all! He is here, in Venice, plying the modest but picturesque calling of a gondolier. I can give you his address—I see him every day! In the entire annals of our history there is absolutely no circumstance so entirely free from all manner of doubt of any kind whatever! Listen, and I'll tell you all about it.

SONG — GRAND INQUISITOR.

I stole the Prince, and I brought him here
　And left him, gaily prattling
With a highly respectable gondolier,

Who promised the Royal babe to rear,
And teach him the trade of a timoneer
    With his own beloved bratling.

Both of the babes were strong and stout,
    And, considering all things, clever.
Of that there is no manner of doubt—
No probable, possible shadow of doubt—
    No possible doubt whatever.

Time sped, and when at the end of a year
    I sought that infant cherished,
That highly respectable gondolier
Was lying a corpse on his humble bier—
I dropped a Grand Inquisitor's tear—
    That gondolier had perished!

A taste for drink, combined with gout,
    Had doubled him up for ever.
Of *that* there is no manner of doubt—
No probable, possible shadow of doubt—
    No possible doubt whatever.

But owing, I'm much disposed to fear,
    To his terrible taste for tippling,
That highly respectable gondolier
Could never declare with a mind sincere
Which of the two was his offspring dear,
    And which the Royal stripling!

Which was which he could never make
    out,
    Despite his best endeavour.
Of *that* there is no manner of doubt—
No probable, possible shadow of doubt—
    No possible doubt whatever.

The children followed his old career—
    (This statement can't be parried)
Of a highly respectable gondolier:
Well, one of the two (who will soon be here)—
But *which* of the two is not quite clear—
    Is the Royal Prince you married!

Search in and out and round about
    And you'll discover never
A tale so free from every doubt—
All probable, possible shadow of doubt—
    All possible doubt whatever!

CASILDA. Then do you mean to say that I am married to one of two gondoliers, but it is impossible to say which?

DON ALHAMBRA. Without any doubt of any kind whatever. But be reassured, the nurse to whom your husband was entrusted is the mother of the musical young man who is such a past-master of that delicately modulated instrument (*indicating the drum*). She can, no doubt, establish the King's identity beyond all question.

LUIZ. Heavens, how did he know that?

DON ALHAMBRA. My young friend, a Grand Inquisitor is always up to date. (*To* CASILDA.) His mother is at present the wife of a highly respectable and old-established brigand, who carries on an extensive practice in the mountains around Cordova. Accompanied by two of my emissaries, he will set off at once for his mother's address. She will return with them, and if she finds any difficulty in making up her mind, the persuasive influence of the torture chamber will jog her memory.

RECITATIVE.

CASILDA. But, bless my heart, consider my position!
    I am the wife of one, that's very clear;
But who can tell, except by intuition,
    Which is the Prince, and which the Gondolier?

DON ALHAMBRA. Submit to Fate without unseemly wrangle:
    Such complications frequently occur—
Life is one closely complicated tangle:
    Death is the only true unraveller!

QUINTETTE.

CASILDA, DUCHESS, LUIZ, DUKE, INQUISITOR.

Try we life-long, we can never
    Straighten out life's tangled skein,

Why should we, in vain endeavour,
　Guess and guess and guess again?
　　Life's a pudding full of plums,
　　Care's a canker that benumbs.
Wherefore waste our elocution
On impossible solution?
Life's a pleasant institution,
　Let us take it as it comes!

Set aside the dull enigma,
　We shall guess it all too soon;
Failure brings no kind of stigma—
　Dance we to another tune!
　　String the lyre and fill the cup,
　　Lest on sorrow we should sup.
Hop and skip to Fancy's fiddle,
Hands across and down the middle—
Life's perhaps the only riddle
　That we shrink from giving up!

(*Exeunt all except* GRAND INQUISITOR *into
Ducal Palace. Chorus of Gondoliers heard
without.*)

*Enter Procession of Gondoliers and Contadine,
crossing the stage.*

CHORUS.

Bridegroom and bride!
　Knot that's insoluble,
　Voices all voluble
Hail it with pride.
Bridegroom and bride!
　Hail it with merriment;
　It's an experiment
Frequently tried.

Bridegroom and bride!
　Bridegrooms all joyfully,
　Brides, rather coyfully,
Stand at their side.
Bridegroom and bride!
　We in sincerity,
　Wish you prosperity,
Bridegroom and bride!

Enter MARCO *with* GIANETTA, *and* GIUSEPPE
with TESSA.

SONG — TESSA.

When a merry maiden marries,
Sorrow goes and pleasure tarries;
　Every sound becomes a song,
　All is right and nothing's wrong!
From to-day and ever after
Let our tears be tears of laughter.
　Every sigh that finds a vent
　Be a sigh of sweet content!
When you marry merry maiden,

Then the air with love is laden;
　Every flower is a rose,
　　Every goose becomes a swan,
　Every kind of trouble goes
　　Where the last year's snows have gone!
Sunlight takes the place of shade
When you marry merry maid!

When a merry maiden marries
Sorrow goes and pleasure tarries;
　Every sound becomes a song—
　All is right, and nothing's wrong.
Gnawing Care and aching Sorrow
Get ye gone until to-morrow;
　Jealousies in grim array,
　Ye are things of yesterday!
When you marry merry maiden,
Then the air with joy is laden;
　All the corners of the earth
　　Ring with music sweetly played,
　Worry is melodious mirth,
　　Grief is joy in masquerade;
Sullen night is laughing day—
All the year is merry May!

GIUSEPPE. And now our lives are going to begin in real earnest! What's a bachelor? A mere nothing—he's a chrysalis. He can't be said to live—he exists.

MARCO. What a delightful institution marriage is! Why have we wasted all this time? Why didn't we marry ten years ago?

TESSA. Because you couldn't find anybody nice enough.

GIANETTA. Because you were waiting for *us*.

MARCO. I suppose that *was* the reason. We were waiting for you without knowing it. (DON AL-HAMBRA *comes forward.*) Hallo!

GIUSEPPE. If this gentleman is an undertaker, it is a bad omen.

DON ALHAMBRA. Good morning. Festivities of some sort going on?

GIUSEPPE (*aside*). He *is* an undertaker! (*Aloud.*) No—a little unimportant family gathering. Nothing in *your* line.

DON ALHAMBRA. Somebody's birthday, I suppose?

GIUSEPPE. Yes, mine!

TESSA. And mine!

GIANETTA. And mine!

MARCO. And mine!

DON ALHAMBRA. Curious coincidence! And how old may you be?

TESSA. It's a rude question—but about ten minutes.

DON ALHAMBRA. Surely you are jesting?

TESSA. In other words, we were married about ten minutes since.

DON ALHAMBRA. Married! You don't mean to say you are married?

MARCO. Oh yes, we are married.

DON ALHAMBRA. What, both of you?

GIANETTA. All four of us.

DON ALHAMBRA (aside). Bless my heart, how extremely awkward!

GIANETTA. You don't mind, I suppose?

TESSA. You were not thinking of either of us for yourself, I presume? Oh, Giuseppe, look at him —he was! He's heartbroken!

DON ALHAMBRA. No, no, I wasn't! I wasn't! (Aside.) What will the Duke say?

GIUSEPPE. Now, my man (slapping him on the back), we don't want anything in your line to-day, and if your curiosity's satisfied—

DON ALHAMBRA. You mustn't call me your man. It's a liberty. I don't think you know who I am.

GIUSEPPE. Not we, indeed! We are jolly gondoliers, the sons of Baptisto Palmieri, who led the last revolution. Republicans, heart and soul, we hold all men to be equal. As we abhor oppression, we abhor kings: as we detest vain-glory, we detest rank: as we despise effeminacy, we despise wealth. We are Venetian gondoliers—your equals in everything except our calling, and in that at once your masters and your servants.

DON ALHAMBRA. Bless my heart, how unfortunate! One of you may be Baptisto's son, for anything I know to the contrary; but the other is no less a personage than the only son of the late King of Barataria.

ALL. What!

DON ALHAMBRA. And I trust—I trust it was that one who slapped me on the shoulder and called me his man!

GIUSEPPE. One of us a king!
MARCO. Not brothers!
TESSA. The King of Barataria! } Together.
GIANETTA. Well, who'd have thought it!
MARCO. But which is it?

DON ALHAMBRA. What does it matter? As you are both Republicans, and hold kings in abhorrence, of course you'll abdicate at once (going).

TESSA and GIANETTA. Oh, don't do that! (MARCO and GIUSEPPE stop him.)

GIUSEPPE. Well, as to that, of course there are kings and kings. When I say that I detest kings, I mean I detest bad kings.

DON ALHAMBRA. I see. It's a delicate distinction.

GIUSEPPE. Quite so. Now I can conceive a kind of king—an ideal king—the creature of my fancy, you know—who would be absolutely unobjectionable. A king, for instance, who would abolish taxes and make everything cheap, except gondolas—

MARCO. And give a great many free entertainments to the gondoliers—

GIUSEPPE. And let off fireworks on the Grand Canal, and engage all the gondolas for the occasion—

MARCO. And scramble money on the Rialto among the gondoliers.

GIUSEPPE. Such a king would be a blessing to his people, and if I were a king, that is the sort of king I would be.

DON ALHAMBRA. Come, I'm glad to find your objections are not insuperable.

MARCO and GIUSEPPE. Oh, they're not insuperable.

TESSA and GIANETTA. No, they're not insuperable.

GIUSEPPE. Besides, we are open to conviction. Our views may have been hastily formed on insufficient grounds. They may be crude, ill-digested, erroneous. I've a very poor opinion of the politician who is not open to conviction.

TESSA (to GIANETTA). Oh, he's a fine fellow!

GIANETTA. Yes, that's the sort of politician for my money!

DON ALHAMBRA. Then we'll consider it settled. Now, as the country is in a state of insurrection, it is absolutely necessary that you should assume the reins of Government at once; and, until it is ascertained which of you is to be king, I have arranged that you will reign jointly, so that no question can arise hereafter as to the validity of any of your acts.

MARCO. As one individual?

DON ALHAMBRA. As one individual.

GIUSEPPE (linking himself with MARCO). Like this?

DON ALHAMBRA. Something like that.

MARCO. And we may take our friends with us, and give them places about the Court?

DON ALHAMBRA. Undoubtedly.

MARCO. I'm convinced!

GIUSEPPE. So am I!

TESSA. Then the sooner we're off the better.

GIANETTA. We'll just run home and pack up a few things (going)—

DON ALHAMBRA. Stop, stop—that won't do at all—we can't have any ladies. (Aside.) What will Her Majesty say!

ALL. What!

DON ALHAMBRA. Not at present. Afterwards, perhaps. We'll see.

GIUSEPPE. Why, you don't mean to say you are going to separate us from our wives!

DON ALHAMBRA (aside). This is very awkward! (Aloud.) Only for a time—a few months. After all, what is a few months?

TESSA. But we've only been married half an hour! (Weeps.)

SONG — GIANETTA.

Kind sir, you cannot have the heart
    Our lives to part
  From those to whom an hour ago
    We were united!
Before our flowing hopes you stem,
    Ah, look at them,
  And pause before you deal this blow,
    All uninvited!
You men can never understand,
    That heart and hand
Cannot be separated when
    We go a-yearning;
You see, you've only women's eyes
    To idolize,
And only women's hearts, poor men,
    To set *you* burning!
Ah me, you men will never understand
That woman's heart is one with woman's
    hand!

Some kind of charm you seem to find
    In womankind—
  Some source of unexplained delight
    (Unless you're jesting),
But what attracts you, I confess,
    I cannot guess,
  To me a woman's face is quite
    Uninteresting!
If from my sister I were torn,
    It could be borne—
I should, no doubt, be horrified,
    But I could bear it;—
But Marco's quite another thing—
    He is my King,
He has my heart and none beside
    Shall ever share it!
Ah me, you men will never understand
That woman's heart is one with woman's
    hand!

FINALE.

RECITATIVE — GRAND INQUISITOR.

Do not give way to this uncalled-for grief!
Your separation will be very brief.
  To ascertain which is the King

And which the other,
To Barataria's Court I'll bring
  His foster-mother;
Her former nurseling to declare
  She'll be delighted.
That settled, let each happy pair
  Be reunited.

MARCO, GIUSEPPE, Viva! His argument is strong!
TESSA, GIANETTA. Viva! We'll not be parted
        long!
        Viva! It will be settled soon!
        Viva! Then comes our hon-
        eymoon!
        (*Exit* DON ALHAMBRA.)

QUARTETTE.

TESSA, GIANETTA, MARCO, GIUSEPPE.

GIANETTA. Then one of us will be a Queen,
    And sit on a golden throne,
      With a crown instead
      Of a hat on her head,
    And diamonds all her own!
  With a beautiful robe of gold and green,
    I've always understood;
      I wonder whether
      She'd wear a feather?
    I rather think she should!

ALL.   Oh! 'tis a glorious thing, I ween,
    To be a regular Royal Queen!
    No half-and-half affair, I mean,
    But a right-down regular Royal Queen!

MARCO. She'll drive about in a carriage and pair,
    With the King on her left-hand side,
      And a milkwhite horse,
      As a matter of course,
    Whenever she wants to ride!
  With beautiful silver shoes to wear
    Upon her dainty feet;
      With endless stocks
      Of beautiful frocks
    And as much as she wants to eat!

ALL. Oh! 'tis a glorious thing, I ween, &c.

TESSA. Whenever she condescends to walk,
    Be sure she'll shine at that,
      With her haughty stare,
      And her nose in the air,
    Like a well-born aristocrat!
  At elegant high society talk
    She'll bear away the bell,
      With her "How de do?"
      And her "How are you?"
    And her "Hope I see you well!"

ALL. Oh! 'tis a glorious thing, I ween, &c.

GIUSEPPE. And noble lords will scrape and bow,

And double them into two,
    And open their eyes
    In blank surprise
At whatever she likes to do.
And everybody will roundly vow
    She's fair as flowers in May,
    And say, "How clever!"
    At whatsoever
She condescends to say!

ALL.   Oh! 'tis a glorious thing, I ween,
    To be a regular Royal Queen—
    No half-and-half affair, I mean,
    But a right-down regular Queen!

Enter Chorus of Gondoliers and Contadine.

CHORUS.

Now, pray, what is the cause of this remarkable
    hilarity?
This sudden ebullition of unmitigated jollity?
Has anybody blessed you with a sample of his
    charity—
Or have you been adopted by a gentleman
    of quality?

MARCO *and* GIUSEPPE.   Replying, we sing
    As one individual.
As I find I'm a king;
    To my kingdom I bid you all.
I'm aware you object
    To pavilions and palaces,
But you'll find I respect
    Your Republican fallacies.

CHORUS.   As they know we object

To pavilions and palaces,
How can they respect
    Our Republican fallacies?

MARCO *and* GIUSEPPE.

For every one who feels inclined,
Some post we undertake to find
Congenial with his peace of mind—
    And all shall equal be.

The Chancellor in his peruke—
The Earl, the Marquis, and the Dook,
The Groom, the Butler, and the Cook—
    They all shall equal be.

The Aristocrat who banks with Coutts,
The Aristocrat who hunts and shoots,
The Aristocrat who cleans our boots—
    They all shall equal be!

The Noble Lord who rules the State—
The Noble Lord who cleans the plate—
The Noble Lord who scrubs the grate—
    They all shall equal be!

The Lord High Bishop orthodox—
The Lord High Coachman on the box—
The Lord High Vagabond in the stocks—
    They all shall equal be!
    Sing high, sing low,
    Wherever they go,
    They all shall equal be!

CHORUS.   Sing high, sing low,
    Wherever they go,
    They all shall equal be!

The Earl, the Marquis, and the Dook,
The Groom, the Butler, and the Cook,
The Aristocrat who banks with Coutts,
The Aristocrat who cleans the boots,
The Noble Lord who rules the State,
The Noble Lord who scrubs the grate,
The Lord High Bishop orthodox,
The Lord High Vagabond in the stocks—
    Sing high, sing low,
    Wherever they go,
    They all shall equal be!

Then hail! O King,
    Whichever you may be,
To you we sing,
    But do not bend the knee.
It may be thou—
    Likewise it may be thee—
So hail! O King,
    Whichever you may be!

MARCO *and* GIUSEPPE (*together*).

Then let's away—our island crown awaits me—
Conflicting feelings rend my soul apart!

The thought of Royal dignity elates me,
  But leaving thee behind me breaks my heart!
      (*Addressing* TESSA *and* GIANETTA.)

TESSA *and* GIANETTA (*together*).

Farewell, my love; on board you must be get-
    ting;
  But while upon the sea you gaily roam,
Remember that a heart for thee is fretting—
  The tender little heart you've left at home!

GIANETTA. Now, Marco dear,
      My wishes hear:
        While you're away,
      It's understood
      You will be good,
        And not too gay.
      To every trace
      Of maiden grace
        You will be blind,
      And will not glance
      By any chance
        On womankind!
      If you are wise,
      You'll shut your eyes
        Till we arrive,
      And not address
      A lady less
        Than forty-five.
      You'll please to frown
      On every gown
        That you may see;
      And, O my pet,
      You won't forget
        You've married me!

  O my darling, O my pet,
  Whatever else you may forget,
  In yonder isle beyond the sea,
  O don't forget you've married me!

TESSA. You'll lay your head
      Upon your bed
        At set of sun.
      You will not sing
      Of anything
        To any one.
      You'll sit and mope
      All day, I hope,
        And shed a tear
      Upon the life
      Your little wife
        Is passing here.
      And if so be
      You think of me,
        Please tell the moon:
      I'll read it all
      In rays that fall
        On the lagoon:

      You'll be so kind
      As tell the wind
        How you may be,
      And send me words
      By little birds
        To comfort me!

And O my darling, O my pet,
Whatever else you may forget,
In yonder isle beyond the sea,
O don't forget you've married me!

CHORUS.
(*during which a xebeque is hauled alongside
the quay*).

Then away we go to an island fair
  That lies in a Southern sea:
We know not where, and we don't much care,
  Wherever that isle may be.

THE MEN (*hauling on boat*). One, two, three,
          Haul!
      One, two, three,
          Haul!
      One, two, three,
          Haul!
      With a will!

ALL. Then away we go, &c.

SOLO — MARCO.

  Away we go
    To a balmy isle,
  Where the roses blow
    All the winter while,

ALL. Then pull, yeo ho! and again yeo ho!
            (*Hoisting sail.*)

And again yeo ho! with a will!
  When the breezes are a-blowing,
  Then our ship will be a-going,
When they don't we shall all stand still!

And away we go to the island fair,
  That lies in a southern sea,

We
They } know not where, and { we
they } don't much
              care,

Wherever that isle may be!

The men embark on the xebeque, MARCO *and*
GIUSEPPE *embracing* GIANETTA *and* TESSA. *The
girls wave a farewell to the men as the
curtain falls.*

END OF ACT I.

ACT II.

SCENE. — *Pavilion in the Court of Barataria.* MARCO *and* GIUSEPPE, *magnificently dressed,
are seated on two thrones, occupied in cleaning the crown and the sceptre. The gondoliers
are discovered dressed, some as courtiers, officers of rank, &c., and others as private soldiers
and servants of various degrees. All are enjoying themselves without reference to social distinctions—some playing cards, others throwing dice, some reading, others playing cup and
ball, "moro," &c.*

CHORUS.

Of happiness the very pith
    In Barataria you may see:
A monarchy that's tempered with
    Republican Equality.
This form of government we find
The beau ideal of its kind—
A despotism strict, combined
    With absolute equality!

MARCO *and* GIUSEPPE.

Two kings, of undue pride bereft,
    Who act in perfect unity,
Whom you can order right and left
    With absolute impunity.
Who put their subjects at their ease
By doing all they can to please!
And thus, to earn their bread-and-cheese,
    Seize every opportunity.

MARCO. Gentlemen, we are much obliged to you
for your expressions of satisfaction and good-feel-
ing. We are delighted, at any time, to fall in with
sentiments so charmingly expressed.

GIUSEPPE. At the same time there is just one
little grievance that we should like to ventilate.

ALL (*angrily*). What!

GIUSEPPE. Don't be alarmed—it's not serious.
It is arranged that, until it is decided which of us
two is the actual King, we are to act as one person.

GIORGIO. Exactly.

GIUSEPPE. Now, although we act as *one* person,
we are, in point of fact, *two* persons.

ANNIBALE. Ah, I don't think we can go into that.
It is a legal fiction, and legal fictions are solemn
things. Situated as we are, we can't recognize two
independent responsibilities.

GIUSEPPE. No; but you can recognize two independent appetites. It's all very well to say we act
as one person, but when you supply us with only
one ration between us, I should describe it as a
legal fiction carried a little too far.

ANNIBALE. It's rather a nice point. I don't like
to express an opinion off-hand. Suppose we reserve it for argument before the full Court?

MARCO. Yes, but what are we to do in the meantime?

ANNIBALE. I think we may make an interim order for double rations on their Majesties' entering
into the usual undertaking to indemnify in the
event of an adverse decision?

GIORGIO. That, I think, will meet the case. But
you must work hard—stick to it—nothing like
work.

GIUSEPPE. Oh, certainly. We quite understand
that a man who holds the magnificent position of
King should do something to justify it. We are
called "Your Majesty," we are allowed to buy
ourselves magnificent clothes, our subjects frequently nod to us in the streets, the sentries always
return our salutes, and we enjoy the inestimable
privilege of heading the subscriptions to all the
principal charities. In return for these advantages
the least we can do is to make ourselves useful
about the Palace.

SONG — GIUSEPPE.

Rising early in the morning,
    We proceed to light our fire,
Then our Majesty adorning
    In its workaday attire,
        We embark without delay
        On the duties of the day.

First, we polish off some batches
Of political despatches,
    And foreign politicians circumvent;
Then, if business isn't heavy,
We may hold a Royal *levée,*
    Or ratify some Acts of Parliament.
Then we probably review the household
        troops—
With the usual "Shalloo humps!" and "Shalloo
        hoops!"
Or receive with ceremonial and state
An interesting Eastern potentate.
    After that we generally
    Go and dress our private *valet*—
(It's a rather nervous duty—he's a touchy little
        man)—
    Write some letters literary
    For our private secretary—
He is shaky in his spelling, so we help him if
        we can.
    Then, in view of cravings inner,
    We go down and order dinner;
Then we polish the Regalia and the Coronation
        plate—
    Spend an hour in titivating
    All our Gentlemen-in-Waiting;
Or we run on little errands for the Ministers of
        State.
    Oh, philosophers may sing
    Of the troubles of a King;
Yet the duties are delightful, and the privileges
        great;
    But the privilege and pleasure
    That we treasure beyond measure
Is to run on little errands for the Ministers of
        State!

After luncheon (making merry
On a bun and glass of sherry),
    If we've nothing in particular to do,
We may make a Proclamation,
Or receive a Deputation—
    Then we possibly create a Peer or two.
Then we help a fellow-creature on his path
With the Garter or the Thistle or the Bath.
Or we dress and toddle off in semi-State
To a festival, a function, or a *fête.*
    Then we go and stand as sentry
    At the Palace (private entry),

Marching hither, marching thither, up and down
        and to and fro,
    While the warrior on duty
    Goes in search of beer and beauty
(And it generally happens that he hasn't far
        to go).
    He relieves us, if he's able,
    Just in time to lay the table,
Then we dine and serve the coffee, and at half-
        past twelve or one,
    With a pleasure that's emphatic,
    We retire to our attic
With the gratifying feeling that our duty has
        been done!
    Oh, philosophers may sing
    Of the troubles of a King,
But of pleasures there are many and of troubles
        there are none;
    And the culminating pleasure
    That we treasure beyond measure
Is the gratifying feeling that our duty has been
        done!
    (*Exeunt all but* MARCO *and* GIUSEPPE.)

GIUSEPPE. Yet it really is a very pleasant existence. They're all so extraordinarily kind and considerate. You don't find them wanting to do this,
or wanting to do that, or saying "It's my turn
now." No, they let us have all the fun to ourselves,
and never seem to grudge it.

MARCO. It makes one feel quite selfish. It almost
seems like taking advantage of their good nature

GIUSEPPE. How nice they were about the double rations.

MARCO. Most considerate. Ah! there's only one thing wanting to make us thoroughly comfortable —the dear little wives we left behind us three months ago.

GIUSEPPE. It *is* dull without female society. We can do without everything else, but we can't do without that.

MARCO. And if we have that in perfection, we have everything. There is only one recipe for perfect happiness.

SONG — MARCO.

Take a pair of sparkling eyes,
  Hidden, ever and anon,
    In a merciful eclipse—
Do not heed their mild surprise—
  Having passed the Rubicon.
    Take a pair of rosy lips;
Take a figure trimly planned—
  Such as admiration whets
    (Be particular in this);
Take a tender little hand,
  Fringed with dainty fingerettes,
    Press it—in parenthesis;—
Take all these, you lucky man—
Take and keep them, if you can!

Take a pretty little cot—
  Quite a miniature affair—
    Hung about with trellised vine,
Furnish it upon the spot
  With the treasures rich and rare
    I've endeavoured to define.
Live to love and love to live—
  You will ripen at your ease,
    Growing on the sunny side—
Fate has nothing more to give.
  You're a dainty man to please
    If you are not satisfied.
Take my counsel, happy man;
Act upon it, if you can!

Enter Chorus of Contadine, running in, led by
FIAMETTA *and* VITTORIA. *They are met by all the
Ex-Gondoliers, who welcome them heartily.*

CHORUS OF CONTADINE.

Here we are, at the risk of our lives,
From ever so far, and we've brought your
  wives—
And to that end we've crossed the main,
And we don't intend to return again!

FIAMETTA. Though obedience is strong,
  Curiosity's stronger—
    We waited for long,

Till we couldn't wait longer.

VITTORIA. It's imprudent, we know,
  But without your society
Existence was slow,
  And we long for variety—

ALL. So here we are, at the risk of our lives,
  From ever so far, and we've brought your
    wives—
  And to that end we've crossed the main,
  And we don't intend to return again!

Enter TESSA *and* GIANETTA. *They rush to the
arms of* GIUSEPPE *and* MARCO.

GIUSEPPE.	Tessa!	
TESSA.	Giuseppe!	} *Embrace.*
GIANETTA.	Marco!	
MARCO.	Gianetta!	

TESSA *and* GIANETTA (*alternate lines*).

After sailing to this island—
  Tossing in a manner frightful,
We are all once more on dry land—
  And we find the change delightful,
As at home we've been remaining—
  We've not seen you both for ages,
Tell me, are you fond of reigning?—
  How's the food, and what's the wages?
Does your new employment please ye?—
  How does Royalizing strike you?
Is it difficult or easy?—
  Do you think your subjects like you?
I am anxious to elicit,
  Is it plain and easy steering?
Take it altogether, is it—
  Better fun than gondoliering?

CHORUS. We shall all go on requesting,
  Till you tell us, never doubt it,
Everything is interesting,
  Tell us, tell us all about it!

Is the populace exacting?
  Do they keep you at a distance?
All unaided are you acting,
  Or do they provide assistance?
When you're busy, have you got to
  Get up early in the morning?
If you do what you ought not to,
  Do they give the usual warning?
With a horse do they equip you?
  Lots of trumpeting and drumming?
Do the Royal tradesmen tip you?
  Ain't the livery becoming!
Does your human being inner
  Feed on everything that nice is?
Do they give you wine for dinner?
  Peaches, sugar-plums, and ices?

CHORUS.   We shall all go on requesting
          Till you tell us, never doubt it;
          Everything is interesting,
          Tell us, tell us all about it!

MARCO. This is indeed a most delightful surprise!

TESSA. Yes, we thought you'd like it. You see, it was like this: After you left we felt very dull and mopey, and the days crawled by, and you never wrote; so at last I said to Gianetta, "I can't stand this any longer; those two poor Monarchs haven't got any one to mend their stockings or sew on their buttons or patch their clothes—at least, I hope they haven't—let us all pack up a change and go and see how they're getting on." And she said "Done," and they all said "Done"; and we asked old Giacopo to lend us his boat, and *he* said "Done"; and we've crossed the sea, and, thank goodness, *that's* done; and here we are, and —and—*I've* done!

GIANETTA. And now—which of you is King?

TESSA. And which of us is Queen?

GIUSEPPE. That we sha'n't know until Nurse turns up. But never mind that—the question is, how shall we celebrate the commencement of our honeymoon? Gentlemen, will you allow us to offer you a magnificent banquet?

ALL. We will!

GIUSEPPE. Thanks very much; and what do you say to a dance?

TESSA. A banquet *and* a dance! Oh, it's too much happiness!

CHORUS.

We will dance a cachucha, fandango, bolero,
Old Xeres we'll drink—Manzanilla, Montero—
For wine, when it runs in abundance, enhances
The reckless delight of that wildest of dances!
      To the pretty pitter-pitter-patter,
      And the clitter-clitter-clitter-clatter—
          Clitter—clitter—clatter,
          Pitter—pitter—patter—
We will dance a cachucha, fandango, bolero;
Old Xeres we'll drink—Manzanilla, Montero;
For wine, when it runs in abundance, enhances
The reckless delight of that wildest of dances!

CACHUCHA. *The dance is interrupted by the unexpected appearance of* DON ALHAMBRA, *who looks on with astonishment.* MARCO *and* GIUSEPPE *appear embarrassed. The others run off.*

DON ALHAMBRA. Good evening. Fancy ball?

GIUSEPPE. No, not exactly. A little friendly dance. That's all.

DON ALHAMBRA. But I saw a groom dancing, and a footman!

GIUSEPPE. Yes. That's the Lord High Footman.

DON ALHAMBRA. And, dear me, a common little drummer boy!

MARCO. Oh no! That's the Lord High Drummer Boy.

DON ALHAMBRA. But surely, surely the servant's-hall is the place for these gentry?

GIUSEPPE. Oh dear no! *We* have appropriated the servant's-hall. It's the Royal Apartment, and we permit no intruders.

MARCO. We really must have some place that we can call our own.

DON ALHAMBRA (*puzzled*). I'm afraid I'm not quite equal to the intellectual pressure of the conversation.

GIUSEPPE. You see, the Monarchy has been remodelled on Republican principles. All departments rank equally, and everybody is at the head of his department.

DON ALHAMBRA. I see.

MARCO. I'm afraid you're annoyed.

DON ALHAMBRA. No. I won't say that. It's not quite what I expected.

GIUSEPPE. I'm awfully sorry.

MARCO. So am I.

GIUSEPPE. By the by, can I offer you anything after your voyage? a plate of macaroni and a rusk?

DON ALHAMBRA (*preoccupied*). No, no—nothing—nothing.

GIUSEPPE. Obliged to be careful?

DON ALHAMBRA. Yes—gout. You see, in every

Court there are distinctions that must be observed.

GIUSEPPE (*puzzled*). There are, are there?

DON ALHAMBRA. Why, of course. For instance, you wouldn't have a Lord High Chancellor play leapfrog with his own cook.

GIUSEPPE. Why not?

DON ALHAMBRA. Because a Lord High Chancellor is a personage of great dignity, who should never, under any circumstances, place himself in the position of being told to tuck in his tuppenny, except by noblemen of his own rank.

GIUSEPPE. Oh, I take you.

DON ALHAMBRA. For instance, a Lord High Archbishop might tell a Lord High Chancellor to tuck in his tuppenny, but certainly not a cook.

GIUSEPPE. Not even a Lord High Cook?

DON ALHAMBRA. My good friend, that is a rank that is not recognized at the Lord Chamberlain's office. No, no, it won't do. I'll give you an instance in which the experiment was tried.

SONG — DON ALHAMBRA.

There lived a King, as I've been told,
In the wonder-working days of old,
When hearts were twice as good as gold,
    And twenty times as mellow.
Good-temper triumphed in his face,
And in his heart he found a place
For all the erring human race
    And every wretched fellow.
When he had Rhenish wine to drink
It made him very sad to think
That some, at junket or at jink,
    Must be content with toddy.
He wished all men as rich as he
(And he was rich as rich could be),
So to the top of every tree
    Promoted everybody.

MARCO *and* GIUSEPPE. Now, that's the kind of
        King for me—
    He wished all men as rich as he,
    So to the top of every tree
        Promoted everybody!

DON ALHAMBRA. Lord Chancellors were cheap
        as sprats,
    And Bishops in their shovel hats
    Were plentiful as tabby cats—
        In point of fact, too many.
    Ambassadors cropped up like hay,
    Prime Ministers and such as they
    Grew like asparagus in May,
        And Dukes were three a penny.
    On every side Field Marshals gleamed,
    Small beer were Lords Lieutenant deemed,
    With Admirals the ocean teemed

All round his wide dominions.
    And Party Leaders you might meet
    In twos and threes in every street,
    Maintaining, with no little heat,
        Their various opinions.

MARCO *and* GIUSEPPE. Now that's a sight you
        couldn't beat—
    Two Party Leaders in each street
    Maintaining, with no little heat,
        Their various opinions!

DON ALHAMBRA. That King, although no one
        denies
    His heart was of abnormal size,
    Yet he'd have acted otherwise
        If he had been acuter.
    The end is easily foretold,
    When every blessed thing you hold
    Is made of silver, or of gold,
        You long for simple pewter.
    When you have nothing else to wear
    But cloth of gold and satins rare,
    For cloth of gold you cease to care—
        Up goes the price of shoddy.
    In short, whoever you may be,
    To this conclusion you'll agree,
    When everyone is somebodee,
        Then no one's anybody!

MARCO *and* GIUSEPPE. Now that's as plain as
        plain can be,
    To this conclusion we agree—
    When every one is somebodee,
        Then no one's anybody!

TESSA *and* GIANETTA *enter unobserved. The two girls, impelled by curiosity, remain listening at the back of the stage.*

DON ALHAMBRA. And now I have some important news to communicate. His Grace the Duke of Plaza-Toro, Her Grace the Duchess, and their beautiful daughter Casilda—I say their beautiful daughter Casilda—have arrived at Barataria, and may be here at any moment.

MARCO. The Duke and Duchess are nothing to us.

DON ALHAMBRA. But the daughter—the beautiful daughter! Aha! Oh, you're a lucky fellow, one of you!

GIUSEPPE. I think you're a very incomprehensible old gentleman.

DON ALHAMBRA. Not a bit—I'll explain. Many years ago when you (whichever you are) were a baby, you (whichever you are) were married to a little girl who has grown up to be the most beautiful young lady in Spain. That beautiful young lady will be here to claim you (whichever you are) in half an hour, and I congratulate that one (whichever it is) with all my heart.

MARCO.   Married when a baby!

TESSA *and* GIANETTA (*aside*).   Oh!

GIUSEPPE.   But we were married three months ago!

DON ALHAMBRA.   One of you—only one. The other (whichever it is) is an unintentional bigamist.

MARCO *and* GIUSEPPE (*bewildered*).   Oh dear me!

TESSA *and* GIANETTA (*coming forward*).   Well, upon my word!

DON ALHAMBRA.   Eh? Who are these young people?

TESSA.   Who are we? Why their wives, of course. We've just arrived.

DON ALHAMBRA.   Their wives! Oh dear, this is very unfortunate. Oh dear, this complicates matters! Dear, dear, what will the Duke say?

GIANETTA.   And do you mean to say that one of these Monarchs was already married?

TESSA.   And that neither of us will be a Queen?

DON ALHAMBRA.   That is the idea I intended to convey. (TESSA *and* GIANETTA *begin to cry*.)

GIUSEPPE (*to* TESSA).   Tessa, my dear, dear child—

TESSA.   Get away! perhaps it's you!

MARCO (*to* GIANETTA).   My poor, poor little woman!

GIANETTA.   Don't! Who knows whose husband you are?

TESSA.   And pray, why didn't you tell us all about it before they left Venice?

DON ALHAMBRA.   Because if I had, no earthly temptation would have induced these gentlemen to leave two such extremely fascinating and utterly irresistible little ladies! (*Aside.*) Neatly put!

TESSA.   There's something in that.

DON ALHAMBRA.   I may mention that you will not be kept long in suspense, as the old lady who nursed the royal child is at present in the Torture Chamber, waiting for me to interview her.

GIUSEPPE.   Poor old girl! Hadn't you better go and put her out of her suspense?

DON ALHAMBRA.   Oh no—there's no hurry—she's all right. She has all the illustrated papers. However, I'll go and interrogate her, and, in the meantime, may I suggest the absolute propriety of your regarding yourselves as single young ladies? (*Exit.*)

TESSA.   Well, here's a pleasant state of things!

MARCO.   Delightful. One of us is married to two young ladies, and nobody knows which; and the other is married to one young lady whom nobody can identify!

GIANETTA.   And one of us is married to one of you, and the other is married to nobody.

TESSA.   But which of you is married to which of us, and what's to become of the other? (*About to cry.*)

GIUSEPPE.   It's quite simple. Two husbands have managed to acquire three wives. Three wives—two husbands (*reckoning up*). That's two-thirds of a husband to each wife.

TESSA.   O Mount Vesuvius, here we are in arithmetic! My good sir, one can't marry a vulgar fraction!

GIUSEPPE.   You've no right to call me a vulgar fraction.

MARCO.   We are getting rather mixed. The situation is entangled. Let's try and comb it out.

QUARTETTE.

MARCO, GIUSEPPE, TESSA, GIANETTA.

In a contemplative fashion
    And a tranquil frame of mind,
Free from every kind of passion,
    Some solution let us find.
Let us grasp the situation,
    Solve the complicated plot—
Quiet, calm deliberation
    Disentangles every knot.

TESSA.	THE OTHERS.
I, no doubt, Giuseppe wedded— That's, of course, a slice of luck. He is rather dunder-headed, Still, distinctly, he's a duck.	In a contempla- tive fashion, &c.

GIANETTA.	THE OTHERS.
I, a victim too of Cupid, Marco married—that is clear. He's particularly stupid, Still, distinctly, he's a dear.	Let us grasp the situation, &c.

MARCO.	THE OTHERS.
To Gianetta I was mated; I can prove it in a trice: Though her charms are over- rated Still I own she's rather nice.	In a contempla- tive fashion, &c.

GIUSEPPE.	THE OTHERS.
I to Tessa, willy-nilly, All at once a victim fell. She is what is called a silly, Still she answers pretty well.	Let us grasp the situation, &c.

MARCO.   Now when we were pretty babies
            Some one married us, that is clear—

GIANETTA.   And if I can catch her
            I'll pinch her and scratch her,
            And send her away with a flea in her ear.

GIUSEPPE.   He, whom that young lady married,
            To receive her can't refuse.

TESSA.   If I overtake her
            I'll warrant I'll make her
            To shake in her aristocratical shoes!

GIANETTA (to TESSA).   If she married your Giu-
            seppe,
            You and he will have to part—

TESSA (to GIANETTA).   If I have to do it
            I'll warrant she'll rue it—
            I'll teach her to marry the man of my
            heart!

TESSA (to GIANETTA).   If she married Messer
            Marco
            You're a spinster, that is plain—

GIANETTA (to TESSA).   No matter—no matter
            If I can get at her
            I doubt if her mother will know her
            again!

ALL.   Quiet, calm deliberation
            Disentangles every knot!
                        (*Exeunt, pondering.*)

MARCH. *Enter procession of Retainers, heralding approach of* DUKE, DUCHESS, *and* CASILDA. *All three are now dressed with the utmost magnificence.*

CHORUS.

With ducal pomp and ducal pride
    (Announce these comers,
        O ye kettle-drummers!)
Comes Barataria's high-born bride.
    (Ye sounding cymbals clang!)
She comes to claim the Royal hand—
    (Proclaim their Graces,
        O ye double basses!)
Of the King who rules this goodly land.
    (Ye brazen brasses bang!)

DUKE.   This polite attention touches
            Heart of Duke and heart of Duchess,

DUCHESS.   Who resign their pet
            With profound regret.

DUKE.   She of beauty was a model
            When a tiny tiddle-toddle,

DUCHESS.   And at twenty-one
            She's excelled by none!

ALL.   With ducal pomp and ducal pride, &c.

DUKE (*to his attendants*).   Be good enough to inform His Majesty that His Grace the Duke of Plaza-Toro, Limited, has arrived, and begs—

CASILDA.   Desires—

DUCHESS.   Demands—

DUKE.   And demands an audience. (*Exeunt attendants.*) And now, my child, prepare to receive the husband to whom you were united under such interesting and romantic circumstances.

CASILDA.   But which is it? There are two of them!

DUKE.   It is true that at present His Majesty is a double gentleman; but as soon as the circumstances of his marriage are ascertained, he will, *ipso facto,* boil down to a single gentleman—thus presenting a unique example of an individual who becomes a single man and a married man by the same operation.

DUCHESS (*severely*). I have known instances in which the characteristics of both conditions existed concurrently in the same individual.

DUKE. Ah, he couldn't have been a Plaza-Toro.

CASILDA. Well, whatever happens, I shall of course be a dutiful wife, but I can never love my husband.

DUKE. I don't know. It's extraordinary what unprepossessing people one can love if one gives one's mind to it.

DUCHESS. I loved your father.

DUKE. My love—that remark is a little hard, I think? Rather cruel, perhaps? Somewhat uncalled-for, I venture to believe?

DUCHESS. It was very difficult, my dear; but I said to myself, "That man is a Duke, and I *will* love him." Several of my relations bet me I couldn't, but I did—desperately!

SONG — DUCHESS.

On the day when I was wedded
    To your admirable sire,
I acknowledge that I dreaded
    An explosion of his ire.
I was overcome with panic—
For his temper was volcanic,
    And I didn't dare revolt,
    For I feared a thunderbolt!
I was always very wary,
    For his fury was ecstatic—
His refined vocabulary
    Most unpleasantly emphatic.
        To the thunder
            Of this Tartar
        I knocked under
            Like a martyr;
        When intently
            He was fuming,
        I was gently
            Unassuming—
        When reviling
            Me completely,
        I was smiling
            Very sweetly:
Giving him the very best, and getting back the
    very worst—
That is how I tried to tame your great progenitor—at first!

    But I found that a reliance
        On my threatening appearance,
    And a resolute defiance
        Of marital interference,
    And a gentle intimation
    Of my firm determination
        To see what I could do
        To be wife and husband too,

Was all that was required
    For to make his temper supple,
And you couldn't have desired
    A more reciprocating couple.
        Ever willing
            To be wooing,
        We were billing—
            We were cooing;
        When I merely
            From him parted
        We were nearly
            Broken-hearted—
        When in sequel
            Reunited,
        We were equal-
            Ly delighted:
So with double-shotted guns and colours nailed
    unto the mast,
I tamed your insignificant progenitor—at last!

CASILDA. My only hope is that when my husband sees what a shady family he has married into he will repudiate the contract altogether.

DUKE. Shady? A nobleman shady, who is blazing in the lustre of unaccustomed pocket-money? A nobleman shady, who can look back upon ninety-five quarterings? It is not every nobleman who is ninety-five quarters in arrear—I mean, who can look back upon ninety-five of them! And this, just as I have been floated at a premium! Oh fie!

DUCHESS. Your Majesty is surely unaware that directly your Majesty's father came before the public he was applied for over and over again.

DUKE. My dear, her Majesty's father was in the habit of being applied for over and over again— and very urgently applied for, too—long before he was registered under the Limited Liability Act.

RECITATIVE — DUKE.

To help unhappy commoners, and add to their
    enjoyment,
Affords a man of noble rank congenial employment;
Of our attempts we offer you examples illustrative:
The work is light, and, I may add, it's most
    remunerative!

DUET — DUKE *and* DUCHESS.

DUKE.   Small titles and orders
             For Mayors and Recorders
         I get—and they're highly delighted—
DUCHESS.   They're highly delighted!
DUKE.   M.P.'s baronetted,
             Sham Colonels gazetted,
         And second-rate Aldermen knighted—
DUCHESS.   Yes, Aldermen knighted.

DUKE.   Foundation-stone laying
           I find very paying:
        It adds a large sum to my makings—
DUCHESS.   Large sum to his makings.
DUKE.   At charity dinners
           The best of speech spinners,
        I get ten per cent. on the takings—
DUCHESS.   One-tenth of the takings.

DUCHESS. I present any lady
          Whose conduct is shady
       Or smacking of doubtful propriety—
DUKE.   Doubtful propriety.
DUCHESS. When Virtue would quash her,
          I take and whitewash her,
       And launch her in first-rate society—
DUKE.   First-rate society!
DUCHESS. I recommend acres
          Of clumsy dressmakers—
       Their fit and their finishing touches—
DUKE.   Their finishing touches.
DUCHESS. A sum in addition
          They pay for permission
       To say that they make for the Duchess—
DUKE.   They make for the Duchess!

DUKE.   Those pressing prevailers,
           The ready-made tailors,
       Quote me as their great double-barrel—
DUCHESS.   Their great double-barrel.
DUKE.   I allow them to do so,
           Though Robinson Crusoe
       Would jib at their wearing apparel!
DUCHESS.   Such wearing apparel!
DUKE.   I sit, by selection,
           Upon the direction
       Of several Companies bubble—
DUCHESS.   All Companies bubble!
DUKE.   As soon as they're floated
           I'm freely bank-noted—
       I'm pretty well paid for my trouble!
DUCHESS.   He's paid for his trouble!

DUCHESS. At middle-class party
          I play at *écarté*—
       And I'm by no means a beginner—
DUKE (*significantly*).   She's not a beginner.
DUCHESS. To one of my station
          The remuneration—
       Five guineas a night and my dinner—
DUKE.   And wine with her dinner.
DUCHESS. I write letters blatant
          On medicines patent—
       And use any other you mustn't—
DUKE.   Believe me, you mustn't—

DUCHESS. And vow my complexion
          Derives its perfection
       From somebody's soap—which it doesn't—
DUKE (*significantly*).   It certainly doesn't!

DUKE.   We're ready as witness
           To any one's fitness
       To fill any place or preferment—
              A place or preferment.
DUCHESS. We're often in waiting
          At junket or *fêting*,
       And sometimes attend an interment—
DUKE.   We like an interment.
BOTH.   In short, if you'd kindle
           The spark of a swindle,
       Lure simpletons into your clutches—
              Yes; into your clutches.
           Or hoodwink a debtor
           You cannot do better
DUCHESS. Then trot out a Duke or a Duchess—
DUKE.   A Duke or a Duchess!

              Enter MARCO *and* GIUSEPPE.

DUKE. Ah! their Majesties. (*Bows with great ceremony.*)

MARCO.   The Duke of Plaza-Toro, I believe?

DUKE. The same. (MARCO *and* GIUSEPPE *offer to shake hands with him. The* DUKE *bows ceremoniously. They endeavour to imitate him.*) Allow me to present—

GIUSEPPE. The young lady one of us married? (MARCO *and* GIUSEPPE *offer to shake hands with her.* CASILDA *curtsies formally. They endeavour to imitate her.*)

CASILDA. Gentlemen, I am the most obedient servant of one of you. (*Aside.*) Oh, Luiz!

DUKE. I am now about to address myself to the gentleman whom my daughter married; the other may allow his attention to wander if he likes, for what I am about to say does not concern him. Sir, you will find in this young lady a combination of excellences which you would search for in vain in any young lady who had not the good fortune to be my daughter. There is some little doubt as to which of you is the gentleman I am addressing, and which is the gentleman who is allowing his attention to wander; but when that doubt is solved, I shall say (still addressing the attentive gentleman), "Take her, and may she make you happier than her mother has made me."

DUCHESS. Sir!

DUKE. If possible. And now there is a little matter to which I think I am entitled to take exception. I come here in State with Her Grace the Duchess and Her Majesty, my daughter, and what do I find? Do I find, for instance, a guard of honour to receive me? No. The town illuminated? No. Refreshment provided? No. A Royal Salute fired? No. Triumphal arches erected? No. The bells set ringing? Yes—one—the Visitors', and I rang it myself. It is not enough.

GIUSEPPE.   Upon my honour, I'm very sorry; but, you see, I was brought up in a gondola, and my ideas of politeness are confined to taking off my hat to my passengers when they tip me.

DUCHESS.   That's all very well, but it is not enough.

GIUSEPPE.   I'll take off anything else in reason.

DUKE.   But a Royal Salute to my daughter—it costs so little.

CASILDA.   Papa, I don't want a Salute.

GIUSEPPE.   My dear sir, as soon as we know which of us is entitled to take that liberty she shall have as many salutes as she likes.

MARCO.   As for guards of honour and triumphal arches, you don't know our people—they wouldn't stand it.

GIUSEPPE.   They are very off-hand with us—very off-hand indeed.

DUKE.   Oh, but you mustn't allow that—you must keep them in proper discipline, you must impress your Court with your importance. You want deportment—carriage—manner—dignity. There must be a good deal of this sort of thing—(*business*)—and a little of this sort of thing—(*business*)—and possibly just a *soupçon* of this sort of thing!—(*business*)—and so on. Oh, it's very useful, and most effective. Just attend to me. You are a King—I am a subject. Very good—

QUINTETTE.

DUKE, DUCHESS, CASILDA, MARCO, GIUSEPPE.

DUKE.   I am a courtier grave and serious
Who is about to kiss your hand:
Try to combine a pose imperious
With a demeanour nobly bland.

MARCO *and* GIUSEPPE.   Let us combine a pose
imperious
With a demeanour nobly bland.
(*MARCO and GIUSEPPE endeavour to carry out
his instructions.*)

DUKE.   That's, if anything, *too* unbending—
Too aggressively stiff and grand;
(*They suddenly modify their attitudes.*)
Now to the other extreme you're tending—
Don't be so deucedly condescending!

DUCHESS *and* CASILDA.   Now to the other extreme
you're tending—
Don't be so dreadfully condescending!

MARCO *and* GIUSEPPE.   Oh, hard to please some
noblemen seem!
At first, if anything, *too* unbending;
Off we go to the other extreme—
Too confoundedly condescending!

DUKE.   Now a gavotte perform sedately—
Offer your hand with conscious pride;
Take an attitude not too stately,
Still sufficiently dignified.

MARCO *and* GIUSEPPE.   Now for an attitude not
too stately,
Still sufficiently dignified.
(*They endeavour to carry out his instructions.*)

DUKE (*beating time*).
Oncely, twicely—oncely, twicely—
Bow impressively ere you glide.
(*They do so.*)
Capital both—you've caught it nicely!
That is the sort of thing precisely!

DUCHESS *and* CASILDA.   Capital both—they've
caught it nicely!
That is the sort of thing precisely!

MARCO *and* GIUSEPPE.   Oh, sweet to earn a noble-
man's praise!
Capital both—we've caught it nicely!
Supposing he's right in what he says,
This is the sort of thing precisely!

GAVOTTE. *At the end exeunt* DUKE *and* DUCHESS,
leaving CASILDA *with* MARCO *and* GIUSEPPE.

GIUSEPPE (*to* MARCO).   The old birds have gone away and left the young chickens together. That's called tact.

MARCO.   It's very awkward. We really ought to tell her how we are situated. It's not fair to the girl.

GIUSEPPE.   Undoubtedly, but I don't know how to begin. (*To* CASILDA.) A—Madam—

CASILDA.   Gentlemen, I am bound to listen to you; but it is right to tell you that, not knowing I was married in infancy, I am over head and ears in love with somebody else.

GIUSEPPE.   Our case exactly! *We* are over head and ears in love with somebody else! (*Enter* TESSA *and* GIANETTA.) In point of fact, with our wives!

CASILDA.   Your wives! Then you are married?

TESSA.   It's not our fault, you know. We knew nothing about it. We are sisters in misfortune.

CASILDA.   My good girls, I don't blame you. Only before we go any further we must really arrive at some satisfactory arrangement, or we shall get hopelessly complicated.

QUINTETTE.

MARCO, GIUSEPPE, TESSA, GIANETTA, CASILDA.

ALL.   Here is a fix unprecedented!
   Here are a King and Queen ill-starred!
   Ever since marriage was first invented
   Never was known a case so hard!

MARCO *and* GIUSEPPE. I may be said to have
   been bisected,
   By a profound catastrophe!

GIANETTA, TESSA, CASILDA. Through a calamity
   unexpected
   I am divisible into three!

ALL.   O moralists all,
   How can you call
   Marriage a state of unitee,
   When excellent husbands are bisected,
   And wives divisible into three?

Enter DON ALHAMBRA, *followed by* DUKE, DUCH-
ESS, *and all the Chorus.*

FINALE.

RECITATIVE — DON ALHAMBRA.

Now let the loyal lieges gather round—
The Prince's foster-mother has been found!
She will declare, to silver clarion's sound,
The rightful King—let him forthwith be
  crowned!

CHORUS. She will declare, &c.

DON ALHAMBRA *brings forward* INEZ, *the Prince's
foster-mother.*

TESSA. Speak, woman, speak—
DUKE.   We're all attention!
GIANETTA. The news we seek—
CASILDA.   This moment mention.
DUCHESS. To us they bring—
DON ALHAMBRA. His foster-mother.
MARCO. Is he the King?
GIUSEPPE. Or this my brother?
ALL. Speak, woman, speak, &c.

RECITATIVE — INEZ.

The Royal Prince was by the King entrusted
To my fond care, ere I grew old and crusted;
When traitors came to steal his son reputed,
My own small boy I deftly substituted!
The villains fell into the trap completely—
I hid the Prince away—still sleeping sweetly;
I called him "son" with pardonable slyness—
His name, Luiz! Behold his Royal Highness!

Sensation. LUIZ *ascends the throne, crowned and
robed as King.*

CASILDA (*rushing to his arms*). Luiz!
LUIZ. Casilda! (*Embrace.*)

ALL. Is this indeed the King?
    Oh, wondrous revelation!
   Oh, unexpected thing!
    Unlooked-for situation!
      (*They kneel.*)

MARCO, GIANETTA, GIUSEPPE, TESSA.
   This statement we receive
    With sentiments conflicting;
   Our thoughts rejoice and grieve,
    Each other contradicting;
   To those whom we adore
    We can be reunited—
   On one point rather sore,
    But, on the whole, delighted!

LUIZ. When others claimed thy dainty hand,

I waited—waited—waited—waited,

DUKE.   As prudence (so I understand)
    Dictated—tated—tated—tated.

CASILDA.   By virtue of our early vow
    Recorded—corded—corded—corded,

DUCHESS.   Your pure and patient love is now
    Rewarded—warded—warded—warded.

ALL.   Then hail, O King of a Golden Land,
    And the high-born bride who claims his hand—
    The past is dead, and you gain your own,
    A royal crown and a golden throne!

MARCO *and* GIUSEPPE.
    Once more *gondolieri,*
    Both skilful and wary,
    Free from this quandary
      Contented are we.
    From Royalty flying,
    Our gondolas plying
    And merrily crying
      Our *"premé," "stalì!"*

ALL.   So good-bye cachucha, fandango, bolero—
    We'll dance a farewell to that measure—
    Old Xeres, adieu—Manzanilla—Montero—
    We leave you with feelings of pleasure!

CURTAIN.

Postscript

As with *The Yeomen*, Gilbert made a vast number of changes in the lyrics of *The Gondoliers* after the first-night performance.

On page 352, in the duet for Marco and Giuseppe, all texts since the third edition change the line "To ladies devoted" to read "To beauty devoted."

On page 354 it is interesting to note that the Girls' chorus commencing "To these gallant *gondolieri*" has been altered to repeat Gianetta's verse exactly.

The most important distinction between the first-edition text and all other editions (including that of the vocal score) is the presence of the ballad for Luiz (page 356), "Thy wintry scorn I dearly prize . . ." Sung by Wallace Brownlow on the first night, a short time later it was dropped by Gilbert in favor of a substitute duet immediately preceded by four lines of recitative for Casilda. The complete Recitative and Duet, as appearing in the latest editions of the libretto and in modern productions, is given here:

RECITATIVE AND DUET—CASILDA *and* LUIZ.

O rapture, when alone together
   Two loving hearts and those that bear them
May join in temporary tether,
   Though Fate apart should rudely tear them!

CASILDA. Necessity, Invention's mother,
   Compelled me to a course of feigning—
But, left alone with one another,
   I will atone for my disdaining!

        Ah, well-beloved,
        Mine angry frown
        Is but a gown
        That serves to dress
        My gentleness!

LUIZ.   Ah, well-beloved,
        Thy cold disdain,
        It gives no pain—
        'Tis mercy, played
        In masquerade!

BOTH.   Ah, well-beloved, &c.

The "Bridegroom and bride!" Chorus on page 359 has been cut in half by eliminating the middle eight lines of the original sixteen.

On page 362, in the close of the chorus to Marco and Giuseppe's duet, the line "The Lord High Vagabond in the stocks—" becomes "The Vagabond in the stocks—" from the third edition on. And the subsequent chorus—"Then hail! O King . . ."—is cut to five lines, retaining the first four lines of the original eight and repeating the first line.

The close of the first act, after the male chorus, hauling on the boat, sing the line "With a will!", is completely changed in modern production and librettos:

ALL. When the breezes are blowing
   The ship will be going,
      When they don't we shall all stand still!
   Then away we go to an island fair,
   We know not where, and we don't much care,
      Wherever that isle may be.

        SOLO—MARCO

Away we go to a balmy isle,
Where the roses blow all the winter while.

ALL (*hoisting sail*).
   Then away we go to an island fair
      That lies in a southern sea;
   Then away we go to an island fair;
      Then away, then away, then away!

On page 365, near the close of Giuseppe's song, "Rising early in the morning," the third and subsequent editions make a slight (and, it would seem, unnecessary) change in replacing the word "troubles" with "worries," so that the resulting line reads: "But of pleasures there are many and of worries there are none."

Several similar minor changes were made in the rest of the act, particularly in the Chorus preceding the Cachucha (page 367).

On page 374, immediately preceding the Finale, after the last line of the Quintette ("And wives divisible into three?") the third and later editions add the following lines:

ALL.   O moralists all,
             How can you call
             Marriage a state of union true?

CAS., GIA., TESS. One-third of myself is married to
             half of ye or you,

MAR. & GIU.   When half of myself has married
             two-thirds of ye or you?

The eight-line duet in the Finale—"Once more *gondolieri* . . ."—is removed from Marco and Giuseppe and is now for "All" to sing.

Utopia (Limited)

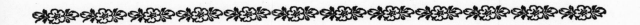

Introduction

"THE RINGING CHEERS which on the fall of the curtain upon *Utopia* (*Limited*) on Saturday night greeted Mr. Gilbert and Sir Arthur Sullivan, as hand in hand they stepped to the footlights, bore ample testimony to the delight of the audience in welcoming back to the Savoy, the author and composer who during the past sixteen years have given the public so much hearty and innocent pleasure." Thus, in his lead sentence, the *Daily News* reviewer caught the joy and pathos of that most sentimental of all Gilbert and Sullivan first nights.

October 7, 1893, was a night of reconciliation and reunion at the Savoy; and if this limited reconciliation seemed Utopian to the cheering faithful, it was appropriate that the offspring of the welcome reunion should have been titled *Utopia* (*Limited*). The thirty-seven-year-old, red-bearded music critic of the *World* wrote:

Pleasant it is to see Mr. Gilbert and Sir Arthur Sullivan working together again full brotherly. . . . The twain still excite the expectations of the public as much as ever. How *Trial by Jury* and *The Sorcerer* surprised the public, and how *Pinafore, The Pirates,* and *Patience* kept the sensation fresh, can be guessed by the youngest man from the fact that the announcement of a new Savoy opera always throws the middle-aged play-goer into the attitude of expecting a surprise. As for me [continued George Bernard Shaw], I avoid this attitude, if only because it is a middle-aged one. Still, I expect a good deal that I would not have hoped for when I first made the acquaintance of comic opera.

"Let us rejoice," beamed the *Daily Graphic,* "over the happy termination of the interregnum which followed the production of *The Gondoliers,* and hail the prosperous restoration of the historic triumvirate of Gilbert, Sullivan, and Carte." G.B.S.

made a more specific and characteristically satiric reference to those almost four years between:

They should be on the best of terms; for henceforth Sir Arthur can always say, "Any other librettist would do just as well: look at *Haddon Hall*" [librettist, Sydney Grundy]; whilst Mr. Gilbert can retort, "Any other musician would do just as well: look at *The Mountebanks*" [composer, Alfred Cellier]. Thus have the years of divorce cemented the happy reunion at which we all assisted last Saturday.

Never was a stage performance viewed through such roseate bifocals of sentiment and expectation. The audience came to cheer and to be delighted, not to criticize. According to the *Sunday Times* the following morning, "It was a first night of first nights. The house was crammed with 'all London,' a term that means (at this season of the year) any number of critics and all who are left to represent that rather mixed community usually termed 'Society.' There was not a place in the house that had not its seat-holder, and the unreserved parts of the theatre were besieged from an early hour in the afternoon." The *Morning Leader* reported that the queuing started at ten a.m. and that those in line spent the long vigil in singing tunes from the other operas. Those who arrived for their reserved seats just before curtain-time included (wrote Mrs. Papillon for *Vanity Fair*): Lady Ormonde with her two daughters ("and Lady Ormonde looked very pretty in black, with pale blue, and wrapped in an Indian mantle," to which *Brighton Society* added, "wearing some magnificent diamonds"), Lord William Nevill and Lady Nevill, Lord Granby (an "inveterate first-nighter"), and the Brazilian Minister (who was the guest of the ever-present Mrs. Ronalds, together with her mother and Mrs. Moreton Frewen). "Jessie Bond sat near Mr. and Mrs. George Grossmith in the stalls," Mrs. Papillon recorded. And she also noted the presence of Mrs. Arthur Lewis and her daughters (if all of Kate Terry's brood were there it was a party of five, not counting papa). *Brighton Society* made special mention of Mrs. Jack Leslie who "looked, to the full, as handsome as her better-known sister, Lady Randolph Churchill." And as a climax, "on the tier above, Madame Melba was gorgeous in dark green."

The audience set the mood of the evening from the moment the composer was observed threading his way through the orchestra pit to the podium. One and all who left any written record of this scene (including Sir Arthur, himself) described the ovation as "tremendous." "Pleasant expectation was at its highest," wrote the *Standard*'s reviewer, "and the reception accorded to the most popular of English composers when he appeared to take the conductor's chair strikingly proved in what estimation he and his works are held."

The rise of the curtain divulged the first of Hawes Craven's two scenes: "The Utopian palm-grove in Act I is a tropical landscape of bewildering splendour," commented the *Daily Graphic,* where, the *Daily News* added, "under the tall palms which shade them from the tropical blue sky, a party of girls clad in rainbow-coloured gowns, recline in hammocks or on the ground, 'dreaming of nothingness,' while one of their number (a part which a sweet-voiced young understudy, Miss Howell-Hersee, a daughter of the well-known English vocalist, Madame Rose Hersee, was suddenly called upon to play) sings melodiously of Lazyland."

Both the souvenir program and the less elaborate one, as well as the librettos in the audience's hands that night, gave the minor role of Phylla to Miss Florence Easton. This was not, however, correct. Miss Easton was indisposed and her part was taken by Miss Howell-Hersee, whose success in a short solo of the opening chorus ("The song of the birds") was appreciated and accurately reviewed by at least two critics (the *Globe* and the *Daily News*). Thereafter her name appeared correctly in the Dramatis Personae until November 7, when Miss Easton returned to the cast.

At least three numbers in Act One were so vociferously received that encores were given. The first of these was Lady Sophy's song, "Bold-faced ranger," "deliciously sung by Miss Rosina Brandram in her old-fashioned English Quaker costume," as the *Sunday Times* put it. The second and third were both in the finale, which the same reviewer thought contained "some of the best fun and best music in the act." One was, as would naturally be expected, the song by Captain Corcoran with its quotation from *H.M.S. Pinafore.* After Lawrence Gridley sang the line "We never run a ship ashore!"—to quote the *Daily News,* "The inquiry 'What, never?' was irresistible, and loud cheers greeted a quotation from the familiar chorus . . . an idea for which, by the way, Sir A. Sullivan can advance the illustrious precedent of Mozart in the Supper Scene of *Don Giovanni.*" The cheers evoked by this echo of an old favorite probably served to parry from most of the audience a thrust at pride in the Senior Service that was neither missed nor relished by the *Daily Graphic:* "We are glad to meet with our old friend Captain Corcoran again, and the quotation from *Pinafore* fairly brought down the house. But it is nothing short of a lamentable error in taste which has prompted Mr. Gilbert to indulge in sarcastic allusions to the steering and running aground of ships of war within a few months after the loss of H.M.S. *Victoria.*" (The rarity of such topical reference in Gilbert librettos is an important factor in the permanence of their appeal. Who but naval archivists recall the disastrous collision during manoeuvres off Tripoli on June 22, 1893, when the H.M.S. *Victoria* was sunk by the H.M.S. *Camperdown?*) The third of these first-act encores was Mr. Goldbury's Company Promoter's song, "Some seven men form an Association," in which Scott Fishe—"one of Mr. Carte's most promising discoveries," according to G.B.S.—scored a decided hit.

"Whispers there may have been," commented the *Daily News,* "that the pruning knife might judiciously be applied to certain scenes in the first act, which is far too long, and at times does not go so briskly as it ought." The *Globe* was more blunt: "It was recognized that the first act (which plays for an hour and three quarters) would be better for being shortened." (A handsome understatement, even for an Englishman: its playing time is exceeded in current operatic repertoire only by the first act of *Die Götterdämmerung!*) Both author and composer must have shared this feeling, at least in part, well in advance of the first night. They had already cut from the first act at least one entire song, which happened to be the best solo number the opera had afforded their new leading lady, Cleveland-born soprano, Miss Nancy McIntosh. This had been omitted from performance at the public dress rehearsal the night of October 6, and the intended permanence of this omission is clear from the fact that the song had already been cut from the libretto that was ready for the first-night audience. That "Youth is a boon avowed" is included in this First-Night Edition text (see page 398) is due to the fact that it was reinstated for the first-night performance—even though not in the printed libretto—and most certainly was sung by Miss McIntosh on that occasion, as was specifically mentioned in the reviews of the *Observer,* the *Standard,* and the *Globe.* The latter went so far as to praise "Youth is a boon avowed" as "one of Sir Arthur Sullivan's best works," and to state that Miss McIntosh sang it "with genuine pathos."

"The second act takes place in a Moorish Hall," wrote the *Daily News* critic, "a veritable fairy palace, illuminated by some hundreds of incandescent lamps." D'Oyly Carte and designer Craven were still exploiting the ever-increasing dramatic possibilities of this still-novel though now twelve-year-old stage lighting. The *Sunday Times* described the palace Throne Room as "a magnificent effulgence of the electric light." The *Daily Graphic* found that this interior setting "shows Utopian art to be even more dazzlingly beautiful than Utopian scenery."

The *Sunday Times* praised the second act as stronger than the first, and the *Globe* recorded that it "gave universal satisfaction." There were two high spots: The first, the Cabinet Council in the manner of Christy's Minstrels, was a huge comic success; the second, the Drawing Room—described by the *Sunday Times* as "a splendid pageant and an accurate picture [that] will attract all London"—was a visual triumph.

The Cabinet Council, as recalled in detail by the *Daily News,* "is one of the funniest incidents in the piece. The chairs are arranged in a semicircle, and in accordance with the practice, if not of the Court of St. James's, at any rate of St. James's Hall. [This was quoted almost verbatim from the libretto. St. James's Hall, Piccadilly, was the home of the Christy Minstrels.] The various court officials produce banjos and fiddles, tambourines and bones, and a side-splitting burlesque of the Christy Minstrels starts, Mr. Rutland Barrington dancing a breakdown and singing alto in the approved style. A double encore rewarded this skit." Of Sullivan's burlesqued minstrel accompaniment, the *Pall Mall Gazette* noted that "a sudden outburst of 'Johnny get your gun' has a laughter all its own in store for the audience." The *Sunday Times* added: "This irresistible skit might have been encored half-a-dozen times." The lone dissenting voice was a particularly bitter attack by *Punch:*

Is this the remarkably original creation of the united intellects of Messrs. Gilbert and Sullivan? Have they ever heard of, or did either of them ever see a burlesque entitled *Black-Eye'd Susan . . . ?* [This piece, which had played over six hundred nights at the Royalty Theatre back in 1866-67, featured a minstrel-show court-martial scene.] Imitation being the sincerest flattery, the author of *Black-Eye'd Susan* must be indeed gratified by this tribute to his original success paid by the librettist and the composer of *Utopia,* and having no further use for this particular bit of humour, he will, no doubt, be willing to make a present of it, free of charge, for nightly use, to the distinguished Savoyards as a practical congratulation to the pair of them on their return to the scene of some of their former triumphs.

It remains only to be reminded that Frank Burnand, author of *Black-Eye'd Susan,* was Francis Cowley Burnand, *Punch*'s managing editor, librettist-rival for the collaborating hand of composer Arthur Sullivan from his pre-Gilbert days.

The Drawing-Room scene, in modern stage vernacular, was played straight. It was not, as some later criticism has indicated, a comic travesty, mocking Queen Victoria's receptions. In this scene, in the words of the *Daily News* review, "contrary to expectation, no sort of parody is attempted. The Royal household and the various Court officials, correct to a button, occupy their proper places, and amid the strains of a stately gavotte, a procession of ladies in such wondrous Court costumes that no mere male would be bold enough to describe them, pass across the stage, every detail of the presentation being carried out practically as at Buckingham Palace. The scene is a very handsome one, but the exact purpose of its introduction into comic opera is not quite apparent." Herein Gilbert unwittingly foreshadowed a device that has since become a staple of musical comedy and revue technique—the costume spectacle, in which humor, romance, and even plot (if any) temporarily give way to an eye-filling pageant against a background of music. That such a scene could be boring to some audience members—in 1893 as in the present day—was abundantly clear in the *Pall Mall Gazette*'s concise comment: "The crowning weakness of a weary business is the reproduction of a Court reception, as dull as it would be possible for a real Court ceremonial to be." But G.B.S. reacted otherwise: "I cannot vouch for its verisimilitude, as I have never, strange as it may appear, been present at a Drawing-Room; but that is exactly why I enjoyed it, and why the majority of the Savoyards will share my appreciation of it." Shaw was right in his prediction of the audience reaction. "The Drawing-Room scene," raved the *Sunday Times,* "superbly managed, brought down a hearty round of applause. . . . The handsome throne-room, with its dazzling glitter of incandescent lamps and the glorious army of rich uniforms and gowns, produced an impression quite unprecedented in the annals of Savoy comic opera." Indeed, one impression this particular scene produced was quite likely a substantial part of the unprecedented total cost of *Utopia (Limited),* a staggering £7,200, of which more than £5,000 was attributable to costumes, accessories, and "hand-props."

Meticulous stage-master Gilbert—just as he had insisted on scrupulous, detailed accuracy in the rigging of *H.M.S. Pinafore* and in the score of regimental uniforms in *Ruddygore*—had spared no pains to be "correct to the button" in this Court reception. Rutland Barrington, who played King Paramount, recalled: "It was great fun for the company on the days when we had a lady professor of deportment attending rehearsals to teach us how to bow." Nor in this scene did Gilbert, the mordant satirist, ruffle any royal plumage; in fact he slyly made a suggestion for improvement that received royal acceptance. It was Barrington's costume in the Cabinet Council scene that unintentionally trespassed. Thomas F. Dunhill sheds light at first-hand on these speculations; he writes that he

> . . . was told by Gilbert himself that the only matter to which the Prince of Wales (King Edward VII) took exception, on seeing the opera, was the appearance of King Paramount in a British Field-Marshal's uniform, wearing the Order of the Garter, a combination which he alone, of all living men, was entitled to wear! Needless to say, the Garter was removed and all was well. Moreover, Gilbert was extremely proud of the effect of one little line in his dialogue [See page 409] . . .

> LORD DRAMALEIGH.   One or two judicious innovations, I think?
> MR. GOLDBURY.   Admirable. The cup of tea and the plate of mixed biscuits were a cheap and effective inspiration.

> It seems that at Queen Victoria's "Drawing-Rooms" it had not been the custom to provide refreshments of any kind, but after the Prince had seen *Utopia Ltd.,* this omission (a serious one, since the proceedings were often terribly lengthy) was actually remedied forthwith.

Near the close of the opera, in a twist of Gilbertian topsy-turvyism, the lovely, fragile, Dresdenesque Miss McIntosh had lines in her "Government by Party!" speech that the *Daily Graphic* regarded as "about the bitterest thing Mr. Gilbert

"Friends Again," the cover illustration of the PALL MALL BUDGET, *October 12, 1893.*

has ever penned." He must have yielded to this point of view for he soon cut the most savage of his aspersions from the offending speech.

The finale heard on the first night, as described by the *Sunday Times,* "is of course very short, and 'Rule Britannia' is an appropriate feature in the music." It dissatisfied both collaborators, as well as the critics, and was replaced in the middle of the following week. (See page 414.)

And now, with the descent of the second-act curtain, came the moment the entire audience had been anticipating with a sentimental fervor that had permitted only rapturous enjoyment for eye and ear throughout the long evening. Obeying the shouted demands for "Author!" and "Composer!" Gilbert and Sullivan made their appearances from opposite sides of the stage. The cheering was deafening, and increased to a roar when the haggard, sickly Sullivan shook hands at stage-center with the hobbling, gout-wracked Gilbert. This was, after all, the real performance of the occasion. "There were many enthusiastic demonstrations on Saturday night," wrote the *Daily Graphic,* "but none more genuine or tumultuous." The *Sunday Times* reviewer also pictured the spirit of this moment: "Sir Arthur Sullivan and Mr. Gilbert came forward, and shaking each other by the hand, the old comrades bowed their thanks and retired; then, after Mr. Charles Harris [the stage director] and Mr. D'Oyly Carte had also been called, the popular *collaborateurs* were compelled to come forth once more to acknowledge another hearty demonstration."

The production that night apparently showed all the pace, polish, and disciplined detail of past Gilbert-trained Savoy first nights. "The faultless stage-management of the whole production," commented the *Sunday Times,* "reflects immense credit upon Mr. Gilbert and Mr. Charles Harris. . . . The Original Comic Opera goes as merrily as a marriage bell; and this is the more remarkable as the Savoy Company has lost many of its most prominent members. . . . In spite of these secessions from the original troupe, the opera went last night with all the old 'go,' and new faces were greeted with nearly as much heartiness as features that had grown familiar behind the same footlights from year to year." The *Daily Graphic* agreed, "If we except an occasional lapse of memory on the part of two of the principal performers, *Utopia* went with wonderful smoothness from beginning to end."

Chief among the newcomers was, of course, the tall and beautiful American, Miss McIntosh, who, in the role of Princess Zara, to the *Daily Graphic*'s eye "looked the part to perfection." But this was her stage debut and it is not hard to understand why, as leading lady, she was clearly too nervous to do herself justice, either vocally (in which department later critics gave her good marks) or as an actress—a field where even the concentrated personal tutoring of Gilbert could not wholly serve as substitute for stage experience. In this connection G.B.S. wrote: "She spoke her part admirably, and, by dint of natural tact, managed to make a positive advantage of her stage-inexperience, so that she won over the audience in no time."

Veteran Rutland Barrington, as King Paramount, was described by *Punch* as "the life and soul of the show." The *Daily Graphic* held that, as Lady Sophy, "Miss Rosina Brandram never sang with greater charm of voice. . . . She presented a perfect picture of primness and prudery . . . and played the part like a true comedian." Lady Sophy, however, was not a satisfactory role. The character had been a collaborative bone of contention between Gilbert and Sullivan. The latter was for grace and dignity; the former for something more caricatured. Their resulting compromise, like most creative compromises, lacked distinction.

From the thousands of words written by first-night reviewers, when the sense is sifted from the sentimentality, it is Gilbert who comes off the poorer of the two reunited craftsmen:

It is always a melancholy business when a writer is driven to imitate himself [wrote the *Pall Mall Gazette*'s critic, who during the whole performance had kept his powder dry of the sentimental]. *Utopia (Limited)* is a mirthless travesty of the work with which [Gilbert's] name is most generally associated. . . . The earlier works indeed were inspired by a common spirit, constructed according to the same formula, but the spirit did not flag, the formula did not seem to be mechanical, the result did not seem to be monotonous. With *Utopia (Limited)* it is different. The philosophy of inversion, of veiled cynicism, of sugared suggestion which had served his turn through a dozen operas suddenly fails him with the ominous number. The quips, whims, jests, the theory of topsy-turvy, the principle of paradox, the law of the unlikely, seem to have grown old in a single night. . . . Mr. Gilbert has failed to make the old seem new. It does not follow that Mr. Gilbert's fancy is exhausted, that Mr. Gilbert's humour has run dry. . . . There is no reason why Mr. Gilbert should not again write a brilliant book for a comic opera. There are many reasons why he should. But for the moment he has failed, and failed conspicuously.

Perhaps the difference between *should* and *could* in this appraisal was already beyond attainment for Gilbert. His 57-year-old creative ego was undergoing a transformation. From the Gilbert who took his work seriously he was becoming Gilbert who took himself seriously. It cannot be dispelled as coincidence that 1890-91 saw two of three significant, completely different yet basically related symptoms of this change-of-life. He bought and settled down in an imposing (and for Gilbert perhaps even ostentatious) country estate, Grim's Dyke. He permitted tongue and temper to steer him into open breach with his two associates, a course the more dextrous Gilbert through fifteen years of partnership with men very different from himself had often managed to avoid. And later, in 1897, he redrew, with infinitely less charm, two hundred of his original *Bab Ballads* illustrations on the pretext that they had "erred gravely in the direction of unnecessary extravagance." In these years Bab had become W. S. Gilbert, Justice of the Peace for his suburban squiredom in Middlesex. It would have been topsy-turvydom indeed if the Magistrate could have done Bab's work, and such "law of the unlikely" by applying "the principle of paradox" is found only in the first dozen Gilbert and Sullivan operas.

"And what shall we say of Sir Arthur Sullivan's share in the new music?" queried the *Sunday Times* critic. "Not, perhaps, that he has excelled all past achievements, for that would mean little less than a miracle where comic opera is concerned. But the well of melody still yields abundantly, and the sources of the musician's inventive power are as though untouched." The exacting G.B.S. observed:

I enjoyed the score of *Utopia* more than that of any of the previous Savoy operas. . . . The orchestral work is charmingly humorous; and as I happen to mean by this only what I say, perhaps I had better warn my readers not to infer that *Utopia* is full of buffooneries with the bassoon and piccolo, or of patter and tum-tum. Whoever can listen to such caressing wind parts—zephyr parts, in fact—as those in the trio for the King and the two Judges in the first act, without being coaxed to feel pleased and amused, is not fit even for treasons, stratagems, and spoils; whilst anyone whose ears are capable of taking in more than one thing at a time must be tickled by the sudden busyness of the orchestra as the city man takes up the parable. I also confidently recommend those who go into solemn academic raptures over themes "in diminution" to go and hear how prettily the chorus of the Christy Minstrel song (borrowed from the plantation dance, "Johnnie, get a gun") is used, very much in diminution, to make an exquisite mock-banjo accompaniment. In these examples we are on the plane, not of the bones and tambourine, but of Mozart's accompaniments to *"Soave sia il vento"* in *Così fan tutte* and the entry of the gardener in *Le Nozze di Figaro.*

Try as they did to tell a story of unqualified success, most of the favorable reviews on Sunday and Monday, October 8 and 9, left evidence of doubt, even though this evidence was often conflicting. The *Sunday Times* predicted: "That *Utopia* (*Limited*) will enjoy a long run is not at all unlikely, but it will benefit by compression, particularly in the first act. . . ." Rutland Barrington's recollection showed even more uncertainty: "Although a success, it did not achieve one of the old-fashioned Savoy runs, and I rather incline to think that this may have been in some measure due to the second act, which was not as full of fun as usual . . . indeed, the more I think about it the less I understand why it did not run longer." Perhaps the opening sentences of the *Globe*'s Monday morning review state the case as it should be, with just the right amount between the lines: "The world already knows that the new Gilbert-Sullivan opera is a triumph for all concerned. It is not by any means a perfect work of art; it has its drawbacks and its limitations. But these were not dwelt upon by Saturday night's gathering. Everybody was glad to see Mr. Gilbert, Sir Arthur Sullivan, and Mr. Carte working together again; everybody was prejudiced in favour of the production; and everybody joined in making it a success."

OCTOBER 7. *Production of "Utopia Limited" at the Savoy Theatre 8.15 p.m. I shockingly nervous as usual—more than usual. Went into the orchestra at 8.15 sharp. My ovation lasted 65 seconds! Piece went wonderfully well—not a hitch of any kind, and afterwards G. and I had a double call.*

ARTHUR SULLIVAN'S DIARY

An Original Comic Opera,

IN TWO ACTS,

ENTITLED

Utopia (Limited)

OR,

THE FLOWERS OF PROGRESS.

Dramatis Personae.

KING PARAMOUNT THE FIRST, *King of Utopia*   MR. RUTLAND BARRINGTON.

SCAPHIO   }   *Judges of the Utopian Supreme Court*   }   MR. W. H. DENNY.

PHANTIS   MR. JOHN LE HAY.

TARARA, *The Public Exploder*   MR. WALTER PASSMORE.

CALYNX, *The Utopian Vice-Chamberlain*   MR. BOWDEN HASWELL.

IMPORTED FLOWERS OF PROGRESS.

LORD DRAMALEIGH, *A British Lord Chamberlain*   MR. SCOTT RUSSELL.

CAPTAIN FITZBATTLEAXE, *First Life Guards*   MR. CHARLES KENNINGHAM.

CAPTAIN SIR EDWARD CORCORAN, K.C.B., *of the Royal Navy*   MR. LAWRENCE GRIDLEY.

MR. GOLDBURY, *A Company Promoter—afterwards Comptroller of the Utopian Household*   MR. SCOTT FISHE.

SIR BAILEY BARRE, Q.C., M.P.   MR. ENES BLACKMORE.

MR. BLUSHINGTON, *of the County Council*   MR. HERBERT RALLAND.

THE PRINCESS ZARA, *Eldest Daughter of King Paramount*   MISS NANCY MCINTOSH.

THE PRINCESS NEKAYA   }   *Her Younger Sisters*   }   MISS EMMIE OWEN.

THE PRINCESS KALYBA   MISS FLORENCE PERRY.

THE LADY SOPHY, *Their English Gouvernante*   MISS ROSINA BRANDRAM.

SALATA   }   MISS EDITH JOHNSTON.

MELENE   }   *Utopian Maidens*   }   MISS MAY BELL.

PHYLLA   MISS HOWELL-HERSEE.

ACT I. — A Utopian Palm Grove.

ACT II. — Throne Room in King Paramount's Palace.

Utopia (Limited)

OR,

THE FLOWERS OF PROGRESS.

ACT I.

Scene. — A Utopian Palm Grove in the gardens of King Paramount's *Palace, showing a picturesque and luxuriant tropical landscape, with the sea in the distance.* Salata, Melene, Phylla, *and other Maidens discovered, lying lazily about the stage and thoroughly enjoying themselves in lotos-eating fashion.*

Opening Chorus.

In lazy languor—motionless,
We lie and dream of nothingness;
    For visions come
    From Poppydom
      Direct at our command:
Or, delicate alternative,
In open idleness we live,
    With lyre and lute
    And silver flute,
      The life of Lazyland!

Solo — Phylla.

The song of birds
    In ivied towers;
      The rippling play
      Of waterway;
The lowing herds;
      The breath of flowers;
      The languid loves
      Of turtle doves—
These simple joys are all at hand
Upon thy shores, O Lazyland!

Chorus. In lazy languor, &c.

Enter Calynx.

Calynx. Good news! Great news! His Majesty's eldest daughter, Princess Zara, who left our shores five years since to go to England—the greatest, the most powerful, the wisest country in the world—has taken a high degree at Girton, and is on her way home again, having achieved a complete mastery over all the elements that have tended to raise that glorious country to her present pre-eminent position among civilized nations!

Salata. Then in a few months Utopia may hope to be completely Anglicized?

Calynx. Absolutely and without a doubt.

Melene (*lazily*). We are very well as we are. Life without a care—every want supplied by a kind and fatherly monarch, who, despot though he be, has no other thought than to make his people happy—what have we to gain by the great change that is in store for us?

Salata. What do we have to gain? English institutions, English tastes, and oh, English fashions!

Calynx. England has made herself what she is because, in that favoured land, every one has to think for himself. Here we have no need to think, because our monarch anticipates all our wants, and our political opinions are formed for us by the journals to which we subscribe. Oh, think how much more brilliant this dialogue would have been, if we had been accustomed to exercise our reflective powers! They say that in England the conversation of the very meanest is a coruscation of impromptu epigram!

Enter Tarara *in a great rage.*

Tarara. Lalabalele talala! Callabale lalabalica falahle!

Calynx (*horrified*). Stop—stop, I beg! (*All the ladies close their ears.*)

TARARA. Callamalala galalate! Caritalla lalabalee kallalale poo!

LADIES. Oh, stop him! stop him!

CALYNX. My Lord, I'm surprised at you. Are you not aware that His Majesty, in his despotic acquiescence with the emphatic wish of his people, has ordered that the Utopian language shall be banished from his court, and that all communications shall henceforward be made in the English tongue?

TARARA. Yes, I'm perfectly aware of it, although —(*suddenly presenting an explosive "cracker"*). Stop—allow me.

CALYNX (*pulls it*). Now, what's that for?

TARARA. Why, I've recently been appointed Public Exploder to His Majesty, and as I'm constitutionally nervous, I must accustom myself by degrees to the startling nature of my duties. Thank you. I was about to say that although, as Public Exploder, I am next in succession to the throne, I nevertheless do my best to fall in with the royal decree. But when I am overmastered by an indignant sense of overwhelming wrong, as I am now, I slip into my native tongue without knowing it. I am told that in the language of that great and pure nation, strong expressions do not exist, consequently when I want to let off steam I have no alternative but to say, "Lalabalele molola lililah kallalale poo!"

CALYNX. But what is your grievance?

TARARA. This—by our Constitution we are governed by a Despot who, although in theory, absolute—is, in practice, nothing of the kind—being watched day and night by two Wise Men whose duty it is, on his very first lapse from political or social propriety, to denounce him to me, the Public Exploder, and it then becomes my duty to blow up His Majesty with dynamite—allow me (*presenting a cracker which CALYNX pulls*). Thank you—and, as some compensation to my wounded feelings, I reign in his stead.

CALYNX. Yes. After many unhappy experiments in the direction of an ideal Republic, it was found that what may be described as a Despotism tempered by Dynamite provides, on the whole, the most satisfactory description of ruler—an autocrat who dares not abuse his autocratic power.

TARARA. That's the theory—but in practice, how does it act? Now, do you ever happen to see the *Palace Peeper?* (*Producing a "Society" paper.*)

CALYNX. Never even heard of the journal.

TARARA. I'm not surprised, because His Majesty's agents always buy up the whole edition; but I have an aunt in the publishing department, and she has supplied me with a copy. Well, it actually teems with circumstantially convincing details of the King's abominable immoralities! If this high-class journal may be believed, His Majesty is one of the most Heliogabalian profligates that ever disgraced an autocratic throne! And *do* these Wise Men denounce him to me? Not a bit of it! They wink at his immoralities! Under the circumstances I really think I am justified in exclaiming "Lalabalele molola lililah kalabalele poo!" (*All horrified.*) I don't care—the occasion demands it. (*Exit.*)

March. Enter Guard, escorting SCAPHIO *and* PHANTIS.

CHORUS.

O make way for the Wise Men!
    They are prizemen—
Double-first in the world's university!
For though lovely this island
    (Which is *my* land),
She has no one to match them in *her* city.
They're the pride of Utopia—
    Cornucopia
Is each in his mental fertility.
O they never make blunder,
    And no wonder,
For they're triumphs of infallibility!

DUET — SCAPHIO *and* PHANTIS.

In every mental lore
    (The statement smacks of vanity),
We claim to rank before
    The wisest of humanity.
As gifts of head and heart
    We wasted on "utility,"
We're "cast" to play a part
    Of great responsibility.

Our duty is to spy
    Upon our King's illicities,
And keep a watchful eye
    On all his eccentricities.
If ever a trick he tries
    That savours of rascality,
At our decree he dies
    Without the least formality.

We fear no rude rebuff,
    Or newspaper publicity;
Our word is quite enough,
    The rest is electricity.
A pound of dynamite
    Explodes in his auriculars;
It's not a pleasant sight—
    We'll spare you the particulars.

It's force all men confess,
    The King needs no admonishing—
We may say its success
    Is something quite astonishing.

Our despot it imbues
    With virtues quite delectable:
He minds his P's and Q's,—
    And keeps himself respectable.

Of a tyrant polite
He's a paragon quite.
He's as modest and mild
In his ways as a child;
And no one ever met
With an autocrat, yet,
So delightfully bland
To the least in the land!

CHORUS.   So make way for the wise men, &c.

Exeunt all but SCAPHIO *and* PHANTIS. PHANTIS *is pensive.*

SCAPHIO.   Phantis, you are not in your customary exuberant spirits. What is wrong?

PHANTIS.   Nothing—nothing—a little passing anxiety, that's all.

SCAPHIO.   Why, what have we to be anxious about? Are not all our little secret commercial ventures doing tremendously? Our time bargains, our cheap wine business, our Army clothing concern, our Matrimonial agency, our Exchange and Mart?

PHANTIS.   Hush—pray be careful! If it should ever be known that these are our speculations, and that we have compelled the King to place his Royal authority and influence at our disposal for their advancement, we should be ruined!

SCAPHIO.   As to our Society paper—why its circulation has increased tenfold since we compelled His Majesty to contribute every week a couple of columns of disreputable attacks on his own moral character! As to our theatre, why, since we insisted on his writing a grossly personal Comic Opera, in which he is held up, nightly, to the scorn and contempt of overwhelming thousands, we have played to double prices!

PHANTIS.   Your keen commercial instincts have been invaluable to us; but my anxiety has nothing to do with our unacknowledged business ventures. Scaphio, I think you once told me that you have never loved?

SCAPHIO.   Never! I have often marvelled at the fairy influence which weaves its rosy web about the faculties of the greatest and wisest of our race; but I thank Heaven I have never been subjected to its singular fascination. For, O Phantis! there is that within me that tells me that when my time *does* come, the convulsion will be tremendous! When *I* love, it will be with the accumulated fervour of sixty-six years! But I have an ideal—a semi-transparent Being, filled with an inorganic pink jelly—and I have never yet seen the woman who approaches within measurable distance of it. All are opaque—opaque—opaque!

PHANTIS.   Keep that ideal firmly before you, and love not until you find her. Though but fifty-five, I am an old campaigner in the battlefields of Love; and, believe me, it is better to be as you are, heart-free and happy, than as I am—eternally racked with doubting agonies! Scaphio, the Princess Zara returns from England to-day!

SCAPHIO.   My poor boy, I see it all.

PHANTIS.   Oh! Scaphio, she is so beautiful. Ah! you smile, for you have never seen her. She sailed for England three months before you took office.

SCAPHIO.   Now tell me, is your affection requited?

PHANTIS.   I do not know—I am not sure. Sometimes I think it is, and then come these torturing doubts! I feel sure that she does not regard me with absolute indifference, for she could never look at me without having to go to bed with a sick headache.

SCAPHIO.   That is surely something. Come, take heart, boy! you are young and beautiful. What more could maiden want?

PHANTIS.   Ah! Scaphio, remember she returns from a land where every youth is as a young Greek god, and where such poor beauty as I can boast is seen at every turn.

SCAPHIO.   Be of good cheer! Marry her, boy, if so your fancy wills, and be sure that love will come.

PHANTIS (*overjoyed*).   Then you will assist me in this?

SCAPHIO.   Why, surely! Silly one, what have you to fear? We have but to say the word, and her father must consent. Is he not our very slave? Come, take heart. I cannot bear to see you sad.

PHANTIS.   Now I may hope, indeed! Scaphio, you have placed me on the very pinnacle of human joy!

DUET — SCAPHIO *and* PHANTIS.

SCAPHIO.   Let all your doubts take wing—
    Our influence is great.
If Paramount our King
    Presume to hesitate,
      Put on the screw,
        And caution him
      That he will rue
        Disaster grim
      That must ensue
        To life and limb,
      Should he pooh-pooh
        This harmless whim.

BOTH.   This harmless whim—this harmless whim,

It is, as $\left\{ \begin{matrix} I \\ you \end{matrix} \right\}$ say, a harmless whim.

PHANTIS (*dancing*).   Observe this dance

Which I employ
When I, by chance,
Go mad with joy.
What sentiment
Does this express?

(PHANTIS *continues his dance while* SCAPHIO
vainly endeavours to discover its meaning.)

Supreme content
And happiness!

BOTH.   And happiness—and happiness—
Of course it does—and happiness!

PHANTIS.   Your friendly aid conferred,
I need no longer pine.
I've but to speak the word,
And lo! the maid is mine!
I do not choose
To be denied.
Or wish to lose
A lovely bride—
If to refuse
The King decide,
The Royal shoes
Then woe betide!

BOTH.   Then woe betide—then woe betide!
The Royal shoes then woe betide!

SCAPHIO (*dancing*).   This step to use
I condescend
Whene'er I choose
To serve a friend.
What it implies
Now try to guess;

(SCAPHIO *continues his dance while* PHANTIS
is vainly endeavouring to discover its meaning.)

It typifies
Unselfishness!

BOTH (*dancing*).   Unselfishness! Unselfishness!
Of course it does—unselfishness!
This step to use
We condescend! &c.
(*Exeunt* SCAPHIO *and* PHANTIS.)

March. Enter KING PARAMOUNT, *attended by
guards and nobles, and preceded by girls dancing
before him.*

CHORUS.

Quaff the nectar—cull the roses—
Gather fruit and flowers in plenty!
For our King no longer poses—
Sing the songs of *far niente!*
Wake the lute that sets us lilting,
Dance a welcome to each comer;
Day by day our year is wilting—
Sing the sunny songs of summer!
La, la, la, la!

SONG — KING.

A King of autocratic power we—
A despot whose tyrannic will is law—
Whose rule is paramount o'er land and sea,
A Presence of unutterable awe!
But though the awe that I inspire
Must shrivel with imperial fire
All foes whom it may chance to touch,
To judge by what I see and hear,
It does not seem to interfere
With popular enjoyment, much.

CHORUS.   No, no—it does not interfere
With our enjoyment much.

KING.   Stupendous when we rouse ourselves to
strike—
Resistless when our tyrant thunder peals—
We often wonder what obstruction's like,
And how a contradicted monarch feels!
But as it is our Royal whim
Our Royal sails to set and trim
To suit whatever winds may blow,
What buffets contradiction deals,
And how a thwarted monarch feels,
We probably shall never know.

CHORUS.   No, no—what thwarted monarch feels
You'll never, never know.

RECITATIVE — KING.

My subjects all, it is your wish emphatic
That all Utopia shall henceforth be modelled
Upon that glorious country called Great
Britain—

To which some add—but others do not—Ireland.

ALL.   It is!

KING.   That being so, as you insist upon it,
   We have arranged that our two younger daughters
   Who have been "finished" by an English Lady—
   (*Tenderly.*) A grave, and good, and gracious English Lady—
   Shall daily be exhibited in public,
   That all may learn what, from the English standpoint,
   Is looked upon as maidenly perfection!
   Come hither, daughters!

Enter NEKAYA *and* KALYBA. *They are twins, about fifteen years old; they are very modest and demure in their appearance, dress, and manner. They stand with their hands folded and their eyes cast down.*

CHORUS.   How fair! how modest! how discreet!
      How bashfully demure!
         See how they blush, as they've been taught,
         At this publicity unsought!
      How English and how pure!

DUET — NEKAYA *and* KALYBA.

BOTH.   Although of native maids the cream,
      We're brought up on the English scheme—
         The best of all
         For great and small
         Who modesty adore.

NEKAYA.   For English girls are good as gold,
      Extremely modest (so we're told),
      Demurely coy—divinely cold—

KALYBA.   And we are that—and more.

      To please papa, who argues thus—
      All girls should mould themselves on us
         Because we are,
         By furlongs far
         The best of all the bunch,
      We show ourselves to loud applause
      From ten to four without a pause—

NEKAYA.   Which is an awkward time because
      It cuts into our lunch.

BOTH.   Oh, maids of high and low degree,
      Whose social code is rather free,
      Please look at us and you will see
      What good young ladies ought to be!

NEKAYA.   And as we stand, like clockwork toys,
      A lecturer whom papa employs
         Proceeds to praise
         Our modest ways

And guileless character—

KALYBA.   Our well-known blush—our downcast eyes—
   Our famous look of mild surprise

NEKAYA.   (Which competition still defies)—

KALYBA.   Our celebrated "Sir!!!"
   Then all the crowd take down our looks
   In pocket memorandum books.
         To diagnose
         Our modest pose
         The Kodaks do their best:

NEKAYA.   If evidence you would possess
   Of what is maiden bashfulness,
   You only need a button press—

KALYBA.   And *we* do all the rest.

Enter LADY SOPHY—*an English lady of mature years and extreme gravity of demeanour and dress. She carries a lecturer's wand in her hand. She is led on by the* KING, *who expresses great regard and admiration for her.*

RECITATIVE — LADY SOPHY.

This morning we propose to illustrate
A course of maiden courtship, from the start
To the triumphant matrimonial finish.

(*Through the following song the two princesses illustrate in gesture the description given by* LADY SOPHY.)

SONG — LADY SOPHY.

   Bold-faced ranger
   (Perfect stranger)
Meets two well-behaved young ladies.
   He's attractive,
   Young and active—

Each a little bit afraid is.
    Youth advances,
    At his glances
To their danger they awaken;
    They repel him
    As they tell him
He is very much mistaken.
Though they speak to him politely,
Please observe they're sneering slightly,
Just to show he's acting vainly.
This is Virtue saying plainly,
    "Go away, young bachelor,
    We are not what you take us for!"
When addressed impertinently,
English ladies answer gently,
    "Go away, young bachelor,
    We are not what you take us for!"

    As he gazes,
    Hat he raises,
Enters into conversation.
    Makes excuses—
    This produces
Interesting agitation.
    He, with daring,
    Undespairing,
Gives his card—his rank discloses—
    Little heeding
    This proceeding,
They turn up their little noses.
Pray observe this lesson vital—
When a man of rank and title
His position first discloses,
Always cock your little noses.
    When at home, let all the class
    Try this in the looking-glass.

English girls of well-bred notions,
Shun all unrehearsed emotions,
    English girls of highest class
    Practise them before the glass.

    His intentions
    Then he mentions.
Something definite to go on—
    Makes recitals
    Of his titles,
Hints at settlements, and so on.
    Smiling sweetly,
    They, discreetly,
Ask for further evidences:
    Thus invited,
    He, delighted,
Gives the usual references.
This is business. Each is fluttered
When the offer's fairly uttered.
"Which of them has his affection?"
He declines to make selection.
    Do they quarrel for his dross?
    Not a bit of it—they toss!
Please observe this cogent moral—
English ladies never quarrel.
    When a doubt they come across,
    English ladies always toss.

RECITATIVE — LADY SOPHY.

The lecture's ended. In ten minutes' space
'Twill be repeated in the market-place!
    (*Exit, followed by* NEKAYA *and* KALYBA.)

CHORUS.

Quaff the nectar—cull the roses—
    Bashful girls will soon be plenty!

Maid who thus at fifteen poses
Ought to be divine at twenty!
    (*Exit* CHORUS. *Manet* KING.)

KING. I requested Scaphio and Phantis to be so good as to favour me with an audience this morning. (*Enter* SCAPHIO *and* PHANTIS.) Oh, here they are!

SCAPHIO. Your Majesty wished to speak with us, I believe. You—you needn't keep your crown on, on our account, you know.

KING. I beg your pardon (*removes it*). I always forget that! Odd, the notion of a King not being allowed to wear one of his own crowns in the presence of two of his own subjects.

PHANTIS. Yes—bizarre, is it not?

KING. Most quaint. But then it's a quaint world.

PHANTIS. Teems with quiet fun. I often think what a lucky thing it is that you are blessed with such a keen sense of humour!

KING. Do you know, I find it invaluable. Do what I will, I *cannot* help looking at the humorous side of things—for, properly considered, everything has its humorous side—even the *Palace Peeper* (*producing it*). See here—"Another Royal Scandal," by Junius Junior. "How long is this to last?" by Senex Senior. "Ribald Royalty," by Mercury Major. "Where is the Public Exploder?" by Mephistopheles Minor. When I reflect that all these outrageous attacks on my morality are written by me, at your command—well, it's one of the funniest things that have come within the scope of my experience.

SCAPHIO. Besides, apart from that, they have a quiet humour of their own which is simply irresistible.

KING (*gratified*). Not bad, I think. Biting, trenchant sarcasm—the rapier, not the bludgeon—that's my line. But then it's so easy—I'm such a good subject—a bad King but a good Subject—ha! ha! —a capital heading for next week's leading article! (*Makes a note.*) And then the stinging little paragraphs about our Royal goings-on with our Royal Second Housemaid—delicately sub-acid, are they not?

SCAPHIO. My dear King, in that kind of thing no one can hold a candle to you.

KING (*doubtfully*). Ye—yes. You refer, of course, to the literary quality of the paragraphs?

SCAPHIO. Oh, of course—

KING. Because the essence of the joke lies in the fact that instead of being the abominable profligate they suggest, I'm one of the most fastidiously respectable persons in my whole dominions!

PHANTIS. But the crowning joke is the Comic Opera you've written for us—"King Tuppence, or A Good Deal Less than Half a Sovereign"— in which the celebrated English tenor, Mr. Wilkinson, burlesques your personal appearance and gives grotesque imitations of your Royal peculiarities. It's immense!

KING. Ye—es—That's what I wanted to speak to you about. Now I've not the least doubt but that even *that* has its humorous side, too—if one could only see it. As a rule, I'm pretty quick at detecting latent humour—but I confess I do *not* quite see where it comes in, in this particular instance. It's so horribly personal!

SCAPHIO. Personal? Yes, of course it's personal —but consider the antithetical humour of the situation.

KING. Yes. I—I don't think I've quite grasped that.

SCAPHIO. No? You surprise me. Why, consider: During the day, thousands tremble at your frown; during the night (from 8 to 11), thousands roar at it. During the day your most arbitrary pronouncements are received by your subjects with abject submission—during the night, they shout with joy at your most terrible decrees. It's not every monarch who enjoys the privilege of undoing by night all the despotic absurdities he's committed during the day.

KING. Of course! Now I see it! Thank you very much. I was sure it had its humorous side, and it was very dull of me not to have seen it before. But, as I said just now, it's a quaint world.

PHANTIS. Teems with quiet fun.

KING. Yes. Properly considered, what a farce life is, to be sure!

SONG — KING.

First you're born—and I'll be bound you
Find a dozen strangers round you.
"Hallo," cries the new-born baby,
"Where's my parents? which may they be?"
    Awkward silence—no reply—
    Puzzled baby wonders why!
Father rises, bows politely—
Mother smiles (but not too brightly)—
Doctor mumbles like a dumb thing—
Nurse is busy mixing something.—
    Every symptom tends to show
    You're decidedly *de trop*—

ALL. Ho! ho! ho! ho! ho! ho! ho! ho!
        Time's teetotum,
            If you spin it,
        Gives its quotum
            Once a minute.
        I'll go bail
        You hit the nail,
        And if you fail

The deuce is in it!

KING.   You grow up, and you discover
　　　　What it is to be a lover.
　　　　Some young lady is selected—
　　　　Poor, perhaps, but well-connected,
　　　　　　Whom you hail (for Love is blind)
　　　　　　As the Queen of fairy kind.
　　　　Though she's plain—perhaps unsightly,
　　　　Makes her face up—laces tightly,
　　　　In her form your fancy traces
　　　　All the gifts of all the graces.
　　　　　　Rivals none the maiden woo,
　　　　　　So you take her and she takes you!

ALL.   Ho! ho! ho! ho! ho! ho! ho! ho!
　　　　　　Joke beginning,
　　　　　　　　Never ceases,
　　　　　　Till your inning
　　　　　　　　Time releases,
　　　　　　On your way
　　　　　　You blindly stray,
　　　　　　And day by day
　　　　　　　　The joke increases!

KING.   Ten years later—Time progresses—
　　　　Sours your temper—thins your tresses;
　　　　Fancy, then, her chain relaxes;
　　　　Rates are facts and so are taxes.
　　　　　　Fairy Queen's no longer young—
　　　　　　Fairy Queen has got a tongue.
　　　　Twins have probably intruded—
　　　　Quite unbidden—just as you did—
　　　　They're a source of care and trouble—
　　　　Just as you were—only double.
　　　　　　Comes at last the final stroke—
　　　　　　Time has had his little joke!

ALL.   Ho! ho! ho! ho! ho! ho! ho! ho!
　　　　　　Daily driven
　　　　　　　　(Wife as drover)
　　　　　　Ill you've thriven—
　　　　　　　　Ne'er in clover:
　　　　　　Lastly, when
　　　　　　Three-score and ten
　　　　　　(And not till then),
　　　　　　　　The joke is over!
　　　　Ho! ho! ho! ho! ho! ho! ho! ho!
　　　　　　Then—and then
　　　　　　　　The joke is over!
(*Exeunt* SCAPHIO *and* PHANTIS. *Manet* KING.)

KING (*putting on his crown again*).   It's all very
well. I always like to look on the humorous side
of things; but I do *not* think I ought to be required
to write libels on my own moral character. Naturally, I see the joke of it—anybody would—but
Zara's coming home to-day; she's no longer a
child, and I confess I should *not* like her to see
my Opera—though it's uncommonly well written;

and I should be sorry if the *Palace Peeper* got into
her hands—though it's certainly smart—very
smart indeed. It is almost a pity that I have to buy
up the whole edition, because it's really too good
to be lost. And Lady Sophy—that blameless type
of perfect womanhood! Great Heavens, what
would *she* say if the Second Housemaid business
happened to meet *her* pure blue eye!

Enter LADY SOPHY.

LADY SOPHY.   My monarch is soliloquizing. I will
withdraw (*going*).

KING.   No—pray don't go. Now I'll give you fifty
chances, and you won't guess whom I was thinking of.

LADY SOPHY.   Alas, sir, I know too well. Ah!
King, it's an old, old story, and I'm well nigh
weary of it! Be warned in time—from my heart I
pity you, but I am not for you! (*Going.*)

KING.   But hear what I have to say.

LADY SOPHY.   It is useless. Listen. In the course
of a long and adventurous career in the principal
European Courts, it has been revealed to me that
I unconsciously exercise a weird and supernatural
fascination over all Crowned Heads. So irresistible
is this singular property, that there is not a European Monarch who has not implored me, with
tears in his eyes, to quit his kingdom, and take my
fatal charms elsewhere. As there is not a civilized
king who is sufficiently single to realize my ideal
of Abstract Respectability, I extended my sphere
of action to the Islands of the South Pacific—only
to discover that the monarchs of those favoured
climes are at least as lax in their domestic arrangements as the worst of their European brethren. As
time was getting on it occurred to me that by
descending several pegs in the scale of Respectability I might qualify your Majesty for my hand.
Actuated by this humane motive and happening
to possess Respectability enough for Six, I consented to confer Respectability enough for Four
upon your two younger daughters—but although I
have, alas, only Respectability enough for Two
left, there is still, as I gather from the public press
of this country (*producing the "Palace Peeper"*),
a considerable balance in my favour.

KING (*aside*).   Da—! (*Aloud.*) May I ask how
you came by this?

LADY SOPHY.   It was handed to me by the officer
who holds the position of Public Exploder to your
Imperial Majesty.

KING.   And surely, Lady Sophy, surely you are
not so unjust as to place any faith in the irrespon-
sible gabble of the Society press!

LADY SOPHY (*referring to paper*).   I read on the
authority of Senex Senior that your Majesty was
seen dancing with your Second Housemaid on the

Oriental Platform of the Tivoli Gardens. That is untrue?

KING. Absolutely. Our Second Housemaid has only one leg.

LADY SOPHY (suspiciously). How do you know that?

KING. Common report, I give you my honour.

LADY SOPHY. It may be so. I further read—and the statement is vouched for by no less an authority than Mephistopheles Minor—that your Majesty indulges in a bath of hot rum-punch every morning. I trust I do not lay myself open to the charge of displaying an indelicate curiosity as to the mysteries of the royal dressing-room when I ask if there is any foundation for this statement?

KING. None whatever. When our medical adviser exhibits rum-punch it is as a draught, not as a fomentation. As to our bath, our valet plays the garden hose upon us every morning.

LADY SOPHY (shocked). Oh, pray—pray spare me these unseemly details. Well, you are a Despot—have you taken steps to slay this scribbler?

KING. Well, no—I have not gone so far as that. After all, it's the poor devil's living, you know.

LADY SOPHY. It is the poor devil's living that surprises me. If this man lies, there is no recognized punishment that is sufficiently terrible for him.

KING. That's precisely it. I—I am waiting until a punishment is discovered that will exactly meet the enormity of the case. I am in constant communication with the Mikado of Japan, who is a leading authority on such points; and, moreover, I have the ground plans and sectional elevations of several capital punishments in my desk at this moment. Oh, Lady Sophy, as you are powerful, be merciful!

DUET — KING and LADY SOPHY.

KING.   Subjected to your heavenly gaze
            (Poetical phrase),
        My brain is turned completely.
            Observe me now,
            No Monarch, I vow,
            Was ever so far afflicted!

LADY SOPHY. I'm pleased with that poetical
            phrase,
        "A heavenly gaze,"
        But though you put it neatly,
            Say what you will,
            These paragraphs still
            Remain uncontradicted.
        Come, crush me this contemptible worm
            (A forcible term),
        If he's assailed you wrongly.

        The rage display,
        Which, as you say,
            Has moved your Majesty lately.

KING.   Though I admit that forcible term,
        "Contemptible worm,"
        Appeals to me most strongly,
            To treat this pest
            As you suggest
            Would pain my Majesty greatly.

LADY SOPHY.   This writer lies!
KING.   Yes, bother his eyes!
LADY SOPHY.   He lives, you say?
KING.   In a sort of a way.
LADY SOPHY.   Then have him shot.
KING.   Decidedly not.
LADY SOPHY.   Or crush him flat.
KING.   I cannot do that.
BOTH.   O royal Rex,
        {My / Her} blameless sex
            Abhors such conduct shady.
        {You / I} plead in vain,
        {You / I} never will gain
            Respectable English lady!

(Dance of repudiation by LADY SOPHY. Exit, followed by KING.)

March. Enter all the Court, heralding the arrival of the PRINCESS ZARA, who enters, escorted by CAPTAIN FITZBATTLEAXE and four troopers, all in the full uniform of the First Life Guards.

CHORUS.

    Oh, maiden, rich
        In Girton lore,
    That wisdom which
        We prized before,
    We do confess

Is nothingness,
And rather less,
　　Perhaps, than more.
On each of us
　　Thy learning shed.
On calculus
　　May we be fed.
And teach us, please,
To speak with ease
All languages,
　　Alive and dead!

SOLO — PRINCESS and CHORUS.

ZARA.　Five years have flown since I took wing—
　　Time flies, and his footstep ne'er re-
　　tards—
I'm the eldest daughter of your king.

TROOPERS.　And we are her escort—First Life
　　Guards!
On the royal yacht,
　　When the waves were white,
In a helmet hot
　　And a tunic tight,
And our great big boots,
　　We defied the storm:
For we're not recruits,
　　And his uniform
A well-drilled trooper ne'er discards—
And we are her escort—First Life Guards!

ZARA.　These gentlemen I present to you,
　　The pride and boast of their barrack-yards;
They've taken, O! such care of me!

TROOPERS.　For we are her escort—First Life
　　Guards!
When the tempest rose,
　　And the ship went so—
Do you suppose
　　We were ill? No, no!
Though a qualmish lot
　　In a tunic tight,
And a helmet hot,
　　And a breastplate bright
(Which a well-drilled trooper ne'er discards),
We stood as her escort—First Life Guards!

FULL CHORUS.

Knightsbridge nursemaids—serving fairies—
Stars of proud Belgravian airies;
At stern duty's call you leave them,
Though you know how that must grieve them!

ZARA.　Tantantarara-rara-rara!
FITZBATTLEAXE.　Trumpet-call of Princess Zara!
CHORUS.　That's trump-call, and they're all trump
　　cards—
　　They are her escort—First Life Guards!

ENSEMBLE.

CHORUS.	ZARA and FITZBATTLE-AXE (aside).
LADIES.	
Knightsbridge nurse-maids, &c.	Oh! the hours are gold,
	And the joys untold,
	When my eyes behold
MEN.	My beloved Princess;
When soldier seeks, &c.	And the years will seem
	But a brief day-dream,
	In the joy extreme
	Of our happiness!

FULL CHORUS. Knightsbridge nursemaids, serving fairies, &c.

Enter KING, PRINCESSES NEKAYA *and* KALYBA, *and* LADY SOPHY. *As the* KING *enters the escort present arms.*

KING. Zara! my beloved daughter! Why, how well you look, and how lovely you have grown! (*Embraces her.*)
ZARA. My dear father! (*Embracing him.*) And my two beautiful little sisters! (*Embracing them.*)
NEKAYA. Not beautiful.
KALYBA. Nice-looking.
ZARA. But first let me present to you the English warrior who commands my escort, and who has taken, O! such care of me during the voyage—Captain Fitzbattleaxe!

TROOPERS.　　　　　The First Life Guards.
　　When the tempest rose,
　　And the ship went so—

CAPTAIN FITZBATTLEAXE *motions them to be silent. The Troopers place themselves in the four corners of the stage, standing at ease, immovably, as if on sentry. Each is surrounded by an admiring group of young ladies, of whom they take no notice.*

KING (*to* CAPTAIN FITZBATTLEAXE). Sir, you come from a country where every virtue flourishes. We trust that you will not criticise too severely such shortcomings as you may detect in our semi-barbarous society.
FITZBATTLEAXE (*looking at* ZARA). Sir, I have eyes for nothing but the blameless and the beautiful.
KING. We thank you—he is really very polite! (LADY SOPHY, *who has been greatly scandalised by the attentions paid to the Lifeguardsmen by the young ladies, marches the* PRINCESSES NEKAYA *and* KALYBA *towards an exit.*) Lady Sophy, do not leave us.
LADY SOPHY. Sir, your children are young, and, so far, innocent. If they are to remain so, it is

necessary that they be at once removed from the contamination of their present disgraceful surroundings. (*She marches them off.*)

KING (*whose attention has thus been called to the proceedings of the young ladies—aside*). Dear, dear! They really shouldn't. (*Aloud.*) Captain Fitzbattleaxe—

FITZBATTLEAXE. Sir.

KING. Your Troopers appear to be receiving a troublesome amount of attention from those young ladies. I know how strict you English soldiers are, and I should be extremely distressed if anything occurred to shock their puritanical British sensitiveness.

FITZBATTLEAXE. Oh, I don't think there's any chance of that.

KING. You think not? They won't be offended?

FITZBATTLEAXE. Oh no! They are quite hardened to it. They get a good deal of that sort of thing, standing sentry at the Horse Guards.

KING. It's English, is it?

FITZBATTLEAXE. It's particularly English.

KING. Then, of course, it's all right. Pray proceed, ladies, it's particularly English. Come, my daughter, for we have much to say to each other.

ZARA. Farewell, Captain Fitzbattleaxe! I cannot thank you too emphatically for the devoted care with which you have watched over me during our long and eventful voyage.

DUET — ZARA *and* CAPT. FITZBATTLEAXE.

ZARA. Ah! gallant soldier, brave and true

In tented field and tourney,
I grieve to have occasioned you
So very long a journey.
A British soldier gives up all—
His home and island beauty—
When summoned by the trumpet-call
Of Regimental Duty!

ALL.   Tantantarara-rara-rara!
Trumpet-call of Princess Zara!

ENSEMBLE.

CHORUS. MEN.	FITZBATTLEAXE *and* ZARA (*aside*).
A British warrior gives up all, &c.	Oh my joy, my pride, My delight to hide, Let us sing, aside, What in truth we feel.
LADIES. Knightsbridge nurse-maids, &c.	Let us whisper low Of our love's glad glow, Lest the truth we show We would fain conceal.

FITZBATTLEAXE.   Such escort duty, as his due,
To young Lifeguardsman falling,
Completely reconciles him to
His uneventful calling.
When soldier seeks Utopian glades
In charge of Youth and Beauty,
Then pleasure merely masquerades
As Regimental Duty!

ALL.   Tantantarara-rara-rara!
Trumpet-call of Princess Zara!

ENSEMBLE.

CHORUS. MEN.	FITZBATTLEAXE *and* ZARA (*aside*).
A British warrior, &c.	Oh the hours are gold And the joys untold When my eyes behold My beloved Princess;
WOMEN. Knightsbridge nurse-maids, &c.	And the year will seem But a brief day-dream In the joy extreme Of our happiness!

Exeunt KING *and* PRINCESS *in one direction, Lifeguardsmen and crowd in opposite direction. Enter, at back,* SCAPHIO *and* PHANTIS, *who watch the* PRINCESS *as she goes off.* SCAPHIO *is seated, shaking violently, and obviously under the influence of some strong emotion.*

PHANTIS. There—tell me, Scaphio, is she not beautiful? Can you wonder that I love her so passionately?

SCAPHIO. No. She is extraordinarily—miraculously lovely! Good heavens, what a singularly beautiful girl!

PHANTIS. I knew you would say so!

SCAPHIO. What exquisite charm of manner! What surprising delicacy of gesture! Why she's a goddess! a very goddess!

PHANTIS (*rather taken aback*). Yes—she's—she's an attractive girl.

SCAPHIO. Attractive? Why, you must be blind! —She's entrancing—enthralling! Her walk—her smile—her play of feature! What eyes—what lips! Why, it's bewildering—dazzling—intoxicating! (*Aside*). God bless my heart, what's the matter with me?

PHANTIS (*alarmed*). Yes. You—you promised to help me to get her father's consent, you know.

SCAPHIO. Promised! Yes, but the convulsion has come, my good boy! It is she—my ideal! My ideal, did I say?

PHANTIS (*much disconcerted*). Yes, you said so.

SCAPHIO. Then I lied, for by all that's dazzling I had no conception that the world contained such transcendent loveliness! Why, what's this? (*Staggering*.) Phantis! Stop me—I'm going mad—mad with the love of her! What an eye! what an ear! what shoulders!

PHANTIS. Scaphio, compose yourself, I beg. The girl is perfectly opaque! Besides, remember—each of us is helpless without the other. You can't succeed without my consent, you know.

SCAPHIO. And you dare to threaten? Oh ungrateful! When you came to me, palsied with love for this girl, and implored my assistance, did I not unhesitatingly promise it? And this is the return you make? Out of my sight, ingrate! (*Aside*.) Dear! dear! what is the matter with me?

Enter CAPT. FITZBATTLEAXE *and* ZARA.

ZARA. Dear me. I'm afraid we are interrupting a *tête-à-tête*.

SCAPHIO (*breathlessly*). No, no. You come very appropriately. To be brief, we—we love you—this man and I—madly—passionately!

ZARA. Sir!

SCAPHIO. And we don't know how we are to settle which of us is to marry you.

FITZBATTLEAXE. Zara, this is very awkward.

SCAPHIO (*very much overcome*). I—I am paralyzed by the singular radiance of your extraordinary loveliness. I know I am incoherent. I never was like this before—it shall not occur again. I—shall be fluent, presently.

ZARA (*aside*). Oh, dear Captain Fitzbattleaxe, what *is* to be done?

FITZBATTLEAXE (*aside*). Leave it to me—I'll manage it. (*Aloud.*) It's a common situation. Why not settle it in the English fashion?

BOTH. The English fashion? What is that?

FITZBATTLEAXE. It's very simple. In England, when two gentlemen are in love with the same lady, and until it is settled which gentleman is to blow out the brains of the other, it is provided, by the Rival Admirers' Clauses Consolidation Act, that the lady shall be entrusted to an officer of Household Cavalry as stakeholder, who is bound to hand her over to the survivor (on the Tontine principle) in a good condition of substantial and decorative repair.

SCAPHIO. Reasonable wear and tear and damages by fire excepted?

FITZBATTLEAXE. Exactly.

PHANTIS. Well, that seems very reasonable. (*To* SCAPHIO.) What do you say—Shall we entrust her to this officer of Household Cavalry? It will give us time.

SCAPHIO (*trembling violently*). I—I am not at present in a condition to think it out coolly—but if he *is* an officer of Household Cavalry, and if the Princess consents—

ZARA. Alas, dear sirs, I have no alternative—under the Rival Admirers' Clauses Consolidation Act!

FITZBATTLEAXE. Good—then that's settled.

QUARTETTE.

FITZBATTLEAXE, ZARA, SCAPHIO, *and* PHANTIS.

FITZBATTLEAXE. It's understood, I think, all round
That, by the English custom bound,
I hold the lady safe and sound
　　In trust for either rival,
Until you clearly testify
By sword or pistol, by and by,
Which gentleman prefers to die,
　　And which prefers survival.

ENSEMBLE.

SCAPHIO *and* PHANTIS.	ZARA *and* FITZBATTLEAXE (*aside*).
It's clearly understood, all round,	We stand, I think, on safish ground;
That, by your English custom bound,	Our senses weak it will astound
He holds the lady safe and sound	If either gentleman is found
In trust for either rival,	Prepared to meet his rival.
Until we clearly testify	Their machinations we defy;

SCAPHIO *and* PHANTIS.

By sword and pistol, by
    and by,
Which gentleman pre-
    fers to die,
    And which prefers
        survival.

PHANTIS (*aside to* FITZBATTLEAXE).
    If I should die and he should live,
    To you, without reserve, I give
    Her heart so young and sensitive,
    And all her predilections.

SCAPHIO (*aside to* FITZBATTLEAXE).
    If he should live and I should die,
    I see no kind of reason why
    You should not, if you wish it, try
        To gain her young affections.

ENSEMBLE.

SCAPHIO *and* PHANTIS
(*angrily to each other*).

If I should die and you
    should live,
To this young officer I
    give
Her heart so soft and
    sensitive,
    And all her predilec-
        tions.
If you should live and I
    should die,
I see no kind of reason
    why
He should not, if he
    chooses, try
    To win her young
        affections.

ZARA *and* FITZBATTLE-
AXE (*aside*).

We won't be parted,
    you and I—
Of bloodshed each is
    rather shy—
    They both prefer sur-
        vival!

FITZBATTLEAXE *and*
ZARA (*aside*).

As both of us are posi-
    tive
That both of them in-
    tend to live,
There's nothing in the
    case to give
    Us cause for grave
        reflections.
As both will live and
    neither die,
I see no kind of reason
    why
I should not, if I wish it,
    try
    To gain your young
        affections!

(*Exeunt* SCAPHIO *and* PHANTIS *together*.)

DUET — ZARA *and* FITZBATTLEAXE.

ENSEMBLE.   Oh admirable art!
        Oh neatly-planned intention!
        Oh happy intervention—
            Oh well-constructed plot!
    When sages try to part
        Two loving hearts in fusion,
        Their wisdom's a delusion,
            And learning serves them not!

FITZBATTLEAXE.   Until quite plain
        Is their intent,
        These sages twain
        I represent.
    Now please infer
        That, nothing loth,

You're henceforth, as it were,
        Engaged to marry both—
    Then take it that I represent the two—
    On that hypothesis, what would you do?

ZARA (*aside*).   What would I do? what would I do?
    (*to* FITZBATTLEAXE).   In such a case,
        Upon your breast,
        My blushing face
            I think I'd rest—   (*doing so*).
        Then perhaps I might
            Demurely say—
        "I find this breastplate bright
            Is sorely in the way!"
    That is, supposing it were true
    That I'm engaged to both—and both were
        you!

ENSEMBLE.   Our mortal race
        Is never blest—
    There's no such case
        As perfect rest;
    Some petty blight
        Asserts its sway—
    Some crumpled roseleaf light
        Is always in the way!
        (*Exit* FITZBATTLEAXE. *Manet* ZARA.)

ZARA (*looking off, in the direction in which* SCA-
PHIO *and* PHANTIS *have gone*). Poor, trusting,
simple-minded, and affectionate old gentlemen!
I'm really sorry for them! How strange it is that
when the flower of a man's youth has faded, he

seems to lose all charm in a woman's eyes; and how true are the words of my expurgated Juvenal:

> "—*Festinat decurrere velox*
> *Flosculus, angustæ, miseræque brevissima vitæ*
> *Portio!*"

Ah, if we could only make up our minds to invest our stock of youth on commercial principles instead of squandering it at the outset, old age would be as extinct as the Dodo!

Song — Zara.

Youth is a boon avowed—
A gift of priceless worth
To rich and poor allowed—
With which all men at birth—
The lowly and the proud—
Are equally endowed.
But sorrow comes anon,
For Man's a prodigal
Who madly lives upon
His little capital.
And this, alas, goes on
Till every penny's gone:
He finds himself, at Life's concluding stage,
With no Youth left to comfort his old age!

Ah, dame improvident,
If you, in very sooth
In infancy had lent
Your Capital of Youth
At four or five per cent—
(As Nature doubtless meant),
Resolved, within your breast,
To do as others do
Who Capital invest,
And live a lifetime through,
With modest comfort blest,
Upon the interest—
You might be still in girlhood's mid-career
A merry madcap maid of fourscore year!

Enter King.

KING. My daughter! At last we are alone together.

ZARA. Yes, and I'm glad we are, for I want to speak to you very seriously. Do you know this paper?

KING (*aside*). Da——! (*Aloud.*) Oh, yes—I've —I've seen it. Where in the world did you get this from?

ZARA. It was given to me by Lady Sophy—my sisters' governess.

KING (*aside*). Lady Sophy's an angel, but I do sometimes wish she'd mind her own business! (*Aloud.*) It's—ha! ha!—it's rather humorous.

ZARA. I see nothing humorous in it. I only see that you, the despotic King of this country, are made the subject of the most scandalous insinuations. Why do you permit these things?

KING. Well, they appeal to my sense of humour. It's the only really comic paper in Utopia, and I wouldn't be without it for the world.

ZARA. If it had any literary merit I could understand it.

KING. Oh, it *has* literary merit. Oh, distinctly, it has literary merit.

ZARA. My dear father, it's mere ungrammatical twaddle.

KING. Oh, it's not ungrammatical. I can't allow that. Unpleasantly personal, perhaps, but written with an epigrammatical point that is very rare nowadays—very rare indeed.

ZARA (*looking at cartoon*). Why do they represent you with such a big nose?

KING (*looking at cartoon*). Eh? Yes, it *is* a big one! Why, the fact is that, in the cartoons of a comic paper, the size of your nose always varies inversely as the square of your popularity. It's the rule.

ZARA. Then you must be at a tremendous discount, just now! I see a notice of a new piece called "King Tuppence," in which an English tenor has the audacity to personate you on a public stage. I can only say that I am surprised that any English tenor should lend himself to such degrading personalities.

KING. Oh, he's not really English. As it happens he's a Utopian, but he calls himself English.

ZARA. Calls himself English?

KING. Yes. Bless you, they wouldn't listen to any tenor who didn't call himself English.

ZARA. And you permit this insolent buffoon to caricature you in a pointless burlesque! My dear father—if you were a free agent, you would never permit these outrages.

KING (*almost in tears*). Zara—I—I admit I am not altogether a free agent. I—I am controlled. I try to make the best of it, but sometimes I find it very difficult—very difficult indeed. Nominally a Despot, I am, between ourselves, the helpless tool of two unscrupulous Wise Men, who insist on my falling in with all their wishes and threaten to denounce me for immediate explosion if I remonstrate! (*Breaks down completely.*)

ZARA. My poor father! Now listen to me. With a view to remodelling the political and social institutions of Utopia, I have brought with me six Representatives of the principal causes that have tended to make England the powerful, happy and blameless country which the consensus of European civilization has declared it to be. Place yourself unreservedly in the hands of these gentlemen, and they will reorganize your country on a footing that will enable you to defy your persecutors. They are all now washing their hands after their journey. Shall I introduce them?

KING. My dear Zara, how can I thank you? I will consent to anything that will release me from the abominable tyranny of these two men. (*Calling*.) What ho! Without there! (*Enter* CALYNX.) Summon my court without an instant's delay! (*Exit* CALYNX.)

FINALE.

Enter everyone, except the Flowers of Progress.

CHORUS.

Although your Royal summons to appear
    From courtesy was singularly free,
Obedient to that summons we are here—
    What would your Majesty?

RECITATIVE — KING.

My worthy people, my beloved daughter
Most thoughtfully has brought with her from England
The types of all the causes that have made
That great and glorious country what it is.

CHORUS.   Oh joy unbounded!

SCAPHIO, TARARA, *and* PHANTIS (*aside*). Why, what *does* this mean?

RECITATIVE — ZARA.

Attend to me, Utopian populace,
    Ye South Pacific Island viviparians;
All, in the abstract, types of courtly grace,
Yet, when compared with Britain's glorious race,
    But little better than half-clothed barbarians!

CHORUS.

That's true—we South Pacific viviparians,
    Contrasted when
    With Englishmen,
Are little better than half-clothed barbarians!

Enter all the Flowers of Progress, led by FITZ-BATTLEAXE.

SOLO — ZARA.
(*Presenting* CAPT. FITZBATTLEAXE.)

When Britain sounds the trump of war
    (And Europe trembles),
The army of that conqueror
    In serried ranks assembles;
'Tis then this warrior's eyes and sabre gleam
    For our protection—

He represents a military scheme
    In all its proud perfection!

FITZBATTLEAXE.   Yes—yes—
I represent a military scheme
    In all its proud perfection!

CHORUS.   Ulahlica! Ulahlica! Ulahlica!

SOLO — ZARA.
(*Presenting* SIR BAILEY BARRE, Q.C., M.P.)

A complicated gentleman allow me to present,
Of all the arts and faculties the terse embodiment,
He's a great Arithmetician who can demonstrate with ease
That two and two are three, or five, or anything you please;
An eminent Logician who can make it clear to you
That black is white—when looked at from the proper point of view;
A marvellous Philologist who'll undertake to show
That "yes" is but another and a neater form of "no."

SIR BAILEY.   Yes—yes—yes—
Oh "yes" is but another and a neater form of "no."
All preconceived ideas on any subject I can scout,
And demonstrate beyond all possibility of doubt,
That whether you're an honest man or whether you're a thief
Depends on whose solicitor has given me my brief.

CHORUS.   Yes—yes—yes—
That whether you're an honest man, &c.
Ulahlica! Ulahlica! Ulahlica!

SOLO — ZARA.
(*Presenting* LORD DRAMALEIGH *and County Councillor.*)

What these may be, Utopians all,
    Perhaps you'll hardly guess—
They're types of England's physical
    And moral cleanliness.
This is a Lord High Chamberlain
    Of purity the gauge—
He'll cleanse our Court from moral stain
    And purify our Stage.

LORD DRAMALEIGH.   Yes—yes—yes—
    Court reputations I revise,
    And presentations scrutinize,
    New plays I read with jealous eyes,
    And purify the Stage.

CHORUS.   Yes—yes—yes—
    New plays, &c.

ZARA.   This County Councillor acclaim,
        Great Britain's latest toy—
    On anything you like to name
        His talents he'll employ—
    All streets and squares he'll purify
        Within your city walls,
    And keep meanwhile a modest eye
        On wicked music halls.

COUNCILLOR.   Yes—yes—yes—
    In towns I make improvements great,
    Which go to swell the County Rate—
    I dwelling-houses sanitate,
        And purify the Halls!

CHORUS.   Yes—yes—yes—
    He'll dwelling-houses, &c.
    Ulahlica! Ulahlica! Ulahlica!

SOLO — ZARA.
(*Presenting* MR. GOLDBURY.)

A Company Promoter this, with special edu-
    cation,
Which teaches what Contango means and also
    Backwardation—
To speculators he supplies a grand financial
    leaven,
Time was when *two* were company—but now
    it must be seven.

MR. GOLDBURY.   Yes—yes—yes—
    Stupendous loans to foreign thrones
        I've largely advocated;
    In ginger-pops and peppermint-drops
        I've freely speculated;
    Then mines of gold, of wealth untold,
        Successfully I've floated,
    And sudden falls in apple-stalls
        Occasionally quoted:
    And soon or late I always call
        For Stock Exchange quotation—
    No schemes too great and none too small
        For Companification!

CHORUS.   Then soon or late, &c.
    Ulahlica! Ulahlica! Ulahlica!

SOLO — ZARA.
(*Presenting* CAPT. SIR EDWARD CORCORAN, R.N.)

    And lastly I present
        Great Britain's proudest boast,
    Who from the blows
    Of foreign foes
        Protects her sea-girt coast—
    And if you ask him in respectful tone,
    He'll show you how you may protect your
        own!

SOLO — CAPTAIN CORCORAN.

I'm Captain Corcoran, K.C.B.,
I'll teach you how we rule the sea,
    And terrify the simple Gauls;
And how the Saxon and the Celt
Their Europe-shaking blows have dealt
With Maxim gun and Nordenfelt
    (Or will, when the occasion calls).
If sailor-like you'd play your cards,
Unbend your sails, and lower your yards,
    Unstep your masts—you'll never want 'em
        more.
Though we're no longer hearts of oak,
Yet we can steer and we can stoke,
And, thanks to coal, and thanks to coke,
    We never run a ship ashore!

ALL.   What never?

CAPTAIN.   No, never!

ALL.   What, *never?*

CAPTAIN.   Hardly ever!

ALL.   Hardly ever run a ship ashore!
    Then give three cheers, and three cheers
        more,
    For the tar who never runs his ship ashore;
    Then give three cheers, and three cheers
        more,
    For he never runs his ship ashore!

CHORUS.

All hail, ye types of England's power—
    Ye heaven enlightened band!
We bless the day, and bless the hour
    That brought you to our land.

QUARTETTE.

Ye wanderers from a mighty State,
Oh teach us how to legislate—
Your lightest word will carry weight
    In our attentive ears.
Oh, teach the natives of this land
(Who are not quick to understand)
How to work off their social and
    Political arrears!

FITZBATTLEAXE.   Increase your army!

DRAMALEIGH.   Purify your Court!

CAPTAIN. Get up your steam and cut your canvas
    short!

SIR BAILEY. To speak on both sides teach your
    sluggish brains!

COUNCILLOR. Widen your thoroughfares, and
    flush your drains!

MR. GOLDBURY. Utopia's much too big for one
    small head—

I'll float it as a Company Limited!

KING.   A Company Limited? What may that be?
  The term, I think, is new to me.

CHORUS.   A Company Limited? &c.

SCAPHIO, PHANTIS, *and* TARARA (*aside*).
  What does he mean? What does he mean?
    Give us a kind of clue!
  What does he mean? What does he mean?
    What is he going to do?

SONG — MR. GOLDBURY.

Seven men form an Association,
  (If possible, all Peers and Baronets).
They start off with a public declaration
  To what extent they mean to pay their debts.
That's called their Capital: if they are wary
  They will not quote it at a sum immense.
The figure's immaterial—it may vary
  From eighteen million down to eighteen-
    pence.
    I should put it rather low;
    The good sense of doing so
  Will be evident at once to any debtor.
    When it's left to you to say
    What amount you mean to pay,
  Why, the lower you can put it at, the better.

CHORUS.   When it's left to you to say, &c.

They then proceed to trade with all who'll trust
    'em,
  Quite irrespective of their capital

(It's shady, but it's sanctified by custom);
  Bank, Railway, Loan, or Panama Canal.
You can't embark on trading too tremendous—
  It's strictly fair, and based on common
    sense—
If you succeed, your profits are stupendous—
  And if you fail, pop goes your eighteenpence.
    Make the money-spinner spin!
    For you only stand to win,
  And you'll never with dishonesty be twitted.
    For nobody can know,
    To a million or so,
  To what extent your capital's committed!

CHORUS.   No, nobody can know, &c.

If you come to grief, and creditors are craving,
  (For nothing that is planned by mortal head
Is certain in this Vale of Sorrow—saving
  That one's Liability is Limited)—
Do you suppose that signifies perdition?
  If so, you're but a monetary dunce—
You merely file a Winding-Up Petition,
  And start another Company at once!
    Though a Rothschild you may be
    In your own capacity,
  As a Company you've come to utter sor-
    row—
    But the Liquidators say,
    "Never mind—you needn't pay,"
  So you start another company to-morrow!

CHORUS.   But the Liquidators say, &c.

RECITATIVE.

KING. Well, at first it strikes us as dishonest,
 But if it's good enough for virtuous England—
 The first commercial country in the world—
 It's good enough for us.

SCAPHIO, PHANTIS, *and* TARARA (*aside to* KING.)
 You'd best take care—
 Please recollect *we* have not been consulted.

KING (*not heeding them*). And do I understand
 you that Great Britain
 Upon this Joint Stock principle is governed?

MR. GOLDBURY. We haven't come to that, ex-
 actly—but
 We're tending rapidly in that direction.
 The date's not distant.

KING (*enthusiastically*). We will be before you!
 We'll go down to Posterity renowned
 As the First Sovereign in Christendom
 Who registered his Crown and Country under
 The Joint Stock Company's Act of Sixty-Two.

ALL. Ulahlica! Ulahlica! Ulahlica!

SOLO — KING.

Henceforward, of a verity,
 With Fame ourselves we link—
 We'll go down to Posterity,
 Of sovereigns all the pink!

SCAPHIO, PHANTIS, *and* TARARA (*aside to* KING).
 If you've the mad temerity
 Our wishes thus to blink,
 You'll go down to Posterity
 Much earlier than you think!

TARARA (*correcting them*). He'll go *up* to Posterity,
 If *I* inflict the blow!

SCAPHIO *and* PHANTIS (*angrily*). He'll go *down*
 to Posterity,

We think we ought to know!

TARARA (*explaining*). He'll go *up* to Posterity,
 Blown up with dynamite!

SCAPHIO *and* PHANTIS (*apologetically*). He'll go
 up to Posterity
 Of course he will, you're right!

ENSEMBLE.

KING, LADY SOPHY, NEKAYA, KALYBA, CALYNX, *and* CHORUS.	SCAPHIO, PHANTIS, *and* TARARA (*aside*).
Henceforward of a verity With fame ourselves we link, And go down to Posterity, Of sovereigns all the pink!	If he has the temerity Our wishes thus to blink, He'll go up to Posterity Much earlier than they think!

FITZBATTLEAXE *and* ZARA (*aside*).

Who love with all sincerity,
 Their lives may safely link;
 And as for our Posterity—
 We don't care what they think!

CHORUS.

Let's seal this mercantile pact—
 The step we ne'er shall rue—
 It gives whatever we lacked—
 The statement's strictly true.
 All hail, astonishing Fact!
 All hail, Invention new—
 The Joint Stock Company's Act—
 The Act of Sixty-Two!

CURTAIN.

ACT II.

SCENE. — *Throne Room in the Palace. Night.* FITZBATTLEAXE *discovered, singing to* ZARA.

RECITATIVE — FITZBATTLEAXE.

Oh Zara, my beloved one, bear with me!
 Ah, do not laugh at my attempted C!
 Repent not, mocking maid, thy girlhood's
 choice—
 The fervour of my love affects my voice!

SONG — FITZBATTLEAXE.

A tenor, all singers above,
 (This doesn't admit of a question),
 Should keep himself quiet,
 Attend to his diet
 And carefully nurse his digestion:

But when he is madly in love
　　It's certain to tell on his singing—
　　　　You can't do chromatics
　　　　With proper emphatics
　　When anguish your bosom is wringing!
When distracted with worries in plenty,
And his pulse is a hundred and twenty,
And his fluttering bosom the slave of mistrust is,
A tenor can't do himself justice.
　　　　Now observe—(*sings a high note*),
You see, I can't do myself justice!

I could sing, if my fervour were mock,
　　It's easy enough if you're acting—
　　　　But when one's emotion
　　　　Is born of devotion
　　You mustn't be over-exacting.
One ought to be firm as a rock
　　To venture a shake in *vibrato,*
　　　　When fervour's expected
　　　　Keep cool and collected
　　Or never attempt *agitato.*
But, of course, when his tongue is of leather,
And his lips appear pasted together,
And his sensitive palate as dry as a crust is,
A tenor can't do himself justice.
　　　　Now observe—(*sings a cadence*),
It's no use—I can't do myself justice!

ZARA. Why, Arthur, what *does* it matter? When the higher qualities of the heart are all that can be desired, the higher notes of the voice are matters of comparative insignificance. Who thinks slightly of the cocoanut because it is husky? Besides (*demurely*), you are not singing for an engagement; (*putting her hand in his*) you have that already!

FITZBATTLEAXE. How good and wise you are! How unerringly your practised brain winnows the wheat from the chaff—the material from the merely incidental!

ZARA. My Girton training, Arthur. At Girton all is wheat, and idle chaff is never heard within its walls! But tell me, is not all working marvellously well? Have not our Flowers of Progress more than justified their name?

FITZBATTLEAXE. We have indeed done our best. Captain Corcoran and I have, in concert, thoroughly remodelled the sister-services—and upon so sound a basis that the South Pacific trembles at the name of Utopia!

ZARA. How clever of you!

FITZBATTLEAXE. Clever! not a bit. It's as easy as possible when the Admiralty and Horse Guards are not there to interfere. And so with the others. Freed from the trammels imposed upon them by idle Acts of Parliament, all have given their natural talents full play and introduced reforms which, even in England, were never dreamt of!

ZARA. But perhaps the most beneficent change of all has been effected by Mr. Goldbury, who, discarding the exploded theory that some strange magic lies hidden in the number Seven, has applied the Limited Liability principle to individuals, and every man, woman, and child is now a Company Limited with liability restricted to the amount of his declared Capital! There is not a christened baby in Utopia who has not already issued his little Prospectus!

FITZBATTLEAXE. Marvellous is the power of a Civilization which can transmute, by a word, a Limited Income into an Income (*Limited*).

ZARA. Reform has not stopped here—it has been applied even to the costume of our people. Discarding their own barbaric dress, the natives of our land have unanimously adopted the tasteful fashions of England in all their rich entirety. Scaphio and Phantis have undertaken a contract to supply the whole of Utopia with clothing designed upon the most approved English models —and the first Drawing Room under the new state of things is to be held here this evening.

FITZBATTLEAXE. But Drawing Rooms are always held in the afternoon.

ZARA. Ah, we've improved upon that. We all look so much better by candle-light! And when I tell you, dearest, that my court train has just arrived, you will understand that I am longing to go and try it on.

FITZBATTLEAXE. Then we must part?

ZARA. Necessarily, for a time.

FITZBATTLEAXE. Just as I wanted to tell you, with all the passionate enthusiasm of my nature, how deeply, how devotedly I love you!

ZARA. Hush! Are these the accents of a heart that really feels? True love does not indulge in declamation—its voice is sweet, and soft, and low. The west wind whispers when he woos the poplars!

DUET — ZARA *and* FITZBATTLEAXE.

ZARA. Words of love too loudly spoken
  Ring their own untimely knell;
  Noisy vows are rudely broken,
   Soft the song of Philomel.
  Whisper sweetly, whisper slowly,
   Hour by hour and day by day;
  Sweet and low as accents holy
   Are the notes of lover's lay!

BOTH. Sweet and low, &c.

FITZBATTLEAXE. Let the conqueror, flushed with
   glory,
  Bid his noisy clarions bray;
  Lovers tell their artless story
   In a whispered virelay.
  False is he whose vows alluring
   Make the listening echoes ring;
  Sweet and low when all-enduring,
   Are the songs that lovers sing!

BOTH. Sweet and low, &c.   (*Exit* ZARA.)

Enter KING, *dressed as Field Marshal.*

KING. To a Monarch who has been accustomed to the uncontrolled use of his limbs, the costume of a British Field Marshal is, perhaps, at first, a little cramping. Are you sure that this is all right? It's not a practical joke, is it? No one has a keener sense of humour than I have, but the First Statutory Cabinet Council of Utopia (*Limited*) must be conducted with dignity and impressiveness. Now, where are the other five who signed the Articles of Association?

FITZBATTLEAXE. Sir, they are here.

Enter LORD DRAMALEIGH, CAPTAIN CORCORAN, SIR BAILEY BARRE, MR. BLUSHINGTON, *and* MR. GOLDBURY *from different entrances.*

KING. Oh! (*Addressing them.*) Gentlemen, our daughter holds her first Drawing Room in half an hour, and we shall have time to make our half-yearly report in the interval. I am necessarily unfamiliar with the forms of an English Cabinet Council—perhaps the Lord Chamberlain will kindly put us in the way of doing the thing properly, and with due regard to the solemnity of the occasion.

DRAMALEIGH. Certainly—nothing simpler. Kindly bring your chairs forward—His Majesty will, of course, preside.

They range their chairs across stage like Christy Minstrels. KING *sits* C., LORD DRAMALEIGH *on his* L., MR. GOLDBURY *on his* R., CAPT. CORCORAN L. *of* LORD DRAMALEIGH, CAPT. FITZBATTLEAXE R. *of* MR. GOLDBURY, MR. BLUSHINGTON *extreme* R., SIR BAILEY BARRE *extreme* L.

KING. Like this?

DRAMALEIGH. Like this.

KING. We take your word for it that this is all right. You are not making fun of us? This is in accordance with the practice at the Court of St. James's?

DRAMALEIGH. Well, it is in accordance with the practice at the Court of St. James's Hall.

KING. Oh! It seems odd, but never mind.

SONG — KING.

Society has quite forsaken all her wicked
 courses,

Which empties our police courts, and abolishes divorces.

CHORUS. Divorce is nearly obsolete in England.

KING. No tolerance we show to undeserving rank and splendour;
For the higher his position is, the greater the offender.

CHORUS. That's a maxim that is prevalent in England.

KING. No peeress at our Drawing Room before the Presence passes
Who wouldn't be accepted by the lower-middle classes.
Each shady dame, whatever be her rank, is bowed out neatly.

CHORUS. In short, this happy country has been
    Anglicized completely!
    It really is surprising
    What a thorough Anglicizing
    We have brought about—Utopia's quite another land;
    In her enterprising movements,
    She is England—with improvements,
    Which we dutifully offer to our motherland!

KING. Our city we have beautified—we've done it willy-nilly—
And all that isn't Belgrave Square is Strand and Piccadilly.

CHORUS. We haven't any slummeries in England!

KING. We have solved the labour question with discrimination polished,
So poverty is obsolete and hunger is abolished—

CHORUS. We are going to abolish it in England.

KING. The Chamberlain our native stage has purged, beyond a question,
Of "risky" situation and indelicate suggestion;
No piece is tolerated if it's costumed indiscreetly—

CHORUS. In short, this happy country has been

Anglicized completely!
    It really is surprising, &c.

KING. Our Peerage we've remodelled on an intellectual basis,
Which certainly is rough on our hereditary races—

CHORUS. We are going to remodel it in England.

KING. The Brewers and the Cotton Lords no longer seek admission,
And Literary Merit meets with proper recognition—

CHORUS. As Literary Merit does in England!

KING. Who knows but we may count among our intellectual chickens
Like you, an Earl of Thackeray and p'r'aps a Duke of Dickens—
Lord Fildes and Viscount Millais (when they come) we'll welcome sweetly—

CHORUS. In short, this happy country has been
    Anglicized completely!
    It really is surprising, &c.

(*At the end all rise and replace their chairs.*)

KING. Now then, for our First Drawing Room. Where are the Princesses? What an extraordinary thing it is that since European looking-glasses have been supplied to the Royal bed-rooms my daughters are invariably late!

DRAMALEIGH. Sir, their Royal Highnesses await your pleasure in the Ante-Room.

KING. Oh. Then request them to do us the favour to enter at once.

MARCH.—*Enter all the Royal Household, including (besides the Lord Chamberlain) the Vice-Chamberlain, the Master of the Horse, the Master of the Buckhounds, the Lord High Treasurer, the Lord Steward, the Comptroller of the Household, the Lord-in-Waiting, the Groom-in-Waiting, the Field Officer in Brigade Waiting, the Gold and Silver Stick, and the Gentlemen Ushers. Then enter the three Princesses (their trains carried by*

Pages of Honour), LADY SOPHY, *and the Ladies-in-Waiting.*

KING. My daughters, we are about to attempt a very solemn ceremonial, so no giggling, if you please. Now, my Lord Chamberlain, we are ready.

DRAMALEIGH. Then, ladies and gentlemen, places if you please. His Majesty will take his place in front of the throne, and will be so obliging as to embrace all the *débutantes.* (LADY SOPHY *much shocked.*)

KING. What—must I really?

DRAMALEIGH. Absolutely indispensable.

KING. More jam for the *Palace Peeper!*

The KING *takes his place in front of the throne, the* PRINCESS ZARA *on his left. The two younger Princesses on the left of* ZARA.

KING. Now, is every one in his place?

DRAMALEIGH. Every one is in his place.

KING. Then let the revels commence.

Enter the ladies attending the Drawing Room. They give their cards to the Groom-in-Waiting, who passes them to the Lord-in-Waiting, who passes them to the Vice-Chamberlain, who passes them to the Lord Chamberlain, who reads the names to the KING *as each lady approaches. The ladies curtsey in succession to the* KING *and the three Princesses, and pass out. When all the presentations have been accomplished, the* KING, *Princesses, and* LADY SOPHY *come forward, and all the ladies re-enter.*

RECITATIVE — KING.

This ceremonial our wish displays
To copy all Great Britain's courtly ways.
Though lofty aims catastrophe entail,
We'll gloriously succeed or nobly fail!

CHORUS (*unaccompanied*).

Eagle high in cloudland soaring—
Sparrow twittering on a reed—
Tiger in the jungle roaring—
Frightened fawn in grassy mead—
Let the eagle, not the sparrow,
Be the object of your arrow—
Fix the tiger with your eye—
Pass the fawn in pity by.
Glory then will crown the day—
Glory, glory, anyway!
(*Then exeunt all.*)

Enter SCAPHIO *and* PHANTIS, *now dressed as judges in red and ermine robes and undress wigs. They come down stage melodramatically—working together.*

DUET — SCAPHIO *and* PHANTIS.

SCAPHIO. With fury deep we burn—

PHANTIS.   We do—
We fume with smothered rage.
These Englishmen who rule supreme,
Their undertaking they redeem
By stifling every harmless scheme
In which we both engage—

SCAPHIO.   They do—
In which we both engage.

BOTH (*with great energy*). For this mustn't be, and this won't do,
If you'll back me, then I'll back you;
Let's both agree, and we'll pull things through,
For this mustn't be, and this won't do.
No, this won't do,
No, this won't do,
No, this mustn't be,
And this won't do.

Enter the KING.

KING. Gentlemen, gentlemen—really! This unseemly display of energy within the Royal Precincts is altogether unpardonable. Pray, what do you complain of?

SCAPHIO (*furiously*). What do we complain of? Why, through the innovations introduced by the Flowers of Progress, all our harmless schemes for making a provision for our old age are ruined. Our Matrimonial Agency is at a standstill, our Cheap Sherry business is in bankruptcy, our Army Clothing contracts are paralyzed, and even our Society paper, the *Palace Peeper,* is practically defunct!

KING. Defunct? Is that so? Dear, dear, I am truly sorry.

SCAPHIO. Are you aware that Sir Bailey Barre has introduced a law of libel by which all editors of scurrilous newspapers are publicly flogged—as in England? And six of our editors have resigned in succession! Now, the editor of a scurrilous paper can stand a good deal—he takes a private thrashing as a matter of course—it's considered in his salary—but no gentleman likes to be publicly flogged.

KING. Naturally. I shouldn't like it myself.

PHANTIS. Then our Burlesque Theatre is absolutely ruined!

KING. Dear me. Well, theatrical property is not what it was.

PHANTIS. Are you aware that the Lord Chamberlain, who has his own views as to the best means of elevating the national drama, has declined to license any play that is not in blank verse and three hundred years old—as in England?

SCAPHIO. And as if that wasn't enough, the County Councillor has ordered a four-foot wall to be built up right across the proscenium, in case of fire—as in England.

PHANTIS. It's so hard on the company—who are liable to be roasted alive—and this has to be met by enormously increased salaries—as in England.

SCAPHIO. You probably know that we've contracted to supply the entire nation with a complete English outfit. But perhaps you do *not* know that, when we send in our bills, our customers plead liability limited to a declared capital of eighteenpence, and apply to be dealt with under the Winding-up Act—as in England?

KING. Really, gentlemen, this is very irregular. If you will be so good as to formulate a detailed list of your grievances in writing, addressed to the Secretary of Utopia (*Limited*), they will be laid before the Board, in due course, at their next monthly meeting.

SCAPHIO. Are we to understand that we are defied?

KING. That is the idea I intended to convey.

PHANTIS. Defied! We are defied!

SCAPHIO (*furiously*). Take care—you know our powers. Trifle with us, and you die!

TRIO — SCAPHIO, PHANTIS, *and* KING.

SCAPHIO. If you think that when banded in unity,
We may both be defied with impunity,
    You are sadly misled of a verity!

PHANTIS. If you value repose and tranquility,
You'll revert to a state of docility,
    Or prepare to regret your temerity!

KING. If my speech is unduly refractory
You will find it a course satisfactory
    At an early Board meeting to show it up.
Though if proper excuse you can trump any,
You may *wind* up a Limited Company,
    You cannot conveniently *blow* it up!

(SCAPHIO *and* PHANTIS *thoroughly baffled.*)

KING (*dancing quietly*). Whene'er I chance to baffle you,
    I, also, dance a step or two—
    Of this now guess the hidden sense:

(SCAPHIO *and* PHANTIS *consider the question as* KING *continues dancing quietly—then give it up.*)
    It means—complete indifference.

ALL THREE (*dancing quietly*). Indifference—indifference—
    Of course it does—indifference!
    You } might have guessed its hidden sense.
    We
    It means complete indifference!

KING (*dancing quietly*), SCAPHIO *and* PHANTIS (*dancing furiously*). As we've a dance for every mood
    With *pas de trois* we will conclude.
    What this may mean you all may guess—

SCAPHIO *and* PHANTIS.   {It typifies remorseless-
ness!
KING.   It means unruffled cheerfulness!

(KING *dances off placidly as* SCAPHIO *and*
PHANTIS *dance furiously.*)

PHANTIS (*breathless*). He's right—we are helpless! He's no longer a human being—he's a Cor-
poration, and so long as he confines himself to his
Articles of Association we can't touch him! What
are we to do?

SCAPHIO. Do? Raise a Revolution, repeal the
Act of Sixty-Two, reconvert him into an individual, and insist on his immediate explosion!
(TARARA *enters.*) Tarara, come here; you're the
very man we want.

TARARA. Certainly, allow me. (*Offers a cracker
to each; they snatch them away impatiently.*)
That's rude.

SCAPHIO. We have no time for idle forms. You
wish to succeed to the throne?

TARARA. Naturally.

SCAPHIO. Then you won't unless you join us. The
King has defied us, and, as matters stand, we are
helpless. So are you. We must devise some plot
at once to bring the people about his ears.

TARARA. A plot?

PHANTIS. Yes, a plot of superhuman subtlety.
Have you such a thing about you?

TARARA (*feeling*). No, I think not. No. There's
one on my dressing-table.

SCAPHIO. We can't wait—we must concoct one
at once, and put it into execution without delay.
There is not a moment to spare!

TRIO — SCAPHIO, PHANTIS, *and* TARARA.

ENSEMBLE.   With wily brain, upon the spot
A private plot we'll plan,
The most ingenious private plot
Since private plots began.
That's understood. So far we've got
And, striking while the iron's hot,
We'll now determine like a shot
The details of this private plot.

SCAPHIO. I think we ought—(*whispers*).

PHANTIS *and* TARARA. Such bosh I never heard!

PHANTIS. Ah! happy thought!—(*whispers*).

SCAPHIO *and* TARARA. How utterly dashed absurd!

TARARA. *I'll* tell you how—(*whispers*).

SCAPHIO *and* PHANTIS. Why, what put that in
your head?

SCAPHIO. I've got it now—(*whispers*).

Oh, take him away to bed!

PHANTIS.   Oh, put him to bed!
TARARA.   Oh, put him to bed!
SCAPHIO.   What! put *me* to bed?
PHANTIS *and* TARARA. Yes, put him to bed!
SCAPHIO. But, bless me, don't you see—
PHANTIS.   Do listen to me, I pray—
TARARA. It certainly seems to me—
SCAPHIO.   Bah—this is the only way!
PHANTIS. It's rubbish absurd you growl!
TARARA.   You talk ridiculous stuff!
SCAPHIO.   You're a drivelling barndoor owl!
PHANTIS.   You're a vapid and vain old muff!

ALL (*coming down to audience*).
So far we haven't quite solved the plot—
They're not a very ingenious lot—
But don't be unhappy
It's still on the *tapis*
We'll presently hit on a capital plot!

SCAPHIO. Suppose we all—(*whispers*).
PHANTIS.   Now *there* I think you're right.
Then we might all—(*whispers*).
TARARA.   That's true—we certainly might.
I'll tell you what—(*whispers*).
SCAPHIO.   We will if we possibly can.
Then on the spot—(*whispers*).
PHANTIS *and* TARARA. Bravo! a capital plan!
SCAPHIO. That's exceedingly neat and new!
PHANTIS.   Exceedingly new and neat.
TARARA. I fancy that that will do.
SCAPHIO.   It's certainly very complete.
PHANTIS. Well done, you sly old sap!
TARARA.   Bravo, you cunning old mole!
SCAPHIO. You very ingenious chap!
PHANTIS.   You intellectual soul!

ALL (*coming down, and addressing audience*).
At last a capital plan we've got;
Never mind why and never mind what:
It's safe in my noddle—
Now off we will toddle,
And slyly develop this capital plot!
(*Business. Exeunt* SCAPHIO *and* PHANTIS *in
one direction, and* TARARA *in the other.*)

Enter LORD DRAMALEIGH *and* MR. GOLDBURY.

DRAMALEIGH. Well, what do you think of our
first South Pacific Drawing Room? Allowing for
a slight difficulty with the trains, and a little want
of familiarity with the use of the rouge-pot, it was,
on the whole, a meritorious affair?

GOLDBURY. My dear Dramaleigh, it redounds infinitely to your credit.

DRAMALEIGH. One or two judicious innovations, I think?

GOLDBURY. Admirable. The cup of tea and the plate of mixed biscuits were a cheap and effective inspiration.

DRAMALEIGH. Yes—my idea, entirely. Never been done before.

GOLDBURY. Pretty little maids, the King's youngest daughters, but timid.

DRAMALEIGH. That'll wear off. Young.

GOLDBURY. *That'll* wear off. Ha! here they come, by George! And without the Dragon! What can they have done with her?

Enter NEKAYA *and* KALYBA, *timidly.*

NEKAYA. Oh, if you please, Lady Sophy has sent us in here, because Zara and Captain Fitzbattle-axe are going on, in the garden, in a manner which no well-conducted young ladies ought to witness.

DRAMALEIGH. Indeed, we are very much obliged to her Ladyship.

KALYBA. Are you? I wonder why.

NEKAYA. Don't tell us if it's rude.

DRAMALEIGH. Rude? Not at all. We are obliged to Lady Sophy because she has afforded us the pleasure of seeing you.

NEKAYA. I don't think you ought to talk to us like that.

KALYBA. It's calculated to turn our heads.

NEKAYA. Attractive girls cannot be too particular.

KALYBA. Oh pray, pray do not take advantage of our unprotected innocence.

GOLDBURY. Pray be reassured—you are in no danger whatever.

DRAMALEIGH. But may I ask—is this extreme delicacy—this shrinking sensitiveness—a general characteristic of Utopian young ladies?

NEKAYA. Oh, no; we are crack specimens.

KALYBA. We are the pick of the basket. *Would* you mind not coming quite so near? Thank you.

NEKAYA. And please don't look at us like that; it unsettles us.

KALYBA. And we don't like it. At least, we *do* like it; but it's wrong.

NEKAYA. *We* have enjoyed the inestimable privilege of being educated by a most refined and easily-shocked English lady, on the very strictest English principles.

GOLDBURY. But my dear young ladies—

KALYBA. Oh don't! You mustn't. It's too affectionate.

NEKAYA. It really does unsettle us.

GOLDBURY. Are you really under the impression that English girls are so ridiculously demure? Why, an English girl of the highest type is the best, the most beautiful, the bravest, and the brightest creature that Heaven has conferred upon this world of ours. She is frank, open-hearted and fearless, and never shows in so favourable a light as when she gives her own blameless impulses full play!

NEKAYA *and* KALYBA. Oh, you shocking story!

GOLDBURY. Not at all. I'm speaking the strict truth. I'll tell you all about her.

SONG — MR. GOLDBURY.

A wonderful joy our eyes to bless,
In her magnificent comeliness,
Is an English girl of eleven stone two,
And five foot ten in her dancing shoe!
　She follows the hounds, and on she pounds—
　　The "field" tails off and the muffs diminish—
　Over the hedges and brooks she bounds,
　　Straight as a crow, from find to finish.
　At cricket, her kin will lose or win—
　　She and her maids, on grass and clover,
　Eleven maids out—eleven maids in—
　　And perhaps an occasional "maiden over"!
Go search the world and search the sea,
Then come you home and sing with me
There's no such gold and no such pearl
As a bright and beautiful English girl!

With a ten-mile spin she stretches her limbs,
She golfs, she punts, she rows, she swims—
She plays, she sings, she dances, too,
From ten or eleven till all is blue!
　At ball or drum, till small hours come,
　　(Chaperon's fan conceals her yawning)
　She'll waltz away like a teetotum,
　　And never go home till daylight's dawning.
　Lawn tennis may share her favours fair—
　　Her eyes a-dance and her cheeks a-glowing—
　Down comes her hair, but what does she care?
　　It's all her own and it's worth the showing!
　　Go search the world, &c.

Her soul is sweet as the ocean air,
For prudery knows no haven there;
To find mock-modesty, please apply
To the conscious blush and the downcast eye.
　Rich in the things contentment brings,
　　In every pure enjoyment wealthy,
　Blithe as a beautiful bird she sings,
　　For body and mind are hale and healthy.
　Her eyes they thrill with right good-will—
　　Her heart is light as a floating feather—

As pure and bright as the mountain rill
  That leaps and laughs in the Highland
    heather!
  Go search the world, &c.

QUARTETTE.

NEKAYA.   Then I may sing and play?
DRAMALEIGH.   You may!
KALYBA.   And I may laugh and shout?
GOLDBURY.   No doubt!
NEKAYA.   These maxims you endorse?
DRAMALEIGH.   Of course!
KALYBA.   You won't exclaim "Oh fie!"
GOLDBURY.   Not I!

GOLDBURY.   Whatever you are—be that:
        Whatever you say—be true:
          Straightforwardly act—
          Be honest—in fact
          Be nobody else but *you*.

DRAMALEIGH.   Give every answer pat—
        Your character true unfurl;
          And when it is ripe,
          You'll then be a type
          Of a capital English girl!

ALL.   Oh sweet surprise—oh dear delight,
        To find it undisputed quite,
        All musty, fusty rules despite,
        That Art is wrong and Nature right!

NEKAYA.   When happy I,
        With laughter glad
          I'll wake the echoes fairly,
        And only sigh
          When I am sad—
          And that will be but rarely!

KALYBA.   I'll row and fish,
        And gallop, soon—
          No longer be a prim one—
        And when I wish
          To hum a tune,
          It needn't be a hymn one?

GOLDBURY *and* DRAMALEIGH.   No, no!
          It needn't be a hymn one!

ALL (*dancing*).   Oh, sweet surprise and dear de-
          light
        To find it undisputed quite—
        All musty, fusty rules despite—
        That Art is wrong and Nature right!
                    (*Dance, and off.*)

Enter LADY SOPHY.

RECITATIVE — LADY SOPHY.

Oh, would some demon power the gift impart

To quell my over-conscientious heart—
Unspeak the oaths that never had been spoken,
And break the vows that never shall be broken!

SONG — LADY SOPHY.

When but a maid of fifteen year,
    Unsought—unplighted—
Short petticoated—and, I fear,
    Still shorter-sighted—
I made a vow, one early spring,
That only to some spotless king
Who proof of blameless life could bring,
    I'd be united.
For I had read, not long before,
Of blameless kings in fairy lore,
And thought the race still flourished here—
        Well, well—
I was a maid of fifteen year!

The KING *enters and overhears this verse.*

Each morning I pursued my game
    (An early riser);
For spotless monarchs I became
    An advertiser:
But all in vain I searched each land,
So, kingless, to my native strand
Returned, a little older, and
    A good deal wiser!
I learnt that spotless King and Prince
Have disappeared some ages since—
Even Paramount's angelic grace—
        Ah, me!—
Is but a mask on Nature's face!
                (KING *comes forward.*)

RECITATIVE.

KING.   Ah, Lady Sophy—then you love me!
          For so you sing—

LADY SOPHY (*indignant and surprised*).
        No, by the stars that shine above me,
            Degraded King!
                (*Producing "Palace Peeper."*)
        For while these rumours, through the city
            bruited,
        Remain uncontradicted, unrefuted,
        The object thou of my aversion rooted,
            Repulsive thing!

KING.   Be just—the time is now at hand
                When truth may published be,
            These paragraphs were written and
                Contributed by me!

LADY SOPHY.   By you? No, no!
KING.   Yes, yes, I swear, by me!
            I, caught in Scaphio's ruthless toil,
                Contributed the lot!

LADY SOPHY.   And *that* is why you did not boil
                 The author on the spot!

KING.   And *that* is why I did not boil
           The author on the spot!

LADY SOPHY.   I *couldn't* think why you did not
                 boil!

KING.   But *I* know why I did not boil
           The author on the spot!

DUET — LADY SOPHY *and* KING.

LADY SOPHY.   Oh the rapture unrestrained
                 Of a candid retractation!
           For my sovereign has deigned
                 A convincing explanation—
           And the clouds that gathered o'er,
                 All have vanished in the distance,
           And of Kings of fairy lore
                 One, at least, is in existence!

KING.   Oh, the skies are blue above,
                 And the earth is red and rosal,
           Now the lady of my love
                 Has accepted my proposal!
           For that *asinorum pons*
                 I have crossed without assistance,
           And of prudish paragons
                 One, at least, is in existence!

KING *and* LADY SOPHY *dance gracefully. While this is going on,* LORD DRAMALEIGH *enters unobserved with* NEKAYA *and* MR. GOLDBURY *with* KALYBA. *Then enter* ZARA *and* CAPT. FITZBATTLEAXE. *The two girls direct* ZARA'S *attention to the* KING *and* LADY SOPHY, *who are still dancing affectionately together. At this point the* KING *kisses* LADY SOPHY, *which causes the Princesses to make an exclamation. The* KING *and* LADY SOPHY *are at first much confused at being detected, but eventually throw off all reserve, and the four couples break into a wild Tarantella, and at the end exeunt severally.*

Enter excitedly TARARA, *meeting* SCAPHIO *and* PHANTIS.

SCAPHIO.   Well—how works the plot? Have you done our bidding? Have you explained to the happy and contented populace the nature of their wrongs, and the desperate consequences that must ensue if they are not rectified?

TARARA.   I have explained nothing. I have done better—I have made an affidavit that what they supposed to be happiness was really unspeakable misery—and they are furious! You know you can't help believing an affidavit.

SCAPHIO.   Of course—an admirable thought! Ha! they come!

Enter all the male Chorus, in great excitement, from various entrances, followed by the female Chorus.

CHORUS.

Upon our sea-girt land,
At our enforced command,
Reform has laid her hand
      Like some remorseless ogress—
And make us darkly rue
The deeds she dared to do—
And all is owing to
      Those hated Flowers of Progress!

      So down with them!
      So down with them!
      Reform's a hated ogress.
      So down with them!
      So down with them!
      Down with the Flowers of Progress!

Flourish. Enter KING, *his three daughters,* LADY SOPHY, *and the* FLOWERS OF PROGRESS.

KING.   What means this most unmannerly irruption?
      Is this your gratitude for boons conferred?

SCAPHIO.   Boons? Bah! a fico for such boons, say we!
      These boons have brought Utopia to a standstill!
      Our pride and boast—the Army and the Navy—
      Have both been reconstructed and remodelled
      Upon so irresistible a basis
      That all the neighbouring nations have disarmed—
      And War's impossible! Your County Councillor
      Has passed such drastic Sanitary laws
      That all the doctors dwindle, starve, and die!
      The laws, remodelled by Sir Bailey Barre,
      Have quite extinguished crime and litigation:
      The lawyers starve, and all the jails are let
      As model lodgings for the working-classes!
      In short—
      Utopia, swamped by dull Prosperity,
      Stifled with benefits, all English-born,
      Demands that these detested Flowers of Progress
      Be sent about their business, and affairs
      Restored to their original complexion!

KING (*to people*).   Is this your will?

ALL.   It is—it is. Down with the Flowers of Progress!

KING (*to* ZARA).   My daughter, this is a very unpleasant state of things. What is to be done?

ZARA.   I don't know—there's something wrong. I don't understand it.

KING. Is everything at a standstill in England? Is there no litigation there? no bankruptcy? no poverty? no squalor? no sickness? no crime?

ZARA. Plenty; it's the most prosperous country in the world! We must have omitted something.

KING. Omitted something? Yes, that's all very well, but—

(SIR BAILEY BARRE *whispers to* ZARA.)

ZARA (*suddenly*). Of course! Now I remember! Why, I had forgotten the most important, the most vital, the most essential element of all!

KING. And that is?—

ZARA. Government by Party! Introduce that great and glorious element—at once the bulwark and foundation of England's greatness—and all will be well! No political measures will endure, because one Party will assuredly undo all that the other Party has done; inexperienced civilians will govern your Army and your Navy; no social reforms will be attempted, because out of vice, squalor, and drunkenness no political capital is to be made; and while grouse is to be shot, and foxes worried to death, the legislative action of the country will be at a standstill. Then there will be sickness in plenty, endless lawsuits, crowded jails, interminable confusion in the Army and Navy, and, in short, general and unexampled prosperity!

ALL. Ulahlica! Ulahlica!

PHANTIS (*aside*). Baffled!

SCAPHIO. But an hour *will* come!

KING. Your hour has come already—away with them, and let them wait my will! (SCAPHIO *and* PHANTIS *are led off in custody*.) From this moment, Government by Party is adopted, with all its attendant blessings; and henceforward Utopia will no longer be a Monarchy (Limited), but, what is a great deal better, a Limited Monarchy!

FINALE.

KING.   When Monarch of barbaric land,
　　　　For self-improvement burning,
　　　Foregathers with a glorious band
　　　　Of sweetness, light, and learning—
　　　A group incalculably wise—
　　　　Unequalled in their beauty—
　　　Their customs to acclimatize
　　　　Becomes a moral duty.

ZARA (*to* FITZBATTLEAXE). Oh gallant soldier,
　　　　brave and true
　　　In tented field and tourney,
　　　I trust you'll ne'er regret that you
　　　　Embarked upon this journey.

FITZBATTLEAXE. To warriors all may it befall
　　　To gain so pure a beauty,
　　　When they obey the trumpet call
　　　　Of Regimental Duty!

CURTAIN.

Postscript

MOST OF THE CUTS AND CHANGES made between the first night's libretto of *Utopia* (*Limited*) and later versions were in Act II. The lone exception affecting a lyric was the elimination of the second verse of King Paramount's song (page 388), "Stupendous when we rouse ourselves to strike," together with the repeat of the chorus. (The critic of the *Pall Mall Gazette* considered this song "almost a failure.")

The song for Princess Zara, "Youth is a boon avowed" (page 398), did not appear in the libretto of the first night, nor, for that matter, in any published libretto. Its words have been preserved, fortunately, in the American deposit copyright copy (deposited October 9, 1893) where it was discovered by the late bibliographer and enthusiastic Gilbert and Sullivan collector, Carroll A. Wilson. As it was most certainly sung by Miss McIntosh in the first night's performance, it has been included in this First Night libretto text.

To understand why it was omitted from the published first edition of the libretto one must resort to speculation. It is clear from all contemporary accounts of the first night that Miss McIntosh was visibly and audibly nervous at this her stage debut. At the public rehearsal on the preceding evening she was also reported as showing nervousness. It seems likely that both Gilbert and Sullivan were well aware of their new soprano's weakness during the latter stages of rehearsal; and they must also have recognized that their first act was over-long. Putting these two considerations together—if a cut was to be made in the first act that in no way affected the plot, this song could be removed. And it might even have been felt by librettist and composer that Miss McIntosh had quite enough to do on stage from her entrance solo with chorus, through two duets and a quartet, prior to "Youth is a boon avowed."

It was her misfortune that this number happened to be her best solo opportunity. The London correspondent for the *Liverpool Echo*, who attended the public rehearsal the night before the première, wrote: "The audience were mainly on the *qui vive* to hear Miss Nancy McI. . . . Her chief song was, however, omitted and in the various duets, etc. she showed nervousness." So, as the plan at this final moment before production was to eliminate this song, naturally the last-minute alterations in the libretto text followed suit. After the public rehearsal it is likely that Miss McIntosh pleaded with Gilbert to reinstate her best number. She was certainly very beautiful and must have been equally persuasive. Furthermore, as Gilbert—of the two collaborators—was the sponsor of her career, he quite possibly felt that the removal of her best solo bit was an admission by him of her professional incompetence. So Miss McIntosh won her chance to sing this song on the first night, even though it was not in the audience's libretto nor was it to be one of Chappell's separately published vocal music titles. In the copy of the original score belonging to the D'Oyly Carte Opera Company, the numbers skip from No. 10 (Duet, Zara and Fitzbattleaxe) to No. 12 (Finale), leaving No. 11 significantly missing.

Modern versions of the opera in the Macmillan and the Random House collected editions omit entirely Zara's immediately preceding soliloquy—beginning "Poor, trusting, simple-minded, and affectionate old gentlemen!"—between the exit of Fitzbattleaxe and the entrance of her father; but in the third edition of the libretto only the one sentence following her quotation from Juvenal is cut.

Among other cuts in dialog, Gilbert yielded to the critical reaction against Zara's "Government by Party!" speech (page 412) and removed the offending portion: "inexperienced civilians will govern your Army and your Navy; no social reforms will be attempted, because out of vice, squalor, and drunkenness no political capital is to be made."

As already noted, the *Sunday Times* and *Daily News* found the Finale short, and the *Daily Graphic* added "even insignificant." Gilbert himself had been dissatisfied with it and it had "displeased" Sullivan. They had had trouble with it from the beginning. Gilbert's original meter had defied Sullivan's efforts to set it. According to Herbert Sullivan, "Gilbert realized the difficulty" and "suggested that Sullivan should compose the music first, and he would then write words to fit it. This was about the only occasion in which any music of one of their operas was set down before the words." Sullivan, working from his summer place at Weybridge, composed the Finale music and sent it to Gilbert, who had returned to Grim's Dyke from Homburg where he had been under treatment for severe gout. On September 26, 1893, he wrote Sullivan: "I got up at seven this morning and polished off the new finale before breakfast. Here it is. It is mere doggerel, but words written to an existing tune are nearly sure to be that. I am sorry to lose the other finale, but I quite see your difficulty and that it can't be helped. You can chop this about just as you please. . . ." This was only ten days before the first night. Both collaborators must have felt that this would have to do, and it was this Finale that was printed in the first edition of the libretto.

But probably after further reflection, under the impact of press criticism from the public rehearsal and first night, Gilbert must have written a third Finale over Sunday, October 8, which Sullivan set the following day. This was first substituted in the Savoy performance four days later (according to Sullivan's biographers), in other words on Friday evening, October 13; and it is this rewritten Finale that appears in the second and subsequent editions of the libretto. Thus the "insignificant" Finale of the first edition was heard on only five performances, after which the following version took its place:

FINALE.

ZARA. There's a little group of isles beyond the wave—
    So tiny, you might almost wonder where it is—
That nation is the bravest of the brave,
    And cowards are the rarest of all rarities.
The proudest nations kneel at her command;
    She terrifies all foreign-born rapscallions;
And holds the peace of Europe in her hand
    With half a score invincible battalions!

    Such, at least, is the tale
    Which is borne on the gale,
        From the island which dwells in the sea.
    Let us hope, for her sake,
    That she makes no mistake—
        That she's all she professes to be!

KING. Oh may we copy all her maxims wise,
    And imitate her virtues and her charities;
And may we, by degrees, acclimatize
    Her Parliamentary peculiarities!
By doing so, we shall, in course of time,
    Regenerate completely our entire land—
Great Britain is that monarchy sublime,
    To which some add (but others do not) Ireland.
    Such, at least, is the tale, &c.

THE GRAND DUKE

Introduction

"THE NEW SAVOY OPERA. A GILBERT-SULLIVAN 'GHOEST' "?—so read the headline of the *Musical Standard*'s long review of the fourteenth Gilbert and Sullivan first-night, as the critic went on to explain—"In Mr. Gilbert's libretto one of the characters, for the sake of rhyme, pronounces ghost as 'ghoest,' and we may be pardoned if we call *The Grand Duke* a 'ghoest' of Gilbert and Sullivan opera. . . ." Indeed, it was doubly appropriate that this critic should have selected "ghost" as the theme of his opening remarks. For if the fare on the Savoy stage the night of Saturday, March 7, 1896, was insubstantial, out front there was a ghost of another kind. Certainly most of those who crammed D'Oyly Carte's theatre for this occasion were subconsciously aware that there would never be another Gilbert and Sullivan first night. This melancholy recognition can be read between the lines of even rave reviews. And the very number of such over-enthusiastic notices undoubtedly stemmed from the omnipresence of that wraith of sentimentality.

Then, if the figure is to be carried further, there was the inevitable comparison with triumphs of the past, thirteen ghosts of memory of which the most corpuscular had enjoyed a second enthusiastic revival terminating a mere three nights before. Stout and very un-"ghoestly" fellow, *The Mikado!* The lead sentences of the *Times* itself set the pattern of these reviews:

The welcome accorded to a new Gilbert and Sullivan opera increases, perhaps not unnaturally, with each member of the famous series, and its warmth is all the greater on account of the regrettable intermissions in the partnership. But the former works themselves are, as usual, the severest critics of the newer; and, in the case of the opera produced on Saturday night, the recent revival of the best of the whole set inevitably provokes awkward comparisons. *The Grand Duke* is not by any means another *Mikado*, and, though it is far from being the least attractive of

the series, signs are not wanting that the rich vein which the collaborators and their various followers have worked for so many years is at last dangerously near exhaustion. This time the libretto is very conspicuously inferior to the music. There are still a number of excellent songs, but the dialogue seems to have lost much of its crispness. . . .

On the other hand, the *Daily Chronicle* in an enthusiastic and lengthy review still felt that Gilbert could do no wrong: "His lyrics, as well as the spoken dialogue, teem with those quaint turns of expression expected from Mr. Gilbert, and which an average audience would perhaps not accept from anyone else." And of the composer: "Had Arthur Sullivan a reputation to make for vocal melody and graceful instrumentation, he could scarcely have submitted a better sample of workmanship than *The Grand Duke*. His music has all the olden attractiveness. . . . For the time being he is the Sullivan of *H.M.S. Pinafore, The Mikado,* and *The Gondoliers.*"

In early August 1895 Sullivan had received from Gilbert the outline for the plot of their final collaboration. "My dear Gilbert," he wrote on August 11 (a letter quoted by Hesketh Pearson), "I have studied the sketch plot very carefully, and like it even more than I did when I heard it first on Thursday. It comes out as clear and bright as possible. I shall be very pleased to set it, and am prepared to begin (as soon as you have anything ready for me) and have written Carte to tell him so. I return the MS registered. Don't let the monkeys get at it. They might forestall Justin McCarthy in the *Pall Mall* and tear it to pieces!" Sullivan's joke was not prophetic. Gilbert was successful in saving his manuscript from destruction by his pet ring-tailed lemurs; and critic McCarthy of the *Pall Mall Gazette* did not tear *The Grand Duke* to pieces in his review seven months later, but wrote that "it may claim to stand in the front rank of comic operas."

The winter months of collaboration had not gone well. Both author and composer had demonstrated they could not make magic except together. It was as though the precious formula of transmutation had been torn evenly in half and divided between them. The failure of their personal relations made their latter-day efforts to get along together stiff and self-conscious. The failure of their separate professional efforts made each man try too hard to write and to compose in the manner he regarded as his erstwhile successful self. Inevitably the result on a personal level was to wear thin the artifice of their daily working relations. And on the professional level each virtually parodied himself, Gilbert becoming over-Gilbertian and Sullivan nearly super-Sullivanesque. The end product of such over-personal concern must have been clear to the critical fraternity on the occasion of the public dress-rehearsal held on Friday, March 6. Just as they had arranged for *Utopia (Limited),* the partners had an invited audience of close friends and press in the Savoy for this final rehearsal, which was said to have proceeded without interruption as though it had been a public performance.

The following evening the usual gala first-night audience was on hand to fill every available space. According to the *Sunday Times,* the new opera was "received with the utmost enthusiasm by a crowded house. The audience was, if possible, more brilliant than at any previous Savoy première, and celebrities were to be seen on every hand. In Mrs. Ronalds' box were the Lord Chamberlain and Lady Lathom and the Brazilian Minister. . . ." The latter had been Mrs. Ronalds' guest at the first night of *Utopia (Limited).* There

were the inevitable society first-nighters such as Lord and Lady Londesborough and Lord and Lady Donoughmore (the former with Lord Bingham, occupying the stage-box opposite Mrs. Ronalds), Sir Francis and Lady Lockwood (well-known caricaturist and *Punch* contributor who had served as Solicitor General the preceding year), Sir Douglas Straight (editor of the *Pall Mall Gazette*), Sir John Charles Robinson (fine-arts authority, Her Majesty's Surveyor of Pictures), Lord and Lady Shand (Baron Shand was a Scottish lawyer and member of the Judicial Committee of the Privy Council), the perennial Savoyard connoisseur Frederick Andrew Inderwick, Q.C., Lord Marcus Beresford, Lady Lister Kaye, Sir Rivers and Lady Wilson, as always at important Savoy performances, Mr. and Mrs. Arthur Lewis and their four daughters, and the newly knighted Sir Eyre Massey Shaw (erstwhile "type of true love" immortalized in *Iolanthe*)—all these notables, and more, were recorded by the *Sunday Times* reporter.

Appropriate top professionals in the audience included Mr. and Mrs. Bancroft (actor-manager); George Edwardes (who had left his Savoy management position to operate the Gaiety Theatre) and his wife Julia Gwynne (a former Savoy principal); Jessie Bond, who assuredly needed no introduction at the Savoy; the Arthur Pineros, Signor Tosti, actress Kate Rorke, and Ernest Ford (who had conducted Sullivan's lone grand opera, *Ivanhoe*).

The cover of the Savoy Theatre programs for the evening of March 7, 1896, featured both in color and in brown ink "the ancient arms of the Savoy" —a two-headed eagle within an armorial shield— and noted that the composer was conducting.

"On taking his place in the conductor's seat," continued the thorough *Sunday Times,* "Sir Arthur Sullivan had a splendid reception, the applause being loud and prolonged." The overture was described by the *Times* as "a string of tunes that are likely to be most popular." Then the curtain rose on "the magnificent mediaeval 'set' representing the market-place of Speisesaal," a triumph of design by Mr. Harford.

"The first act," in the *Times'* estimation, "contains a number of pretty choruses, some concerted vocal numbers as effective as usual, and a capital march of the chamberlains, all neatly finished and in strict conformity with the pattern established for such things a good many years ago. That form of instrumental humour, in which Sir Arthur Sullivan has delighted ever since the famous 'bassoon joke' in *The Sorcerer,* finds excellent opportunity in a song (page 434) in which the grand duke describes his ailments, to the accompaniment of some orchestral symptoms so realistic as to be al-

*"The Ancient Arms of the Savoy," from the cover
of the Savoy Theatre program, March 7, 1896.*

most painful." To the ear of the *Era* this particular example of "the composer's clever treatment of the orchestra . . . is carried almost to excess." It made this reviewer, for one, feel more than "a little bit queer."

The *Sunday Times* gave particular praise to the first-act finale, which "went with wonderful spirit, and though the act had played over an hour and a half, there was not the slightest sense of weariness or languor when the curtain fell. . . . The whole of the finale to the first act shows Sir Arthur Sullivan at his best . . . the jolly hornpipe tune . . . brings down the curtain 'with a snap.' " It seems clear that the "snap" was too long delayed. Even the ecstatic *Sunday Times* conceded parenthetically of this finale, "It will stand slight condensation." *Punch* stated bluntly, "About a third of the first act . . . might be omitted with advantage." And *Modern Society* showed almost too casual restraint by remarking merely that "the finale to the first act is of the customary length." It occupies, in point of fact, thirty-four pages in the vocal score, which makes it second only to that of *Iolanthe*.

That there were too many encores, and that this may have been Sullivan's fault, seems apparent from *Punch*'s acid pleasantry: "Also for the conductor to catch at the slightest possible indication of a wish to encore is a mistake. 'When in doubt, play trumps'—but don't give an encore." The first of these, Ludwig's sausage-roll song (page 424), according to the *Daily Chronicle* "capitally sung by Mr. Rutland Barrington, started a series of requests for repetition which Sir Arthur Sullivan . . . frequently had difficulty in repressing." Regarding Gilbert's sausage-roll plot-adjunct, the critic for the *Musical Standard* felt "the idea is not really funny, and it is enlarged upon to wearisomeness." In exchanging his magic lozenge for a sausage-roll Gilbert had not improved his formula. "The humour of the 'kipper,' " remarked the reviewer for *City*, "has for a long time held an honoured place [he resisted saying "role"] in music hall patter; now we have the humour of the sausage roll at the Savoy. I do not greatly prefer the latter form of wit myself."

It was in the second act that most critics conceded both collaborators made the best showing. "Song after song is good here," said the *Musical Standard*. Sullivan's opening chorus in this act won universal approbation from the press. "No number last night was more warmly applauded 'on its merits,' " wrote the *Sunday Times* critic, "than the superb processional chorus sung as the curtain rises on the lovely picture of the Grand Ducal Hall. This massive and impressive piece—worthy in every respect of the pen that wrote the choruses in *The Martyr of Antioch*—was splendidly given by the Savoy choristers." And from the *Times* came perceptive and unusually glowing words of praise: "It is a good many years since the composer has given us anything so fine as the opening chorus of the second act, with a sham-Greek refrain, a melody so spontaneous, dignified, and original that it seems hardly suited to its surroundings, or to the taste of most of the audience." With these last words the *Times* was almost certainly touching the subtle weakness inherent in the composer's overly self-conscious effort in this opera. Was this processional chorus an integral and appropriate part of a comic opera? . . . or was it a subconsciously motivated shift of Sullivan to a serious music creation bound to focus more attention on the composer even at the expense of its comic opera surroundings? A columnist writing under the caption "Stage Whispers" for the *Man of the World* posed the question in another way: "The opening chorus of the second act is the finest thing in the opera and I do not know what the audience was thinking of on Saturday night not to insist on a repetition of it." The *Times* had the answer.

Again in the second act, Barrington scored with "At the outset I may mention" (page 439). "This song was among the most notable 'hits' on Saturday night," held the *Daily Chronicle,* "the audience showing a desire for a second encore." Its success bore out the *Sunday Times* appraisal that "perhaps the most taking solos are the patter-songs, which are not only more numerous than usual, but simply astonishing in their variety." The *Era* made the same point, only with a good-humored jibe, in commenting of Sullivan—"he displays his customary facility in many—perhaps too many—patter-songs. As a wag has said, 'the patternity of these is never doubtful.'"

Just as the *Sunday Times* had recorded that "the charm of the music was even more strongly felt in the second act," so did the *Musical Standard* note: "Mr. Gilbert is decidedly at his best in the first half of the second act, when we have left the tiresome Statutory Duet and Sausage Rolls far behind us." Even so, the same critic moaned: "If the opera could only be compressed, for it becomes very wearisome in places."

The Herald's song (page 446), the only solo effort for Mr. Jones Hewson, was what in modern vernacular is termed a sleeper. It quite unexpectedly caught both press and audience. Dubbed by the *Times* "one of the most taking things in the opera, it was deservedly encored." But from the Herald's song to the close the performance dragged. The humor of the Roulette Song (page 448), for example, passed unnoticed. As Sullivan wrote in reply to critic Vernon Blackburn's post-dress-rehearsal comments, on the very day of the première: "I purposely tried to hit the French Café Chantant style (*tout ce qu'il y a de plus canaille*) and I fear I have succeeded but too well!!" It mirrored its prototype too closely for those who could not recognize the original.

"At the close Sir Arthur Sullivan, Mr. Gilbert, and Mr. D'Oyly Carte were summoned to receive the congratulations of a large and distinguished audience," reported the *Era*. "The performance, of course," in the opinion of the *Musical Standard,* "was characterized by all the care for detail which we expect at the Savoy, where the prince of stage managers, Mr. W. S. Gilbert, reigns supreme. The acting of the chorus gives wonderful life and go to the production, and nowhere, not even at Bayreuth, is the like to be seen."

The *Daily Chronicle* held that "no preceding Savoy opera has received better interpretation than *The Grand Duke.*" In the cast, "Rutland Barrington, as the depository of all the traditions of Gilbert and Sullivan opera, has the chief part of the comedian, Ludwig," wrote the *Man of the World*. "Fancy Barrington in Greek costume; Barrington as Agamemnon, in a breastplate and nothing else to speak of but a big Louis Quatorze wig," the same enthusiast continued; "he is figuratively and literally, immense." And the *Times,*

Cartoon monument to Rutland Barrington, in PUNCH, *March 21, 1896.*

in less colorful prose, agreed with this verdict. *Modern Society* thought Barrington "certainly admirable; but there is a little too much of him." And the man himself (in *Rutland Barrington, by Himself*) admitted: "The veriest glutton for work might have been satisfied with my part in this opera, about the longest and most hard-working I have ever undertaken, and yet one in which I failed to find too many chances of scoring."

To the eye and ear of the *Man of the World,* Rosina Brandram, the other Savoy veteran, was "as purely delightful as ever as the middle-aged party, without whom no Gilbert and Sullivan opera is complete."

"Walter Passmore, in the character of the stingy and dyspeptic grand duke," in earning the *Times'* cautiously qualified notice, "comes nearer to Mr. Grossmith's level than he has done yet, and his delivery of the songs is in some respects very good." The *St. James Budget* thought him "very funny in the first act, but in the second [he] has practically nothing to do."

"As the soubrette, Lisa, Florence Perry is delicious," judged the *Man of the World,* "but why does so sweet a morsel seek to add an inch to her altitude by wearing such monstrously ugly high heels to her shoes? The song, 'Take care of him —he's much too good to live' (page 440), is one of the jewels of the piece, and it could not possibly have been delivered in better style."

But it was a foreign star who dominated the final first night of this most British of theatrical companies and who in a thoroughly Gilbertian sense imparted to his casting that touch of topsy-turvyism the dramatist had previously accorded his librettos. Mme. Ilka von Palmay, Countess Kinsky, had made her first London appearance the preceding season in the Saxe-Coburg Company. She had played in *Patience* and *Yeomen* on the continent, as well as singing both Yum-Yum and (wearing tights) Nanki-Poo in German *Mikado* productions. Now her return to London was triumphant. "The histrionic success of the piece is the English actress, Julia Jellicoe, of Mme. Ilka von Palmay," was the opinion of the *Musical Standard;* "It was a whimsical idea to make the Germans in the opera speak pure English, and to give the part of the Englishwoman to a German singer. . . . Mme. von Palmay has a pleasing voice of rare freshness, and her acting quite lifted the piece when she was on stage." The *Sunday Times* added: "Her quaint accent and merry glances, not to speak of her vivacious acting and genuine sense of humour or her piquant singing, made an instant effect." But the *Times* rumbled, ungallantly: "The distinguished Hungarian soubrette has considerably improved and toned down her method, or possibly she is fortunately hampered by her incomplete command of English. Her voice, though far from pleasing, is used with much art, and her delivery of the song in the second act, with its *cantabile* beginning and brilliant close, fully deserved the encore it received on Saturday."

Her British colleague, Barrington, had the last and significant word on this casting: "By this time much of the all-English atmosphere, which on former days had been so strenuously insisted on, had evaporated, so it was no surprise to find in our new *prima donna* a foreigner who was reputed to have taken high rank in her profession in her own country, though I never found out if this was earned entirely by her artistic capabilities or enhanced to a certain extent by the fact of her being Countess Ilka von Palmay."

Although there were notices of unqualified praise to offset those highly critical, what real success there was that night was clearly more Sullivan's than Gilbert's. "Mr. Gilbert has stood still, but Sir Arthur Sullivan has advanced. That is the gist of it," said the *Man of the World* in "Stage Whispers." "Sir Arthur Sullivan has done better than his librettist," wrote the *Musical Standard*'s critic, "and perhaps would have done better still if he had not been dullened by that Sausage Roll." And, in contradistinction, the *City*'s verdict was: "In my opinion *The Grand Duke* is a very unworthy successor of *The Pirates of Penzance* and *Patience,* both in the words and music. . . . Mr. Gilbert has lost all his gaiety and nearly all his old brilliance. He appears to rhyme with more facility than ever, but there is little point in his lines now; they are merely rhyme without reason. Nor is the spoken dialogue at all exhilarating."

But, as Isaac Goldberg put it, "The last curtain had fallen upon the greatest collaboration in the history of the modern stage." And it was with appreciation and gratitude that the *Theatre* magazine reviewer approached the delicate subject of passing judgment: "That the new Savoy opera is a great success there can be no possible doubt. It may have faults; it may be inferior to more than one of its predecessors; but the fact remains that *The Grand Duke* is from first to last a delightful entertainment. It makes one glad that there are such men in the world as W. S. Gilbert and Arthur Sullivan—glad, above all, that they are once more pulling together in 'double harness.' "

"The reign of *The Grand Duke* at the Savoy is not likely to be interrupted for several months" was the best the *Daily Chronicle* could venture. It was, in fact, performed only 123 times (the shortest first run of any of the fourteen operas except *Thespis*) and, in the words of Mr. Dunhill, "in justice to Sullivan's memory, as well as Gilbert's, it is to be hoped that it will never be heard again." Sullivan himself appears privately to have blamed Gilbert for the failure. In a letter he wrote Frank Burnand from Monte Carlo at midnight, March 12, five days after the première, he confessed: "Why reproach me? *I* didn't write the book!! . . . I arrived here yesterday dead beat, and feel better already. Another week's rehearsal with W.S.G. and I should have gone raving mad. I had already ordered some straw for my hair." Tragically enough, in a letter written to his close friend Mrs. Bram Stoker only two days after the first night, on Monday, March 9, Gilbert gave indication—also private—that he recognized the failure as his own: "Thank you very much for your kind letter. I have had rather a bad time of it, but now that the baby is born I shall soon recover. I pick up very quickly (thank God!) after these little events. I'm not at all a proud Mother, and I never want to see the ugly misshapen little brat again!"

MARCH 7. *Began new opera "Grand Duke" at ¼ past eight—usual reception. Opera went well; over at 11.15. Parts of it dragged a little, dialogue too redundant, but success great and genuine I think. Thank God opera is finished and out.*

ARTHUR SULLIVAN'S DIARY

A New and Original Comic Opera,

IN TWO ACTS,

THE
GRAND DUKE

OR,

THE STATUTORY DUEL.

Dramatis Personae.

RUDOLPH, *Grand Duke of Pfennig Halbpfennig*	MR. WALTER PASSMORE.
ERNEST DUMMKOPF, *A Theatrical Manager*	MR. C. KENNINGHAM.
LUDWIG, *His Leading Comedian*	MR. RUTLAND BARRINGTON.
DR. TANNHÄUSER, *A Notary*	MR. SCOTT RUSSELL.
THE PRINCE OF MONTE CARLO	MR. SCOTT FISHE.
VISCOUNT MENTONE	MR. CARLTON.
BEN HASHBAZ, *A Costumier*	MR. WORKMAN.
HERALD	MR. JONES HEWSON.
THE PRINCESS OF MONTE CARLO, *betrothed to Rudolph*	MISS EMMIE OWEN.
THE BARONESS VON KRAKENFELDT, *betrothed to Rudolph*	MISS ROSINA BRANDRAM.
JULIA JELLICOE, *An English Comédienne*	MDME. ILKA VON PALMAY.
LISA, *A Soubrette*	MISS FLORENCE PERRY.

OLGA		MISS MILDRED BAKER.
GRETCHEN		MISS RUTH VINCENT.
BERTHA	*Members of Ernest Dummkopf's Company*	MISS JESSIE ROSE.
ELSA		MISS ETHEL WILSON.
MARTHA		MISS BEATRICE PERRY.

CHAMBERLAIN, NOBLES, ACTORS, ACTRESSES, &C.

ACT I. — Public Square of Speisesaal.

ACT II. — Hall in the Grand Ducal Palace.

DATE. — 1750.

THE GRAND DUKE

OR,

THE STATUTORY DUEL.

———

ACT I.

SCENE. — *Market Place of Speisesaal, in the Grand Duchy of Pfennig Halbpfennig. A well, with decorated iron-work, up* L.C. GRETCHEN, BERTHA, OLGA, MARTHA, *and other members of* ERNEST DUMMKOPF'S *theatrical company are discovered, seated at several small tables, enjoying a repast in honour of the nuptials of* LUDWIG, *his leading comedian, and* LISA, *his soubrette.*

CHORUS.

Won't it be a pretty wedding?
    Doesn't Lisa look delightful?
Smiles and tears in plenty shedding—
    Which in brides of course is rightful.
    One might say, if one were spiteful,
Contradiction little dreading,
    Her bouquet is simply frightful—
Still, it is a pretty wedding!
Oh, it is a pretty wedding!
    Such a pretty, pretty wedding!

ELSA.   If her dress *is* badly fitting,
    Theirs the fault who made her *trousseau.*

BERTHA.   If her gloves *are* always splitting,
    Cheap kid gloves, we know, will do so.

OLGA.   If her wreath *is* all lop-sided,
    That's a thing one's always dreading.

GRETCHEN.   If her hair *is* all untidied,
    Still, it is a pretty wedding!

CHORUS.   Oh, it is a pretty wedding!
    Such a pretty, pretty wedding!

CHORUS.

Here they come, the couple plighted—
    On life's journey gaily start them.
Soon to be for aye united,

Till divorce or death shall part them.

LUDWIG *and* LISA *come forward.*

DUET — LUDWIG *and* LISA.

LUDWIG.   Pretty Lisa, fair and tasty,
    Tell me now, and tell me truly,
Haven't you been rather hasty?
    Haven't you been rash unduly?
Am I quite the dashing *sposo*
    That your fancy could depict you?
Perhaps you think I'm only so-so?
             (*She expresses admiration.*)
    Well, I will not contradict you!

CHORUS.   No, he will not contradict you!

LISA.   Who am I to raise objection?
    I'm a child, untaught and homely—
When you tell me you're perfection,
    Tender, truthful, true, and comely—
That in quarrel no one's bolder,
    Though dissensions always grieve you—
Why, my love, you're so much older
    That, of course, I must believe you!

CHORUS.   Yes, of course, she must believe you!

CHORUS.

If he ever acts unkindly,
Shut your eyes and love him blindly—

[423]

Should he call you names uncomely,
Shut your mouth and love him dumbly—
Should he rate you, rightly—leftly—
Shut your ears and love him deafly.
  Ha! ha! ha! ha! ha! ha! ha!
  Thus and thus and thus alone,
  Ludwig's wife may hold her own!
    (LUDWIG and LISA *sit at table.*)

Enter NOTARY TANNHÄUSER.

NOTARY. Hallo! Surely I'm not late? (*All chatter unintelligibly in reply.*) But, dear me, you're all at breakfast! Has the wedding taken place? (*All chatter unintelligibly in reply.*) My good girls, one at a time, I beg. Let me understand the situation. As solicitor to the conspiracy to dethrone the Grand Duke—a conspiracy in which the members of this company are deeply involved—I am invited to the marriage of two of its members. I present myself in due course, and I find, not only that the ceremony has taken place—which is not of the least consequence—but the wedding breakfast is half eaten—which is a consideration of the most serious importance.

    (LUDWIG and LISA *come down.*)

LUDWIG. But the ceremony has *not* taken place. We can't get a parson!

NOTARY. Can't get a parson! Why, how's that? They're three a penny!

LUDWIG. Oh, it's the old story—the Grand Duke!

ALL. Ugh!

LUDWIG. It seems that the little imp has selected this, our wedding day, for a convocation of all the clergy in the town to settle the details of his approaching marriage with the enormously wealthy Baroness von Krakenfeldt, and there won't be a parson to be had for love or money until six o'clock this evening!

LISA. And as we produce our magnificent classical revival of *Troilus and Cressida* to-night at seven, we have no alternative but to eat our wedding-breakfast before we've earned it. So sit down, and make the best of it.

GRETCHEN. Oh, I should like to pull his Grand Ducal ears for him, that I should! He's the meanest, the cruellest, the most spiteful little ape in Christendom!

OLGA. Well, we shall soon be freed from his tyranny. Tomorrow the Despot is to be dethroned!

LUDWIG. Hush, rash girl! You know not what you say.

OLGA. Don't be absurd! We're all in it—we're all tiled, here.

LUDWIG. That has nothing to do with it. Know ye not that in alluding to our conspiracy without having first given and received the secret sign, you are violating a fundamental principle of our Association?

SONG — LUDWIG.

By the mystic regulation
Of our dark Association,
Ere you open conversation
  With another kindred soul,
  You must eat a sausage-roll!
    (*Producing one.*)

ALL.   You must eat a sausage-roll!

LUDWIG. If, in turn, he eats another,
That's a sign that he's a brother—
Each may fully trust the other.
  It is quaint and it is droll,
  But it's bilious on the whole.

ALL.   Very bilious on the whole.

LUDWIG. It's a greasy kind of pasty,
Which, perhaps, a judgment hasty
Might consider rather tasty:
  Once (to speak without disguise)
  It found favour in our eyes.

ALL.   It found favour in our eyes.

LUDWIG. But when you've been six months feeding
(As we have) on this exceeding
Bilious food, it's no ill-breeding
  If at these repulsive pies
  Our offended gorges rise!

ALL.   Our offended gorges rise!

MARTHA. Oh, bother the secret sign! I've eaten it until I'm quite uncomfortable! I've given it six times already to-day—and (*whimpering*) I can't eat any breakfast!

BERTHA. And it's so unwholesome. Why, we should all be as yellow as frogs if it wasn't for the make-up!

LUDWIG. All this is rank treason to the cause. I suffer as much as any of you. I loathe the repulsive thing—I can't contemplate it without a shudder—but I'm a conscientious conspirator, and if you won't give the sign I will. (*Eats sausage roll with an effort.*)

LISA. Poor martyr! He's always at it, and it's a wonder where he puts it!

NOTARY. Well, now, about *Troilus and Cressida.* What do *you* play?

LUDWIG (*struggling with his feelings*). If you'll be so obliging as to wait until I've got rid of this feeling of warm oil at the bottom of my throat, I'll tell you all about it. (LISA *gives him some brandy.*) Thank you, my love; it's gone. Well, the piece will be produced upon a scale of unexampled magnificence. It is confidently predicted that my appearance as King Agamemnon, in a Louis Quatorze wig, will mark an epoch in the theatrical annals of Pfennig Halbpfennig. I endeavoured to persuade Ernest Dummkopf, our manager, to lend us the classical dresses for our marriage. Think of the effect of a real Athenian wedding procession cavorting through the streets of Speisesaal! Torches burning—cymbals banging—flutes tootling—citharæ twanging—and a throng of fifty lovely Spartan virgins capering before us, all down the High Street, singing "Eloia! Eloia! Opoponax, Eloia!" It would have been tremendous!

NOTARY.   And he declined?

LUDWIG.   He did, on the prosaic ground that it might rain, and the ancient Greeks didn't carry umbrellas! If, as is confidently expected, Ernest Dummkopf is elected to succeed the dethroned one, mark my words, he will make a mess of it.

OLGA.   He's sure to be elected. His entire company has promised to plump for him on the understanding that all the places about the Court are filled by members of his troupe, according to professional precedence.

MARTHA.   I'm sure he'll make a lovely Grand Duke. How he will stage-manage the processions!

GRETCHEN.   And won't it make Julia Jellicoe jealous! That English woman has always rejected his advances, hitherto—but now I fancy the tables will be turned and he'll reject hers. The pretentious little London cockney—there's nobody good enough for her!

LUDWIG.   Bah!—Ernest's a stick—a very stick! And what a part it is! What a chance for an actor who is really a master of stage resource! Why, a Grand Duke of Pfennig Halbpfennig might have a different make-up for every day in the week! Monday, touch-and-go light comedy in lavender trousers and a flaxen wig. Tuesday, irritable old uncle from India. Wednesday, heavy philanthropist with benevolent "bald." Thursday, incisive baronet with diamond ring and cigarette to show it off. Friday, slimy solicitor with club foot and spectacles. Saturday, escaped convict with one eye and a gulp! It's one of those parts that really give a man a chance!

(*He strolls up and off with* LISA, *as* ERNEST *enters in great excitement.*)

BERTHA (*looking off*).   Here comes Ernest Dummkopf. Now we shall know all about it!

ALL.   Well—what's the news? How is the election going?

ERNEST.   Oh, it's a certainty—a practical certainty! Two of the candidates have been arrested for debt, and the third is a baby in arms—so, if you keep your promises, and vote solid, I'm cocksure of election!

OLGA.   Trust to us. But you remember the conditions?

ERNEST.   Yes—all of you shall be provided for, for life. Every man shall be ennobled—every lady shall have unlimited credit at the Court Milliner's, and all salaries shall be paid weekly in advance!

GRETCHEN.   Oh, it's quite clear he knows how to rule a Grand Duchy!

ERNEST.   Rule a Grand Duchy? Why, my good girl, for ten years past I've ruled a theatrical company! A man who can do that can rule anything!

SONG — ERNEST.

Were I a king in very truth,
And had a son—a guileless youth—
    In probable succession;
To teach him patience, teach him tact,
How promptly in a fix to act,
He should adopt, in point of fact,
    A manager's profession.
To that condition he should stoop
    (Despite a too fond mother),
With eight or ten "stars" in his troupe,
    All jealous of each other!
Oh, the man who can rule a theatrical crew,
Each member a genius (and some of them two),
And manage to humour them, little and great,
    Can govern this tuppenny State!

ALL.   Oh, the man, &c.

Both A and B rehearsal slight—
They say they'll be "all right at night"
    (They've both to go to school yet);
C in each act *must* change her dress,
D *will* attempt to "square the press";
E won't play Romeo unless
    His grandmother plays Juliet;
F claims all hoydens as her rights
    (She's played them thirty seasons);
And G must show herself in tights
    For two convincing reasons—
    Two very well-shaped reasons!
Oh, the man who can drive a theatrical team,
With wheelers and leaders in order supreme,
Can govern and rule, with a wave of his fin,
    All Europe—with Ireland thrown in!

ALL.   Oh, the man, &c.   (*Exeunt all but* ERNEST.)

ERNEST.   Elected by my fellow conspirators to be Grand Duke of Pfennig Halbpfennig as soon as the contemptible little occupant of the historical throne is deposed—here is promotion indeed! Why, instead of playing Troilus of Troy for a month, I shall play Grand Duke of Pfennig Halbpfennig for a lifetime! Yet am I happy? No —far from happy! The lovely English *comédienne* —the beautiful Julia, whose dramatic ability is so overwhelming that our audiences forgive even her strong English accent—that rare and radiant being treats my respectful advances with disdain unutterable! And yet, who knows? She is haughty and ambitious, and it may be that the splendid change in my fortunes may work a corresponding change in her feelings towards me!

Enter JULIA JELLICOE.

JULIA. Herr Dummkopf, a word with you, if you please.

ERNEST. Beautiful English maiden—

JULIA. No compliments, I beg. I desire to speak with you on a purely professional matter, so we will, if you please, dispense with allusions to my personal appearance, which can only tend to widen the breach which already exists between us.

ERNEST (*aside*). My only hope shattered! The haughty Londoner still despises me! (*Aloud.*) It shall be as you will.

JULIA. I understand that the conspiracy in which we are all concerned is to develop to-morrow, and that the company is likely to elect you to the throne on the understanding that the posts about the court are to be filled by members of your theatrical troupe, according to their professional importance.

ERNEST. That is so.

JULIA. Then all I can say is that it places me in an extremely awkward position.

ERNEST (*very depressed*). I don't see how it concerns you.

JULIA. Why, bless my heart, don't you see that, as your leading lady, I am bound under a serious penalty to play the leading part in all your productions?

ERNEST. Well?

JULIA. Why, of course, the leading part in this production will be the Grand Duchess!

ERNEST. My wife?

JULIA. That is another way of expressing the same idea.

ERNEST (*aside—delighted*). I scarcely dared even to hope for this!

JULIA. Of course, as your leading lady, you'll be mean enough to hold me to the terms of my agreement. Oh, that's so like a man! Well, I suppose there's no help for it—I shall have to do it!

ERNEST (*aside*). She's mine! (*Aloud.*) But—do you really think you would care to play that part? (*Taking her hand.*)

JULIA (*withdrawing it*). Care to play it? Certainly not—but what am I to do? Business is business, and I am bound by the terms of my agreement.

ERNEST. It's for a long run, mind—a run that may last many, many years—no understudy—

and once embarked upon there's no throwing it up.

JULIA. Oh, we're used to these long runs in England: they are the curse of the stage—but, you see, I've no option.

ERNEST. You think the part of Grand Duchess will be good enough for you?

JULIA. Oh, I think so. It's a very good part in Gerolstein, and oughtn't to be a bad one in Pfennig Halbpfennig. Why, what did you suppose I was going to play?

ERNEST (*keeping up a show of reluctance*). But, considering your strong personal dislike to me and your persistent rejection of my repeated offers, won't you find it difficult to throw yourself into the part with all the impassioned enthusiasm that the character seems to demand? Remember, it's a strongly emotional part, involving long and repeated scenes of rapture, tenderness, adoration, devotion—all in luxuriant excess, and all of the most demonstrative description.

JULIA. My good sir, throughout my career I have made it a rule never to allow private feeling to interfere with my professional duties. You may be quite sure that (however distasteful the part may be) if I undertake it, I shall consider myself professionally bound to throw myself into it with all the ardour at my command.

ERNEST (*aside—with effusion*). I'm the happiest fellow alive! (*Aloud.*) Now—would you have any objection—to—to give me some idea—if it's only a mere sketch—as to how you would play it? It would be really interesting—to me—to know your conception of—of—the part of my wife.

JULIA. How would I play it? Now, let me see—let me see. (*Considering.*) Ah, I have it!

BALLAD — JULIA.

How would I play this part—
        The Grand Duke's Bride?
All rancour in my heart
        I'd duly hide—
    I'd drive it from my recollection
    And 'whelm you with a mock affection,
    Well calculated to defy detection—
That's how I'd play this part—
        The Grand Duke's Bride.

With many a winsome smile
        I'd witch and woo;
With gay and girlish guile
        I'd frenzy you—
    I'd madden you with my caressing,
    Like turtle, her first love confessing—
    That it was "mock," no mortal would be
        guessing,
With so much winsome wile

I'd witch and woo!

Did any other maid
        With you succeed,
I'd pinch the forward jade—
        I would indeed!
    With jealous frenzy agitated
    (Which would, of course, be simulated),
    I'd make her wish she'd never been
        created—
Did any other maid
        With you succeed!

And should there come to me,
        Some summers hence,
In all the childish glee
        Of innocence,
    Fair babes, aglow with beauty vernal,
    My heart would bound with joy diurnal!
    This sweet display of sympathy maternal,
Well, that would also be
        A mere pretence!

My histrionic art,
        Though you deride,
That's how I'd play that part—
        The Grand Duke's Bride!

ENSEMBLE.

ERNEST.	JULIA.
Oh joy! when two glowing young hearts,	My boy, when two glowing young hearts,
From the rise of the curtain,	From the rise of the curtain,
Thus throw themselves into their parts,	Thus throw themselves into their parts,
Success is most certain!	Success is most certain!
If the *rôle* you're prepared to endow	The *rôle* I'm prepared to endow
With such delicate touches,	With most delicate touches,
By the heaven above us, I vow	By the heaven above us, I vow
You shall be my Grand Duchess!	I will be your Grand Duchess! (*Dance.*)

Enter all the Chorus with LUDWIG, NOTARY, *and* LISA—*all greatly agitated.*

EXCITED CHORUS.

My goodness me! what shall we do? Why, what a dreadful situation!
(*To* LUDWIG.) It's all your fault, you booby you—you lump of indiscrimination!
I'm sure I don't know where to go—it's put me into such a tetter—
But this at all events I know—the sooner we are off, the better!

ERNEST. What means this *agitato*? What d'ye seek?
As your Grand Duke elect I bid you speak!

SONG — LUDWIG.

Ten minutes since, I met a chap
    Who bowed an easy salutation—
Thinks I, "This gentleman, mayhap,
    Belongs to our Association."
        But, on the whole,
          Uncertain yet,
        A sausage-roll
          I took and eat—
That chap replied (I don't embellish)
By eating *three* with obvious relish.

CHORUS (*angrily*). Why, gracious powers,
        No chum of ours
    Could eat three sausage-rolls with relish!

LUDWIG. Quite reassured, I let him know
    Our plot—each incident explaining;
That stranger chuckled much, as though
    He thought me highly entertaining.
        I told him all,
          Both bad and good;
        I bade him call—
          He said he would:
I added much—the more I muckled,
The more that chuckling chummy chuckled!

ALL (*angrily*). A bat could see
        He couldn't be
    A chum of ours if he chuckled!

LUDWIG. Well, as I bowed to his applause,
    Down dropped he with hysteric bellow—
And *that* seemed right enough, because
    I *am* a devilish funny fellow.
        Then suddenly,
          As still he squealed,
        It flashed on me
          That I'd revealed
Our plot, with all details effective,
To Grand Duke Rudolph's own detective!

ALL.   What folly fell,
          To go and tell
    Our plot to any one's detective!

CHORUS (*attacking* LUDWIG). You booby dense—
        You oaf immense,
    With no pretence
    To common sense!
    A stupid muff
    Who's made of stuff
    Not worth a puff
    Of candle-snuff!
Pack up at once and off we go, unless we're anxious to exhibit

Our fairy forms all in a row, strung up upon the Castle gibbet!
(*Exeunt Chorus. Manent* LUDWIG, LISA, ERNEST, JULIA, *and* NOTARY.)

JULIA. Well, a nice mess you've got us into! There's an end of our precious plot! All up—pop—fizzle—bang—done for!

LUDWIG. Yes, but—ha! ha!—fancy my choosing the Grand Duke's private detective, of all men, to make a confidant of! When you come to think of it, it's really devilish funny!

ERNEST (*angrily*). When you come to think of it, it's extremely injudicious to admit into a conspiracy every pudding-headed baboon who presents himself!

LUDWIG. Yes—I should never do that. If I were chairman of this gang, I should hesitate to enroll *any* baboon who couldn't produce satisfactory credentials from his last Zoological Gardens.

LISA. Ludwig is far from being a baboon. Poor boy, he could not help giving us away—it's his trusting nature—he was deceived.

JULIA (*furiously*). His trusting nature! (*To* LUDWIG.) Oh, I should like to talk to you in my own language for five minutes—only five minutes! I know some good, strong, energetic English remarks that would shrivel your trusting nature into raisins—only you wouldn't understand them!

LUDWIG. Here we perceive one of the disadvantages of a neglected education!

ERNEST (*to* JULIA). And I suppose you'll never be my Grand Duchess, now!

JULIA. Grand Duchess? My good friend, if you don't produce the piece how can I play the part?

ERNEST. True. (*To* LUDWIG.) You see what you've done.

LUDWIG. But, my dear sir, you don't seem to understand that the man ate three sausage-rolls. Keep that fact steadily before you. Three large sausage-rolls.

JULIA. Bah!—Lots of people eat sausage-rolls who are not conspirators.

LUDWIG. Then they shouldn't. It's bad form. It's not the game. When one of the Human Family proposes to eat a sausage-roll, it is his duty to ask himself, "Am I a conspirator?" And if, on examination, he finds that he is *not* a conspirator, he is bound in honour to select some other form of refreshment.

LISA. Of course he is. One should always play the game. (*To* NOTARY, *who has been smiling placidly through this.*) What are you grinning at, you greedy old man?

NOTARY. Nothing—don't mind me. It is always

amusing to the legal mind to see a parcel of lay-men bothering themselves about a matter which to a trained lawyer presents no difficulty whatever.

ALL. No difficulty!

NOTARY. None whatever! The way out of it is quite simple.

ALL. Simple?

NOTARY. Certainly! Now attend. In the first place, you two men fight a Statutory Duel.

ERNEST. A Statutory Duel?

JULIA. A Stat-tat-tatutory Duel! Ach! what a crack-jaw language this German is!

LUDWIG. Never heard of such a thing.

NOTARY. It is true that the practice has fallen into abeyance through disuse. But all the laws of Pfennig Halbpfennig (which are framed upon those of Solon, the Athenian law-giver) run for a hundred years, when (again like the laws of So-lon) they die a natural death, unless, in the mean-time, they have been revived for another century. The Act that institutes the Statutory Duel was passed a hundred years ago, and as it has never been revived, it expires to-morrow. So you're just in time.

JULIA. But what is the use of talking to us about Statutory Duels when we none of us know what a Statutory Duel is?

NOTARY. Don't you? Then I'll explain.

SONG — NOTARY.

About a century since,
    The code of the duello
        To sudden death
        For want of breath
    Sent many a strapping fellow.
The then presiding Prince
    (Who useless bloodshed hated),
        He passed an Act,
        Short and compact,
    Which may be briefly stated:
Unlike the complicated laws
A Parliamentary draughtsman draws,
    It may be briefly stated.

ALL. We know that complicated laws,
    Such·as a legal draughtsman draws,
        Cannot be briefly stated.

NOTARY. By this ingenious law,
    If any two shall quarrel,
        They may not fight
        With falchions bright
    (Which seemed to him immoral);
But each a card shall draw,
    And he who draws the lowest
        Shall (so 'twas said)
        Be thenceforth dead—

In fact, a legal "ghoest"
(When exigence of rhyme compels,
Orthography foregoes her spells,
    And "ghost" is written "ghoest.")

ALL (aside). With what an emphasis he dwells
    Upon "orthography" and "spells"!
        That kind of fun's the lowest.

NOTARY. When off the loser's popped
    (By little legal fiction),
        And friend and foe
        Have wept their woe
    In counterfeit affliction,
The winner must adopt
    The loser's poor relations—
        Discharge his debts,
        Pay all his bets,
    And take his obligations.
In short, to briefly sum the case,
The winner takes the loser's place,
    With all its obligations.

ALL. How neatly lawyers state a case!
    The winner takes the loser's place,
        With all its obligations!

LUDWIG. I see. The man who draws the lowest card—

NOTARY. Dies, *ipso facto,* a social death. He loses all his civil rights—his identity disappears—the Revising Barrister expunges his name from the list of voters, and the winner takes his place, what-ever it may be, discharges all his functions and adopts all his responsibilities.

ERNEST. This is all very well, as far as it goes, but it only protects one of us. What's to become of the survivor?

LUDWIG. Yes, that's an interesting point, be-cause *I* might be the survivor.

NOTARY. The survivor goes at once to the Grand Duke, and, in a burst of remorse, denounces the dead man as the moving spirit of the plot. He is accepted as King's evidence, and, as a matter of course, receives a free pardon. To-morrow, when the law expires, the dead man will, *ipso facto,* come to life again—the Revising Barrister will restore his name to the list of voters, and he will resume all his obligations as though nothing un-usual had happened.

JULIA. When he will be at once arrested, tried, and executed on the evidence of the informer! Candidly, my friend, I don't think much of your plot!

NOTARY. Dear, dear, dear, the ignorance of the laity! My good young lady, it is a beautiful maxim of our glorious Constitution that a man can only die once. Death expunges crime, and when he comes to life again, it will be with a clean slate.

ERNEST. It's really very ingenious.

LUDWIG (*to* NOTARY). My dear sir, we owe you our lives!

LISA (*aside to* LUDWIG). May I kiss him?

LUDWIG. Certainly not: you're a big girl now. (*To* ERNEST.) Well, miscreant, are you prepared to meet me on the field of honour?

ERNEST. At once. By Jove, what a couple of fire-eaters we are!

LISA. Ludwig doesn't know what fear is.

LUDWIG. Oh, I don't mind this sort of duel!

ERNEST. It's not like a duel with swords. I hate a duel with swords. It's not the blade I mind—it's the blood.

LUDWIG. And I hate a duel with pistols. It's not the ball I mind—it's the bang.

NOTARY. Altogether it is a great improvement on the old method of giving satisfaction.

QUINTETTE.

LUDWIG, LISA, NOTARY, ERNEST, JULIA.

Strange the views some people hold!
　　Two young fellows quarrel—
Then they fight, for both are bold—
Rage of both is uncontrolled—
Both are stretched out, stark and cold!
　　Prithee where's the moral?
　　　　Ding dong! Ding dong!
There's an end to further action,
And this barbarous transaction
Is described as "satisfaction"!
　　Ha! ha! ha! ha! satisfaction!
　　　　Ding dong! Ding dong!
Each is laid in churchyard mould—
Strange the views some people hold!

Better than the method old,
　　Which was coarse and cruel,
Is the plan that we've extolled.
Sing thy virtues manifold
(Better than refinèd gold),
　　Statutory Duel!
　　　　Sing song! Sing song!
Sword or pistol neither uses—
Playing card he lightly chooses,
And the loser simply loses!
　　Ha! ha! ha! ha! simply loses.
　　　　Sing song! Sing song!
Some prefer the churchyard mould!
Strange the views some people hold!

NOTARY (*offering a card to* ERNEST). Now take a card and gaily sing
How little you care for Fortune's rubs—

ERNEST (*drawing a card*). Hurrah, hurrah! I've drawn a King!

ALL. 　　　　He's drawn a King!
　　　　He's drawn a King!
Sing Hearts and Diamonds, Spades and Clubs!

ALL (*dancing*). He's drawn a King!
　　　　How strange a thing!
An excellent card—his chance it aids—
Sing Hearts and Diamonds, Spades and Clubs—
Sing Diamonds, Hearts and Clubs and Spades!

NOTARY (*to* LUDWIG). Now take a card with heart of grace—
(Whatever our fate, let's play our parts).

LUDWIG (*drawing card*). Hurrah, hurrah!—I've drawn an Ace!

ALL. 　　　　He's drawn an Ace!

He's drawn an Ace!
Sing Clubs and Diamonds, Spades and
    Hearts!

ALL (*dancing*). He's drawn an Ace!
            Observe his face—
Such very good fortune falls to few—
Sing Clubs and Diamonds, Spades and
    Hearts—
Sing Clubs, Spades, Hearts and Diamonds
    too!

NOTARY. That both these maids may keep their
    troth,
And never misfortune them befall,
I'll hold 'em as trustee for both—

ALL.   He'll hold 'em both!
                He'll hold 'em both!
Sing Hearts, Clubs, Diamonds, Spades and
    all!

ALL (*dancing*). By joint decree
            As $\left\{\begin{array}{c}\text{our}\\\text{your}\end{array}\right\}$ trustee

This Notary $\left\{\begin{array}{c}\text{we}\\\text{you}\end{array}\right\}$ will now install—

In custody let him keep $\left\{\begin{array}{c}\text{their}\\\text{our}\end{array}\right\}$ hearts,

Sing Hearts, Clubs, Diamonds, Spades and all!
(*Dance and exeunt* LUDWIG, ERNEST, *and*
    NOTARY *with the two Girls.*)

March. Enter the seven Chamberlains of the
GRAND DUKE RUDOLPH.

CHORUS OF CHAMBERLAINS.

The good Grand Duke of Pfennig Halbpfennig,
Though, in his own opinion, very very big,
In point of fact he's nothing but a miserable
    prig,
Is the good Grand Duke of Pfennig Halbpfen-
    nig!

Though quite contemptible, as every one agrees,
We must dissemble if we want our bread and
    cheese,
So hail him in a chorus, with enthusiasm big,
The good Grand Duke of Pfennig Halbpfennig!

Enter the GRAND DUKE RUDOLPH. *He is meanly
and miserably dressed in old and patched clothes,
but blazes with a profusion of orders and decora-
tions. He is very weak and ill, from low living.*

SONG — RUDOLPH.

A pattern to professors of monarchial auton-
    omy,
I don't indulge in levity or compromising *bon-
    homie,*

But dignified formality, consistent with econ-
    omy,
    Above all other virtues I particularly prize.
I never join in merriment—I don't see joke or
    jape any—
I never tolerate familiarity in shape any—
This, joined with an extravagant respect for
    tuppence ha'penny,
    A keynote to my character sufficiently
        supplies.

(*Speaking.*) Observe. (*To Chamberlains.*) My
    snuff-box!
(*The snuff-box is passed with much ceremony
from the Junior Chamberlain, through all the
others, until it is presented by the Senior Chamberlain to* RUDOLPH, *who uses it.*)
That incident a keynote to my character sup-
    plies.

ALL. That incident, &c.

RUDOLPH. I weigh out tea and sugar with preci-
    sion mathematical—
Instead of beer, a penny each—my orders are
    emphatical—
(Extravagance unpardonable, any more than
    that I call),
    But, on the other hand, my Ducal dignity
        to keep—
All Courtly ceremonial—to put it comprehen-
    sively—
I rigidly insist upon (but not, I hope, offen-
    sively)
Whenever ceremonial can be practised inex-
    pensively—
    And, when you come to think of it, it's
        really very cheap!
(*Speaking.*) Observe. (*To Chamberlains.*) My
    handkerchief!
(*Handkerchief is handed by Junior Chamber-
lain to the next in order, and so on until it
reaches* RUDOLPH, *who is much inconvenienced
    by the delay.*)
It's sometimes inconvenient, but it's always very
    cheap!

ALL. It's stately and impressive, &c.

RUDOLPH. My Lord Chamberlain, as you are
aware, my marriage with the wealthy Baroness
von Krakenfeldt will take place to-morrow, and
you will be good enough to see that the rejoicings
are on a scale of unusual liberality. Pass that on.
(*Chamberlain whispers to Vice-Chamberlain, who
whispers to the next, and so on.*) The sports will
begin with a Wedding Breakfast Bee. The leading
pastry-cooks of the town will be invited to compete, and the winner will not only enjoy the satisfaction of seeing his breakfast devoured by the

Grand Ducal pair, but he will also be entitled to have the Arms of Pfennig Halbpfennig tattoo'd between his shoulder-blades. The Vice-Chamberlain will see to this. All the public fountains of Speisesaal will run with Gingerbierheim and Currantweinmilch at the public expense. The Assistant Vice-Chamberlain will see to this. At night, everybody will illuminate; and as I have no desire to tax the public funds unduly, this will be done at the inhabitants' private expense. The Deputy Assistant Vice-Chamberlain will see to this. All my Grand Ducal subjects will wear new clothes, and the Sub-Deputy Assistant Vice-Chamberlain will collect the usual commission on all sales. Wedding presents (which, on this occasion, should be on a scale of extraordinary magnificence) will be received at the Palace at any hour of the twenty-four, and the Temporary Sub-Deputy Assistant Vice-Chamberlain will sit up all night for this purpose. The entire population will be commanded to enjoy themselves, and with this view the Acting-Temporary Sub-Deputy Assistant Vice-Chamberlain will sing comic songs in the Market Place from noon to nightfall. Finally, we have composed a Wedding Anthem, with which the entire population are required to provide themselves. It can be obtained from our Grand Ducal publishers at the usual discount price, and all the Chamberlains will be expected to push the sale. (*Chamberlains bow and exeunt.*) I don't feel at all comfortable. I hope I'm not doing a foolish thing in

getting married. After all, it's a poor heart that never rejoices, and this wedding of mine is the first little treat I've allowed myself since my christening. Besides, Caroline's income is very considerable, and as her ideas of economy are quite on a par with mine, it ought to turn out well. Bless her tough old heart, she's a mean little darling! Oh, here she is, punctual to her appointment!

Enter BARONESS VON KRAKENFELDT.

BARONESS.   Rudolph! Why, what's the matter?

RUDOLPH.   Why, I'm not quite myself, my pet. I'm a little worried and upset. I want a tonic. It's the low diet, I think. I am afraid, after all, I shall have to take the bull by the horns and have an egg with my breakfast.

BARONESS.   I shouldn't do anything rash, dear. Begin with a jujube. (*Gives him one.*)

RUDOLPH (*about to eat it, but changes his mind*). I'll keep it for supper. (*He sits by her and tries to put his arm round her waist.*)

BARONESS.   Rudolph, don't! What in the world are you thinking of?

RUDOLPH.   I was thinking of embracing you, my sugarplum. Just as a little cheap treat.

BARONESS.   What, here? In public? Really you appear to have no sense of delicacy.

RUDOLPH.   No sense of delicacy, Bon-bon!

BARONESS.   No. I can't make you out. When you courted me, all your courting was done publicly in the Market Place. When you proposed to me, you proposed in the Market Place. And now that we're engaged you seem to desire that our first *tête-à-tête* shall occur in the Market Place! Surely you've a room in your Palace—with blinds—that would do?

RUDOLPH.   But, my own, I can't help myself. I'm bound by my own decree.

BARONESS.   Your own decree?

RUDOLPH.   Yes. You see, all the houses that give on the Market Place belong to me, but the drains (which date back to the reign of Charlemagne) want attending to, and the houses wouldn't let—so, with a view of increasing the value of the property, I decreed that all love-episodes between affectionate couples should take place, in public, on this spot, every Monday, Wednesday, and Friday, when the band doesn't play.

BARONESS. Bless me, what a happy idea! So moral too! And have you found it answer?

RUDOLPH.   Answer? The rents have gone up fifty per cent., and the sale of opera glasses (which is a Grand Ducal monopoly) has received an extraordinary stimulus! So, under the circumstances, *would* you allow me to put my arm round your waist? As a source of income. Just once!

BARONESS. But it's so very embarrassing. Think of the opera glasses!

RUDOLPH. My good girl, that's just what I *am* thinking of. Hang it all, we must give them *something* for their money! What's that?

BARONESS (*unfolding paper, which contains a large letter, which she hands to him*). It's a letter which your detective asked me to hand to you. I wrapped it up in yesterday's paper to keep it clean.

RUDOLPH. Oh, it's only his report! That'll keep. But, I say, you've never been and bought a newspaper?

BARONESS. My dear Rudolph, do you think I'm mad? It came wrapped round my breakfast.

RUDOLPH (*relieved*). I thought you were not the sort of girl to go and buy a newspaper! Well, as we've got it, we may as well read it. What does it say?

BARONESS. Why—dear me—here's your biography! "Our Detested Despot!"

RUDOLPH. Yes—I fancy that refers to me.

BARONESS. And it says—Oh it can't be!

RUDOLPH. What can't be?

BARONESS. Why, it says that although you're going to marry me to-morrow, you were betrothed in infancy to the Princess of Monte Carlo!

RUDOLPH. Oh yes—that's quite right. Didn't I mention it?

BARONESS. Mention it! You never said a word about it!

RUDOLPH. Well, it doesn't matter, because, you see, it's practically off.

BARONESS. Practically off?

RUDOLPH. Yes. By the terms of the contract the betrothal is void unless the Princess marries before she is of age. Now, her father, the Prince, is stony-broke, and hasn't left his house for years for fear of arrest. Over and over again he has implored me to come to him to be married—but in vain. Over and over again he has implored me to advance him the money to enable the Princess to come to me—but in vain. I am very young, but not as young as that; and as the Princess comes of age at two to-morrow, why at two to-morrow I'm a free man, so I appointed that hour for our wedding, as I shall like to have as much marriage as I can get for my money.

BARONESS. I see. Of course, if the married state is a happy state, it's a pity to waste any of it.

RUDOLPH. Why, every hour we delayed I should lose a lot of you and you'd lose a lot of me!

BARONESS. My thoughtful darling! Oh, Rudolph, we ought to be very happy!

RUDOLPH. If I'm not, it'll be my first bad investment. Still there *is* such a thing as a slump even in Matrimonials.

BARONESS. I often picture us in the long, cold, dark December evenings, sitting close to each other and singing impassioned duets to keep us warm, and thinking of all the lovely things we could afford to buy if we chose, and, at the same time, planning out our lives in a spirit of the most rigid and exacting economy!

RUDOLPH. It's a most beautiful and touching picture of connubial bliss in its highest and most rarefied development!

DUET — BARONESS *and* RUDOLPH.

BARONESS. As o'er our penny roll we sing,
  It is not reprehensive
 To think what joys our wealth would bring
 Were we disposed to do the thing
  Upon a scale extensive.
 There's rich mock-turtle—thick and clear—

RUDOLPH (*confidentially*). Perhaps we'll have it
  once a year!

BARONESS (*delighted*). You *are* an open-handed
  dear!

RUDOLPH. Though, mind you, it's expensive.

BARONESS. No doubt it *is* expensive.

BOTH. How fleeting are the glutton's joys!
  With fish and fowl he lightly toys,

RUDOLPH. And pays for such expensive tricks
 Sometimes as much as two-and-six!

BARONESS (*surprised*). As two-and-six?

RUDOLPH.   As two-and-six.

BOTH. Sometimes as much as two-and-six!

It gives him no advantage, mind—
For you and he have only dined.

BARONESS. And you remain, when once it's
down,
A better man by half-a-crown!

RUDOLPH (*doubtfully*). By half-a-crown?

BARONESS (*decisively*). By half-a-crown.

BOTH. Yes, two-and-six is half-a-crown.
(*Dancing*). Then let us be modestly merry,
And rejoice with a derry down derry,
For to laugh and to sing
No extravagance bring—
It's a joy economical, very!

BARONESS. Although, as you're of course aware
(I never tried to hide it),
I moisten my insipid fare
With water—which I can't abear—

RUDOLPH. Nor I—I can't abide it.

BARONESS. This pleasing fact our souls will cheer,
With fifty thousand pounds a year
We *could* indulge in table beer!

RUDOLPH (*incredulously*). Get out!

BARONESS. We could—I've tried it!

RUDOLPH. God bless my soul, she's tried it!

BOTH. Oh, he who has an income clear
Of fifty thousand pounds a year
Can purchase all his fancy loves—

BARONESS. Conspicuous hats—

RUDOLPH. Two-shilling gloves—

BARONESS (*doubtfully*). Two-shilling gloves?

RUDOLPH (*positively*). Two-shilling gloves—

BOTH. Cheap shoes and ties of gaudy hue,
And Waterbury watches, too—
And think that he could buy the lot
Were he a donkey—

RUDOLPH. Which he's *not!*

BARONESS. Oh no, he's *not!*

RUDOLPH. Oh no, he's *not!*

BOTH. That kind of donkey he's *not!*
(*Dancing*). Then let us be modestly merry,
And rejoice with a derry down derry.
For to laugh and to sing
Is a rational thing—
It's a joy economical, very! (*Exit* BARONESS.)
RUDOLPH. Oh, now for my detective's report.
(*Opens letter.*) What's this! Another conspiracy!
A conspiracy to depose *me!* And my private detective was so convulsed with laughter at the notion of a conspirator selecting him for a confidant
that he was physically unable to arrest the malefac-
tor! Why, it'll come off! This comes of engaging a
detective with a keen sense of the ridiculous! For
the future I'll employ none but Scotchmen. And
the plot is to explode to-morrow! My wedding
day! Oh, Caroline, Caroline! (*Weeps.*) This is
perfectly frightful! What's to be done? I don't
know! I ought to keep cool and think, but you
can't think when your veins are full of hot soda
water, and your brain's fizzing like a firework, and
all your faculties are jumbled in a perfect whirlpool of tumblication! And I'm going to be ill! I
know I am! I've been living too low, and I'm going to be very ill indeed!

SONG — RUDOLPH.

When you find you're a broken-down critter,
Who is all of a trimmle and twitter,
With your palate unpleasantly bitter,
As if you'd just eaten a pill—
When your legs are as thin as dividers,
And you're plagued with unruly insiders,
And your spine is all creepy with spiders,
And you're highly gamboge in the gill—
When you've got a beehive in your head,
And a sewing machine in each ear,
And you feel that you've eaten your bed,
And you've got a bad headache *down here*—
When such facts are about,
And these symptoms you find
In your body or crown—
Well, you'd better look out,
You may make up your mind
You had better lie down!

When your lips are all smeary—like tallow,
And your tongue is decidedly yellow,
With a pint of warm oil in your sw*a*llow,
And a pound of tin-tacks in your chest—
When you're down in the mouth with the
vapours,
And all over your new Morris papers
Black-beetles are cutting their capers,
And crawly things never at rest—
When you doubt if your head is your own,
And you jump when an open door slams—
Then you've got to a state which is known
To the medical world as "jim-jams."
If such symptoms you find
In your body or head,
They're not easy to quell—
You may make up your mind
You are better in bed,
For you're not at all well!
(*Sinks exhausted and weeping at foot of well.*)

Enter LUDWIG.

LUDWIG. Now for my confession and full pardon. They told me the Grand Duke was dancing duets in the Market Place, but I don't see him. (*Sees* RUDOLPH.) Hallo! Who's this? (*Aside.*) Why, it *is* the Grand Duke!

RUDOLPH (*sobbing*). Who are you, sir, who presume to address me in person? If you've anything to communicate, you must fling yourself at the feet of my Acting Temporary Sub-Deputy Assistant Vice-Chamberlain, who will fling himself at the feet of his immediate superior, and so on, with successive foot-flingings through the various grades—your communication will, in course of time, come to my august knowledge.

LUDWIG. But when I inform your Highness that in me you see the most unhappy, the most unfortunate, the most completely miserable man in your whole dominion—

RUDOLPH (*still sobbing*). *You* the most miserable man in my whole dominion? How can you have the face to stand there and say such a thing? Why, look at me! Look at me! (*Bursts into tears.*)

LUDWIG. Well, I wouldn't be a cry-baby.

RUDOLPH. A cry-baby? If you had just been told that you were going to be deposed to-morrow, and perhaps blown up with dynamite for all I know, wouldn't *you* be a cry-baby? I do declare, if I could only hit upon some cheap and painless method of putting an end to an existence which has become insupportable, I would unhesitatingly adopt it!

LUDWIG. You would? (*Aside.*) I see a magnificent way out of this! By Jupiter, I'll try it! (*Aloud.*) Are you, by any chance, in earnest?

RUDOLPH. In earnest? Why, look at me!

LUDWIG. If you are really in earnest—if you really desire to escape scot free from this impending—this unspeakably horrible catastrophe—without trouble, danger, pain, or expense—why not resort to a Statutory Duel?

RUDOLPH. A Statutory Duel?

LUDWIG. Yes. The Act is still in force, but it will expire to-morrow afternoon. You fight—you lose —you are dead for a day. To-morrow, when the Act expires, you will come to life again and resume your Grand Duchy as though nothing had happened. In the meantime, the explosion will have taken place and the survivor will have had to bear the brunt of it.

RUDOLPH. Yes, that's all very well, but who'll be fool enough to *be* the survivor?

LUDWIG (*kneeling*). Actuated by an overwhelming sense of attachment to your Grand Ducal person, I unhesitatingly offer myself as the victim of your subjects' fury.

RUDOLPH. You do? Well, really that's very hand-some. I daresay being blown up is not nearly as unpleasant as one would think.

LUDWIG. Oh, yes it is. It mixes one up, awfully!

RUDOLPH. But suppose I were to lose?

LUDWIG. Oh, that's easily arranged. (*Producing cards.*) I'll put an Ace up my sleeve—you'll put a King up yours. When the drawing takes place, I shall seem to draw the higher card and you the lower. And there you are!

RUDOLPH. Oh, but that's cheating.

LUDWIG. So it is. I never thought of that (*going*).

RUDOLPH (*hastily*). Not that I mind. But I say —you won't take an unfair advantage of your day of office? You won't go tipping people, or squandering my little savings in fireworks, or any nonsense of that sort?

LUDWIG. I am hurt—really hurt—by the suggestion.

RUDOLPH. You—you wouldn't like to put down a deposit, perhaps?

LUDWIG. No. I don't think I should like to put down a deposit.

RUDOLPH. Or give a guarantee?

LUDWIG. A guarantee would be equally open to objection.

RUDOLPH. It would be more regular. Very well, I suppose you must have your own way.

LUDWIG. Good. I say—we must have a devil of a quarrel!

RUDOLPH. Oh, a devil of a quarrel!

LUDWIG. Just to give colour to the thing. Shall I give you a sound thrashing before all the people? Say the word—it's no trouble.

RUDOLPH. No, I think not, though it would be very convincing and it's extremely good and thoughtful of you to suggest it. Still, a devil of a quarrel!

LUDWIG. Oh, a devil of a quarrel!

RUDOLPH. No half-measures. Big words—strong language—rude remarks. Oh, a devil of a quarrel!

LUDWIG. Now the question is, how shall we summon the people?

RUDOLPH. Oh, there's no difficulty about that. Bless your heart, they've been staring at us through those windows for the last half hour!

FINALE.

RUDOLPH. Come hither, all you people—
　　When you hear the fearful news,
　All the pretty women weep'll,
　　Men will shiver in their shoes.

LUDWIG. And they'll all cry "Lord, defend us!"
　　When they learn the fact tremendous
　　That to give this man his gruel

In a Statutory Duel—

BOTH.   This plebeian man of shoddy—
  This contemptible nobody—
    Your Grand Duke does not refuse!

*During this, Chorus of men and women have en-
tered, all trembling with apprehension under the
impression that they are to be arrested for their
complicity in the conspiracy.*

CHORUS.

With faltering feet,
    And our muscles in a quiver,
Our fate we meet
    With our feelings all unstrung!
If our plot complete
    He has managed to diskiver,
There is no retreat—
    We shall certainly be hung!

RUDOLPH (*aside to* LUDWIG).
  Now *you* begin and pitch it strong—walk into
  me abusively—

LUDWIG (*aside to* RUDOLPH).
  I've several epithets that I've reserved for you
  exclusively.
  A choice selection I have here when you are
  ready *to* begin.

RUDOLPH.   Now *you* begin—
LUDWIG.   No, *you* begin—
RUDOLPH.   No, *you* begin—
LUDWIG.   No, *you* begin!
CHORUS (*trembling*).   Has it happed as we ex-
    pected?
  Is our little plot detected?

DUET — RUDOLPH *and* LUDWIG.

RUDOLPH (*furiously*).
  Big bombs, small bombs, great guns and little
    ones!
    Put him in a pillory!
    Rack him with artillery!
LUDWIG (*furiously*).
  Long swords, short swords, tough swords and
    brittle ones!
    Fright him into fits!
    Blow him into bits!
RUDOLPH.   You muff, sir!
      You lout, sir!
LUDWIG.   Enough, sir!
      Get out, sir!   (*Pushes him.*)
RUDOLPH.   A hit, sir?
      Take that, sir!   (*Slaps him.*)
LUDWIG (*slapping* RUDOLPH).
    It's tit, sir,
    For tat, sir!

CHORUS (*appalled*).   When two doughty heroes
    thunder,
  All the world is lost in wonder;
    When such men their temper lose,
    Awful are the words they use!

LUDWIG.   Tall snobs, small snobs, rich snobs
    and needy ones!
RUDOLPH (*jostling him*).
      Whom are you alluding to?
LUDWIG (*jostling him*).
      Where are you intruding to?
RUDOLPH.   Fat snobs, thin snobs, swell snobs and
    seedy ones!
LUDWIG.   I rather think you err.
    To whom do you refer?
RUDOLPH.   To you, sir!
LUDWIG.   To me, sir?
RUDOLPH.   I do, sir!
LUDWIG.   We'll see, sir!
RUDOLPH.   I jeer, sir!
    (*Makes a face at* LUDWIG.)   Grimace, sir!
LUDWIG.   Look here, sir—
    (*Makes a face at* RUDOLPH.)   A face, sir!

CHORUS (*appalled*).   When two heroes, once pa-
    cific,
  Quarrel, the effect's terrific!
    What a horrible grimace!
    What a paralysing face!

ALL.   Big bombs, small bombs, &c.

LUDWIG *and* RUDOLPH (*recit.*).   He has insulted
    me, and, in a breath,
  This day we fight a duel to the death!
NOTARY (*checking them*).   You mean, of course,
    by duel (*verbum sat.*),
  A Statutory Duel.
ALL.   Why, what's that?
NOTARY.   According to established legal uses,
  A card apiece each bold disputant chooses—
  Dead as a doornail is the dog who loses—
  The winner steps into the dead man's shoeses!
ALL.   The winner steps into the dead man's
    shoeses!
RUDOLPH *and* LUDWIG.   Agreed! Agreed!
RUDOLPH.   Come, come—the pack!
NOTARY (*producing one*).   Behold it here!
RUDOLPH.   I'm on the rack!
LUDWIG.   I quake with fear!
    (NOTARY *offers card to* LUDWIG.)
LUDWIG.   First draw to you!
RUDOLPH.   If that's the case,
  Behold the King! (*Drawing card from
      his sleeve.*)

LUDWIG (*same business*).   Behold the Ace!

CHORUS.   Hurrah, hurrah! Our Ludwig's won,
And wicked Rudolph's course is run—
So Ludwig will as Grand Duke reign
Till Rudolph comes to life again—

RUDOLPH.   Which will occur to-morrow!
I come to life to-morrow!

GRETCHEN (*with mocking curtsey*).
My Lord Grand Duke, farewell!
A pleasant journey, very,
To your convenient cell
In yonder cemetery!

LISA (*curtseying*).   Though malcontents abuse
you,
We're much distressed to lose you!
You were, when you were living,
So liberal, so forgiving!

BERTHA.   So merciful, so gentle!
So highly ornamental!

OLGA.   And now that you've departed,
You leave us broken-hearted!

ALL (*pretending to weep*).   Yes, truly, truly,
truly, truly—
Truly broken-hearted!
Ha! ha! ha! ha! ha! ha! (*Mocking him.*)

RUDOLPH (*furious*).   Rapscallions, in penitential
fires,
You'll rue the ribaldry that from you falls!
To-morrow afternoon the law expires,
And then—look out for squalls!
(*Exit* RUDOLPH, *amid general ridicule.*)

CHORUS.   Give thanks, give thanks to wayward
fate—
By mystic fortune's sway,
Our Ludwig guides the helm of State
For one delightful day!

(*To* LUDWIG.)   We hail you, sir!
We greet you, sir!
Regale you, sir!
We treat you, sir!
Our ruler be
By fate's decree
For one delightful day!

NOTARY.   You've done it neatly! Pity that your
powers
Are limited to four-and-twenty hours!

LUDWIG.   No matter, though the time will quickly
run,
In hours twenty-four much may be done!

SONG — LUDWIG.

Oh, a monarch who boasts intellectual graces
Can do, if he likes, a good deal in a day—
He can put all his friends in conspicuous places,
With plenty to eat and with nothing to pay!
You'll tell me, no doubt, with unpleasant grim-
aces,
To-morrow, deprived of your ribbons and laces,
You'll get your dismissal—with very long
faces—
But wait! on that topic I've something to say!
(*Dancing.*)   I've something to say—I've some-
thing to say—I've something to
say!
Oh, our rule shall be merry—I'm not an
ascetic—
And while the sun shines we will get up
our hay—
By a pushing young Monarch, of turn en-
ergetic,
A very great deal may be done in a day!

CHORUS.   Oh, his rule will be merry, &c.

(*During this,* LUDWIG *whispers to* NOTARY,
who writes.)

For instance, this measure (his ancestor drew
it),   (*Alluding to* NOTARY.)
This law against duels—to-morrow will die—
The Duke will revive, and you'll certainly rue
it—
He'll give you "what for" and he'll let you
know why!
But in twenty-four hours there's time to renew
it—
With a century's life I've the right to imbue it—
It's easy to do—and, by Jingo, I'll do it!
(*Signing paper, which* NOTARY *presents.*)
It's done! Till I perish your Monarch am I!
Your Monarch am I—your Monarch am I—
your Monarch am I!
Though I do not pretend to be very
prophetic,
I fancy I know what you're going to
say—
By a pushing young Monarch, of turn
energetic,
A very great deal may be done in a day!

ALL (*astonished*).   Oh, it's simply uncanny, his
power prophetic—
It's perfectly right—we *were* going to
say.
By a pushing, &c.

Enter JULIA, *at back.*

LUDWIG (*recit.*).   This very afternoon—at two
(about)—
The Court appointments will be given out.
To each and all (for that was the condition)
According to professional position!

ALL.   Hurrah!

JULIA (*coming forward*). According to professional position?

LUDWIG.   According to professional position!

ALL.   Then, horror!

JULIA.   Why, what's the matter? What's the matter? What's the matter?

SONG — JULIA (LISA *clinging to her*).

Ah, pity me, my comrades true,
Who love, as well I know you do,
This gentle child,
To me so fondly dear!

ALL.   Why, what's the matter?

JULIA.   Our sister-love so true and deep
From many an eye unused to weep
Hath oft beguiled
The coy, reluctant tear!

ALL.   Why, what's the matter?

JULIA.   Each sympathetic heart 'twill bruise
When you have learnt the frightful news
(Oh, will it not?)
That I must now impart!

ALL.   Why, what's the matter?

JULIA.   Her love for him is all in all!
Ah, cursed fate! that it should fall
Unto *my* lot
To break my darling's heart!

ALL.   Oh, *that's* the matter!

LUDWIG.   What means our Julia by those fateful looks?
Please do not keep us all on tenter-hooks—
Now, what's the matter?

JULIA.   Our duty, if we're wise,
We never shun.
This Spartan rule applies
To every one.
In theatres, as in life,
Each has her line—
This part—the Grand Duke's wife
(Oh agony!) is mine!
A maxim new I do not start—
The canons of dramatic art
Decree that this repulsive part
(The Grand Duke's wife)
Is mine!

LISA (*appalled, to* LUDWIG). Can that be so?

LUDWIG.   I do not know—
But time will show
If that be so.

CHORUS.   Can that be so? &c.

LISA (*recit.*).   Be merciful!

DUET — LISA *and* JULIA.

LISA.   Oh, listen to me, dear—
I love him only, darling!
Remember, oh, my pet,
On him my heart is set!
This kindness do me, dear—
Nor leave me lonely, darling!
Be merciful, my pet,
Our love do not forget!

JULIA.   Now don't be foolish, dear—
You couldn't play it, darling!
It's "leading business," pet,
And you're but a soubrette.
So don't be mulish, dear—
Although I say it, darling,
It's not your line, my pet—
I play that part, you bet!
I play that part—
I play that part, you bet!
(LISA *overwhelmed with grief.*)

NOTARY.   The lady's right. Though Julia's engagement
Was for the stage meant—
It certainly frees Ludwig from his
Connubial promise.
Though marriage contracts—or whate'er you call 'em—
Are very solemn,
Dramatic contracts (which you all adore so)
Are even more so!

ALL.   That's very true!
Though marriage contracts, &c.

SONG — LISA.

The die is cast,
My hope has perished!
Farewell, O Past,
Too bright to last,
Yet fondly cherished!
My light has fled,
My hope is dead,
Its doom is spoken—
My day is night,
My wrong is right
In all men's sight—
My heart is broken! (*Exit, weeping.*)

LUDWIG (*recit.*). Poor child, where will she go? What will she do?

JULIA.   *That* isn't in your part, you know.

LUDWIG (*sighing*).   Quite true!
(*With an effort.*) Depressing topics we'll not touch upon—
Let us begin as we are going on!
For this will be a jolly Court, for little and for big!

ALL. Sing hey, the jolly jinks of Pfennig Halbpfennig!

LUDWIG. From morn to night our lives shall be
as merry as a grig!

ALL. Sing hey, the jolly jinks of Pfennig Halbpfennig!

LUDWIG. All state and ceremony we'll eternally
abolish—
We don't mean to insist upon unnecessary
polish—
And, on the whole, I rather think you'll find
our rule tollolish!

ALL. Sing hey, the jolly jinks of Pfennig Halbpfennig!

JULIA. But stay—your new-made Court
Without a courtly coat is—
We shall require
Some Court attire,
And at a moment's notice.
In clothes of common sort
Your courtiers must not grovel—
Your new *noblesse*
Must have a dress

Original and novel!

LUDWIG. Old Athens we'll exhume!
The necessary dresses,
Correct and true
And all brand-new
The company possesses:
Henceforth our Court costume
Shall live in song and story,
For we'll upraise
The dead old days
Of Athens in her glory!

ALL. Yes, let's upraise
The dead old days
Of Athens in her glory!

ALL. Agreed! Agreed!
For this will be a jolly Court for little and for
big! &c.
(*They carry* LUDWIG *round stage and deposit
him on the ironwork of well.* JULIA *stands by
him, and the rest group round them.*)

ACT DROP.

ACT II.

SCENE. — *Entrance Hall of the Grand Ducal Palace, the next morning. Enter a procession
of the members of the theatrical company* (*now dressed in the costumes of* Troilus and Cressida), *carrying garlands, playing on pipes, cithand, and cymbals, and heralding the return
of* LUDWIG *and* JULIA *from the marriage ceremony, which has just taken place.*

CHORUS.

As before you we defile,
Eloia! Eloia!
Pray you, gentles, do not smile
If we shout, in classic style,
Eloia!
Ludwig and his Julia true
Wedded are each other to—
So we sing, till all is blue,
Eloia! Eloia!
Opoponax! Eloia!

Wreaths of bay and ivy twine,
Eloia! Eloia!
Fill the bowl with Lesbian wine,
And to revelry incline—
Eloia!
For as gaily we pass on
Probably we shall, anon,
Sing a Diergeticon—
Eloia! Eloia!
Opoponax! Eloia!

RECITATIVE — LUDWIG.

Your loyalty our Ducal heartstrings touches:
Allow me to present your new Grand Duchess.
Should she offend, you'll graciously excuse
her—
And kindly recollect *I* didn't choose her!

SONG — LUDWIG.

At the outset I may mention it's my sovereign
intention
To revive the classic memories of Athens at
its best,
For the company possesses all the necessary
dresses
And a course of quiet cramming will supply
us with the rest.
We've a choir hyporchematic (that is, ballet-
operatic)
Who respond to the *choreutæ* of that cultivated age,

And our clever chorus-master, all but captious
  criticaster,
Would accept as the *choregus* of the early
  Attic stage.
This return to classic ages is considered in their
  wages,
Which are always calculated by the day or
  by the week—
And I'll pay 'em (if they'll back me) all in
  oboloi and *drachmæ*,
Which they'll get (if they prefer it) at the
  Kalends that are Greek!

(*Confidentially to audience.*)

    At this juncture I may mention
      That this erudition sham
    Is but classical pretension,
      The result of steady "cram":
    Periphrastic methods spurning,
    To this audience discerning
    I admit this show of learning
      Is the fruit of steady "cram"!

CHORUS. Periphrastic methods, &c.

In the period Socratic every dining-room was
  Attic
  (Which suggests an architecture of a topsy-
  turvy kind),
There they'd satisfy their thirst on a *recherché*
  cold ἄριστον,
Which is what they called their lunch—and
  so may you, if you're inclined.
As they gradually got on, they'd τρέπεσθαι πρὸς
  τὸν πότον
  (Which is Attic for a steady and a conscien-
  tious drink).
But they mixed their wine with water—which
  I'm sure they didn't oughter—
And we modern Saxons know a trick worth
  two of that, I think!
Then came rather risky dances (under certain
  circumstances)
  Which would shock that worthy gentleman,
  the Licenser of Plays,
Corybantian mani*ac* kick—Dionysiac or Bac-
  chic—
And the Dithryambic revels of those undec-
  orous days.

(*Confidentially to audience.*)

    And perhaps I'd better mention,
      Lest alarming you I am,
    That it isn't our intention
      To perform a Dithyramb—
    It displays a lot of stocking,
    Which is always very shocking,
    And of course I'm only mocking
      At the prevalence of "cram."

CHORUS. It displays a lot, &c.

Yes, on reconsideration, there are customs of
  that nation
  Which are not in strict accordance with the
  habits of our day,
And when I come to codify, their rules I mean
  to modify,
  Or Mrs. Grundy, p'r'aps, may have a word
  or two to say.
For they hadn't macintoshes or umbrellas or
  goloshes—
  And a shower with their dresses must have
  played the very deuce,
And it must have been unpleasing when they
  caught a fit of sneezing,
  For, it seems, of pocket-handkerchiefs they
  didn't know the use.
They wore little underclothing—scarcely anything—or no-thing—
  And their dress of Coan silk was quite transparent in design—
Well, in fact, in summer weather, something
  like the "altogether."
And it's *there,* I rather fancy, I shall have to
  draw the line!

(*Confidentially to audience.*)

    And again I wish to mention
      That this erudition sham
    Is but classical pretension,
      The result of steady "cram."
    Yet my classic love aggressive
    (If you'll pardon the possessive)
    Is exceedingly impressive
      When you're passing an exam.

CHORUS. Yet his classic love, &c.
  (*Exeunt* CHORUS. *Manent* LUDWIG, JULIA, *and*
                       LISA.)

LUDWIG (*recit.*). Yes, Ludwig and his Julia are
  mated!
For when an obscure comedian, whom the law
  backs,
  To sovereign rank is promptly elevated,
He takes it with its incidental drawbacks!
  So Julia and I are duly mated!
(LISA, *through this, has expressed intense dis-
    tress at having to surrender* LUDWIG.)

SONG — LISA.

Take care of him—he's much too good to live!
  With him you must be very gentle:
Poor fellow, he's so highly sensitive,
  And O, so sentimental!
Be sure you never let him sit up late
  In chilly open air conversing—
Poor darling, he's extremely delicate,
  And wants a deal of nursing!

LUDWIG. I want a deal of nursing!

LISA. And O, remember this—
    When he is cross with pain,
    A flower and a kiss—
    A simple flower—a tender kiss
    Will bring him round again!

His moods you must assiduously watch:
    When he succumbs to sorrow tragic,
Some hardbake or a bit of butter-scotch
    Will work on him like magic.
To contradict a character so rich
    In trusting love were simple blindness—
He's one of those exalted natures which
    Will only yield to kindness!

LUDWIG. I only yield to kindness!

LISA. And O, the bygone bliss!
    And O, the present pain!
    That flower and that kiss—
    That simple flower—that tender kiss
    I ne'er shall give again!
                (*Exit, weeping.*)

JULIA. And now that everybody has gone, and we're happily and comfortably married, I want to have a few words with my new-born husband.

LUDWIG (*aside*). Yes, I expect you'll often have a few words with your new-born husband! (*Aloud.*) Well, what is it?

JULIA. Why, I've been thinking that as you and I have to play our parts for life, it is most essential that we should come to a definite understanding as to how they shall be rendered. Now, I've been considering how I can make the most of the Grand Duchess.

LUDWIG. Have you? Well, if you'll take my advice, you'll make a very fine part of it.

JULIA. Why, that's quite *my* idea.

LUDWIG. I shouldn't make it one of your hoity-toity vixenish viragos.

JULIA. You think not?

LUDWIG. Oh, I'm quite clear about that. I should make her a tender, gentle, submissive, affectionate (but not too affectionate) child-wife—timidly anxious to coil herself into her husband's heart, but kept in check by an awestruck reverence for his exalted intellectual qualities and his majestic personal appearance.

JULIA. Oh, that is your idea of a good part?

LUDWIG. Yes—a wife who regards her husband's slightest wish as an inflexible law, and who ventures but rarely into his august presence, unless (which would happen seldom) he should summon her to appear before him. A crushed, despairing violet, whose blighted existence would culminate (all too soon) in a lonely and pathetic death-scene! A fine part, my dear.

JULIA. Yes. There's a good deal to be said for your view of it. Now there are some actresses whom it would fit like a glove.

LUDWIG (*aside*). I wish I'd married one of 'em!

JULIA. But, you see I *must* consider my temperament. For instance, my temperament would demand some strong scenes of justifiable jealousy.

LUDWIG. Oh, there's no difficulty about that. You shall have *them*.

JULIA. With a lovely but detested rival—

LUDWIG. Oh, *I'll* provide the rival.

JULIA. Whom I should stab—stab—stab!

LUDWIG. Oh, I wouldn't stab her. It's been done to death. I should treat her with a silent and contemptuous disdain, and delicately withdraw from a position which, to one of your sensitive nature, would be absolutely untenable. Dear me, I can see you delicately withdrawing, up centre and off!

JULIA. *Can* you?

LUDWIG. Yes. It's a fine situation—and in your hands, full of quiet pathos!

DUET — LUDWIG *and* JULIA.

LUDWIG. Now Julia, come,
    Consider it from
        This dainty point of view—
    A timid tender
    Feminine gender,
        Prompt to coyly coo—
    Yet silence seeking
    Seldom speaking
        Till she's spoken to—
    A comfy, cosy,
    Rosy-posy
        Innocent *ingenoo!*
        The part you're suited to—
        (To give the deuce her due)
        A sweet (O, jiminy!)

Miminy-piminy
Innocent inge*noo!*

ENSEMBLE.

LUDWIG.	JULIA.
The part you're suited to—	I'm much obliged to you,
(To give the deuce her due)	I don't think that would do—
A sweet (O, jiminy!)	To play (O, jiminy!)
Miminy-piminy,	Miminy-piminy,
Innocent inge*noo!*	Innocent inge*noo!*

JULIA. You forgot my special magic
      (In a high dramatic sense)
Lies in situations tragic—
      Undeniably intense.
As I've justified promotion
      In the histrionic art,
I'll submit to you my notion
      Of a first-rate part.

LUDWIG. Well, let us see your notion
      Of a first-rate part.

JULIA (*dramatically*).
    I have a rival! Frenzy-thrilled,
      I find you both together!
My heart stands still—with horror chilled—
      Hard as the millstone nether!
Then softly, slyly, snaily, snaky—
Crawly, creepy, quaily, quaky—
      I track her on her homeward way,
      As panther tracks her fated prey!

(*Furiously.*) I fly at her soft white throat—
      The lily-white laughing leman!
On her agonized gaze I gloat
      With the glee of a dancing demon!
My rival she—I have no doubt of her—
So I hold on—till the breath is out of her!
      —till the breath is out of her!

And then—Remorse! Remorse!
O cold unpleasant corse,
      Avaunt! Avaunt!
That lifeless form
      I gaze upon—
That face, still warm
      But weirdly wan—
Those eyes of glass
      I contemplate—
And then, alas,
      Too late—too late!
I find she is—your Aunt!

(*Shuddering.*) Remorse! Remorse!
Then, mad—mad—mad!
      With fancies wild—chimerical—
Now sorrowful—silent—sad—

Now, hullaballoo hysterical!
      Ha! ha! ha! ha!
But whether I'm sad or whether I'm glad,
Mad! mad! mad! mad!

This calls for the resources of a high-class art,
    And satisfies my notion of a first-rate part!
      (*Exit* JULIA.)

Enter all the Chorus, hurriedly, and in great excitement.

CHORUS.

Your Highness, there's a party at the door—
    Your Highness, at the door there is a party—
      She says that we expect her,
      But we do not recollect her,
For we never saw her countenance before!

With rage and indignation she is rife,
    Because our welcome wasn't very hearty—
      She's as sulky as a super,
      And she's swearing like a trooper,
O, you never heard such language in your life!

Enter BARONESS VON KRAKENFELDT, *in a fury.*

BARONESS. With fury indescribable I burn!
    With rage I'm nearly ready to explode!
There'll be grief and tribulation when I learn
    To whom this slight unbearable is owed!
For whatever may be due I'll pay it double—
There'll be terror indescribable and trouble!
    With a hurly-burly and a hubble-bubble
I'll pay you for this pretty episode!

ALL. Oh, whatever may be due she'll pay it double!—
    It's very good of her to take the trouble—
    But we don't know what she means by "hubble-bubble"—
No doubt it's an expression *à la mode.*

BARONESS (*to* LUDWIG).
    Do you know who I am?

LUDWIG (*examining her*). I don't;
    Your countenance I can't fix, my dear.

BARONESS. This proves I'm not a sham.
    (*Showing pocket-handkerchief.*)

LUDWIG (*examining it*). It won't:
    It only says "Krakenfeldt, Six," my dear.

BARONESS. Express your grief profound!

LUDWIG. I sha'n't!
    This tone I never allow, my love.

BARONESS. Rudolph at once produce!

LUDWIG. I can't;
    He isn't at home just now, my love.

BARONESS (*astonished*). He isn't at home just now!

ALL. He isn't at home just now,
  (*Dancing derisively.*) He has an appointment particular, very—
    You'll find him, I think, in the town cemetery;
    And that's how we come to be making so merry,
    For he isn't at home just now!

BARONESS. But bless my heart and soul alive, it's impudence personified!
  I've come here to be matrimonially matrimonified!

LUDWIG. For any disappointment I am sorry unaffectedly,
  But yesterday that nobleman expired quite unexpectedly—

ALL (*sobbing*). Tol the riddle lol!
    Tol the riddle lol!
  Tol the riddle, lol the riddle, lol lol lay!
    (*Then laughing wildly.*) Tol the riddle, lol the riddle, lol lol lay!

BARONESS. But this is most unexpected. He was well enough at a quarter to twelve yesterday.

LUDWIG. Yes. He died at half-past eleven.

BARONESS. Bless me, how very sudden!

LUDWIG. It *was* sudden.

BARONESS. But what in the world am I to do? I was to have been married to him to-day!

ALL (*singing and dancing*). For any disappointment we are sorry unaffectedly,
  But yesterday that nobleman expired quite unexpectedly—
    Tol the riddle lol!

BARONESS. Is this Court Mourning or a Fancy Ball?

LUDWIG. Well, it's a delicate combination of both effects. It is intended to express inconsolable grief for the decease of the late Duke and ebullient joy at the accession of his successor. *I* am his successor. Permit me to present you to my Grand Duchess. (*Indicating* JULIA.)

BARONESS. Your Grand Duchess? Oh, your Highness! (*Curtseying profoundly.*)

JULIA (*sneering at her*). Old frump!

BARONESS. Humph! A recent creation, probably?

LUDWIG. We were married only half-an-hour ago.

BARONESS. Exactly. I thought she seemed new to the position.

JULIA. Ma'am, I don't know who you are, but I flatter myself I can do justice to *any* part on the very shortest notice.

BARONESS. My dear, under the circumstances you are doing admirably—and you'll improve with practice. It's so difficult to be a lady when one isn't born to it.

JULIA (*in a rage, to* LUDWIG). Am I to stand this? Am I not to be allowed to pull her to pieces?

LUDWIG (*aside to* JULIA). No, no—it isn't Greek. Be a violet, I beg.

BARONESS. And now tell me all about this distressing circumstance. How did the Grand Duke die?

LUDWIG. He perished nobly—in a Statutory Duel.

BARONESS. In a Statutory Duel? But that's only a civil death!—and the Act expires to-night, and then he will come to life again!

LUDWIG. Well, no. Anxious to inaugurate my reign by conferring some inestimable boon on my people, I signalized this occasion by reviving the law for another hundred years.

BARONESS. For another hundred years! Am I to understand that you, having taken upon yourself all Rudolph's responsibilities, will occupy the Grand Ducal throne for the ensuing century?

LUDWIG. If I should live so long.

BARONESS. Set the merry joy-bells ringing! Let festive epithalamia resound through these ancient halls! Cut the satisfying sandwich—broach the exhilarating Marsala—and let us rejoice to-day, if we never rejoice again!

LUDWIG. But I don't think I quite understand. We have already rejoiced a good deal.

BARONESS. Happy man, you little reck of the extent of the good things you are in for. When you killed Rudolph you adopted all his overwhelming responsibilities. Know then that I, Caroline von Krakenfeldt, am the most overwhelming of them all!

LUDWIG. But stop, stop—I've just been married to somebody else!

JULIA. Yes, ma'am, to somebody else, ma'am! Do you understand, ma'am? To somebody else!

BARONESS. Do keep this young woman quiet; she fidgets me!

JULIA. Fidgets you!

LUDWIG (*aside to* JULIA). Be a violet—a crushed, despairing violet!

JULIA. Do you suppose I intend to give up a magnificent part without a struggle?

LUDWIG. My good girl, she has the law on her side. Let us both bear this calamity with resignation. If you must struggle, go away and struggle in the seclusion of your chamber.

CHORUS.

Now away to the wedding we go,
    So summon the charioteers—
No kind of reluctance they show
    To embark on their married careers.
Though Julia's emotion may flow
    For the rest of her maidenly years,
To the wedding we eagerly go,
    So summon the charioteers!

Now away, &c.
(*All dance off to wedding except* JULIA.)

RECITATIVE — JULIA.

So ends my dream—so fades my vision fair!
Of hope no gleam—distraction and despair!
My cherished dreams, the Ducal throne to
    share,
That aim supreme has vanished into air!

SONG — JULIA.

Broken every promise plighted—
    All is darksome—all is dreary.
Every new-born hope is blighted!
    Sad and sorry—weak and weary!
Death the Friend or Death the Foe,
Shall I call upon thee? No!
I will go on living, though
    Sad and sorry—weak and weary!

No, no! Let the bygone go by!
    No good ever came of repining:
If to-day there are clouds o'er the sky,
    To-morrow the sun may be shining!
      To-morrow, be kind,
      To-morrow, to me!
      With loyalty blind
      I curtsey to thee!
To-day is a day of illusion and sorrow,
So *viva* To-morrow, To-morrow, To-mor-
    row!
    God save you, To-morrow!
    Your servant, To-morrow!
God save you, To-morrow, Tomorrow,
    To-morrow!   (*Exit* JULIA.)

Enter ERNEST.

ERNEST. It's of no use—I can't wait any longer. At any risk I must gratify my urgent desire to know what is going on. (*Looking off.*) Why, what's that? Surely I see a wedding procession winding down the hill, dressed in my *Troilus and Cressida* costumes! That's Ludwig's doing! I see how it is—he found the time hang heavy on his hands, and is amusing himself by getting married to Lisa. No—it can't be to Lisa, for here she is!

Enter LISA.

LISA (*not seeing him*). I really cannot stand seeing my Ludwig married twice in one day to somebody else!

ERNEST. Lisa!   (LISA *sees him, and stands as if transfixed with horror.*)

ERNEST. Come here—don't be a little fool—I want you.   (LISA *suddenly turns and bolts off.*)

ERNEST. Why, what's the matter with the little donkey? One would think she saw a ghost! But if he's not marrying Lisa, whom *is* he marrying? (*Suddenly.*) Julia! (*Much overcome.*) I see it all! The scoundrel! He had to adopt all my responsibilities, and he's shabbily taken advantage of the situation to marry the girl I'm engaged to! But no, it can't be Julia, for here *she* is!

Enter JULIA.

JULIA (*not seeing him*). I've made up my mind. I won't stand it! I'll send in my notice at once!

ERNEST. Julia! Oh, what a relief!
    (JULIA *gazes at him as if transfixed.*)

ERNEST. Then you've not married Ludwig? You are still true to me?

    (JULIA *turns and bolts in grotesque horror.*
    ERNEST *follows and stops her.*)

ERNEST. Don't run away! Listen to me. Are you all crazy?

JULIA (*in affected terror*). What would you with me, spectre? Oh, ain't his eyes sepulchral! And ain't his voice hollow! What are you doing out of your tomb at this time of day—apparition?

ERNEST. I do wish I could make you girls understand that I'm only technically dead, and that physically I'm as much alive as ever I was in my life!

JULIA. Oh, but it's an awful thing to be haunted by a technical bogie!

ERNEST. You won't be haunted much longer. The law must be on its last legs, and in a few hours I shall come to life again—resume all my social and civil functions, and claim my darling as my blushing bride!

JULIA. Oh—then you haven't heard?

ERNEST. My love, I've heard nothing. How could I? There are no daily papers where I come from.

JULIA. Why, Ludwig challenged Rudolph and won, and now *he's* Grand Duke, and he's revived the law for another century!

ERNEST. What! But you're not serious—you're only joking!

JULIA. My good sir, I'm a light-hearted girl, but I don't chaff bogies.

ERNEST. Well, that's the meanest dodge I ever heard of!

JULIA. Shabby trick, *I* call it.

ERNEST. But you don't mean to say that you're going to cry off!

JULIA. I really can't afford to wait until your time is up. You know, I've always set my face against long engagements.

ERNEST. Then defy the law and marry me now. We will fly to your native country, and I'll play broken-English in London as you play broken-German here!

JULIA. No. These legal technicalities cannot be defied. Situated as you are, you have no power to make me your wife. At best you could only make me your widow.

ERNEST. Then be my widow—my little, dainty, winning, winsome widow!

JULIA. Now what would be the good of that? Why, you goose. I should marry again within a month!

DUET — ERNEST and JULIA.

ERNEST.   If the light of love's lingering ember
        Has faded in gloom,
  You cannot neglect, O remember,
        A voice from the tomb!
  That stern supernatural diction
  Should act as a solemn restriction,
  Although by a mere legal fiction
        A voice from the tomb!

JULIA (in affected terror).
  I own that that utterance chills me—
        It withers my bloom!
  With awful emotion it thrills me—
        That voice from the tomb!
  Oh, spectre, won't anything lay thee?
  Though pained to deny or gainsay thee,
  In this case I cannot obey thee,
        Thou voice from the tomb!

  (Dancing). So, spectre appalling,
        I bid you good-day—
  Perhaps you'll be calling
        When passing this way.
  Your bogeydom scorning,
  And all your love-lorning,
  I bid you good-morning,
        I bid you good-day.

ERNEST (furious).   My offer recalling,
        Your words I obey—
  Your fate is appalling,
        And full of dismay.
  To pay for this scorning
  I give you fair warning
  I'll haunt you each morning,
        Each night, and each day!

(Repeat Ensemble, and exeunt in opposite directions.)

Re-enter the Wedding Procession of LUDWIG and BARONESS, dancing.

CHORUS.

Now bridegroom and bride let us toast
  In a magnum of merry champagne—
Let us make of this moment the most,
  We may not be so lucky again.
So drink to our sovereign host
  And his highly intelligent reign—
His health and his bride's let us toast
  In a magnum of merry champagne!

BRINDISI — BARONESS.

Come, bumpers—aye, ever-so-many—
  And then, if you will, many more!
This wine doesn't cost us a penny,
  Though it's Pomméry, Seventy-four!
Old wine is a true panacea
  For every conceivable ill,
When you cherish the soothing idea
  That somebody else pays the bill!
Old wine is a pleasure that's hollow
  When at your own table you sit,
For you're thinking each mouthful you swallow
  Has cost you a threepenny bit!

CHORUS.   So bumpers—aye, ever-so-many—
    And then, if you will, many more!
  This wine doesn't cost us a penny,
    Though it's Pomméry, Seventy-four!

I once gave an evening party
  (A sandwich and cut-orange ball)
But my guests had such appetites hearty,
  That I couldn't enjoy it at all!
I made a heroic endeavour
  To look unconcerned, but in vain,
And I vowed that I never—oh never—
  Would ask anybody again!
But there's a distinction decided—
  A difference truly immense—
When the wine that you drink is provided
  At somebody else's expense.

CHORUS.   So bumpers—aye, ever-so-many—
    The cost we may safely ignore!
  For the wine doesn't cost us a penny,
    Though it's Pomméry, Seventy-four!
      (Exit BARONESS. March heard.)

LUDWIG (recit.).   Why, who is this approaching,
    Upon our joy encroaching?
    Some rascal come a-poaching
    Who's heard that wine we're broaching?

ALL.   Who may this be?
        Who may this be?
    Who is he? Who is he? Who is he?

Enter HERALD.

HERALD.　The Prince of Monte Car*lo*,
　　　From Mediterranean water,
　　Has come here to bestow
　　　On you his beautiful daughter.
　　They've paid off all they owe,
　　　As every statesman ought*er*—
　　That Prince of Monte Car*lo*
　　　And his be-*eau*tiful daughter!

CHORUS.　The Prince of Monte Car*lo*, &c.

HERALD.　The Prince of Monte Car*lo*,
　　　Who is so very partick*lar*,
　　Has heard that you're also
　　　For ceremony a stick*ler*—
　　Therefore he lets you know
　　　By word of mouth auric'*lar*—
　　(That Prince of Monte Car*lo*
　　　Who is so very partick*lar*)—

CHORUS.　The Prince of Monte Car*lo*, &c.

HERALD.　That Prince of Monte Car*lo*,
　　　From Mediterranean water,
　　Has come here to bestow
　　　On you his be-*eau*tiful daughter!

LUDWIG (*recit.*).　His Highness we know not—
　　　　nor the locality
　　In which is situate his Principality;
　　But, as he guesses by some odd fatality,
　　This *is* the shop for cut and dried for-
　　　　mality!
　　　Let him appear—
　　　He'll find that we're
　　Remarkable for cut and dried formality.
(*Reprise of March. Exit* HERALD. LUDWIG
　　　　　　　beckons his Court.)

LUDWIG.　I have a plan—I'll tell you all the plot
　　　of it—
　　He wants formality—he shall have a lot of it!
　　　(*Whispers to them, through symphony.*)
　　Conceal yourselves, and when I give the cue,
　　Spring out on him—you all know what to do!
(*All conceal themselves behind the draperies
　　　　　　that enclose the stage.*)

Pompous March. Enter the PRINCE *and* PRINCESS
OF MONTE CARLO, *attended by six theatrical-
looking nobles and the Court Costumier.*

DUET — PRINCE *and* PRINCESS.

PRINCE.　We're rigged out in magnificent array
　　　(Our own clothes are much gloomier)
　　In costumes which we've hired by the day
　　From a very well-known costumier.

COSTUMIER (*bowing*).　*I* am the well-known cos-
　　tumier.

PRINCESS.　With a brilliant staff a Prince should
　　　make a show
　　　(It's a rule that never varies),
　　So we've engaged from the Theatre Monaco
　　Six supernumeraries.

NOBLES.　We're the supernumeraries.

ALL.　　　At a salary immense,
　　　　　Quite regardless of expense,
　　Six supernumeraries!

PRINCE.　They do not speak, for they break our
　　　grammar's laws,
　　And their language is lamentable—
　　And they never take off their gloves, because
　　Their nails are not presentable.

NOBLES.　Our nails are not presentable!

PRINCESS.　To account for their shortcomings
　　　manifest,
　　We explain, in a whisper bated,
　　They are wealthy members of the brewing in-
　　　terest,
　　To the Peerage elevated.

NOBLES.　To the Peerage elevated.

ALL.　 {They're / We're} very, very rich
　　　　　And accordingly, as sich,
　　To the Peerage elevated.

PRINCE.　Well, my dear, here we are at last—just
in time to compel Duke Rudolph to fulfil the terms
of his marriage contract. Another hour and we
should have been too late.

PRINCESS.　Yes, papa, and if you hadn't fortunately discovered a means of making an income
by honest industry, we should never have got
here at all.

PRINCE.　Very true. Confined for the last two
years within the precincts of my palace by an
obdurate bootmaker who held a warrant for my
arrest, I devoted my enforced leisure to a study
of the doctrine of chances—mainly with the view
of ascertaining whether there was the remotest
chance of my ever going out for a walk again—
and this led to the discovery of a singularly fascinating little round game which I have called
Roulette, and by which, in one sitting, I won no
less than five thousand francs! My first act was to
pay my bootmaker—my second, to engage a good
useful working set of second-hand nobles—and
my third, to hurry you off to Pfennig Halbpfennig
as fast as a *train de luxe* could carry us!

PRINCESS.　Yes, and a pretty job-lot of second-
hand nobles you've scraped together!

PRINCE (*doubtfully*).　Pretty, you think? Humph!

I don't know. I should say tol-lol, my love—only tol-lol. They are not wholly satisfactory. There is a certain air of unreality about them—they are not convincing.

COSTUMIER. But, my goot friend, vhat can you expect for eighteenpence a day!

PRINCE. Now take this Peer, for instance. What the deuce do you call *him?*

COSTUMIER. Him? Oh, he's a swell—he's the Duke of Riviera.

PRINCE. Oh, he's a Duke, is he? Well, that's no reason why he should look so confoundedly haughty. (*To Noble.*) Be affable, sir! (*Noble takes attitude of affability.*) That's better. Now (*passing to another*) here's a nobleman's coat all in holes!

COSTUMIER (*to Noble*). Vhat a careless chap you are! Vhy don't you take care of the clo's? These cost money, these do! D'ye think I stole 'em?

PRINCE. It's not the poor devil's fault—it's yours. I don't wish you to end our House of Peers, but you might at least mend them. (*Passing to another.*) Now, who's this with his moustache coming off?

COSTUMIER. Why, you're Viscount Mentone, ain't you?

NOBLE. Blest if I know. (*Turning up sword belt.*) It's wrote here—yes, Viscount Mentone.

COSTUMIER. Then vhy don't you say so? 'Old yerself up—you ain't carryin' sandwich boards now. (*Adjusts his moustache and hat—a handkerchief falls out.*)

PRINCE. And we may be permitted to hint to the Noble Viscount, in the most delicate manner imaginable, that it is not the practice among the higher nobility to carry their handkerchiefs in their hats.

NOBLE. I ain't got no pockets.

PRINCE. Then tuck it in here. (*Sticks it in his breast.*) Now, once for all, you Peers—when His Highness arrives, don't stand like sticks, but appear to take an intelligent and sympathetic interest in what is going on. You needn't say anything, but let your gestures be in accordance with the spirit of the conversation. Now take the word from me. Affability! (*Attitude.*) Submission! (*Attitude.*) Surprise! (*Attitude.*) Shame! (*Attitude.*) Grief! (*Attitude.*) Joy! (*Attitude.*) That's better! You can do it if you like!

PRINCESS. But, papa, where in the world is the Court? There is positively no one here to receive us!

PRINCE. Well, my love, you must remember that we have taken Duke Rudolph somewhat by surprise. These small German potentates are famous for their scrupulous adherence to ceremonial observances, and it may be that the etiquette of this Court demands that we should be received with a certain elaboration of processional pomp—which Rudolph may, at this moment, be preparing.

PRINCESS. I can't help feeling that he wants to get out of it. First of all you implored him to come to Monte Carlo and marry me there, and he refused on account of the expense. Then you implored him to advance us the money to enable us to go to him—and again he refused, on account of the expense. He's a miserly little wretch—that's what he is.

PRINCE. Well, I shouldn't go so far as to say that. I should rather describe him as an enthusiastic collector of coins—of the realm—and we must not be too hard upon a numismatist if he feels a certain disinclination to part with some of his really very valuable specimens. It's a pretty hobby: I've often thought I should like to collect some coins myself.

PRINCESS. Papa, I'm sure there's some one behind that curtain. I saw it move!

PRINCE. Then no doubt they are coming. Now mind, you Peers—haughty affability combined with a sense of what is due to your exalted ranks, or I'll fine you half a franc each—upon my soul I will!

Gong. The curtains fly back and the Court are discovered. They give a wild yell and rush on to the stage dancing wildly, with PRINCE, PRINCESS, and Nobles, who are taken by surprise at first, but eventually join in a reckless dance. At the end all fall down exhausted.

LUDWIG. There, what do you think of that? That's our official ceremonial for the reception of visitors of the very highest distinction.

PRINCE (*puzzled*). It's very quaint—very curious indeed. Prettily footed, too. Prettily footed.

LUDWIG. Would you like to see how we say "good-bye" to visitors of distinction? That ceremony is also performed with the foot.

PRINCE. Really, this tone—ah, but perhaps you have not completely grasped the situation?

LUDWIG. Not altogether.

PRINCE. Ah, then I'll give you a lead over. (*Significantly.*) I am the father of the Princess of Monte Carlo. Doesn't that convey any idea to the Grand Ducal mind?

LUDWIG (*stolidly*). Nothing definite.

PRINCE (*aside*). H'm—very odd! Never mind—try again! (*Aloud.*) This is the daughter of the Prince of Monte Carlo. Do you take?

LUDWIG (*still puzzled*). No—not yet. Go on—don't give it up—I daresay it will come presently.

PRINCE. Very odd—never mind—try again. (*With sly significance.*) Twenty years ago! Little doddle doddle! *Two* little doddle doddles! Happy father—hers and yours. Proud mother—yours and hers! Hah! *Now* you take? I see you do! I see you do!

LUDWIG. Nothing is more annoying than to feel that you're not equal to the intellectual pressure of the conversation. I wish he'd say something intelligible.

PRINCE. You didn't expect me?

LUDWIG (*jumping at it*). No, no. I grasp that—thank you very much. (*Shaking hands with him.*) No, I did *not* expect you!

PRINCE. I thought not. But ha! ha! at last I have escaped from my enforced restraint. (*General movement of alarm.*) (*To crowd, who are stealing off.*) No, no—you misunderstand me. I mean I've paid my debts! And how d'you think I did it? Through the medium of Roulette!

ALL. Roulette?

LUDWIG. Now you're getting obscure again. The lucid interval has expired.

PRINCE. I'll explain. It's an invention of my own —the simplest thing in the world—and what is most remarkable, it comes just in time to supply a distinct and long-felt want! I'll tell you all about it.

(*Nobles bring forward a double Roulette table, which they unfold.*)

SONG — PRINCE.

Take my advice—when deep in debt,
Set up a bank and play Roulette!
At once distrust you surely lull,
And rook the pigeon and the gull.
The bird will stake his every franc
In wild attempt to break the bank—
But you may stake your life and limb
The bank will end by breaking him!

(*All crowd round and eagerly stake gold on the board.*)

Allons, encore—
    Garçons, fillettes—
Vos louis d'or
    Vos roues d'charette!
        Holà! holà!
Mais faites vos jeux—
    Allons, la classe—
    Le temps se passe—

La banque se casse—
Rien n'va plus! Rien n'va plus! Rien
    n'va plus!
Le dix-sept noir, impair et manque!
Holà! holà! vive la banque!
For every time the board you spin,
Be sure the bank is bound to win!

CHORUS.   For every time, &c.
    (*During Chorus,* PRINCESS *and* COSTUMIER
        rake in all the stakes.)

PRINCE.   A cosmic game is this Roulette!
    The little ball's a true coquette—
    A maiden coy whom "numbers" woo—
    Whom six-and-thirty suitors sue!
    Of all complexions, too, good lack!
    For some are red and some are black,
    And some must be extremely green,
    For half of them are not nineteen!
                (*All stake again.*)

Allons, encore—
    Garçons, fillettes—
Vos louis d'or
    Vos roues d'charette!
        Holà! holà!
Mais faites vos jeux—
    Allons, la foule!
    Ça roule—ça roule
    Le temps s'écoule—
Rien n'va plus! Rien n'va plus! Rien
    n'va plus!
Le trente-cinq rouge—impair et passe!
Très bien, étudiants de la classe—
The moral's safe—when you begin
Be sure the bank is bound to win!

CHORUS.   The moral's safe, &c.
        (PRINCE *rakes in all the stakes.*)

PRINCE.   The little ball's a flirt inbred—
    She flirts with black—she flirts with red;
    From this to that she hops about
    Then back to this as if in doubt.
    To call her thoughtless were unkind—
    The child is making up her mind,
    For all the world like all the rest,
    Which *prétendant* will pay the best!

Allons, encore—
    Garçons, fillettes—
Vos louis d'or—
    Vos roues d'charette!
        Holà! holà!
    Mais faites vos jeux—
        Qui perte fit
        Au temps jadis
        Gagne aujourd'hui!
Rien n'va plus! Rien n'va plus! Rien
    n'va plus!

Tra, la, la, la! le double zéro!
Vous perdez tout, mes nobles héros—
Where'er at last the ball pops in,
Be sure the bank is bound to win!

CHORUS.   *Tra, la, la, la! le double zéro, &c.*
    (PRINCE *gathers in the stakes. Nobles fold up
        table and take it away.*)

LUDWIG.   Capital game.—Haven't a penny left!

PRINCE.   Pretty toy, isn't it? Have another turn?

LUDWIG.   Thanks, no. I should only be robbing
you.

PRINCESS (*affectionately*).   Do, dearest—it's such
fun!

BARONESS.   Why, you forward little hussy, how
dare you? (*Takes her away from* LUDWIG.)

LUDWIG.   You mustn't do that, my dear—never
in the presence of the Grand Duchess, I beg!

PRINCESS (*weeping*).   Oh, papa, he's got a Grand
Duchess!

LUDWIG.   *A* Grand Duchess! My good girl, I've
got three Grand Duchesses!

PRINCESS.   *Three* Grand Duchesses! But let us
understand each other. Am I not addressing the
Grand Duke Rudolph?

LUDWIG.   Not at all. You're addressing another-
guess sort of Grand Duke altogether.

PRINCESS.   This comes of not asking the way.
We've mistaken the turning and got into the
wrong Grand Duchy.

PRINCE.   But—let us know where we are. Who
the deuce is this gentleman?

LISA.   He's the gentleman I married yesterday—

JULIA.   He's the gentleman I married this morning—

BARONESS.   He's the gentleman I married this
afternoon—

PRINCESS.   Well, I'm sure! Papa, let's go away—
this is not a respectable Court.

PRINCE.   All these Grand Dukes have their little
fancies, my love. This Potentate appears to be collecting wives. It's a pretty hobby—I should like to
collect a few myself. This (*admiring* BARONESS)
is a charming specimen—an antique, I should say
—of the early Merovingian period, if I'm not mistaken; and here's another—a Scotch lady, I think
(*alluding to* JULIA), and (*alluding to* LISA) a little
one thrown in. Two half-quarters and a make-
weight! (*To* LUDWIG.) Have you such a thing as a
catalogue of the Museum?

PRINCESS.   But this is getting serious. If this is not
Rudolph, the question is, where in the world is he?

LUDWIG.   No—the question is, where *out* of the
world is he? And *that's* a very curious question,
too!

PRINCE *and* PRINCESS. What do you mean?

LUDWIG (*pretending to weep*). The Grand Duke Rudolph—died yesterday!

PRINCE *and* PRINCESS. What!

LUDWIG. Quite suddenly—of—of—a cardiac affection.

PRINCE *and* PRINCESS. Of a cardiac affection?

LUDWIG. Yes, a pack-of-cardiac affection. He fought a Statutory Duel with me and lost, and I took over all his engagements—including this imperfectly preserved old lady, to whom he has been engaged for the last three weeks.

PRINCESS. Three weeks! But I've been engaged to him for the last twenty years!

BARONESS, LISA, *and* JULIA. Twenty years!

PRINCE (*aside*). It's all right, my love—they can't get over that. (*Aloud.*) He's yours—take him, and hold him as tight as you can!

PRINCESS. My own! (*Embracing* LUDWIG.)

LUDWIG. Here's another!—the fourth in four-and-twenty hours! Would anybody else like to marry me? You, ma'am—or you—anybody! I'm getting used to it!

{ BARONESS. But let me tell you, ma'am—
{ JULIA. Why, you impudent little hussy—
{ LISA. Oh, here's another—here's another! (*Weeping.*)

PRINCESS. Poor ladies, I'm very sorry for you all; but, you see, I've a prior claim. Come, away we go—there's not a moment to be lost!

CHORUS (*as they dance towards exit*).

Away to the wedding we'll go
  To summon the charioteers,
Though her rival's emotion may flow
  In the form of impetuous tears—
(*At this moment* RUDOLPH, ERNEST, *and* NOTARY *appear. All kneel in astonishment.*)

RECITATIVE.
RUDOLPH, ERNEST, *and* NOTARY.

Forbear! This may not be!
  Frustrated are your plans!
With paramount decree
  The Law forbids the banns!

ALL. The Law forbids the banns!

SONG — RUDOLPH.

(*Furiously.*) Well, you're a pretty kind of fellow, thus my life to shatter, O!
My dainty bride—my bride elect—you wheedle and you flatter, O!
You fascinate her tough old heart with vain and vulgar patter, O!

And eat my food and drink my wine—especially the latter, O!

ALL.   The latter, O!
        The latter, O!
  Especially the latter, O!

RUDOLPH. But when compared with other crimes, for which your head I'll batter, O!
        This flibberty gibberty
        Kind of a liberty
    Scarcely seems to matter, O!

For O, you vulgar vagabond, you fount of idle chatter, O!
You've done a deed on which I vow you won't get any fatter, O!
You fancy you've revived the Law—mere empty brag and clatter, O!
You can't—you shan't—you don't—you won't—you thing of rag and tatter, O!

ALL.   Of tatter, O!
        Of tatter, O!
  You thing of rag and tatter, O!

RUDOLPH. For this you'll suffer agonies like rat in clutch of ratter, O!
        This flibberty gibberty
        Kind of a liberty
    's quite another matter, O!

ALL.   This flibberty gibberty
        Kind of a liberty
    's quite another matter, O!
(RUDOLPH *sinks exhausted into* NOTARY's *arms.*)

LUDWIG. My good sir, it's no use your saying that I can't revive the Law, in face of the fact that I *have* revived it.

RUDOLPH. You didn't revive it! You couldn't revive it! You—you are an impostor, sir—a tuppenny rogue, sir! You—you never were, and in all human probability never will be—Grand Duke of Pfennig Anything!

ALL. What!!!

RUDOLPH. Never—never, never! (*Aside.*) Oh, my internal economy!

LUDWIG. That's absurd, you know. I fought the Grand Duke. He drew a King, and I drew an Ace. He perished in inconceivable agonies on the spot. Now, as that's settled, we'll go on with the wedding.

RUDOLPH. It—it isn't settled. You—you can't. I —I—(*to* NOTARY). Oh, tell him—tell him! I can't!

NOTARY. Well, the fact is, there's been a little mistake here. On reference to the Act that regulates Statutory Duels, I find it is expressly laid down that Ace shall count invariably as lowest!

ALL. As lowest!

RUDOLPH (*breathlessly*). As lowest—lowest— lowest! So *you're* the ghoest—ghoest—ghoest! (*Aside.*) Oh, what *is* the matter with me inside here!

ERNEST. Well, Julia, as it seems that the Law hasn't been revived—and as, consequently, I shall come to life in about three minutes—(*consulting his watch*)—

JULIA. My objection falls to the ground. (*Resignedly.*) Very well. But will you promise to give me some strong scenes of justifiable jealousy?

ERNEST. Justifiable jealousy! My love, I couldn't do it!

JULIA. Then I won't play.

ERNEST. Well, well, I'll do my best! (*They retire up together.*)

LUDWIG. And am I to understand that, all this time, I've been a dead man without knowing it?

BARONESS. And that I married a dead man without knowing it?

PRINCESS. And that I was on the point of marrying a dead man without knowing it? (*To* RUDOLPH, *who revives.*) Oh, my love, what a narrow escape I've had!

RUDOLPH. Oh—you are the Princess of Monte Carlo, and you've turned up just in time! Well, you're an attractive little girl, you know, but you're as poor as a rat!

PRINCE. Pardon me—there you mistake. Accept her dowry—with a father's blessing! (*Gives him a small Roulette board, then flirts with* BARONESS.)

RUDOLPH. Why, what do you call this?

PRINCESS. It's my little Wheel of Fortune. I'll tell you all about it. (*They retire up, conversing.*)

LISA. That's all very well, but what is to become of *me?* (*To* LUDWIG.) If you're a dead man— (*Clock strikes three.*)

LUDWIG. But I'm not. Time's up—the Act has expired—I've come to life—the parson is still in attendance, and we'll all be married directly.

ALL. Hurrah!

FINALE.

Happy couples, lightly treading,
   Castle chapel will be quite full!
Each shall have a pretty wedding,
   As, of course, is only rightful,
   Though the bride be fair or frightful.
Contradiction little dreading,
   This will be a day delightful—
Each shall have a pretty wedding!
   Such a pretty, pretty wedding!
   Such a pretty wedding!

All dance off to get married as the

CURTAIN FALLS.

Postscript

THE COPYRIGHT NOTICE at the bottom of the front wrapper and title page of the *Grand Duke* libretto (and the corresponding notice in the vocal score) represents the only use of Sullivan's knighthood title, "Sir," in contemporary official Gilbert and Sullivan billing.

Like *Thespis,* the first opera of their collaboration, Gilbert and Sullivan's last opera never had an American performance by an authorized professional company. It has never enjoyed a revival in England, although a revival of *Utopia, Ltd.* was seriously considered by Rupert D'Oyly Carte shortly before his death. Only at this writing (1975) is there a new official production text of *The Grand Duke*—and still no commercial recording—which rather limits the usefulness of a detailed description of differences between the first and second editions. Suffice to say, in Act I there is a major cut in the Duet on pages 433–34, and Julia's song on page 438 is condensed; and in Act II the Brindisi for the Baroness and chorus is omitted (page 445), the entire Roulette Song of the Prince is cut, and Rudolph's song following the Recitative on page 450 is omitted.

A comparison of the first-night text or second-edition text with the texts of the vocal score or of the Macmillan and the Random House editions would serve no useful purpose here. There are many seemingly arbitrary agreements and disagreements. And although the vocal score appears to have been the basis for the infrequent amateur productions that form the only American audience experience with this opera, there is no consistency in this quarter. The American première of *The Grand Duke* put on by M.I.T. students in 1901 at the Hollis Theatre, Boston, as well as the Philadelphia Savoy Opera Company's production in 1938, included both the Brindisi and the Roulette Song, while the Blue Hill Troupe's offering in New York, 1937, included the Roulette Song but omitted the Brindisi. In contradistinction, both the Macmillan and Random House editions print the Brindisi but omit the Roulette Song.

The American copyright deposit copy of the *Grand Duke* libretto appears never to have been published, although a second copy exists in the Theater Collection of the Harvard College Library. As this text was deposited in the Library of Congress on March 5, 1896 (ascertained by the late Carroll Wilson), it must clearly have been the product of a draft rehearsal-copy at least two or three weeks earlier than the London first night. The way Gilbert and Sullivan worked, that was almost long enough for a complete rewrite! So it is not surprising to find in this American libretto considerable material that is not contained in any published English edition.

For example: Rudolph apparently started out as Wilhelm, and his Grand Duchy was *Hesse-Halbpfennig.* (The M.I.T. students' American first performance had used Hesse-Halbpfennig.) One can readily understand the likelihood that Gilbert and Sullivan felt this might be too close to *lèse-majesté,* as there actually was a William, grandson of George III, who became Grand Duke of Hesse-Cassel. And this Grand Duke was actually nicknamed "Halbpfennig" for his greedy financial practices. Hence the change to Rudolph and *Pfennig-*Halbpfennig.

The patter-song for Rudolph on page 434 has, of course, been likened to its more distinguished predecessor, the Lord Chancellor's "Nightmare Song" from *Iolanthe.* But for *The Grand Duke,* Gilbert drew from his file of unused or slightly-used literary efforts a song about the Jim-jams that he had written for *The Mountebanks* in collaboration with Alfred Cellier a little more than four years before. Late in the pre-production period of *The Mountebanks,* Cellier had died with the music for the second act still not completed. Specifically there were three lyrics that had not been set and so were not in the published English libretto. Apparently one of these, the song of the Jim-jams, was sent by Chappell to their New York agents as part of the text for the American libretto of *The Mountebanks.*

As he frequently borrowed from himself, it is easy to understand why Gilbert chose to include this ex-*Mountebanks* song in *The Grand Duke,* and from the foregoing history it can be deduced that in so doing he forgot (or did not know) that the song, though unpublished in England, had been published in America four years earlier. This would account for what must have been a very late substitution—some time between the middle of February and the first few days of March—of his rewritten lyric on the same theme with nearly all the same comic ideas and similar metrical structure.

The ill-fated lyric that in England was not used in two different operas, although included in the prepublication librettos of both, deserves a better fate. So it is reproduced here from the American *Mountebanks* libretto, "as performed by The Lillian Russell Opéra Comique Company, at Garden City, New York":

When your clothes, from your hat to your socks,
   Have tickled and scrubbed you all day;
When your brain is a musical box
   With a barrel that turns the wrong way;
When you find you're too big for your coat,
   And a great deal too small for your vest,
With a pint of warm oil in your throat,
   And a pound of tin-tacks in your chest;
When you've got a beehive in your head,
   And a sewing machine in each ear;
And you feel that you've eaten your bed,
   And you've got a bad headache down here;
When your lips are like underdone paste,
   And you're highly gamboge in the gill;
And your mouth has a coppery taste,
   As if you'd just bitten a pill;
    And whatever you tread,
     From a yawning abyss
      You recoil with a yell,—
   You are better in bed,
    For, depend upon this,
     You are not at all well.

When everything spins like a top
   And your stock of endurance gives out;
If some miscreant proposes a chop
   (Mutton-chop, with potatoes and stout),

When your mouth is of flannel—like mine—
   And your teeth not on terms with their stumps,
And spiders crawl over your spine,
   And your muscles have all got the mumps;
When you're bad with the creeps and the crawls,
   And the shivers, and shudders, and shakes,
And the pattern that covers the walls
   Is alive with black-beetles and snakes;
When you doubt if your head is your own,
   And you jump when an open door slams,
And you've got to a state which is known
   To the medical world as "jim-jams,"—
    If such symptoms you find
     In your body or head
      They're not easy to quell
   You may make up your mind
    That you're better in bed,
     For you're not at all well!

The original Jim-jams song and the other two unused *Mountebanks* lyrics were misleadingly included by the late Townley Searle in his collection of *Lost Bab Ballads* (Putnam, 1932), as were some verses not even authored by Gilbert, let alone Bab! The proper *Grand Duke* patter-song, "When you find you're a broken-down critter," as performed on March 7, 1896, was included by Gilbert in his 1898 edition of *The Bab Ballads and Songs of a Savoyard* under the title, "Out of Sorts."

The wonder-working triumvirate, as drawn by Alfred Bryan for the
ENTR'ACTE ANNUAL, *1894.*

Encore

THE FIRST NIGHTS OF THE FIRST REVIVALS

"ENCORE means sing-it-again!" snorted Gilbert when, in a rash moment, Rutland Barrington presumed to ask the author to write a special encore-verse to the Policemen's Song, "When the enterprising burglar's not a-burgling."

To the delectation of London theatregoers, *Trial by Jury* had been sung again, either as curtain raiser or afterpiece, on and off since its original production. But with *The Sorcerer* the Gilbert and Sullivan operas took on a rhythmic pattern that precluded for a full seven years the necessity and even the advisability of a revival. The creative energy of Gilbert and his ability to spark one "New and Original" operatic libretto after another to kindle Sullivan's amazing gift of melody, had struck a success stride.

D'Oyly Carte was far too smart to interrupt such a paying pace with an encore. A new G. & S. opera could be counted on to run for at least a year. And the pattern of experience at the Opéra Comique and later at the Savoy showed that in one year's time—"and a little bit over"— Carte could get its successor written, set to music, and in rehearsal before the bloom had worn off his previous box-office attraction. This periodicity followed from *The Sorcerer* to *Pinafore*, to *Patience*, to *Iolanthe*, and to *Princess Ida.* Between these first runs there were only brief intervals of from four to ten days for final rehearsals.

Clearly there was no occasion for the three partners to think in terms of revivals. Yet, as each new opera was met by the inevitable comparison with its predecessors, the public interest in an encore became increasingly apparent, and the business possibilities latent in London revivals increasingly propitious. Memories were mellow. The time was ripe. With hindsight one can applaud the fact that *Princess Ida*'s short first run broke the magic rhythm of new productions and allowed the first triumph of that hardiest of perennials—the Gilbert and Sullivan revival.

THE SORCERER & TRIAL BY JURY

First Revival

October 11, 1884 through March 12, 1885

150 Performances

The shorter-than-usual run of *Princess Ida* caught D'Oyly Carte and his author-composer partners without a new work. The *Observer* stated the con-

dition and its solution with a partiality that suggested press-agentry: "After a long and most prosperous run *Princess Ida* was replaced at the Savoy Theatre last night, not by the new opera which Sir Arthur Sullivan and Mr. Gilbert have in preparation [i.e., *The Mikado*], but by *The Sorcerer,* which first came before the public in 1877. If the revival was intended merely as a stopgap it will probably fail to fulfill the expectations of the management, for judging by its reception last night the piece will run as long as *Princess Ida* or *Patience* itself."

Neither *Trial by Jury* nor *The Sorcerer* had ever before been given at the Savoy. That D'Oyly Carte used good showmanship in electing to revive his first Gilbert and Sullivan successes was made clear by the same *Observer* critic: "*The Sorcerer* went last night infinitely better than it did when it was originally presented seven years ago. Its humour was more keenly enjoyed; its music seemed to be far more highly appreciated. . . . The probable causes of this attitude of the public towards a work which must be thoroughly familiar in almost all of its points . . . may be briefly defined as a species of educational advance both before and behind the footlights. The composer and author have since 1877 educated not only the performers engaged in the serious interpretation of fantastic nonsense, but the public asked to amuse itself with burlesque of the most consistent and elaborate order."

Richard Temple, Rutland Barrington, and George Grossmith were the only cast members who had created their roles in the original production, although Rosina Brandram had served as Mrs. Howard Paul's understudy for Lady Sangazure. Durward Lely was the tenor, Leonora Braham the soprano, Jessie Bond and Ada Doree respectively Constance and Mrs. Partlet. "The chorus of peasantry," commented the *Observer,* ". . . is so largely increased as to enable wholly new effects to be accomplished after the manner of grand opera, especially at the commencement of the second act."

It was, in fact, at the opening of the second act that the opera had its only drastic revision. As described by the *Times,* "A certain continuity of the action is, however, established by means of the villagers, who, having sunk into magic slumber when the curtain falls after the first act, are still lying on the stage when it rises upon the second. A characteristic song and dance which they perform on awakening and finding themselves entangled in the meshes of love appeared also new. A ballad for the tenor, 'Thou hast the power,' must be called a less welcome addition, if addition it was, for we have not the original libretto before us. In any case it should be cut out, although it was very well sung by Mr. Lely."

This critic's suspicion was correct; the ballad for Alexis at the opening of the second act was not new. It was recognized properly by the *Topical Times* reviewer, who wrote that it "was believed by many of those present to be an innovation; as a matter of fact it was in the original score, but was cut out after the first performance." The first act suffered only the loss of a verse of Constance's first aria. Lady Sangazure's ballad, "In days gone by," had been cut from that act after the original production first night. (See page 70.)

There appear to have been two souvenir programs for the occasion, as well as the regular Savoy paper program. A possible explanation may be that one was for ladies (with a sunset view on its cover) and the other for gentlemen (its cover featuring a turbaned Moor smoking a hookah). All three programs carried the date and the information that "On this occasion the Two Operas will be conducted by the COMPOSER." The libretto, specially prepared by Chappell for this double bill, contained both texts in the one volume, each preceded by a Dramatis Personae for the revival.

At the end of *The Sorcerer,* reported the *Daily Chronicle,* "The audience on Saturday when the curtain fell did not cease their applause until Sir Arthur Sullivan, who conducted, came forward with Mr. Gilbert."

"After a rather extended interval, during which" —according to the *Observer*—"the gallery showed signs of good-natured patience by indulging in a little melody on its own account, Sir Arthur Sullivan . . . reappeared in his place, and once more presided over the rendering of his burlesque cantata, *Trial by Jury,* which may be regarded as the seed from which he and Mr. Gilbert have grown all their joint successes." The *Daily Chronicle* felt: "Its performance on Saturday suffered from the very late hour at which the curtain rose. The audience wanted to see the entertainment to the end, but were anxious respecting the trains and omnibuses. Notwithstanding this distraction of interest, doubtless as patent to the actors as to the assemblage facing them, the piece passed off merrily, and amid many signs of renewed gratification." Naturally there were no principals of the original cast on stage. The role of the Judge was played by Barrington, who—popular though he was—could not dim the memory of Fred Sullivan's original portrayal in the mind's eye of several critics.

Gilbert added an elaborate transformation scene and some closing lines (see page 43). As described by the *Standard*—"When the Judge has settled the difficulty by declaring his intention of marrying the deserted lady himself, a sort of pantomimic change occurs. The Judge becomes a species of legal Harlequin, the Plaintiff Columbine, and so amid red fire and much applause the curtain falls." (See cut on opposite page.)

Both Gilbert and Sullivan were urged by the audience to take their second curtain call of the evening at the conclusion of *Trial by Jury.*

Sullivan, in his diary, noted: ". . . Went to the Savoy to conduct the *Sorcerer* and *Trial by Jury*—magnificent house—most brilliant and enthusiastic reception of the opera. Excellently performed."

H.M.S. PINAFORE
First Revival
November 12, 1887, through March 10, 1888
120 Performances

The Mikado had played from March of '85 until the end of 1886, and in January of '87 was followed by *Ruddygore.* One week after the close of *Ruddygore,* the Savoy Theatre enjoyed its first production of *Pinafore* and the Nautical Comic Opera its first London revival. It was received, reported the *Times,* "by a large and distinguished audience with all the signs of cordial welcome which one offers to an old friend after a long separation." Gilbert had his own explanation for the nine years' absence of *Pinafore,* when interviewed in January 1887 by the *Pall Mall Budget.* He said they had run the opera too long for its own good at the time of the original production.

"Looking back upon the long line of these operettas," continued the *Times,* "one cannot help congratulating Mr. Gilbert and Sir Arthur Sullivan upon their achievement of having supplied London with innocent enjoyment for an uninterrupted space of ten years, to say nothing of the travelling companies which have spread their fame over the length and breadth of England, the United States, and latterly the Continent of Europe. . . . In addition to creating a style of art of their own, Mr. Gilbert and Sir Arthur Sullivan have also trained a school of actors to perform it. How successful they have been in this respect also, how perfectly their intentions are understood by their interpreters, was proved especially by those members of Saturday's cast who resumed their original parts. . . . A more sublimely official Sir Joseph Porter than Mr. Grossmith, a more comic captain of the Navy than Mr. Rutland Barrington singing to a small guitar by the light of the moon, it would be impossible to imagine. . . . Miss Jessie Bond as a very charming Hebe and Mr. Richard Temple as a desperate Dick Deadeye also repeated former successes, and Miss Brandram as Little Buttercup fully realized the humour of her part. Miss Geraldine Ulmar as Josephine acted with grace and sang with an agreeable voice of considerable compass . . . and Mr. J. G. Robertson atoned for want of stage experience by the pleasant *timbre* of his tenor voice. Chorus and orchestra under the composer's direction were all that could be desired."

The colorful souvenir program used that night was the one designed for *Princess Ida* by Mrs. Alice Havers Morgan. It bore the date and the line—"On this occasion the Opera will be conducted by the Composer." Those in the audience who bought the libretto found a new edition (the fourth) with the current revival cast properly listed on the Dramatis Personae page. On February 14, 1888, a curtain raiser was added to the bill: *Mrs. Jarramie's Genie,* an operetta, libretto by Frank Desprez, music by Alfred and François Cellier.

At the last. "and a good judge too" the gong is struck for the trick
change to Fairyland -
The canopy revolves
The fan pieces behind judge fall
2 Revolving pieces on either side of Judge come round
The rise comes up & covers Bench front
The judge & associate's desks open
The chamber flats are broken & taken away & wings
pushed on.
Cloths in front of Benches & Jury box are let down
And masking for same pushed on
The Jurymen, Counsel, & ladies have blue bells which
they hold over Bridesmaids for Final Picture
At "Oh yes I'm a judge" the Bridesmaids clap their hands a la minstrels
For Final Picture the Plaintiff gets on the Judges back - the two
the two Bridesmaids with counsel & Deft fall right & left while the
remaining Bridesmaids kneel with their arms over their heads.
Red fire. 5 pans on each side. one in each entrance
to be lighted when gong sounds

GRAND TRANSFORMATION SCENE: *Original manuscript stage-directions, though not in Gilbert's hand, from his own prompt-copy of* TRIAL BY JURY *now at the British Museum.*
(*See also illustration on page 43.*)

THE PIRATES OF PENZANCE

First Revival

March 17, 1888, through June 6, 1888

80 Performances

"Pending the completion of the new operetta [i.e., *The Yeomen of the Guard*] on which Mr. Gilbert and Sir Arthur Sullivan are understood to be engaged," wrote the reviewer for the *Times* of Monday, March 19, 1888, "the Savoy Theatre relies upon revivals of earlier favourites, and the *Pinafore,* having run its course, was on Saturday evening followed by *The Pirates of Penzance.* This work, having been first introduced in 1880, was originally perhaps rather less successful than its immediate predecessor; but its reception on Saturday was such that a long and prosperous career may be safely predicted for the revival. The audience was less distinguished than is usually the case at first nights at the Savoy, and the occasion was shorn of much of its interest by the absence of Sir Arthur Sullivan from the conductor's seat. But, on the other hand, there was no falling off in the favour with which Mr. Gilbert's good-humoured and perfectly harmless sallies, and the charming melodies which Sir Arthur Sullivan has wedded to them, were received by the audience."

As veterans in their original roles, the cast contained Grossmith as Major General Stanley, Barrington as the Sergeant of Police, Richard Temple as the Pirate King, and Jessie Bond, who was the Edith of the New York première. But Geraldine Ulmar as Mabel and Rosina Brandram as Ruth could hardly, by that time, be dubbed newcomers, as was Mr. J. G. Robertson, "an agreeable *tenorino* [who] sang well as Frederic" and who did "not as yet show any particular dramatic aptitude," according to the *Times.*

"The policeman's song, rendered with sublime *aplomb* by Mr. Rutland Barrington and his merry men," the review continued, "was accordingly applauded to the echo. In other respects . . . the revival of the *Pirates,* although less elaborately mounted than that of the *Pinafore,* showed all the signs of careful rehearsal under the author's own superintendence, without which a Savoy performance would not be what it is. . . . Talking of colour, we may mention that the blues and reds of the pirates' dresses were positively painful to the eye, and it must be hoped that successive layers of dust will soon tone down their brightness." Attention was called to the fact that "while Major General Stanley's numerous daughters singing in the chorus wear the high-waisted frocks of half a century ago, their sister Mabel appears in a modern dress, including a 'dress improver' [a journalese pat on the bustle, then in high fashion], which might have come from M. Worth's *atelier* yesterday." This purist critic held that one expected a mixture of costumes in Italian opera—naming *Traviata* as an example—but "in an entertainment of Mr. Gilbert's devising . . . such an anomaly should not be tolerated."

The *Theatre* magazine's April 1888 issue hailed the first appearance of this opera at the Savoy as "in every way a brilliant success," and added ruefully, "Arthur Sullivan, alas! was not in his accustomed place, as usual upon such occasions, at the conductor's desk. His state of health has been unsatisfactory for some time past. . . ." Cellier conducted the performance "with care and circumspection" but, oddly, neither his name nor the date appears on the souvenir program of the occasion (again Mrs. Morgan's design). For the balance of the run of the *Pirates* revival, *Mrs. Jarramie's Genie* was played as a curtain raiser, except Saturday matinees, when it was replaced by one of George Grossmith's Drawing-Room Sketches. But for the first night of this revival the *Pirates* was alone on the bill.

With the production of this first revival of THE PIRATES OF PENZANCE, *D'Oyly Carte had presented all thirteen of the extant Gilbert and Sullivan operas at the Savoy Theatre.*

THE MIKADO

First Revival

June 7, 1888, through September 29, 1888

166 Performances

The first night of this first revival of *The Mikado,* which immediately followed the *Pirates* encore, was conducted by François Cellier, as Sullivan was still ailing. Except for J. G. Robertson and Geraldine Ulmar, the cast was identical with that of the original production. After the first night *Mrs. Jarramie's Genie* returned as curtain raiser. This *Mikado* was still going strong when taken off to make way for the première of *The Yeomen of the Guard.*

THE MIKADO

Second Revival

November 6, 1895, through March 4, 1896

127 Performances

Extended

July 11, 1896, through February 17, 1897

226 Performances

The Yeomen had opened in '88, *The Gondoliers* in '89, *Utopia* in '93, and no revivals had intervened. Now, over a year after *Utopia*'s close, Arthur Sullivan was back at the Savoy to conduct the first night of the second revival of *The Mikado*, while he and Gilbert completed their work on *The Grand Duke*. For a souvenir program, Carte reissued the colorful lithographic souvenir that had decorated fifteen months of the *Mikado*'s monumental first run in 1885-1886. There was also a replica of the same program, but on cheaper paper and in black rather than color, presumably for "the gods." Rutland Barrington, Jessie Bond, and Rosina Brandram were present in their original roles. An indulgence slip was circulated among the first-night audience "on behalf of Miss Rosina Brandram, who is suffering from a severe cold." At the outset *The Mikado* was alone on the bill, but in January 1896 Frank Desprez's and Alfred Cellier's *After All* was revived to serve as curtain raiser.

The Grand Duke was presented March 7, but so short was its run, by Savoy standards, that D'Oyly Carte was caught without a replacement when it was taken off on July 10. But one virtue in this brevity was that *The Mikado* had been so very recently in performance, that it could be re-revived without the Savoy's missing a single night. As Sullivan was again in bad health, convalescing in the south of France, the first night of this extended revival was conducted by François Cellier. Initially it was without a curtain raiser, but starting August 15, *Weather or No* (book by Ross and Beach, music by B. L. Selby) was added. The composer was still out of the country on the occasion of the thousandth London performance of this remarkable opera. But a few weeks later he had returned and on Saturday evening, October 31, 1896, a special "thousandth performance" (actually the 1,037th) was celebrated in the best Savoy fashion. According to the *Daily News*, "In honour of the event the composer conducted, and with Mr. Gilbert came before the curtain at the end of the representation." After the author and composer had taken their bows, "Mr. Cellier, to

the regret of everybody, announced that Mr. D'Oyly Carte was too ill to come to the theatre, but had sent his thanks." Save for the absence of one of the triumvirate, that was a truly gala evening. As described by the same *Daily News* reviewer, "The Savoy programme was printed on Japanese fans, and *Gilbert and Sullivan Birthday Books* were presented to every member of the audience. The theatre was prettily decorated with Liberty silks in the Japanese colours, the electric lights were concealed by huge Japanese lanterns, and festoons of chrysanthemums were hung across the box fronts, the proscenium, and the back of the stalls."

THE YEOMEN OF THE GUARD

First Revival

May 5, 1897, through November 20, 1897

186 Performances

After an interlude filled by the brief run of *His Majesty* (libretto by Francis Cowley Burnand of *Cox & Box* fame, music by Sir Alexander Mackenzie—the blind composer's first effort in the field of comic opera), D'Oyly Carte elected to revive *Yeomen*. Only two members of the original 1888 cast were on hand, Richard Temple and the indestructible Rosina Brandram. (Jessie Bond had retired from the stage during the preceding *Mikado* revival.) Ilka von Palmay (see *The Grand Duke*) played Elsie Maynard. Arthur Sullivan conducted the first night of this first revival, and so the program stated. It was the same vertical two-fold affair (with the ancient arms of Savoy on its cover) that had established the new style in Savoy programs six months before, late in the second *Mikado* revival.

THE GONDOLIERS

First Revival

March 22, 1898, through May 21, 1898

62 Performances

Extended

July 18, 1898, through September 17, 1898

63 Performances

Halévy and Offenbach's *The Grand Duchess of Gerolstein* had followed the first *Yeomen* revival into the Savoy. "The most interesting consequence of this . . . ," wrote Cunningham-Bridgeman, "was the opportunity it afforded of drawing comparison between the English and the French masters of light opera. However much opinions in the wider world may have differed regarding the comparative merits of the two composers, it was quite certain that, at the Savoy, Offenbach in all his brilliancy did not succeed in dimming the glory of Sullivan. If, at any time, any playgoer questioned that fact, the enthusiasm which greeted the return of *The Gondoliers* must have convinced them that Sir Arthur Sullivan still reigned King Paramount in the hearts of British music-lovers."

During the run of *The Grand Duchess*, Sullivan had been on the Riviera starting work on *The Beauty Stone* (libretto by Arthur W. Pinero and J. Comyns Carr). So, when D'Oyly Carte decided to replace the fading Offenbach hit with the first revival of *The Gondoliers*, Sullivan was not on hand to conduct the first night, and Cellier took his place. Rosina Brandram, as the Duchess of Plaza-Toro, was the only member of the original cast to participate.

As soon as *The Beauty Stone* was ready, it replaced the revived *Gondoliers*, but for so short a run (only fifty performances) that Carte re-convened his *Gondoliers* company to keep the Savoy open. Again Sullivan was not able to conduct the first night's performance which, as usual under such circumstances, Cellier took over.

THE SORCERER & TRIAL BY JURY

Second Revival

September 22, 1898, through December 31, 1898

102 Performances

After being off the Savoy boards for fourteen years, the double bill of *Sorcerer* and *Trial by Jury* was revived for a second time in order to make capital of the former's twenty-first anniversary. Naturally no member of the original 1877 cast of *The Sorcerer* was in the production, but Rosina Brandram played Lady Sangazure, as she had in the 1884 revival. Cellier conducted the first night, for the composer "was abroad holiday-making." But the real birthday celebration took place on November 17, twenty-one years to a day from the first performance of *The Sorcerer* at the Opéra Comique. Sullivan was on hand to conduct; Gilbert was in the audience. Sullivan's diary shows how far apart the old partners had drifted:

Tremendous house—ditto reception. Opera went very well. Passmore inimitable. Call for Gilbert

and self—we went on together but did not speak to each other. He is mortally offended about *The Beauty Stone*, insisting that I left him out of the theatre on the first night. As he will not allow me to explain that I had nothing whatsoever to do with it, of course there is nothing to be done.

D'Oyly Carte had prepared a souvenir booklet for this anniversary audience, which listed the casts of both 1877 and 1898 productions, with portrait illustrations of both sets of principals.

H.M.S. PINAFORE & TRIAL BY JURY

Second Revival

June 6, 1899, through November 25, 1899

174 Performances

The popular Gilbert and Sullivan double bill had been followed into the Savoy by *Lucky Star,* a new and successful comic opera of mixed international parentage, which had been revised by Helen Lenoir (Mrs. D'Oyly Carte). And then the theatre rang once more to the familiar strains of *Pinafore.* (Of course Little Buttercup was Rosina Brandram.) Sullivan conducted the first night of this second revival, and *Trial by Jury*'s revival was extended to provide an after-piece. This was to be the last first night of a Gilbert and Sullivan opera conducted by the composer.

THE PIRATES OF PENZANCE

Second Revival

June 30, 1900, through November 3, 1900

127 Performances

"The Persian Opera," as Sullivan is said to have called his *Rose of Persia* (libretto by Captain Basil Hood, a descendant of Thomas Hood), was, according to Adair Fitz-Gerald, "a worthy successor of Gilbert's work." It did so well through the first half of 1900 (212 performances) that Carte arranged for a second Hood-Sullivan collaboration. While awaiting it, he gave the *Pirates* its second revival. Rosina Brandram was still Ruth; but Henry Lytton (as Major General Stanley) and Walter Passmore (as the Sergeant of Police) were at their peak of popularity to make the faithful forget the missing Grossmith and Barrington. Sullivan had been summoned to Berlin by the then Kaiser Wilhelm II, so he was not at the conductor's desk for the first night of this *Pirates* revival. Cellier served in his stead.

PATIENCE

First Revival

November 7, 1900, through April 20, 1901

150 Performances

Sullivan started composing his final opera, *The Emerald Isle,* to Basil Hood's libretto, while in Switzerland during August of 1900, but poor health delayed his work. D'Oyly Carte, also seriously ill, arranged for the first revival of *Patience* since its opening success in 1881, in order to keep his theatre active. Gilbert, gradually recovering from a bad siege of gout, had written his old partner a letter that—with the help of Helen D'Oyly Carte—had restored peace. In a rebirth of his old topsy-turviness he dreamed up the idea of having all three of the decrepit partners take a curtain call together at the close of *Patience* on the first night of its revival. Sullivan entered into the spirit of the whimsy, and Helen D'Oyly Carte elaborated it by suggesting that they appear in three wheel chairs. As this prank was being hatched, Sullivan wrote her:

> I thought that if three such frightful wrecks as Gilbert, D'Oyly, and myself were to appear on

the stage at the same time it would create something more than a sensation. It wasn't my intention to come to the first night of *Patience* but if it would really please Gilbert to have me there and to go on with him I will come.

On November 7 the curtain went up on the last first night of a Gilbert and Sullivan opera with all three partners still alive; but, alas! with only two of them present at the Savoy. Arthur Sullivan was mortally sick and unable to attend. He had scrawled a note of regret to Helen D'Oyly Carte, headed "In bed": "Pray tell Gilbert how very much I feel the disappointment. Good luck to you all. Three invalid chairs would have looked very well from the front."

François Cellier conducted. Rosina Brandram was Lady Jane. The *Standard* noted: "It should be added that the interest of last night's revival was increased by the distribution of the remaining copies of the old souvenir books, that were prepared nearly twenty years ago on the 250th performance of *Patience* at the Savoy Theatre." After the final curtain, gouty old Gilbert and sick, feeble D'Oyly Carte hobbled and shuffled onto the stage for the applause they had hoped would be shared by all three. On November 17, Gilbert wrote Sullivan: "The old opera woke up splendidly."

On November 22, 1900, Arthur Sullivan died, followed on April 3, 1901, by his friend and partner Richard D'Oyly Carte. Meanwhile, on January 22, Queen Victoria's monumental reign had ended, and with it the era that had born and nurtured to world-wide acclaim the Gilbert and Sullivan operas.

CURTAIN

Sources

GILBERT & SULLIVAN: *Popular Comic Operas—Librettos*, Chappell & Co., Ltd., London.

ARCHER, William: *Real Conversations*, William Heinemann, London, 1904.

BAILY, Leslie: *The Gilbert & Sullivan Book*, Cassell & Co., Ltd., London, 1952. Revised 1956.

BARRINGTON, Rutland: *Rutland Barrington, by Himself*, Grant Richards, London, 1908.

BOND, Jessie: *The Life and Reminiscences of Jessie Bond*, John Lane, London, 1930.

BRERETON, Austin: *Dramatic Notes, A Chronicle of the London Stage, 1881*. David Bogue, London, 1883.

BROWNE, Edith A.: *W. S. Gilbert* (Stars of the Stage Series), John Lane, The Bodley Head, London, 1907.

CELLIER, François, and Bridgeman, Cunningham: *Gilbert and Sullivan and Their Operas*, Sir Isaac Pitman & Sons, Ltd., London, 1914.

DARK, Sidney, and Grey, Rowland: *W. S. Gilbert: His Life and Letters*, Methuen & Company, Ltd., London, 1923.

DUNHILL, Thomas F.: *Sullivan's Comic Operas, A Critical Appreciation*, Edward Arnold & Co., London, 1928.

DUNN, George E.: *A Gilbert & Sullivan Dictionary*, Oxford University Press, New York, 1926.

FITZ-GERALD, S. J. Adair: *The Story of the Savoy Opera*, Stanley Paul & Co., Ltd., London, 1924.

FITZGERALD, Percy: *The Savoy Opera and the Savoyards*, Chatto & Windus, London, 1894.

GILBERT, W. S.: *Patience; or, Bunthorne's Bride—with new introduction by W. S. Gilbert*, Doubleday, Page & Co., New York, 1902.

GILBERT, W. S.: *Plays & Poems* (with a preface by Deems Taylor), Random House, New York, 1932.

GILBERT, W. S.: *Savoy Operas—Foreword by W. S. Gilbert*, George Bell & Sons, London, 1909.

GILBERT, W. S.: *The Savoy Operas* (complete edition), Macmillan and Co., Ltd., London, 1932.

GILBERT AND SULLIVAN JOURNAL: The Official Publication of the Gilbert & Sullivan Society, London.

GOLDBERG, Isaac: *The Story of Gilbert and Sullivan*, Simon and Schuster, New York, 1928.

GROSSMITH, George: *A Society Clown*, J. W. Arrowsmith, Bristol, 1888.

HALTON, Frederick J.: *The Gilbert and Sullivan Operas, A Concordance*, The Bass Publishers, New York, 1935.

HOLLINGSHEAD, John: *Gaiety Chronicles*, Archibald Constable & Co., London, 1898.
Good Old Gaiety, Gaiety Theatre Company Ltd., London, 1903.

JACOBS, Arthur: *Gilbert and Sullivan* (The World of Music), Max Parrish & Co., Ltd., London, 1951.

KENEALY, Arabella: *Memoirs of Edward Vaughn Kenealy*, J. Long, London, 1908.

KLEIN, Herman: *Musicians and Mummers*, Cassell & Co., Ltd., London, 1925.

LAWRENCE, Arthur: *Sir Arthur Sullivan: Life Story, Letters and Reminiscences*, Herbert S. Stone & Co., Chicago & New York, 1899.

LYTTON, Henry A.: *The Secrets of a Savoyard*, Jarrolds, London, 1922.

PEARSON, Hesketh: *Gilbert, His Life and Strife*, Methuen & Company, Ltd., London, 1957.

REED, E. T.: *Mr. Punch's Animal Land*, Bradbury, Agnew & Co., London, 1898.

SEARLE, Townley: *Sir William Schwenck Gilbert, A Topsy-Turvy Adventure*, Alexander-Ouseley, Ltd., London, 1931.

SHAW, George Bernard: *London Music in 1888-89 as heard by Corno di Bassetto*, Constable & Co., Ltd., London, 1937—*Music in London, 1890-94* (revised and reprinted), Constable & Co., Ltd., London, 1932.

STEEGMULLER, Francis: *Maupassant, A Lion in the Path*, Random House, New York, 1949.

SULLIVAN, Herbert, and Flower, Newman: *Sir Arthur Sullivan, His Life, Letters, & Diaries*, Cassell & Co., Ltd., London, 1927.

WALBROOK, H. M.: *Gilbert & Sullivan Opera, A History and a Comment*, F. V. White & Co., Ltd., London, 1922.

WILLIAMSON, Audrey: *Gilbert & Sullivan Opera, A New Assessment*, Rockliff Publishing Corp., Ltd., London, 1953.

WILSTACH, Paul: *Richard Mansfield—The Man and the Actor*, Chas. Scribner's Sons, New York, 1908.

BRITISH NEWSPAPERS AND MAGAZINES

ACADEMY, THE
BAT, THE
BELL'S LIFE
BIRMINGHAM POST
BRIGHTON SOCIETY
CITIZEN, THE
CITY, THE

DAILY CHRONICLE
DAILY GRAPHIC
DAILY NEWS
DAILY TELEGRAPH
ECHO, THE
ELECTRICAL TIMES, THE
ENGLAND

ENTR'ACTE, THE
ERA, THE
EVENING NEWS
FAN, THE
FIGARO, THE
FUN
GLOBE

BRITISH NEWSPAPERS AND MAGAZINES (*continued*)

AMERICAN NEWSPAPERS AND MAGAZINES

MISCELLANEOUS

PROGRAMS: Royalty Theatre; Opéra Comique; Savoy Theatre; Provincial

POSTERS: Fifth Avenue; Opéra Comique; Royal Bijou Theatre, Paignton; Savoy Theatre; U.S. Tradecard

SHEET MUSIC: Ashdown & Parry; Chappell & Co.

Index of Sources in Order of Use

MOST of the very many quoted passages and other references in the Introductions and Postscripts of this volume are identified, but some are not. In order that the reader may readily identify these, the following index of sources has been prepared. For each of the book's major divisions, each source-title is listed once, in the order of its first use. After each such listing are page numbers and column designations (*a:* left, *b:* right) by which quotations and references from the particular source may be located. Identification of illustration sources follows each list. In a few instances illustrations have been adapted from the originals.